Lecture Notes in Artificial Intelligence 1323

Subseries of Lecture Notes in Computer Science
Edited by J. G. Carbonell and J. Siekmann

Lecture Notes in Computer Science

Edited by G. Goos, J. Hartmanis and J. van Leeuwen

Springer
Berlin
Heidelberg
New York
Barcelona
Budapest
Hong Kong
London
Milan
Paris
Santa Clara
Singapore
Tokyo

Ernesto Costa   Amilcar Cardoso (Eds.)

Progress in Artificial Intelligence

8th Portuguese Conference
on Artificial Intelligence, EPIA-97
Coimbra, Portugal, October 6-9, 1997
Proceedings

 Springer

Series Editors
Jaime G. Carbonell, Carnegie Mellon University, Pittsburgh, PA, USA
Jörg Siekmann, University of Saarland, Saarbrücken, Germany

Volume Editors

Ernesto Coasta
Amilcar Cardoso
Dep. Eng. Informatica
Universidade de Coimbra, Polo II
Pinhal de Marrocos, 3030 Coimbra, Portugal
E-mail: {ernesto, amilcar}@dei.uc.pt

Cataloging-in-Publication Data applied for

Die Deutsche Bibliothek - CIP-Einheitsaufnahme

Progress in artificial intelligence : proceedings / 8th Portuguese
Conference on Artificial Intelligence, EPIA-97, Coimbra, Portugal,
October 6 - 9, 1997. Ernesto Costa ; Amilcar Cardoso (ed.). - Berlin ;
Heidelberg ; New York ; Barcelona ; Budapest ; Hong Kong ;
London ; Milan ; Paris ; Santa Clara ; Singapore ; Tokyo : Springer,
1997
    (Lecture notes in computer science ; Vol. 1323 : Lecture notes in
    artificial intelligence)
    ISBN 3-540-63586-6

CR Subject Classification (1991): I.2

ISBN 3-540-63586-6 Springer-Verlag Berlin Heidelberg New York

© Springer-Verlag Berlin Heidelberg 1997
Printed in Germany

Typesetting: Camera ready by author
SPIN 10545743   06/3142 – 5 4 3 2 1 0   Printed on acid-free paper

Preface

The Portuguese Conference on Artificial Intelligence has been organized, since 1985, under the auspices of the Portuguese Association for Artificial Intelligence (APPIA). Since the first conference, standards have been gradually refined, particularly since the fourth conference, when the EPIA became an international event, English being adopted as the official language.

EPIA'97, the eighth in the series, has reconfirmed the international status of the conference and the high standard of accepted papers. A total of 74 contributions were received from 13 countries. All of them were subject to a (AAAI-style) triple blind peer review. From these contributions, 24 were selected for full presentation and 9 were selected for poster presentation.

EPIA'97 could count on a highly qualified program committee, which included many internationally distinguished researchers covering a wide range of AI areas. Our special thanks go to them all and also to the reviewers, listed elsewhere in these proceedings, for their excellent hard work.

The presence of the invited lecturers Oskar Dressler, Tom Mitchell, Luís Moniz Pereira, and Francisco Varela greatly contributed to broadening the thematic spectrum of the conference. We would like to thank them for their presentations and for the written contributions included in these proceedings. We are also grateful to Pedro Barahona, Félix Costa, Yves Kodratoff, and Daniel O'Leary. Their tutorials made a significant contribution to EPIA97. We will not forget the effort made by Pavel Brazdil, Fernando Moura-Pires, Eugénio Oliveira, and Nick Jennings, who worked very hard to enrich the conference with interesting workshops.

We would also like to thank the following institutions that contributed (financially or otherwise) to the organization of this conference and to the edition of these proceedings:

Companhia de Seguros Fidelidade
Reitoria da Universidade de Coimbra
JNICT - Junta Nacional de Investigação Científica e Tecnológica
Júlio Logrado Figueiredo, Lda.
Digital Equipment Portugal, Lda.
Fundação Calouste Gulbenkian
FLAD - Fundação Luso-Americana para o Desenvolvimento
Câmara Municipal de Coimbra
IPN - Instituto Pedro Nunes
SISCOG - Sistemas Cognitivos
Departamento de Engenharia Informática da Universidade de Coimbra

Particular thanks are due to all those who helped us with the local organization, namely Olga Costa, Carlos Bento, José Luís Ferreira, Paulo Gomes, Francisco Câmara Pereira, Penousal Machado, Miguel Ferrand, and Bernardete Ribeiro. We are also grateful to Maria Ferrand, who contributed with her creativity to the visual image of the conference. Special thanks go to António Raimundo (Companhia de Seguros Fidelidade) – our gratitute to him will last forever. We could not forget either the invaluable support from Vergílio Rocha (Tecnotrom), Graça Martins (EF), and Manuel Cardoso (Sepil). The final thanks go to Springer-Verlag for their help and assistance in producing this book.

Coimbra, August 1997

Ernesto Costa
Amílcar Cardoso

Programme and Conference Co-Chairs

Ernesto Costa
Dep. Eng. Informática
Centro de Informática e Sistemas
Universidade de Coimbra - Polo II
3030 Coimbra, Portugal
Voice: +351 (39) 7000019
Fax: +351 (39) 701266
URL: http://www.dei.uc.pt/~ernesto
E-mail: ernesto@dei.uc.pt

Amílcar Cardoso
Dep. Eng. Informática
Centro de Informática e Sistemas
Universidade de Coimbra - Polo II
3030 Coimbra, Portugal
Voice: +351 (39) 7000015
Fax: +351 (39) 701266
URL: http://www.dei.uc.pt/~amilcar
E-mail: amilcar@dei.uc.pt

Program Committee

Bernardete Ribeiro *(Universidade de Coimbra, Portugal)*
Carlos Bento *(Universidade de Coimbra, Portugal)*
Cristiano Castelfranchi *(Istituto di Psicologia, CNR, Roma, Italia)*
Ernesto Morgado *(Instituto Superior Técnico, Portugal)*
Eugénio Oliveira *(Universidade do Porto, Portugal)*
Gabriel Pereira Lopes *(Universidade Nova de Lisboa, Portugal)*
Helder Araújo *(Universidade de Coimbra, Portugal)*
Helder Coelho *(Universidade de Lisboa, Portugal)*
John Self *(Lancaster University, United Kingdom)*
Larry Medsker *(American University, USA)*
Luís Moniz Pereira *(Universidade Nova de Lisboa, Portugal)*
Luís Monteiro *(Universidade Nova de Lisboa, Portugal)*
Manuela Veloso *(Carnegie-Mellon University, USA)*
Miguel Filgueiras *(Universidade do Porto, Portugal)*
Nuno Mamede *(Instituto Superior Técnico/INESC, Portugal)*
Oskar Dressler *(OCC'M Software GmbH, Germany)*
Pavel Brazdil *(Universidade do Porto, Portugal)*
Pedro Barahona *(Universidade Nova de Lisboa, Portugal)*
Philippe Dague *(Université Paris Nord, France)*
Ramon López de Màntaras *(Institut d'Investigació en Intelligència Artificial, CSIC, Barcelona, España)*
Rosa Viccari *(Universidade Federal de Rio Grande do Sul, Brasil)*
Stefano Nolfi *(Istituto di Psicologia, CNR, Roma, Italia)*
Stuart Shapiro *(State University of New York at Buffalo, USA)*
Takeo Kanade *(Carnegie-Mellon University, USA)*
Xue Mei Wang *(Carnegie-Mellon University, USA)*
Yves Kodratoff *(Université Paris Sud, France)*

Reviewers

Agnar Aamodt
Alexander Kovacec
Alistair E. Campbell
Amedeo Cesta
Amílcar Cardoso
Ana Paiva
Ana P. Rocha
Antoine Cornuejols
António C. R. Costa
Bernardete Ribeiro
Carlos Bento
Carlos Pinto-Ferreira
Carmen B. D'Amico
Cristiano Castelfranchi
Daniel Kayser
Daniel M. Campos
Daniela D'Aloisi
Debra T. Burhans
Enric Plaza
Ernesto Costa
Ernesto Morgado
Eugénio Oliveira
Fabien Torre
Flávio M. Oliveira
Francisco Pereira
François Levy
Gabriel P. Lopes
Gonzalo Escalada-Imáz
Graça Gaspar
Helder Araújo
Helder Coelho

Hervé Mignot
Irene P. Rodriges
João Balsa
João Gama
Joaquim Aparício
Joaquim Reis
John Self
Jorge Dias
Jorge M. Pais
José J. Alferes
José L. Ferreira
José M. Fonseca
José P. Leal
José V. Lima
Larry Medsker
Leonor Melo
Luca Spalazzi
Lúcia M. Giraffa
Luís Caires
Luís Macedo
Luís M. Custódio
Luís Moniz
Luís M. Pereira
Luís Monteiro
Luís P. Reis
Luís Torgo
Manuela Veloso
Marcelo Ladeira
Maria C. Neves
Marie E. Gonçalves

Michael Cox
Michael C. Móra
Michele Sebag
Miguel Filgueiras
Nuno Mamede
Oskar Dressler
Pablo Noriega
Paolo Bouquet
Paul Brna
Paulo Faria
Paulo Gomes
Paulo Reis
Paulo Urbano
Pavel Brazdil
Pedro Barahona
Pedro Soares
Pere Garcia
Peter Struss
Philippe Balbiani
Philippe Dague
Ramon L. Mantaras
Rosario Falcone
Salvador P. Abreu
Stefano Nolfi
Stuart Shapiro
Sylvie Salotti
Takeo Kanade
Tatiana Tambouratzis
Vera L. S. Lima
Xue M. Wang

Table of Contents

Intelligent Tutoring Systems and Training

Knowledge Representation

Multi-Agent Systems and Distributed Artificial Intelligence

Non-Monothonic Reasoning

Problem Solving

Qualitative Reasoning

Temporal Reasoning

Posters (extended abstracts)

Invited Talks

Flexible Proof-Replay with Heuristics

Marc Fuchs

Fakultät für Informatik, TU München
80290 München
Germany
E-mail: fuchsm@informatik.tu-muenchen.de

Abstract. We present a general framework for developing search heuristics for automated theorem provers. This framework allows for the construction of heuristics that are on the one hand able to replay (parts of) a given proof found in the past but are on the other hand flexible enough to deviate from the given proof path in order to solve similar proof problems. We substantiate the abstract framework by the presentation of three distinct techniques for learning search heuristics based on so-called features. We demonstrate the usefulness of these techniques in the area of equational deduction. Comparisons with the renowned theorem prover OTTER validate the applicability and strength of our approach.

1 Introduction

The problem in automated theorem proving is trying to decide whether or not a given (proof) goal λ_{th} is a logical consequence of a given set of axioms Ax. Although this problem is not decidable in general it is possible in many cases to construct algorithms able to recognize each valid goal. These algorithms are usually represented by an inference system where only weak *fairness conditions* have to be satisfied in order to guarantee completeness. But this entails an indeterminism that can only be tackled with heuristics since usually no a priori knowledge exists to help to solve the conflicts caused by the fact that often a lot of inference rules are applicable.

The difficulties in overcoming this indeterminism are the main reason why automated theorem provers are inferior to human mathematicians when trying to prove difficult problems. Thus improvements in automated reasoning systems are needed in order to allow for a more "intelligent" search thus avoiding a complete and exhaustive enumeration of all theorems of a given theory.

A possible method to increase the power of a theorem prover is the use of solved examples to solve new (and harder) problems. Theorem proving by analogy tries to find a proof for a given *target problem* $\wp_T$ by using the proof of a similar *source problem* $\wp_S$. Usually, constructive approaches are applied in order to try to transform inference steps of the source to the target using analogous matches (cp. [11], [2], [9]). But a direct transformation of proof steps normally fails because of differences in the problem descriptions. Sophisticated patching strategies are necessary in order to "fill the gaps" which are not covered by the analogical reasoning.

Therefore, we will focus in this paper on the heuristical use of proofs. We will discuss the advantages of such an approach (cp. [6]), and we will present a general framework for reusing proofs by heuristic means. This framework allows for the construction of heuristics which perform a proof-replay of a given source proof. Moreover, the heuristics offer the flexibility to deviate from the given proof path which is needed in order to solve target problems that are similar to the given source problem.

We demonstrate the applicability of our general framework by the construction of three search-guiding heuristics based on "features". Features describe structural properties of the objects that are manipulated by a theorem prover. By mapping them to numbers they allow for an abstraction of the concrete objects. The choice of features was made according to the good results obtained by using them in different ways before (e.g. [12], [6]). Our methods using features are based on the *nearest-neighbour rule* [4] that is refined in various ways in order to offer sufficient support to guide the search for a new target. We evaluate the performance of our approach with several experiments in the area of equational reasoning using the prover DISCOUNT [1].

2 Automated Deduction with Synthetic Calculi

Problems of automated deduction can in general be specified as follows: From a given set Ax of facts (*axioms*), we must decide whether or not a further fact λ_{th} (*goal*) is a logic consequence of Ax. A proof problem is hence given as $\wp = (Ax, \lambda_{th})$. A fact may be a clause, equation, or a general first or higher-order formula.

A common principle for solving proof problems algorithmically with a synthetic calculus can be described as follows: Essentially, an automated deduction system maintains a set F^P of so-called *potential facts* from which it selects and removes one fact λ at a time. λ is put into the set F^A of *activated facts*, or discarded if it is subsumed by an already existing activated fact $\lambda' \in F^A$ (*forward subsumption*). Activated facts, unlike potential facts, are allowed to produce new facts via the application of given inference rules. The inferred new facts are put into F^P. At the beginning, $F^A = \emptyset$ and $F^P = Ax$. The indeterministic selection or *activation step* is realized by heuristic means. To this end, a search-guiding heuristic $\mathcal{H}$ associates a natural number $\mathcal{H}(\lambda) \in \mathbb{N}$ with each $\lambda \in F^P$. Subsequently, that $\lambda \in F^P$ with the smallest weight $\mathcal{H}(\lambda)$ is selected. This way we do not (costly) control every inference but restrict ourselves to a special choice point (activation step). Good heuristics for selecting the next activated fact usually lead to proofs in a negligible amount of time despite the fact that time is spent on unnecessary inferences.

There are several possibilities for defining the proof obtained by the deduction process. Our first definition of a proof is based on the inference chain performed by the prover resulting in the application of a success inference. Since this inference chain usually contains a lot of unnecessary steps we can extract an inference chain $\mathcal{I}$ by deleting these steps. This inference chain $\mathcal{I}$ is called a *proof*.

Another possibility for defining a proof according to our control strategy is to consider the facts activated by $\mathcal{H}$ during the deduction process. If $\mathcal{H}$ succeeds in proving $\wp$, we obtain a *search protocol* $\mathcal{S} \equiv \lambda_1; \ldots; \lambda_n$ ($n \geq 1$) which contains the activated facts. λ_n concludes the proof. By tracing back the application of inference rules starting with λ_n, all those facts λ_i of S which actually contributed to deducing λ_n can be identified. They are collected together with λ_n in the set P of *positive facts*. The complementary set $N = \{\lambda_1, \ldots, \lambda_n\} \setminus P$ is the set of *negative facts*. By omitting all $\lambda \in N$ from S we obtain a sequence $\mathcal{P} \equiv \lambda_1^+; \ldots; \lambda_m^+$, $\lambda_m^+ \equiv \lambda_n$ and $m \leq n$ which only contains the activation steps that are relevant regarding the deduction of λ_n. Note that S, $\mathcal{P}$, P and N depend on $\mathcal{H}$ and $\wp$, but we shall make this dependency explicit only if it is necessary to avoid confusion. Although $\mathcal{P}$ above all provides instructions on how to attain a proof of $\wp$ by traversing the search space efficiently it is nevertheless a correct chain of reasoning: we therefore also call $\mathcal{P}$ a *proof*. In the following, we denote proofs represented by inference chains by $\mathcal{I}$ whereas proofs represented by activation chains are denoted by $\mathcal{P}$.

When solving a problem $\wp$ with a fixed deduction system we obtain a so-called *proof experience* $\mathcal{E} = (\mathcal{H}, S)$. The quality of a heuristic can be measured by using the following notion of redundancy: The redundancy R of a search S performed with heuristic $\mathcal{H}$ is defined by $R = \frac{|N|}{|P|+|N|}$. An optimal heuristic for a problem $\wp$ ($R = 0$) only activates facts which contribute directly to the proof. In practice, we can see that conventional heuristics show a rather high degree of redundancy or even fail when trying to solve more difficult problems. Altogether, there exists a great demand for improvements in search-guiding heuristics.

3   A Heuristical Framework for Proof-Replay

Reusing proofs in order to improve automated theorem proving systems is a difficult task. This is due to the fact that in the area of automated deduction "small differences between problems usually do *not* result in small differences of their solutions". In order to overcome this problem we propose a heuristical usage of past proof experience, more exactly of one given proof, as discussed in [6] in more detail.

Instead of trying to compute a proof $\mathcal{I}_T$ for a new target problem $\wp_T$ we still search for it with a conventional deduction system that uses a source proof $\mathcal{I}_S$ delivered by a heuristic $\mathcal{H}$ and tries to prove $\wp_T$ by using a heuristic based on $\mathcal{H}$ that is further incorporated with information on $\mathcal{I}_S$. Such a heuristic is well suited for solving problems similar to the source problem $\wp_S$ because we can achieve a suitable compromise between flexibility (allowing for small deviations from $\mathcal{I}_S$) and specialization (avoiding useless inferences for the target). The flexibility stems from the "original" heuristic $\mathcal{H}$ which should usually be general enough to work quite well for a large set of problems. We achieve specialization by the incorporation of information on the similar source proof.

In order to realize such reusing of proofs by heuristic means it is sensible to use our second notion of a proof. This is because we assume that only the activation step is controllable according to a heuristic weighting. A heuristic specialized in the source proof can be constructed by weighting all facts $\lambda^+ \in P_S$ which are positive w.r.t. the source proof $\mathcal{P}_S$ smaller than the minimal weighting of a negative fact $\lambda \in N_S$. Furthermore, we should take care that such a heuristic does not give facts $\lambda \notin P_S \cup N_S$ a heuristic weight smaller than the maximal weight of positive facts. This could result in a completely different proof run compared with the proof obtained by $\mathcal{H}$. In particular, it is not guaranteed that such a heuristic will reach the goal (in an acceptable time limit) because the activation of positive facts could be delayed by the activation of facts $\lambda \notin P_S \cup N_S$. The following technique of *flexible proof-specialization* of a heuristic keeps these requirements in mind and offers a general framework for constructing search-guiding heuristics using information on a specific source proof. We choose the approach to penalize facts $\lambda \notin P_S$ with a penalty function ω. Thus, we get the following definition of an ω-specialization of a heuristic $\mathcal{H}$.

Definition 1. Let $\wp$ be a solved proof problem with proof experience $\mathcal{E}$ and proof $\mathcal{P}$ given over a set of facts $\mathcal{O}$. Furthermore, let S be the sequence of facts activated by heuristic $\mathcal{H}$ while searching for $\mathcal{P}$. P denotes the set of positive facts. Let $\omega : \mathcal{O} \to \mathbb{N}$ be a (penalty) function. We call the search heuristic $\mathcal{H}_\omega$ defined by $\mathcal{H}_\omega(\lambda) = \mathcal{H}(\lambda) + \omega(\lambda)$ an ω-*specialization* of $\mathcal{H}$ (w.r.t. $\mathcal{E}$) if $\omega(\lambda^+) = 0 \ \forall \lambda^+ \in P$.

ω is a function used to estimate whether a fact to be judged by some heuristic $\mathcal{H}_\omega$ contributes to a proof or not. It is the main task of ω to allow an ordinal weighting on the facts by $\omega(\lambda_1) > \omega(\lambda_2)$ iff λ_2 has a higher probability of usefulness for a proof than λ_1. In order to construct heuristics specialized in a proof also an appropriate cardinal weighting is necessary. The degree of specialization of a heuristic $\mathcal{H}_\omega$ in a proof $\mathcal{P}$ heavily depends on the values ω assigns to negative facts. We represent the degree of specialization achieved when using ω by the notion of *e-consistency*:

Definition 2. Let $\wp$ be a source problem with proof experience $\mathcal{E} = (\mathcal{H}, S)$ obtained by deduction system $\mathcal{D}$. Let $\mathcal{P}$ be the proof extractable from $\mathcal{E}$. P and N denote the sets of the positive and negative facts, respectively. Let $e \in [0; 100]$ be a constant. Furthermore, let $\mathcal{H}_\omega^+ = \max\{\mathcal{H}_\omega(\lambda^+) : \lambda^+ \in P\}$. An ω-specialization $\mathcal{H}_\omega$ is said to be *e-consistent* with $\mathcal{E}$ if $|\{\lambda : \lambda \in N \wedge \mathcal{H}_\omega(\lambda) > \mathcal{H}_\omega^+\}| \geq \frac{e}{100} \cdot |N|$.

Thus, an ω-specialization $\mathcal{H}_\omega$ being 100-consistent with $\mathcal{E}$ (associated with problem $\wp$) excludes all of the negative facts from the search and obtains the proof $\mathcal{P}$ without any redundancy. Smaller consistency-values with $\mathcal{E}$ increase the overhead that still remains when using $\mathcal{H}_\omega$ for proving $\wp$. The following theorem summarizes the effect of the usage of an ω-specialization $\mathcal{H}_\omega$ being e-consistent with proof experience $\mathcal{E}$.

Theorem 3. *Let $\wp$, $\mathcal{E}$, $\mathcal{P}$, P, and N be as in the previous definition. Let ω be a penalty function such that $\mathcal{H}_\omega$ is an ω-specialization and $\mathcal{H}_\omega$ is e-consistent with $\mathcal{E}$ for some $e \in [0; 100]$. Then it is true that deduction system $\mathcal{D}$ using $\mathcal{H}_\omega$ proves $\wp$ with proof $\mathcal{P}'$ equal to $\mathcal{P}$. Furthermore, the set of positive facts P' is given by $P' = P$. For the redundancy R' of the search S' performed with $\mathcal{H}_\omega$ it holds $R' \leq \frac{\eta \cdot |N|}{|P| + \eta \cdot |N|}$ whereby $\eta = \frac{100 - e}{100}$. Particularly, it holds $R' < R$ if $e > 0$ where R denotes the redundancy of the search obtained using $\mathcal{H}$.*

Note that it can be sensible to allow for some redundancy (use $\mathcal{H}_\omega$ that is not 100-consistent with $\mathcal{E}$) in order to avoid "over-specialization". Over-specialization arises mainly because of our inability to develop a penalty function ω which judges all facts appropriate while searching for a proof of a new target (cf. the following section). The "intelligence" or practical success of an ω-specialization (e-consistent with a proof experience belonging to a source problem $\wp_S$) in solving target problems $\wp_T$ similar to $\wp_S$ is heavily influenced by the realization of ω. A naive realization, e.g. $\omega(\lambda) = pen\_fac \cdot (1 - \chi_{P_S}(\lambda))$ (χ_{P_S} denotes the characteristic function of the positive facts w.r.t. the source proof) allows a solution of the source problem to be found more quickly (with increasing pen_fac). But it offers no real support for the solution of targets which are similar but not equal to $\wp_S$. The reason for this is that ω only favors facts *syntactically* equal to positive facts of the source. A better solution would be to favour facts that share some properties with positive facts and hence are *structurally* equal to them. Hence, we are interested in the detection of more general tendencies what positive or negative really means.

Due to positive experience obtained with so-called features in the past (e.g., [12], [6]) we want to instantiate our abstract framework described above with some concrete realizations of ω based on features. In the following section we introduce the feature concept, and then we discuss three different techniques which can be used to develop penalty functions based on features.

4 Heuristical Proof-Specialization with Features

As discussed in the previous section we want to realize "intelligent" penalty functions by using features. Features describe structural properties of facts. We want to restrict ourselves to represent such properties by functions $f : \mathcal{O} \to \mathbb{Z}$ where $\mathcal{O}$ is the set of facts. We call f a *feature*, the value $f(\lambda)$ is called the *feature value* of λ w.r.t. f. In order to allow for a better distinction between positive and negative facts and to detect properties typical for useful and useless facts, it is sensible to use several (distinct) features $f_1, \ldots, f_n$. Hence, we represent a fact λ by its *feature value vector* $(f_1(\lambda), \ldots, f_n(\lambda))$. We assume that a fixed sequence of features $f_1, \ldots, f_n$, is given and we define $FV(\lambda) = (f_1(\lambda), \ldots, f_n(\lambda))$.

In the following we are looking for penalty functions ω based on features that estimate whether a fact might contribute to a proof of a target problem $\wp_T$ or not. As usual let $\wp_S$ be a solved source problem and $\mathcal{E} = (\mathcal{H}, \mathcal{S})$ be a proof experience. P_S, N_S denote the sets of positive and negative facts, respectively. A common principle for classifying an element in artificial intelligence is to use so-called nearest-neighbour techniques (cp. [4]). The nearest-neighbour rule (NNR) in our context allows for a fact λ to take on the "class" (positive, negative) of a "nearest" fact $\lambda' \in P_S \cup N_S$ according to some predefined distance measure d (based on features) as the class of λ. But since we want to use a function ω not only for classifying elements, but also for an estimation of probabilities, we modify this technique by explicitly using distances to the nearest positive and negative facts. In the following, we present three different techniques stemming from the NNR that are based on the explicit use of distance measures in order to rate facts. We start with a simple distance measure (constructed by hand)

and study the effects arising from the use of more and more information on the source proof which is used to *learn* appropriate distance measures automatically.

A Penalty Function Based on the Euclidean Distance: Our first technique to construct a penalty function ω_1 uses a distance measure $d : \mathcal{O} \times \mathcal{O} \rightarrow \mathbb{R}$. $d(\lambda_1, \lambda_2)$ is based on the Euclidean distance of the feature value vectors of the facts λ_1 and λ_2. Implicit weightings of features resulting from different ranges are avoided by *standardizing* the feature values as described in [5] in more detail. If we assume a target $\wp_T$ similar to a source problem $\wp_S$ it is sensible to consider facts λ similar to at least one positive fact "at the feature level" to be positive but only if no negative facts exist whose feature values are similar to λ.

We restrict ourselves to the consideration of one positive fact, namely the fact $\lambda^+ \in P_S$ which has the smallest difference d w.r.t. λ. We do so because we cannot assume that all positive facts contain similar or even equal feature value vectors. Therefore, we would risk giving (deducible) positive facts $\lambda^+ \in P_S$ a penalty although they are the most likely to contribute to a proof of the target problem $\wp_T$. Furthermore, we do not take all negative facts into consideration. Experience shows that it is not sensible to regard the distance of negative facts which are very dissimilar to λ. This way we only use the distances of the k ($k \in \mathbb{N}$, $k > 0$) nearest negative facts w.r.t. a fact λ whose usefulness we want to estimate. Let $d_1, \ldots, d_k$ be these distances. Using a constant factor $f_{pen} \in \mathbb{R}$ our realization of the function ω_1 is as follows:

$$\omega_1(\lambda) = \left\lfloor f_{pen} \cdot \frac{\min\{d(\lambda, \lambda^+) : \lambda^+ \in P_S\}}{1 + \sum_{j=1}^{k} (2^{-j} \cdot d_j)} \right\rfloor$$

The factor f_{pen} controls the redundancy still remaining if we try to solve $\wp_S$ with (ω_1-specialization) $\mathcal{H}_{\omega_1}$ within the limits given by the ability of the features to distinguish the negative from the positive facts. This means that an increase of f_{pen} can at most result in an e_{max}-consistency with proof experience $\mathcal{E}$ where e_{max} is the percentage of negative facts containing a different feature value vector from all positive facts. Note that it is sensible to allow for some redundancy (even if possibly $e_{max} = 100$) since it could be the case that a fact λ is needed although it is a rather high distance away from positive facts. If we do not allow for some redundancy this possibly causes a rather large factor f_{pen}. But this can result in a weight $\mathcal{H}_{\omega_1}(\lambda)$ that makes an activation of λ impossible within an acceptable amount of time. Therefore, we try to find a compromise between a sufficient degree of specialization and flexibility.

In order to find an appropriate setting of f_{pen} we consider the value e_{max} that is the maximal value e that allows for an e-consistency of $\mathcal{H}_{\omega_1}$ w.r.t. $\mathcal{E}$. If this value e_{max} is rather low it is sensible to fully exploit the given potential for eliminating negative facts from the search for the source proof. But if e_{max} is rather high it could be better to allow for more redundancy. A possible compromise is to use $e_{f_s} = \min\{e_{max}, e_f\}$ for a given constant $e_f < 100$. Utilizing e_{f_s} a possible method is to set f_{pen} as the minimal factor that allows for an ω_1-specialization of $\mathcal{H}$ that is e_{f_s}-consistent with $\mathcal{E}$. In our experiments settings of e_f in the range of $[70; 90]$ reached the best results.

Learning a Weighted Distance Measure: Since we want to estimate the quality of a fact λ by using its feature value vector the technique previously used is surely justified. But our technical realization can be furthermore improved. Indeed, we have developed a measure without implicit weightings of features but we do not explicitly consider the importance of certain features according to their ability to distinguish positive from negative facts. Hence, we should try to use an *explicit weighting* of features w.r.t. their assumed importance. This way we use the distance measure $d_{a_1,\ldots,a_n} : \mathcal{O} \times \mathcal{O} \to \mathbb{R}$ parameterized by $(a_1,\ldots,a_n) \in \mathbb{N}^n$ when using features $f_1,\ldots,f_n$. It is defined by $d_{a_1,\ldots,a_n}(\lambda_1,\lambda_2) = (\sum_{i=1}^{n} a_i(x_i - y_i)^2)^{\frac{1}{2}}$ if $FV(\lambda_1) = (x_1,\ldots,x_n)$ and $FV(\lambda_2) = (y_1,\ldots,y_n)$. Important features can get a higher influence on the distance value than less important features by giving them a higher coefficient. Furthermore, features f_i associated with coefficient a_i with $a_i = 0$ can be neglected so as to contribute to a higher degree of abstraction compared with the method described above. The use of $d_{a_1,\ldots,a_n}$ also offers some advantages w.r.t. the computation time when compared with d. Since we can define the coefficients in such a way that a small (Euclidean) distance to negative facts (which are distinguishable from positive facts) results in a high distance, no explicit consideration of negative facts is needed. Altogether, a possible realization of a penalty function ω_2 is

$$\omega_2(\lambda) = \lfloor \min\{d_{a_1,\ldots,a_n}(\lambda,\lambda^+) : \lambda^+ \in P_S\}\rfloor$$

Using this realization the coefficients control the importance of distinct features as well as the remaining redundancy when proving the source problem $\wp_S$. Finally, we have to discuss how an appropriate setting of the coefficients $a_1,\ldots,a_n$ can be achieved. It is clear that this setting should not be chosen by a human reasoner but has to be learned automatically. Due to the lack of space we cannot explain our method in detail. But in order to give a rough idea how to compute coefficients we should clarify what the "importance" of a feature means. A feature f is said to be important if it is able to distinguish the negative from the positive facts w.r.t. the feature values of f. Hence, if a small increase in the coefficient associated with a feature f results in a rather high increase of the values $\omega_2(\lambda)$ of a high number of negative facts f can be considered to be quite important. For a more detailed description of our method we refer to [6] where a similar technique is used to compute coefficients for a heuristic that weights distances between feature values of facts and so-called permissible feature values. Similar to our first method the algorithm for computing coefficients uses a parameter e_f. This constant is responsible for controlling the percentage of negative facts that disappear from the search for the source proof which is carried out with $\mathcal{H}_{\omega_2}$ as described before.

Abstraction from Positive Feature Value Vectors: Similar to the previous technique we want to recognize relevant features in order to construct a penalty function ω_3 that rates the distance of a fact λ to the nearest positive fact $\lambda^+ \in P_S$ w.r.t. the relevant features. But compared with the technique described above we even want to pay more attention to the source proof in order to learn an appropriate distance measure. This way we try to find out for *every positive fact* which deviations from its feature value vector can cause problems and which are harmless. The central idea is only to penalize deviations from "positive feature value vectors" that are quite similar to the feature values of negative facts. This idea is similar to the concepts applied to find the coefficients $a_1, \ldots, a_n$ of our second method but here we want to consider each positive fact separately.

This way we abstract from the actual positive facts and only represent each of them by one "positive (contiguous) area" containing the positive fact. The facts in these areas all are considered to be positive. As implied above the construction of these positive areas is influenced by the negative facts. We are interested in a rather high abstraction from a positive fact that is consistent with the negative facts, i.e. no negative fact should be contained in a positive area. The function ω_3 is intended to rate the distance of a fact to the nearest positive area instead of the distance to the nearest positive fact.

In order to substantiate these abstract principles we should at first choose an appropriate structure of a positive area. We have chosen the approach to represent a positive area $A_{\lambda+}$ associated with a positive fact λ^+ in the following way (assuming features $f_1, \ldots, f_n$): $A_{\lambda+} = A_{\lambda+, a_1, \ldots, a_n, \epsilon} = \{\lambda \in \mathcal{O} : \sum_{i=1}^{n} a_i \cdot (f_i(\lambda^+) - f_i(\lambda))^2 \leq \epsilon^2\}$.[1] It holds $a_i \in \mathbb{R}$, $a_i \geq 0$, $1 \leq i \leq n$, and $\epsilon \in \mathbb{R}$, $\epsilon \geq 0$. If $a_i > 0$, $\forall i \in \{1, \ldots, n\}$, then $A_{\lambda+}$ represents all facts whose feature value vectors are placed in the n-dimensional ellipse that is parameterized by $a_1, \ldots, a_n$, ϵ and its center $FV(\lambda^+)$. Note, however, that it is explicitly allowed to use $a_i = 0$ for a feature f_i. In this way we can completely abstract from some features in order to measure distances to certain positive facts.

In order to define a penalty function ω_3 we assume the existence of a positive area $A_{\lambda+}$ for each positive fact $\lambda^+ \in P_S$. A possible definition of ω_3 is

$$\omega_3(\lambda) = \lfloor \min\{d_A(\lambda, A_{\lambda+}) : \lambda^+ \in P_S\} \rfloor$$

d_A is a distance measure based on features where $d_A(\lambda^+, A_{\lambda+}) = 0 \ \forall \lambda^+ \in P_S$. Altogether, our definition of ω_3 allows for proof specializations of given source proofs. In the sequel we shall show how positive areas can be learned and how to construct an appropriate distance measure d_A.

At first we want to take a closer look at the construction of positive areas. A positive area $A_{\lambda+}$, $\lambda^+ \in P_S$, is defined by the parameters $a_1, \ldots, a_n$ and ϵ. Thus we are looking for settings of these parameters. A sensible method is to displace the learning of $A_{\lambda+}$ to the maximization of a function $\varphi_{\lambda+} = \varphi_{\lambda+}(a_1, \ldots, a_n, \epsilon)$. The function value of $\varphi_{\lambda+}$ should measure the degree of abstraction from λ^+ that is consistent with the negative facts. Since the size of the set $A_{\lambda+}$ is usually infinite we have to use another value in order to measure the degree of abstraction from λ^+ obtained by using $A_{\lambda+}$. Thus we use a value that approximates the size of the n-dimensional ellipse defined by $FV(\lambda^+)$, $a_1, \ldots, a_n$ and ϵ. We define

$$\varphi_{\lambda+}(a_1, \ldots, a_n, \epsilon) = \begin{cases} \frac{\epsilon^n}{\prod_{i=1}^{n}(\sqrt{a_i}+1)} & ; A_{\lambda+, a_1, \ldots, a_n, \epsilon} \cap N_S = \emptyset \\ 0 & ; otherwise \end{cases}$$

---

[1] Naturally, the coefficients $a_1, \ldots, a_n, \epsilon$ belong to a certain $\lambda^+ \in P_S$ but in the following we will not make this dependency explicit.

$\varphi_{\lambda^+}(a_1, \ldots, a_n, \epsilon)$ is large if the corresponding area $A_{\lambda^+, a_1, \ldots, a_n, \epsilon}$ is large and contains only positive facts. We have used a simulated annealing algorithm SA in order to learn coefficients separately for each positive fact. This algorithm starts to learn $a_1, \ldots, a_n$, ϵ for a fixed positive fact λ^+ with the initial setting $a_1 = \ldots = a_n = 1$. ϵ is set to the greatest value that satisfies that no negative fact is contained in A_{λ^+}. We restricted the solution space of the following maximization process performed by the SA to a discrete universe (a $n+1$-dimensional regular grid) that contains the initial setting.

In order to construct a distance measure d_A we rate the distance between a fact λ and an area A_{λ^+} with the help of the Euclidean distance between "$FV(\lambda)$ and the ellipses defined by A_{λ^+}". It is impossible to give here an exact definition of the measure. Similar to the previous method the learning process of d_A is controlled by a parameter e_f which limits the degree of e-consistency reached by the ω_3-specialization $\mathcal{H}_{\omega_3}$ w.r.t. the proof experience $\mathcal{E}$.

5 Features in the Area of Equational Deduction

In this section we briefly introduce equational reasoning by unfailing completion. We have chosen this area to evaluate our concepts with some experiments. Since the techniques presented before heavily depend on the quality of the features we discuss afterwards how features should be construed within the context of equational reasoning.

5.1 Unfailing Completion

Equational reasoning deals with the following problem: Does it hold $Ax \models u = v$ for a given set $Ax = \{s_i = t_i : 1 \leq i \leq n, n \in \mathbb{N}\}$ of equations (of terms over a fixed signature sig) and a goal $u = v$? The completion method by Knuth and Bendix ([8], extended to unfailing completion, [3]) has proven to be quite successful for solving this problem.

Basically, completion uses the extension rule *critical-pair-generation* and the contraction rule *reduction*. A basis for the completion procedure is a so-called reduction ordering $\succ$ that is used to restrict the applicability of the inference rules and avoids cycles. Both, critical-pair-generation and reduction depend heavily on the reduction ordering to be applied during the completion process. To solve problems algorithmically using unfailing completion an algorithm based on the principles described in section 2 is applicable. It is possible to realize the completion procedure in such a way that the only indeterminism that remains is which generated critical pair should be used for further inferences.

5.2 Features for Equations

In order to construct features for equations we should take care that the equational relation is symmetric. The equations $u = v$ and $v = u$ should obtain equal feature value vectors. But we should not neglect the fact that equations can become oriented equations (rules) during the proof process. This is important since we should not, e.g., make two rules $l \rightarrow r$ and $l' \rightarrow r'$ equal (or similar) at the abstraction level of feature value vectors even if l and r' as well as r and l' are quite similar. Considering the role the rules can play in the proof process (especially if l and l' as well as r and r' are quite dissimilar) they should not contain similar feature values. Thus a feature should on the one hand ignore the physical ordering of the equations produced by the deduction system. But on the other hand a feature should take the reduction ordering into account.

We choose the approach to *standardize* the equations according to the used reduction ordering, and then use the standardized equations in order to compute feature values. The process of standardizing an equation is carried out by reordering the equation w.r.t. a total ordering of terms. Let $\succ$ be a fixed reduction ordering. Furthermore, let $\rho_\succ$ be a relation on the given set of terms that includes $\succ$ ($\succ\,\subseteq\,\rho_\succ$). Moreover, it should hold for $u \not\equiv v$ that $\rho_\succ(u,v)$ or $\rho_\succ(v,u)$ but not both (simultaneously). $\rho_\succ$ can easily be defined using $\succ$ and any total ordering defined on terms used to orient equations which are not orientable by $\succ$. Using $\rho_\succ$ we define $Norm_{\rho_\succ}(u = v) = (u = v)$ if $u \equiv v$ or $\rho_\succ(u,v)$ and $Norm_{\rho_\succ}(u = v) = (v = u)$ otherwise. We define standardized features $f_{\rho_\succ}$ according to a feature f by $f_{\rho_\succ}(u = v) = f(Norm_{\rho_\succ}(u = v))$.

If $\succ$ denotes the reduction ordering used to prove the chosen source problem it is sensible to choose a reduction ordering $\succ'\supseteq\succ$ in order to solve a similar though not equal target problem. This is necessary in order to allow for similar inferences as well for the use of the feature values to estimate whether facts, similar to positive facts at the feature level, can contribute to inferences similar to the positive inferences of the source proof.

Finally, we want to give a brief overview of the features which we have used. The features only consider syntactical properties of the given facts. Altogether, we used 15 fixed features and 4 feature schemata applied for each function symbol. Due to lack of space we cannot describe the features we used in detail. An example of a feature is the number of function symbols introduced by an (oriented) equation. A feature scheme is, e.g. the number of occurrences of a specific function symbol in an equation.

6 Experiments with DISCOUNT

We carried out several experiments with the equational prover DISCOUNT. We report on experiments in the domains of Robbins algebra and group theory of the TPTP library [13] v.1.2.1 (ROB and GRP domain). We tried to solve the problems in both domains that are not solvable with conventional heuristics of DISCOUNT within 10 minutes using a SPARCstation 10 ("hard problems"). A comparison with the renowned OTTER prover [10] demonstrates the quality of our learning approach.

Methodology: In order to use the concepts previously introduced source proofs are needed that are in a way similar to the target problems that we want to solve. In general it is a non trivial task to choose a source problem appropriate for a given target problem. But since we only apply a heuristical reuse of proofs the choice of a source problem is not as problematic as if we had chosen a "constructive" approach.

Therefore, in order to solve the 13 (universally quantified) problems of the ROB domain that are not solvable with a conventional DISCOUNT heuristic we

Table 1. Results in the ROB and GRP domain ("hard" problems)

GRP domain	OTTER	$max_{\omega_1^G}$	$max_{\omega_2^G}$	$max_{\omega_3^G}$
successes	3	15	15	15
acc. runtime	15008	8082	7992	8412
'winner'	3	4	11	0
ROB domain	OTTER	$add_{\omega_1^R}$	$add_{\omega_2^R}$	$add_{\omega_3^R}$
successes	6	4	4	5
acc. runtime	4426	5600	5479	4859
'winner'	5	0	0	1

used only one source proof, namely ROB003-1 which is the hardest problem solvable by the conventional *add* heuristic. *add* simply counts the number of functions and variables of an equation. Similarly, in the GRP domain (more exactly in the area of lattice ordered groups) we chose only the proof for problem GRP179-1. We can specialize the heuristic *max* in this proof. *max* computes the maximum of the weights of the left hand side and right hand side of an equation where weight corresponds to the number of functions and variables. In the area of "standard" groups DISCOUNT only fails for two problems which also remained unsolved after employing learned heuristics. Hence, in the following we only consider the 28 problems in the area of lattice ordered groups that cannot be solved with conventional DISCOUNT heuristics (within 10 minutes).

Outgoing from the proof of ROB003-1, obtained using *add*, we learned three penalty functions ω_1^R, ω_2^R, and ω_3^R according to the three techniques developed before. Although one can construct 100-consistent ω_i^R-specializations of *add*, $i = 1, 2, 3$, we allowed for some redundancy by using $e_f = 80$ when learning the penalty functions. This setting performed best in our experiments. Similarly, we specialized *max* in the proof of GRP179-1. The learning process was executed using $e_f = 80$. We learned the penalty functions ω_1^G, ω_2^G, and ω_3^G.

Experimental Results: The heuristics $add_{\omega_i^R}$ and $max_{\omega_i^G}$ were applied to perform experiments in the ROB and GRP domain, respectively. The orderings used for the target problems are equal to the orderings used to solve their related source problems (lexicographical path orderings). Table 1 gives an overview about our results. For each domain we depict the number of successful proof runs and the accumulated run time (in seconds) counting failures with 600 seconds. All times are measured on a SPARCstation 10. The entry of the row 'winner' denotes the number of proof runs in which the learned heuristics or OTTER performed better than the other techniques.

Altogether, we can improve the performance of DISCOUNT significantly. Although OTTER still performs better than our learning approach in the area of Robbins algebra we could increase the number of successful proofs of DISCOUNT in this area from 5 to 10. Now the success rate of DISCOUNT almost reaches that from OTTER (11 problems solved). We can also improve the results of DISCOUNT in the GRP domain. Using the conventional heuristics and the learned heuristics we are now able to solve 93 of 105 problems in the area of lattice ordered groups (78 problems solved without learning). OTTER can only solve 79 problems.

Comparing our different techniques one can see that neither technique is consistently better than the other. But a general tendency is that heuristics based on ω_1 or ω_2 seem to show a higher degree of specialization. Therefore they perform fairly well in the area of lattice ordered groups where the problems are more similar than in the robbins algebra. But in some cases where more flexibility is needed (to allow for deviations from the source proof) ω_3 improves on the performance of the other heuristics by offering a higher degree of abstraction from the positive facts. Therefore, the use of this penalty functions allows for the construction of heuristics in the domain of robbins algebra that are clearly superior to the heuristics based on the other simpler learning schemes.

7 Conclusions and Future Work

We have presented a framework for flexible proof-replay with heuristics. We substantiated this framework by the development of three realizations based on features. Experiments in two domains underline the applicability of our approach. Although DISCOUNT is clearly inferior to OTTER when its inference rate is considered, we nearly achieved the results of OTTER in the ROB domain in which DISCOUNT performed quite badly before. This, together with the fact that we could solve problems in the GRP domain that were out of range before, is a sign that our approach is well suited for controlling theorem provers.

An interesting topic for future work is the use of techniques other than features to learn appropriate penalty functions. The use of connectionist approaches is imaginable. The so-called *folding architecture* together with the *backpropagation through structure* learning scheme [7] seems to be appropriate to allow for an even better learning of penalty functions.

References

1. **Avenhaus, J.; Denzinger, J.; Fuchs, Matt.**: DISCOUNT: *A system for distributed equational deduction*, Proc. 6th RTA, Kaiserslautern, FRG, 1995, LNCS 914, pp. 397–402.
2. **Brock, B.; Cooper, S.; Pierce, W.**: *Analogical reasoning and proof discovery*, Proc. CADE 9, Argonne, IL, USA, 1988, LNCS 310, pp. 454–468.
3. **Bachmair, L. ; Dershowitz, N. ; Plaisted, D.A.**: *Completion without Failure*, Coll. on the Resolution of Equations in Algebraic Structures, Austin (1987), Academic Press , 1989.
4. **Cover, T.M. ; Hart P.E.**: *Nearest Neighbor pattern classification*, IEEE, Transactions on Information Theory 13, pp. 21-27, 1967.
5. **Fuchs, M.**: *Flexible Proof-Replay with Heuristics*, LSA-Report, LSA-97-03E, University of Kaiserslautern, 1997.
6. **Fuchs, Matt.**: *Experiments in the Heuristic Use of Past Proof Experience*, Proc. CADE 13, New Brunswick, NJ, USA, 1996.
7. **Goller, C. ; Küchler, A.**: Learning Task-Dependent Distributed Representations by Backpropagation Through Structure, Proc. ICNN-96, 1996.
8. **Knuth, D.E. ; Bendix, P.B.**: *Simple Word Problems in Universal Algebra*, Computational Algebra, J. Leech, Pergamon Press, 1970, pp. 263-297.
9. **Kolbe, T.; Walther, C.**: *Reusing proofs*, Proc. 11th ECAI '94, Amsterdam, HOL, 1994, pp. 80–84.
10. **McCune, W.W.**: *OTTER 3.0 reference manual and guide*, Techn. report ANL-94/6, Argonne Natl. Laboratory, 1994.
11. **Owen, S.**: *Analogy for automated reasoning*, Academic Press, 1990.
12. **Suttner, C.; Ertel, W.**: *Automatic acquisition of search-guiding heuristics*, Proc. CADE 10, Kaiserslautern, FRG, 1990, LNAI 449, pp. 470–484.
13. **Sutcliffe, G.; Suttner, C.B.; Yemenis, T.**: *The TPTP Problem Library*, Proc. CADE 12, Nancy, Springer LNAI 814, pp. 252-266, 1994

Flexible Re-enactment of Proofs*

Matthias Fuchs

Center for Learning Systems and Applications (LSA)
Fachbereich Informatik, Universität Kaiserslautern
Postfach 3049, 67653 Kaiserslautern, Germany
E-mail: fuchs@informatik.uni-kl.de

Abstract. We present a method for making use of past proof experience called flexible re-enactment (FR). FR is actually a search-guiding heuristic that uses past proof experience to create a search bias. Given a proof $\mathcal{P}$ of a problem solved previously that is assumed to be similar to the current problem $\mathcal{A}$, FR *searches* for $\mathcal{P}$ and in the "neighborhood" of $\mathcal{P}$ in order to find a proof of $\mathcal{A}$.
This heuristic use of past experience has certain advantages that make FR quite profitable and give it a wide range of applicability. Experimental studies substantiate and illustrate this claim.

1 Introduction

Automated deduction is essentially a search problem that gives rise to potentially infinite search spaces because of general undecidability. Despite these unfavorable conditions state-of-the-art theorem provers have gained a remarkable level of performance mainly due to (problem-specific) search-guiding heuristics and advanced implementation techniques. Nevertheless theorem provers can hardly rival a mathematician when it comes to proving "challenging" theorems. The main reason for this fact is also a major shortcoming of theorem provers: Unlike humans, theorem provers lack the ability to learn. Learning, however, is a key ability in any form of human problem solving, in particular in theorem proving.

The necessity to equip theorem provers with learning capabilities has been recognized quite early. But learning for theorem proving causes much more difficulties than learning in other areas of artificial intelligence because the premise that *"small changes of the problem cause small changes of its solution"* is not fulfilled at all. In theorem proving tiny variations of a problem specification can result in significant changes of the solution (proof). This circumstance complicates matters substantially.

Learning methods based on analogous proof transformation (e.g., [3, 2, 14, 18]) basically attempt to transform a *source proof* of a *source problem* solved previously into a *target proof* of a given *target problem* to be solved. Mostly, the mainly *deterministic* transformation procedure centers on some kind of analogy mapping obtained by comparing source and target problem. The transformation

---

* This work was supported by the *Deutsche Forschungsgemeinschaft (DFG)*.

may include abstraction and planning steps. Occasionally, a little search may be involved in order to patch failures of the transformation procedure (e.g., [2]).

The prevailing determinism has the advantage that analogous proof transformation can be quite fast. The downside, however, is that source and target problem have to be very similar so that the source proof can be transformed into a target proof mainly with deterministic actions. For this reason, methods based on analogous proof transformation are preferably applied to inductive theorem proving. There, the inherent proof structures provide a suitable platform for such methods. However, for theorem proving in domains without any (recognizable) structure, these methods appear to be inappropriate.

An alternative approach to learning for theorem proving is to incorporate problem-solving experience into the search-guiding heuristic (e.g., [20, 23, 8, 11, 6]). That is, when solving a target problem, the source problem is in some way exploited by the search-guiding heuristic. The theorem prover still conducts a search, but the heuristic is biased towards a certain area of the search space depending on the source proof and on the way it is utilized by the heuristic. This approach has the advantage that the demands on similarity between source and target problem do not have to be as high as for methods based on proof transformation. Naturally we incur the usual overhead of search caused by exploring areas of the search space that do not contribute to the proof eventually found.

In this paper we investigate a method for incorporating past proof experience into a search-guiding heuristic called *flexible re-enactment* (FR). FR basically attempts to re-enact the source proof *via search, if* possible. Flexibility is achieved by also searching in the "neighborhood" of the source proof or by using some "standard" (non-learning) heuristic if the trace of the source proof is (temporarily) lost. Both re-enactment and flexibility are combined in a monolithic structure that allows for shifting smoothly between flexibility and re-enactment depending on the search space encountered.

FR was first introduced in [11]. In this paper we present a systematic experimental evaluation of FR that illustrates its performance and range of applicability. Furthermore, we counter a frequent and unjustified criticism of FR, namely to be a costly disguise for adding the source proof (in the form of lemmas) to the axiomatization of the target problem.

2 Theorem Proving

Theorem provers can attempt to accomplish a task in various ways. We focus here on so-called *saturation-based theorem provers*. This type of theorem prover is very common and is employed by provers based on the resolution method (e.g., [4]) or the Knuth-Bendix completion procedure (e.g., [1]). The principle working method of such a prover is to infer facts by applying given rules of inference, starting with a given set Ax of axioms, until the *goal* λ_G (the theorem to be proved) can be shown to be a logical consequence of Ax. A proof problem $\mathcal{A}$ is hence specified by $\mathcal{A} = (Ax, \lambda_G)$.

The prover maintains two sets of facts, the set F^A of *active facts* and the set F^P of *passive* or *potential facts*. In the beginning, $F^A = \emptyset$ and $F^P = Ax$. In the *selection* or *activation step* a fact $\lambda \in F^P$ is selected, removed from F^P, and put into F^A unless there is a fact $\lambda' \in F^A$ that subsumes λ (in symbols $\lambda' \lhd \lambda$) in which case λ is simply discarded. Note that $\lambda \equiv \lambda'$ (syntactic identity modulo renaming variables) implies $\lambda' \lhd \lambda$ (and of course $\lambda \lhd \lambda'$). If λ is indeed activated (put into F^A), all (finitely many) inferences involving λ are applied exhaustively, and inferred facts are added to F^P. Facts in F^P are so to speak known to be inferable (from F^A), but are not yet considered to be actually inferred.

The activation step is the only inherently indeterministic step in the proof procedure just sketched. Commonly, a heuristic $\mathcal{H}$ is employed to resolve the indeterminism at the (inevitable) expense of introducing search. $\mathcal{H}$ associates a natural number $\mathcal{H}(\lambda) \in \mathbb{N}$ (a *weight*) with each $\lambda \in F^P$ which is called "weighting λ with $\mathcal{H}(\lambda)$". The fact with the smallest weight $\mathcal{H}(\lambda)$ is next in line for activation. Ties are usually broken in compliance with the FIFO strategy.

The search-guiding heuristic $\mathcal{H}$ is pivotal for efficiency. The quality of $\mathcal{H}$ can be measured in terms of redundant search effort. The sequence $S \equiv \lambda_1; \ldots; \lambda_n$ of facts activated by $\mathcal{H}$ describes the search behavior of $\mathcal{H}$. Assuming that such a *search protocol* S represents a successful search, the last fact λ_n of S concluded the proof. By tracing back the application of inference rules starting with λ_n we can identify all those facts that actually contributed to concluding the proof. These facts are called *positive facts* and are collected in the set P of positive facts. The remaining facts constitute the set N of negative facts and represent redundant search effort. The set P obtained when solving a source problem represents past proof experience. It is utilized by FR as described in the following section in order to reduce redundant search effort.

3 Flexible Re-enactment

Similarity between two proof problems A and B can occur in many variations. For instance, a considerable number of the facts that contribute to a proof of A are also useful for proving B (or vice versa). This means in our terminology that the associated sets of positive facts share many facts. FR attempts to exploit such a similarity.

Assuming that a target problem $\mathcal{A}_T$ and a source problem $\mathcal{A}_S$ are similar in the way just described, it is reasonable to concentrate on deducing facts when attempting to prove $\mathcal{A}_T$ that also played a role in finding the source proof of $\mathcal{A}_S$, namely the set P_S of positive facts. When proving $\mathcal{A}_T$, FR prefers a $\lambda \in F^P$ (by giving it a relatively small weight FR(λ)) if λ "bears significant resemblance" with a fact in P_S. Such a λ is called a *focus fact*. Depending on how strong the preference of focus facts is, FR will activate focus facts as soon as they appear in F^P and give little attention to other facts while there are focus facts. (If all source axioms occur in the target axiomatization, this essentially means that FR will re-enact the source proof.)

Although we assume the proofs of $\mathcal{A}_T$ and $\mathcal{A}_S$ to share many positive facts, a few of the facts useful for proving $\mathcal{A}_S$ may lead to focus facts that do not contribute to the proof of $\mathcal{A}_T$ eventually found. Besides the redundant search effort caused by these *irrelevant* focus facts, the crucial difficulty is to find the (non-focus) facts not needed for proving $\mathcal{A}_S$, but necessary for proving $\mathcal{A}_T$. These "missing" facts have to supplement the *relevant* focus facts, i.e., the focus facts that do contribute to the target proof. It is very likely that the missing facts are descendants[2] of relevant focus facts considering that the relevant focus facts already established the core of a proof and that there are only a few steps needed to conclude the proof. It is reasonable to assume that "taking the reasoning process a few steps further in the direction given by the focus facts", i.e., that also preferring their descendants will be profitable. Immediate descendants should be preferred the most. In the sequel we give a formal definition of FR.

3.1 Details of FR

For the definition of FR the notions 'difference' and 'distance' are pivotal. First, we define the *difference diff* between two facts λ and λ' to formalize the notion 'focus fact'.

$$diff(\lambda, \lambda') = \begin{cases} 0, & \lambda \lhd \lambda' \\ 100, & \text{otherwise.} \end{cases}$$

For the time being, we content ourselves with this simple definition of difference that centers on subsumption. Note that the values 0 and 100 are somewhat arbitrary but intuitive hints of percentages, denoting "perfect similarity" and "no similarity at all", respectively. As we shall see, the restriction of *diff* to $\mathbb{N}_{100} = \{0, 1, \dots, 100\}$ entails that all further computations will produce values from $\mathbb{N}_{100}$ which makes computations more transparent.

diff is used to find out whether a given fact λ is a focus fact. We define

$$\mathcal{D}(\lambda) = \min\left(\{diff(\lambda, \lambda') \mid \lambda' \in P_S\}\right).$$

Hence, $\mathcal{D}(\lambda)$ returns the minimal difference between a given fact λ (target) and the positive facts (source). If $\mathcal{D}(\lambda) = 0$ then λ is considered to be a focus fact, which complies with the ideas from above.

Now recall that also descendants of focus facts are to be favored. The preference given to them should, however, decrease with their distance from focus facts. The *distance* $d(\lambda)$ of a given fact λ measures distance, roughly said, in terms of the number of inference steps separating λ from ancestors which are focus facts. It depends on the distance of the immediate ancestors of λ from focus facts (if λ is not an axiom) and $\mathcal{D}(\lambda)$:

$$d(\lambda) = \begin{cases} \psi\Big(q, \mathcal{D}(\lambda)\Big), & \lambda \text{ is an axiom} \\ \psi\Big(d(\lambda_1), \mathcal{D}(\lambda)\Big), & \lambda_1 \text{ is the (only) immediate ancestor of } \lambda \\ \psi\Big(\gamma\big(d(\lambda_1), d(\lambda_2)\big), \mathcal{D}(\lambda)\Big), & \lambda_1 \text{ and } \lambda_2 \text{ are immediate ancestors of } \lambda. \end{cases}$$

---

[2] When applying an inference rule to facts $\lambda_1, \dots, \lambda_m$, thus producing a fact λ, the facts $\lambda_1, \dots, \lambda_m$ are the *(immediate) ancestors* of the *(immediate) descendant* λ.

The first argument of ψ represents the distance of the immediate ancestors. It is simply given as the distance of the immediate ancestor if there is just one immediate ancestor. If λ is an axiom (i.e., there are no ancestors), this value is specified by a parameter $q \in \mathbb{N}_{100}$. If λ has two immediate ancestors, then γ computes this value. (Note that $d(\lambda)$ is defined if λ has zero, one, or two immediate ancestors which is sufficient for most deduction systems. If the number of immediate ancestors should be in excess of two, then a weighted average of the ancestors' distances can be employed, for instance.) We chose a parameterized γ employing a parameter $q_1 \in [0; 1]$. Depending on q_1, the result of γ ranges between the minimum and the maximum of the distances of the immediate ancestors:

$$\gamma(x, y) = \min(x, y) + \lfloor q_1 \cdot (\max(x, y) - \min(x, y)) \rfloor .$$

Using $q_1 = 0$ or $q_1 = 1$, γ computes the minimum or maximum, respectively. With $q_1 = 0.5$, γ computes the (integer part of the)[3] average.

The distance of immediate ancestors (or q) and $\mathcal{D}$ are combined by ψ yielding $d(\lambda)$. ψ should—for obvious reasons—satisfy the following criteria: On the one hand, $d(\lambda)$ should be minimal (i.e., 0) if $\mathcal{D}(\lambda) = 0$, in which case λ itself is a focus fact. On the other hand, the value produced by ψ should increase (reasonably) with the values obtained from γ and $\mathcal{D}$ in order to reflect the (growing) remoteness of λ from focus facts (and, in a way, from the source proof). As a matter of fact, γ already satisfies the latter criterion. Therefore, ψ is in parts identical to γ. It also uses a parameter $q_2 \in [0; 1]$.

$$\psi(x, y) = \begin{cases} 0, & y = 0 \\ \min(x, y) + \lfloor q_2 \cdot (\max(x, y) - \min(x, y)) \rfloor, & \text{otherwise.} \end{cases}$$

The remaining task consists in designing FR so that it offers a reasonable degree of specialization in (i.e., focus on) the source proof that is paired with an acceptable degree of flexibility, i.e., the ability to cope with a target problem with a proof that requires minor to moderate deviations from the source proof. The use of d already provides sufficient specialization by directing the search towards the source proof. Its rudimentary flexibility can be enhanced by combining it with some "standard" ("general purpose") heuristic $\mathcal{H}$. Among several sensible alternatives we picked the following:

$$\text{FR}(\lambda) = (d(\lambda) + p) \cdot \mathcal{H}(\lambda), \quad p \in \mathbb{N}.$$

The parameter p controls the effect of $d(\lambda)$ on the final weight $\text{FR}(\lambda)$. $d(\lambda)$ will be dominant if $p = 0$. In this case, if $d(\lambda) = 0$, $\text{FR}(\lambda)$ will also be 0 regardless of $\mathcal{H}(\lambda)$. As p grows, $\mathcal{H}$ increasingly influences the final weight, thus mitigating the inflexibility of the underlying method, namely using $d(\lambda)$ *alone* as a measure for the suitability of a fact λ. For very large p, the influence of $d(\lambda)$ becomes negligible, and FR basically degenerates into $\mathcal{H}$.

---

[3] We restrict our computations to $\mathbb{N}$, because there is no gain in "high precision arithmetic" when dealing with weighting functions, but there would be a loss in efficiency w.r.t. computation time.

3.2 Range of Applicability

FR is most suitable in situations where each source axiom is "covered" by a target axiom, i.e., for each source axiom λ' there is a target axiom λ so that $\lambda \lhd \lambda'$. Then FR can conduct a search guided by the source proof in the sense that FR can re-enact the source proof (or a more general proof) *without search* since, for each positive fact, there will be a focus fact subsuming it. The re-enacted source proof or, more precisely, the focus facts constituting the source proof, can serve as a basis for finding the target proof by searching in the "neighborhood" of the source proof, i.e., in particular by focusing on immediate descendants of focus facts (cp. subsection 4.2, case 1). (If additionally the source goal λ_S subsumes the target goal λ_T then plain re-enactment will succeed.) Under these conditions it is sound to add the positive facts as lemmas to the target axiomatization. Therefore, FR has often been mistaken for a costly disguise for adding lemmas. Subsection 4.2 will show that this criticism is not justified. Moreover, subsection 4.2 will demonstrate that FR is also useful in case source and target axiomatizations do not agree "obviously", i.e., agreement (logical equivalence) cannot be checked with simple (syntactic) subsumption criteria. Under these conditions it is not sound to add the positive facts of the source proof to the target axiomatization because it is not known whether they are logical consequences of the target axiomatization.

Hence, FR is very versatile and covers a wide range of applicability. Nevertheless we want to point out that FR does of course not prove useful if source and target problem are not "similar enough", i.e., the sets of positive facts do not share enough facts. In other words, there are too few relevant focus facts that do not suffice to supply the core of a target proof. In addition, too many irrelevant focus facts hamper the search. (Naturally, relevant and irrelevant focus facts can only be identified at the end of a successful search.) In this case focusing on the source proof will be counterproductive. Hence it is important to find a suitable source problem. This difficulty is not addressed in this paper (see [12] or [5] instead). Here, we want to show that—when given a suitable source problem—FR allows for solving target problems that pose serious difficulties or cannot be handled at all without FR.

4 Experiments

We conducted our experimental studies with a theorem prover for problems of *condensed detachment* (CD). Subsection 4.1 explains the basics of CD and motivates this choice. We want to point out, however, that we have also successfully applied FR to equational reasoning (cp. [5]). The results of our experiments with CD are summarized in section 4.2.

4.1 Condensed Detachment

CD allows for studying logic calculi with automated deduction systems. (See [24] and [15] for motivation and a detailed theoretical background.) There is only one inference rule (also denoted by CD) that manipulates first-order terms which we shall also call facts. The set of terms (facts) $Term(\mathcal{F}, \mathcal{V})$ is defined as usual, involving a finite set $\mathcal{F}$ of function symbols and an enumerable set $\mathcal{V}$ of variables.

CD (in its basic form) is defined for a distinguished binary function symbol $f \in \mathcal{F}$. CD allows us to deduce $\sigma(t)$ from two given facts $f(s, t)$ and s' if σ is the most general unifier of s and s'. A proof problem $\mathcal{A} = (Ax, \lambda_G)$ hence consists in deducing λ_G from Ax with continuous applications of CD. Subsumption is merely a matching problem, i.e., $\lambda \lhd \lambda'$ if (and only if) there is a match σ so that $\sigma(\lambda) \equiv \lambda'$.

CD fits the theorem proving framework given in section 2. Despite the simplicity of CD the arising proof problems can be very hard, sometimes even exceeding the limits of state-of-the-art provers. Therefore, CD is widely acknowledged as a testing ground for new ideas. It has been (and still is) used for this purpose quite frequently (e.g., [19, 26, 16, 21, 27, 11]). Furthermore, CD offers problems of a varying degree of difficulty, almost continuously ranging from (nearly) trivial to (very) challenging. This constellation is important if we want to employ learning techniques (like FR).

For the experiments we used the theorem prover 'CODE' ([7]) that realizes CD based on the concepts introduced in section 2. CODE has a standard ("general purpose") heuristic $\mathcal{W}$ at its disposal that computes the weight $\mathcal{W}(\lambda)$ of a fact $\lambda \in F^P$ as $\mathcal{W}(\lambda) = c_\delta \cdot \delta(\lambda) + c_w \cdot w(\lambda)$, $c_\delta, c_w \in \mathbb{N}$. $w(\lambda)$ is equal to twice the number of function symbols occurring in λ plus the number of variables in λ. $\delta(\lambda)$ is the *level* or *depth* of λ: $\delta(\lambda) = 0$ if λ is an axiom; otherwise $\delta(\lambda)$ is the maximum of the levels of the immediate ancestors of λ plus 1. Furthermore, we set $\mathcal{W}(\lambda) = 0$ if $\lambda \lhd \lambda_G$. Consequently, facts subsuming the goal and hence concluding the proof are activated immediately (cp. [9] or [10]).

$\mathcal{W}$ is quite a successful heuristic in particular when taking into account the component δ reasonably (e.g., $c_\delta = 2$, $c_w = 1$). We use $\mathcal{W}$ as the standard heuristic required by FR, i.e., $FR(\lambda) = (d(\lambda) + p) \cdot \mathcal{W}(\lambda)$. Here, we always set the coefficients $c_\delta = 0$ and $c_w = 1$, thus ignoring the level for reasons explained in [9]. Based on extensive experiments (cp. [9]) the remaining parameters of FR are set as follows: $p = 20$, $q_1 = 0.75$, $q_2 = 0.25$, $q = 0$.

4.2 Experimental Results

We examined FR in the light of problems LCL040-1 through LCL072-1 (problems 1-33 in [16]) and problems LCL109-1 through LCL116-1 (problems 55–62 in [16]). These problems have the property emphasized in the preceding subsection which is important for learning, namely to offer a varying degree of difficulty that ranges from rather simple to challenging. They are a part of the public TPTP problem library ([22]) version 1.2.1. (Note that the problems in the TPTP are given in CNF, a form suitable for resolution-based or tableaux-oriented theorem provers. The CNF "encoding" of problems of CD is not needed for CODE.) We consider here mainly those problems that pose some difficulties for CODE when using $\mathcal{W}$ to control the search. The performance of $\mathcal{W}$ with respect to the problems above (for various settings of the parameters c_δ and c_w) was thoroughly investigated in

Table 1. Case 1.

Target	Source	FR	FFU	RFF	lemmas	lemmas*	$\mathcal{W}$
058	060	23s (519)	89%	100%	—	5s (362)	25s (710)
060	058	8s (328)	95%	93%	—	12s (533)	26s (733)
071	070	4s (235)	75%	94%	—	3s (230)	—
	072	7s (366)	58%	100%	—	3s (254)	
068	067	4s (227)	72%	95%	2s (193)	2s (225)	68s (982)
	069	20s (629)	77%	100%	—	—	
114	113	3s (234)	83%	91%	12s (513)	10s (482)	—
116	113	5s (314)	78%	95%	14s (541)	10s (492)	—

[9] (see also [10]) and compared with the performance of the renowned theorem prover OTTER ([17]) as reported in [16]. This comparison showed that $\mathcal{W}$ can control the search so well that CODE clearly outperforms OTTER even though CODE is inferior to OTTER in terms of inferences per second. Therefore, it is not easy at all for FR to improve on $\mathcal{W}$.

In the sequel we examine the three interesting cases regarding the axiomatizations and the goals of target and source problems $\mathcal{A}_T = (Ax_T, \lambda_T)$ and $\mathcal{A}_S = (Ax_S, \lambda_S)$:

1. Identical axiomatization ($Ax_T = Ax_S$), but different goals (i.e., neither $\lambda_S \lhd \lambda_T$ nor $\lambda_T \lhd \lambda_S$);
2. Different axiomatizations (Ax_T and Ax_S may share some axioms, but one axiomatization is not a subset of the other), but the same goal ($\lambda_S \lhd \lambda_T$);
3. Different axiomatizations and different goals;

(We omit the fourth case "*the same axiomatization and the same goal*" because then plain re-enactment suffices and always succeeds very fast.)

Note that only for case 1 it is sound to add positive facts of the source proof as lemmas to Ax_T. Therefore, we shall consider this possibility only for case 1. Table 1 displays our experiments concerning case 1. The first two columns list target and source problems, respectively. (The names are abbreviated, e.g., 058 instead of LCL058-1.) The source problems were chosen according to some simple, automatable criteria. (This is not a relevant issue in this paper. See [12] instead.) Note that we employed source proofs found by $\mathcal{W}$ whenever possible in order to avoid creating particularly similar proofs with FR. For instance, we did *not* use the proof of LCL058-1 found by FR using a proof of LCL060-1 when proving LCL060-1 with FR (and source LCL058-1).

The results of FR are given in column 'FR'. The entries display run-time (approximate CPU time in seconds obtained on a SPARCstation 10) and the number of activation steps (i.e., the length of the search protocol) in parentheses. This number gives us a rough idea of the search effort. (The length of the search protocol usually does not correlate well with the length of the proof eventually found. This is also not an issue here since we are only interested in *some* proof, not necessarily a short one.)

Column 'FFU' shows the "focus fact usage", i.e., the share (relevant) focus facts have of the target proof, given as an approximate percentage. Column 'RFF' shows the share which facts that account for relevant focus facts have of the source proof. This value hence gives us an idea of how many facts of the source proof proved useful for finding the target proof. Consider, for instance, target problem LCL071-1 and source problem LCL070-1. The target proof consists of 20 facts. 15 of the 20 facts are focus facts. Hence, FFU is $15/20 = 75\%$. These 15 relevant focus facts go back to 15 facts in the source proof. Since 16 facts constitute the source proof, RFF is $15/16 \approx 94\%$.

The values of RFF listed in table 1 indicate that it is important that RFF is rather high. Given case 1 (equal source and target axiomatization) this is understandable considering that the share $100\% - \text{RFF}$ of the source proof will definitely give rise to irrelevant focus facts that may disarrange the search. Large values of FFU indicate that a large part of the target proof goes back to re-enactment and hence could be found rather efficiently.

When adding the positive facts of the source proof as lemmas to the axiomatization of the target problem, CoDE employed $\mathcal{W}$ with $c_\delta = 2$ and $c_w = 1$ to guide the search. (This parameter setting turned out to be generally useful during the experiments reported on in [9].) The results of utilizing lemmas in this manner are listed in column 'lemmas'. The entries again show run-time and length of the search protocol. The entry '—' signifies that no proof was found within one hour.

A slight modification of lemma usage is to assign the weight 0 to all axioms (including added lemmas) so that they are immediately activated. Column 'lemmas*' shows that this modification is crucial in order to make adding lemmas competitive. The improvements are understandable because we can thus coerce re-enactment and hence simulate the obviously profitable re-enactment part of FR. Nonetheless, table 1 does not reveal any significant advantage of adding lemmas compared to FR. As a matter of fact, adding lemmas can cause a failure when FR still succeeds (cp. target LCL068-1, source LCL069-1). An opposite observation (failure of FR, success of adding lemmas) has so far not been made. This leads us to conclude that the "hierarchical" search induced by the distance measure d is pivotal. (Note, however, that the component δ of $\mathcal{W}$ (switched off for FR) also allows for taking into account distance or depth, but in a much cruder way than d does. Basically, the ancestor with maximal depth determines the depth of a descendant. The depth of the other ancestor has no effect.)

The last column of table 1 lists the results of $\mathcal{W}$ as a point of reference. The generally useful parameter setting ($c_\delta = 2$ and $c_w = 1$) fails for all target problems of table 1 (and also of tables 2 and 3). (Recall that the selected problems are the ones that cause difficulties for $\mathcal{W}$.) The successful runs of $\mathcal{W}$ were obtained with $c_\delta = 0$ and $c_w = 1$—the setting that also FR employs. These experiments show that FR enables CoDE to prove problems quite fast which it could not handle with $\mathcal{W}$ and one of the two mentioned parameter settings. (There are,

Table 2. Case 2.

Target	Source	FR	FFU	RFF	$\mathcal{W}$
054	042	118s	31%	79%	—
058	045	4s	23%	82%	25s
045	058	< 1s	95%	51%	—
042	054	< 1s	84%	55%	—

Table 3. Case 3.

Target	Source	FR	FFU	RFF	$\mathcal{W}$
042	058	—	—	—	—
	060	126s	82%	95%	
045	060	22s	76%	41%	—
058	042	18s	20%	42%	25s
060	042	—	—	—	26s
	045	11s	18%	82%	

however, two different and very problem-specific parameter settings for problems LCL068-1 and LCL071-1 that allow $\mathcal{W}$ to prove these problems. See [9].)

Experiments regarding cases 2 and 3 are summarized by tables 2 and 3. These tables are organized like table 1 without the columns concerning lemmas since the soundness of adding lemmas is—as mentioned earlier—not guaranteed for cases 2 and 3. As a matter of fact, for case 2 adding lemmas is completely pointless since the goal itself would be added as a lemma.

Considering tables 2 and 3 we can again observe that FR allows CoDe to solve problems rather quickly which were out of reach when using $\mathcal{W}$. The two bottom rows of table 2 indicate that FR can also cope with situations where large parts of the target proof go back to quite a small part of the source proof (i.e., large FFU, but rather small RFF). Note that—due to different axiomatizations—it is not necessarily the case that the share 100% − RFF of the source proof entails irrelevant focus facts. The results concerning problems LCL042-1, LCL058-1, and LCL060-1 in different roles as source and target problems (cp. tables 1 and 2) reveal that—quite expectedly—FR is not "symmetric". That is, a proof of a problem A found by FR when using a source problem B does not guarantee to find a proof of B when using A as source.

Due to space limitations we cannot present proof listings which illustrate properties of FR. See [13] instead.

5 Discussion

We presented a method called flexible re-enactment (FR) that exploits past proof experience with heuristic means. When searching for the (target) proof of a given proof problem, FR *attempts* to re-enact a given source proof by *searching* for the facts that constitute the source proof. Flexibility is achieved by also searching in the "neighborhood" of the source proof, i.e., by also preferring descendants of the facts constituting the source proof. Experiments have demonstrated that FR allows for solving problems that could not be handled before.

The similarity between the source and target proof required so that FR or in other words a "flexible, search-based re-enactment of the source proof" can succeed is basically reflected by the number (or percentage) of facts constituting the source proof that are also useful for a target proof: the more, the better. But such a kind of similarity can only be assessed *a posteriori*. Hence, *a priori* similarity can only be estimated with "heuristic indicators" such as, for instance, the percentage of source axioms that are also present in the target axiomatization. Simple, easy to check criteria like this can already produce remarkable results (cp. [12]) which supports our belief that selecting an appropriate source problem can be automated reasonably (see also [5]). Naturally, in order to be independent of symbol names, methods for finding a suitable renaming of symbols must be available (cf. [5]). Thus, for FR similarity is kind of a "loosely" defined notion that perforce cannot and does not play as important a role as it does, e.g., in [14]. There, similarity is a clearly defined central notion, but—probably a common trade-off—restricts applicability.

FR is not limited to the use of just one source proof. The design of FR allows us to exploit an arbitrary number of source proofs. But the usefulness of more than one source proof is questionable ("a jack of all trades, but master of none"). Redundant search effort might become a problem that outweighs possible advantages like having available more focus facts which undoubtedly increases the chance of having the "right" ones. Nonetheless, exploiting a pool of proof experience rather than one piece also has certain advantages (cp. [6] where sophisticated abstraction techniques are used).

Finally, FR can of course also be employed for *proof checking* and *proof completion*. Proof checking corresponds to plain re-enactment. Proof completion means that the given positive facts represent the "skeleton" of a source proof with a few intermediate steps missing. Under these conditions the positive facts will give rise only to relevant focus facts. Thus, FR can search for the missing intermediate steps *without* being confused and possibly misguided by irrelevant focus facts which makes things easier than in general applications of FR.

In [25] the *hints strategy* (HS) has been investigated as to its usefulness for proof checking, proof completion, and also for proof finding. Hints basically are the counterparts of the positive facts of a source proof. HS and FR have commonalities, but also have different features and design concepts. In order to search for (or complete) a proof with certain properties, HS also allows for *avoiding* (instead of focusing on) hints—a feature that was not an objective when designing FR. But when it comes to searching for a (target) proof without such constraints, FR subsumes HS in particular because of its ability to deal sensibly with non-focus facts that are descendants of focus facts, thus exploiting a source proof beyond mere re-enactment—a concept not present in HS.

References

1. **Bachmair, L.; Dershowitz, N.; Plaisted, D.**: *Completion without Failure*, Coll. on the Resolution of Equations in Algebraic Structures, Austin, TX, USA (1987), Academic Press, 1989.
2. **Brock, B.; Cooper, S.; Pierce, W.**: *Analogical Reasoning and Proof Discovery*, Proc. CADE-9, Argonne, IL, USA, 1988, Springer LNCS 310, pp. 454–468.
3. **Bundy, A.**: *The Use of Explicit Plans to Guide Inductive Proofs*, Proc. CADE-9, Argonne, IL, USA, 1988, Springer LNCS 310, pp. 111–120.

4. **Chang, C.L.; Lee, R.C.**: *Symbolic Logic and Mechanical Theorem Proving*, Academic Press, 1973.

5. **Denzinger, J.; Fuchs, M.; Fuchs, Marc**: *High Performance ATP Systems by Combining Several AI Methods*, SEKI Report SR-96-09, University of Kaiserslautern, 1996, http://www.uni-kl.de/AG-AvenhausMadlener/fuchs.html.

6. **Denzinger, J.; Schulz, S.**: *Learning Domain Knowledge to Improve Theorem Proving*, Proc. CADE-13, New Brunswick, NJ, USA, 1996, Springer LNAI 1104, pp. 62–76.

7. **Fuchs, D.; Fuchs, M.**: *CODE: A Powerful Prover for Problems of Condensed Detachment*, Proc. CADE-14, Townsville, AUS, 1997, Springer LNAI, to appear.

8. **Fuchs, M.**: *Learning Proof Heuristics by Adapting Parameters*, Proc. 12th ICML, Tahoe City, CA, USA, 1995, Morgan Kaufmann, pp. 235–243.

9. **Fuchs, M.**: *Experiments in the Heuristic Use of Past Proof Experience*, SEKI Report SR-95-10, University of Kaiserslautern, 1996, obtainable via WWW at http://www.uni-kl.de/AG-AvenhausMadlener/fuchs.html.

10. **Fuchs, M.**: *Powerful Search Heuristics Based on Weighted Symbols, Level, and Features*, Proc. FLAIRS-96, Key West, FL, USA, 1996, pp. 449–453.

11. **Fuchs, M.**: *Experiments in the Heuristic Use of Past Proof Experience*, Proc. CADE-13, New Brunswick, NJ, USA, 1996, Springer LNAI 1104, pp. 523–537.

12. **Fuchs, M.**: *Towards Full Automation of Deduction: A Case Study*, SEKI Report SR-96-07, University of Kaiserslautern, 1996, obtainable via WWW at http://www.uni-kl.de/AG-AvenhausMadlener/fuchs.html.

13. **Fuchs, M.**: *Flexible Re-enactment of Proofs*, SEKI Report SR-97-01, Univ. of Kaiserslautern, 1997, http://www.uni-kl.de/AG-AvenhausMadlener/fuchs.html.

14. **Kolbe, T.; Walther, C.**: *Reusing Proofs*, Proc. 11th ECAI '94, Amsterdam, HOL, 1994, pp. 80–84.

15. **Łukasiewicz, J.**: *Selected Works*, L. Borkowski (ed.), North-Holland, 1970.

16. **McCune, W.; Wos, L.**: *Experiments in Automated Deduction with Condensed Detachment*, Proc. CADE-11, Saratoga Springs, NY, USA, 1992, Springer LNAI 607, pp. 209–223.

17. **McCune, W.**: *OTTER 3.0 reference manual and guide*, Techn. report ANL-94/6, Argonne Natl. Laboratory, 1994.

18. **Melis, E.**: *A Model of Analogy-driven Proof-plan Construction*, Proc. 14th IJCAI, Montreal, CAN, AAAI Press, 1995, pp. 182–189.

19. **Peterson, G.J.**: *An Automatic Theorem Prover for Substitution and Detachment Systems*, Notre Dame J. of Formal Logic, Vol. 19, No. 1, Jan. 1976, pp. 119–122.

20. **Slagle, J.R.; Farrell, C.D.**: *Experiments in Automatic Learning of a Multipurpose Heuristic Program*, Comm. of the ACM, Vol. 14, No. 2, 1971, pp. 91–99.

21. **Slaney, J.**: *SCOTT: A Model-guided Theorem Prover*, Proc. IJCAI '93, Chambery, FRA, 1993, AAAI Press, pp. 109–114.

22. **Sutcliffe, G.; Suttner, C.; Yemenis, T.**: *The TPTP Problem Library*, Proc. CADE-12, Nancy, FRA, 1994, Springer LNAI 814, pp. 252–266.

23. **Suttner, C.; Ertel, W.**: *Automatic Acquisition of Search-guiding Heuristics*, Proc. CADE-10, Kaiserslautern, FRG, 1990, Springer LNAI 449, pp. 470-484.

24. **Tarski, A.**: *Logic, Semantics, Metamathematics*, Oxford University Press, 1956.

25. **Veroff, R.**:, *Using Hints to Increase the Effectiveness of an Automated Reasoning Program: Case Studies*, JAR **16**:223–239, 1996.

26. **Wos, L.**: *Meeting the Challenge of Fifty Years of Logic*, JAR **6**:213–232, 1990.

27. **Wos, L.**: *Searching for Circles of Pure Proofs*, JAR **15**:279–315, 1995.

Inference Rights for Controlling Search in Generating Theorem Provers

Dirk Fuchs

Fachbereich Informatik, Universität Kaiserslautern
Postfach 3049, 67653 Kaiserslautern
Germany
E-mail: dfuchs@informatik.uni-kl.de

Abstract. We investigate the usage of so-called inference rights. We point out the problems that arise from the inflexibility of existing approaches to heuristically control the search of automated deduction systems, and we propose the application of inference rights that are well-suited for controlling the search more flexibly. Moreover, inference rights allow for a mechanism of "partial forgetting" of facts that is not realizable in the most controlling aproaches. We study theoretical foundations of inference rights as well as the integration of inference rights into existing inference systems. Furthermore, we present possibilities to control such modified inference systems in order to gain efficiency. Finally, we report on experimental results obtained in the area of condensed detachment.

1 Introduction

The original task of a theorem prover is to check efficiently if a goal is a logic consequence of a given set of axioms. If we want to use generating calculi (e.g. resolution) to fulfill this task the usual proceeding is to modify the given start state of facts (the axioms and the goal) with rules for generation and deletion of facts until an end state is reached. A common way to control the application of the rules of a calculus is to use heuristic methods. Experiments have shown that heuristic control of the search is a viable approach (see, e.g., [3]).

In spite of this fact some problems still remain: unfortunately experience tells us that even automated theorem provers with good heuristics do many more unnecessary steps than are needed for a proof. Performing unnecessary inference steps in order to delete or to manipulate facts increases the run time a little bit, but does not lead to a dramatic change of the proof run. The generation of useless facts, however, can entail aggravating consequences. Since usually it cannot be tested whether facts are really needed in order to prove the goal such facts persist throughout the search. Because of the fact that these generated facts can take part in further inferences more unnecessary facts can and will be generated. This way the number of facts that are not needed for a proof grows dramatically and often makes it impossible for the prover to prove the goal within given limits of time or space.

One method that is—in our opinion—well-suited to deal with the mentioned problems is the integration of so-called *inference rights* into existing inference systems. Thus, certain inferences can only take place if all facts involved in it have the right to perform it. By utilizing inference rights it is possible to refine the common saturation strategies and to control inferences more flexibly. Especially the problems previously mentioned can be tackled with inference rights. It is possible, e.g., to prevent facts that possibly do not contribute to the proof from generating inferences. This way, such inferences are delayed for a certain period of time and possibly unnecessary offspring cannot be generated. This shows that by means of inference rights some kind of "partial forgetting" can be realized. Facts that possibly do not contribute to a proof are not deleted and hence totally forgotten, but only certain inferences using these facts are omitted.

In the following, we shall describe at first basics of generating theorem provers and especially the area of *condensed detachment* we chose to experiment in with inference rights. After that, we introduce in section 3 inference rights and give some remarks on the way in which they can be incorporated into already existing inference systems. Furthermore, we propose a method well-suited for controlling such modified inference systems. In section 4 we instantiate our abstract framework in the area of condensed detachment. Experimental results obtained with these techniques are presented in this section, too. We conclude the paper with a summary of our work and propose some possible future extensions.

2 Basics of Automated Theorem Provers

The problem in automated theorem proving is given as follows: Given a set of facts Ax (axioms), is a further fact λ_G (goal) a logic consequence of the axioms? A fact may be a clause, equation, or a general first or higher-order formula. The definition of "logic consequence" depends heavily on the concrete domain one is interested in.

Commonly, automated theorem provers utilize certain *calculi* for accomplishing the task mentioned above. *Analytic calculi* attempt to recursively break down and transform a goal into sub-goals that can finally be proven immediately with the axioms. *Generating calculi* go the other way by continuously producing logic consequences from Ax until a fact covering the goal appears. We shall here concentrate on generating calculi.

Typically a generating calculus contains several inference rules which can be applied to a subset of the given facts (search state). Expansion inference rules are able to synthesize a new fact from known ones and add these facts to the current set. Contracting inference rules allow for the deletion of facts or replacing facts by other ones.

A common principle to solve proof problems algorithmically with a generating calculus is employed by most systems (algorithm GTP: generating theorem prover): Essentially, a theorem prover maintains a set F^P of so-called *potential* or *passive facts* from which it selects and removes one fact λ at a time. After the application of some contracting inference rules on λ, it is put into the set F^A of *activated facts*, or discarded if it was deleted by a contracting rule (*forward subsumption*). Activated facts are, unlike potential facts, allowed to produce new facts via the application of expanding inference rules. The inferred new facts are put into F^P. We assume the expanding rules to be exhaustively applied on the elements of F^A. Initially, $F^A = \emptyset$ and $F^P = Ax$. The indeterministic selection or *activation step* is realized by heuristic means resulting in a search. To this end, a search-guiding heuristic $\mathcal{H}$ associates a natural number $\mathcal{H}(\lambda) \in I\!N$ with each $\lambda \in F^P$. Subsequently, that $\lambda \in F^P$ with the smallest weight $\mathcal{H}(\lambda)$ is selected. Ties are usually broken according to the FIFO-strategy ("*first in–first out*").

A typical example for generating calculi is the inference system $\mathcal{CD}$ which contains the inference rule *condensed detachment* (CondDet) (see [10] and [5] for motivation and a theoretical background). Since $\mathcal{CD}$ contains only one expanding and one contracting inference rule it is very simple. But nevertheless resulting proof problems can be very challenging. Therefore, condensed detachment was chosen as a test domain by several researchers before ([12], [6], [8], [13]) and the choice of condensed detachment as our test domain surely is justified. The rules of the inference system $\mathcal{CD}$ manipulate first-order terms. These terms are defined as usual, involving a finite set $\mathcal{F}$ of function symbols and an enumerable set of variables $\mathcal{V}$. The inference system $\mathcal{CD}$ is defined as follows:

Definition 1 The inference system $\mathcal{CD}$.
Let $f \in \mathcal{F}$ be a distinguished binary function symbol. Then $\mathcal{CD}$ contains the rules

(Subsum) $\Lambda \cup \{s,t\} \vdash \Lambda \cup \{s\}$; $\exists$ substitution $\sigma : \sigma(s) \equiv t$

(CondDet) $\Lambda \cup \{s,t\} \vdash \Lambda \cup \{s,t,u\}$; $s \equiv f(s',u'), \sigma = mgu(s',t), u \equiv \sigma(u')$

We denote $\Lambda \vdash \Lambda'$ if Λ' can be derived from Λ by the application of one inference rule. A sequence $(\Lambda_i)_{i\geq 0}$ with $\Lambda_j \vdash \Lambda_{j+1}$ $(j \geq 0)$ is called a $\mathcal{CD}$-derivation. A term t is $\mathcal{CD}$-derivable from Λ_0 if (and only if) a $\mathcal{CD}$-derivation $(\Lambda_i)_{i\geq 0}$ and an index j exist such that $t \in \Lambda_j$. t is called $\mathcal{CD}$-provable from Λ_0 iff a $\mathcal{CD}$-derivable term t' and a substitution σ exist such that $\sigma(t') \equiv t$. A proof problem $\wp = (Ax, t)$ is solvable iff t is $\mathcal{CD}$-provable from Ax. An important property of $\mathcal{CD}$-derivations is the *fairness*: we call a $\mathcal{CD}$-derivation $(\Lambda_i)_{i\geq 0}$ fair iff for each $\mathcal{CD}$-derivable term t a j, σ exists such that $t' \in \Lambda_j$ and $\sigma(t') \equiv t$. In the case that an algorithm only produces fair $\mathcal{CD}$-derivations each solvable proof problem can be solved with the help of the algorithm.

We have described before how to solve proof problems algorithmically. It is interesting in which way algorithms or heuristics have to be construed in order to produce only fair $\mathcal{CD}$-derivations. The following theorem formulates demands on a heuristic $\mathcal{H}$. Its proof can be found in [2].

Theorem 2 Fairness of a $\mathcal{CD}$-derivation.
The algorithm GTP *produces fair $\mathcal{CD}$-derivations if the associated heuristic guarantees that each fact being passive at one moment is activated or subsumed and discarded after a finite period of time.*

Such heuristics can be construed quite easily, e.g. a heuristic $\mathcal{H}$ is fair if the set $M_z = \{\lambda \in Term(\mathcal{F}, \mathcal{V}) : H(\lambda) = z\}$ is finite for each natural number z. It is to be emphasized that the efficiency of the algorithm strongly depends on the heuristic and that the quality of heuristics depends on the given proof problem.

3 Basics of Inference Rights

3.1 Discussion of the Algorithm GTP

If we take a closer look at GTP we can at first recognize that the algorithm allows for a simple control of applications of the inference rules. Furthermore, GTP facilitates the control of rule applications because only one decision point exists—the choice of potential facts—which can easily be controlled by heuristics.

Nevertheless, the simple and inflexible scheme of GTP has some disadvantages. Because of the fact that the next fact to be activated is selected out of an ever growing set of facts and that only a few of these facts contribute to a proof, it is very probable that an unnecessary fact is selected and activated. Such a fact λ remains in the set F^A which often has serious consequences. On the one hand more unnecessary facts are generated because λ can be involved in a lot of applications of expanding inference rules in future. Thus, a lot of computation time is wasted. On the other hand, if such unnecessary descendants of λ are activated in future, the number of facts that do not contribute to a proof can grow enormously. Since a large number of facts entails a high demand for memory and computation time it is possible that the proof is unnecessarily delayed.

Another main disadvantage of GTP is that no further investigation of activated facts—e.g. with respect to new information—takes place. Thus, no a posteriori knowledge can be incorporated into the algorithm. The following example gives a rough overview of how such a posteriori knowledge could be utilized: Usually a lot of different proofs for a given proof problem exist. Thus, it is reasonable to search for short proof runs, i.e. proof runs where only few steps not contributing to the proof are performed. In the case that a fact λ has been activated which is involved in the application of many expanding inference steps it possibly does not contribute to short proof runs because a lot of possibly unnecessary "offspring" is generated. A modification of the search state which, e.g., forces λ to be involved only in contracting but not in expanding inferences could be the right way to cope with this problem. This is not an option in GTP, however, because *all* kinds of inferences are exhaustively applied to active facts.

All in all it is sensible to preserve the main principles of GTP—the division of the inferred facts into F^A and F^P and the use of heuristics in order to activate facts—because of the advantages mentioned before. To deal with the disadvantages the two following aspects should be integrated into the algorithm: In order to integrate a posteriori knowledge the facts $\lambda \in F^A$ should be analyzed periodically. This way it should be possible to detect unnecessary facts, i.e. facts which do not contribute to any proof, or at least facts that possibly do not contribute to short proof runs. The second step should be the "restructuring" of the current search state so as to avoid generating too many facts. (Problem 26 in [11].) Nevertheless, such a restructuring must neither destroy the simplification power of the system of activated facts nor the completeness. Such a restructuring could be achieved by "partial forgetting" of unnecessary facts. This means that the information on the activation of unnecessary facts is not totally forgotten, i.e. possibly unnecessary facts are not deleted, but such facts are forgotten in such a manner that they cannot take part in certain inferences.

We will only sketch the first aspect because the detection of unnecessary facts depends on the concrete calculus (see section 4) and so-called *referees* ([1]) are known to be fairly well-suited for judging facts. In the following, we shall hence concentrate on the second aspect, i.e. on the question how partial forgetting and hence a better control can be achieved. Our solution to this very issue are *inference rights* which allow for a finer grained control of inferences.

3.2 Inference Rights

The main idea of inference rights is to enrich the facts an inference system works on with rights to perform inferences. The intended use of these rights is as follows: If a fact is assumed to be unnecessary or not contributing to short proof runs the generation power of this fact is restricted. This is achieved by retracting the right to take part in expanding inferences. Additional conditions on the algorithm, however, are necessary to guarantee that finally all necessary inferences are performed. Thus, it should be possible to recover rights to perform inferences. Our method to model inference rights is to use annotations to a fact that determine the inferences in which a fact is allowed to be involved in:

Definition 3 Inference Right, Fact with Inference Right.
Let I be an inference system, and $\mathcal{I}$ be the set of inference rules. Let λ be a fact. An inference right w.r.t. I is a set $C \subseteq \mathcal{I}$. A fact with inference right is a pair (λ, C). In the following, we write $\lambda|C$ instead of (λ, C).

We give some remarks on the way inference rights can be incorporated into already existing inference systems. At first, inference rules do not work on sets of facts Λ any longer but on facts with rights $\Lambda^{\mathcal{R}}$. The rights stem from the original inference system and are subsets of the original inference rules. They restrict the applicability of inference rules. The expanding inference rule

$$\textbf{(Exp)} \quad \Lambda \cup \{\lambda_1, \ldots, \lambda_n\} \vdash \Lambda \cup \{\lambda_1, \ldots, \lambda_n, \lambda\}; P(\lambda_1, \ldots, \lambda_n)$$

could be, e.g., modified in the following manner:

$$\textbf{(Exp}^{\mathcal{R}}) \quad \Lambda^{\mathcal{R}} \cup \{\lambda_1|C_1, \ldots, \lambda_n|C_n\} \vdash \Lambda^{\mathcal{R}} \cup \{\lambda_1|C_1, \ldots, \lambda_n|C_n, \lambda|\mathcal{I}\}; P(\lambda_1, \ldots, \lambda_n)$$
$$\wedge \forall i, 1 \leq i \leq n : \textbf{Exp} \in C_i$$

So, facts can only be involved in an inference if they have the right to perform it. Moreover, further rules are necessary which are only needed to handle rights:

$$\textbf{(Retract}^{\mathcal{R}}) \quad \Lambda^{\mathcal{R}} \cup \{\lambda|D\} \vdash \Lambda^{\mathcal{R}} \cup \{\lambda|C\}; C \subset D$$

$$\textbf{(Recover}^{\mathcal{R}}) \quad \Lambda^{\mathcal{R}} \cup \{\lambda|C\} \vdash \Lambda^{\mathcal{R}} \cup \{\lambda|D\}; C \neq \mathcal{I} \wedge C \subset D$$

The rule $\textbf{Retract}^{\mathcal{R}}$ is needed, e.g., to forbid facts to perform the generation of facts. The rule $\textbf{Recover}^{\mathcal{R}}$ is needed to add rights. In the area of condensed detachment this is necessary to allow for fair derivations (cf. section 4).

Note that inference rights offer only an abstract framework to enrich facts with further information. An important question is now in which way such an extended inference system should be controlled. Such a control should allow for a gain of efficiency in comparison with the original inference mechanism. Moreover, completeness should be guaranteed. Since these aspects depend mainly on the concrete inference system one is interested in, we will discuss them in the following section in more detail.

In the following, we will nevertheless give a rough idea of how inference rights could be used. Algorithm $GTP^{\mathcal{R}}$—utilizing inference rights—is an extension of GTP, i.e. it divides the facts into F^A and F^P and performs inferences as described before. The main difference is that active facts are periodically judged and bad facts are determined. Then, inference rule $\texttt{Retract}^{\mathcal{R}}$ is applied to these facts so as to forbid them to produce new ones via expanding inferences ("deactivation"). This way, certain facts are partially forgotten and not allowed to generate new facts. If we deactivate facts that do not contribute to any proof unnecessary offspring of these facts is avoided. If we deactivate facts that are able to generate a lot of facts it is possible that shorter proof runs occur. In order to preserve completeness it is necessary that all inferences (needed for completeness) which are delayed for a certain period of time finally take place. To this end, it is convenient to note which facts were involved in an application of the rule $\texttt{Retract}^{\mathcal{R}}$. Thus, one can apply $\texttt{Recover}^{\mathcal{R}}$ on such facts after a certain period of time and perform the inferences delayed before. The technical realization could be as follows: We introduce a *recover set* F^R and move, after the application of $\texttt{Retract}^{\mathcal{R}}$ on an active fact λ, this fact from F^A to F^R. The facts from F^R can be utilized for contracting but not for expanding inferences. Furthermore, the facts from F^R are possible candidates for activation steps, i.e. facts are not only selected from F^P but also periodically from F^R. If a fact $\lambda \in F^R$ is selected its inference rights are set to $\mathcal{I}$ via $\texttt{Recover}^{\mathcal{R}}$. After that it is processed analogously to a selected potential fact, i.e. inferences delayed previously can be performed.

A crucial step with regard to performance is the selection of facts from F^R. If we select facts too frequently, i.e. they are not forgotten for a long time, expanding inferences where bad facts are involved in are delayed for a short time only, and we hence cannot expect to gain much efficiency. But if we select facts from F^R only very seldom and deactivate a fact that really contributes to a proof it is possible that important inferences are delayed for a long time and hence the runtime increases. Thus, a good compromise between these extremes has to be achieved. At least it is necessary that all facts from F^R are finally selected in order to preserve completeness (cf. section 4).

4 Inference Rights and Condensed Detachment

So far we have introduced inference rights as a general framework to modify inference systems. This modification is necessary in order to achieve a better control especially of the expanding inference rules. Since the concrete realization depends on the calculus one is interested in we have only given a few remarks on the way how to control such an inference system. Therefore, this section describes more precisely in which way inference rights can be utilized. We chose condensed detachment as a first test domain because the inference system $\mathcal{CD}$ used in this area is rather typical for generating provers.

At first it is necessary to integrate inference rights into the inference system $\mathcal{CD}$ resulting in a new inference system $\mathcal{CD}^{\mathcal{R}}$. The next step is to present a concrete algorithm for controlling $\mathcal{CD}^{\mathcal{R}}$. Note that we are still interested in solving $\mathcal{CD}$ proof problems and need an algorithm that is able to solve them. We describe a basic algorithm—using an abstract function β in order to detect unnecessary facts—and give sufficient conditions on the algorithm to guarantee that it only produces fair derivations. Finally, we introduce a possible realization of function β for judging facts and use this function in some experiments.

4.1 The Inference System $\mathcal{CD}^{\mathcal{R}}$

The inference system $\mathcal{CD}^{\mathcal{R}}$ is an extension of $\mathcal{CD}$. Therefore, the inference rules CondDet and Subsum must be adapted in order to work with facts with inference rights. Furthermore, the rules $\text{Retract}^{\mathcal{R}}$ and $\text{Recover}^{\mathcal{R}}$ are necessary to deal with rights (cf. section 3). In this context the set of inference rights is given as $\mathcal{R} = \{M : M \subseteq \mathcal{I} = \{\text{CondDet}, \text{Subsum}\}\}$. The following definition introduces the inference system $\mathcal{CD}^{\mathcal{R}}$.

Definition 4 The inference system $\mathcal{CD}^{\mathcal{R}}$.
Let $f \in \mathcal{F}$ be a distinguished binary function symbol. Then $\mathcal{CD}^{\mathcal{R}}$ contains

$(\text{Subsum}^{\mathcal{R}}) \quad \Lambda^{\mathcal{R}} \cup \{s|C_1, t|C_2\} \vdash \Lambda^{\mathcal{R}} \cup \{s|C_1\}; \exists \sigma : \sigma(s) \equiv t \wedge \text{Subsum} \in C_1$

$(\text{CondDet}^{\mathcal{R}}) \quad \Lambda^{\mathcal{R}} \cup \{s|C_1, t|C_2\} \vdash \Lambda^{\mathcal{R}} \cup \{s|C_1, t|C_2, u|\mathcal{I}\}; (s \equiv f(s', u'),$
$\sigma = mgu(s', t), u \equiv \sigma(u')) \wedge \text{CondDet} \in C_1, C_2$

$(\text{Recover}^{\mathcal{R}}) \quad \Lambda^{\mathcal{R}} \cup \{s|C_1\} \vdash \Lambda^{\mathcal{R}} \cup \{s|C_2\}; C_1 \neq \mathcal{I} \wedge C_1 \subset C_2$

$(\text{Retract}^{\mathcal{R}}) \quad \Lambda^{\mathcal{R}} \cup \{s|C_1\} \vdash \Lambda^{\mathcal{R}} \cup \{s|C_2\}; C_2 \subset C_1$

Inference system $\mathcal{CD}^{\mathcal{R}}$ follows exactly the principles pointed out in section 3. The expanding inference rule $\text{CondDet}^{\mathcal{R}}$ can only be applied if both facts that take part in it have the right to perform it. In order to subsume a fact it is only necessary to have the subsumption right. Note that it is not required that the fact to be subsumed has this inference right. Inference rules $\text{Retract}^{\mathcal{R}}$ and $\text{Recover}^{\mathcal{R}}$ are exactly the same as described before.

In analogy to section 2 we write $\Lambda_i^{\mathcal{R}} \vdash \Lambda_{i+1}^{\mathcal{R}}$ if $\Lambda_{i+1}^{\mathcal{R}}$ can be derived from $\Lambda_i^{\mathcal{R}}$ by the application of one inference rule. $(\Lambda_i^{\mathcal{R}})_{i \geq 0}$ is called a $\mathcal{CD}^{\mathcal{R}}$-derivation iff $\Lambda_j^{\mathcal{R}} \vdash \Lambda_{j+1}^{\mathcal{R}} \forall j \geq 0$. A fact with inference right $t|C$ is $\mathcal{CD}^{\mathcal{R}}$-derivable from $\Lambda_0^{\mathcal{R}}$ iff a $\mathcal{CD}^{\mathcal{R}}$-derivation $(\Lambda_i^{\mathcal{R}})_{i \geq 0}$ and an index j exist such that $t|C \in \Lambda_j^{\mathcal{R}}$. We call a $\mathcal{CD}^{\mathcal{R}}$-derivation $(\Lambda_i^{\mathcal{R}})_{i \geq 0}$ fair iff for each $\mathcal{CD}$-derivable fact t there exists a j, σ such that $t'|C \in \Lambda_j^{\mathcal{R}}$ and $\sigma(t') \equiv t$. Note that by means of fair $\mathcal{CD}^{\mathcal{R}}$-derivations it is possible to solve $\mathcal{CD}$ proof problems. It is only necessary to perform $\mathcal{CD}^{\mathcal{R}}$-derivations until a fact appears that subsumes the goal. The right is ignored in that case since it is only needed to circumvent certain inferences during the inference process.

4.2 An Algorithm for Controlling $\mathcal{CD}^{\mathcal{R}}$

In the following, we introduce an algorithm that allows to control $\mathcal{CD}^{\mathcal{R}}$ easily and to solve $\mathcal{CD}$ proof problems very efficiently. Note that our algorithm is only one of a lot of different possible ones. In general, there might be many different ways in which way the new rules provided by the inference system can be utilized.

Basic Algorithm: In order to construe an algorithm for controlling $\mathcal{CD}^{\mathcal{R}}$ it is sensible to employ the algorithm GTP$^{\mathcal{R}}$ as described in section 3. Thus, it is still possible to perform the activation steps heuristically. As described in section 3, GTP$^{\mathcal{R}}$ employs the inference rights to restrict the applicability of inference rules. This restriction takes place in such a manner that activated facts which do not appear to be contributing to a proof or only contribute to long proof runs are "deactivated" periodically. Thus, they are not allowed to be involved in expanding, but only in contracting inferences. To this end, a function β is needed that determines the active facts that behave "badly" w.r.t. a certain criterion. More exactly, $\beta(F^A) = \{\lambda_1|\mathcal{I}, \ldots, \lambda_m|\mathcal{I}\} \subseteq F^A$, i.e. β selects a fixed number of active facts. The realization of algorithm GTP$^{\mathcal{R}}$—well-suited for proving $\mathcal{CD}$ proof problems—uses β to determine the facts to be deactivated (see figure 1).

```
begin
    F^A := ∅, F^R := ∅, F^P := {ax|I : ax ∈ Ax}, cnt := 0
    while F^P ∪ F^R ≠ ∅
        if cnt = n
            S := β(F^A)
            forall λ|I ∈ S
                F^A := F^A \ {λ|I}, F^R := F^R ∪ {λ|I \ {CondDet}}
            cnt := 0
        select λ|C ∈ F^P ∪ F^R with minimal H(λ)
        if λ|C ∈ F^P : F^P := F^P \ {λ|C}
        else F^R := F^R \ {λ|C}, C := I
        if λ|C was selected from F^P ∧ ∃λ'|D ∈ F^A ∪ F^R, σ: σ(λ') ≡ λ:
            delete λ|C
        else
            if μ(λ) ≡ λ_G for a μ: "proof found"
            M := {λ' : λ' CondDet descendant of λ, λ̃; λ̃|I ∈ F^A}
            F^P := F^P ∪ {λ'|I : λ' ∈ M}
            F^A := F^A ∪ {λ|C}, cnt := cnt + 1
    "proof failed"
end
```

Fig. 1. Algorithm GTP$^{\mathcal{R}}$

As one can see, algorithm GTP$^{\mathcal{R}}$ is instantiated in the following aspects: The periodical deactivation of facts is realized in such a manner that the function β determines—after a fixed number n of activation steps—a fixed number m of active facts that should not take part in expanding inferences any longer. In our experiments we employed a number m that is a certain percentage d of the number of activation steps n. The deactivation is achieved via Retract$^{\mathcal{R}}$. The fact $\lambda|C$ originating from the application of Retract$^{\mathcal{R}}$ is moved from the set

F^A to the recover set F^R. After that, it can only take part in $\mathtt{Subsum}^R$ but not in $\mathtt{CondDet}^R$. In order to achieve that expanding inferences using λ are only delayed but not strictly forbidden, inference rule $\mathtt{Recover}^R$ must be applied later, i.e. $\lambda|C$ has to be activated again. To this end it is sensible to select the facts that should be activated from $F^P \cup F^R$. As we have mentioned previously the duration a fact $\lambda|C$ remains in F^R influences heavily the performance of a prover. We chose the search-guiding heuristic $\mathcal{H}$ for accomplishing the task of selecting facts from F^R. Thus, we prefer small facts w.r.t. $\mathcal{H}$ that are possibly more important for the proof. Moreover, utilizing $\mathcal{H}$ for selection of facts allows to preserve completeness (see below). It is reasonable, however, to change the heuristic weight $\mathcal{H}(\lambda)$ of a fact $\lambda \in F^R$ to $\gamma \cdot \mathcal{H}(\lambda)$, $\gamma \in \mathbb{N}$, $\gamma > 1$. Otherwise it might be often the case that a fact that was deactivated is activated immediately.

Fairness of $\mathcal{CD}^R$-derivations: In order to guarantee fairness of $\mathcal{CD}$-derivations performed by algorithm GTP we formalized theoretical demands on algorithm GTP which were sufficient to achieve fairness, namely that potential facts must not remain passive infinitely long. Furthermore, we gave remarks on the way how these demands could be realized. Thus, we formalized some conditions on the heuristic responsible for the activation of facts. In the following, we will hence deal with the same aspects w.r.t. $\mathcal{CD}^R$ and GTP^R.

Intuitively, the following precondition should be sufficient to preserve fairness of derivations: In order to guarantee that all inferences are finally performed potential facts must not stay in F^P infinitely long. But since GTP^R allows for the deactivation of active facts, i.e. to insert them into the recover set F^R, we must also guarantee that these facts do not remain in F^R infinitely long. Furthermore, we have to consider the following problem: If an infinite cycle of activation and deactivation of two facts occurs, i.e. each time one fact is deactivated before the other fact is activated, descendants of these facts will never be generated. In order to circumvent such cycles it has to be forbidden that a fact is deactivated infinitely often. We formalize this as follows: Precondition $\mathcal{P}$ on algorithm GTP^R holds true iff the algorithm is constructed in such a way (the heuristic and the deactivation function β are realized in such a manner) that no fact—being element of F^P or F^R at a certain point in time—stays infinitely long in F^P or F^R, respectively, *and* that no fact $\lambda|\mathcal{I}$ is deactivated infinitely often. Precondition $\mathcal{P}$ is indeed sufficient to entail fair derivations:

Theorem 5 Fairness of a $\mathcal{CD}^R$-derivation.
Let $\mathcal{P}$ be fulfilled. Then algorithm GTP^R produces only fair $\mathcal{CD}^R$-derivations.

Again, the proof of the theorem can be found in [2]. In order to fulfill precondition $\mathcal{P}$ it is at first necessary to employ a heuristic $\mathcal{H}$ which finally selects all of the potential facts and the facts from the recover set. In section 2 we showed in which way we can construct such heuristics. Moreover, we must avoid that an active fact $\lambda|\mathcal{I}$ is deactivated infinitely often. To this end, it is sensible to enrich each fact with a natural number that counts how often the respective fact has been deactivated. If a threshold of c_{max} is exceeded β is not allowed to select λ. Hence, λ cannot be deactivated in future.

Determination of bad facts: As we have described before β selects—after a number of n activations—a set of facts $\{\lambda_1|\mathcal{I},\ldots,\lambda_m|\mathcal{I}\}$ from the set of active facts. It is reasonable to forbid β to select the following kinds of facts: At first facts whose number of deactivations has exceeded a certain threshold must not be selected for fairness reasons (see before). Furthermore, due to our experiments it is wise to forbid the deactivation of axioms. In the following, we will describe in which way β determines bad facts among the remaining ones. Remember, that we denote facts as bad if they contribute to no or only long proof runs.

Facts being involved in a lot of expanding inferences but only in a few contracting inferences contribute with a high probability to long proof runs. This is mainly because of the fact that they generate a lot of offspring. If this offspring is not needed for the proof the prover is forced to waste a lot of computation time to handle such facts. Hence, facts that possibly contribute to long proof runs can be detected by counting the inferences they were involved in. The detection of facts that are not needed in any proof is much more difficult and in general undecidable. Despite of the undecidability the probability is rather high to detect facts that are unnecessary for proving the goal. This is mainly due to the fact that in successful proof runs usually only a few activated facts ($\leq 5\%$) are needed. Moreover, experiments have shown that facts needed for a proof are often quite general, i.e. they subsume a lot of deduced facts, and often have a small weight according to the heuristic of the prover ([1]). If we choose facts that have not subsumed many other facts or have a high weight according to the heuristic it is quite probable that these facts are not needed for a proof.

If we assume that we want to select facts periodically after n activations, i.e. at the moments $\tau_{0,n}, \tau_{1,n}, \ldots$, we can define the function $\beta = \beta_{\tau_{i,n}}{}^1$ for the selection of bad facts at moment $\tau_{i,n}$ as follows. Let $\mathcal{H}$ be the used heuristic, let $|gen_{\Delta\tau_{i,n}}(\lambda)|$ and $|del_{\Delta\tau_{i,n}}(\lambda)|$ be the number of facts that were generated and discarded, respectively, using λ in the period between $\tau_{i-1,n}$ and $\tau_{i,n}$. Then set

$$\beta_{\tau_{i,n}}(\lambda) := |del_{\Delta\tau_{i,n}}(\lambda)| - |gen_{\Delta\tau_{i,n}}(\lambda)| - \mathcal{H}(\lambda)$$

A small value of $\beta_{\tau_{i,n}}$ is a sign that a fact λ behaves badly because a lot of facts have been generated but only a few facts have been subsumed.

4.3 Experimental Results

In order to perform an experimental evaluation we used the condensed detachment prover CoDe ([4]) as our basic prover. We integrated into this program that originally used algorithm GTP inference rights employing the techniques presented in section 4. We applied CoDe to problems stemming from the area of logic calculi which McCune and Wos tackled in [6] with their renowned prover OTTER. These problems can also be found in the TPTP library ([9]) version 1.2.1, namely in the LCL domain. In order to show that the speed-ups

---

[1] Note that the function β depends strongly on the moment it is applied on the set of active facts. However, we make this dependency explicit only if it is necessary to avoid confusion.

achieved with our techniques are not due to the weakness of our basic prover we compare the results obtained with CODE with those of OTTER. The results with CODE were obtained on a SPARCstation ELC, the results with OTTER on a SPARCstation 1+ which is a comparable machine. The results of OTTER depicted in table 1 are extracted from [6], and were achieved by the best of six different heuristics. The results of CODE were obtained with heuristic ϖ (see [3]). CODE employing $GTP^{\mathcal{R}}$ was parameterized in the following manner: Every $n = 50$ activation steps m facts were deactivated, with $m = d\%$ of n (d can be found in table 1). The parameter γ was set to the value 2.

The table 1 compares the results obtained with CODE and OTTER. Columns 2 and 3 show the run time (in seconds) and the number of activations needed by heuristic ϖ, the next six columns show the corresponding values if we deactivate a certain percentage d of the activated facts. Column 10 displays the run time needed when using OTTER. Table 1 shows that algorithm $GTP^{\mathcal{R}}$ which utilizes inference rights outperforms GTP. If we deactivate only a small percentage of the activated facts the speed-ups are rather low, but if we increase the number of deactivated facts we can achieve higher speed-ups. In table 1 we can find one problem where deactivation of facts causes longer run-times because important facts were deactivated. But such a situation is quite improbable and the proof could still be found because we do not loose completeness by deactivation.

Example	GTP(ϖ)		$GTP^{\mathcal{R}}(d=10\%)$		$GTP^{\mathcal{R}}(d=20\%)$		$GTP^{\mathcal{R}}(d=30\%)$		OTTER
	time	activ.	time	activ.	time	activ.	time	activ.	
LCL006-1	43	544	36	534	32	532	27	528	244
LCL016-1	47	554	41	557	34	541	30	466	151
LCL045-1	60	670	53	665	43	644	32	615	1467
LCL058-1	59	710	54	710	46	708	37	703	423
LCL060-1	63	733	59	733	49	733	40	726	509
LCL068-1	121	982	109	983	89	977	148	1217	257
LCL069-1	80	773	73	774	61	774	25	501	5
LCL070-1	55	715	47	715	37	693	21	568	480
LCL071-1	55	687	51	687	36	665	33	656	511
LCL072-1	95	826	84	826	72	825	39	613	224
LCL111-1	79	852	68	852	56	835	45	832	5
LCL113-1	64	737	55	737	46	731	37	725	1468

Table 1. GTP vs. $GTP^{\mathcal{R}}$

If we take a closer look at the problems where we achieved speed-ups we can recognize that in nearly all cases the "real" proof of the goal did not change, i.e. the sequence of activated facts, ordered w.r.t. the moment of their activation, remained unchanged. This shows that our deactivation function is indeed well-suited in judging facts. Although the real proof did not change we could achieve speed-ups. These speed-ups stem from the following two aspects: On the one hand table 1 shows that when using $GTP^{\mathcal{R}}$ instead of GTP often less activation steps had to be performed. This is mainly due to the fact that after the deactivation of unnecessary facts their unnecessary offspring was not generated and hence not activated. On the other hand we find examples where speed-ups occured although the number of activation steps did not decrease. This is possible because if we use GTP^R instead of GTP the period of time needed for one activation step is shorter: Due to the periodical deactivation the number of facts that take part in time consuming expanding inferences increases only slightly.

5 Conclusion and Future Work

Automated deduction systems have reached a considerable level of performance. Nevertheless, the use of conventional approaches to control deduction systems— heuristic control of the search and exhaustive application of inference rules (saturation strategy)—is sometimes problematic. Because of the difficulty to discover an appropriate heuristic for a lot of different examples it is very probable to employ a heuristic which activates many facts not contributing to a proof. This entails much overhead due to the common saturation strategy.

Our approach of controlling the search by means of inference rights can help to deal better with these problems. Integration of inference rights into already existing inference systems makes it possible to achieve a more flexible control of the search and hence to reduce the amount of time for processing unnecessary facts. Despite of the fact that they cause a small overhead our experimental results in the area of condensed detachment were fairly satisfactory.

In order to substantiate our work with further results future work should deal with experiments in different calculi. In particular we have to consider the fact that most calculi contain more inference rules as only one rule for generating and one rule for deleting of facts. Hence, further research is necessary to find out whether restricting the applicability of such rules via inference rights is sensible.

References

1. Denzinger, J.; Fuchs, D.: *Referees for Teamwork*, Proc. FLAIRS '96, Key West, FL, USA, 1996, pp. 454–458.
2. Fuchs, D.: *Inference Rights for Controlling Search in Generating Theorem Provers*, SEKI Report SR-96-12, University of Kaiserslautern, 1996.
3. Fuchs, M.: *Powerful Search Heuristics Based on Weighted Symbols, Level and Features*, Proc. FLAIRS '96, Key West, FL, USA, 1996, pp. 449–453.
4. Fuchs, D., Fuchs, M.: *CoDe: A Powerful Prover for Problems of Condensed Detachment*, Proc. CADE-14, Townsville, Australia, 1997, to appear.
5. Łukasiewicz, J.: *Selected Works*, L. Borkowski (ed.), North-Holland, 1970.
6. McCune, W.; Wos, L.: *Experiments in Automated Deduction with Condensed Detachment*, Proc. CADE-11, Saratoga Springs, NY, USA, 1992, LNAI 607, pp. 209–223.
7. McCune, W.: *OTTER 3.0 Reference Manual and Guide*, Techn. Report ANL-94/6, Argonne Natl. Laboratory, 1994.
8. Slaney, J.: *SCOTT: A Model-Guided Theorem Prover*, Proc. IJCAI '93, Chambery, FRA, 1993, pp. 109–114.
9. Sutcliffe, G.; Suttner, C.; Yemenis, T.: *The TPTP Problem Library*, Proc. CADE-12, Nancy, FRA, 1994, LNAI 814, pp. 252–266.
10. Tarski, A.: *Logic, Semantics, Metamathematics*, Oxford University Press, 1956.
11. Wos, L.: *Automated Reasoning: 33 Basic Research Problems*, Prentice-Hall, 1988.
12. Wos, L.: *Meeting the Challenge of Fifty Years of Logic*, JAR 6, 1990, pp. 213-232.
13. Wos, L.: *Searching for Circles of Pure Proofs*, JAR 15, 1995, pp. 279-315.

A Retrieval Method for Exploration of a Case Memory

Paulo Gomes[1,2]

Carlos Bento[2]

[1] ISEC - Instituto Superior de Engenharia
de Coimbra
Quinta da Nora, 3030 Coimbra
pgomes@sun.isec.pt

[2] CISUC - Centro de Informática e
Sistemas da Universidade de Coimbra
Polo II, 3030 Coimbra
{pgomes|bento}@eden.dei.uc.pt

Abstract

The reminding of old episodes useful for generation of new solutions is a crucial task in case-based design. Another important process in creative design is the exploration of the case library, in order to find design alternatives.

In this paper we present an index structure for exploration of a memory containing design cases. We represent cases as Structure-Behavior-Function (SBF) models. This representation allows an adequate understanding of the design, enabling case retrieval at a functional level.

We propose a retrieval method capable of exploring the case library. This method has two different algorithms, which are driven by case adaptation. Retrieved cases will be used for adaptation, in this sense, the usefulness of cases is defined accordingly to the adaptation operation that will take place by the adaptation module.

1.   Introduction

Design is a complex activity that is generally ill-structured and requires a great amount of different types of knowledge (Reich 91). It comprises creation of a structure complying with a set of functional specifications and constraints (Tong & Sriram 92).

Design can be divided into routine and non-routine design (Gero 94). We use the term *routine design* when the designer is *a priori* acquainted with the necessary knowledge. In this way routine design comprises parametric variations of old designs. *Non-routine design* involves two sub-classes: (1) innovative and (2) creative design. In *innovative design* a new artefact is generated from a known class of designs, but differs from previous class artefacts in some substantive way. This can occur, for instance, in terms of value(s) assigned to the design variables which are specific to the new solution. In *creative design* the space of possible design alternatives is expanded through the use of new design variables. This takes place when the space of potential designs is extensive and is not entirely defined by the knowledge available to the user. In creative design the process of specifying the design requirements is also viewed as an important phase (Tong & Sriram 92 , Kolodner & Wills 93).

Designers use old solutions when dealing with new design problems. While in routine design old solutions are applied nearly unchanged, in non-routine design old designs are reused in novel ways broadening the space of design solutions. This is the approach pursued in case-based design and the one on the basis of various creative design systems (Kolodner and Wills 93, Gomes et. al. 96).

In creative design the index structure used for episode retrieval must allow for the exploration of a case memory instead of searching for a specific case. Various systems in this area use conventional memory structures, ranging from hierarchical structures (Maher and Zhao 93, Sycara and Navinchandra 91,93) to model-based indexing schemes (Goel 92). The work presented in this paper follows a distinct approach to case memory organization. We propose a memory structure having in mind the exploration of the case library, and retrieval algorithms for case mutation and thematic abstraction which take advantage of this memory structure.

Within our framework cases are indexed by functional keys taken from SBF models. In addition to these indexes, the case structure comprises links between episodes like in Protos (Bareiss 89). A link defines a relation between two cases in terms of functional differences. The mutation strategy, which is an adaptation method explores the case library using links between cases. The thematic abstraction algorithm uses a taxonomy of functions to explore the case library. These two retrieval algorithms make an exploration of the case library using different relations between cases, thus performing exploration at different levels. In our framework the retrieval process is guided by the type of adaptation strategy used for generation of a new design. This retrieval algorithm retrieves cases that will be mutated (one or more elements of the case will be modified).

One of the creative design characteristics is the transfer of ideas from designs that have no surface similarities, but which have abstract similarities. This can happen between different domains, or it can happen in the same domain of application. To deal with this kind of situations it is used the thematic abstraction adaptation strategy. This strategy uses a process of knowledge transfer between the old case and the new problem (analogy).

The following section presents the case representation used in our work. Section three describes the case memory organisation. In section four we present three versions of the retrieval algorithm. Section five shows an example of the differences between the algorithm versions. In section six we compare our approach to other works. Finally some conclusions are presented and we propose plans for future work.

2. Case Representation

Within our framework *design episodes* are represented in the form of SBF models (Goel 92, Stroulia et al. 92). These models are based on the component-substance ontology developed by Bylander and Chandrasekaran (Bylander and Chandrasekaran 85). A case comprises three different parts: (1) problem specification - function; (2) explanation - behavior; (3) design solution - structure.

The problem specification comprises a set of *high level functionalities* (HLF) and a set of *functional specifications* (FS) which must be held by the design. The explanation is in the form of a causal structure, representing the design behavior. The case solution describes the design structures that accomplish the functionalities described in the target problem.

A design problem is represented by a tree of functionalities, where leaves are FSs and the high levels in the tree represent HLFs. HLFs are abstract functionalities, used to help the user in specifying the design problem. Each leaf in the tree represents a FS a schema comprising the following slots: *Given*: The initial behavior state; *Makes*: The final behavior state; *By-Behavior*: Behavior constraints; *Stimulus*: External stimulus to the design; *Provided*: Structural constraints.

Figure 1b specifies the functionalities associated with the digital circuit sketched in figure 1a. This circuit has a HLF comprising two FSs: f(A*B) ∧ f(~A+~B). The description of function f(A*B) comprises the final and initial behavioral states (*Makes* and *Given* slots). The *Makes* slot describes the demand for a substance Data, located in AND1, named Output, with value A*B. The *Given* slot defines the initial conditions, which comprise the existence of a substance Data located in AND1, named Input1, with value A, and a substance Data located in AND1, named Input2, with value B.

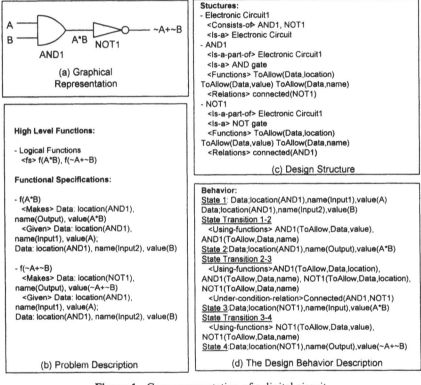

Figure 1 - Case representation of a digital circuit.

The *design solution* is in the form of a hierarchy of device structures. Each structure can be viewed as a set of device structures where substances can flow through. The structure schema is as follows:

- *Is-a-part-of*: the super structure of the structure.
- *Consists-of*: the sub-structures of the structure.
- *Is-a*: the class of the structure.
- *Relations*: structural relations with other structures.
- *Properties*: structure properties.
- *Functions*: the structure primitive functions.

Figure 1c describes the design structure for the digital circuit in figure 1a which comprises an AND and a NOT gate. The description comprises three structures. The first one describes the Electronic Circuit1, consisting in AND1 and NOT1, and the class of the structure Electronic Circuit. The description of structures AND1 and NOT1 refers to a superstructure Electronic Circuit1, to the class of the structure AND/NOT gate, to the primitive functions performed by each structure, and to relations with other structures.

A *case explanation* describes the causal behavior of the design in terms of directed graphs (DGs). The nodes of a DG represent behavioral states and the edges represent state transitions. A *behavioral state* can be composed by one or more substance schemas. A *substance schema* characterises the properties and the property values of a substance. A *state transition* represents the conditions under which the transition between behavioral states occurs. A state transition is represented by a schema with the following slots:

- *Using-functions*: the primitive component's functions that allow the state transition.
- *Under-condition-relation*: structural relations necessary to perform the state transition.
- *Domain-principle*: domain principles or laws responsible for the state transition.
- *Under-condition-component*: component conditions that must be observed.
- *Under-condition-substance*: substance conditions that must be observed.
- *Under-condition-transition*: other state transitions that are influential to the state transition.

Figure 1d presents the digital circuit's behavior. It comprises four behavioral states and three state transitions. In figure 1 there are two substance schemas associated with State1 representing the properties of Data substances. Substance Data is located in AND1, named Input1, with value A. State1 comprises also another substance of the same type, in the same location, named Input2, with value B. Transition 1-2 expresses that the transformation from State1 to State2 is due to the primitive function of AND1, allowing Data to change value and name. The remainder of the description has an analogous form.

3.   Memory Structure

The memory structure that supports case retrieval comprises two substructures: (1) a tree of HLFs and FSs, and (2) a graph, whose nodes represent cases, and whose links describe functional differences between cases (see figure 2). In the tree of HLFs and FSs, HLFs are at higher levels of the tree and FSs are leafs of the tree. The tree of functions links the FSs to cases. The FSs are used as indexes for selection of the starting cases. The starting cases have at least one FSs in common with the target problem. These cases are then used as starting points for exploration of the case graph.

In figure 2 a link from FS f(A*B) to *Case1* is shown, meaning that the problem description of *Case1* contains FS f(A*B). *Case1* is indexed by f(A*B) and f(A+B), and possibly by other FSs.

In figure 2 *Case1* is connected to *Case2* by the *Differences1-2* link. This link represents the differences in the problem description between *Case1* and *Case2*.

A difference link is only created when the cases it connects have at least one FS in common. A difference link connecting two cases, comprises three parts:

- The set of FSs that belong to the first case but don't belong to the second one.
- The set of FSs that belong to the second case but don't belong to the first one.
- The set of FSs common to both cases.

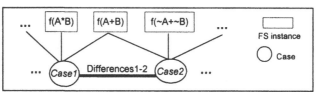

Figure 2 - Example of a memory structure.

Case links are automatically generated, when a new case is stored in the case library. In the next section we describe how case retrieval is performed using this memory structure.

4. Case Retrieval

Reminding of useful experiences is a critical purpose in a case-based system. Although in case retrieval accuracy is important, in case-based creative reasoning exploration of several alternative solutions is also a main goal. Within our framework accuracy is achieved by the use of FS indexes, and space exploration takes place through the use of difference links.

The FSs defined in the target problem are used as probes to retrieve the set of starting cases. Then a best starting case is selected as a starting point in the search space. This case is selected by the number of FSs in common with the new problem. The search space is represented by the graph of cases. Exploration is performed using the difference links necessary to go from one case to another.

An important feature of the exploration process is that cases are selected accordingly to the adaptation strategy that will be used for generation of the new solution. The retrieval algorithm explores the case graph searching for cases with features suitable for the adaptation method that will be applied. This makes retrieval an adaptation-guided process. This kind of adaptation-guided process is different from the one performed in Déjà Vu (Smyth e Keane 95) as within our framework we use three adaptation strategies. Furthermore Déjà Vu is a specific domain application, which enables the system to have specific knowledge on the adaptation rules, while in our system this is not possible *a priori*.

The adaptation strategies considered within our framework are: mutation, case abstraction, and composition. The mutation strategy comprises the modification of one or more case attributes. It is a one-case strategy, as a new solution is produced from a single case. Case abstraction is also a one-case strategy, and consists on the use of a case taxonomy to generalize or specialize an old design creating a new one. The composition strategy deals with one or multiple cases. It splits and/or merges case pieces generating new solutions - it is a multi-case strategy. Due to space constraints, only the retrieval process for the case mutation is shown here.

4.1 Case Retrieval for Mutation

The process begins with the best starting case (the one indexed by the greater number of FSs common to the new problem). Then the system searches the case graph for episodes candidate for generation of a new design. The selected cases are given to the adaptation module, which tries to build new solutions from these cases. The solutions have to be validated by the user. If the user does not accept any of these solutions, the retrieval module begins a new cycle of exploration of the case graph, starting from the cases in the previous iteration (see figure 3).

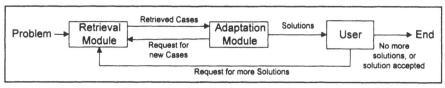

Figure 3 - The reasoning cycle.

Three versions of the algorithm were developed: continuous search, prune search without backtracking, and prune search with backtracking. Prune search without and with backtracking are evolution's of the continuous search algorithms. It performs a continuous exploration of the case library. The other two algorithms make a controlled search in the case library by retrieving only n cases at each iteration. Number n is the prune factor. The backtracking mechanism makes the difference between the pruning versions. In case of dead-ends the backtracking mechanism presented in one of the pruning versions makes possible to return to cases left behind by the search algorithm.

Two lists of cases are considered through the cycles comprising the retrieval process. One is the list of cases that were explored by the algorithm (*Seen_Cases*). The other list comprises cases that were explored but were not expanded (*Unexpanded_Cases*). A case is expanded if all the cases with links from it belong to *Seen_Cases*. The next subsections presents each of the algorithm versions.

4.2 Continuous Search Algorithm

In figure 4 we present the continuous search algorithm. The process starts with the best start case (*Start_Case*). In the first iteration the *Unexpanded_Cases* and the *Seen_Cases* lists are initialized with the start case (lines 2 and 3 in figure 4). Then the *Start_Case* is given to the adaptation module (line 4).

If the process is not complete at the end of the first iteration, two situations may occur. One takes place when the *Unexpanded_Cases* list is empty (test in line 6) and there are no more starting cases (test in line 7). Within this circumstance the algorithm returns "end_of_search" (line 8), because it has no more cases to expand, and no more starting cases to begin exploring the graph of cases in a different location. If there are more starting cases, then a start case is selected from the list of starting cases (line 10), is added to *Seen_Cases* (line 11), and the process resumes with a non-empty *Unexpanded_Cases* list (line 12).

If *Unexpanded_Cases* contains cases, then the best case from this list is selected (*Expand_Case* in line 15). This case is the one with more FSs in common with the target problem in the *Unexpanded_Cases* list. Then the *Expand_Case*, is expanded (line 16). The result of this expansion is a list of cases (*Retrieved_Cases*).

The *Retrieved_Cases* list has no common cases with the *Seen_Cases* list. The algorithm then removes the *Expand_Case* from *Unexpanded_Cases* (line 17), and ranks the *Retrieved_Cases* (line 18). The ranking procedure is defined in subsection 4.5. Then the *Retrieved_Cases* are added to *Unexpanded_Cases* and to *Seen_Cases* (lines 19 and 20). Finally in line 21 the *Retrieved_Cases* are returned to the adaptation module.

```
1. IF first_iteration THEN
2.      Unexpanded_Cases=Start_Case
3.      Seen_Cases=Start_Case
4.      Return Start_Case
5. ELSE
6.      IF Unexpanded_Cases=∅ THEN
7.          IF Start_Cases=∅ THEN
8.              Return end_of_search
9.          ELSE
10.             Unexpanded_Cases=best case (Start_Case1) form Start_Cases AND must not be a
member                    of Seen_Cases
11.             Add Start_Case1 to Seen_Cases
12.             Call the retrieval algorithm again
13.         END IF
14. ELSE
15.     Select best case (Expand_Case) from Unexpanded_Cases
16.     Retrieved_Cases=Cases with direct links with the Expand_Case that don't belong to
            Seen_Cases
17.     Remove Expand_Case from Unexpanded_cases
18.     Rank Retrieved_Cases
19.     Add Retrieved_Cases to Unexpanded_Cases
20.     Add Retrieved_Cases to Seen_Cases
21.     Return Retrieved_Cases
22.   END IF
23. END IF
```

Figure 4 - The Continuous Search Algorithm.

4.3   Prune Search Algorithm (without Backtracking)

As stated before, this version is a modification of the continuous search algorithm. Figure 5 presents part of the algorithm. Lines 1 to 18 are exactly equal to the previous algorithm, the difference resides on lines 19 to 22.

```
19.     Retrieved_Cases1=The first nth (prune factor) cases from Retrieved_Cases
20.     Add Retrieved_Cases1 to Seen_Cases
21.     Add Retrieved_Cases1 to Unexpanded_Cases
22.     Return Retrieved_Cases1
23.   END IF
24. END IF
```

Figure 5 - Part of the Prune Search Algorithm without Backtracking.

After selecting the best case from *Unexpanded_Cases* (line 15), expanding the *Expand_Case* (line 16), removing it from *Unexpanded_Cases* (line 17), and ranking the *Retrieved_Cases* (line 18), the algorithm chooses only the best nth cases from *Retrieved_Cases* (line 19). This results in the *Retrieved_Cases1* list. The number of cases in *Retrieved_Cases1* is determined by the prune factor, which is a parameter defined by the user. Then cases in *Retrieved_Cases1* are added to

Seen_Cases and to *Unexpanded_Cases* (lines 20 and 21), and returned to the adaptation module (line 22).

This version is named 'without backtracking' because cases in *Retrieved_Cases* which are not in *Retrieved_Cases1* are not added to *Unexpanded_Cases*, thus not being explored again unless they are reached by a different path.

4.4   Prune Search Algorithm (with Backtracking)

Like in the previous algorithm, the prune search algorithm with backtracking is based on the continuous search algorithm. Figure 6 presents the pseudo-code lines which differ from the continuous version. Lines 1 to 18 are equal to the previous two algorithms.

This algorithm differs from the prune search without backtracking in lines 20 and 21. *Retrieved_Cases* are added to *Seen_Cases* and to *Unexpanded_Cases*, instead of *Retrieved_Cases1*. One consequence of this difference from the last two algorithms, is that, cases which were not retrieved but were explored, can be expanded. They were ignored in the retrieval but they still can act as exploration departure points in the case graph. In the prune search without backtracking they can only be expanded if they can be reached by a different path. This happens because they were added to *Seen_Cases* in the backtracking version.

19.	*Retrieved_Cases1*=The first nth (prune factor) cases from *Retrieved_Cases*
20.	Add *Retrieved_Cases* to *Seen_Cases*
21.	Add *Retrieved_Cases* to *Unexpanded_Cases*
22.	Return *Retrieved_Cases1*
23.	END IF
24. END IF	

Figure 6 - Part of the Prune Search Algorithm with Backtracking.

4.5   Ranking Cases

Retrieved cases are ranked based on two things: the score of the case they were reached from, and the difference link with that case. The score is the number of FSs in common with the problem, which is computed in the following way: Case1 is the case we want to score, Case0 is the case from which Case1 was reached, N0 is the score of Case0, N1 is the score of Case1 (the one we want to calculate), #FSs0 is the number of FSs in Case0 which are present in the problem and are not present in Case1, #FSs1 is the number of FSs in Case1 which are present in the problem and are not present in Case0, then $N1 = N0 - \#FSs0 + \#FSs1$. #FSs0 and #FSs1 are given by the difference link between Case1 and Case0 (see section 3). Using this method for score calculation only the information in the difference link is used, which takes less computational resources than normal nearest neighbor metrics.

5.   Example

In this section we describe an example of each version of the retrieval algorithms. The retrieval algorithms are implemented in a system called CREATOR. This system is a case-based design system in the domain of digital circuit design. The case library used for tests contains fifty cases (case0 to case49). Cases represent digital circuits implementing logical functions. These logical functions are the FSs.

The example we present comprises a new problem specifying three FSs: f(A*B + C*D) ∧ f(A*B) ∧ f(C*D).

Each version of the algorithm performed 44 iterations. It run until there were no more cases to expand, and all the starting cases were seen. In Figure 8 we present the retrieved cases in each iteration. From the algorithm run 44 cases were expanded (the number of iterations).

The continuous search version began with *case3* as the starting case. It is the case that matches perfectly the target problem (see figure 7). If the goal of the system was to retrieve the best case, the algorithm would stop at this point. But we are interested in doing the exploration of the case library looking for alternative solutions. The graph (see figure 8a) of the continuous version displays an irregular retrieval of cases, in which it can be seen a decrease on the number of retrieved cases.

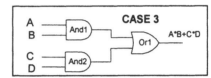

Figure 7 - Graphical representation of the start case.

The prune search algorithm (without backtracking) began with *case3* as the starting case. The prune factor used was 2. This means that the maximum number of cases that can be retrieved in each iteration is two. As can be seen by the data in figure 8b, a more moderate retrieval of cases is achieved.

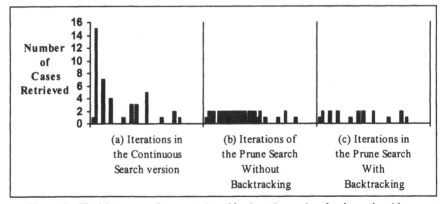

Figure 8 - The histogram of cases retrieved by iteration, using the three algorithms.

The other prune search version starts with the same case of the other versions. The prune factor is also two. At a first look it might appear that data in Figure 8c does not agree with data in Figure 8b, because the prune search with the backtracking version uses a backtrack mechanism to go back to cases that were pruned, thus making possible to retrieve more cases than the non-backtracking version. But this is not true for this example. This happens because cases have many links, connecting them with various cases, thus making possible to reach the same case by various alternative paths. So, a path to a case that was not explored, can be pruned, but there are other paths to reach it. In the backtracking version the difference is that the case is added to the *Seen_Cases* list, though disabling it to be retrieved further ahead in the algorithm.

If the graph of cases would have few links between cases the situation would be the opposite one. The backtracking version would reach more cases due to its backtracking mechanism, and the non-backtracking version would not because the only path available would have been pruned. These two situations show that there are increased advantages in using the prune search with backtracking when the number of links between cases is high. On the other side, when the number of links between cases is low the backtracking version is more useful.

6. Related Work

In the core of this work is the adaptation strategies which are defined by Rosenman and Gero (Rosenman and Gero 93). The selected design is based on the closest, or at least a good match with the target problem. Developed systems that address this kind of case retrieval are, CADSYN (Maher, Balachandran and Zhang 95), KRITIK (Goel 91, 92), and IM-RECIDE (Gomes et. al. 96). In most of the systems this is viewed as normal adaptation, but other adaptation strategies exist.

CADSYN is a domain-independent case-based reasoner that retrieves and adapts design cases using a combination of case memory and generalized design knowledge in the form of system definitions and constraints. Like in CREATOR, cases are indexed by their functionalities. The ranking process is similar to the one in CREATOR. The main difference with our system is that it does not perform exploration of the case library, but it can decompose the current problem into sub-problems. Our retrieval algorithm for the mutation adaptation strategy is not prepared for this situation, but the retrieval algorithm for case composition is specially dedicated to this problem. The user is quite involved in the whole design process, like in CREATOR.

KRITIK is a case-based system for designing physical devices. It uses case-based reasoning for design retrieval and model-based reasoning for case adaptation. Case representation in CREATOR is based in KRITIK's case representation. Cases are indexed by the functionalities they exhibit (like in CREATOR). The main difference resides in the lack of the exploration process. KRITIK retrieves only the best case in the case library and tries to adapt it to the target problem.

IM-RECIDE is a creative case-based shell for development of expert systems. This system focus on the exploration of the case library by a clustering of cases. Each cluster of cases, called spaces, is defined by the properties of the cases it comprises. Thus searching for design alternatives is done through the use of spaces. The main difference with CREATOR is the case representation. IM-RECIDE deals with cases imperfectly described and explained, CREATOR uses a model based representation for cases. Another difference is the lack of an index structure. This deteriorates the system performance. IM-RECIDE uses a retrieval metric instead of an index scheme.

7. Discussion and Future Work

We described a retrieval process driven by case adaptation. This process is based on a memory structure capable of supporting exploration of the case library for generation of design alternatives. We use two retrieval algorithms to perform case retrieval: a mutation-driven and a thematic abstraction-driven algorithm.

In this paper we stress the importance of exploring the case library in order to obtain alternative designs. Each of the algorithms is suited for a specific type of case graph. If abstract relations can be established between case functionalities, than the thematic abstraction retrieval algorithm is more suited. When the functional similarities are more important then the mutation retrieval algorithm seems to perform better. The topology of the case library and similarities between cases are also important for choosing a suited algorithm.

One important observation is that, with the increase of the number of iterations, the retrieved cases are less similar to the new problem. This is a normal situation in exploration. More useless cases are retrieved, as well as cases more difficult to adapt, but the probability of finding a more creative solutions increases.

At this moment we are starting the implementation of adaptation strategies and rules. We are also exploring various ways of performing case validation.

8. Acknowledgments

This research was partially supported by a MSc. grant to the first author from JNICT (PRAXIS XXI BM 6563 95).

9. References

(Bareiss 89) Bareiss, R ed. 1989. Exemplar-Based Knowledge Acquisition - A Unified Approach to Concept Representation, Classification, and Learning. San Diego, CA: Academic Press

(Bylander and Chandrasekaran 85) Bylander,T., and Chandrasekaran, B. 1985. Understanding Behavior Using Consolidation. In Proceedings of the Ninth International Joint Conference on Artificial Intelligence.

(Gero 94) Gero, J. 1994. Computational Models of Creative Design Processes. In T. Dartnall (ed.), AI in Creativity. Kluwer, Dordrecht, pp. 269-281.

(Goel 91) Goel, A. 1991. A Model-Based Approach to Case Adaptation. In Proceedings of the 13th Annual Conference of the Cognitive Science Society, CogSci91, August, Chicago, Illinois, USA.

(Goel 92) Goel, A. 1992. Representation of Design Functions in Experience-Based Design. Intelligent Computer Aided Design. D. Brown, M. Waldron, and H. Yoshikawa (eds.). Elsevier Science Publishers.

(Gomes et al. 96) Gomes, P., Bento, C., Gago, P., and Costa, E. 1996. Towards a Case-Based Model for Creative Processes. In Proceedings of the 12th European Conference on Artificial Intelligence. John Willey & Sons.

(Kolodner and Wills 93) Kolodner, K., and Wills, L. 1993. Case-Based Creative Design. In AAAI Spring Symposium on AI+Creativity, Stanford, CA.

(Maher and Zhao 93) Maher, M., and Zhao, F. 1993. Dynamic Associations for Creative Engineering Design. Moddeling Creativity and knowledge-Based Creative Design, John Gero, and Mary Lou Maher (eds.). Lawrence Erlbaum Associates, pp.329-351.

(Maher, Balachandran, and Zhang 95) Maher, M., Balachandran, M., and Zhang, D. 1995. Case-Based Reasoning in Design. Lawrence Erlbaum Associates.

(Reich 91) Reich, Y. 1991. Design Knowledge Acquisition: Task Analysis and a Partial Implementation. Knowledge Acquisition: An International Journal of Knowledge Acquisition for Knowledge-Based System 3(3):234-254.

(Rosenman and Gero 93) Rosenman, M., and Gero, J. 1993. Creativity in Design Using a Design Prototype Approach. Modeling Creativity and Knowledge-Based Creative Design, John Gero and Mary Lou (eds.). Lawrence Erlbaum Associates, pp. 111-137.

(Smyth e Keane 95) Smyth, B., e Keane, M., 1995. Experiments on Adaptation-Guided Retrieval in Case-Based Design. Em Proceedings of the International Conference on Case-Based Reasoning, ICCBR95. Springer. Sesimbra, Portugal.

(Stroulia et al. 92) Stroulia, E., Shankar, M., Goel, A., and Penberthy, L. 1992. A Model-Based Approach to Blame Assignment in Design. In Proceedings of the 2nd International Conference on AI in Design.

(Sycara and Navinchadra 91) Sycara, K., and Navinchandra, D. 1991. Influences: A Thematic Abstraction for Creative Use of Multiple Cases. In Proceedings of the first European Workshop on Case-Based Reasoning.

(Sycara and Navinchandra 93) Sycara, K., and Navinchandra, D. 1993. Case Representation and Indexing for Innovative Design Reuse. In Proceedings of the Workshop of the 13th International Joint Conference on Artificial Intelligence, France.

(Tong and Sriram 92) Tong, C., and Sriram, D. eds. 1992. Artificial Intelligence in Engineering Design, Vol. I. Academic Press.

Incremental Concept Evolution Based on Adaptive Feature Weighting

Udo Hahn & Manfred Klenner

Text Knowledge Engineering Lab, Freiburg University
Werthmannplatz 1, D-79085 Freiburg, Germany
http://www.coling.uni-freiburg.de/

Abstract. We provide a model of concept drift by which concept classes are automatically updated according to the dynamics of change in the underlying learning environment. Instances with a well-defined degree of feature similarity are incrementally grouped together to form so-called concept versions. A comparative empirical evaluation of the versioning system VERGENE, which is built on these premises, demonstrates its effectiveness for properly dealing with concept drift phenomena in medium-sized knowledge bases.

1 The Dynamics of Concept Change and Text Understanding

Most work in the field of computational concept learning presupposes that the goal concept to be learned is stable over time, i.e., that its concept description does not change while learning proceeds. In real-world learning situations, however, concept drift is a natural phenomenon which must be accounted for by the learning machinery. The procedure we propose for tracking such concept drift phenomena produces a generational stratification of the underlying concept class description in terms of concept versions. Each version stands for a particular stage of the conceptual evolution of its corresponding concept class. This is expressed by constraints which define a particular "standard" holding at that developmental state.

Although this versioning methodology is not limited to a special application, it has been developed and evaluated as part of SYNDIKATE, a text understanding system which is geared for knowledge base synthesis from test reports in the information technology domain [8]. Its parsing component is closely coupled with conceptual integrity constraints at the knowledge representation level [7]. These constraints directly restrict permitted mappings from the surface text to conceptual representations which capture the content of the text under analysis. The more specific these constraints, the stronger the effect on search space reductions as required, e.g., for ambiguity and anaphora resolution, and the more accurate is the knowledge properly extracted from the texts. From this, one may easily conclude that systematic changes in permitted value intervals not made explicit at the knowledge representation level lead to a continuously degrading performance of the text understander as the most recent texts are entered into the system. These texts actually reflect the newest standards currently valid in the domain, while a (non-versioned) knowledge base of the domain represents the more or less aging or already dated ones. Thus, the natural language understanding component will necessarily run into severe problems if these changes are not propagated to the level of domain representations.

2 A Model for Concept Versioning

Our approach to concept versioning is located between unsupervised concept learning paradigms like conceptual clustering [6] and supervised learning algorithms like IBL [2]. As in conceptual clustering, the task is to form classes (in this case, versions) out of a stream of instances. However, unlike conceptual clustering but similar to supervised learning the version learner starts with a training set of instances (hence, we supply *a priori* classified instances of a generic concept class). The "classes" to be learned are situated at the so-called version layer which mediates between the generic concept class subsuming the instances and the instances themselves.

The versions of a concept group the instances according to their "quality" which in our domain often coincides with – but is not fully determined by – their recency.[1] Thus, the quality of instances needs to be assessed. We here provide a knowledge-based evaluation scheme in terms of (hierarchically ordered) progress models of the domain (cf. also [13]). A *progress model* of a concept specifies for each attribute its type ("symbolic" or "numerical", i.e., "discrete" or "continuous") and its developmental tendency ("increasing", "decreasing" or "unspecified" for numerical, "dynamic" or "static" for symbolic attributes). If the progress model indicates, e.g., a tendency for increasing values for a particular numerical attribute, a high value in the data set signals higher quality than a low one. A symbolic attribute considered "dynamic" is expected to vary (shrink or augment) its values, while a static one does not. However, time-invariant attributes (i.e., attributes with static or undefined tendencies) may become variant and *vice versa*. Thus, the initially supplied specifications in the progress model are only tentative and will be automatically adapted (cf. Section 2.1).

In our model, concept drift is not captured by changes at the local level of a single attribute but at the global level of the combined changes of instance distances. At this global level, the local changes accumulate to a (monotonic) increase of a measure we refer to as *instance quality* (cf. Section 2.2). Technically, the distance of an instance to some evaluation fixpoint is measured. Considering well-defined points on this distance scale, version boundaries can be established, thus separating obsolete from up-to-date instances (cf. Section 2.3). Currently, we approximate this quality growth of instances by a linear development function $D(t) = a_0 + a_1 t$, where a_0 denotes the (quality) offset, a_1 the (linear) growth rate and t the position of an instance in the stream of instances (t serves as an index on the set of instances ordered by the quality measure).

The starting point for quality diagnosis (approximation of the function D) is a *training set* TS of instances I, which is selected to form the initial version of the concept. The size of the training set is a parameter of the system. Most systems that cope with concept drift rely on such a parameterized "window" defined over the size of instances (cf. [14,12,21]). The instances of TS, first, are ordered in qualitatively increasing order according to the distances of their relevant attributes to the respective bottom values of the first version V (which is derived by inductive generalization from TS). Initially, all unspecified or static attributes are considered irrelevant, while the other attributes are

---

[1] We assume a *large-scale* temporal ordering on the entire set of instances, which in our case comes with the ordering of computer magazines according to the publishing year. However, the articles of the annual set are entered into the system in an arbitrary order.

considered relevant (cf. Section 2.1 for relevance updates). In a second step, the (pairwise) quality increase between any two adjacent instances is weighted such that quality increases from the upper spectrum of the ordered distance list are favored, while those at the lower end tend to be lessened. From the weighted sum of these quality increases, the mean quality increase $\overline{QI}$ of the training set is derived. This measure turns out to be crucial for versioning decisions (cf. Section 2.2).

2.1 The Role of Feature Weights in Versioning: Relevance Updating

The relevance of a feature (attribute) is usually defined as its ability to predict the class membership of an instance. In the case of concept *drift*, the relevance of an attribute, however, is defined in terms of its disposition to *change in time*: *time-varying* attributes are relevant, while time-invariant ones are not. This is due to the fact that the values of time-varying attributes indicate the most recent developmental stages and thus are *version predictors*, while those of invariant attributes are, in the extreme case, randomly distributed over all versions. In our approach, the relevance of an attribute has initially to be specified in the progress model. Relevant attributes are assigned a development tendency and a weight of *1*, while irrelevant ones, initially, are weighted with *0*, i.e., they do not contribute to versioning and classification decisions with respect to the initial version.

Let VR_A be the global value range of a (continuous) numerical attribute A over all versions $Vers$, i.e., the lower and upper bound of VR_A enclose all version-specific value ranges. $Sub_A \sqsubset VR_A$, the maximal non-overlapping region of a version-specific value range $VR_{A,V}$, then satisfies the following condition: $VR_{A,V} \sqcap Sub_A = Sub_A \wedge \forall W \in Vers \backslash V : VR_{A,W} \sqcap Sub_A = \emptyset$ (the operators $\sqsubset$ and $\sqcap$ denote the inclusion and intersection of intervals, respectively; $\emptyset$ stands for the empty interval).[2] "Maximal" means that there exist no larger subinterval Int_A with $Sub_A \sqsubset Int_A$ that satisfies the same condition as Sub_A. $NOV_{A,V}$, the *local non-overlap rate* of a version V, can then be defined as:

$$NOV_{A,V} := \frac{length(Sub_A)}{length(VR_{A,V})} \tag{1}$$

where $length(VR_{A,V}) := |L_{A,V} - U_{A,V}|$, i.e., the length of the interval spanned by the lower value bound $L_{A,V}$ of $VR_{A,V}$ to its upper value bound $U_{A,V}$. The *global non-overlap rate* NOV_A is defined by the ratio of the length of all overlap-free subintervals of VR_A and the length of VR_A. Given the definition of $NOV_{A,V}$, the *local overlap rate* $OV_{A,V}$ can be defined as: $OV_{A,V} := 1 - NOV_{A,V}$.

The relevance of an attribute may change over time. This is captured in our model by a feature weighting method that alters the initial feature weights in the course of learning for relevant as well as irrelevant attributes. Increasing (decreasing) relevance of an irrelevant (relevant) attribute is reflected by the increased (decreased) NOV. If these changes of an attribute's relevance pass a certain threshold, its developmental tendency needs to be adapted, too. A relevant attribute that converges towards *0* should then be

---

[2] Analogous definitions can be easily formulated for discrete and symbolic attributes, but these are omitted from the following presentation.

assigned the tendency *"unspecified"*, while any irrelevant attribute that transforms into a relevant one should be characterized in terms of whether its values are increasing or decreasing. For a relevant attribute to be considered irrelevant, a low threshold value ($NOV_{A,V} = 0.1$) must be reached, while for irrelevant attributes to become relevant an increase of their NOV to at least 0.5 is required. In both cases, however, the threshold value must be passed for a certain time period (currently, the span of a version). This prevents the system from relevance oscillation due to only temporary value alternations. The tendency, $Tend_A$, of an initially irrelevant attribute A that is getting relevant is, e.g., induced with the aid of a simple heuristic (for real-valued attributes):

$$Tend_A := \begin{cases} increasing & if\ U_{A,v} > U_{A,v-1}\ and\ L_{A,v} > L_{A,v-1} \\ decreasing & if\ U_{A,v} < U_{A,v-1}\ and\ L_{A,v} < L_{A,v-1} \\ unspecified\ else \end{cases} \quad (2)$$

We conducted some preliminary experiments on learning attribute relevance. Since in our data sets no changes of attribute relevance actually occurred, we simulated this situation by considering relevant attributes to be irrelevant (we assigned them *unspecified* tendencies). Fig. 1 illustrates a typical scenario in this experimental setting. In Fig. 1a) the original NOV developments of two of the six relevant attributes (LINE-FREQUENCY and BANDWIDTH) of the concept MONITOR are given (starting with instance 20, the last instance of the training set). After versioning (instance 24), both relevant attributes temporarily drop to about 0.5 (caused by an overlap of the initial value ranges of the new version). While LINE-FREQUENCY recovers to a high relevance level after a few learning steps (0.9), BANDWIDTH ends up with a NOV of 0.4. Such a decrease, if it occurs within a certain range, does not neccessarily indicate a loss of relevance. More often it reflects a difference in the dynamics of change of the relevant attributes, since the rates of development of several relevant attributes do not necessarily correlate. Fig. 1b) shows the corresponding NOVs under the experimental condition that LINE-FREQUENCY is considered irrelevant. Its initial NOV (*0*) increases to 0.9 immediately after a versioning process. Later on, it decreases to 0.7 and increases again up to 0.9. Compared with Fig. 1a), it is on the average of lower relevance (indicated by a lower mean NOV). On the other hand, the mean NOV of BANDWIDTH which is

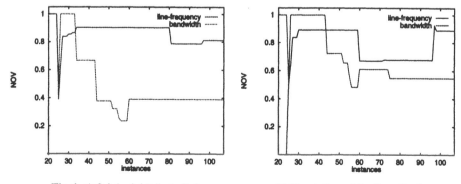

Fig. 1. a) Original Attribute Relevance   b) Simulation of Attribute Irrelevance

tentatively considered the only relevant attribute in this setting is higher under condition *b)* than under condition *a)*. This increase is due to the dominant role of BANDWIDTH as the sole relevant attribute for two versions (LINE-FREQUENCY becomes relevant only at the transition from the second to the third version, after instance 60). We have some experimental evidence that relevance updates of attributes are likely to be traced by the NOV measure. However, more experiments are needed to further clarify its validity and to identify the most significant constraints for relevance updating.

2.2 Version Formation and Quality Evaluation

Version descriptions are generated by inductive generalization from instances, whether initially (and non-incrementally) from the training set TS or in subsequent (incremental) learning steps as a result of the integration of new instances. Part of the integration of a new instance is the quality reevaluation of the version that incorporates the new instance. If the version quality reaches a given threshold, a successor version to the current one is built. The quality of a version is determined from the weighted mean of the distance increases between the instances of the version. Distance increase is a *directed* distance measure that operates with a version boundary used as a fixpoint for distance assessment. The distance of each instance I to the lower bound of its version V is called the bottom distance $BD_{I,V}$ (BD_V is the increasingly ordered set of all $BD_{I,V}$s). The lower boundaries of a version V are derived from the value range $VR_{A,V}$ of each attribute and the attribute's tendency specified in the progress model. Let I_A be the value of instance I for attribute A and $VR_{A,V} = [L_{A,V}, U_{A,V}]$; $L_{A,V} = I_{A,1}$ and $U_{A,V} = I_{A,n}$ from the ordered list of n instance values $Is_{A,V}$, where $I_{A,i} < I_{A,i+1}$, for $i = 1, \ldots, n-1$. With respect to the qualitative evaluation of instances, the version's value range, $VR_{A,V}$, must be interpreted in terms of a bottom value, $B_{A,V}$, and a top value, $T_{A,V}$. For increasing numerical attributes the *bottom value* $B_{A,V}$ of a value range $VR_{A,V}$ equals $L_{A,V}$, while for decreasing ones it equals $U_{A,V}$ (similarly is the *top value* $T_{A,V}$ defined).

The knowledge about the lower quality bounds of a version is used to impose a quality-based ordering on the instances of a version V, by considering for each attribute the distances an instance has to the bottom values of V. The *bottom distance* $BD_{I,V}$ of instance I of version V with respect to each of its attributes A is defined as follows:

$$BD_{I,V} := \sum_A dist(B_{A,V}, I_A) * NOV_A \qquad (3)$$

For numerical attributes, e.g., the function *dist* is defined as:

$$dist(B_{A,V}, I_A) := \frac{|B_{A,V} - I_A|}{length(VR_{A,V})} \qquad (4)$$

BD_V, the increasingly ordered set of all $BD_{I,V}$s, is determined for each version to characterize its *version quality*. The quality of a version is computed by taking the pairwise sum of its quality increases between any two adjacent instances on the quality ordering induced by $BD_{I,V}$, i.e., the sum of the differences on BD_V. The weighted mean *quality increase* $\overline{QI}_V$ is determined from BD_V as follows:

$$\overline{QI}_V := \frac{\sum_{i=1}^{|BD_V|-1} |BD_{i,V} - BD_{i+1,V}| * i}{\sum_{i=1}^{|BD_V|-1} i} \qquad (5)$$

where i is the position index on BD_V that serves as a weight for the recency of a distance. According to this definition, we favor qualitatively superior data items which express the current development stages over inferior ones. The $\overline{QI}_V$ measure then can be used as a quality index for the evaluation of the quality of future versions, too. Except for the initial version whose quality index is determined from the training set TS, in later stages all other $\overline{QI}_V$s are derived from the (system-generated) most recent version. This happens whenever that version has reached the versioning threshold as determined by the $\overline{QI}_{V-1}$ of its predecessor version V-1.

2.3 Versioning

A new version with index $V+1$ is created, if the quality increase of the most recent version V reaches the quality threshold determined by its predecessor V-1 (except for the first version which has no predecessor). The following criterion applies:

$$DS_{V-1} * \overline{QI}_{V-1} \leq |BD_{1,V} - BD_{n,V}| * \frac{NOV_{VQ-1}}{NOV_{VQ}} \qquad (6)$$

$BD_{1,V}$ is the first, $BD_{n,V}$ is the last element from BD_V; $DS_{V-1} := |BD_{V-1}| - 1$ denotes the number of developmental steps for the preceding version V-1. $DS_{V-1} * \overline{QI}_{V-1}$ characterizes the quality threshold that the most recent version must reach, before versioning is allowed to occur. The non-overlap rate NOV_{VQ} of the whole version cluster VQ is defined as:

$$NOV_{VQ} := \frac{\sum_A NOV_A}{|A|} \qquad (7)$$

In each learning state, the *version cluster* VQ comprises all versions generated so far. If in the course of learning a new version is formed, it is added to VQ. Consequently, the NOV of the augmented VQ (usually) differs from its predecessor. In order to compare the quality of a version V derived from a BD_V of version cluster VQ to the one predicted from a BD_{V-1} of version cluster VQ-1, their non-overlap rates must be assimilated (cf. the rightmost ratio in expression (6)): a decreasing non-overlap rate yields a ratio greater than one, i.e., the quality of V is lifted, while given an increasing one the quality of V is lowered, accordingly.

Generally, if the versioning threshold of a version V is reached, the "best" instance of V (in terms of its distance on the quality scale) is selected to be the first instance of the new version $V+1$. The *initialization of a new version* is a knowledge-based generalization process. The version boundaries for the relevant attributes of a new version are determined from the upper bounds of its predecessor version and the values of the new version's first instance. For an increasing relevant attribute, e.g., the following criterion is used to determine the initial value range of the new version:

$$VR_{A,V+1} = \begin{cases} [I_A, U_{A,v}] \; if \; I_A < U_{A,v} \\ [U_{A,v}, I_A] \; if \; I_A \geq U_{A,v} \end{cases} \qquad (8)$$

This generalization part of a versioning process is justified by the attributes' tendencies specified in the progress model: the values are expected to develop in the predicted direction. Accordingly, the *best* possible value range for the new version is the one that spans an interval between the boundaries of the last version and the instance values of the new version. Discriminative initial value ranges are important, since a new version competes with former ones for the integration of new instances, a process which depends (among other things) on the relative distance to a version's value ranges.

2.4 Integration of New Instances

Conceptual clustering systems attempt to maximize intra-class similarity and inter-class dissimilarity. Since concept versions are refinements of a single generic concept, they (usually) share the type and number of attributes. Hence, the possibility of overlapping value ranges is quite high. Sophisticated criteria are needed when integrating new instances into existing versions in order to avoid undesirable overlapping rates that, in turn, drastically diminish the discriminative power of the whole version cluster. We here provide a measure called *quality development QD*. An instance is integrated into the version with the best, i.e., highest QD. The *quality development QD* of a version V, given an instance I to be integrated, is defined as:

$$QD_{V,I} := \frac{1}{|A|} \sum_A diff(VR_{A,v}, I_A) * QC(V, I, A) \qquad (9)$$

where QC, the *quality change*, is defined as:

$$QC(V, I, A) := \begin{cases} NOV_A & if \; \Delta OV_{A,v} = 0 \land NOV_A \neq 0 \\ \Delta OV_{A,v} & if \; NOV_A = 0 \land \Delta OV_{A,v} \neq 0 \\ NOV_A * \Delta OV_{A,v} & else \end{cases} \qquad (10)$$

The overlap change is defined as $\Delta OV_{A,v} := (OV_{A,v} - OV_{A,v \oplus I_A})$, with $OV_{A,v}$ being the overlap rate for the value range $VR_{A,v}$ prior to the integration of I_A, and $OV_{A,v \oplus I_A}$ being the overlap rate after the integration of I_A into version V. The function $diff$ is defined as follows (for continuous values):

$$diff([L_{A,v}, U_{A,v}], I_A) := \begin{cases} 0 & if \; L_{A,v} \leq I_A \leq U_{A,v} \\ \frac{L_{A,v} - I_A}{length([L_{A,v}, U_{A,v}])} & if \; I_A < L_{A,v} \\ \frac{I_A - U_{A,v}}{length([L_{A,v}, U_{A,v}])} & if \; U_{A,v} < I_A \end{cases} \qquad (11)$$

QD consists of a distance value, a global (NOV_A) and a local weight ($\Delta OV_{A,v}$). If NOV_A is high (say, close to 1), i.e., attribute A has almost overlap-free value ranges, a given value distance and local rate change (ΔOV) is fully taken into account. On the other hand, any change on the basis of a low NOV_A, whether increasing or decreasing, only partially contributes to the decision into which version a new instance should be integrated. Note that the distance of a value and the resulting change of overlap effected by the integration of this value are often, but not always, proportional to each other. Hence, the need to consider both criteria in the definition of QD.

3 Empirical Evaluation

We have implemented a versioning system called VERGENE, which is based on the principles outlined in Section 2. The experimental results we here discuss are based on three data sets: one from the information technology, another from the automobile domain (see Table 1).[3] Only recently, we have started to consider a third domain, viz. household appliances like washing machines, dishwashers, etc.

concept	abbrev.	# of attributes (relevant)	# of instances
washing machine	wm	3 (2)	122
hard disk	hd	6 (2)	119
notebook	nb	7 (3)	192
personal computer	pc	6 (3)	144
laser writer	lw	10 (8)	103
monitor	mon	10 (7)	104
desk top publishing	dtp	7 (1)	65
automobile	car5	8 (1)	390

Table 1. Data Sets: Household Appliances, Information Technology, Automobiles

For an evaluation of VERGENE, we compared it on the basis of these data with the results generated by two well-known machine learning (ML) systems, viz. COBWEB [6], an incremental conceptual clustering system, and AUTOCLASS [19], a non-incremental probabilistic clustering system. Additionally, we analyzed the data with a standard statistical clustering program (BAVERAGE (average-linkage-between-groups) with quadratic Euclidean distance). None of these systems need domain-specific background knowledge as VERGENE (moderately) does, viz. the attribute development tendencies supplied by the progress model. On the other hand, two of them (AUTOCLASS and BAVERAGE) are non-incremental (in contrast to the incremental learning mode of VERGENE). We considered a comparison with COBWEB fairly reasonable, since it has been explicitly characterized as being able to cope with concept drift (cf. [6], p.44).

The evaluation of the results for each system was carried out relative to a third ML system, viz. IBL (NTGrowth [2]). The basic evaluation strategy was to let IBL define the gold standard for the test accuracy. On the basis of the different version descriptions that were generated by VERGENE, COBWEB, AUTOCLASS, and BAVERAGE for each of the eight major concept classes in the entire data set, IBL was used to assign each test instance to that version considered "most similar". So every time IBL assigns an instance to the same version as one of the four competing systems, IBL confirms

---

[3] The automobile data set was taken from the UCI ML repository [16]. We partitioned it into four subsets according to the attribute HORSEPOWERS and assumed MILES PER GALLON to be a time-variant attribute (tendency: increasing).

their division into versions. IBL's test accuracy then can be interpreted as its *confirmation rate* relative to the cluster quality. For our experiments, the training set was equal to the test set (cf. [11] for a similar setting). Fig. 2 gives the results of this evaluation. The entire automobile data set from UCI is referred to as CAR5, while CAR1 to CAR4 are the classes extracted from the original data set as specified in footnote 3.

The result of COBWEB for CAR4 was dropped, since it produced, for this data set, a totally unfavorable result (one version for each instance). This poor performance is a by-product of an instance ordering (very common in our data sets) that poses, in principle, serious problems to COBWEB, *viz.* only slightly differing instances (low discrimination) follow each other. More preferable to COBWEB is an ordering with sharp contrasts (high discrimination) between successive instances. The solid line in Fig. 2 shows the results obtained

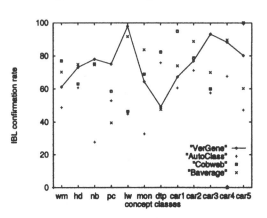

Fig. 2. IBL Confirmation Rates

by VERGENE. All points above (below) this curve indicate results of the competing systems that have higher (lower) scores. None of the systems is clearly superior to the others. With regard to the mean confirmation rate for each system, VERGENE was confirmed with a rate of 75.4%, followed by COBWEB (73.2%), BAVERAGE (72.0%), and AUTOCLASS (53.9%). We interpret these data such that the results of VERGENE are favorable when compared to those of other systems with respect to *classification accuracy*. However, they do not yield an assessment for the problem-specific merits we expect our learning scheme to have on properly dealing with drifting concepts.

Such a problem-specific evaluation dimension is the overlap rate between versions. While VERGENE has been tuned to minimize this rate, it was by no means evident whether the other systems could compete with VERGENE's results on this dimension, although they consider the maximization of inter-cluster dissimilarity a general goal. We tested the *actual overlap* rate $OV_{act} := \frac{|MPI|}{|Is|}$, where MPI denotes the set of instances with more than one parent version, and Is stands for the entire set of instances. To obtain class descriptions for COBWEB, AUTOCLASS and BAVERAGE, we constructed generalizations of the extensional classes derived by AUTOCLASS and BAVERAGE, while the number of classes in COBWEB was determined by the number of nodes directly below the root node. The left side of Fig. 3 shows the results of the *actual* class overlap measured by OV_{act}. The points above the solid curve which depicts VERGENE's performance indicate worse results, while those below it indicate better ones. On the average VERGENE's overlap rate is 12.6, followed by COBWEB (26.8), AUTOCLASS (28.8) and BAVERAGE (37.5).

We also used the global non-overlap rate NOV_A to measure the *potential overlap* OV_{pot} between versions: $OV_{pot} := \frac{\sum_A 1 - NOV_A}{|Vers|}$. While actual overlap is determined

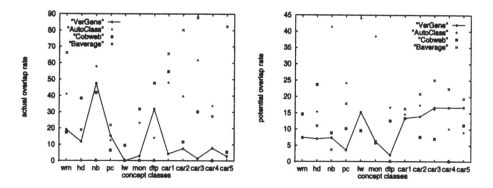

Fig. 3. Evaluation Based on Actual and Potential Overlap

relative to a given data set (it measures the percentage of real overlap), the potential overlap ratio measures the amount of overlapping regions of a version cluster normalized by the number of versions. It characterizes for each attribute the extent to which its version-specific value ranges overlap between the versions. The greater the potential overlap, the greater the risk of a high actual overlap in other data sets. The right side of Fig. 3 gives the results of this comparison. They point to the same direction as for the actual overlap, though they are less distinctive (cf. also Table 2 for a summary based on the mean values of all concept classes in the test set). Summing up, VERGENE receives substantial support from the empirical data, and tends to outperform the competing system with respect to the effectiveness of versioning for the data under scrutiny.

	IBL Confirmation	Actual Overlap	Potential Overlap
VerGene	75.4	12.6	10.3
COBWEB	73.2	26.8	11.3
BAVERAGE	72.0	37.5	13.3
AUTOCLASS	53.9	28.8	21.8

Table 2. Summary of the Evaluation Data

4 Related work

Langley's work on a general theory of discrimination learning [15] is embedded in the framework of production systems. In this environment, concept drift results in the weakening of previously valid production rules and the creation and strengthening of new ones. Contrary to that, STAGGER [17] uses Bayesian statistics to cope with concept drift. The underlying learning procedure distinguishes between noise and genuine concept drift. Both systems realize incremental concept learning (as we do), but both, just like more recent work [21], also rely on the presence of negative instances in the learning process (usually not contained in our data). There are also a number of papers from the field of computational learning theory on concept drift – non-incremental paradigms like [9], and incremental ones like [14]. Common to all these approaches is that obsolete instances are abandoned in the course of concept drift and only the latest concept "version" is maintained. From our point of view, this is an undesirable feature, since knowledge about prior concept versions is often necessary (e.g., when reasoning about the dynamics or quality of progress in the given domain). The model we here propose extends our own previous work on concept drift [13] mainly with respect to the introduction of a mechanism for the update of feature relevance (cf. Section 2.1) and the incorporation of a weighting scheme for quality increase (cf. Section 2.2).

COBWEB ([6]) has also been tested for its capability to cope with drifting concepts. However, as Kilander and Jansson [12] correctly observe, concept drift "coincide[s] with those (instance) orderings that are least suitable" (ibid., p.245) for an incremental clustering system. They augment COBWEB with a new control procedure (resulting in COBBIT) in order to overcome these limitations. But they add other – as the authors admit – "undesirable properties" to COBBIT. One of these is that training instances may possibly get lost in the course of concept drift, which is precluded in our model.

As Wettscherek *et al.* [20] remark, most of the feature weighting algorithms in use – whether they are based on conditional probabilities [3], on information theory [4], or on and genetic algorithms [10,18] – employ a global weighting scheme by assuming "that feature relevance is invariant over the instance space" (ibid, p.12). This assumption is nevertheless too strong in the presence of concept drift. On the other hand, purely local measures have also disadvantages [5] (e.g., they obscure feature information and are quite brittle). We propose a mixed mode, incorporating a local and global weight function (QD) similar to GCM-ISW [1]. However, due to incomparable learning environments, totally different weight types are used (overlap rates *vs.* probability estimates).

5   Conclusions

In this paper, we have presented a concept learning model that accounts for concept change based on a feature weighting scheme. It incorporates mechanisms for the identification and maintenance of concept versions, i.e., concept class descriptions under which similar instances can be subsumed. This model combines aspects of unsupervised learning (such as conceptual clustering) and supervised learning (e.g., IBL). Version descriptions are generated by inductive generalization from instances as a result of the integration of new instances into a version. Based on the notion of "version quality" (a feature-based similarity measure), either version descriptions are updated as new instances are integrated, or a successor version to the currently valid one is built. The model incorporates quantitative numerical and qualitative symbolic attributes. Comparative evaluation experiments indicate that the versioning system VERGENE built on these premises works effectively and tends to outperform well-known ML clustering systems such as COBWEB or AUTOCLASS with respect to the versioning task.

We currently plan to continue our work in two directions. At the methodological level, an open issue is the identification of *new* attributes which contribute to versioning processes. Also the description of changes of attribute relevance and the proper determination of development tendencies of items that are getting relevant still have not been fully accounted for by the current model. At the empiricial level, we plan to extend our experiments such that the effects of missing version descriptions on the effectiveness of the text parser can be explicitly traced, thus, providing experimental evidence for the necessity of versioning systems in large-scale natural language applications [8].

References

1. D. W. Aha and R. L. Goldstone. Concept learning and flexible weighting. In *Proc. of the 14th Annual Conf. of the Cognitive Science Society*, pages 534–539. L. Erlbaum, 1992.
2. D. W. Aha, D. Kibler, and M. Albert. Instance-based learning algorithms. *Machine Learning*, 6:37–66, 1991.
3. R. H. Creecy, B. M. Mansand, S. J. Smith, and D. L. Waltz. Trading MIPS and memory for knowledge engineering. *Communications of the ACM*, 35:48–64, 1992.
4. W. Daelemans and A. van den Bosch. Generalization performance of backpropagation learning on a syllabification task. In *Proc. of the TWLT 3 – Connectionism and Natural Language Processing*, pages 27–37, 1992.
5. K. Fukunaga and T. Flick. An optimal global nearest neighbor metric. *IEEE Transactions on Pattern Analysis and Machine Intelligence*, 6:314–318, 1984.
6. J. H. Gennari, P. Langley, and D. Fisher. Models of incremental concept formation. *Artificial Intelligence*, 40(1/3):11–61, 1989.
7. U. Hahn, S. Schacht, and N. Bröker. Concurrent, object-oriented natural language parsing: the PARSETALK model. *Int'l. Journal of Human-Computer Studies*, 41(1/2):179–222, 1994.
8. U. Hahn and K. Schnattinger. Deep knowledge discovery from natural language texts. In *KDD '97 – Proc. of the 3rd Int'l. Conf. on Knowledge Discovery and Data Mining*, 1997.
9. D. P. Helmbold and P. M. Long. Tracking drifting concepts by minimizing disagreements. *Machine Learning*, 14(1):27–45, 1994.
10. J. D. Kelly and L. Davis. A hybrid genetic algorithm for classification. In *IJCAI '91 – Proc. of the 12th Int'l. Joint Conf. on Artificial Intelligence*, pages 645–650, 1991.
11. D. Kibler, D. W. Aha, and M. Albert. Instance-based prediction of real-valued attributes. *Computational Intelligence*, 5:51–57, 1989.
12. F. Kilander and C. G. Jansson. COBBIT: a control procedure for COBWEB in the presence of concept drift. In *ECML '93 – Proc. of the European Conf. on Machine Learning*, pages 245–261, 1993.
13. M. Klenner and U. Hahn. Concept versioning: a methodology for tracking evolutionary concept drift in dynamic concept systems. In *ECAI '94 – Proc. of the 11th European Conference on Artificial Intelligence*, pages 473–477. J. Wiley, 1994.
14. T. Kuh, T. Petsche, and R. Rivest. Incrementally learning time-varying half-planes. *Neural Information Processing Systems*, 4, 1992.
15. P. Langley. A general theory of discrimination learning. In D. Klahr, P. Langley, and R. Neches, editors, *Production System Models of Learning and Development*, pages 99–161. MIT Press, 1987.
16. P. M. Murphy and D. W. Aha. Automobile database from the UCI repository. <http://www.ics.uci.edu/~mlearn/MLRepository.html>, 1994.
17. J. C. Schlimmer and R. H. Granger. Incremental learning from noisy data. *Machine Learning*, 1(3):317–354, 1986.
18. D. Skalak. Protoype and feature selection by sampling and random mutation hill climbing algorithms. In *Proc. of the 11th Int'l. Machine Learning Conference*, pages 293–301, 1994.
19. J. Stutz and P. Cheeseman. AutoClass: a Bayesian approach to classification. In J. Skilling and S. Sibisi, editors, *Maximum Entropy and Bayesian Methods*. Kluwer, 1994.
20. D. Wettscherek, D. W. Aha, and T. Mohri. A review and comparative evaluation of feature weighting methods for lazy learning algorithms. Technical Report AIC-95-012, Washington, DC: Naval Research Laboratory, Navy Center for Appl. Res. in Artificial Intelligence, 1995.
21. G. Widmer. Combining robustness and flexibility in learning drifting concepts. In *ECAI '94 – Proc. of the 11th European Conference on Artificial Intelligence*, pages 468–472, 1994.

A 0-1 Quadratic Knapsack Problem for Modelizing and Solving the Constraint Satisfaction Problems

Mohamed ETTAOUIL

Département de Mathématiques et Informatique de Fès-Saïss
et Laboratoire d'Informatique de Paris-Nord, LIPN, URA CNRS n° 1507
Université Sidi Mohammed Ben Abdellah , Faculté des Sciences et Techniques Fès -Saïss
B.P. 2202 Fès, Maroc   fax. : +212(5) 60.82.14

Abstract

A constraint satisfaction problem CSP consists of assigning values to variables which are subject to a set of constraints. This problem can be modelized as a 0-1 quadratic knapsack problem. We show that a CSP has a solution if and only if the value of the optimization problem is null. A branch-and-bound method exploiting this representation is presented. At each node, a lower bound given naturally by the value of dual problem may be improved by a new Lagrangean heuristic. An upper bound is computed by satisfying the quadratic constraint. The theoritical results presented are used for filtring the associated subproblem and for detecting quickly a solution or a failure. The simulation results assess the effectiveness of the theoretical results shown in this paper.

Keywords : Constraint Satisfaction Problem; 0-1 quadratic Knapsack problem; duality; heuristics;   Branch-and-bound.

1. Introduction

Constraint satisfaction problems CSP involve the assignment of values to variables which are subject to a set of constraints. This problem arises in several applications in artificial intelligence.

Classically, a binary CSP is represented by a constraint graph [3,15]. We propose a new way for modelizing and solving CSP. We show that a CSP can be modelized as a 0-1 quadratic knapsack problem subject to quadratic constraint. Then some theoretical results establishing the links between a CSP and its associated optimization problem are presented. As for any hard optimization problem, a reasonable way of handling the 0-1 quadratic knapsack problem is to try to derive a heuristic approach that solves it suboptimally and that, if possible, yields a good tradeoff between the quality of the solutions, the compute time and the memory requirements.

A branch-and-bound method exploiting this representation is presented. It follows the same scheme developed by the Forward-Checking procedure. At each node, a lower bound given naturally by the value of dual problem may be improved by a new Lagrangean heuristic. We also propose a new method for computing a good upper bound. This method is based on satisfying the quadratic constraint, the obtained feasible solution is improved by an exchange procedure. The evaluation of each node can detecte a solution or failure. The classical filtering used in the forward-checking procedure (elimination of values inconsistent with value of the last instantiated variable) can be exploited by the optimization problem for obtaining a good evalution of the nodes during the search. Hence, this leads to reduce considerably the search space.

In the next section we introduce a new optimization model for the CSP. Section 3 presents some theoretical results and algorithms for computing upper and lower bounds. Section 4 shows how to incorporate the previous results and algorithms into a branch-and-bound scheme. Finally we evaluate the complexity of heuristics, reduction and checking consistency.

2. Modelization

The constraint satisfaction problem (CSP) introduced by Montanari [16] is the following task : We are given a finite set of variables $X = \{x_1,..., x_n\}$ in which each variable x_i in a discrete set D_i explicitly defined for i=1,..., n, and a set of constraints C defined on X (each constraint C_{ij} between the variables x_i and x_j is defined by its relation R_{ij}), does there exist an assignment of variables satisfying the set C of constraints?

In the following we want to present a new formulation of the CSPs problem.
To each variable x_i of the CSP we introduce di (di=$|D_i|$) binary variables x_{ik} k=1,...,di such that :

$$x_{ik} = \begin{cases} 1 & \text{if } x_i = v_k \quad v_k \in D_i \\ 0 & \text{otherwise} \end{cases}$$

Since each variable x_i must be assigned to exactly one of the n domains the following set of equations has to be satisfied $\sum_{k=1}^{di} x_{ik} = 1$ for all i=1,..,n   (1)

The modelization process of the constraint satisfaction problem (CSP) to a 0-1 quadratic knapsack problem leads to a complex formula with a lot of indices on variables, which can seen very hard to understand. We prefer to discribe this process by an example.

Example :

We are given a constraint satisfaction problem (CSP), with $X = \{x_1,x_2,x_3\}$ and $D=\{D_1,D_2,D_3\}$ where $D_1=\{v_1,v_2,v_3\}$, $D_2=\{v_1,v_2\}$ and $D_3=\{v_1,v_2,v_3\}$. Each constraint C_{ij} between the variables x_i and x_j is defined by its relation R_{ij} (R_{ij} is a subset of the cartesian product $D_i x D_j$ specifying the compatible values between x_i and x_j). $R_{12}=\{(v_1,v_2), (v_2,v_1), (v_3,v_1),(v_3,v_2)\}$,
$R_{13}=\{(v_1,v_2),(v_2,v_1),(v_3,v_3),(v_3,v_1)\}$,

and $R_{23} = \{ (v_1, v_1), (v_1, v_2), (v_2, v_1), (v_2, v_3) \}$.

If C_{ij} is a constraint between two variables x_i and x_j defined by its relation R_{ij} of the CSP, for each couple (v_r, v_s) such that $\neg R_{ij}(v_r, v_s)$ we generate a constraint:

$$x_{ir} x_{js} = 0 \qquad (2)$$

These constraints can be aggregated in a single constraint :

$$f(x) = x_{11}x_{21} + x_{12}x_{22} + x_{11}x_{31} + x_{11}x_{33} + x_{12}x_{32} + x_{12}x_{33} + x_{13}x_{32} + x_{21}x_{33}$$
$$+ x_{22}x_{32} = 0 \qquad (3)$$

The constraints (1) imply that

$$x_{11} = 1 - x_{12} - x_{13},$$
$$x_{21} = 1 - x_{22},$$
$$x_{31} = 1 - x_{32} - x_{33}.$$

By substitution in the equation (3), we obtain :

$$f(x) = 2 - 2 x_{12} - 2 x_{13} - x_{22} + x_{33} - x_{32} + 2x_{12}x_{22} + 2 x_{12}x_{32} + x_{12}x_{33}$$
$$+ 2x_{13}x_{32} + x_{13}x_{22} + x_{22}x_{32} - x_{22}x_{33} = 0 \qquad (4)$$

The constraints $x_{12} + x_{13} \leq 1$, $x_{22} \leq 1$ and $x_{32} + x_{33} \leq 1$ can be rewritten as follows

$$: g(x) = x_{22} + x_{12}x_{13} + x_{32}x_{33} \leq 1 \qquad (x_{12}x_{13} = 0, \ x_{32}x_{33} = 0) \qquad (5)$$

Thus, the CSP problem is equivalent to the following system

$$\begin{cases} f(x) = 0 \\ g(x) \leq 1 \end{cases} \qquad (**)$$

The CSP has a solution if and only if the quadratic system has one.

Finally, we consider the following 0-1 quadratic knapsack problem :

$$(QK) \qquad \text{Min } f(x)$$
$$\text{subject to } g(x) \leq 1$$

Theorem 1.

Consider the 0-1 quadratic knapsack problem (QK). The value $v(QK)$ is equal to 0 if and only if the constraint satisfaction problem CSP has a solution.

Proof.

By construction of the system the value of the problem (QK) is nonnegative. The value $v(QK)$ is equal to 0 if and only if there exists a solution of the system $(**)$. Then, the CSP has a solution if and only if the value $v(QK)$ is equal to 0. ◆

The theorem 1 is valid for any binary CSP and the equivalent quadratic system can be obtained easily following the above modelization. Without loss of generality, as we observed above, we will consider in this paper the following problem :

$$(QK) \qquad \text{Min } f(x) = \left(q_0 + \sum_{i=1}^{N} q_i x_i + \sum_{\substack{i,j=1 \\ i<j}}^{N} q_{ij} \, x_i x_j \right)$$

$$\text{subject to } g(x) = \sum_{i=1}^{N} a_i x_i + \sum_{\substack{i,j=1 \\ i<j}}^{N} a_{ij} \, x_i x_j \leq b$$

$$x_i \in \{0,1\} \quad \text{for all} \quad i = 1,...,N$$

where q_0, q_i, q_{ij}, a_i and a_{ij} are integer constants and N the number of binary variables of the (QK) problem (N is bounded by nd where d=max{di, i=1,..,n})

$$0 < b < \sum_{i=1}^{N} a_i + \sum_{\substack{i,j=1 \\ i<j}}^{N} a_{ij} \quad , \quad a_{ij} \geq 0 \ (1 \leq i < j \leq N),$$

Based on this formulation we will develop heuristics for an approximative solution of the problem. Before studying the 0-1 quadratic knapsack problem, let us introduce the following notation : if (P) is an optimization problem, then v(P) will be its optimal value.

3. Resolution of the 0-1 quadratic knapsack problem (QK)

Many methods of reduction to equivalent forms and of linearization have been proposed [1,10,18]. Some particular cases are solvable in polynomial time. Moreover, although the duality in nonlinear programming had created many interests. Few efforts are consacreted by his algorithmic using. Our work related to the solution of (QK) is part of theoretical and algorithmic. Based on the information provided by the approximated or optimal solution of the dual problem and the best upper bound. We show how these bounds can be efficiently used for solving the 0-1 quadratic Knapsack problem (QK) by a branch-and-bound method. The optimality of the generated solution can be proved at different levels : first, when the optimal solution of the Lagrangean dual is feasible solution for (QK); second, when the duality gap is equal zero; finally, during the final enumeration if it involves exploring a limited number of nodes of the binary solution tree.

3.1 Equivalent Forms

The (QK) problem can be solved after transformation into a linear program equivalent to mixt variables. Balas and Mazzola[1], Watters[18], have proved that any quadratic program (more generally polynomial) in 0-1 variables can be reduced into 0-1 linear program by the new variables and new constraints adding. This equivalence has the inconvenience to increase considerably the constraints system eight. Glover and woolsey[10] have proposed to replace the bivalent variables by continues non negative variables by introducing others constraints. In general thoses problems are NP-complete and for solving them, we use heuristic methods.

3.2 Unconstrained quadratic 0-1 Programming

Some different approaches for this problem have been presented : Barahona et al. [2] proposed a cut generation technique, and Branch and Bound techniques were discussed by Billonnet and Sutter [4] using the best lower plane, by Pardalos and Rodgers [17] using first order approximations, by Kalanhari and Bagchi [11] using a concave formulation, and by Carter [5] using a convex formulation. Classicaly, the quadratic 0-1 optimization problems is solved by the Branch-and-Bound method. It is well known that this method uses two bounds (a lower and upper bound) for pruning the search space. The size of the search tree depends on the quality of these bounds.

3.3 Computation of a lower bound

For reasons due to an increase of difficulty going from linear to nonlinear constraint, we have chosen to solve the Lagrangean relaxation dual problem. Dualizing the nonlinear constraint with a nonnegative muliplier λ, we obtain the dual function :

$w(\lambda) = \text{Min}\{\varphi(\lambda, x) \text{ subject to } x \in \{0,1\}^N\}$ where $\varphi(\lambda, x) = f(x) + \lambda(g(x) - b)$.

It is well known [9,13,17] that w is a convex piecewise linear function and that $w(\lambda) \leq V(QK) \ \forall \ \lambda \in IR_+$. Therefore, in order to obtain the best lower bound we have to solve the dual problem :

(DK) $\qquad$ Max $w(\lambda)$; $\lambda \geq 0$.

This bound is first used to see whether a CSP has a solution or has no solution (theorem 2 and 4), and in addition to filter the CSP.

3.3.1 Basic theoretical results

The representation of the CSP by 0-1 quadratic optimization problem puts in interaction all constraints of the problem, and the problem can considered globally during the search, and the quantity of knowledge inferred can be more important than if it were considered partially. Classical properties of the duality can detect that the CSP has no solution. Moreover, the notion of saddle point associated with some complementary assumptions can also detect that the CSP has a solution.

Theorem 2.

Let $(\underline{\lambda}, \underline{x})$ be an approximated solution generated during the resolution of the dual problem (DK). If $\varphi(\underline{\lambda}, \underline{x}) > 0$ then the CSP problem has no solution.

Proof.

If $(\underline{\lambda}, \underline{x})$ be an approximate solution generated during the resolution of the dual problem (DK), such that $\varphi(\underline{\lambda}, \underline{x}) > 0$ then $0 < \varphi(\underline{\lambda}, \underline{x}) \leq v(DK) \leq v(QK)$ The theorem 1. imply that the CSP problem has no solution. $\qquad \blacklozenge$

The following corollary is an immediate consequence of theorem 2.

Corollary 1.

Let $(\underline{\lambda}, \underline{x})$ be an optimal solution of the dual problem (DK).

If $\varphi(\underline{\lambda}, \underline{x}) > 0$ then the CSP problem has no solution.

Now, before stating another criterion to know whether the CSP has a solution by using the notion of saddle point [7,8,14], let us recall some classical results about this notion :

Given any mathematical programming problem

$\qquad \qquad$ Min $f(x)$

(P) $\qquad \qquad$ subjet to $g_i(x) \leq 0 \qquad i \in \{1,....,m\}$

$\qquad \qquad x \in X \qquad (X \subset IR^n)$.

and its associated Lagrangean function $\varphi(\lambda, y) = f(x) + \sum_{i=1}^{m} \lambda_i g_i(x) \quad \lambda \in IR_+^m$.

Definition

Let $y \in X$ and $\mu \in IR_+^m$ we say that (μ, y) is a saddle point of $\varphi(\lambda, x)$ if

(i) $\varphi(\mu, y) \leq \varphi(\mu, x)$ $\forall x \in X$

(ii) $\varphi(\lambda, y) \leq \varphi(\mu, y)$ $\forall \lambda \in IR_+^m$.

The main characteristics of a saddle point is given by the following theorem :

Theorem 3. [14]

(μ, y) is a saddle point of $\varphi(\lambda, x)$ if and only if

(i) $\varphi(\mu, y) = \underset{x \in X}{Min} \; \varphi(\mu, x)$

(ii) $\mu_i g_i(y) = 0$ $\forall i \in \{1, ..., m\}$

(iii) $g_i(y) \leq 0$ $\forall i \in \{1, ..., m\}$.

Corollary 2. [14]

If (μ, y) is a saddle point of $\varphi(\lambda, x)$, then y is an optimal solution of (P).

The following theorem can detected a solution of the CSP problem.

Theorem 4.

Let $(\underline{\lambda}, \underline{x})$ be an optimal solution of the dual problem (DK).

If   (i) $(\underline{\lambda}, \underline{x})$ is a saddle point of $\varphi(\lambda, x)$

       (ii) $\varphi(\underline{\lambda}, \underline{x}) = 0$

then the CSP problem has a solution.

Proof.

Let $(\underline{\lambda}, \underline{x})$ be an optimal solution of the dual problem (DK),

then $v(DK) = \varphi(\underline{\lambda}, \underline{x}) = \underset{\lambda \geq 0}{Max} \; \underset{x \in \{0,1\}^N}{Min} \; \varphi(\lambda, x)$

$\varphi(\underline{\lambda}, \underline{x}) = f(\underline{x}) + \underline{\lambda}(g(\underline{x}) - b)$

Since $(\underline{\lambda}, \underline{x})$ is a saddle point of $\varphi(\lambda, x)$ (hypothesis (i)), and by (theorem 3),

we have $\underline{\lambda}(g(\underline{x}) - b) = 0$, then $\varphi(\underline{\lambda}, \underline{x}) = f(\underline{x})$

By corollary 2, $\underline{x}$ is an optimal solution of (QK)

$v(QK) = f(\underline{x}) = \varphi(\underline{\lambda}, \underline{x}) = 0$ (hypothesis (ii)).

The value $v(QK)$ of the problem (QK) is equal to 0 if and only if the constraint satisfaction problem CSP has a solution (Theorem 1). $\blacklozenge$

3.3.2 Lagrangean heuristic

The lower bound of $v(QK)$ given naturally by the value of Lagrangean dual may be improved by a new Lagrangean heuristic which consists in generating an increasing finite sequence of the values of the Lagrangean function. Let $\underline{\lambda}$ be an approximated or optimal solution of the dual problem and $w(\underline{\lambda})$ its value. Let $\underline{x}$ be the optimal solution of the unconstrained quadratic 0-1 programming

Min $\varphi(\underline{\lambda}, x)$ subject to $x \in \{0,1\}^N$ [2,4,5,7,11,17]. For all index $j=1,..,N$, compute $\psi_j = \varphi(\underline{\lambda}, (\underline{x}_1, .., 1-\underline{x}_j,.., \underline{x}_N))$ in order to construct the set $I = \{ j / \psi_j > w(\underline{\lambda}) \}$. Setting $S_j = \{ x \in \{0,1\}^N / \varphi(\underline{\lambda}, x) \leq w(\underline{\lambda}) \}$, by definition of the function φ, no solution contained in S_j is better than $w(\underline{\lambda})$. Thus we are sur that the subset S_j does not contain any optimal solution. Let $\psi_i = \text{Inf}\{\psi_j / j \in I\}$. Then the variable x_i should be fixed to $1 - \underline{x}_i$. These fixations will allow a reduction of the size problem (QK) before solving it by a branch-and-bound procedure. Hence, as soon as variables have been fixed by any of the tests, we try to compute the optimal solution of the dual of the new current subproblem.

Let J0, J1 be the sets of variables assigned respectively to 0 and 1, and J2 the set of variables non-assigned.

Algorithm IMPROVE 1 : Generating a good lower bound is a key goal in this procedure.

J0 $\leftarrow$ empty; J1 $\leftarrow$ empty; J2 $\leftarrow$ {1,...,N};

Let $(\underline{\lambda}, \underline{x})$ be an approximated or optimal solution generated during the resolution of the dual problem (DK);

    if $\varphi(\underline{\lambda}, \underline{x}) > 0$ **then** return the CSP problem has no solution (theorem 2)
        endif
    if $(\underline{\lambda}, \underline{x})$ is a saddle point of $\varphi(\lambda, x)$ and $\varphi(\underline{\lambda}, \underline{x}) = 0$ **then** return the
        CSP problem has a solution (theorem 4) **endif**

(Improvement of the lower bound LB = $\varphi(\underline{\lambda}, \underline{x})$)

while a failure or a solution of the CSP has not detected **do**
    for all index $j = 1$ to N **do**
        compute $\psi_j = \varphi(\underline{\lambda}, (\underline{x}_1,.., 1-\underline{x}_j,.., \underline{x}_N))$ in order to construct the set
        $I = \{ j / \psi_j > \varphi(\underline{\lambda}, \underline{x}) \}$
        if the set I is nonempty **then**
        $\psi_i \leftarrow \text{Inf} \{ \psi_j / j \in I \}$ and $x_i \leftarrow 1 - \underline{x}_i$ **endif**
        update the sets J0, J1 and J2
        update the terms q_0, q_i, a_0, a_i $(x_i \leftarrow 1 - \underline{x}_i)$
    endfor
endwhile

In addition, in many cases the optimal dual solution solves (QK) when either it is a feasible solution or the associated optimal value v(DK) is equal to the value of a current feasible solution of (QK).

3.4 Computation of an upper bound

A first upper bound is computed by satisfying the quadratic constraint (i.e. solving the unconstrained quadratic 0-1 programming : (Q) Min g(x) subject to $x \in \{0,1\}^N$, this paticular case is solvable in polynomial time [6]). Assume the set of feasible solutions F(QK) is nonempty. Let $y \in$ F(QK) then Min { g(x) subject to $x \in \{0,1\}^N$ } $\leq$ g(y) $\leq$ b, this inequality prove that all optimal solution of the problem (Q) is a feasible solution of (QK).

Proposition 1.

Let y be an optimal solution of (Q). If g(y) = Min {g(x) subject to $x \in \{0,1\}^N$} > b then the set of feasible solutions is empty.

Proof.

$g(y) = $ Min { g(x) subject to $x \in \{0,1\}^N$ } $\leq$ g(x) $\quad \forall x \in \{0,1\}^N$

$g(y) > b \Rightarrow g(x) > b \ \forall x \in \{0,1\}^N$ then the set of feasible solutions is empty. $\quad \blacklozenge$

3.4.1 Improvement of the feasible solution

This stage consists in generating a decrease finite sequence of the values of the objective function. Let y be the optimal solution of the unconstrained quadratic 0-1 programming (Q). If y is a feasible solution, then set UB = f(y). For all $j \in \{1,..,N\}$, compute $f_j = f(y_1,...,1-y_j,...,y_N)$ and $g_j = f(y_1,...,1-y_j,...,y_N)$.

By setting $I = \{j \ / \ g_j \leq b$ and $f_j < UB\}$. If I is empty, then no improvement is possible. the current feasible solution is stored if not compute $f_i = $ Inf { $f_j / j \in I$ }. Then the variable x_i is fixed to $1-y_i$, and UB takes the value f_i and a new iteration is executed.

Algorithm IMPROVE 2: generating a good feasible solution is a key goal in this procedure. Let y be the optimal solution of the optimization problem

    (Q):   Min g(x) subject to $x \in \{0,1\}^N$;

    if g(y) > b **then** the set of feasible solutions is empty **endif**

    if g(y) $\leq$ b **then** y is feasible for the quadratic Knapsack problem (QK) **endif**

while y satisfy the quadratic constraint (g(x) $\leq$ b) **do**

Let UB= f(y) a first upper bound

for i = 1 to N **do**

    compute $f_j = f(y_1,..,1-y_j,..,y_N)$ and $g_j = g(y_1,...,1-y_j,...,y_N)$ in order to construct

    the set $I = \{j / g_j \leq b$ et $f_j < UB \}$;

    if the set I is nonempty and $f_i = $ Inf { $f_j / j \in I$} **then** $x_i \leftarrow 1-y_i$; UB $\leftarrow f_i$

endif

endfor

$x = (y_1,..,1-y_i,...,y_n)$ is a good feasible solution and UB an upper bound of the value v(QK)

endwhile

3.5. Reduction of the size problem CSP.

The main idea of this filter is to try to reduce as much as possible the initial size of the CSP, and the same time, to exploite the new representation (problem (QK)) for obtaining a good evalution of the nodes during the search. We first apply the classical filtering like in the Forward-Checking procedure, after the instantiation of some variables of a given CSP, we eliminate all directely inconsistent values with the value of the last variable instantiated. Then, some binary variables of the optimization problem (QK) will be assigned to 0 or 1. The values are reported on the 0-1 quadratic Knapsack problem (QK). Based on the information provided by the approximated or optimal solution of the dual problem and the best upper bound, values of some binary variables of the problem (QK) can be deduced.

Let us assume that some variables of the CSP are instantiated, then some binary variables of (QK) will be assigned to 0 or 1. Let $(\underline{\lambda},\underline{x})$ be an approximated solution generated during the resolution of the dual problem (DK$_{J2}$).

For each index $j \in J2$, compute $\psi_j = \varphi(\underline{\lambda}, (\underline{x}_1,...,1-\underline{x}_j,...,\underline{x}|_{J2}))$, then each variable x_j such that $\psi_j > UB$ should be fixed and equal $\underline{x}_j$ (UB an upper bound).

Algorithm FILTER : a procedure for filtering CSP during the search (the Forward-Checking procedure).

D={ $D_1, D_2, .., D_n$ }, X the set of non-instantiated variables

    choose a variable x_i from X

    choose a value v_r from D_i

    instantiate x_i to v_r

    delete v_r from D_i

    J0 ← empty; J1 ← {ir}

consistency ← true

while consistency **do**

    for each x_j : $C(x_i, x_j)$ **do**

        for each value v_s in D_j **do**

            if $\neg R_{ij}(v_r, v_s)$ **then** delete v_s from

            J0 ← J0 U {js} **endif**

            if D_j is empty **then** return **endif**

update the sets J0, J1 and J2

consistency ← **Algorithm** REDUCE

        endfor

    endfor

endwhile

Algorithm REDUCE : this procedure reduce the size of the 0-1 quadratic Knapsack problem (QK). (J2 the set of variables non-assigned)

Let $(\underline{\lambda}, \underline{x})$ be an approximated or optimal solution generated during the resolution of the dual problem (DK$_{J2}$).

if $\varphi(\underline{\lambda}, \underline{x}) > 0$ **then** return the CSP problem has no solution **endif**
while a failure or a solution of the CSP has not detected **do**
    for all index $j = 1$ to N **do**
      compute $\psi_j = \varphi(\underline{\lambda}, (\underline{x}_1, .., 1-\underline{x}_j, .., \underline{x}|_{J2}))$
        if $\psi_j > UB$ **then** x_j should be fixed and equal $\underline{x}_j$ **endif**
    endfor
endwhile

The search of the solution to a CSP exploits simultaneously the domain of variables, the relations and its associated modelization with a 0-1 quadratic Knapsack problem (QK) in complementary way.

4. Search a solution of the CSP Problem
The theoretical results proposed above are used at each node of the search tree for filtering the associated subproblem and for detecting quickly a solution or a failure. In the following section, we present the treatment performed at the node of the search tree.

4.1 Partial enumeration of The reduced problem
All the above ingredients are used repeatedly until reduction fails or the size of the current subproblem is less than or equal to a given threshold. Then the enumeration of the solutions of the reduced problem is performed by a branch-and-bound algorithm, whose characteristics are the following. Let $(\underline{\lambda}, \underline{x})$ be an approximated solution generated during the resolution of the dual problem (DK_{J2}).
For each index $j \in J2$, compute $\psi_j = \varphi(\underline{\lambda}, (\underline{x}_1, .., 1-\underline{x}_j, .., \underline{x}|_{J2}))$ in ordre to construct the set $I = \{ j \mid \psi_j > v(DK_{J2})\}$. At each node of the tree, we compute a bounds (LB and UB), if $UB < LB$ or $LB > 0$, then we backtrack; otherwise we branch on the tree variable x_i such that $\psi_i = Min \{ \psi_j / j \in I\}$.

5. Complexity analysis
In this section we evaluate the complexity of heuristics, reduction and checking consistency. Given a CSP with n variables, m constraints, and d the size of the largest domains of its variables. The complexity of the heuristics (Improvement phasis of the lower and an upper bound) and reduction are in $O(|J2|^2)$, $|J2|$ is bounded by nd. The complexity of checking consistency of the Span is linear in the number of its quadratic terms, it is bounded by md^2.
The advantage of our method is the use of the constraints of the problem in an active way to infer a knowledge about the problem. In fact, the representation puts in interaction all constraints, and then the problem can be considered globally during the search, and the quantity of knowledge inferred can be more important than if it were considered partially.

6. Computational experiments

In order to assess the effectiveness of the theoretical results shown in this paper, and the advantage of the new modelization. The preliminary numerical experiments were performed on randomly generated test CSP problems (with a relatively small number of variables, containing 5 to 20 variables). The computing of a solution consists of 2 phases. During the first phasis we apply the classical filtering like in the Forward-Checking procedure; we eliminate all directely inconsistent values with the value of the last variable instantiated. Then, some binary variables will be assigned to 0 or 1. The values are reported on the 0-1 quadratic Knapsack problem (QK). In the second phasis, the obtained optimization problems were also solved with the duality, heuristics, size reduction, subgradient algorithm, Ford-Furkelson algorithm for the unconstrained 0-1 quadratic problems and a branch-and-bound procedure. It should be noted that at the end of the reduction phasis, 10 test problems are solved exactly because the dual solves the primal and 20 other test problems are reduced to a 0-1 quadratic Knapsack problems.

For the 20 last 0-1 quadratic Knapsack problem, the absolute values of the coefficients q_i and q_{ij} of the objective function are integers distributed between 0 and 20, and the coefficients a_i and a_{ij} of the quadratic constraint are integers distributed between 0 and 20, while b is an integer between 1 and $\sum_{i=1}^{N} a_i + \sum_{\substack{i,j=1 \\ i<j}}^{N} a_{i,j}$.

Our Lagrangean heuristic is indeed very efficient for solving the 0-1 quadratic Knapsak problems up to N = 40 (number of binary variables). It is important to note that the objective of these simulations is to assess the effectiveness of the theoretical results of the theorems (2), (4) and heuristics (i.e. detecting a solution or a failure), and not to compare (in view of the time complexity) our results with those obtained using other heuristics or exact methods. The preliminary results that have been obtained suggest that the proposed algorithm is promising as an efficient method for solving the CSP problem.

Many elements of the reduction phase can be improved, such as heuristics, duality techniques and coefficient reduction. Numerical experiments are in progress for searching adequate values of parameters such as the threshold value of the branch-and-bound, and to select the tools that perform the best tradeoff between reduction quality and time complexity.

Conclusion

We have presented a new modelization (problem (QK)) for the constraint satisfaction problem (CSP). A branch-and-bound method is proposed for solving this problem. The representation of a CSP by a 0-1 quadratic knapsack problem allows the evaluation of each node of the search tree. This evaluation integrated in the propagation process allows the deduction of an important knowledge about the CSP during the search. Then a solution or failure may be detected prematuraly.

References

[1] Balas E., Mazzola J.B.(1984), "Nonlinear 0-1 programming linearisation techniques", Mathematical programming 30, 1-21.

[2] Barahona F., Jüngler M. and Reinelt G.(1989), "Experiments in quadratic 0-1 program-ming", Mathematical programming 44, 127-137.

[3] Bessière C.(1994),"Arc-consistency and arc-consistency again", Research note,Vol. 65

[4] Billionnet A., Sutter A.(1992)," Persistency in quadratic 0-1 optimization", Mathematical programming 54, 115-119.

[5] Carter M.W.(1984), "The indefinite 0-1 Quadratic problem", Discrete Applied Mathematics, 7, 23-44.

[6]Crama Y.(1989), " Recognition problems for special classes of polynomials in 0-1 variables", Mathematical programming 44, 127-137.

[7] Ettaouil M. (1994),"Satisfaction de contraintes non linéaire en vatiables 0-1 et outils de la programmation quadratique",Thèse d'Université, Université Paris 13.

[8] Ettaouil M., Plateau G.(1996), "An exact algorithm for the nonlinear 0-1 constraint Satisfaction problem", Rapport de recherche LIPN 96-10, Université Paris 13.

[9] Geoffrion A. M. (1974),"The Lagrangian relaxation for integer programming", Mathematical Programming Study 2, 82-114.

[10] Glover F., Woolsey E.(1974), "Converting the 0-1 polynomial programming problem to 0-1 linear program", Operations research 22, 180-182.

[11] Kalanhari B. and Bagchi A.(1990),"An algorithm for quadratic 0-1 programs", Naval Research Logistic, 37, 527-538.

[12] Martello S., Toth P.(1977), "An upper bound for the 0-1 Knapsack problem and a branch and bound algorithm", European Journal of Operations Research 1,169-175.

[13] Michelon P. et Maculan N.(1991), "Lagrangean methods for 0-1 quadratic problems", Discrete Applied Mathematics 42, 257-269.

[14] Minoux M. (1983), "Programmation Mathématique ", Tome 2 Dunod.

[15] Mohr R. and Henderson T. C.(1986), "Arc and path consistency revisid" Artificial Intelligence 28-2.

[16] Montanari U.(1974), "Networks of constraints : Fundamental proprieties and applications to picture processing", Information Sciences, Vol. 7 N°2, 95-132.

[17] Pardalos P.M., Rogers G.P.(1990),"Computational Aspects of a Branch and Bound algorithm for quadratic 0-1 programming", Computing, 45, 131-144.

[18] Watters L.J. (1967), "Reduction of integer polynomial programming problems to zero-one linear programming problems", Operations Research 15, 1171-1174.

An Algorithm for Solving Systems of Linear Diophantine Equations in Naturals

Ana Paula Tomás and Miguel Filgueiras

LIACC & DCC, Universidade do Porto, Portugal
R. do Campo Alegre 823, 4150 Porto, Portugal
email: {apt,mig}@ncc.up.pt

Abstract. A new algorithm for finding the minimal solutions of systems of linear Diophantine equations has recently been published. In its description the emphasis was put on the mathematical aspects of the algorithm. In complement to that, in this paper another presentation of the algorithm is given which may be of use for anyone wanting to implement it.

1 Introduction

It is known since about 1900 that the monoid $\mathcal{M}$ of nonnegative integral solutions of the system of linear Diophantine equations (1)

$$AX = 0, \quad A \text{ a } m \times n \text{ integral matrix}, X \in \mathbb{N}^n \tag{1}$$

is finitely generated, there existing a unique finite subset of $\mathcal{M}$ such that $\mathcal{M}$ is the set of linear nonnegative integral combinations of the solutions in that subset, which we shall denote by $\mathcal{H}(\mathcal{M})$. The solutions in $\mathcal{H}(\mathcal{M})$ are the nonnull solutions of (1) that are minimal in the component-wise ordering given by $(u_1, \ldots, u_n) \preceq (v_1, \ldots, v_n)$ iff $u_i \leq v_i$ for all i. Problems as (1) arise in several different contexts, e.g., Constraint Programming, Integer Programming, Combinatorics, Rewriting Systems, and Abstract Interpretation. In some situations, solving means finding just one solution (as for instance, an optimal solution for some cost function). The problem of finding all the minimal solutions of (1) has been investigated by Elliott [4] and MacMahon [9] in the beginning of this century, and more recently by several other researchers ([7, 8, 2, 1, 11, 10, 3, 6, 5]) when it was found to be related to areas such as AC-unification, word problems, Petri Nets.

It should be noted that the problem belongs to the NP-complete complexity class, although it may be checked in polynomial time whether it is satisfiable. The algorithm presented here is polynomial when the solution space is planar. However, in the general case, the number of minimal solutions is exponential in the size of the system matrix. This number may be so large that a complete representation of the solution set by the set of minimal solutions will be of no practical interest. In term rewriting applications, and more specifically in some associative-commutative unification algorithms based on solving systems of Diophantine equations, a system with about twenty minimal solutions may render the unification problem intractable. In fact, solving an AC-problem may involve solving more than one system of equations, and furthermore, to consider, at intermediate steps, subsets of the set of minimal solutions found.

The existing algorithms follow rather distinct approaches (see [15] for a brief survey). For instance, in general terms, the algorithm by Contejean and Devie [1], proceeds by increasing components one by one checking whether some solution is reached. In order to ensure termination, the components that can be incremented at a given step are selected following a criterion whose fundamental idea is that a move aims at improving, in some sense, the residue of a node. The algorithm by Domenjoud [3] uses the fact that the solutions of (1) in nonnegative real numbers define a polyhedral cone, $\mathcal{H}(\mathcal{M})$ being a subset of the finite set of $\mathbb{N}$-solutions that are rational nonnegative combinations with coefficients ≤ 1 of maximal subsets of linearly independent smallest $\mathbb{N}$-solutions generating the extreme rays of the cone. It uses a procedure for finding those combinations that give $\mathbb{N}$-solutions.

In our view the Slopes Algorithm, described here, is closer to the nature of the problem being solved. Its mathematical foundations give a better insight into the structure of the problems. This may be useful in identifying classes of problems for which one of the algorithms is more appropriate than another, as well as in improving the search.

The paper is organized as follows. We first recall some of the mathematical concepts involved, then give an outline of the Slopes Algorithm and proceed to see in detail each of its main steps.

2 Some Background

Given $A \in \mathbb{Z}^{m \times n}$, the set of the nonnegative real solutions of $AX = 0$ is a pointed convex polyhedral cone $\mathcal{C}$, which we call *the solution cone*. When $\mathcal{C}$ is non-degenerated, $\mathcal{C}$ is the convex hull of its extreme rays (i.e., 1-dimensional faces) which are finitely many. Each extreme ray is given by $\{\alpha r_i \mid \alpha \in \mathbb{R}_0^+\}$ where $0 \neq r_i \in \mathbb{N}^n$ is some minimal solution of minimal support of (1). The support of x is supp $x = \{i \mid x_i \neq 0\}$, the x_i's being the coordinates of x wrt the canonical basis of $\mathbb{R}^n$. By definition, supp $X = \cup_{x \in X}$ supp x, for all $X \subseteq \mathbb{R}^n$. It is known that the faces of $\mathcal{C}$, together with the improper face $\mathcal{C}$, form a lattice under inclusion, the so-called face lattice. This lattice is isomorphic to the lattice of the supports of the faces under inclusion. Each face $\mathcal{F}$ of $\mathcal{C}$ is a pointed convex polyhedral cone whose extreme rays are extreme rays of $\mathcal{C}$. That is, if $\mathcal{R}_{\mathcal{C}} = \{r_1, \ldots, r_p\}$ is the set of minimal solutions of minimal support, then $\mathcal{C} = cone\mathcal{R}_{\mathcal{C}} = \{\sum_{i=1}^{p} \alpha_i r_i \mid \alpha_i \in \mathbb{R}_0^+\}$, and for each face $\mathcal{F} \subset \mathcal{C}$ we have $\mathcal{F} = cone\mathcal{R}_{\mathcal{F}}$ for some $\mathcal{R}_{\mathcal{F}} \subset \mathcal{R}_{\mathcal{C}}$. The dimension of $\mathcal{F}$, denoted by dim $\mathcal{F}$, is the dimension of the linear subspace generated by $\mathcal{R}_{\mathcal{F}}$. A cone $\mathcal{F}$ is called *simplicial* if its extreme rays are linearly independent. If $\mathcal{R}_{\mathcal{F}}$ is some subset of $\mathcal{R}_{\mathcal{C}}$, then a necessary and sufficient condition for $cone\mathcal{R}_{\mathcal{F}}$ to be a face of $\mathcal{C}$ is that there exists no $r \in \mathcal{R}_{\mathcal{C}} \backslash \mathcal{R}_{\mathcal{F}}$ such that supp$\mathcal{R}_{\mathcal{F}} = $ supp$(\mathcal{R}_{\mathcal{F}} \cup \{r\})$. Moreover, if $\mathcal{F}'$ is a face of $\mathcal{F}$, and $\mathcal{F}'$ precedes immediately $\mathcal{F}$, then $\mathcal{F}'$ is called a facet of $\mathcal{F}$ and dim $\mathcal{F} = $ dim $\mathcal{F}' + 1$.

Algorithms that compute the solutions of minimal support and the face lattice are given in sections 4 and 5, respectively.

Example 1 The solution cone C of $AX = 0$ where

$$A = \begin{bmatrix} -1 & 1 & 0 & 1 & 1 & -2 & 1 & 0 & 2 \\ 2 & -1 & 0 & 1 & -2 & -1 & 2 & 1 & 2 \\ 0 & -2 & -2 & 2 & 1 & -1 & 2 & 0 & 0 \\ 0 & -2 & -1 & 1 & 0 & 1 & 0 & -2 & 2 \\ 0 & 0 & 0 & -2 & 0 & -1 & 2 & 2 & -2 \end{bmatrix}$$

is 4-dimensional with eight extreme rays defined by the minimal support solutions $r_1, \ldots, r_8$.

$$
\begin{aligned}
r_1 &= (\ 20\ 16\ \ 0\ \ 0\ 22\ \ 22\ \ 16\ \ 0\ \ 5\ ) \\
r_2 &= (\ \ 4\ \ 0\ \ 0\ \ 0\ 14\ \ 14\ \ \ 0\ 16\ \ 9\ ) \\
r_3 &= (\ \ 7\ \ 0\ 20\ \ 6\ 16\ \ 14\ \ 13\ \ 0\ \ 0\ ) \\
r_4 &= (\ 20\ \ 0\ 16\ \ 0\ 26\ \ 10\ \ \ 8\ \ 0\ \ 3\ ) \\
r_5 &= (\ \ 0\ \ 7\ \ 5\ \ 5\ \ 4\ \ 14\ \ 12\ \ 0\ \ 0\ ) \\
r_6 &= (\ \ 0\ 96\ \ 0\ 40\ 22\ 142\ 116\ \ 0\ \ 5\ ) \\
r_7 &= (\ \ 0\ \ 0\ \ 7\ \ 3\ \ 4\ \ \ 6\ \ \ 5\ \ 1\ \ 0\ ) \\
r_8 &= (\ \ 0\ \ 0\ \ 0\ \ 8\ 62\ \ 86\ \ \ 4\ 96\ 49\ )
\end{aligned}
$$

The cross sections of the six 3-dimensional faces (i.e., facets) of C are schematically as follows, the two on the top-left being simplicial.

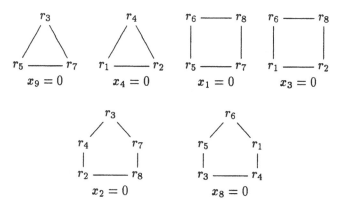

Each pointed convex polyhedral cone $\mathcal{F}$ may be decomposed into simplicial cones of dimension dim $\mathcal{F}$ and such that the intersection of any two cones in the decomposition is a common face of both. We refer to such a decomposition as a *triangulation* of $\mathcal{F}$. It is possible to triangulate $\mathcal{F}$ in such a way that the extreme rays of the cones in the triangulation are extreme rays of $\mathcal{F}$ (e.g., [13]). We shall be considering only triangulations as such, and in section 6 an algorithm to compute such a triangulation is presented. From the characterization of the monoid $\mathcal{M}$ given by Stanley in [13], it may be deduced that if $s \in \mathcal{M}$ is a minimal solution lying in the interior of a simplicial face $\mathcal{F} = cone\{r_1, \ldots, r_k\}$ then

$s = \sum_{i=1}^{k} \alpha_i r_i$ with $\alpha_i \in \mathbb{Q}$ and $0 < \alpha_i < 1$ (this result was stated independently by Domenjoud in [3]). When $\mathcal{F}$ is not simplicial, the same can be said about minimal solutions lying in the interior of each cone in a triangulation of $\mathcal{F}$. In particular, this result is useful to deduce upper bounds on the components of minimal solutions in the interior of a given face $\mathcal{F}$ from the minimal solutions of minimal support that generate the extreme rays of $\mathcal{F}$, i.e., from $\mathcal{R}_{\mathcal{F}}$.

Example 2 (Example 1 continued.) From the latter remarks, and the triangulation schematically shown below on the left, it follows that any minimal solution in the interior of $\mathcal{F} = cone\{r_2, r_3, r_4, r_7, r_8\}$ lies in the interior of either $cone\{r_2, r_4, r_7\}$ or $cone\{r_2, r_7, r_8\}$, since $x_8 < 1$ for minimal solutions in the interior of $cone\{r_3, r_4, r_7\}$. Thus, for any minimal solution in the interior of $\mathcal{F}$, a strict upper bound on x_i is $max\{(r_2 + r_4 + r_7)_i, (r_2 + r_7 + r_8)_i\}$. In particular, we see that $x_4 < 11$. The label on each 2-dimensional face indicates the component that is null for solutions lying in that face, either than x_2.

Bounds deduced for each subcone
$$r_3 + r_4 + r_7 = (\ 27\ 0\ 43\ \ 9\ 46\ \ 30\ 26\ \ \ 1\ \ 3\ )$$
$$r_2 + r_4 + r_7 = (\ 24\ 0\ 23\ \ 3\ 44\ \ 30\ 13\ \ 17\ 12\ )$$
$$r_2 + r_7 + r_8 = (\ \ 4\ 0\ \ 7\ 11\ 80\ 106\ \ 9\ 113\ 58\ )$$

The following 4-dimensional simplicial cones make a triangulation of $\mathcal{C}$:

$$cone\{r_1, r_2, r_4, r_7\},\ cone\{r_2, r_6, r_7, r_8\},\ cone\{r_1, r_2, r_6, r_7\},$$
$$cone\{r_1, r_5, r_6, r_7\},\ cone\{r_3, r_4, r_5, r_7\},\ cone\{r_1, r_4, r_5, r_7\}.$$

3   The Slopes Algorithm

The general idea of the Slopes algorithm [15] is to visit all faces of the solution cone $\mathcal{C}$, searching for minimal solutions lying in the interior of each face (including $\mathcal{C}$, which is the top of the face lattice). The faces are explored in increasing order of dimension. The solutions in the interior of a face $\mathcal{F}$ are the solutions in *positive* integers (i.e., positive solutions) of the subsystem $A_{\mathcal{F}}X_{\mathcal{F}} = 0$ where $A_{\mathcal{F}}$ is obtained from A by keeping just the columns A^i such that $i \in supp\mathcal{F}$, and $X_{\mathcal{F}}$ resulting from X in a similar way. To compute these solutions, some of the variables in $X_{\mathcal{F}}$ are given values through enumeration. For each tuple of values, a problem of the form (2) is solved to find values for the remaining variables.

$$aX = By + Cz + V, \quad a > 0, \ B, C \in \mathbb{N}^r, V \in \mathbb{Z}^r \qquad (2)$$

The minimal (X, y, z) in $\mathbb{N}^{r+2}$ satisfying (2) are well characterized [15], there existing efficient algorithms to compute them.

We shall now explain how (2) is obtained from $A_{\mathcal{F}}X_{\mathcal{F}} = 0$. It is shown in [15] that any system of the form $AX = 0$ with a *positive* solution and whose solution cone is at least two dimensional, is equivalent to (3),

$$\begin{cases} aX_0 & = A_{11}X_1 + A_{12}X_2 \\ a'X_3 = & A_{22}X_2 \end{cases} \tag{3}$$

where all the coeffices are integers, $a > 0$, $A_{11} \in \mathbb{N}^{r \times p}$, X is partitioned into X_0, X_1, X_2, X_3 (possibly, X_2 or X_3 are empty). In fact, suppose $A \in \mathbb{Z}^{m \times n}$, and let $\mathcal{C}$ be the solution cone. Always, $\mathrm{rank}A = n - \dim\mathcal{C}$. To give the system form (3), consider some simplicial face $\mathcal{F}$ of $\mathcal{C}$ (e.g., all 2-dimensional faces are simplicial). Given $\mathrm{supp}\mathcal{F}$, $p = \dim\mathcal{F} \geq 2$, and $\mathcal{R}_{\mathcal{F}} = \{r_1, \ldots, r_p\}$, identify X_1 with $\{x_{i_k} \mid 1 \leq k \leq p\}$ where $i_k \in \mathrm{supp}\, r_k$ and $i_k \notin \mathrm{supp}(\mathcal{R}_{\mathcal{F}} \backslash \{r_k\})$, and X_0 with $X_{\mathcal{F}} \backslash X_1$. Let A_{X_0} be the submatrix of A consisting of the columns that correspond to X_0. This submatrix is full column rank, and $r = \mathrm{rank}A_{\mathcal{F}} = \mathrm{rank}A_{X_0}$. Now, either $r = \mathrm{rank}A$ and the system is given the form $aX_0 = A_{11}X_1 + A_{12}X_2$, by diagonalization of A_{X_0}. Or, $r < \mathrm{rank}A$, and $\mathrm{rank}A - r$ variables from $X \backslash X_{\mathcal{F}}$ are selected so that $\mathrm{rank}(A_{X_0}A_{X_3}) = \mathrm{rank}A$, and $(A_{X_0}A_{X_3})$ is given a diagonal form to obtain (3).

By enumerating the values of variables in X_2 and of all those in X_1 but two (which we denote by y and z), the values of X_0, y, and z may be found by solving a problem as (2). We denote by W all the variables in $(X_1 \backslash \{y, z\}) \cup X_2$.

Example 3 Consider again the previous example. For solutions in $cone\{r_2, r_3, r_4, r_7, r_8\}$ the value of x_2 is null, and the subsystem may be written, wrt $\mathcal{F} = cone\{r_2, r_4\}$, as

$$\begin{cases} 16x_1 & = 20x_3 + 4x_8 - 48x_4 \\ 16x_5 & = 26x_3 + 14x_8 - 44x_4 \\ 16x_6 & = 10x_3 + 14x_8 + 4x_4 \\ 16x_7 & = 8x_3 + 0x_8 + 8x_4 \\ 16x_9 = & 3x_3 + 9x_8 - 10x_4 \end{cases}$$

For each value of x_4, with $1 \leq x_4 < 11$, the problem reduces to (2).

The method developed in [15] for solving $AX = 0$ is:

```
compute sols of minimal support;
compute the face lattice;
find minimal sols in 2-dimensional faces;
for all k with 2 < k <= dim(Top)
  for each k-dimensional face F
    triangulate F to deduce bounds on sols;
    give the subsystem the form  aX = By + Cz + DW;
    compute the basic spacings;
    enumerate values of all variables in W and
      for each tuple solve aX = By + Cz + V  where V = DW.
```

We shall now go on to explain each of the steps of the algorithm in more detail. In the sequel all gcd's are taken to be positive.

4   The Solutions of Minimal Support

The computation of the solutions of minimal support can be made in several ways. In our implementation we used an algebraic method that is fast enough for the examples we have. It is based on the fact that any such solution is a solution of some subsystem involving M+1 columns of A, which is assumed of full row rank with M rows.

```
for each combination C of M+1 matrix columns do
   compute s[1], ..., s[M+1] with
   s[k] = det(Ck)  where Ck is C leaving out column k;
   if not all s[k] are null and all the components of
   (s[1],-s[2], ... (-1)^M*s[M+1]) are of same sign Sgn
   then Sgn*(s[1],..., (-1)^M*s[M+1])/gcd(s[1],..., s[M+1])
       are the components of a solution of minimal support
       corresponding to the columns of the matrix in C,
       the other components being null.
```

In the implementation we first compute all the determinants for combinations of M columns of the given matrix. Such combinations can be represented in a compact way by bit masks; moreover, with matrix dimensions less than 20, there are less than $2^{20} = 2048$ possible combinations and it is feasible to have an array of determinant values directly indexed by the masks. For accessing the matrix elements we keep an array of column indices.

5   Computing the Lattice of Faces

The maximal face (top node) in the lattice is described by the set of all extreme rays (solutions of minimal support). Each extreme ray is a 1-dimensional face. These facts are used to start the computation of the lattice, in which we do not include the bottom element. We call *layer* a set of faces of same dimension.

If there is only one extreme ray, the top node of the lattice is the only one to be created and contains it. If this is not the case, the algorithm starts by creating the top node of the lattice and faces for the extreme rays setting their dimension to 1. Then it proceeds by forming new faces through combining an already created face with each extreme ray. During this process a dimension is assigned to the new face and adjustments to the dimensions of other faces may have to be made. When no new face can be formed, each face (different from the maximal one) is inserted in the layer corresponding to its dimension. Finally, each layer is visited and the faces in it are linked to their subfaces in the next (lower) layer, and the top node is linked to the faces in the upper layer.

This algorithm can be described as follows:

```
set Top to a new face containing all extreme rays;
if there is only one extreme ray stop;
for each extreme ray create a new face of dimension 1;
combine each extreme ray with each created face f =/= Top
  if resulting face is Top or is f do nothing
  else if resulting face exists then
    if its dimension < dim(f)+1
    then set its dimension to  dim(f)+1
    else do nothing;
  else (resulting face is new)
    set F to a new face;
    set dim(F) to  1+max { dim(F') | F' is subface of F };
    for each face F' with F a subface of F'
      set dim(F') to  max(dim(F)+1, dim(F'));
set all layers to empty;
for each face f =/= Top
  insert f into Layer[dim(f)];
set dim(Top) to 1+maximum dimension found;
for each i>1, i<dim(Top)
  for each face f in Layer[i]
    for each face f' in Layer[i-1]
      if f' is subface of f
      then link f to f';
for each face f in upper layer  link Top to f.
```

6   Triangulating a Face

The result of the computation is a set of cones, each being represented by the set of its extreme rays. The algorithm has two parameters: the face to triangulate and a set of selected rays (empty on the first call). It begins by a test on whether the given face is simplicial, in which case a new cone, given by the union of the current set of extreme rays with the extreme rays in the face, obtains. Otherwise, an extreme ray in the face is selected (as described below) and added to the set of rays, and recursive calls are made on each facet of the given face such that it does not contain the selected ray.

There are no constraints on the selection of an extreme ray. However, choosing different rays may lead to different triangulations and possibly to different bounds (derived from them) on the values of variables. We use as heuristics the selection of the ray with least sum of components. For representing sets of extreme rays we use bit masks, so that set operations are very efficient.

```
set SC to empty;
call triang(Face, {}),
```

```
where triang(F, Sel_Rays) is
  if F is simplicial
  then  set SC to  SC U {Sel_Rays U rays_of(F)}
  else
    select a vertex R of F;
    for all f, f a facet of F, R not in f
      call triang(f, {R} U Sel_Rays).
```

7 Solving $aX = By + Cz + V$

Solving $aX = By + Cz + V$, where $B, C \in \mathbb{N}^m$, $a \in \mathbb{N}\setminus\{0\}$, is related to solving $By + Cz + V \equiv 0 \pmod{a}$ with $By + Cz + V \in \mathbb{N}^m$. So, reduce $(B\ C)$ to $\begin{pmatrix} t_{11} & 0 & 0 \dots 0 \\ t_{12} & t_{22} & 0 \dots 0 \end{pmatrix}^t$, which we denote by $\begin{pmatrix} T \\ 0 \end{pmatrix}$, by performing elementary row transformations (similar to the computation of Hermite normal form [12]) and reducing the elements modulo a along the process. Let $U \in \mathbb{Z}^{m \times m}$ be the matrix of transformations, i.e., $U(B\ C) \equiv \begin{pmatrix} T \\ 0 \end{pmatrix} \pmod{a}$.

7.1 When $V = 0$

Since $(X, y, z) \in \mathbb{N}^{m+2}$ is a minimal solution of $aX = By + Cz$ iff $(y, w) \in \mathbb{N}^2$ is a minimal nonnull solution of

$$t_{11}y + a/\gcd(a, t_{22})t_{12}w \equiv 0 \pmod{a} \qquad (4)$$

being $z = a/\gcd(a, t_{22})w$, and $X = 1/a(By + Cz)$, the algorithm solves (4).

Example 4 In the example above, the minimal solutions in $cone\{r_2, r_4\}$ correspond to the minimal $(x_3, x_8) \in \mathbb{N}^2$ satisfying $8x_8 \equiv 0 \pmod{16} \wedge x_3 + 3x_8 \equiv 0 \pmod{16}$, or equivalently to the minimal (x_3, w) in $\mathbb{N}^2$ such that $x_3 + 6w \equiv 0 \pmod{16} \wedge x_8 = 2w$.

The minimal nonnull $(y, z) \in \mathbb{N}^2$ satisfying $by + cz \equiv 0 \pmod{a}$, $a > 0$, $b, c \geq 0$, may be found efficiently by the following algorithm, where **mod** gives a nonnegative remainder, and **multiplier(b,a)** computes $m_b > 0$ such that $m_b b + m_a a = \gcd(a, b)$.

```
ymax = a/gcd(a,b);   zmax = a/gcd(a,c);
dz = gcd(a,b)/gcd(a,b,c);
dy = (c*multiplier(b,a)/gcd(a,b,c)) mod ymax;
S =  {(ymax, 0), (0, zmax)};
if  dy = 0 return;
y = ymax-dy;    z = dz;  S = S U {(y, z)};
while  dy > 0
  while  y > dy
    y = y-dy;   z = z+dz;  S = S U {(y, z)};
  aux = dy/y;    dy = dy mod y;    dz = aux*z+dz.
```

The minimal solutions in 2-dimensional faces are computed by this method, since if dim $\mathcal{F} = 2$, then $A_{\mathcal{F}} X_{\mathcal{F}} = 0$ is equivalent to some system of the form $aX = By + Cz$, which is obtained by applying the transformation in Section 3. The algorithm computes just minimal solutions and no superfluous candidates.

7.2 When $V \neq 0$

The general idea is to compute a starting solution, and to move from a given minimal solution s to the next one (in increasing order of z) by adding a suitable spacing to s. Note that, if some solution (X, y, z) found by the method has some null component, (X, y, z, W) is not checked for (global) minimality since it is not in the *interior* of the face being explored.

Computing the basic spacings Rename t_{11} and $t_{12}a/\gcd(a, t_{22})$ to b and c respectively. The so-called set of basic spacings BS is computed by the following method.

```
ymax = a/gcd(a,b);
dw1 = gcd(a,b)/gcd(a,b,c);
dy1 = (c*multiplier(b,a)/gcd(a,b,c)) mod ymax;
compute the set Sp of minimal (dy,u) such that
    (ymax-1)*dy+dy1*u equiv 0 (mod ymax);
dz1 = a/gcd(a,t22)*dw1;
BS = {(1/a*(-dy*B+dz*C),-dy,dz)) | (dy,u) in Sp, dz=dz1*u}.
```

The algorithm described in the previous section is used yielding the elements of Sp in increasing order of u. Thus, BS is assumed to be in increasing order of δ_z (i.e., variation in z).

The starting solution The starting solution is the solution with the least z. Provided $U_i V \equiv 0 \pmod{a}$ for all $3 \leq i \leq m$, and $U_2 V \equiv 0 \pmod{\gcd(a, t_{22})}$, otherwise the problem is unsatisfiable, let

$$z_0 = -U_2 V / \gcd(a, t_{22}) \text{multiplier}(t_{22}, a) \mod a/\gcd(a, t_{22}).$$

Here, U_i stands for the ith row of the matrix of transformations U. Now, the problem is satisfiable iff $\gcd(a, t_{11}, t_{12}a/\gcd(a, t_{22}))$ divides $-U_1 V - t_{12}z_0$. Replace z_0 by $z_0 + a/\gcd(a, t_{22})max(0, \lceil (z_{\min} - z_0)\gcd(a, t_{22})/a \rceil)$, where $z_{\min} = max(0, \{\lceil -v_i/c_i \rceil \mid b_i = 0 \wedge c_i \neq 0\})$, being $B = (b_i)_i$, $C = (c_i)_i$, $V = (v_i)_i$. Let $b = t_{11}$, $c = t_{12}a/\gcd(a, t_{22})$, and $v = -U_1 V - t_{12}z_0$, and compute

$$w_0 = \frac{v M_c}{\gcd(a, b, c)} \mod \delta_w^1 \qquad y_0 = \frac{(v - w_0 c)m_b}{\gcd(a, b)} \mod y_{\max}. \qquad (5)$$

where $y_{\max} = a/\gcd(a, b)$, $\delta_w^1 = \gcd(a, b)/\gcd(a, b, c)$, m_b is multiplier(b, a), and M_c is any integer satisfying $bM_b + cM_c + aM_a = \gcd(a, b, c)$, for some integers M_a, and M_b. The *starting solution* is given by

$$(y_0 + k_0 y_{\max}, z_0 + w_0 a/\gcd(a, t_{22}))$$

with $k_0 = max(0, \{\lceil(-b_i y_0 - c_i(z_0 + w_0 a/ \gcd(a, t_{22})) - v_i)/(b_i y_{max})\rceil \mid b_i \neq 0\})$.
Clearly, for the starting solution,

$$X = 1/a(B(y_0 + k_0 y_{max}) + C(z_0 + w_0 a/ \gcd(a, t_{22})) + V).$$

Note that, $k_0 = z_{min} = y_{min} = 0$ when $V \succeq 0$, where y_{min} is defined as $max(0, \{\lceil -v_i/b_i\rceil \mid b_i \neq 0 \wedge c_i = 0\})$.

Finding the minimal solutions when $V \succeq 0$

```
zmax = a/gcd(a,t12,t22);
dymin = the least nonnull dy;
find starting solution (X,y,z);
check global minimality of the solution found;
while y > dymin and z < zmax
  add the first spacing in BS with dy < y to (X,y,z);
  check global minimality of the solution found.
```

The least positive **dy** is given by the last but one element in **BS**. Note that, if the kth spacing was used, then the spacings that can be used in the subsequent steps are either the kth or the following ones in **BS**.

Finding the minimal solutions when $V \not\succeq 0$

```
Boundz = upper bound on z;
dymin = the least nonnull dy;
dXL1 = dX for the last but one spacing in BS;
dXL  = dX for the last spacing in BS;
find starting solution (X,y,z);
check global minimality of the solution found;
while y >= dymin+ymin and z < Boundz
  if no spacing in BS but the last can be added to (X,y,z);
    t0 = mininum t with  X + t*dXL1 + dXL  nonnegative;
    add t0*(dXL,0,zmax) to (X,y,z);
  else
    add the 1st spacing with dy<=y-ymin, X+dX>=0 to (X,y,z);
  check global minimality of the solution found.
```

Here **Boundz** is some known upper bound on the z-component for the minimal solutions in the interior of the face $\mathcal{F}$, which can be deduced, for instance, from a triangulation.

8   Checking Global Minimality

Global minimality of candidate solutions must be checked by making sure that known bounds for the components were not exceeded and by comparison with minimal solutions computed before. Only solutions with support included in the support of the candidate need to be compared. The isomorphism between the lattice of supports and the lattice of faces is used here: we keep information on which face the minimal solutions belong to and when checking minimality for a candidate for a given face we just compare it with the solutions in the face and in its descendants in the lattice. The representation of the set of solutions for a face in the lattice consists of a pair of indices in the global array of solutions, as the algorithm computes all the solutions for each face consecutively. This leads to the following procedure:

```
if bounds for y or X are violated  return;
for each solution s in current face
   if each component of candidate > component of s  return;
visit recursively, once, each descendant of current face
   and return if there is a solution smaller than candidate;
add candidate as new minimal solution.
```

Candidate solutions found in a given face for the same W are not comparable, so s above can be taken as some solution found for a different W.

9   Conclusion

We have presented, in algorithmic terms, the method for solving systems of linear Diophantine equations described, in mathematical terms, in [15, 14]. This presentation may be useful for those interested in implementing it without delving into the mathematical details.

We have implemented our algorithm in C and compared it with other similar algorithms by applying the statistical method of [6]. The results of the comparison are given in [16] and the conclusion is that for most cases our algorithm is faster.

Our current implementation incorporates some improvements (see [16] for the details), among which

- when the solution cone is simplicial, the system is equivalent to a system of congruences, as deduced from the transformation described in Section 3, and can be solved in a faster way. The minimal solutions may be used to prune effectively the search space.
- rather than reducing a subsystem to the form $aX = By + Cz + DW$ and enumerating W for all possible values, it can be studied whether it is advantageous to change the enumerated variables by performing again a reduction wrt another subface.

References

1. Boudet, A., Contejean E., and Devie, H.: A new AC Unification algorithm with an algorithm for solving systems of Diophantine equations. In Proceedings of the 5th Conference on Logic and Computer Science, IEEE, 289–299, 1990.
2. Clausen, M., and Fortenbacher, A.: Efficient solution of linear Diophantine equations. J. Symbolic Computation, 8, 201–216, 1989.
3. Domenjoud, E.: Outils pour la Déduction Automatique dans les Théories Associatives-Commutatives. Thése de doctorat, Université de Nancy I, 1991.
4. Elliott, E. B.: On linear homogenous Diophantine equations. Quart. J. Pure Appl. Math., 34, 348–377, 1903.
5. Filgueiras, M., and Tomás, A. P.: Fast Methods for Solving Linear Diophantine Equations. In M. Filgueiras, L. Damas (eds.) Progress in Artificial Intelligence — 6th Portuguese Conference on Artificial Intelligence, Lecture Notes in Artificial Intelligence 727, Springer-Verlag, 297–306, 1993.
6. Filgueiras, M., and Tomás, A. P.: A Fast Method for Finding the Basis of Non-negative Solutions to a Linear Diophantine Equation. J. Symbolic Computation, 19, 507–526, 1995.
7. Huet, G.: An algorithm to generate the basis of solutions to homogeneous linear Diophantine equations. Information Processing Letters, 7(3), 1978.
8. Lambert, J.-L.: Une borne pour les générateurs des solutions entières positives d'une équation diophantienne linéaire. Comptes Rendus de l'Académie des Sciences de Paris, t. 305, série I, 39–40, 1987.
9. MacMahon, P.: Combinatory Analysis, 2. Chelsea Publishing Co., 1918.
10. Moulinet-Ossola, C.: Algorithmique des Réseaux et des Systèmes Diophantiens Linéaires. Thése de doctorat, Université de Nice Sophia-Antipolis, 1995.
11. Pottier, L.: Minimal solutions of linear diophantine systems: bounds and algorithms. In R. V. Book (ed.), Proceedings of the 4th International Conference on Rewriting Techniques and Applications, Lecture Notes in Computer Science 488, Springer-Verlag, 162–173, 1991.
12. A. Schrijver, Theory of Linear and Integer Programming, Wiley-Interscience, 1986.
13. Stanley, R.P.: Enumerative Combinatorics, Vol I, The Wadsworth & Brooks/Cole Mathematics Series, 1986.
14. Tomás, A. P., Filgueiras, M.: Solving linear Diophantine equations using the geometric structure of the solution space. In H. Common (ed.), Rewriting Techniques and Applications. Proceedings, Lecture Notes in Computer Science 1232, Springer-Verlag, 269–283, 1997.
15. Tomás, A. P.: On Solving Linear Diophantine Constraints. Tese de Doutoramento, Faculdade de Ciências da Universidade do Porto, 1997.
16. Tomás, A. P., Filgueiras, M.: Exploiting the Geometric Structure of the Solution Space in Solving Linear Diophantine Equations. Internal Report, DCC & LIACC, Universidade do Porto, 1997.

GenSAT: A Navigational Approach

Yury Smirnov and Manuela M. Veloso

School of Computer Science
Carnegie Mellon University
Pittsburgh, PA 15213-3891
{smir, mmv}@cs.cmu.edu

Abstract. GenSAT is a family of local hill-climbing procedures for solving propositional satisfiability problems. We restate it as a navigational search process performed on an N-dimensional cube by a fictitious agent with limited lookahead. Several members of the GenSAT family have been introduced whose efficiency varies from the best in average for randomly generated problems to a complete failure on the realistic, specially constrained problems, hence raising the interesting question of understanding the essence of their different performance. In this paper, we show how we use our navigational approach to investigate this issue. We introduce new algorithms that sharply focus on specific combinations of properties of efficient GenSAT variants, and which help to identify the relevance of the algorithm features to the efficiency of local search. In particular, we argue for the reasons of higher effectiveness of HSAT compared to the original GSAT. We also derive fast approximating procedures based on variable weights that can provide good switching points for a mixed search policy. Our conclusions are validated by empirical evidence obtained from the application of several GenSAT variants to random 3SAT problem instances and to simple navigational problems.

1 Introduction

Recently an alphabetical mix of variants of GSAT [6, 11] has attracted a lot of attention from Artificial Intelligence (AI) researchers: TSAT, CSAT, DSAT, HSAT [3, 5], WSAT [12], WGSAT, UGSAT [2] just to name few. All these local hill-climbing procedures are members of the GenSAT family. Propositional satisfiability (SAT) is the fundamental problem of the class of NP-hard problems, which is believed not to admit solutions that are always polynomial on the size of the problems. Many practical AI problems have been directly encoded or reduced to SAT. GenSAT (see Table 1) is a family of hill-climbing procedures that are capable of finding satisfiable assignments for some large-scale problems that cannot be attacked by conventional resolution-based methods.

GSAT [6, 11] is an instance of GenSAT in which *initial* (see Table 1) generates a random truth assignment, *hill-climb* returns all those variables whose flips[1] give the greatest increase in the number of satisfied clauses and *pick* chooses one of these variables at random [3]. Previous work on the behavior of GSAT and

---

[1] Flip is a change of the current value of a variable to the opposite value.

```
procedure GenSAT (Σ)
  for i:=1 to Max_Tries
    T:= initial(Σ)
    for j:=1 to Max_Flips
      if T satisfies Σ then return T
      else poss-flips := hill-climb(Σ, T)
        ; compute best local neighbors of T
        V := pick(poss-flips) ; pick a variable
        T := T with V's truth assignment inverted
    end
  end
  return "no satisfying assignment found"
```

Table 1. The GenSAT Procedure.

similar hill-climbing procedures [3] identified two distinct search phases and suggested possible improvements for GenSAT variants. HSAT is a specific variant of GenSAT, which uses a queue to control the selection of variables to flip[2]. Several research efforts has attempted to analyze the dominance of HSAT compared with the original GSAT for randomly generated problem instances. We have developed a navigational search framework that mimics the behavior of GenSAT. This navigational approach allows us to re-analyze the reasons of higher effectiveness of HSAT and other hill-climbing procedures by relating it to the number of equally good choices. This navigational approach also suggests strong approximating SAT procedures that can be applied efficiently to practical problems. An approximation approach can be applied to both "easy" and "hard" practical problems, in the former case it will likely to produce a satisfiable assignment, whereas in the latter case it will quickly find an approximate solution. For a standard testbed of randomly generated 3SAT problems, the transition phase between "easy" and "hard" problem instances corresponds to the ratio value of 4.3 between the number of clauses L to the number of variables N [10, 1]. Figure 1 demonstrates the probability of generating a satisfying assignment for random 3SAT problems depending on the L/N-ratio.

An approximate solution can be utilized in problems with time-critical or dynamically changing domains. Interestingly, we found that it also provides a good starting point for a different search policy, i.e. serves as a switching point between distinct search policies within the same procedure. Such an approach can be utilized beneficially in multi-processor/multi-agent problem settings.

Our experiments with randomly generated 3SAT problem instances and realistic navigational problems confirmed the results of our analysis.

---

[2] See Section3 for the definition of HSAT.

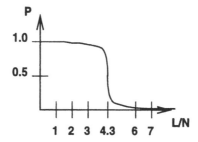

Fig. 1. The transition phase for random 3SAT problems.

2 GenSAT as an Agent-Centered Search

State spaces for boolean satisfiability problems can be represented as N-dimensional cubes, where N is the number of variables. We view GSAT and similar hill-climbing procedures as performing search on these high-dimensional cubes by moving a fictitious agent with limited lookahead. For efficiency reasons, the majority of GSAT-like procedures limit the lookahead of the agent to the neighbors of its current state, i.e., to those vertices of the cube that are one step far from the current vertex. An edge of the cube that links two neighboring vertices within the same face of the cube, corresponds to the flip of a variable. Thus, we reduced the behavior of GSAT to agent-centered search on a high-dimensional cube. Recall, in agent-centered search the search space is explored incrementally by an agent with limited lookahead. Throughout the paper we refer to this navigational version of GenSAT as to NavGSAT.

The worst-case complexity of both informed and uninformed agent-centered search is of the order of the number of vertices, i.e. $O(2^N)$. Moreover, unlike classical AI search where A* is an optimal informed algorithm for an arbitrary admissible heuristic, there are no optimal algorithms for agent-centered search problems[13]. Furthermore, even a consistent, admissible heuristic can become misleading, and an efficient informed agent-centered search algorithm can demonstrate worse performance than the uninformed (zero heuristic) version of the same algorithm [8].

From the algorithmic point of view, the behavior of LRTA* [9], one of the most efficient agent-centered search methods, is close to NavGSAT's behavior. Both methods look for the most promising vertex among neighbors of the current vertex. In addition to selecting a neighbor with the best heuristic value, LRTA* also updates the heuristic value of the current vertex (see Table 2). The efficiency of LRTA* depends on how closely the heuristic function represents the real distance [13]. The vast majority of GSAT-like procedures use the number of unsatisfied (or satisfied) clauses as the guiding heuristic. In general, this heuristic is neither consistent, nor admissible. However, for the most intricate random instances of SAT problems with $L = O(N)$, this heuristic is an $O(N)$ approximation of the real distance. Therefore, ϵ-search [7], a modification of LRTA* that uses approximations of admissible heuristics, applies to SAT problems.

procedure LRTA*(V, E)
Initially, $F(v) := h(v)$ for all $v \in V$.
LRTA* starts at vertex v_{start}:

1. $v :=$ the current vertex.
2. If $v \in Goal$, then STOP successfully.
3. $e := argmin_e F(neighbor(v, e))$.
4. $F(v) := max(F(v), 1 + F(neighbor(v, e)))$.
5. Traverse edge e, update $v := neighbor(v, e)$.
6. Go to 2.

Table 2. Learning Real-Time Algorithm (LRTA*). LRTA* also looks for the most promising vertex among neighbors of the current vertex.

Lemma 1. *After repeated problem-solving trials of a soluble propositional satisfiability problem with N variables and $O(N)$ clauses, the length of the solution of ϵ-search converges to $O(N^2)$.*

Proof: After repeated problem-solving trials the length of a solution of ϵ-search converges to the length of the optimal path multiplied by $(1 + \epsilon)$ [7]. On one hand, the length of the optimal path for a soluble propositional satisfiability problem is $O(N)$. On the other hand, for problems with $L = O(N)$ approximating factor ϵ is also $O(N)$. These two facts imply $O(N^2)$ complexity of the final solution after an unknown number of repeated trials. ∎

Even though the length of a solution of ϵ-search converges to $O(N^2)$ for soluble problem instances, several initial trials can have exponential length. Thus, this approach can be applied only in special circumstances: One is provided possibly exponential memory and possibly exponential time for pre-processing to rebalance the heuristic values, then the complexity of solving of the pre-processed problem is $O(N^2)$. Since this scenario is not always what AI researchers keep in mind when applying GenSAT, we do not consider ϵ-search as a general navigational equivalent of GenSAT. However, in Section 3 we show that one (first) run of ϵ-search coincides completely with the run of HSAT for the majority of soluble SAT problem instances.

Thus, the question of the efficiency of GSAT and similar procedures is reduced to the domain-heuristics relations that guide agent-centered search on an N-dimensional cube. Recent works on changing the usual static heuristic – the number of unsatisfied (satisfied) clauses – to the dynamic weighted sums [2] produced another promising sub-family of GenSAT procedures. Our experiments showed that the "quality" of the usual heuristic varies greatly in different regions of the N-dimensional cube, and as the ratio of L to N grows, this heuristic becomes misleading in some regions of the problem's domain. These experiments identified the need to introduce novel heuristics and better analysis of the existing ones.

3 New Corners or Branching Factor?

We conducted a series of experiments with the ϵ-search version of LRTA* and the number of unsatisfied clauses as the heuristic values for each vertex (corner) of the N-dimensional cube. We found that the combination of a highly connected N-dimensional cube and such prior knowledge forces an agent to avoid vertices with updated (increased in step 4) heuristic values. Exactly the same effect has been achieved by HSAT - a variant of GenSAT. In HSAT flipped variables form a queue, and this queue is used in *pick* to break ties in favor of variables flipped earlier until the satisfying assignment is found or the amount of flips has reached the pre-set limit of *Max_Flips*. Thus, ϵ-search is a navigational analogue of HSAT for soluble problem instances.

Previous research identified two phases of GenSAT procedures: steady hill-climbing and plateau phases [3]. During the plateau phase these procedures perform series of sideway flips keeping the number of satisfied clauses on the same level. The reduction of the number of such flips, i.e. cutting down the length of the plateau, has been identified as the main concern of such procedures. Due to high connectivity of the problem domain and the abundance of equally good choices during the plateau phase, neither HSAT nor ϵ-search re-visit already explored vertices (corners) of the cube for large-scale problems. This property of HSAT has been stated as the reason of its performance advantage for randomly generated problems in comparison with GSAT [5].

To re-evaluate the importance of visiting new corners of the N-dimensional cube, we introduced another hill-climbing procedure, that differs from GSAT only in keeping track of all visited vertices and Never Re-visiting them again, NRGSAT. On all randomly generated 3SAT problems, NRGSAT's performance in terms of flips was identical to GSAT's one. Practically, NRGSAT ran much slower, because it needs to maintain a list of visited vertices and check it before every flip. Based on this experiment, we were able to conclude that exploring new corners of the cube is not that important. This increased our interest in studying further reasons for the performance advantage of HSAT over GSAT.

We focused our attention on *poss-flips* – the number of equally good flips between which GSAT randomly picks [4], or, alternatively, the branching factor of GSAT search during the plateau phase. We noticed that on earlier stages of the plateau phase both GSAT and NRGSAT tend to increase *poss-flips*, whereas HSAT randomly oscillates *poss-flips* around a certain (lower) level. To confirm the importance of *poss-flips*, we introduced *variable weights*[3] as a second heuristic to break ties during the plateau phase of NavGSAT. NavGSAT monitors the number of flips performed for each variable and among all equally good flips in terms of the number of unsatisfied clauses, NavGSAT picks a variable that was flipped the least number of times. In case of second-order ties, they can be broken either randomly, fair – NavRGSAT – or deterministically, unfair, according to a fixed order – NavFGSAT.

---

[3] Weight of each variable is the number of times this variable has been flipped from the beginning of the search procedure. Each flip of a variable increases its weight by one.

Problem	Algorithm	Mean	Median	St.Dev.
100	GSAT	12,869	5326	9515
vars,	HSAT	2631	1273	1175
430	NavFGSAT	3558	2021	1183
clauses	NavRGSAT	3077	1743	1219
1000	GSAT	4569	2847	1863
vars,	HSAT	1602	1387	334
3000	NavFGSAT	1475	1219	619
clauses	NavRGSAT	1649	1362	675
1000	GSAT	7562	4026	3515
vars,	HSAT	3750	2573	1042
3650	NavFGSAT	3928	2908	1183
clauses	NavRGSAT	4103	3061	1376

Table 3. Comparison of number of flips for GSAT, HSAT, NavRGSAT and NavFGSAT.

Both NavRGSAT and NavFGSAT allow to flip back the just flipped variable. Moreover, the latter procedure often forces to do so due to the fixed order of variables. However, the performance of both NavRGSAT and NavFGSAT is very close to HSAT's performance. Table 3 presents median, mean and standard deviation of GSAT, HSAT, NavRGSAT and NavFGSAT for randomly generated 3SAT problems with 100 and 1000 variables and different ratios L to N. We investigated problems of this big size, because they represents the threshold between satisfiability problems that accept solutions by conventional resolution methods, for example Davis-Putnam procedure, and ones that can be solved by GenSAT hill-climbing procedures.

In the beginning of the plateau phase both NavGSAT methods behave similarly to HSAT: Variables flipped earlier are considered last when NavGSAT is looking for the next variable to flip. As more variables gain weight, NavGSAT methods' behavior deviates from HSAT. Both methods can be perceived as an approximation of HSAT.

We identified that a larger number of *poss-flips* is the main reason why GSAT loses to HSAT and NavGSAT on earlier stages of the plateau phase. As the number of unsatisfied clauses degrades, there are less choices for equally good flips for GSAT, and the increase of *poss-flips* is less visible. During earlier sideway flips GSAT picks equally good variables randomly, this type of selection leads to the vertices of the cube with bigger *poss-flips*, where GSAT tends to be "cornered" for a while. Figure 2 presents average amounts of *poss-flips* with the 95%-confidence intervals. The *poss-flips* were summed up for each out of four hill-climbing procedures for every step in the beginning of the plateau phases

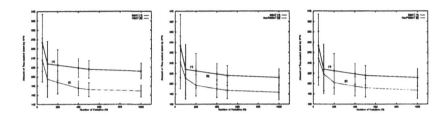

Fig. 2. Comparison of *Poss-Flips* for GSAT, HSAT, NavRGSAT and NavFGSAT.

(from $0.25N$ to N) for a range of problem sizes. Since the number of variables and the interval of measuring grow linearly on N, we present sums of *poss-flips* scaled down by N^2. As it follows from Figure 2, the original GSAT consistently outnumbers all other three procedures during that phase, although its confidence intervals overlap with NavRGSAT and NavFGSAT's confidence intervals.

Figure 3 presents the dynamics of *poss-flips* during a typical run of GSAT. It is easy to see that on early plateaux *poss-flips* tend to grow with some random noise, for example, in Figure 3 second, third and fifth plateaux produced obvious growth of *poss-flips* until drops corresponding to the improvement of the heuristic values and, thus, the end of the plateau. During the first and fourth plateaux, the growth is not that steady though still visible. Even though flips back are prohibited for NRGSAT, it maintains the same property, because of the high connectivity of the problem domain and the abundance of equally good choices.

Figure 4 represents the average percentage of ties for a 3SAT problem with 100 variables and 430 clauses over 100 runs for GSAT and HSAT, and for GSAT and NavRGSAT. The average number of *poss-flips* for GSAT dominates the analogous characteristic for HSAT by a noticeable amount. This type of dominance is similar in the comparison of GSAT with NavRGSAT in the beginning of the plateau phase. In the second part of the plateau phase the number of *poss-flips* for HSAT or NavRGSAT approaches the number of *poss-flips* for GSAT. Lower graph represents second-order ties for NavRGSAT that form a subset of *poss-flips*.

Our experiments confirmed the result obtained in [3] that the whole picture scales up linearly in the number of variables and the number of *poss-flips*. The plateau phase begins after about $0.2N - 0.25N$ steps. By that moment at most a quarter of the variable set has been flipped, and thus NavFGSAT mimics HSAT up to a certain degree. After $2N$ or $3N$ flips, both versions of NavGSAT diverge significantly from HSAT. After these many steps both NavRGSAT and NavFGSAT still maintain random oscillation of *poss-flips*, whereas GSAT tends to promote higher levels of *poss-flips*. Unfortunately, for problems with larger ratio of the number of clauses to the number of variables NavFGSAT is often trapped in an infinite loop. NavRGSAT also may behave inefficiently for such problems: From time to time the policy of NavRGSAT forces it to flip the same variable with a low weight several times in a row to gain the same weight as other variables from the set of *poss-flips*.

Thus, NavGSAT showed that the number of *poss-flips* plays an important

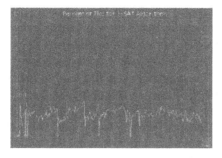

Fig. 3. Dynamics of *Poss-Flips* for GSAT.

Fig. 4. Percentage of *Poss-Flips* for GSAT with HSAT and GSAT with NavRGSAT.

role in improving the efficiency of GenSAT procedures. HSAT capitalizes on this property and therefore constitutes one of the most efficient hill-climbing procedures for random problem instances. However, many real-world satisfiability problems are highly structured and, if applied, HSAT may easily fail due to its queuing policy. NavGSAT suggests another sub-family of GenSAT hill-climbing procedures that does not tend to increase the number of *poss-flips*. Weights of variables and their combinations can be used as a second tie-breaking heuristic to maintain lower level of *poss-flips* and find exact or deliver approximate solutions for those problems for which HSAT fails to solve.

For randomly generated 3SAT problems HSAT proved to be one of the most efficient hill-climbing procedures. There has been reports on HSAT's failures in solving non-random propositional satisfiability problems [5]. We view the non-flexibility of HSAT's queue heuristic as a possible obstacle in solving over-constrained problems. This does not happen in solving random 3SAT problems with low L/N-ratio.

4 Approximate Satisfaction

While running experiments with GSAT, HSAT and other hill-climbing procedures, we noticed that GSAT experiences biggest loss in the performance in the beginning of the plateau phase where the amount of *poss-flips* can be as high as 20-25%. On the other hand, HSAT, NavFGSAT and NavRGSAT behave equally good during the hill-climbing phase and the beginning of the plateau phase. We thus concluded that any of the latter three procedures can be applied to provide fast approximate solutions. For some problems, versions of NavGSAT are not as efficient as HSAT. Nonetheless, we introduced NavFGSAT and NavRGSAT to show that HSAT's queuing policy is not the unique way of improving the efficiency of solving propositional satisfiability problems.

Approximate solutions can be utilized in time-critical problems where the quality of the solution discounts the time spent for solving the problem. NavGSAT can be also applied to problems with dynamically changing domains, when the domain changes can influence the decision making process. Finally, approximate solution provide an excellent starting point for a different search policy. For example, WGSAT and UGSAT [2] utilized a promising idea of the instant heuristic update based on the weight of unsatisfied clauses. An approximate solution provided by HSAT or NavGSAT constitutes an excellent starting point for WGSAT, UGSAT or another effective search procedure of a satisfiable solution, for example, ϵ-search (with heuristic updates). Among others we outline the following benefits of employing HSAT or NavGSAT to deliver a good starting point for another search method:

- Perfect initial assignment with a low number of unsatisfied clauses.
- Absence of hill-climbing phase that, for example, eliminates noise in tracking clause weights.
- Efficient search in both steps of policy-switching approach.
- Convenient point in time to fork search in multi-agent/multi-processor problem scenarios.

Although HSAT, itself, is an efficient hill-climbing procedure for randomly generated problems with a low clause-variable ratio, we expect that HSAT might experience difficulties in more constrained problems. NavGSAT provides another heuristic that guides efficiently in the initial phases. On the other hand, the hill-climbing phase may either produce noise in clause weight bookkeeping or redundant list of vertices with updated heuristics that slows down the performance of ϵ-search. Search with policy switching can benefit significantly from employing efficient procedures in all of its phases.

5 Navigational Problems

To confirm the results of our navigational approach to GSAT, we applied all the discussed above hill-climbing procedures to the following simple navigational problem:

Navigational Problem (NavP): An agent is given a task to find the shortest path that reaches a goal vertex from a starting vertex in an "obstacle-free" rectangular grid.

NavP is a simplistic planning problem. It can be represented as a propositional satisfiability problem with $N = |S| * D$ variables, where S is the set of vertices in the rectangular grid and D is the shortest distance between starting vertex X and goal vertex G. In a correct solution, a variable x_s^d is assigned *True* ($x_s^d = 1$), if s is dth vertex on the shortest path from X to G, and *False* otherwise. There can be only one variable with the *True* value among variables representing grid vertices that are d-far from starting vertex X. This requirement implies $L_1 = \Theta(|S|^2 * D)$ pigeonhole-like constraints:

$$\bigwedge_{d=1}^{D-1} \bigwedge_{s_1 \neq s_2} (\neg V_{s_1}^d \vee \neg V_{s_2}^d)$$

Already these constraints make the domain look "over-constrained," since the ratio of L_1 to N is not asymptotically bounded. Another group of constraints has to force *True*-valued variables to form a continuous path. There can be different ways of presenting such constraints, we chose the easiest and the most natural presentation that does not produce extra variables:

$$\bigwedge_{d=2}^{D-1} \bigvee_{s \in S} (V_s^d \wedge (V_{s_1}^{d-1} \vee V_{s_2}^{d-1} \vee V_{s_3}^{d-1} \vee V_{s_4}^{d-1}))$$

Vertices $s_1, s_2, s_3, s_4 \in S$ are the neighbors of vertex $s \in S$ in the rectangular grid. To reduce the number of variables and clauses, the initial and the goal states are represented by stand-alone single clauses:

$$(V_{s_5}^1 \vee V_{s_6}^1 \vee V_{s_7}^1 \vee V_{s_8}^1) \quad and \quad (V_{s_9}^{D-1} \vee V_{s_{10}}^{D-1} \vee V_{s_{11}}^{D-1} \vee V_{s_{12}}^{D-1}).$$

Vertices $s_5, s_6, s_7, s_8 \in S$ are the neighbors of the starting vertex, $s_9, s_{10}, s_{11}, s_{12} \in S$ are the neighbors of the goal vertex.

Second group of constraints is not presented in the classical CNF form. It is possible to reduce it to 3SAT, but such a reduction will introduce a lot of new variables and clauses and will significantly slow down the performance without facilitating search for a satisfiable assignment. From the point of view of hill-climbing procedures that track clause weights, this would mean only a different initial weight assignment and a linear change in bookkeeping clause weights. Therefore, we decided to stay with the original non-3SAT model and considered each complex conjunction $\bigvee_{s \in S} (V_s^d \wedge (V_{s_1}^{d-1} \vee V_{s_2}^{d-1} \vee V_{s_3}^{d-1} \vee V_{s_4}^{d-1}))$ as a single clause. Together with the starting and goal vertex constraints, the second group contains $L_2 = \Theta(D)$ constraints that force *True*-valued variables to form a continuous path.

It is fairly easy to come up with an initial solution, so that all but one constraint are satisfied. Figure 5 shows one of such solutions that alternates between the goal vertex and one of its neighbors, and the final path that satisfies all the constraints. The original GSAT has complexity that is exponential on D. It performs poorly for such domains, because at every step it has more equally good chances than any other algorithm. HSAT was able to solve "toy" problems with less than 200 variables until its search was under the influence of initial states. For larger problems, after an initial search HSAT used to switch to a

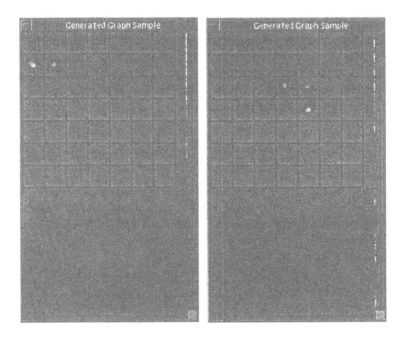

Fig. 5. Initial and final solutions for NavP.

systematic search that avoided changing recently changed vertices. Since HSAT re-started search from both starting and goal vertices on a regular basis, all the variable corresponding to their neighboring vertices has frequently changed their values. Therefore, paths from the opposite direction attempted to avoid changing these variables again. This was one of the domain where the queuing policy of HSAT played against it.

A slightly modified versions of NavFGSAT and NavRGSAT were capable of solving larger problems using Top-Down Depth-First-Search (TDDFS). TDDFS traverses repeatedly the search tree (the set of vertices reachable in D steps) from the root down, each time attempting to visit the least visited vertex from the current vertex or, if possible, unvisited vertex. The only modification of this behavior was that NavGSAT methods alternated roots between the starting vertex and the goal vertex while performing such search.

6 Conclusions

We showed that GenSAT hill-climbing procedures for solving propositional satisfiability problems can be interpreted as navigational, agent-centered search on a high-dimensional cube, NavGSAT. This type of search heavily depends on how well heuristic values represent the actual distance towards the set of goal states. HSAT, one of the most efficient GSAT-like procedures, maintains low level of *poss-flips*. We identified this property as the main benefit of HSAT in comparison with the original GSAT. However, the non-flexibility of HSAT's queuing policy can be an obstacle in solving more constrained problems. We introduced two versions of NavGSAT that also maintain low level of *poss-flips* and can be applied as approximating procedures for time-critical or dynamically changing problems, or serve as a starting phase in search procedures with switching search policies.

Acknowledgements

This research is sponsored in part by the National Science Foundation under grant number IRI-9502548. The views and conclusions contained in this document are those of the authors and should not be interpreted as representing the official policies, either expressed or implied, of the sponsoring organizations or the U.S. government.

References

1. Crawford, J., Auton, L.: Experimental results on the crossover point in satisfiability problems. In *Proceedings of 11th National Conference on Artificial Intelligence (AAAI)* (1993) 21–27
2. Frank, J.: Weighting for Godot: Learning Heuristics for GSAT. In *Proceedings of 13th National Conference on Artificial Intelligence (AAAI)* (1996) 338–343
3. Gent, I., Walsh, T.: Towards an understanding of hill-climbing procedures for SAT. In *Proceedings of 11th National Conference on Artificial Intelligence (AAAI)* (1993) 28–33
4. Gent, I., Walsh, T.: An empirical analysis of search in GSAT. *Journal of Artificial Intelligence Research* 1 (1993) 47–59
5. Gent, I., Walsh, T.: Unsatisfied variables in local search. In J. Hallam, editor, *Hybrid Problems, Hybrid Solutions.* IOS press. (1995)
6. Gu, J.: Efficient local search for very large-scale satisfiability problems. *SIGART Bulletin* 3(1) (1992) 8–12
7. Ishida, T., Shimbo, M.: Improving the learning efficiencies of realtime search.. In *Proceedings of 13th National Conference on Artificial Intelligence (AAAI)* (1996) 338–343
8. Koenig, S., Smirnov, Y.: Graph learning with a nearest neighbor approach. In *Proceedings of the Conference on Computational Learning Theory (COLT)* (1996) 19–28
9. Korf, R.: Real-time heuristic search. *Artificial Intelligence* 42(2-3) (1990) 189–211
10. Mitchell, D., Selman, B., Levesque, H.: Hard and easy distributions of SAT problems. In *Proceedings of 10th National Conference on Artificial Intelligence (AAAI)* (1992) 459–465
11. Selman, B., Levesque, H., Mitchell, D.: A new method for solving hard satisfiability problems. In *Proceedings of 10th National Conference on Artificial Intelligence (AAAI)* (1992) 440–446
12. Selman, B., Kautz, H., Cohen, B.: Noise strategies for improving local search. In *Proceedings of 12th National Conference on Artificial Intelligence (AAAI)* (1994) 337–343
13. Smirnov, Y., Koenig, S., Veloso, M., Simmons, R.: Efficient goal-directed exploration. In *Proceedings of 13th National Conference on Artificial Intelligence (AAAI)* (1996) 292–297

Timetabling Using Demand Profiles

Pedro Soares   and   Nuno J. Mamede

Instituto Superior Técnico/INESC
Technical University of Lisbon
Rua Alves Redol 9, 1000 Lisboa, Portugal
{Pedro.Soares,Nuno.Mamede}@inesc.pt

Abstract. Timetabling problems can be extremely time-consuming when they are solved without any kind of computer assistance. Computer assistance can vary from some intuitive graphical interface to an automated timetabler. Although a good graphical interface may be suitable for small problems, when we consider medium-size or large-size problems only an automated tool can be useful. In this paper we introduce a new paradigm for automated timetabling based on models and techniques developed for scheduling. Scheduling concepts such as activity and resource are translated to the timetabling domain and a general Bardadym's scheduling method, named micro-opportunistic approach, is applied in this novel domain. This approach constructs schedules incrementally and always focus its attention on the most critical decisions, to avoid backtracking. This framework is constraint-based and object-oriented. These two methods allows the easy representation of the timetabling problem and the handling of new timetabling constraints, either "hard" (should be satisfied) or "soft" (should preferably be satisfied).

1 The Timetabling Problem

The timetabling problem is composed by a set of classes, a set of lessons. a set of teachers and a set of classrooms. Each class groups a set of students with a common curriculum and studying together. Each lesson is an indivisible temporal block that joins together one teacher, one classroom, and one or more classes.

We simplify the timetabling model assuming that (i) the set of all lessons can be known in advance or previously determined; and (ii) that all pairs <class, lesson> are known beforehand.[1] Along with these entities there exists some ultimate "hard" requirements:

(i) *Completeness* – All lessons must be completely scheduled. Each one must have a teacher, a classroom and a start time associated;

(ii) *Non-Contradictoriness* – There can be no teacher conflict, no class conflict, and no classroom conflict;

(iii) *Distribution* – A minimum meal break time for each class and teacher must be respected.A maximum of teaching time per day must not be exceeded, both for classes and teachers.

---

[1] In this model, the relation between lessons and classes are considered to be static all over the timetabling process.

And some preferences or "soft" requirements:

(i) *Sequencing* – The number of gaps (or windows) must be as low as possible. The logical structure of courses must be respected (labs must follow lectures, etc.).

(ii) *Classroom fitness* – Classrooms should have enough space for the students.

(iii) *Travel minimization* – All student and teacher travels should be reduced.

(iv) *Uniform distribution* – Lessons with the same subject for the same class(es) must be spread uniformly all over the week.

A complete set of "hard" and "soft" requirements, regarding the timetabling domain can be found in [2].

According to timetabling problem classification [2], the problem here described is the combination of Class-Teacher Timetabling and Classroom-Assignment. The goal is to assign a start time, a teacher and a classroom to each lesson, without violating any "hard" requirement and satisfying as much as possible the "soft" requirements.

2   The Scheduling Model

Although there is not a globally accepted definition of scheduling, this concept can be defined as follows:

Scheduling selects among alternative plans, and assigns resources and times to each activity so that they obey the temporal restrictions of activities and the capacity limitations of a set of shared resources.[6]

In scheduling there are four basic concepts: *time, activity. resource* and *constraint*. Time is an intrinsic characteristic of the scheduling process. what makes scheduling different from planning [27].

An *activity* is a component of a plan that corresponds to an action that will be executed. The duration of the activities can be constant or can vary according to the resource (machine/worker) where they will be executed.[2] An activity has also some resource requirements (which and how many resources it needs) and some special requirements (pre-conditions to its execution).

A *resource* is an entity necessary to the execution of an activity. Each resource has associated a capacity, defined as the number of units available for consumption [18], and its availability in time. Resources with capacity equal to one are called unary resources.

According to these definitions it is possible to view a lesson as an activity; and classrooms, teachers, and class groups as unary resources. A resource can be classified along several dimensions [18]:

(i) *Single capacity vs. multiple capacity* – Whether a resource is an individual resource or a group/pool composed by several individual resources.

---

[2] From now on, we will just consider fixed duration activities because the variable duration activities model is not relevant in the timetabling domain.

(ii) *Single user vs. multiple user* – Whether a resource can "serve" one activity at a time or more than one activity.

(iii) *Renewable vs. non-renewable* – Whether the capacity of the resource is restored after the execution or just consumed.

From this point of view, one classroom can be seen as a single capacity, single user and renewable resource.

In general, a *constraint* limits the possible values of the variables it restricts. In the scheduling domain, a constraint relates activities with activities, and activities with resources, reflecting their interdependencies. Constraints can be "hard" (must be satisfied) or "soft" (should preferably be satisfied).

Typical scheduling constraints include [22]:

Functional (or Physical) constraints – Limiting the types of activities that a specific resource can perform (*e.g.*, a certain machine can not perform a certain task).

Capacity constraints – Restricting the number of activities a resource can process at any given time (*e.g.*, a certain machine can only do two task simultaneously).

Availability constraints – Specifying when each resource is available (*e.g.*, number of shifts available on a group of machines).

Precedence constraints – Stipulating temporal relations between activities (*e.g.*, one task must be completed before another).

Setup constraints – Requiring each particular machine (resource) to be in the proper configuration before performing a particular task (*e.g.*, proper sets of fixtures and tools).

Time-bounded constraints – Specifying for each job an earliest acceptable release date before which the job cannot start (*e.g.*, because raw material cannot arrive earlier) and a due date by which it should ideally be delivered to a customer.

Preferences constraints – Stating user preferences in respect to machine utilization (*e.g.*,low cost, better quality, etc.).

Approaches to solve a scheduling problem can be classified as *constructive* or *reparative*. While the first approach incrementally extends valid partial schedules until a complete schedule is synthesized, the second approach begins with a complete but possible flawed set of assignments and then iteractivelly modifies or repairs those assignments to improve the overall schedule [29].

One of scheduling's major difficulties is known as the *bottleneck* problem. Bottlenecks arise when there are many activities competing for the same resource in the same time interval. In those situations, assigning a start time to one of the competing activities can difficult others activities' time assignments. In spite of that, if several of those activities have temporal constraints (*e.g.*, some activity must be executed after another) the current bottleneck can originate new (even worst) bottlenecks in another resources in another time interval. Bottlenecks are sometimes said to "wander over time" [22].

The ability to detect the emergence of new bottlenecks during the construction of the schedule and revise the current scheduling strategy has been termed *opportunistic scheduling* [22]. In *macro-opportunistic scheduling* [19] it is necessary to schedule an entire bottleneck (or at least a large chunk of it) before being able to switch to another one. In *micro-opportunistic scheduling* [22] there is a constant evaluation of the topology of the problem allowing the scheduler to shift attention from one bottleneck to another, rather than focus on the optimization of a single bottleneck at the expense of the others.

3 Constraint Representation and Heuristic Search

A constraint satisfaction problem [27, 12, 15] is defined by a set V of n variables $\{v_1, v_2, \ldots, v_n\}$, with each variable v_i associated with a domain D_i of possible values; and by a set C of m constraints $c_1, c_2, \ldots, c_m$, between those variables (the arity of each constraint is given by the number of variables it restrains). One solution consists on a tuple of n assignments (one for each variable) satisfying the set C.

A constraint satisfaction problem can be seen as a graph in which each node is a variable (with the corresponding domain), and each arc represents a binary[3] restriction between the connected variables.

Constraint representation has been used in many domains. including job-shop scheduling [7, 22, 14, 17], timetabling [4, 3, 28] computer vision [24] and astronomical observation scheduling [8, 11, 10, 18, 29].

One of the advantages of this representation is that it allows the implementation of consistency enforcement techniques. Using constraints as propagators [26, 9] it is possible to "propagate knowledge" and reduce the domain of others variables. An overview on constraint propagation and consistency methods can be found on [12].

Consider the following example: two variables (X, Y) having the same domain, the interval between 1 and 10, and the constraint "$X + Y < 4$" between them. This constraint can reduce the domains of both variables. because the values that do not guarantee the satisfaction of the constraint can be removed. Using this propagator, the domains of X and Y will become just the values 1 and 2.

This dynamic property can be very useful when combined with search methods. This local propagation can introduce transversal "cuts" in the search space reducing its size as search proceeds. These transversal "cuts" can avoid the *thrashing problem* [15], *i.e.*, repetitive exploration of sub-trees only differing in irrelevant variables.

While this propagation can be used in the manipulation of mandatory constraints, preferences need another approach. Preferences are often used to impose quality in the solution and/or to impose quality in the scheduling process. They form the heuristic information needed to guide the search.

Combining constraint propagation to guarantee consistency. and heuristic search to guide the process. we get *constrained heuristic* search [5].

---

[3] It is possible to convert constraint satisfaction problems with n-ary constraints to another equivalent constraint satisfaction problem with binary constraints [21].

In constraint heuristic search, any search step (assignment) is followed by a consistency enforcement to reduce the domains of the variables. To decide what is the best step, *i.e.*, best assignment, some heuristic measures need to be evaluated. The overall procedure is stated in Figure 1.

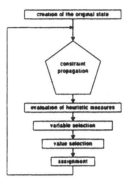

Fig. 1. Constraint Heuristic Search procedure

4 The New Paradigm

The main characteristic of this new timetabling model is that it uses scheduling as a metaphor. Lessons are activities; and teachers, classrooms and classes are resources (required by the lessons). There are also timetabling constraints relating lessons and timetabling resources.

First, we will describe the representation and then the dynamics of micro-opportunistic approach applied to the timetabling domain.

4.1 Representation

To represent the time during the week[4] we use a discrete representation (time slots). The first time slot represents the start of the first day of the week, and the last time slot represents the end of the last day (see Figure 2).

Fig. 2. Time representation

Each lesson *requires* one teacher. *requires* one classroom and *requires* one or more classes. In this model, we assumed that a lesson may alternatively require

---

[4] In our assumptions, the time horizon is the week.

several teachers and several classrooms. Since the relation between lessons and classes is static (see Section 1.) this model does not contemplate *alternative requires* from lessons to classes.

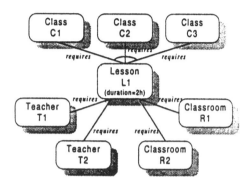

Fig. 3. Representation of require relations between lessons and their resources

In Figure 3, it is stated that lesson $L1$ requires classes $C1$, $C2$ and $C3$ (these classes must have lesson $L1$ simultaneously), requires teacher $T1$ or teacher $T2$, and requires classroom $R1$ or classroom $R2$.

In this AND-OR graph representation [20], nodes represent entities like activity and resource, and arcs represent the *require relationships*. Alternative requirements (OR-Arcs) are represented as multiple links coming from the same node. Non-alternative requirements (AND-Arcs) are represented with arcs connected by a small line. Properties of entities, like the duration of the activity can be expressed inside nodes.

According to the scheduling classifications in Section 2: (i) lessons are fixed duration activities; (ii) teachers, classrooms and classes are unary resources (capacity=1), single-user and renewable. They can only have one lesson at a time and their capacity is restored after the occurrence of each lesson.

In certain cases, teachers have associated a maximum number of teaching hours per week (week load). In those cases, the teacher's model must be augmented with another scheduling resource named energy (multiple-capacity, single-user and non-renewable), necessary to manage their week load.

An object oriented representation of the models for resources (classes, classrooms and teachers) and activities (lessons) can be found in [25].

Regarding "hard" constraints, we identified two major classes for the timetabling domain: *temporal constraints* and *resource utilization constraints*.

A temporal constraint is used to express a temporal relation between two lessons. The set of temporal constraints include (but are not limited to): (i) "at the same time"; (ii) "in the same day"; (iii) "before"; (iv) "just before" and "just after"; (v) "not overlapped".

These binary constraints relate the possible start times of two lessons. All opposite constraints, like "not at the same time", "in different days", "after", "not *just before"* and *"overlapped"* can also be modelled. A large set of temporal operators can be found in [1].

Resource utilization constraints include (but are not limited to): (i) *"requires"*; (ii) *"same teacher"*; (iii) *"same classroom"*.

The first constraint is the basic primitive for activity-resource association. When an activity requires a resource. it means that the resource availability must take into account the activity, and the activity start time can be influenced by the resource availability. Recall that lessons are activities and classes. teachers and classrooms are resources.

The other two constraints, along with their opposite constraints, relate two lessons and are used to restrict the lessons' resource usage. In Figure 4. there is an example containing lessons, resources and constraints.

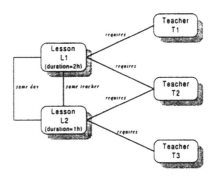

Fig. 4. Example of temporal and resource utilization constraints

This situation is an example of how constraints can be used to restrain the solution space: teacher $T2$ is the only teacher that can satisfy the "same teacher" constraint posted between those two lessons. Teacher $T1$ cannot be $L1$'s teacher and teacher $T3$ cannot be $L2$'s teacher.

The "same day" constraint will force the removal of some values of the domain of the start time variables of $L1$ and $L2$ to guarantee that both lessons occur on the same day.

"Soft" constraints or preferences constitute the heuristic information. or domain knowledge information, that should be used to guide the decision making process and guarantees solution quality. In this model we consider all preferences described in Section 1.

To understand how they are represented and how they are used we need to introduce the *demand profile concept* [22]. A demand profile is a chart that reflects how an activity requires a resource, over time. Figure 5 contains an example of a demand profile expressing that the lesson only requires the resource between time 7 and time 21 and preferably near time 15.

Since class-lesson information is static, *i.e.*, a lesson always requires a class in the same way, the only resources that will have demand profiles are teachers and classrooms.

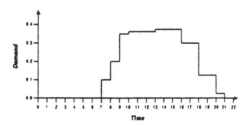

Fig. 5. Example of a demand profile

Since it is necessary to consider various factors like minimizing the number of gaps in timetables, minimizing travel distances inside the campus, etc., a demand profile is created from a weighted sum of other demand profiles (one for each factor). Examples of demand profiles for the timetabling domain will be described in the next section.

4.2 Demand Profiles

Consider the timetabling "soft" requirement classification in Section 1. Although all can be modelled using demand profiles, we selected two to describe in this paper: *reduce gaps* and *classroom fitness*.

Reduce Gaps

Suppose for the sake of simplicity that we are considering just one day (from 8h to 19h).[5] Suppose also that we have already a partial timetable for classroom $C1$ with two lessons already scheduled: $L1$ ($10 \rightarrow 11$) and $L2$ ($17 - 19$). If a two hour lesson $L3$ requires $C1$, it is clear that the valid start times for $L1$ would be the intersection of $L1$'s current start time[6] with $S = \{8, 11 - 15\}$. Consider that the valid start times for $L1$ is the set S. In what respects to gaps, it is clear that if we choose $L3$'s start time to be any value in $\{8, 11, 15\}$ we are not creating any gap; if we choose 12 or 14, we are creating an one hour gap; and finally, if we choose 13 we are creating a two two hour gap. All we need is to create a demand profile that promotes gaps reduction, giving higher values when there is no gaps creation and lower values when new and small gaps appear. Note that, since this is a constructive approach we don't know what will fill a certain gap. If we have a large gap it could be completely filled with other lessons. In the opposite, if we have a small gap, i.e., an one hour gap, and only long duration lessons, for instance two hours lessons, the gap could not be avoided.

In Figure 6, it is represented the demand profile for the case above. Note that $V1$, $V2$ and $V3$ are not quantified but just ordered, because they are parameters of the heuristic, and should be tuned according to each problem.

---

[5] Meals are not considered for simplicity.

[6] Eventually reduced using constraint propagation in constraints associated with the lesson (e.g. same day, same teacher, etc).

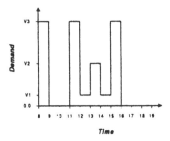

Fig. 6. Demand profile for the reduce gap heuristic

Classroom Fitness

When a lesson alternatively requires different classrooms, it should select the one that fits the number of students that the lesson have.[7] If a lesson is scheduled to a classroom with less seats than the lesson's number of students we have an avoidable situations (should be strongly penalized); if the number of seats is far greater then the number of students we have classroom waste (should be lightly penalized); and finally if the number of seats is not much bigger than the number of students we have a good fit (should not be penalized).

Since time is not relevant in this heuristic, we have flat demand profiles that vary between alternative classrooms.

Suppose we consider the classroom $C1$ of the previous example, and also classrooms $C2$ and $C3$, both with $C1$'s availability. Suppose also that the classroom capacity is 30, 60 and 90, for $C1$, $C2$ and $C3$, respectively. Lesson $L3$ have 55 students and alternatively requires the three classrooms. The three demand profiles for $C1$, $C2$ and $C3$ are the follow in Figure 7.

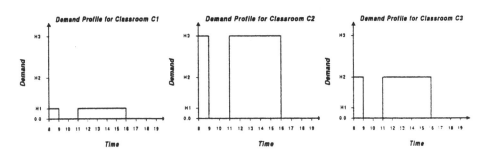

Fig. 7. Demand Profiles for the classroom fitness heuristic.

The demand profile for classroom $C2$ have higher values because it is the lesson's best fit (waste= 5). Classroom $C3$ creates a big waste, and finally class-

---

[7] The number of student of a lesson is the sum of the number of students of the classes associated with this lesson.

room $C1$ have the lower values because of its insufficient capacity. Again $H1$, $H2$ and $H3$ are not quantified but just ordered, because they are parameters of the heuristic, and should be tuned according to each problem.

Demand profiles can also model other problem specific quality measures like travel distance in campus, teacher satisfaction (according to their preferences), etc.. How demand profiles are used will be the focus of the next section.

4.3 Dynamics

Demand profiles are used to guide search. In Constraint Heuristic Search (see Section 3), we need to evaluate some measures to help the decision of the next variable to instantiate. These measures are very important because they have a strong relation with the solution quality and the solving process quality. Solving process quality stands for convergence, good performance and low resource usage.

The basic idea behind our method is that, to avoid bottlenecks, the focus must always be in the most critical decision, *i.e.*, the focus should be in the most contended resource (teacher or room) and on the lesson that most contributes to that contention in time. This technique can avoid bottlenecks and anticipate dead-end situations, minimizing backtracking.

Our algorithm is based on the micro-opportunistic method of micro-Boss [22]. A simplified version of the method is as follows:

1. If all lessons have been scheduled, then stop, else go on to 2.
2. Apply the *consistency enforcing* procedure.
3. If a dead-end is detected, then *backtrack*; else go on to 4.
4. If all the lessons have been scheduled, then stop, else go on to 5.
5. Perform a *look-ahead analysis* to evaluate resource contention over time.
6. Select the most critical pair resource/time.
7. Select the most critical lesson, and identify the most critical assignment.
8. Create a new search state by making the new assignment.
9. Go back to 1.

There are two exit situations: stopping with success (step 4) and stopping with failure (when all search space is exhausted and it is impossible to back-track). Dead-end situations occur when the set of (already made) assignments is incompatible. The consistency enforcement step (step 2) is used to propagate the current information, reducing the domain of the variables. In the *look-ahead analysis* or *heuristic measures evaluation step* (step 5) the algorithm tries to find out what is the next decision to make. Resource contentions over time are evaluated to escape from bottlenecks and guide the search. Look ahead analysis is done using demand profiles.

Look-Ahead Analysis

This step consists of building *individual demand profiles* and *aggregate demand profiles*. Individual demand profiles are computed for each "require" relationship,[8] *i.e.*, each pair lesson-resource. An individual demand profile reflects the subjective probability that a lesson uses that resource as a function of time (see Figure 5).

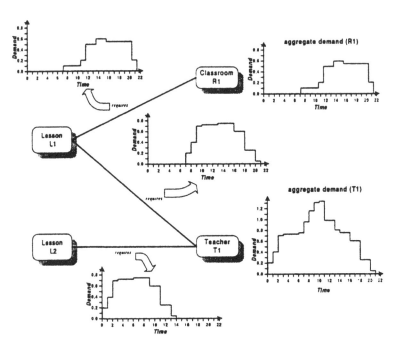

Fig. 8. Aggregate demand profiles

Then, an *aggregate demand profile* is calculated for each resource (teacher and classroom), by summing all individual demand profiles of the lessons that require that resource. For example, if a lesson $L1$ requires classroom $R1$ and teacher $T1$, and lesson $L2$ requires only teacher $T1$, the aggregate demand profile for classroom $R1$ will be only the demand profile associated both with $L1$ and $R1$, and the aggregate demand profile of $T1$ will be the sum of the demand profiles associated with $L1$ and $T1$, and $L2$ and $T1$ (see Figure 8).

Selecting a Critical Decision and an Assignment

This step consists in the identification of the most critical resource/time pair, the identification of the lesson that most contributes to that contention, and making the critical assignment.

The most critical resource/time pair can be detected looking at the aggregate demand profiles.

---

[8] Only "requires" associated with teachers and classrooms. This number can be previously determined.

The resource which has the highest peak in its aggregated demand profile is the most contended resource, and the most contended time is the time slot where that highest contention occurs. In the previous example the most critical resource/time pair is teacher $T1$ at time slot 10.

The lesson that most contributes to that contention can be found looking at all individual demand profiles attached to the critical resource and finding the one with the highest contribution to that contention peak. In the previous example, we can notice that at time slot 10, the contribution of lesson $L1$ is greater than the contribution of $L2$. The critical triple is lesson $L1$, resource $T1$ and time slot 10.

The choice of the lesson assures that the selected lesson is the one whose "preferred reservations" are the most likely to become unavailable if the other lessons contending for the current bottleneck were scheduled first.

At this point, we have identified a critical resource/time pair and also the lesson that has the highest contribution to the resource contention.

One possible way would be to make the time and the resource assignment to the lesson. But other alternatives exist and need to be considered. Since a lesson requires both a teacher and a classroom, one alternative would be not to choose exactly the time slot pointed out, but a time slot in a local temporal window that most satisfies both teacher and classroom requirements of the critical lesson. Another alternative is to do some *look-ahead*, and to choose a time slot in a local temporal window that takes into account all current competitors (in the contented resource). The first way can be classified as a *greedy* decision, while the alternatives can be seen as *altruist* decisions.

In the previous example, the effect of the first alternative would be to force a higher time value (for instance time slot 12), because at that time slot both $L1$'s individual demand profiles for teacher and classrooms have higher values than at time slot 10. The second alternative would also shift the assignment to a higher time value (for instance time slot 12), because the other competitor ($L2$) prefers time slots with lower values.

Since we do not have practical results, the selection of one of these three methods or a combination of all three has to be postponed.

When the assignment is made we go back to the consistency enforcement step and demand profiles must be updated (because lesson start time or resource availability may have changed

4.4 How to represent meals ?

Using this approach, we can easily represent meal breaks. A meal can be modelled as an fixed duration activity that requires a class (or a teacher) only in some time interval. For instance, lunch time could be defined as an one hour period that can slide between 12 a.m. and 2 p.m.. When a meal *requires* a class or a teacher, it means that this requiring relation will force all lessons competing to that resource to "move away", respecting meal time. That assures a dynamic meal that is allowed to balance inside a time interval, using only consistency enforcement.

These fake activities must be created for every meal (both for classes and teachers).

5 Conclusion

In this paper we describe a new paradigm to timetabling based on existing scheduling models.

First we introduce the timetabling problem. A scheduling overview is also introduced to formalize timetabling concept using scheduling representation. Concepts like a lesson can be seen as an activity (in a scheduling sense) and teachers, classes and classroom can also be seen as resources (in a scheduling sense). Since we combine constraint representation, constraint propagation and heuristic search we also described constraint heuristic search [5].

The micro-opportunistic method of Micro-Boss [22] is also translated to the timetabling domain. The result is a flexible framework, both for "hard" and "soft" constraints. We also have showed how we represented meals and two heuristics factors.

Since most concluding remarks can only be made with a real system and practical results, we have already implemented the model described herein. using ILOG Solver [26] and ILOG Scheduler [23]. We are connecting this system to our university database (approximately 7 thousand students, and 950 teachers) to fully test our proposals. We plan to publicize the achieved results in the near future.

Acknowledgement

This work was partially supported by Grant PRAXIS XXI/BM/6861/95 of Junta Nacional de Investigação Científica (JNICT).

References

1. Allen, J.: "Maintaining Knowledge about Temporal Intervals", in Communications of the ACM 26 (11), 1983.
2. Bardadym, V.: "Computer-Aided School and University Timetabling: The New Wave",in Practice and Theory of Automated Timetabling, Burke E. Ross P. (Eds), Springer Verlag, 1996.
3. Evertsz, R.: "The Development of SYLLABUS - An Interactive Constraint-Based Scheduler for Schools and Colleges",in Proceedings of Innovative Applications of Artificial Intelligence, pp. 39-51, AAAI Press, CA, 1991.
4. Feldman, R., Golumbic, M.: "Optimisation algorithms for student scheduling via constraint satisfability" in Computer Journal 33, pp: 356-364. 1990.
5. Fox, M., Sadeh, N., Baykan, C.: "Constrained Heuristic Search",in Proceedings of the International Joint Conference on Artificial Intelligence, pp. 309-316. Morgan Kaufmann Pub. Inc.. 1989.
6. Fox, M., Sadeh, N: "Why Is Scheduling Difficult? A CSP Perspective".in Proceedings of the 9th European Conference on Artificial Intelligence. pp. 754-767. John Wiley and Sons, NY, 1990.

7. Fox, M., Sycara, K.: "The CORTES Project: A Unified Framework for Planning, Scheduling and Control",Darpa Workshop on Innovative Approaches to Planning, Scheduling and Control, pp. 412-421, Morgan Kaufmann Publishers. Inc., San Mateo, CA, 1990.
8. Hansson, O., Mayer A.: "DTS: A Decision-Theoretic Scheduler for Space Telescope Applications",in Intelligent Scheduling, pp. 371-388, Morgan Kaufmann Publishers Inc., San Francisco, CA, 1994.
9. Henz, M., Würtz, J.: "Using Oz for College Timetabling",in Practice and Theory of Automated Timetabling, Burke E, Ross P. (Eds), Springer Verlag, 1996.
10. Johnston, M., Miller G.: "SPIKE: Intelligent Scheduling of Hubble Space Telescope Observations",in Intelligent Scheduling, pp. 391-422, Morgan Kaufmann Publishers Inc., San Francisco, CA, 1994.
11. Johnston, M., Minton S.: "Analyzing a Heuristic Strategy for Constraint-Satisfaction and Scheduling",in Intelligent Scheduling, pp. 257-289, Morgan Kaufmann Publishers Inc., San Francisco, CA, 1994.
12. Kumar, V.: "Algorithms for Constraint-Satisfaction Problems: A Survey",in AI Magazine, Volume 13, Number 1, 1992.
13. Le Pape, C.: "Implementation of Resource Constraints in Ilog Schedule: A Library for the Development of Constraint-Based Scheduling Systems",in Intelligent Systems Engineering, Volume 3, pp. 55-66, 1994.
14. Le Pape, C.: "Scheduling as Intelligent Control of Decision-Making and Constraint Propagation",in Intelligent Scheduling, pp. 67-98, Morgan Kaufmann Publishers Inc., San Francisco, CA, 1994.
15. Mackworth, A.: "Constraint Satisfaction",in Encyclopedia of Artificial Intelligence, Volume 1, S. C. Shapiro (ed.), pp. 205-211, John Wiley and Sons, New York, 1987.
16. Mamede, N., Soares, P.: "University Automated Timetabling".in Proceedings of the Eighteenth International Conference on Information Technology Interfaces. Pula, Croatia, pp 11-19, 1996.
17. Miyashita, K. Sycara, K.: "Adaptive Case-based Control of Schedule Revision",in Intelligent Scheduling, pp. 291-308, Morgan Kaufmann Publishers Inc.. San Francisco, CA, 1994.
18. Muscettola, N.: "HSTS: Integrating Planning and Scheduling",in Intelligent Scheduling, pp. 169-212, Morgan Kaufmann Publishers Inc.. San Francisco. CA, 1994.
19. Ow, P., Smith, S.: "Viewing Scheduling as an Opportunistic Problem-Solving Process",in Annals of Operations Research, Volume 12. pp. 85-108. 1988.
20. Rich, E.: "Artificial Intelligence",McGraw-Hill, 1983.
21. Rossi, F., Petrie, C., Dhar, V.: On the Equivalence of Constraint-Satisfaction Problems, Technical Report ACT-AI-222-89, MCC corp.. Austin. Texas, 1989.
22. Sadeh, N.: "Micro-Opportunistic Scheduling: The Micro-Boss Factory Scheduler",in Intelligent Scheduling, pp. 99-135, Morgan Kaufmann Publishers Inc.. San Francisco, CA, 1994.
23. "Ilog Scheduler User Manual Version 2.2",Ilog, 1996.
24. Shapiro L. and Haralick R. "Structural descriptions and inexact matching",IEEE Trans. Pattern Anal. Mach. Intelligence 3, pp: 504-519. 1981.
25. Soares, P., Mamede, N.: "Micro-Opportunistic Timetabling". Proceedings of the Second International Conference on the Practice and Theory of Automated Timetabling, Toronto, Ontário, Canada (1997).
26. "Ilog Solver User Manual Version 3.2",Ilog, 1996.
27. Sousa, S.: "Escalamento baseado em restrições espaciais e temporais",MSc Thesis, IST, Lisbon, 1997.
28. Yoshikawa, M., Kaneko, K., Nomura, Y., Watanabe, M.: "A Constraint-Based Approach to High-School Timetabling Problems: A Case Study",in Proceedings of the 12th National Conference on Artificial Intelligence. Volume 2. pp. 111-116, AAAI Press, Seattle, 1994.
29. Zweben, M., Daun, B., Davis. E., Deale, M.: "Scheduling and Rescheduling with Iterative Repair", in Intelligent Scheduling, pp. 241-255. Morgan Kaufmann Publishers Inc., San Francisco, CA, 1994.

Intelligent VR Training

Lu Ruqian* Han Ke** Ma Yinghao* Zhang Wenyan* Wang Wenbiao**
(* Institute of Mathematics, Academia Sinica,
** School of Stomatology, Beijing Medical University)

* 100080 Beijing, China.
* email: lrq@mimi.cnc.ac.cn

Abstract

The authors took the stomatology as an application area for using VR techniques in training manual skills. In order to get real data for the shape of the oral cavity, we took complete dentitions from an young male corpse. While keeping their original geometrical shapes and relations to each other intact, we implemented a virtual oral environment with a set of virtual dental operations on this model. The environment was implemented in a style of agent oriented programming. This environment was used in an ICAI system for training stomatology skills.
The way of skill training is planed automatically based on the techniques of fuzzy inference.
Keywords: Intelligent Skill Training,
Virtual Reality,
Stomatology.

1. Introduction

1.1 VR and ICAI Techniques

Most of the conventional ICAI systems are used for teaching knowledge. For example, Scholar, a well-known tutoring system, teaches geography of South America[10]. Another system, Guidon, uses the expert system Mycin to teach knowledge in medicine[10]. There are lots and lots of such systems. However, the concept "knowledge" does not cover the intelligence of a human-being completely. There are other aspects of human intelligence, skill for example. It is relatively easy to teach mental skills to the students. The most common form of such skills is the ability of solving some problems of combined nature, the eight queens problem, the pagoda of Hanoi, the eight puzzle, the magic cube, etc. The skill of users for solving such problems will be enhanced greatly in the process of training.

On the other hand, there has been much fewer work done for training manual skills by using a computer. It is hard to imagine, for example, how a computer can train a person to swim, though it is easy for a computer to tutor a user in some theory of swimming.

In this paper, we advocate the use of virtual reality techniques to train students in manual skills based on our own experiences in den virtual dental operations. The virtual reality techniques, VR techniques for short, have attracted a large amount of attention over the past few years[2],[3],[4]. Being widely applied to many different areas such as military simulation and computer games, it provides also a great perspective of developing new generation ICAI systems. In our case, it provides the students of oral medicine to operate on a virtual patient with a computer.

1.2 Immersive and Non-immersive VR Techniques

Most people are interested mainly in immersive VR techniques which, if successful, could bring about ideal effects. But some of the present technologies supporting immersive VR could not yet satisfy the requirements of high quality VR, e.g., the speed of generating graphics is too slow to get the sense of reality; the graphics generation and the object action could barely get synchronized due to the delay of transmitting information by tracking devices. Moreover, it is very expensive and not natural to use such equipment as HMDs, data gloves, etc. This is especially the case for ICAI systems, because such systems have to be used by a huge group of people, including those of schools and institutions, which will find VR costs hard to afford.

One of the practical solutions is to use non-immersive methods [4], which only require some prevailing I/O devices such as workstations, mouse, joysticks, etc., instead of expensive HMDs, data gloves and tracking devices. Non-immersive VR methods do not cost much, and would not make users feel uncomfortable.

1.3 The VORAL System

This paper introduces a VR based ICAI system, called VORAL (Virtual ORAL). It uses a virtual oral cavity with a complete set of 32 teeth as the basic teaching model. These 32 teeth are taken from the oral cavity of a human body. The students of oral medicine can simulate various kinds of oral operations on this " data oral cavity". For any student's operation which is deviated from the standard ones, VORAL issues a warning to inform the student. Apart from that, VORAL can also make an assessment of the student's global behavior and give hints about the general problem the students has, and about the possible direction of improvement of this student's operation skill. Our experience showed good effects of using this method to teach students.

2. Preparing the Data Teeth

2.1 Approaches Reported in the Literature

In order to use VR techniques in the area of oral medical teaching, the first step is to build a three dimensional model which is a good approximation of the oral cavity of a real human-being.

Our experiment is not the first study about research of VR application in oral medicine. In fact, there are research reports in this aspect[5]. They did build a three dimensional model of an oral cavity with a set of simulation operations on it. But this oral model consists only from simple geometric figures which possess hardly any similarity with the oral cavity of a real human body. In order to get a model approximating a real oral cavity, it is necessary to obtain its real geometrical data. One approach is to get its geometrical model by using laser beam image construction [6]. But what they have got was only the image of a global and integral set of the 32 teeth. It did not include those data of the teeth roots which are buried in the gum, nor those of an individual tooth, nor those of the intern structure of the dental pulp cavity. In a word, their data are incomplete from the point of view of oral anatomy. In United States, people have established the so-called electronic Adam and Eva[7]. They took a frozen male corpse and also a female one, cut them into a set of very thin slices, took pictures of them, and then scanned the pictures into the computer. By three dimensional model rebuilding they have got a complete data man and data woman. We do not have access to such fine slice machines. Even if we did have it, it would not provide us with as good results as were reported in literature, because the size of a tooth is much less than that of a human body.

2.2 Our Approach of Acquiring Real Data

According to what we have set as our goal, we used a grinding machine instead of a slicing one. First, we dissolved a teeth series and got 32 individual teeth. We buried each tooth into a peace of black plastic mold. Around the tooth we inserted two additional needles, vertical to the mold plane, to mark the position of the tooth. We ground the tooth layer by layer. The distance between two layers was about 0.1 mm. Each time a layer of the tooth was ground away, we took a picture of its cross section. Then we inputted the picture series into the computer in order to first get a sequence of two dimensional figures of the tooth sections by pattern recognition, then to get a three dimensional model of the whole tooth by graphics rebuilding. We developed ourselves an algorithm for this sake. It worked quite well. By further data smoothing, surface enveloping and illumination effects processing we obtained a tooth image which approximates a real tooth quite well.

3. Using VR Techniques to Teach Skills

3.1 Functions of VR Skill Training

The VR techniques are used in VORAL to teach oral operation skills mainly in the following way:
(1) On site observation of the three dimensional structure of the in-internal and external shape of the oral cavity and its teeth.
(2) Simulation of various therapy operations on the oral cavity.
(3) Generation of skill exercises, more exactly, generation of special purpose exercises, showing virtual oral diseases of an assumed patient, including simulation of different kinds of damages of the teeth.
These three kinds of jobs of skill teaching are divided into two classes. The first two belong to the class of so-called experiment oriented teaching. This kind of teaching works forwards. Students can perform any kind of operations as they will. The virtual oral environment then calculates the result and presents it to the student. The last one belongs to the class of so-called goal oriented teaching. In this paradigm of VR teaching, the system keeps a student model and produces exercises according to this model. The goal is to improve the skills of the student and asks him/her to perform virtual operations on the assumed patient. After each operation, the system calculates the student's merit and modifies the student model. The teaching is successfully finished when the weakness set of the student model becomes empty. The way of its working is backwards.

The bottom of the excavated hole should be quite smooth. (fuzzy concept)

These standards serve as a basis for measuring the appropriateness of students' operations, and thus the degree of how good they have mastered the skills needed for these operations. The measuring process is based on a fuzzy comparison of student's operation with the relevant standard. The results of the comparison are stored in the student model. This comparison may be made between two numeric values, a numeric value and a fuzzy concept, or two fuzzy concepts. In any case, a transformation in values of membership function is needed to allow a fuzzy comparison. To this end, we need a dictionary of fuzzy concepts, where they are assigned with membership functions which are value distributions over the domains of the relevant concept definitions. For example, the smoothness of a hole bottom is measured with the maximal deviation of that bottom surface from a two dimensional plane. The correspondence between numerical values and fuzzy concepts is given by experts.

As a result of fuzzy comparison, we may get the following judgment in the student model:

Student A always makes too slanting walls of teeth holes.

Student A often damages neighboring teeth when grinding caries.

Here again, the fuzzy concepts "always", "too slanting", "often", "neighboring" etc. should have their corresponding distributions in the dictionary.

The next step is to analysis the student's overall behavior based on the set of individual judgments stored in the student model. The aim of this analysis is to find the inherent reason of the student's failure
on a higher level. There are different kinds of reason possible:

(1) (The student is) not well familiar with the anatomical structure of the teeth

(2) Not well familiar with the principles of processing caries.

(3) Not well familiar with the functions and use of different types of drilling bits.

(4) Not well familiar with the different types of tooth hole excavating, for example the five types of hole preparing according to G.V.Black.

(5) Not well skilled in the processing of some special kind of caries, or caries at some special position.

(6) Technical deviations of personal character, for example, a left_hander.

The judgments about the student's skills and the conclusion about his/her general behavior will be used by VORAL to teach skills to the students. The type of lesson taught depends on the type of conclusion about student's behavior. If the problem of the student is the lack of knowledge (like the case (1) above), then VORAL starts to ask the student more questions and to give theoretical lectures to him/her. On the other hand, if the problem is the lack of necessary skills, then VORAL will generate special exercises which will help the students to improve the skills, by producing virtual oral diseases of an assumed patient, i.e. by generating virtual teeth damages, of which a successful processing will be hardly possible if the student has not overcome his/her relevant weakness.

A skeletal plan will be used to produce the skill exercises. Its structure can be seen in the following:

E-Plan:
Goal: (Main weakness of skill to be overcome)

For the first aspect, on site observation of the three dimensional shape of the oral cavity, VORAL allows the students to observe the teeth both from the external and the internal side. While observing from the internal side, one gets the illusion as if one were traversing the dental pulp cavity oneself. The virtual operations of VORAL include: rotating a tooth and observing it from all directions; pointing to an arbitrary point of the tooth and letting it be cut into two pieces at this point, and observing its cross section; and getting into the intern of the pulp cavity and traveling along its intern wall.

For the second aspect, simulation of dental operations, one can use VORAL to simulate tooth extraction, tooth repairing, tooth grinding, tooth planting, etc. Let us take tooth grinding, which is already implemented in VORAL, as an example. The student can move around the drilling bit in the three dimensional space, to stick it to an appropriate point of a tooth, to change its spatial angle w.r.t. the tooth and to drill the tooth. In order to get a real feeling of the three dimensional operations, VORAL produces special graphics, which provide the student with the desired effect. The student can decide him/her self the choice of different drilling bits, different rotation speeds, and different drilling directions. These parameters determine the speed and the way with which the tooth material is ground away, and the geometric shape of the tooth left after grinding.

For the third aspect, generation of special-purpose VR exercises, VORAL uses a knowledge base which maintains the following components:

(1) A list of standards for each kind of dental operation.

(2) A student model of skills for each apprentice.

(3) A dictionary of fuzzy concepts used in representation of standards and in calculation of students' operation failures.

(4) A skeletal plan of producing students' exercises (random dental damages) according to the student model

Each standard is a summary of dentists' experiences. It can be represented with numerical values or with fuzzy concepts, or both. Each time a student performs an operation, the trace of the operating instrument in the three dimensional space is recorded exactly. Then a fuzzy comparison of the student's behavior with the relevant standard is made. Its result is stored in the student model as a judgment on the student's skill. VORAL then tries to find out all the weakness points of the student from the student model. Based on it, the skeletal plan will be turned into a concrete plan by a automatic planing procedure. New exercises will be produced for the student, aiming at removing one or several of his/her weakness points.

This procedure will be repeated until the set of the student's weakness points becomes empty.

3.2 More About Goal-Oriented Generation of Students' Exercises

In this subsection, we will give a more detailed description about the generation process of students' exercises.

The whole process is based on the principle of fuzzy inference. Let us first have a look at some examples of standards.

The slanting angle of the internal wall of an excavated hole should not be more than 5 degrees . (numerical value)

Subgoals: (Other skill improvements which may be attained through this exercise at the same time)
Type of Job: (To be finished to reach the goal)
Type of Tooth Damage: (To be processed in the job)
Random Procedure: (To be used for producing the virtual damage)
History of the Student's Operations: (For reference)
Whether Repeat: (Yes or No)
Expected use of Instrument: (Device standard)
Expected Strategy of Operation: (Skill standard)
Scoring Rule: (For making judgments after the exercise is done)

4. Agent Oriented VR Environment

In this section, we will describe the implementation scheme of VORAL. It's based on a community of intelligent agents. In 1990, Y.Shoham [8] proposed the concept of agent oriented programming, AOP for short. He considered AOP as a further development of OOP (object oriented programming). An intelligent agent should possess various mental states such as belief, goal, capability, etc. An agent can act on the environment by sensing and sending information, doing inference, making decision, giving commitment, etc. Cone proposed a set of criterion for the intelligent agents [9].They are: 1. communication and negotiation. 2. autonomous stimulus--reaction. 3. robustness in behavior. 4. self improvement and automatic evolution. 5. distributed cooperation.

The implementation of VR requests high degree real time processing and interactively. AOP is especially suited to this area. We have designed and implemented three kinds of agents in VORAL.

4.1 Operation Agents

Each agent of this kind represents a dental operation. They are deviled into two classes. The first class includes domain specific operations, such as tooth extraction, tooth repairing, tooth grinding, etc. The behavior of these agents is determined by the technical standards. The second one includes those of the general server, such as graphic operations, text operations and voice operations.

4.2 Object agents

Each agent of this kind represents a part of the oral cavity organization. For example, a tooth is represented by a tooth agent. Its tooth cover, pulp cavity, tooth root are represented by the corresponding tooth cover agent, pulp cavity agent and tooth root agent, respectively.

The object agents have stimulus--reaction capability. For example, if the tooth grinding agent starts to drill on the tooth cover, then the tooth cover agent will be activated, which will give its reaction: removing a little from its surface part according to the strength and direction of the force acting on it. If the travel agent travels within the dental pulp cavity, then the pulp cavity agent will serve as a travel guide. Depending on the moving direction of the traveler, the pulp cavity agent makes the necessary geometrical movements such as translation, rotation, zooming in, zooming out. At the same time, it passes the corresponding messages about its change in position to the graphics agent which then displays the relevant part of the cavity's shape to the student. At the same time, the pulp cavity agent has yet another job of watching the movement of the traveler. If the latter tries to traverse through the internal wall of the pulp cavity, then this agent will stop the temptation and issues an alarm signal. This function corresponds to exception handling in conventional programming languages. Another example of this function can be seen in tooth extraction. If the tooth extraction agent tries to extract a tooth, then this tooth will immediately check whether the corresponding position of the oral cavity has been anaesthetized and if the anaesthetic is appropriate. When necessary, it will activate the tooth nerve agent which will then issue a signal to designate the patient's painful feeling.

Here, the communication capability among the agents is very important. Another example of this capability is the communication between the tooth cover agent and other agents. When the tooth grinding agent breaks through the tooth cover, the latter sends immediately a message to the pulp cavity agent and activates it. The pulp cavity agent then sends a message to the tooth blood agent which calculates its flowing action and passes the resulting information to the graphics agent to generate the corresponding animation.

The dental operation tools and devices also have their own agents. Their functions are somewhat different than those described above. We will discuss this problem somewhere else.

4.3 System agents

They are managers of various VORAL functions. Their responsibility includes: test and acceptance of student requests, job decomposition and assignment, monitoring the activities of the agents and exception handling, coordination of the activities of agents, maintaining student models, producing exercises, watching and scoring the students' operations, judging about their behavior, etc.

The results of our experiments have shown that the agent oriented method can be well used to enhance the skill teaching in the field of oral medicine while interacting with the students. It has improved the effects of conventional course teaching greatly.

5. Conclusion and future work

VORAL was designed and implemented by a cooperative teamwork of a research institute and an hospital for oral medicine. The authors wish to express their sincere thanks to Go Suing, Lie Dally, Lie Xuefeng, Ji Guangfeng, Liu Lenning and Wang Songxin for their important contribution. Though inspired by some work done elsewhere [5], [7], this paper has shown also results which are completely new and have not been done anywhere else. It is the combination of artificial intelligence, VR techniques, CAI techniques and medical information processing techniques. There is a broad perspective in this direction.

Possible future work includes:

(1) Development of a good dynamic equation as a model for the growing, developing and decaying process of the teeth. The best method is to establish a dynamic equation to describe the general principle of this process, then to let the students substitute different values for the parameters of the equation to observe the influence of these values upon the above mentioned process. These parameters include the time, position and direction of the growing process of the milk teeth, etc.

(2) Improvement of the agents' inference capability, so that they can meet the requirement of solving more complex problems.

(3) We are now using a fixed virtual oral environment. In the future, we will allow random deformation of the teeth shape

(4) Enhancement of the agents' negotiation and cooperation capability, so that many agents can act in a distributed way.

REFERENCES

[1] M.Giardia(Ed.), Interactive Multimedia Learning Environments, Human Factors and Technical Considerations on Design Issues, Springer Verlag, 1992.

[2] R.E.Clark et.al., Research and Theory on Multi-Media Learning Effects, in Interactive Multimedia Learning Environments, pp.19-30, 1992.

[3] R.Pansch, Three Views of VR, An Overview, Computer, 1993, Feb., 79-80.

[4] G.G.Robertson et. al., Non-immersive Virtual Reality, Computer, 1993, Feb., 81-83.

[5] T.Nanbu, S.Tsutsumi et al., CAI by VR System in Clinical Dentistry, Proc. of the Fifth Int. Acad. of Dental Comp. June, 25-26, 1994, Tokyo.

[6] J.Ke, Establishment and Application of Orthodontic Diagnosis-and Design Assisting System of Dental Maxillofacial Deformity, PhD. Thesis, Stomatological College, 1995.

[7] Visible Human Project, USA Reports.

[8] Y.Shoham, Agent Oriented Programming, AI, VOL.60, pp.51-92, 1993.

[9] M.H.Coen et al., A Software Agent Environment and Construction System, TR. 1493, MIT, Cambridge, 1994.

[10] A.Barr, E.A.Feigenbaum, The Handbook of Artificial Intelligence, V.2, Kaufmann, 1982.

Training Strategies and Knowledge Acquisition: Using the Same Reflective Tools for Different Purposes

Christophe CHOQUET, Pierre TCHOUNIKINE & Francky TRICHET
IRIN
Université de Nantes & École Centrale de Nantes
2, rue de la Houssinière - BP 92208
44322 Nantes cedex 03 FRANCE
choquet©irin.univ-nantes.fr

Abstract. The Emma educational system embodies a Knowledge Based System (KBS) that models a problem-solving method defined at an abstract level. In order to allow different explicit problem-solvings, the KBS is based on a Task-Method modelisation. The objectives of this paper are (1) to explain how we take advantage of the flexibility provided by the modelisation by using analysis-modules that can study what the influence of the student's propositions on the rest of the solving is; (2) to highlight that elaborating a knowledge-base that allows such a flexibility requires the use of automated tools that help the modelling-team to keep a precise understanding of how the different notions interact one with another; and (3) to demonstrate that these different tools can be constructed over the same set of reflective primitive modules, modules that are linked to the problem-solving modelisation.

1 Introduction

Emma is an educational system (under construction) that aims at training students in the practice of linear programming as a technique to solve concrete problems (for example economic problems). In accordance with lessons learned from educational systems for technical domains [6],[2] and [11], Emma embodies a Knowledge Based System (KBS) that models a problem-solving method defined at an abstract level. In our case this method is an abstracted modelisation of the one that is taught and practised in classroom: Emma will be used as a support tool, it must not modify the pedagogy around the software.

The system is defined to allow two pedagogic situations:

- The system solves the problem using the method presented in classroom and explicits its solving. The solving is that of an "ideal student".
- The student solves the problem with help from the system. The student controls the solving by selecting an action and/or by producing the results of an action. The system analyses the student's actions to define if they are acceptable and, eventually, provides a feedback.

In both situations the system and the student use the same concepts, those that have been taught and practised in classroom. Here again this "overlay" approach [10] is motivated by the fact that Emma is a support tool, that will be used in a context where students have already used these notions in classroom: students and teachers share the same vocabulary, the system is supposed to allow solving problems within the taught model, and not just any problem solving.

Emma's problem-solving model is defined at an implementation-independent level in terms of Activities (an identified action to achieve) and Methods (a means to achieve an Activity). Activities and Methods are defined by different attributes (e.g. pre-conditions or resources) from which some are used to select, dynamically, what Activity should be considered, and then what Method should be used to achieve it.

This modelling has been elaborated in order to allow the putting into practice of our pedagogical objectives, in particular the fact that the system can analyse and accept different variations of the problem-solving method it uses: choice of a different Activity or Method, production of different results and/or different interpretations of these results. Studying the student's propositions is achieved by using reflective[1] modules that analyse, at run-time, how achieving an action, stating a result or forgetting a result can influence the rest of the problem-solving. This provides the necessary material to decide what teaching strategy should be used. It is more flexible than a model-tracing based on a step-by-step comparison with a predefined set of legal actions, and allows non directive tutoring strategies [5]. As an example, when a student proposes his results, the system can emphasise that a result is not acceptable and why, or that the student has forgotten a result and why this is problematic for the rest of the solving, or on the contrary that given the results proposed by the student one can cut across the method. This is of much more pedagogical value than just saying "this is what you are supposed to do".

On the other hand, the flexibility made possible by the modelisation is difficult to manage for the modelling-team (i.e., the different persons involved in the modelling and the construction of the knowledge base), that must keep the different interrelations between the model notions and the different solvings that they allow in mind.

The objective of this paper is to highlight that taking advantage of the flexibility provided by our modelisation requires analysis-modules to (1) allow the putting into practice of different pedagogical strategies and (2) help the modelling-team to keep a precise understanding of how the different knowledge-base notions interact one with another, but that these different tools can be constructed over a set of reflective primitive modules linked to the problem-solving modelisation.

In Section 2 we describe the modelisation we use in Emma. In Section 3

---

[1] In this paper we call "reflective module" a module that can analyse another part of the system. We use the term "reflective" in order to keep coherent with the terminology proposed by the European Reflect project [7], in some other works this is called "introspection" or "meta" capacities.

we present what analysis tools are necessary for educational purposes and for helping the modelling-team in the knowledge-base construction. In Section 4 we discuss lessons learned from this work and study its generic aspects. It should be noted that, concerning the interaction with the student, we focus here on the tools we use and not on the pedagogic control of their use.

2 The Model

In Emma a typical problem describes a company that must face a command with constraints that it cannot manage. The student must identify the situation (for instance that it is a problem of maximisation of margins) and then solve a linear programming problem. The objective is to make him explicit what activities he must consider and how he can solve them, from the analysis of the problem to the proposition of a solution. As in different works that aim at expliciting a problem-solving method at different levels of abstraction (for instance [1]), we use a modelling that is based on Task (called Activity in Emma) and Method notions.

An Activity is an aspect of the solving that teachers can identify when they present their reasoning process. Examples are "Formalisation of the mathematical situation" or "Solution of a linear programming problem". An Activity is defined by a name, an objective, pre-conditions (the fact that it is pertinent from the point of view of the problem-solving method one teaches), an activation-context (the fact that it is pertinent from the point of view of mathematical constraints), resources (what knowledge must be accessible to achieve it), post-conditions (what strategic aspect has been obtained afterwards) and a set of Methods.

A Method is a possible means to achieve an Activity. Decomposition Methods split an Activity into multiple sub-Activites and operational Methods define what Process can be achieved to effectively achieve an Activity. An Activity can usually be achieved by different Methods. A Method is described by a name, a type (decomposition or operational), resources (what knowledge must be accessible to achieve it), a selection context (when this Method can be used from a mathematical point of view) and a favourable context (the situation where it is particularly adapted, if any). A Process describes concrete low-level manipulations that are not in the scope of what one wants to teach. Figure 1 presents an extract of Emma's Activities and Methods (in italics in the Figure).

Different types of knowledge are used to represent the domain. We will simplify their presentation by dissociating domain knowledge, that denotes information on the solution (e.g. "number of variables is 2" or "the function is linear"), and strategic knowledge, that denotes information on the solving state (e.g. "the mathematical situation is not defined" or "the nature of the function to optimise is defined"). A graph defines the interrelations within domain and strategic knowledge using relations such as "is-a-particular-case", "is-a-possible-value", "are-exclusive-values", "imply" or "are-equivalent". Figure 2 presents an extract of this graph.

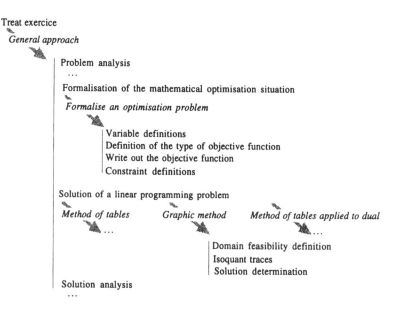

Treat exercice
   General approach

        Problem analysis
        ...

        Formalisation of the mathematical optimisation situation
        Formalise an optimisation problem

           Variable definitions
           Definition of the type of objective function
           Write out the objective function
           Constraint definitions

        Solution of a linear programming problem
        Method of tables   *Graphic method*   *Method of tables applied to dual*
           ...   ...

                                    Domain feasibility definition
                                    Isoquant traces
                                    Solution determination

        Solution analysis
        ...

Fig. 1. Activities and Methods (extract)

Interpretation knowledge is associated to every Activity and Process. This interpretation knowledge is composed of relations of the domain graph. It is used to interpret at an abstract level the results of the Activities and Processes. As an example, when a Process produces "linear-programming-problem certain" it can be interpreted as "problem-optimisation certain" by using an "Is-a" relation. In order to allow different solvings we have dissociated Necessary Interpretations (relations that *must* be considered when the Activity or the Process is finished) and Possible Interpretations (relations that *can* be considered when the Activity or the Process is finished).

The explicit representation of the model allows the system to analyse the pertinency of an Activity (resp. a Method, a result) proposed by the student at two levels. First, from the domain point of view (i.e., from a mathematical point of view): the acceptability can be analysed by checking the resources and activation context for Activities (resp. resources and selection context for Methods), by checking the domain graph for the results. Second, from the perspective of the taught method. For instance if the student states the post-conditions of an Activity, the system can define if this affirmation is impossible (the post-conditions are the result of none of the possible Interpretations), anticipated (some necessary results have not been yet affirmed) or acceptable. Such an analysis can also be achieved for the Activities and Methods by checking their description.

In this paper we do not emphasise pedagogical aspects of the selection of Activities and Methods. This knowledge will be modelled within the same formalism, but is to be managed by other mechanisms that cannot be explicited here. As an example of pedagogical knowledge representation, we will just men-

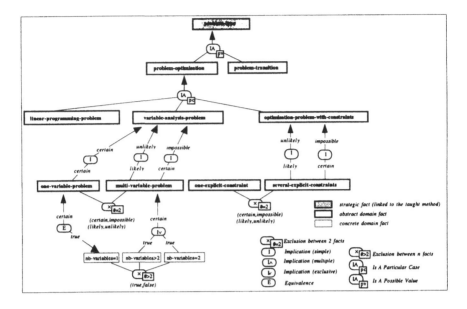

Fig. 2. The domain graph (extract)

tion that a status has been attached to every relation of the domain graph. This status denotes if the relation is "to be explicited" (the student must explicitly say he uses the relation), "to be mentioned" (if the student points out a result that can be reached with such a relation the system accepts but mentions the relation) or "implicit" (the system accepts an implicit use of such a relation). For instance, uses of "imply" between a domain knowledge and a strategic knowledge are to be explicited, uses of "imply" between domain knowledge of the same level are to be mentioned and uses of "are-exclusive-values between two facts" are implicit. This information is not hard-encoded and can be modified, eventually at run-time. It allows the system to reason not only on the correctness of a result, but also on how the result is produced.

3 Dealing with the flexibility enabled by the model

3.1 Flexibility enables different teaching strategies

When the system solves the problem, it selects an Activity (resp. a Method) because its description matches the current state of the solving. The way these slots have been filled denote both mathematical constraints and the problem-solving method one wants to teach (e.g. pre-conditions or favourable context). This method is that of an ideal student, and shortcuts are possible. In our modelisation they are made possible by the differentiation of Necessary and Possible Interpretations. In general, Possible Interpretation allows going a step further that just Necessary Interpretations.

As an example, the Activity "Definition of the type of objective function" aims at defining if the function to optimise is (for instance) a maximisation. While some students can state one is in a maximisation problem from the reading of the exercise, others must write the function to discover it. Nevertheless, if when writing the function they realise that it is linear (this is a Possible Interpretation), one can accept that they don't achieve the "Write out the objective function" Activity, where this is a Necessary Interpretation.

In order to take advantage of this flexibility and dynamically adopt an intelligent behaviour we need different materials.

As an example, let us suppose the student produces a result that would have been produced later on following the "ideal student" method, and that this result is the post-condition of the A Activity. Should one allow the student to ignore the Activity ? First, one must analyse the student's solving in order to define if A can be ignored: did the student produce the results that are defined by the Necessary interpretations attached to A ? if not, could he have produced these results while one of the Activities he has already achieved ? Second, if one makes him ignore the Activity, one must analyse the influence on the rest of the solving. For instance if ignoring the Activity requires inciting the student to produce a result, how will this result be used in the rest of the solving. When this material is obtained one can, using pedagogical knowledge on the domain knowledge (such as for example that this particular interpretation should preferably be studied during a particular Activity), study what strategy should be used, i.e,. how the system should react to the student proposition, such as for example:

- Opportunist behaviour: if the student states the post-conditions of an Activity A before this Activity is undertaken and he has studied all the Necessary Interpretation attached to A, consider that A is no longer to be achieved.
- Incitative behaviour: if the student states part of the results that correspond to an Activity A, incite the student to produce all the Interpretations that can be made, and advocate shortcuts in the method. Considering the fact that all the high-level Activities are systematically decomposed into sub-Activities, two sub-strategies can be used: either use the Possible Interpretation as soon as possible (during the sub-Activites), or be incitative when all the sub-Activities have been achieved (when one finishes the up-level Activity).

3.2 Flexibility requires help for the modelling-team

Elaborating the problem-solving model of an educational system is known as a difficult process [11], [8]. A model such as Emma's is rather complex. Modifying an Activity description or its Interpretation knowledge can heavily influence the solvings the system proposes and accepts. When building the knowledge-base, it is difficult to keep a synthetic understanding of how the different aspects of the model interact one with each other.

As an example, when an interaction situation such as "allow the student not to achieve an Activity" is modelled, the modelling-team must analyse the knowledge-base from this perspective. Analysing the knowledge-base by hand is not possible, and automatic analysis modules must be used. Given an Activity A, one must define all the possible contexts in which it can be considered (i.e., all the possible Methods that define a decomposition that contains A). For each of these contexts one must define the Activities that can precede A, analyse their results and compare them with the objective and the results of A. This allows checking what Activities can possibly be ignored and find possible misconceptions. For instance, given the knowledge-base an Activity can be ignored but this has no sense from a mathematical and/or pedagogical point of view; it is pedagogically interesting to allow an Activity to be ignored but some of its results cannot be produced by a Possible Interpretation of a preceding Activity; etc.

3.3 Analysing if an Activity can be ignored

Modules that allow interactions between the system and the student and modules that help in the construction of the system's knowledge-base have different objectives. Nevertheless, because the notions used in the model (the Activities, the Methods and their description) are represented explicitly in the knowledge-base, modules can be used for both purposes, although with different strategies. Figure 3 presents the principle of the tool that helps the modelling-team study if an Activity can be ignored.

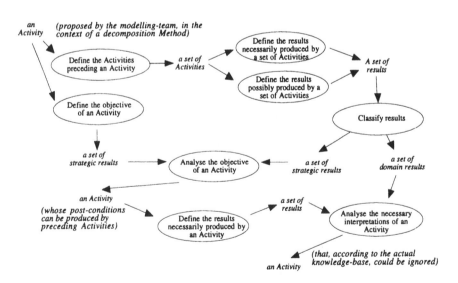

Fig. 3. Inference structure of a tool for the modelling-team

Figure 4 presents the principle of the tool that can be used at run-time to provide the pedagogical control with the material necessary to decide how to behave if it appears that an Activity could be ignored.

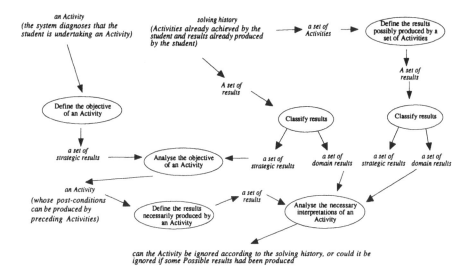

Fig. 4. Inference structure of a tool for dealing with a student's proposition

Analysing these two inference structures, one can see that they are different combinations of the same primitives. These primitives are reflective modules that provide information on the knowledge-base and analysis capacities on this information.

3.4 Reflective tools for analysing the student propositions and helping the modelling-team

Analysing if an Activity can be ignored is but a perspective on Emma's knowledge-base. Exploiting the flexibility provided by the modelisation requires many other analysis tools. Different tools are interesting for both teaching and helping the modelling-team, as for example:

- Analyse the influence of the Interpretation knowledge attached to an Activity on the rest of the solving, and in particular the fact that it is defined as Possible or Necessary Interpretation. This is necessary to justify the system's propositions and study the system's reaction to the student propositions. When constructing the knowledge-base, it appeared that defining when an abstraction step must be taken or should be taken is sometimes difficult. An automated tool can study such aspects in perspective with the rest of the solving and the pedagogical strategies that have been defined. Similar analyses are necessary on the domain graph.
- Study interrelations between the concepts. As an example, considering an Activity that can be achieved by different Methods, it is interesting to analyse the influence of the choice of a Method on the rest of the solving: it can interfere with the selection of a following Activity and/or Method, or on

what type of domain relation (exclusion, implication, etc.) will be used to produce a result.

Some tools essentially address helping the modelling-team, as for example:

- Analyse possible misconceptions, such as for example the fact that an Activity has two possible Methods which description does not allow an explicit choice. Although in some cases two Methods can be interchangeable, when one teaches different Methods they usually have different advantages and/or inconvenients. When acquiring knowledge it appeared that teachers often forget to explicit some preferences that seem obvious to them. Such tools help refining the knowledge-base on such aspects, in a systematical process.
- Study the coherence of pedagogical information attached to the model items. As an example, if one wants a result to be produced only within an explicit process, one must make sure that there is no combination of relations defined as "implicit" that can produce it. Due to the redundancy and the complexity of the domain graph, this can become overly complex.

It appears that all the tools that are used for dealing with the student are pertinent when refining the knowledge-base. At least, they are used to build tools that allow simulating different solvings; such simulations are necessary to deal with the complexity of the model.

4 Discussion

4.1 Lessons learned

As we have argued in Section 3, the same primitives can be used to construct tools that address educational issues and tools that address modelling issues. What these primitives allow are:

- The capacity to access an explicit representation of the model's notions (Activities, Methods, domain relations), their description and how they are used while solving.
- The capacity to simulate different uses of this material: achieve a list of Activities and, for each Activity, the interpretation knowledge one wants; specify a subset of domain relations selected upon different criteria and control their use (e.g. fire the relations by layer or fire only certain types of relations); etc.

This suggests that constructing the corresponding set of modules using a language that allows their connection permits not only the construction of the tools we need to put teaching strategies into action, but also the construction of the tools we need to support the modelling-team when elaborating and refining the knowledge-base. A Task-Method (Activity-Method in Emma's case) modelisation allows an explicit representation of the problem-solving method to teach. Its implementation within an architecture that respects a structural correspondence with the model allows the analysis capacities we need to construct such tools.

4.2 Reusability

Emma is the first system of the Elmer project, that aims at the construction of different systems to support teaching problem-solving in a French technological cursus [3]. For all of these the KBS will be modelled within the Task-Method modelling paradigm.

To implement Emma we have used the DSTM framework, a flexible kernel that implements dynamic selection of Tasks and Methods [9]. DSTM proposes basic definitions of Tasks and Methods, high-level operations (such as select a Task) and a control over them. To implement Emma's model we have modified DSTM in order to match the constraints resulting from our educational objectives, in particular the modification of the Task definition in the Activity definition, the dissociation of Necessary and Possible interpretations and the definition of an explicit relational language for domain knowledge representation.

Emma is thus represented at an abstract (generic) level. Most of the analysis modules we have presented in this paper are linked to the modelling paradigm (in Figures 3 & 4 we have used the term 'Activity' to keep coherent with the rest of the paper, but in fact the reflective modules essentially manipulate DSTM items). They can be used not only for Emma, but, mutandis mutandem, for any system modelled within the DSTM framework. Such modifications can easily be achieved as the implementation is layered. DSTM and the different analysis tools are developed using the knowledge level reflective capacities of the Zola language[4], i.e., the fact that one can define operations that can analyse the different notions of the model.

References

1. Aïmeur E., Frasson C. *Eliciting the learning context in cooperative tutoring systems.* In (P. Brezillon and S. Abu-Hakima eds.) "Working notes of the IJICAI-95 workshop on modelling context in knowledge representation and reasoning", LAFORIA report 95/11 (Paris VI, France):1-11, 1995.
2. Anderson J.R., Boyle C.F., Corbett A.T., Lewis M.W. *Cognitive modeling and intelligent tutoring.* Artificial Intelligence **42**:7-49, 1990.
3. Choquet C., Tchounikine P., Trichet F. *Le projet ELMER : premier rapport* (in French). Research report IRIN-145, Nantes, France, 1996.
4. Istenes Z., Tchounikine P. *Zola: a language to Operationalise Conceptual Models of Reasoning.* Journal of computing and information (special issue ICCI'96) **2**(1):689-706, 1996.
5. Lelouche R., Dion P. *Using the model-tracing methodology in a learning environment with a non-directive tutoring strategy.* Proceedings of Calisce'94:259-268, 1994.
6. Means B., Gott S.P. *Cognitive task analysis as a basis for tutor development: articulating abstract knowledge representations.* In (J. Psotka, L.D. Massey and S.A. Mutter eds.) "ITS: lessons learned", Lawrence Erlbaum Associates Publishers:35-57, 1988.
7. Reinders M., Vinkhuyzen E., Voss A., Akkermans H., Balder J., Bartsch-Sparl B., Bredeweg B., Drouven U., van Harmelen F., Karbach W., Karsen Z., Schreiber G.,

Wielinga B. *A conceptual modelling framework for knowledge-level Reflection.* AI Communications 4(2/3):74-87, 1991.

8. Tchounikine P. *Modelling problem-solving for an educational system.* Intelligent Tutoring Media 7(3-4):83-96, 1997.

9. Trichet F., Tchounikine P. *Reusing a Flexible Task-Method Framework to Prototype a Knowledge Based System.* To appear in the Proceedings of the Seventh International Conference on Software Engineering and Knowledge Engineering (SEKE'97), 1997.

10. Wenger E. *Artificial Intelligence and tutoring systems, computational and cognitive approaches to the communication of knowledge.* Morgan-Kaufman, Los Altos, C.A., 1987.

11. Winkels R., Breuker J. *Modelling expertise for educational purposes.* Proceedings of the International Conference on Tutoring Systems ITS'92:633-641, Montréal, Canada, 1992.

About the Intended Meaning of a Linguistic Negation

Daniel Pacholczyk

LERIA, Université d'Angers, 2 Boulevard Lavoisier,
F-49045 Angers Cedex 01, France

Abstract. In this paper, we present a Model dealing with Linguistic Negation of Nuanced Properties. Our Approach to Negative Information is based upon a Similarity Relation between Nuanced Properties. A Choice Strategy allows the User to explain more explicitly the intended meaning of Linguistic Negations. This Model improves the abilities in Classical Knowledge Management in that a premise or conclusion of a Classical Rule can include Linguistic Negations. Moreover, Default Reasoning can be extended through a Linguistic Approach to Negative Information.

1 Introduction

In this paper, we present a Model dealing with Linguistic Negation of Imprecise Information. Our Approach to Vagueness is essentially based upon Zadeh's Fuzzy Set Theory [18]. Desmontils & Pacholczyk have proposed ([3], [4]) a Model dealing with *Affirmative Information* encoded in a Qualitative way. So, the User can introduce in a Knowledge Base an assertion like « John is *really very* tall ». In order to make the basic terminology clear, this Model is briefly presented in Section 2.

Our purpose here is to improve the abilities of this Model in such a way that the User can also express Knowledge using *Negative Information*. That is to say, he can also assert that «John is *not* small». In such a case, he may refer to the Fuzzy Complement Property «not small», but very often he intends to mean another Property like «*very* tall» or «*really extremely* small». A lot of works on Linguistic Negation have already been proposed. Some authors (see Muller [9], Ladusaw [7], Ducrot & Schaeffer [5], Horn [6], Culioli [2], Lenzen [8], Pearce [11], Pearce & Wagner [12]) have developed *pragmatic* or *formal* methods dealing with Negation of a precise Property. In Section 3, we present the fundamental ideas concerning these Approaches to Negation in Linguistics. Within the Fuzzy Context, the recent paper by Torra [16], some similarities could be found with our Approach.

In many situations, « x is not A » seems to have, in a Fuzzy Context, an equivalent affirmative translation of the form « x is P », where the Property P is defined in the same domain as A, but has a *weak similarity* to A. Some authors have studied *Similarity Relations* (see Tversky [17], Baldwin & Pilsworth [1], Zadeh [20], Ruspini [14], Pacholczyk [10]). We have chosen the weakly transitive Similarity Relation proposed by Pacholczyk [10]. The basic notions leading to the Concept of θ_i-*similarity of Fuzzy Sets* are defined in Sections 4.1 and 4.2. Then, we generate (§ 4.3) a set of ρ-*plausible Linguistic Negations* in the domain. Thus, in Section 5 we can propose to the User an *Interactive Choice Strategy* of « x is P » as interpretation of « x is not A ». We present in Section 6, some Common sense Properties of our Linguistic Negation. Section 7.1 is more particularly devoted to the Interpretation of Rules containing Linguistic Negation like if « Jack is not tall » then « Jack is invisible in a crowd ». Finally, in Section 7.2 we point out that our Concept of Linguistic Negation can be applied in Default Reasoning.

2 Fuzzy Properties Description *via* Fuzzy Operators and Modifiers

In this Section, we briefly describe the Symbolic Representation of Nuanced Properties proposed by Desmontils & Pacholczyk ([3], [4]). They suppose that the Discourse Universe is characterized by a finite number of concepts C_i. A set of Properties P_{ik} is associated with each C_i, whose Description Domain is denoted as D_i. The P_{ik} are said to be the *Basic Properties* connected with C_i.

A finite set of *Fuzzy Modifiers* m_α allows us to define new Properties, denoted as « $m_\alpha P_{ik}$ », whose membership L-R function simply results from P_{ik} by using a translation and a contraction. We can select the following set (Fig. 1): $M_7=\{$extremely little, very little, rather little, moderately ($\varnothing_m$), rather, very, extremely$\}$.

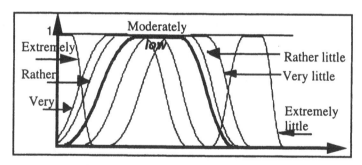

Fig. 1. A plausible set of Fuzzy Modifiers

In order to modify the Precision or Imprecision of each « $m_\alpha P_{ik}$ », we use a finite set of *Fuzzy Operators* f_α defining new Properties « $f_\alpha m_\beta P_{ik}$ ». Their membership L-R functions simply result from the ones of « $m_\beta P_{ik}$ ». The following set F_6 gives us a possible choice of Fuzzy Operators (Fig. 2):

$F_6=\{$vaguely, neighboring, more or less, moderately ($\varnothing_f$), really, exactly $\}$.

Given a Basic Property P_{ik}, a property such as « $f_\alpha m_\beta P_{ik}$ » which requires for its expression the list of linguistic terms (f_α, m_β) can be called a *Nuanced Property*.

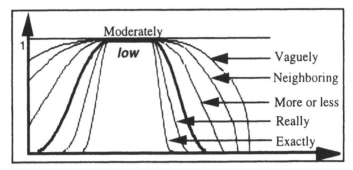

Fig. 2. A plausible set of Fuzzy Operators

3 Negation in Linguistics

In this Section we present the fundamental aspects resulting from the Analysis of Negation proposed in Linguistics (see Muller [14], Culioli [4], Horn [11], Ducrot and Schaeffer [7]).

3.1 Characterization of Linguistic Negation

Many Linguists have pointed out that Negation must be defined within a *Pragmatic Context*. More precisely, saying that « x is not A », the Speaker characterizes as Negation *i)* the *judgement of rejection* and *2)* the *semiologic means* exclusively used to notify this rejection. So, « x is A » is not in Adequation with Discourse Universe, but « x is not A » does not necessarily imply its Adequation with this Universe. It can only be a step in the outcome of this precise Adequation by the Speaker.

3.2 Interpretations of « x is not A »

We have chosen some characteristic cases to present the argumentation of previous linguists leading to the interpretations of « x is not A ».

Linguistic Negation based upon A.

Saying that «John is not tall», the Speaker does not deny a certain height, he simply denies that his height can be high. So, his precise Adequation to Reality can be « John is *extremely little* tall ». In this case, the Speaker refers to the same Property and expresses a weak agreement between « tall » and « *extremely little* tall ».

Marked and not marked Properties.

Let us suppose that three Properties « thin », « big » and « enormous » are associated with the basic concept « weight » (Fig. 3). Then, « x is not thin » can mean that the speaker *1)* rejects « x is thin » and *2)* refers to « x is enormous » or « x is *really* big », but not to « x is *vaguely* big ». It can be noted that « big » and « enormous » have a weak agreement with « thin ». On the other hand, asserting that « x is not big » generally means that « x is thin », that is to say, the affirmative Interpretation is precise and unique. So, linguists distinguish a *marked* property like « thin » from a *not marked* property such as « big ». This distinction is important *since the Negation of not marked Property is explicitly defined.*

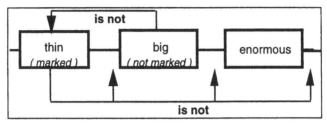

Fig. 3. Negations of Properties associated with the concept « weight »

A new property denoted as « not-A ».

When the Speaker asserts that « Mary is not ugly », this *semblance of Negation* is in fact an *affirmative reference* to the new Property « not-ugly ». So, in some cases, Negation of « A » introduces *a new Basic Property* denoted as « not-A ».

Reference to logical ¬ A.

The interpretation of the assertion « this head-scarf is not green » is « this head-scarf has another color than green ». So, « x is not A » means that « x is P (color) » with P ≠ A. The Property P is exactly ¬A. We can note that between P and A, no similarity can exist.

A simple rejection of « x is A ».

Saying that « John is not guilty », the Speaker *only rejects* the fact « John is guilty ». So, we progress weakly with the adequation of « x is not guilty » to Reality.

4 An Approach to Linguistic Negation *via* Similarity of Fuzzy Sets

4.1 Interpretations of « x is A » and « x is not A »

Scheffe [15] has already pointed out that, linguistically speaking, the statement «x is A» implies a lot of related statements. So, applying this result to Nuanced Properties, «x is A» may be interpreted as one of the statements: «x is $\varnothing_i$ A», «x is really A» or «x is more or less A». As an example, basic Properties such as «low», «average» and « high » can be associated with the particular concept «number of intersection points» (Fig. 4). Then, the statement « x is low » corresponds to one of the following statements : «x is $\varnothing_i$ low», « x is *really* low » and « x is *more or less* low ».

In F_6, we can put : G_1={more or less, $\varnothing_1$, really } and G_2 ={vaguely, neighboring, exactly}. So, more formally we have :

$$« \text{ x is A } » \Leftrightarrow \{ « \text{ x is } f_\alpha \text{ A } » \text{ with } f_\alpha \in G_1 \}.$$

Then, the Negation of « x is A », denoted as « x is not A », can receive the following meaning : the speaker *rejects* all previous interpretations of «x is A», and, *refers to* a Nuanced Property P having a weak agreement with A, and, in such a way that « x is P» is equivalent to the statement « x is not A ». By using our previous

« Nuances », P is « $f_\beta A$ » with $f_\beta \in G_2$, *or* P is « $m_\delta A$ » with $m_\delta \neq \varnothing$, *or* P is « $f_\chi B$ » with $B \neq A$ defined in the same domain and $f_\chi \in F_6$. The main difficulty is then due to the fact that P is not explicitly given.

In the following, we propose to the User a *Choice Method* based upon the notion of Nuanced Similarity of Fuzzy Sets.

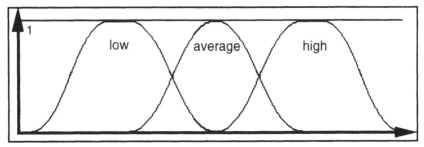

Fig. 4. Basic Properties associated with the Concept « number of intersection points »

4.2 Nuanced Similarity of Fuzzy Sets

Let us recall Lukasiewicz's Implication: $u \rightarrow v = 1$ if $u \leq v$ else $1-u+v$, where the values u and v belong to [0, 1]. The *neighborhood relation* $\mho_\alpha$ is defined in [0, 1] as follows.

Definition 1. u and v are α-*neighboring*, denoted as $u \mathbin{\mho_\alpha} v$, if and only if, Min $\{u \rightarrow v, v \rightarrow u\} \geq \alpha$.

So, we can define the Similarity of Fuzzy Sets.

Definition 2. The Fuzzy sets A and B are said to be α-*neighboring*, and we denote this as $A \approx_\alpha B$, if and only if, $\forall x, \mu_A(x) \mathbin{\mho_\alpha} \mu_B(x)$.

In order to define Linguistic *Nuanced Similarity of Fuzzy Sets*, we have introduced a totally ordered partition of the interval [0, 1]:

$\{I_1, I_2, ..., I_7\} = [0] \cup]0, 0.25] \cup]0.25, 0.33] \cup]0.33, 0.67[\cup [0.67, 0.75[\cup [0.75, 1[\cup [1]$.

We have defined a one-to-one correspondence between these intervals and a *totally ordered set of Linguistic Expressions*: $\{\theta_1, ..., \theta_7\} = \{$not at all, very little, rather little, moderately (or $\varnothing$), rather, very, entirely$\}$.

Finally, we put the following definition of θ_i-similar Fuzzy Sets.

Definition 3. A and B are said to be θ_i-*similar* if and only if, $\alpha \in I_i$ knowing that $\alpha = \text{Max } \{\delta \mid A \approx_\delta B\}$.

4.3 ρ-plausible Linguistic Negations

Definition 4. Let ρ be a real such that $0.33 \geq \rho \geq 0$ and P a property defined in the same domain as A. If P satisfies the following properties:

[P1] : P and A are θ_i-similar with $\theta_i <$moderately (or $\varnothing$),   (Global Property)
[P2] : $\forall x, ((\mu_A(x) = \xi \geq 0.67 + \rho) \Rightarrow (\mu_P(x) \leq \xi - 0.67))$,   (Local Property)
[P3] : $\forall x, ((\mu_P(x) = \xi \geq 0.67 + \rho) \Rightarrow (\mu_A(x) \leq \xi - 0.67))$,   (Local Property)
then « x is P » is said to be a ρ-*plausible Linguistic Negation* of « x is A ».

Remark: We can point out the fact that the values 0.33 and 0.67 are not arbitrarily chosen. The Neighborhood degree is weak if its value is less than 0.33, and strong if its value is greater than 0.67 (§ 3.2). Moreover, the Fuzzy Operators have been defined in such a way that: $\forall f_a \in G_1$, P and $f_a A$ will be θ_1-similar with $\theta_1 \geq$moderately. So, any ρ-plausible solution rejects all previous interpretations of « x is A ».

5 An Interactive Choice Strategy

5.1 Construction of the Sets of ρ-plausible solutions

First, we ask the Speaker for the Possibility of Negation based upon A. So, we can determinate a value of ρ satisfying this condition. If he does not make a Choice, we include Negation based upon A by putting $\rho=0.3$. This being so, we can define and structure the *set of ρ-plausible Linguistic Negations* of A, denoted as **Neg(A,ρ)**, by using successively the following Rules.

Simplicity Principle.

Among the previous ρ-plausible solutions, we define the set **Neg(A,ρ)** of Nuanced Properties P based upon *at most two Nuances of a Basic Property.*

Increasing Similarity.

For each degree θ_i with $\theta_i <$moderately, we define the subset S_i of **Neg(A,ρ)** whose elements P are θ_i-*similar* to A.

Increasing Complexity.

We constitute a partition of each S_i in subsets $S_{i\,P}$ where P is defined in the same Domain as A. The last subset will be $S_{i\,A}$. Moreover, each $S_{i\,P}$ is reorganized in such a way that its elements appear ordered to an increasing *Complexity extent*, that is to say, the number of Nuances (different from $\varnothing$) required in their construction.

Example. The concept being «the number of intersection points», and the associated properties being « low », « average » and « high » (Fig. 4), the Choice Strategy suggests among the elements of **Neg(low, 0.3)** the solutions having 1 as Complexity collected in Figure 5.

Remark: For any Property A, the function of ρ is to increase (or not) the number of Nuanced Negations and to accept (or reject) some Negations based upon A. A first Choice is made among 20 interpretations of « x is not low » when $\rho= 0.3$, and among 10 interpretations when $\rho=0.1$. So, the User can choose, for any ρ, solutions as « high », « extremely high », « exactly average », « really average », and in addition, « extremely low », « really extremely low » and « exactly extremely low » for $\rho= 0.3$. The function of the *mark* i, defined in the following section, is then to select in the previous set the pertinent solutions.

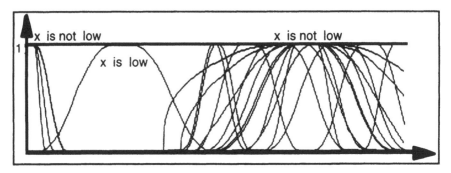

Fig. 5. Linguistic Negations of « x is low » having 1 as Complexity

5.2 The intended Meaning of a Linguistic Negation

The Choice Strategy, based upon the following Rules denoted **M[i]**, allows the User to explain his intended interpretation of a *particular occurrence* of the assertion « x is not A ». In other words, the procedure must be applied to each previous occurrence appearing in a Knowledge Base. So, each occurrence of « x is not A » being explained with the aid of a particular Rule **M[i]**, we associate the *mark* **i** to this particular occurrence.

An interactive Process proposes to the User the following ordered Rules.

M[0] : If the Negation is in fact the *logical Fuzzy Negation* $\neg A$, then :

- if $\neg A$ is a Property defined in the same domain as A, we propose $\neg A$,

- if not, for any P such that $P \subset (\neg A)$, we propose a Choice among the solutions of S_{iP}, i=1,2, ...

M[1] : If the Negation *is based upon* A, we propose a Choice among the solutions of S_{iA}, i=1,2, ...

M[2] : If the Negation *is based upon only one* $P \neq A$, we ask the User for its basic Negation P. Then, his Choice has to be made among the solutions of the previous sets S_{iP}, i=1,2, ...

M[3] : If the Negation can be *based upon B* and C *different from A*, then the User has to retain his interpretation among the solutions of S_{iB} and S_{iC} where i=1,2, ...

M[4] : If the Negation can be based upon *one of all the basic properties*, his interpretation is one of plausible solutions of S_{iP} where i=1,2, ... , for any P.

M[5] : If the Negation *is in fact a New basic Property denoted as not-A*, we must ask the User for its membership L-R function.

M[6] : If the Negation is *simply the rejection* of « x is A », then any element of **Neg**(A, ρ) is a potential solution but he does not choose one of them.

M[7] : If the Negation requires a *Combination based upon two basic Properties B and C*, we ask the User for the Linguistic Operator. So, we propose a Choice among the Combination solutions of S_{iB} and S_{iC}, i=1, 2, ...

M[8] : If no Choice is made with rules **M[0]**-**M[4]** or **M[7]** then the System proposes a *Default Choice*.

Remark: The solutions are always proposed by increasing Complexity.

Remark: This Choice Strategy recovers all interpretations of Linguistic Negations presented in Section 3.

Remark: Using rule **M[6]**, no Choice is made. But, « x is not A » (without explicit translation) is however less than moderately similar to A. Then, an Inference Process based upon Similarity can deduce a conclusion when a Rule contains such an hypothesis. This aspect will be developed in a subsequent paper.

Remark: Note that a lot of works on Linguistic Negation have already been achieved. Among these, the papers by Trillas, Lowen, Ovchinnokov and Esteva are not quoted here since very different points of view are considered. In the recent paper by Torra [16], one will find a closer point of view. But, our Definition and our Treatment of Linguistic Negation of Nuanced Property lead to a different Model. Let us now go into the comparison between our Approach and the one of Torra.

First, we can give their common points of view. Our Set **Neg**(A, ρ) of ρ-plausible Linguistic Negations and the Torra Negative Function have been conceived within a Fuzzy Context in such a way that they lead to results consistent with those intuitively expected in the chosen Domain. In both cases, by using the Torra terminology, this is a function Neg from L to $\mathcal{P}$(L), where L is a given set of Fuzzy Properties (or Linguistic Labels) and $\mathcal{P}$(L) the set of parts of L. Note that our set **Neg**(A, ρ) takes the place of Neg(x). Moreover, in both Approaches the Torra Condition C2 holds, that is to say, if x∈Neg(x') then x'∈Neg(x). In our Model, this property results immediately from the definition of ρ-plausible Linguistic Negation.

We can now point out some essential differences. Indeed, the Model of Torra concerns the sets of Linguistic Labels totally ordered. In our Approach, we refer to Fuzzy Properties for which an order relation is of no importance. This point is enforced by the fact that the Use of Fuzzy Operators and Modifiers in the combinations of the Basic Properties creates difficulties in making a total Order. Note that our Nuanced Properties being automatically defined, the User has not to define their L-R membership functions, he has only to supply the L-R membership functions of the Basic Properties associated with each Concept. In other words, the Context of our Analysis seems to be more general that the one of Torra. We can now examine the Torra Conditions C0 and C1. Linguists have pointed out that a Linguistic Negation can be simply the rejection of « x is A ». In other words, Neg(x) can be an empty Set. Moreover, the Basic Properties, associated with the concept « height », being « low », « medium » and « high », linguists accept that Neg(medium)={low, high} (in our System, Nuanced Properties based upon these Basic Properties). In this case, Neg(x) is not a Convex Function. So, our analysis based upon Natural Language does not require the Torra Condition C0. We can also recall that a Linguistic Negation can induce a new Basic Property. So, the set of Linguistic Labels cannot be considered as completely defined, and it is not sure that the order can be preserved. By using the previous Basic Properties, The Linguistic Analysis accepts the following results: Neg(medium)={low, high}and Neg(low)={medium, high}. Then, if we add the following order :low<medium<high, it is obvious that the condition C1 fails in this case.

So, it appears clearly that, the Contexts of both Analyses are basically different, and the Concept of Negation by Torra, fulfilling more restrictive conditions, can be viewed as a particular restriction to ordered Labels of our Concept of Negation.

6 General Properties of previous Linguistic Negation

In this Section, we point out the fact that our Linguistic Negation satisfies some Common sense properties of Negation.

Proposition 1. *Given a Fuzzy Property A, « x is A » does not automatically define the Knowledge about « x is not A ».*

Proof. This property results directly from our construction Process of Linguistic Negation. Knowing exactly A does not imply, as does the Logical Negation, precise Knowledge of its Negation, since most of them require complementary information, as the mark of the property, and a Choice among possible interpretations. □

Proposition 2. *Given a Fuzzy Property A, its double Negation does not generally lead to A.*

Proof. Using Figure 3, the User can choose « x is thin » as the interpretation of « x is not big », and « x is enormous » as the negation of « x is thin ». □

Proposition 3. *If « x is P » is a ρ-plausible Linguistic Negation of « x is A », then « x is A » is a ρ-plausible Linguistic Negation of « x is P ». Moreover, « x is A » is a ρ-plausible double Negation of « x is A ».*

Proof. This properties result from the definition of ρ-plausible Negation. □

Proposition 4. *Given the Rule « if « x is A » then « y is B » », we can deduce that « if « y is not B » then « z is A' » » where A' is a ρ-plausible Negation of A.*

Proof. This property results from the definition of ρ-plausible Linguistic Negation. □

Remark: The previous Approach to Linguistic Negation gives us a *Pragmatic Model* leading to results consistent with those intuitively expected, and this, within the Context of Nuanced Fuzzy Properties. Its integration in Many-valued Predicate Logics is actually being examined. Our objective in due course is to define a new Adequate Fuzzy Negation Operator having Properties like the one proposed in a logical Approach to the Negation of Precise assertions (see Lenzen [8], Pearce [11], Pearce & Wagner [12]). At this point, we can point out that Propositions 1-4 give us the first results as the Basis of a possible formalization within Many-valued Logics.

7 Reasoning *via* Linguistic Negation

7.1 Classical Deductive Process

The presence of Negations in the Facts or Classical Rules does not generally modify the use of the existing Deductive Process.

Example. In following Figures 6 and 7, we have collected Properties associated with the concepts « height » and « appearance ». The arrows specifying the directions of the plausible Negations result from the marks associated with the basic Properties. The Nuances of the intended Meanings of Linguistic Negations appear in brackets.

Let us now analyse Rules containing Linguistic Negations.
1 : if « Jack is not tall » then « Jack is not visible in a crowd ». It results from User interpretation that we obtain the following equivalent Rule : if « Jack is small » then « Jack is invisible in a crowd ».
2 : if « Jack is not small » then « Jack is visible in a crowd». Let us suppose that the User has selected « Jack is really very tall » as the intended meaning of « Jack is not small ». So, the initial Rule is equivalent to : if « Jack is really very tall » then « Jack is visible in a crowd ».
3 : if « Jack is not small » then « Jack is not invisible in a crowd ».The previous Choice gives us : if « Jack is really very tall » then « Jack is not invisible in a crowd ». If « Jack is not invisible in a crowd » receives as its meaning « Jack is extremely visible in a crowd », we obtain : if « Jack is really very tall » then « Jack is extremely visible in a crowd ».

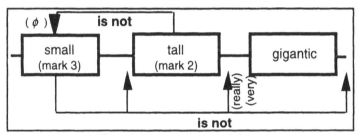

Fig. 6. The concept « height »

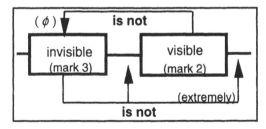

Fig. 7. The concept « appearance »

Remark: It is obvious that information does not generally correspond with the Premise of Rules. As an example, the Knowledge Base can contain Facts like «Jack is exactly small », « Jack is more or less small », « Jack is really very tall » or « Jack is rather tall ». It is clear that some Rules lead to deductions in terms of Basic Properties by using the first or third Facts. But, it is not the case with the second or fourth Facts. In other words, a Deductive Process founded upon some Generalized Modus Ponens Rule (like Zadeh's [19]) creates difficulty in making useful Deductions in terms of the Basic Properties of the Discourse Universe. Note that we are actually achieving a variant of Zadeh's deductive Process *via* the previous Similarity of Nuanced Properties.

7.2 Default Reasoning

Our Approach to Negative Information can be applied to Default Reasoning (Reiter [13]). Let us suppose that a Default Rule has the following form :« x is A »: **P** «x is B»/«x is B», where **P** «x is B» means that «x is B» is Consistent with the current Knowledge Base. Our Linguistic Negation can define the Consistency Condition : «x is B» is Consistent iff a Linguistic Negation of «x is B» does not belong to the Knowledge Base. This Approach to Default Reasoning through a Linguistic Negation is actually on Study. At this point, we simply give an illustration of its possible use.

Example. Put the Default Rule: « x is a boy »: **P** «x is small»/«x is small», and suppose that the Linguistic Negation of «x is small» results from the Rule **M[4]**. So, knowing only that « x is a boy », we initially infer that « x is small ». If the Knowledge Base latter contains the Fact « x is rather tall » (that is to say, a plausible Linguistic Negation of « x is small »), then we reject the previous Deduction « x is small » and the deductions resulting from this hypothesis.

8 Conclusion

We have presented an Approach to Linguistic Negation of Nuanced Properties based upon a Similarity Relation and we have proposed a Choice Strategy improving the abilities in the Management of a Knowledge Base. Indeed, the User can refer to Linguistic Negations either in Classical or Default Rules, since this Strategy allows him to explain their implicit meanings.

References

1. Baldwin J. F., Pilsworth B. W.: Axiomatic approach to implication for approximate reasoning with fuzzy logic. Fuzzy Sets and Systems 3 (1980) 193-219
2. Culioli A.: Pour une linguistique de l'énonciation: Opérations et Représentations. Tome 1 Ophrys Eds. Paris (1991)
3. Desmontils E., Pacholczyk D.: Apport de la théorie des ensembles flous à la modélisation déclarative en Synthèse d'images. Proc. LFA'96 Nancy (1996) 333-334
4. Desmontils E., Pacholczyk D.: Modélisation déclarative en Synthèse d'images: traitement semi-qualitatif des propriétés imprécises ou vagues. Proc. AFIG'96 Dijon (1996) 173-181
5. Ducrot O., Schaeffer J.-M. et al.: Nouveau dictionnaire encyclopédique des sciences du langage. Seuil Paris (1995)
6. Horn L.R.: A Natural History of Negation. The Univ. of Chicago Press (1989)
7. Ladusaw W.A.: Negative Concord and « Made of Judgement ». Negation, a notion Focus. H. Wansing, W. de Gruyter eds. Berlin (1996) 127-144
8. Lenzen W.: Necessary Conditions for Negation Operators. Negation, a notion in Focus. H. Wansing, W. de Gruyter eds. Berlin (1996) 37-58
9. Muller C.: La négation en français. Publications romanes et françaises Genève (1991)

10. Pacholczyk D.: Contribution au traitement logico-symbolique de la connaissance. Thèse d'Etat Paris 6 (1992)
11. Pearce D.: Reasoning with negative information II: Hard Negation, Strong Negation and Logic Programs. LNAI **619** Berlin (1992) 63-79
12. Pearce D., Wagner G.: Reasoning with negative information I: Hard Negation, Strong Negation and Logic Programs, Language, Knowledge, and Intentionality: Perspectives on the Philosophy of J. Hintikka. Acta Philosophica Fennica **49** (1990) 430-453
13. Reiter R.: A Logic for Default Reasoning. Artificial Intelligence **13** (1980) 81-132
14. Ruspini E. H.: The Semantics of vague knowledge. Rev. int. De Systémique **3:4** (1989) 387- 420
15. Scheffe P.: On foundations of reasoning with uncertain facts and vague concepts. Fuzzy Reasoning and its Applications (1981) 189-216
16. Torra V.: Negation Functions Based Semantics for Ordered Linguistic Labels. Int. Jour. of Intelligent Systems **11** (1996) 975-988
17. Tversky A.: Features of Similarity. Psychological Review **4** (1977)
18. Zadeh L.A.: Fuzzy Sets. Inform. and Control **8** (1965) 338-353
19. Zadeh L.A.: PRUF-A meaning representation language for natural languages. Int. J. Man-Machine Studies **10:4** (1978) 395-460
20. Zadeh L.A.: Similarity relations and Fuzzy orderings. Selected Papers of L. A. Zadeh **3** (1987) 387-420

Integration of Inheritance in SNePS

H. Sofia Pinto

Instituto Superior Técnico
Departamento de Eng. Mecânica, Grupo de Inteligência Artificial
Av. Rovisco Pais, 1096 Lisboa, Portugal
sofia@gia.ist.utl.pt

Abstract. This paper presents a solution to two problems of inheritance theories in general: the confusion between classes and properties, and the inability to distinguish, just by looking at a link, if it was derived or introduced by the user. SNePS's (Semantic Network Processing System) inheritance system, the system where we developed a solution to both these problems, is a credulous mixed inheritance system where paths are built bottom-up and conflicts are solved with off-path preemption. This system is integrated in a general purpose representation system with general inference capabilities, SNePS [10,11]. Its unique features include a finer division of concepts and links, reification of links, the association of adequate justifications to all the conclusions, the representation of the assumptions raised, and the identification and adequate treatment of conflicts. All these features make it unique and an overall clearer system. Our system was specified using a direct (topological) approach (in contrast to translational approaches where information in the system is translated into an appropriate logic).

1 Introduction

Inheritance is based on an extended notion of a taxonomic hierarchy to which inference mechanisms are added. A taxonomic hierarchy consists of classes connected through class superclass links, forming a tree. In this hierarchy most specific classes are represented at the lower levels of the tree and the more general at the upper levels. Besides the obvious advantage of a higher power of abstraction, inheritance is a useful and conceptually correct model to express our knowledge about the world and provides a more compact way of information storage which is associated with a faster information search process.

In AI, taxonomic hierarchies are extended with the representation of instances (Tweety, Fig. 1), with the possibility of connecting each class or instance to several others, forming an acyclic graph (Tweety is both a bird and a domestic animal, Fig. 1), with the representation of properties in the hierarchy (the property of flying, Fig. 1), and with the possibility of representing exceptions (Tweety does not fly, Fig. 1). The inference mechanism allows information associated with the upper levels of the hierarchy to be inherited by (transferred to) the lower levels. The most important idea on the way information is inherited is that information concerning lower levels of the hierarchy is preponderant over

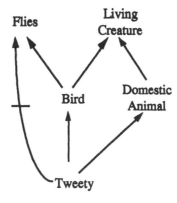

Fig. 1. An AI hierarchy.

information concerning the upper levels, since lower levels convey more specific information.

In this paper we discuss some of the problems of inheritance systems and the new ideas introduced by SNePS's inheritance system to solve those problems: a finer division of links and the association of an adequate justification to all the conclusions derived from the initial network. These new ideas make it a rather unique inheritance system.

2 Notions and problems of inheritance

In inheritance systems there are two types of concepts: instances and classes. Classes include both true classes (classes of objects) and those classes that represent classes of objects that possess a certain property. We should stress that, although in natural language they are represented as different kinds of entities – classes are usually expressed as nouns (the class of birds), and properties are usually expressed as adjectives (a flying bird) –, in inheritance systems, they are both represented as classes and this may be a problem. Between concepts there are links, usually named as IS-A, that correspond to two kinds of relations: *membership* and *subset*. Links can also be classified according to two other orthogonal classifications: *polarity*, that corresponds to positive and negative statements, and *certainty*, that is subdivided into defeasible and strict (Fig. 2). A defeasible link, represented by →, corresponds to a relation to which one knows that there are exceptions (there are some birds that do not fly, although one generally assumes that if a particular individual is a bird it flies) and a strict link, represented by ⇒, corresponds to a relation to which there are no exceptions.

A defeasible link connecting two classes corresponds to a statement of the form "Typically this class is a subclass of that one". There is no precise meaning associated to the link connecting an instance to a class but one usually associates

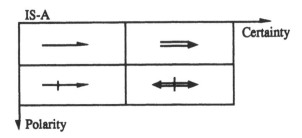

Fig. 2. Kinds of links in inheritance systems.

it with "Given this particular object it is more natural to classify it as belonging to that class". This ambiguous semantics is also a problem. The certainty of the links allowed in a given inheritance system provides one possible classification for the system. Those systems that allow both strict and defeasible links are named mixed inheritance systems.

SNePS's inheritance system is based on the work of Touretzky, Horty, and Thomason (TH&T) [1,13,3,14]. In TH&T's direct (topological) approach, links can be connected to form paths. Each path supports one conclusion. However, one can not see this fact as an argument to believe in the conclusion to which that path constitutes an argument for: in Fig. 1, although a path, stating that Tweety flies (because it is a bird and typically birds fly), can be built, this is not a reason to believe in it, since the same hierarchy has information to build a path (with only one link) that is an argument to the opposite conclusion. This kind of conflict is solved by means of a preemption notion [13,8] that states that information concerning lower levels of the hierarchy (representing more specific information) is preponderant over information concerning its upper levels (representing more general information). If this conflict still can not be solved by means of preemption, then one can follow one of two approaches: either one is using a skeptical approach and one doesn't compromise itself with conflicting information or one is using a credulous approach in which two extensions are created. In the skeptical approach the only believed consequences are those that are not conflicted or that are not derived from conflicted conclusions. In the credulous approach the consequences of what was found plus one of the conflicting conclusions and its consequences are added to each one of the extensions built. We should stress that all extensions are equally plausible.

In the beginning of this section we mentioned that the confusion between classes and properties could lead to some problems. Let us suppose that we have Bus1111 ⇒ Bus ⇒ Orange ⇒ Bright Color ⇒ Color. We are stating that the Bus1111 (an instance) is a Bus (a true class), that Buses are Orange (a property), that Orange is a Bright Color (a true class) and that a Bright Color is a subclass (a possible classification) of Color (a true class) (example from [5]). From this network we can conclude that Bus1111 is Orange (property), Bus1111 is a Bright Color (class), and Bus1111 is a Color (class). This last two conclusions, Bus1111 is an instance of Bright Color and Bus1111 is an instance of Color, are orthodox and not easily acceptable. What we should have was, on one side, `Bus1111 ⇒ Bus ⇒ Orange`, that is, knowledge about buses, and on the other, `Orange ⇒ Bright Color ⇒ Color`, that is, knowledge about colors. Note that in this case Orange is both a property and an instance. The paths built from both pieces of network should not be concatenated, remaining as two independent lines of reasoning [5], one about buses and the other about colors.

Other problems of inheritance systems, in general, are: (1) they don't distinguish between information introduced in the system from information derived by the system, and (2) they are unable to represent the assumptions raised when using defeasible links. This can be important when we want to know why we should accept one conclusion.

3 A new approach

We discuss both the representational and inferential aspects of SNePS's inheritance system [5-7]. Under the representational aspects we discuss the finer division of links and concepts, the semantics associated to each kind of link allowed, and show how links are represented. Under the inferential aspects we discuss how links can be combined to build paths that correspond to meaningful lines of reasoning, how a justification of one conclusion is built, how this justification enables the distinction between what was derived and what was introduced by the user, and, finally, how assumptions, are represented.

3.1 Representational aspects

Classes in an inheritance network include both true classes and properties. This can lead to some confusion and possibly to some orthodox conclusions as we've already seen in 2. To solve this problem we introduced a finer division on concepts, separating classes from properties into two different concepts. The concepts allowed were divided into instances, classes, and properties.

We also introduced a finer division on the links between these concepts, as shown in Fig. 3. Besides distinguishing those links between an instance and a class, and between two classes, we also distinguish those links between an instance and a property, and a class and a property, introducing another dimension on the classification of links.

The main advantage of this division is that, when asked for the properties of an instance, these are found immediately, and there is a clear distinction between the classes to which it belongs to and the properties that it possesses (and similarly when asked for the properties of a class).

For each one of these links a precise meaning was supplied [5], even for the foggy case of a defeasible link beginning in an instance. For example, suppose we see an animal that looks like a leopard but we are not sure if it's a leopard, a cheetah, a jaguar or some other feline. Since we are not sure about our knowledge we raise an assumption, making a sort of a guess, about that instance. In the case

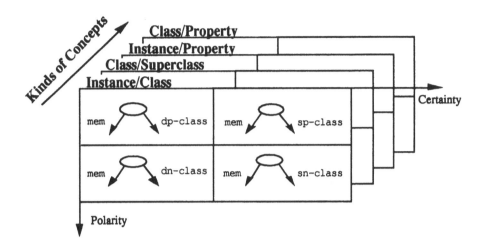

Fig. 3. A new dimension on links in SNePS's inheritance system

of a defeasible link beginning in a concept representing a class we are making a generalization: typically felines are dangerous but there may be some exceptions like the cat.

Another particularity of SNePS's inheritance system regards the way links are represented in the system. In SNePS [10,11] nodes represent concepts, and the system can only talk about information that is represented as a node. Thus, if the relationship between two concepts is represented as a node (for instance, between an instance and its class, or between a class and its superclass) then SNePS is able to talk about the relation established between those concepts. For this reason, the inheritance links are represented as nodes. This is a rather unique feature of this system, when comparing it with the other inheritance systems in the literature, since they always represent inheritance relationships as links. The set of pre-defined arcs emanating from a node representing a link defines the kind of relation that is being established and the nodes pointed by those arcs represent the concepts involved in that link. Defeasible links use the prefix **d** and strict links use the prefix **s**. Positive links use the prefix **p** and negative links use the prefix **n**. For example, if we see a particular bird that is always playing and moving around then it seems logic to assume that this particular bird is young. This would be represented in SNePS's inheritance system by a node with arcs **dp-mem-has-prop** and **prop**, Fig. 4, pointing, respectively, to a node representing the particular bird we are talking about (an atomic node labelled "Tweety") and to a node representing the property of being young (an atomic node labelled "Young").

The property of being able to talk about its nodes would allow SNePS to speak about the meaning of having a certain link represented in the knowledge base, provided that enough information was represented in the system. This is possible because SNePS is a general purpose representation system with gen-

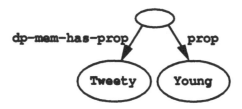

Fig. 4. An example of a link in SNePS

eral inference capabilities and links are represented as nodes. Therefore we can represent knowledge about inheritance links.

3.2 Inferential aspects

We developed a set of rules for combining links in order to build paths[1]. These rules take into account the kinds of links involved, and consequently the kinds of concepts involved. The paths built are arguments that univocally determine the conclusions that can be derived from them. For example, we can build a path beginning in an instance stating that it belongs to a certain class, then add one or more links stating that a class is a subclass of another, and finally add a link stating that the elements of the last class have(n't) a certain property. From this path one can conclude that the instance has(n't) that property. The polarity and the degree of certainty of the conclusion is determined by the polarity and the degree of certainty of the links traversed. Moreover, there are restrictions to the links that can be added to a path, concerning the kinds of concepts involved in order to get a meaningful argument to some conclusion. For example:

1. In the case of a positive path ending in a property, after the node representing the property no more links can be added, since we cannot talk about properties (the relations involved in inheritance don't allow us to say nothing more about properties). This will prevent orthodox conclusions as the ones discussed in 2 (rule 1, Fig. 5);
2. In the case of a negative path ending in a property, new strict positive links may be added since that corresponds to "moving downwards" on another branch of the hierarchy, provided that an instance isn't reached. After the negative link stating that the members of a class don't have a certain property one can add a strict positive link stating that all members of another class must have that very same property. What is being added to the path is the intuitive notion that if the members of a class (say C1) don't have a property and all members of another class (say C2) must have that property then, no members of C1 can be members of C2. This is illustrated in the example presented in section 4. This path can be extended provided that only strict, positive links are added and an instance isn't reached. This is

---

[1] An earlier version of these rules was presented in [5]

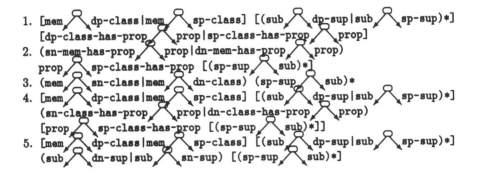

Fig. 5. Rules to build compound paths in SNePS's inheritance system

one of the rules defined by TH&T adapted to the new division of concepts and links, taking into account the links and the line of reasoning that is being followed (rules 2 and 4, Fig. 5).

The set of rules to build compound paths is represented in Fig. 5, using an extended BNF notation where (x)* represents at least one time x, [y] means that y is optional and z | w means that either z or w. The algorithm used by this system to find all paths that can be built from a given network begins by taking all links and builds simple paths with them. It then proceeds by finding all paths that can be built by concatenating a link to the end of the path. This operation is repeated until the closure of the concatenation operation is found. [9] shows that building paths bottom-up (as in our case), for defeasible inheritance networks, is P-hard while building them top-down would be NP-hard. Although, as far as we know, results for mixed inheritance systems still haven't been established [2] hints that this complexity results will be maintained.

From the links on the network several paths can be built and it may be the case that some of them support the same conclusion. A possible conclusion is an association between one conclusion and the paths built from the network that support that conclusion. Note that a conclusion is the link that can be concluded from a path for which this latter constitutes an argument. It should also be stressed that the conclusion takes into account not only the kinds of concepts in the beginning and in the end of the path, but also the links present in the path. From the set of possible conclusions found, one proceeds in an analogous way as [1] in order to compute the extensions from the network[2].

SNePS associates each proposition with a justification. A justification [4] is composed of an origin tag, stating whether the proposition was introduced as an hypothesis or derived from other propositions, and an origin set that represents the hypotheses from which it derives. We can introduce hypotheses (their justification states their condition and includes itself as its origin), reason from

---

[2] Our inheritance system is a credulous mixed inheritance system where conflicts are solved with off-path preemption [8]. Credulous extensions are due to Touretzky [13]

them to generate new propositions (whose justification contains all hypotheses used in their derivation), and whenever a contradiction is detected the system identifies the hypotheses underlying the contradiction. In SNePS's inheritance system every conclusion that can be built from a path has a justification[3], even if that conclusion is not believed because there are valid reasons to believe in the opposite conclusion. The justification is built from the path found supporting that conclusion, taking into account the links involved [7][4]. This is another innovation of our system since, to the best of our knowledge, no other mixed inheritance system associates justifications to the conclusions found[5].

Let us see how this justification should be built. Every time we add a strict link to a path this link should appear in the justification to the conclusion since there are no doubts or exceptions to it and we are using it to derive the conclusion. Therefore we should add the hypotheses underlying the link to the origin set. But when we add a defeasible link the solution is not so simple. A defeasible link presupposes an assumption, that is, there is an assumption underlying it (I assume that that animal is a leopard). When we add a defeasible link to a path we are taking that assumption as applicable to our line of reasoning. This means that we have to represent another kind of information in the system besides links: the assumptions raised and applied in the lines of reasoning made by the system (through the paths that were built). So, in this case, the justification to the conclusion includes the hypotheses underlying the defeasible link and its assumptions. See [7] for the formal specification of justifications.

Assumptions are represented as nodes. The nodes representing assumptions are distinguished by the pair of pre-defined arcs used: **d-arg** and **d-supp**. According to the concepts involved in the defeasible link there may be two kinds of assumptions.

1. If the link begins in an instance we are making a guess about its class or property. In this case the meaning of the assumption states that we are raising the assumption underlying the node pointed by the **d-supp** arc (the node representing the link), and that this assumption is being taken as applicable to the instance represented by the node pointed by the **d-arg** arc (that is, the beginning of that link and consequently of the path since instances can only appear in the beginning of paths).

2. If the link begins in a class we are making a generalization. In this case the meaning of the assumption states that we are generalizing, represented by the node pointed by the **d-supp** arc (the node representing the link), and that this generalization is being applicable to the entity represented by the

---

[3] If a different path for the same conclusion is found we can have more than one justification associated to the same conclusion.

[4] An earlier version appeared in [5]

[5] [12] describes a defeasible inheritance system where every conclusion has an ATMS justification associated. However, her work was published after [5] was concluded, where an earlier version of our ATMS justifications for SNePS's mixed inheritance system was presented.

node pointed by the **d-arg** arc (that is, the node in the beginning of the path in which this link is).

Nodes representing assumptions must also have a justification. We choose to have an "hyp" origin tag. However this is a justified assumption since there are reasons in the system to raise this and not some other assumption. For this reason, this hypothesis depends not only from itself (as other hypotheses) but also from the line of reasoning being made (for which the path constitutes an argument). This means that the origin set contains not only the assumption but also every link (represented by a node) in the path built that precedes this particular link for which we are building the underlying assumption. In fact, the links that take place before the guess or generalization are responsible for the fact that this (the guess or the generalization) and not some other assumption was raised. The subsequent links in the path have no role whatsoever since they are added to the path after the link for which we are building the assumption. We should stress that when determining the justification of the node representing the justified assumption (that is being taken as applicable) there may be strict and/or defeasible links.

Since every proposition in SNePS's inheritance system, as well as in SNePS, has associated its adequate justifications, there is a clear distinction between information introduced directly by the user from information derived by the system. Moreover, in the case of derived information there is a clear and easy identification of what was involved in its derivation. Another important role played by justifications is in the identification of the hypotheses underlying one contradiction. In inheritance systems two kinds of conflicts may arise: those that can be solved from the topological notion of preemption and the notion of extension (that come from defeasible information) and those that are true contradictions (that come from strict information). While the first are treated by SNePS's inheritance system, that creates the appropriate extensions, the latter are recognized by SNePS as contradictions and are treated accordingly by SNePS's contradiction handler.

4 Example

We are going to discuss a classical example of mixed inheritance, shown in Fig. 6. Note that we have represented this example as close as possible to its representation in other inheritance systems. Herman is a Pennsylvania Dutch speaker (M1). Every Pennsylvania Dutch speaker is also a German speaker (M2) because Pennsylvania Dutch is a German dialect. Typically those who speak German are *not* American (M4). Typically native Pennsylvania Dutch speakers are born in Pennsylvania (M3). Everyone born in Pennsylvania is American (M5). From these hypotheses the inheritance system derives the following nodes:

```
(M6 (mem Herman) (sp-class Native-German-Speaker))
Justification: der {M1 M2}
```

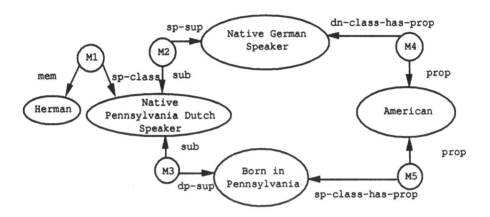

Fig. 6. An example of a mixed inheritance network in SNePS

```
(M7   (mem Herman) (dp-class Born-in-Pennsylvania))
Justification: der {M1 M3 M8}

(M9   (dn-class-has-prop Native-Pennsylvania-Dutch-Speaker)
      (prop American))
Justification: der {M2 M4 M10}

(M11  (dp-class-has-prop Native-Pennsylvania-Dutch-Speaker)
      (prop American))
Justification: der {M3 M5 M12}

(M13  (sub Native-German-Speaker)
      (dn-sup Born-in-Pennsylvania))
Justification: der {M4 M5 M14}

(M15  (sub Native-Pennsylvania-Dutch-Speaker)
      (dn-sup Born-in-Pennsylvania))
Justification: der {M2 M4 M5 M10}

(M16  (dp-mem-has-prop Herman) (prop American))
Justification: der {M1 M3 M5 M8}

(M17  (dn-mem-has-prop Herman) (prop American))
Justification: der {M1 M2 M4 M18}

(M19  (mem Herman) (dn-class Born-in-Pennsylvania))
Justification: der {M1 M2 M4 M5 M18}
```

M6 represents the proposition "Herman is a Native-German-Speaker". This conclusion was found from M1 and M2 (rule 1, Fig. 5). M7 represents the proposition "I assume Herman was Born-in-Pennsylvania" that was derived from M1, M3 (rule 1, Fig. 5) and the assumption represented by node M8, described later. M9 represents the proposition that "Typically those who are Native-Pennsylvania-Dutch-Speaker aren't American" that was derived from M2 and M4 (rule 4, Fig. 5) and the assumption represented by node M10. The assumptions referred in the justifications are:

```
(M8   (d-arg Herman) (d-supp M3))
Justification: hyp {M1 M3 M8}


(M10  (d-arg Native-Pennsylvania-Dutch-Speaker) (d-supp M4))
Justification: hyp {M2 M4 M10}


(M12  (d-arg Native-Pennsylvania-Dutch-Speaker) (d-supp M3))
Justification: hyp {M3 M12}


(M14  (d-arg Native-German-Speaker) (d-supp M4))
Justification: hyp {M4 M14}


(M18  (d-arg Herman) (d-supp M4))
Justification: hyp {M1 M2 M4 M18}
```

For instance, node M8 represents the assumption that "Typically Native Pennsylvania Dutch Speakers are born in Pennsylvania", represented by M3, can be applied to Herman. M10 represents the assumption that "Typically those who speak German are not American", represented by M4, can be applied to Native Pennsylvania Dutch Speakers.

The only extension found from the network, as discussed in [1], is:

```
((M1! M11 M13 M16 M2! M3! M4! M5! M6! M7))
```

5   Conclusions

With the introduction of a finer division of available concepts and links, a meaning for the links, and precise rules for combining those links we have a clearer system than other inheritance systems. Every proposition in the network has a justification associated enabling the distinction between information introduced directly by the user from information derived by the system. We also have a clear distinction between plausible and certain conclusions from the justifications associated with every conclusion. Certain conclusions have in their justifications the information used directly in their derivation (the links). Plausible conclusions have in their justifications, not only the information used directly to make those conclusions but also the assumptions made and taken as applicable. We can easily identify the assumptions raised and the information used to derive one conclusion through their justification. Assumptions are also represented in the system. In our system there is a reification of links since they are represented as nodes and, provided that we have introduced enough information in the system, the system can talk about the meaning of having one link represented in the network. Inheritance links have a precise, pre-defined meaning for SNePS.

Finally, conflicts are detected and treated accordingly. There are two kinds of conflicts: those that can be solved from the topological notion of preemption and the notion of extension (that come from defeasible information) and those that are true contradictions (that come from strict information). While the first are treated by the inheritance system, the latter are treated by the contradiction handler of SNePS.

Acknowledgments

I would like to thank António Leitão for his useful comments. I would also like to thank the rest of GIA's members for their support.

References

1. Horty, J. F., "A Credulous Theory of Mixed Inheritance", *Inheritance Hierarchies in Knowledge Representation and Programming Languages*, M. Lenzerini, D. Nardi and M. Simi, eds., New York: John Wiley & Sons, pp. 13-28, 1991.
2. Horty, J. F., "Some Direct Theories of Nonmonotonic Inheritance", *Handbook of Logic in Artificial Intelligence and Logic Programming, Vol 3*, D. Gabbay, C. Hogger and T. Thomason, Oxford: Oxford Science Publications
3. Horty, J. F. and Thomason, R. H., "Mixing Strict and Defeasible Inheritance", *Proceedings of AAAI-88*, San Mateo: Morgan Kaufmann, pp. 427-432, 1988.
4. Martins, J.P. and Shapiro, S.C., "A Model for Belief Revision", *Artificial Intelligence* 35(1), pp. 25-79, 1988.
5. Pinto, H. Sofia, "Formalização da Herança em SNePS", Tese de Mestrado, Instituto Superior Técnico, Departamento de Engenharia Electrotécnica e Computadores, Lisboa, 1992.
6. Pinto, H. Sofia and Martins, J.P., "Inheritance in SNePS*", presented at the *Third Annual SNePS Workshop*, Buffalo, N.Y., 1994.
7. Pinto, H. Sofia, "A Herança no SNePS", Relatório Técnico GIA 96/01, Grupo de Inteligência Artificial do Instituto Superior Técnico, 1996.
8. Sandewall, E., "Nonmonotonic inference rules for multiple inheritance with exceptions", *Proceedings of IEEE-86*, 74, pp 1345-1353, 1986.
9. Selman, B. and Levesque, H. J. "The Tractability of Path-Based Inheritance", *Proceedings of IJCAI-89*, San Mateo: Morgan Kaufmann, pp. 1140-1145, 1989.
10. Shapiro, Stuart C., "The SNePS semantic network processing system", *Associative Networks: The Representation and Use of Knowledge by Computers*, N. V. Findler, New York: Academic Press, pp. 179-203, 1979.
11. Shapiro, S. C. and The SNePS Implementation Group, *SNePS 2.3 User's Manual*, Department of Computer Science, SUNY at Buffalo, NY, 1995.
12. Stein, L.A., "Resolving ambiguity in nonmonotonic inheritance hierarchies", *Artificial Intelligence* 55, pp. 259-310, 1992.
13. Touretzky, D.S., *The Mathematics of Inheritance Systems*, Los Angeles: Morgan Kaufmann, 1986.
14. Touretzky, D.S., Thomason, R.H. and Horty, J.F., "Skeptic's Menagerie: Conflictors, Preemptors, Reinstaters and Zombies in Nonmonotonic Inheritance", *Proceedings of IJCAI-91*, Los Altos: Morgan Kaufmann, pp. 478-483, 1991.

Measures of Uncertainty and Independence Concept in Different Calculi*

Jiřina Vejnarová

Laboratory of Intelligent Systems, University of Economics
Ekonomická 957, CZ-148 00 Prague
and
Institute of Information Theory and Automation
Academy of Sciences of the Czech Republic
Pod vodárenskou věží 4, CZ-182 08 Prague
Czech Republic

Abstract. This contribution studies the relationship between measures of uncertainty and the independence (or noninteractiveness) concepts in probability theory, Dempster-Shafer theory and possibility theory. Although *Shannon entropy* is very strong tool when studying independence and conditional independence relations in probability theory, its nonprobabilistic counterparts (i.e. *amount of uncertainty* in Dempster-Shafer theory and *measure of nonspecificity* in possibility theory) seem not to play this role, which is demonstrated by simple examples. Moreover, it is argued, why amount of uncertainty — although used in possibility theory — is not appropriate measure of uncertainty within this framework.

1 Introduction

Since probability theory has been the only mathematical tool at our disposal for uncertainty quantification and processing for three centuries, many important theoretical as well as practical achievments have been reached in this field. Nevertheless, during the last thirty years some new mathematical tools alternative to probability theory have emerged. Their aims are to treat either the cases, when the nature of uncertainty in question does not meet the demands requested by probability theory, or the cases in which probabilistic approaches are based on too strong and hardly assurable (or even verifiable) conditions. These theories are, among others, Dempster-Shafer theory and possibility theory.

Probability theory has always served as a source of inspiration for the development of nonprobabilistic calculi dealing with uncertainty and such calculi have been continually confronted with probability theory and mathematical statistics from various points of view. It has been found out that probability theory is the most powerfull tool namely for the description of not only isolated uncertain

---

* The work on this paper was partially supported by Grant no. VS96008 of the Minisry of Education of the Czech Republic.

phenomena (random events in probabilistic terms) but also complicated structures of them and their mutual relations. At this moment let us remind the well-known notion of stochastical independence.

When studying problems of stochastical independence or more general conditional independence in probability theory, the mutual information or conditional mutual information, which are based on the notion of Shannon entropy, play important roles. Since measures of uncertainty have been studied in the frameworks of Dempster-Shafer theory and possibility theory from the early 1980's, we will deal with them from the viewpoint of their ability to express the independence and conditional independence relations.

2 Terminology and Notation

2.1 Dempster-Shafer Theory

The purpose of this section is to introduce briefly the basic terminology and notation connected with Dempster-Shafer theory ([20, 6]).

Let X be a finite set called *frame of discernment*, $\mathcal{P}(X)$ the power set of X and

$$m : \mathcal{P}(X) \longrightarrow [0, 1]$$

a *basic assignment* (or basic probability assignment). This mapping must satisfy two requirements

$$m(\emptyset) = 0 \quad \text{and} \quad \sum_{A \subseteq X} m(A) = 1 \ . \tag{1}$$

Every set $A \in \mathcal{P}(X)$ for which $m(A) \neq 0$ is called a *focal element* and the pair $(\mathcal{F}, m)$, where $\mathcal{F}$ is the set of all focal elements, is called a *body of evidence*.

With each basic assignment m a pair of measures, *belief* and *plausibility*, is associated. They are defined for all $A \in \mathcal{P}(X)$ by

$$Bel(A) = \sum_{B \subseteq A} m(B) \ ,$$
$$Pl(A) = \sum_{B \cap A \neq \emptyset} m(B) \ .$$

Clearly

$$Bel(A) \leq Pl(A) \ .$$

As it is well-known, belief measure (or a plausibility measure) becomes *probability measure* when all focal elements are singletons. In this case $Bel(A) = Pl(A)$ for all $A \in \mathcal{F}$ and the basic assignment corresponds to the discrete probability distribution.

To investigate concepts analogous to independence, it is necessary to study the body of evidence defined on the Cartesian product of two frames of discernment. That is, we will deal with basic assignment of the form

$$m : \mathcal{P}(X \times Y) \longrightarrow [0, 1] \ ,$$

where X and Y denote frames of discernment of two distinct areas of interest (e.g. two investigated variables), which may be connected in some way. This basic assignment is called *joint basic assignment*.

For every joint basic assignment defined on $X \times Y$ the marginal basic assignment

$$m_X(A) = \sum_{C:\Pi_X(C)=A} m(C)$$

can be obtained for all $A \in \mathcal{P}(X)$ ($\Pi_X(C)$ being the projection of set $C \subset X \times Y$ to X), and $m_Y(B)$ for all $B \in \mathcal{P}(Y)$ is defined analogously.

Bodies of evidence $(\mathcal{F}_X, m_X)$ and $(\mathcal{F}_Y, m_Y)$ are called *noninteractive* according to Dempster-Shafer theory (see e.g. [12]) if and only if

$$m(A \times B) = m_X(A) \cdot m_Y(B) \ , \tag{2}$$

for all $A \in \mathcal{F}_X$ and $B \in \mathcal{F}_Y$; and $m(C) = 0$ for all $C \neq A \times B$. That is, two marginal bodies of evidence are noninteractive if and only if the only focal elements are Cartesian products of focal elements of the marginal bodies of evidence and m is determined from m_X and m_Y by Eq. (2). It is evident, that the noninteractiveness is the counterpart of stochastical independence in the framework of Dempster-Shafer theory[2].

2.2 Possibility Theory

Possibility theory [2] may be viewed as a special Dempster-Shafer theory that deals only with nested bodies of evidence [12]. To utilize this fact, let us introduce a convenient notation.

Assume that $X = \{x_1, x_2, \ldots, x_n\}$ and let $\{A_1, A_2, \ldots, A_k\}, k \leq n$ be a system of *nested* subsets (i.e. for all $i, j = 1, \ldots, k$ either $A_i \subset A_j$ or $A_i \supset A_j$) that contains all focal elements of a possibility measure[3] (i.e. plausibility measure on this nested body of evidence). That is, $m(A) = 0$ for each $A \notin \{A_1, A_2, \ldots, A_k\}$. Let

$$r_i = r(x_i) = \sum_{j:x_i \in A_j} m(A_j)$$

for all $i = 1, 2, \ldots, n$. The n-tuple $\mathbf{r} = (r_1, r_2, \ldots, r_n)$ fully characterizes the possibility distribution, by which the possibility measure is defined.

From the *joint possibility distribution* $r(x, y)$, defined on the Cartesian product $X \times Y$, we can obtain the marginal possibility distribution

$$r_X(x) = \max_{y \in Y} r(x, y)$$

and analogously $r_Y(y)$.

---

[2] Another approach using commonality functions can be found in [22, 24].

[3] Possibility measures are usually defined in a different way, but this definition expresses the relation to Dempster-Shafer theory.

Two bodies of evidence are *noninteractive* according to possibility theory (see e.g. [12]) if and only if

$$r(x, y) = \min\{r(x), r(y)\}$$

for all $x \in X, y \in Y$. Let us note, that although marginalization is a special case of the one in Dempster-Shafer theory, the noninteractiveness notions are different.

3 Classical Measures of Uncertainty

The first measure of uncertainty was proposed by Hartley [9]. This measure is defined by the formula

$$I(A) = \log_2 |A| \ ,$$

where $|A|$ is the cardinality of a set $A \subset X$. This entropy depends only on the size of the set in question and has no connection with the probability theory.

Within the framework of probability theory the *Shannon entropy* [21]

$$H(p_1, \ldots, p_n) = -\sum_{i=1}^{n} p_i \ \log_2 \ p_i \ ,$$

$(p_1, \ldots, p_n$ being values of a probability distribution of a discrete random variable) has been used as a measure of expected information (or uncertainty, if you like). It is the only function which satisfies all requirements (see e.g. [1]), which are generally taken as necessary for a meaningfull measure of uncertainty. Though there are other entropies (or, more precisely, classes of entropies), the Shannon entropy is the best-known and most widely used one.

4 Measures of Uncertainty in Dempster-Shafer Theory

4.1 Measure of Nonspecificity

The measure, which generalizes Hartley measure, is called *nonspecificity* (see e.g. [19]) and is expressed by function N defined by the formula

$$N(m) = \sum_{A \in \mathcal{F}} m(A) \log_2 |A| \ ,$$

where $|A|$ denotes the cardinality of a focal element A.

Since the focal elements of a discrete probability distributions are singletons, $N(m) = 0$ for each distribution and, consequently, the function N has no connection with the Shannon entropy. There were several suggestions how to generalize Shannon entropy within Dempster-Shafer theory. Some of them are set forth bellow.

4.2 Entropy-like Mesures

Any of these measures (summarized in the following table[4]) has the form

$$U(m) = - \sum_{A \in \mathcal{F}} m(A) \; \log_2 f_U(A) \; . \qquad (3)$$

measure of	U	$f_U(A)$	reference
dissonance	E	$Pl(A)$	[27]
confusion	C	$Bel(A)$	[10]
discord	D	$\sum_{B \in \mathcal{F}} m(B) \frac{|A \cap B|}{|B|}$	[15]
strife	S	$\sum_{B \in \mathcal{F}} m(B) \frac{|A \cap B|}{|A|}$	[14]
	GP	$\sum_{B \in \mathcal{F}} m(B) \frac{|A \div B|}{|A \cup B|}$	[5]

4.3 Total Uncertainties

Lamata and Moral [16] suggested to combine a measure of nonspecificity with the measure of dissonance to obtain the total measure of uncertainty $T(m) = N(m) + E(m)$. In [15] the measure of total uncertainty was defined as the sum $ND(m) = N(m) + D(m)$ of measures of nonspecificity and discord and in [14] the measure of total uncertainty was defined analogously as the sum $NS(m) = N(m) + S(m)$ of nonspecificity and strife.

Another measure of total uncertaity TU, which can be expressed by (3) with $f_{TU}(A) = \frac{m(A)}{|A|}$ was suggested by Pal et al. [17] and generalized by Ramer et al. [18] to the class of measures $TU_k(m) = -\frac{1}{k}TU(m)$.

4.4 Desired Properties

As stressed in [7], any meaningful measure of total uncertainty in the framework of Dempster-Shafer theory should satisfy certain requirements that are considered essential on intuitive grounds. They are:

1. If m is probability distribution, U collapses to Shannon entropy, i.e. it has the form
   $$U(m) = - \sum_{x \in X} m(\{x\}) \log_2 m(\{x\}) \; .$$

2. If m has only one focal element, i.e. there exists a set A such that $m(A) = 1$, U collapses to Hartley measure.

3. The *range* of U is defined by the inequalities
   $$0 \leq U(m) \leq \log_2 |X| \; .$$

---

[4] $\div$ denotes the symetric difference, i.e. $A \div B = (A \cup B) - (A \cap B)$.

4. *Additivity:* if $(\mathcal{F}_X, m_X)$ and $(\mathcal{F}_Y, m_Y)$ are noninteractive bodies of evidence (i.e. Eq. (2) holds), then

$$U(m) = U(m_X) + U(m_Y) \ .$$

5. *Subadditivity:* for arbitrary body of evidence $(\mathcal{F}, m)$ and corresponding marginal bodies of evidence

$$U(m) \leq U(m_X) + U(m_Y) \ . \tag{4}$$

None of the measures stated above satisfies all the required properties. C, TU, TU_k do not have the proper range, GP is not additive. It seemed that the measure of nonspecificity (which is the only one satisfying the subadditivity requirement) should be combined with some subadditive entropy-like measure to get a reasonable measure of total uncertainty. Although much effort was paid to this problem (which is obvious even from this brief overview), none measure possessing the subadditivity property has been found.

4.5 Amount of Uncertainty

A novel approach has been proposed by Harmanec and Klir [7]. A new measure called *amount of uncertainty* is defined as follows.

Let X be a frame of discernment, m a basic assignment on $\mathcal{P}(X)$ and p a probability distribution on X. The amount of uncertainty AU contained in m is then

$$AU(m) = \max \left\{ -\sum_{x \in X} p(x) \log_2 p(x) \right\} \ , \tag{5}$$

where the maximum is taken over all probability distributions p that satisfy the constraints

$$Bel(A) \leq \sum_{x \in A} p(x) \leq Pl(A) \tag{6}$$

for all $A \subseteq X$.

This measure satisfies requirements 1–5 (see e.g. [7]) and therefore it seems to be the only candidate for the counterpart of Shannon entropy in the framework of Dempster-Shafer theory. Let us note that this is not entropy-like measure, but the measure of total uncertainty. Unfortunately, it is not expressed explicitly and therefore some optimizing procedure for finding the maximum entropy distribution satisfying (6) is necessary. An algorithm can be found in [8], theoretical (and more general) grounds e.g. in [11].

5 Entropy and Independence

5.1 Probability Theory

It is well-known that the subadditivity requirement (4) is satisfied by Shannon entropy and moreover the equality holds if and only if the variables X and Y are independent (see e.g. [3]). Note that this property is somewhat stronger than the subadditivity and additivity requirements, respectively. Hence the mutual information $I(X;Y)$ defined as

$$I(X;Y) = H(X) + H(Y) - H(XY) ,$$

can be used in order to be judged whether the variables are independent or not. We will call this property *strict subadditivity*.

A more general property of the Shannon entropy, from which (4) immediately follows, is the *submodularity property*:

$$H(XYZ) + H(X) \leq H(XY) + H(XZ) . \tag{7}$$

An equivalent form of this inequality is

$$I(Y;Z|X) = H(XY) + H(XZ) - H(XYZ) - H(X) \geq 0 ,$$

and the equality holds if and only if Y and Z are conditionally independent on each value x of X (see e.g. [3]). In coherence with the preceding notions we will call this property, which is used in studying conditional independence relations (see e.g.[23]), *strict submodularity*.

It seems to us, if the notion of independence is substituted by the noninteractiveness one, that the meaningful measures of uncertainty within the Dempster-Shafer theory and possibility theory should satisfy these properties as well.

5.2 Dempster-Shafer Theory

As mentioned in 4.4 the only meaningful measure of uncertainty within the framework of Dempster-Shafer theory seems to be the amount of uncertainty (5), which is the only one satisfying the requirements 1–5, i.e. including the subadditivity property. Unfortunately, it is not strictly subadditive, which is demonstrated in the following example.

Example 1. Let $X = \{x, \overline{x}\}$ and $Y = \{y, \overline{y}\}$ be two frames of discernment and m be the basic assignment on the product set $X \times Y$ defined as follows

$$m(\{[x,y], [x,\overline{y}], [\overline{x},y]\}) = \alpha, \quad 0 < \alpha \leq \frac{3}{4}$$

and

$$m(X \times Y) = 1 - \alpha ,$$

the values of remaining sets being zero. Hence, the marginal basic assignments on X and Y are

$$m_X(X) = 1, \qquad\qquad m_Y(Y) = 1 .$$

It is evident that $(\mathcal{F}_X, m_X)$ and $(\mathcal{F}_Y, m_Y)$ are not noniteractive. One can easily verify that the maximum entropy distributions satisfying the inequalities (6) are

$$p(x,y) = p(x,\overline{y}) = p(\overline{x},y) = p(\overline{x},\overline{y}) = \frac{1}{4} ,$$

$$p_X(x) = p_X(\overline{x}) = \tfrac{1}{2} \ ,$$
$$p_Y(y) = p_Y(\overline{y}) = \tfrac{1}{2} \ ,$$

and the corresponding amounts of uncertainty $AU(m_X)$, $AU(m_Y)$ and $AU(m)$:

$$AU(m_X) = \log_2 2 \ = AU(m_Y) \ ,$$
$$AU(m) = \log_2 4 \ .$$

Therefore we obtain

$$AU(m_X) + AU(m_Y) - AU(m) = 0 \ ,$$

but $(\mathcal{F}_X, m_X)$ and $(\mathcal{F}_Y, m_Y)$ are not noninteractive bodies of evidence, i.e. the inequality (4) (for AU instead of U) cannot be used as the noninteractiveness criterion. $\diamond$

Moreover, the amount of uncertainty does not possess the submodularity property (7), which is demonstrated in the next example.

Example 2. Let $X = \{x, \overline{x}\}$, $Y = \{y, \overline{y}\}$ and $Z = \{z, \overline{z}\}$ be three frames of discernment and m be the basic assignment on the product set $X \times Y \times Z$ defined as follows

$$m(\{[x, y, z]\}) = \alpha, \qquad 0 < \alpha \le \frac{1}{5},$$

and

$$m(\{[x, y, z], [\overline{x}, y, z], [x, \overline{y}, z], [x, y, \overline{z}], [x, \overline{y}, \overline{z}]\}) = 1 - \alpha$$

(the values of basic assignment of the other subsets of $X \times Y \times Z$ being zero). The marginal basic assignments on $X \times Y$, $X \times Z$ and X are:

$$m_{XY}(\{[x, y]\}) = \alpha \ ,$$
$$m_{XY}(\{[x, y], [\overline{x}, y], [x, \overline{y}]\}) = 1 - \alpha \ ,$$
$$m_{XZ}(\{[x, z]\}) = \alpha \ ,$$
$$m_{XZ}(\{[x, z], [\overline{x}, z], [x, \overline{z}]\}) = 1 - \alpha \ ,$$
$$m_X(\{x\}) = \alpha \ ,$$
$$m_X(\{x, \overline{x}\}) = 1 - \alpha \ ,$$

respectively. It can be easily found that the maximum entropy probability distributions satisfying the inequalities (6) are[5]

$$p([x, y, z]) = p([\overline{x}, y, z]) = p([x, \overline{y}, z]) = p([x, y, \overline{z}]) = p([x, \overline{y}, \overline{z}]) = \frac{1}{5} \ ,$$

$$p_{XY}([x, y]) = p_{XY}([\overline{x}, y]) = p_{XY}([x, \overline{y}]) = \tfrac{1}{3} \ ,$$
$$p_{XZ}([x, z]) = p_{XZ}([\overline{x}, z]) = p_{XZ}([x, \overline{z}]) = \tfrac{1}{3} \ ,$$
$$p_X(x) = p_X(\overline{x}) = \tfrac{1}{2} \ ,$$

---

[5] Let us note that p_{XY}, p_{XZ} and p_X are not marginals of p, but maximum entropy probability distributions corresponding to m_{XY}, m_{XZ} and m_X, respectively.

and the corresponding amounts of uncertainty are

$$AU(m) = \log_2 5 \ ,$$
$$AU(m_{XY}) = \log_2 3 \ = AU(m_{XZ}) \ ,$$
$$AU(m_X) = \log_2 2 \ .$$

Therefore we obtain

$$AU(m_{XY}) + AU(m_{XZ}) - AU(m) - AU(m_X) = \log_2 \frac{3 \cdot 3}{5 \cdot 2} \ ,$$

which is less then zero. $\diamond$

5.3 Possibility Theory

In spite of the fact that possibility theory can be viewed as a special Dempster-Shafer theory dealing only with nested bodies of evidence, the amount of uncertainty seems not be to a meaningful measure of uncertainty within this framework (although used e.g. in [8]). For this, there are two reasons:

The first one is quite intuitive. Although probability theory and possibility theory can be viewed as special Dempster-Shafer theories, they are almost completely disjoint (the only exception is the case of one point frame of discernment, which is terribly trivial). Therefore it seems that there is no reason to "approximate" the possibility distributions by the probability ones.

The second one is rather practical. The noninteractiveness notions are very different and therefore even the additivity requirement is not satisfied for the amount of uncertainty in possibility theory, which is shown in the next example.

Example 3. Let $\mathbf{r}_X = \left(1, \frac{1}{2}\right)$ and $\mathbf{r}_Y = \left(1, \frac{1}{4}\right)$ be two distributions corresponding to two noninteractive bodies of evidence, i.e.

$$\mathbf{r}_{XY} = \left(1, \frac{1}{2}, \frac{1}{4}, \frac{1}{4}\right) \ .$$

The probabilities maximizing (5) under (6) (corresponding to $\mathbf{r}_{XY}, \mathbf{r}_X$ and $\mathbf{r}_Y$ respectively) are

$$\mathbf{p}_{XY} = \left(\frac{1}{2}, \frac{1}{4}, \frac{1}{8}, \frac{1}{8}\right) \ ,$$
$$\mathbf{p}_X = \left(\frac{1}{2}, \frac{1}{2}\right) \ ,$$
$$\mathbf{p}_Y = \left(\frac{3}{4}, \frac{1}{4}\right) \ ,$$

and the corresponding amounts of uncertainty:

$$AU(\mathbf{r}_{XY}) = \frac{1}{2} \cdot \log_2 2 + \frac{1}{4} \cdot \log_2 4 + \frac{1}{4} \cdot \log_2 8 = \frac{7}{4} \cdot \log_2 2 \ ,$$
$$AU(\mathbf{r}_X) = \log_2 2 \ ,$$
$$AU(\mathbf{r}_Y) = \frac{1}{4} \cdot \log_2 4 + \frac{3}{4} \cdot \log_2 \frac{4}{3} = 2 \cdot \log_2 2 - \frac{3}{4} \cdot \log_2 3 \ .$$

Therefore we obtain

$$AU(\mathbf{r}_{XY}) - AU(\mathbf{r}_X) - AU(\mathbf{r}_Y) = -\frac{5}{4} \cdot \log_2 2 + \frac{3}{4} \cdot \log_2 3 = \frac{1}{4} \cdot \log_2 \frac{27}{32} \ ,$$

which is not equal to zero, although X and Y are nonintreactive. ◇

Therefore the measure of nonspecificity N seems to be a more appropriate one, although it is not the measure of total uncertainty. As already claimed in [4, 26], entropy-like measures do not play any important role in possibility theory. Their values are negligible in comparison with the value of the measure of nonspecificity. It seems to be intuitively sound: the entropy-like measures can be viewed as measures of conflict among focal elements and since the bodies of evidence are nested, they should be at least almost conflict-free. Moreover, it has already been proven in [13] that this measure satisfies, among others, all requirements set forth in 4.4 (with the exception of the first one, which is not so important — cf. above).

Although the use of this measure is both intuitively and practicaly justified, the submodularity property (7) is not satisfied yet.

Example 4. Let X, Y, Z and m be defined in the same way as in Example 2. Let us note that the focal elements are nested. Now we can obtain the values of nonspecificity measure

$$\begin{aligned} N(m) &= (1 - \alpha) \log_2 5 \ , \\ N(m_{XY}) &= (1 - \alpha) \log_2 3 \ = N(m_{XZ}) \ , \\ N(m_X) &= (1 - \alpha) \log_2 2 \ , \end{aligned}$$

and therefore we have

$$N(m_{XY}) + N(m_{XZ}) - N(m) - N(m_X) = (1 - \alpha) \log_2 \frac{3 \cdot 3}{5 \cdot 2} \ ,$$

which is again less then zero for every $\alpha < 1$. ◇

But the measure of nonspecificity is strictly subadditive, which immediatelly follows from the proof of Theorem 1 in [25] and the nested character of focal elements.

6 Conclusions

The aim of this paper was not to criticize measures of uncertainty in Dempster-Shafer theory and possibility theory but to compare their abilities to express independence and conditional independence relations with the one of Shannon entropy in probability theory.

It has been shown that neither the amount of uncertainty in Dempster-Shafer theory nor the measure of nonspecificity in possibility theory satisfy the submodularity property. This property (a generalization of the subadditivity one) is satisfied by Shannon entropy and used, among others, when studying the conditional independence relations within probability theory. Though the subadditivity property is possessed by these measures, only the measure of nonspecificity is strictly subadditive, and therefore the inequality (4) can be used as the noninteractiveness criterion within possibility theory, in contrast to the amount of uncertainty within Dempster-Shafer theory. However, these results are highly unsatisfactory. We can conceive of two strategies to address this issue:

1. We may search for yet another measure of total uncertainty in Dempster-Shafer theory as well as in possibility theory, a function that would be strictly submodular (strict subadditivity follows immediately from this property) in addition to possesing all other desired properties (proper range, collapsibility to Shannon entropy and Hartley measure, etc.).

2. We may give up the idea of the role of measures of uncertainty in this kind of problems in both Dempster-Shafer theory and possibility theory and to concentrate our attention to another methods.

Unfortunately, at this moment it seems that more promising is the second strategy. We realized that many functions have been suggested to play the role of Shannon entropy in Dempster-Shafer theory and possibility theory. But none of them (with the exception of the amount of uncertainty and measure of nonspecificity) possessed the subadditivity property. To find the measure satisfying properties from 4.4 required a great effort and therefore some measure possesing these more restrictive properties does not seem to us highly likely to be found soon.

These are only some of our thoughts regarding the relation between the measures of uncertainty and the independence concept in various calculi. Their deeper investigation, which is beyond the scope of this paper, will be one topic of our future research.

References

1. Aczél, J., Daróczy, Z.: *On measures of information and their characterizations*, Academic Press, New York, San Francisco, London, 1975.
2. Dubois, D., Prade H.: *Possibility theory.* Plenum Press, New York, 1988.
3. Gallager, R.R.: *Information Theory and Reliable Communication*, New York, Wiley, 1968.
4. Geer, J. F., Klir, G.J.: Discord in possibility theory. *Intern. J. of General Systems*, **19** (1991), 119–132.
5. George, T., Pal, N.R.: Quantification of conflict in Dempster-Shafer framework: a new approach." *Intern. J. of General Systems*, **24** (1996), 407–423.
6. Guan, J. W., Bell, J.W.: *Evidence Theory and Applications* (Vol. 1). North-Holland, Amsterdam and New York, 1991.
7. Harmanec, D., Klir G.J.: Measuring total uncertainty in Dempster-Shafer theory: a novel approach. *Intern. J. of General Systems*, **22** (1994), 405–419.

8. Harmanec, D., Resconi, G., Klir, G.J. and Pan, Y.: On the computation of the uncertainty measure for the Dempster-Shafer theory. *Intern. J. of General Systems*, **25** (1996), 153–163.

9. Hartley, R.V.L.: Transmission of information. *The Bell Systems Technical J.*, **7** (1928), 535–563.

10. Höhle, V.: Entropy with respect to plausibility measures. *Proc. 12th IEEE Symp. on Multiple-Valued Logic*, Paris, 167–169.

11. Jaffray, J.Y.: On the maximum-entropy probability which is consistent with convex capacity. *Intern. J. of Uncertainty, Fuzziness and Knowledge-Based Systems*, **3** (1995), 27–33.

12. Klir, G.J., Folger, T.A.: *Fuzzy Sets, Uncertainty, and Information*. Prentice Hall, Englewood Cliffs, NJ, 1988.

13. Klir, G.J., Mariano, M.: On the uniqueness of possibilistic measure of uncertainty and information. *Fuzzy sets and systems*, **24** (1987), 197–219.

14. Klir, G.J., Parviz, P. A note on the measure of discord. *Proc. Eighth Conf. on Uncertainty in AI* (D. Dubois et al., editors), San Mateo, California, Morgan Kaufman, 1992, 138–141.

15. Klir, G.J., Ramer, A.: Uncertainty in the Dempster-Shafer theory: A critical re-examination. *Intern. J. General Systems* **18** (1990), 155–166.

16. Lamata, M.T., Moral, S.: Measures of entropy in the theory of evidence. *Intern. J. of General Systems*, **14** (1988), 297–305.

17. Pal, N.R., Bezdek, J.C., Hemasinha, R.: Uncertainty measures for evidential reasoning II: A new measure of total uncertainty. *Intern. J. of Approximate Reasoning*, **8** (1993), 1–16.

18. Ramer, A., Diamond P., Padet, C.: Total Uncertainty Revisited. *Intern. J. of General Systems* (submitted).

19. Ramer, A.: Uniqueness of information measure in the theory of evidence. *Fuzzy Sets and Systems* **24** (1987), 193–196.

20. Shafer, G.: *A Mathematical Theory of Evidence*. Princeton University Press, Princeton, 1976.

21. Shannon, C.E.: The mathematical theory of communication. *The Bell System Technical J.*, **27** (1948), 379–423, 623–665.

22. Shenoy, P.P.:Conditional independence in valuation-based systems. *Intern. J. of Approximate Reasoning*, **10** (1994), 203–234.

23. Studený, M.: Multiinformation and the problem of characterization of conditional independence relations. *Problems of Control and Information Theory*, **18** (1989), 3–16.

24. Studený, M.: Formal properties of conditional independence in different calculi of AI. *Symbolic and Quantitative Approaches to Reasoning and Uncertainty* (M. Clarke, R. Kruse and S. Moral eds.), Lecture Notes in Computer Science 747, Springer-Verlag, 341–348.

25. Vejnarová, J.: A few remarks on measures of uncertainty in Dempster-Shafer theory. *Intern. J. of General Systems*, **22** (1994), 233–243.

26. Vejnarová, J., Klir, G.J.: Measure of strife in Dempster-Shafer theory. *Intern. J. of General Systems*, **22** (1993), 25–42.

27. Yager, R.: Entropy and specificity in a mathematical theory of evidence. *Intern. J. of General Systems*, **9** (1983), 249–260.

A Multi-Agent Approach to First-Order Logic

Guilherme Bittencourt
Isabel Tonin

Laboratório de Controle e Microinformática
Departamento de Engenharia Elétrica
Universidade Federal de Santa Catarina
88040-900 - Florianópolis - SC - Brazil
E-mail: { gb | isabel }@lcmi.ufsc.br

Abstract. This paper presents a hierarchical heterogeneous multi-agent society based on a hypercube parallel architecture able to manage, in a distributed way, a first-order logic knowledge base and to draw inferences from it. The knowledge base is structured into theories, composed by sets of formulas. The adopted internal representation of these theories consists of both canonical forms of the formulas that define them. The inference method underlying the deductive capabilities of the architecture is based on the fact that the two canonical forms of a set of formulas can used as a generalized inference rule, giving rise to a complete logical inference method. A prototype of the proposed knowledge representation system, where concurrence is sequentially simulated, has been implemented in Common Lisp/CLOS.

Content Areas: Agent-Oriented Programming, Automated Reasoning, Knowledge Representation, Theorem Proving.

1 Introduction

Any knowledge representation system based in first-order logic has to face some inherent difficulties: (i) the radical modularity of the language, where each sentence is an eternal independent truth, (ii) the locality of the proof methods, where the context of the inference is not taken into account, and (iii) the combinatorial explosion, i.e., the fact that the space and time needed to solve a first-order logic inference problem grow exponentially with the size of the problem.

The extreme modularity gave rise to knowledge representation methods where part of the structure of the represented knowledge is captured into the formalism (e.g., *frames* and *semantic nets* [5]). In theorem proving research, inference methods that use global context information (and heuristic knowledge) to guide the proofs were also proposed (e.g., *Graph Resolution* [10] and the *Connection Method* [1]). But the combinatorial explosion is inherent to logical proof methods and, as the problems get bigger, the use of concurrence is the only chance to escape the hardware limitations of a single computer.

Concurrence can be obtained through parallel computers or through distributed architectures. In the former case, some theorem proving methods were successfully adapted to parallel computers [16], but usually logical inference procedures are not easy to parallelize. Another solution is to design special algorithms for specific parallel architectures (e.g., [8], [18]). Also in the domain of logic programming languages, research has been undertaken to devise methods for the parallelization of the program execution procedure (e.g., [7], [9]). In the later case, the recent advances in *Distributed Artificial Intelligence* [20] have been applied in the development of some logic-based systems (e.g., [19], [15], [14], [17]).

In this paper, we describe a knowledge representation system and its underlying architecture. The system supports a first-order logic language and presents theorem proving and logic programming capabilities. These capabilities are implemented by a society of computational agents. More specifically, a hierarchical heterogeneous multi-agent society [12] that consists of a group of reactive agents, organized in a hypercube parallel architecture, controlled by a cognitive agent, which is also responsible for the interaction with the user.

The paper is organized as follows. In Section 2, we define the functionalities of the proposed system and sketch the global structure of its underlying architecture. In Sections 3 and 4, the two main modules of the architecture – the hypercube society and the control/interface agent – are described. Finally, in Section 5, some possible extensions of the architecture are proposed.

2 A Knowledge Representation System

Consider the first-order language $L(P, F, C)$, where P, F and C are finite sets of predicate, function and constant symbols, respectively. In what follows, we adopt the usual definitions of *term, literal, clause, dual clause, subsumption* and *(well-formed) formula* (e.g., [11]). We call $\mathcal{L}$ the set of all well-formed formulas and $\mathcal{T}$ the set of all terms in language L. Let also $\mathcal{F} = \mathcal{F}_1 \cup ... \cup \mathcal{F}_n$ be the set of all possible literals in language L, in such a way that all literals in $\mathcal{F}_i$ are built up from the predicate symbol $P_i \in P$.

The proposed knowledge representation system contains an internal knowledge base that, differently from the usually monolithic logical knowledge bases, is structured into *theories*. A theory is defined simply as a set of well-formed formulas, i.e., a subset of $\mathcal{L}$. We associate each theory with a *theory symbol* $T_i \in \aleph$. The external behavior of the system can be defined by two primitives, whose intended semantics is the following:

- TELL : given a theory name in $\aleph$ and a set of logical formulas in $\mathcal{L}$, this primitive stores the formulas in the knowledge base and associates with them the given theory name.
- ASK : given a set of theory names and a logical formula, this primitive verifies if the given formula can be proved from the formulas in all the theories whose names appear in the given set of names, producing the relevant substitutions if the given logical formula presents variables.

Given a set of well-formed formulas $W \subset \mathcal{L}$, there are algorithms for converting it into a formula W_c, in clause form, and into a formula W_d, in dual clause form, such that $W \Leftrightarrow W_c \Leftrightarrow W_d$. To transform a formula from one clause form to the other, only the properties of the logical operators are needed[1].

In the system's knowledge base, the internal representation of a theory consists of *both* canonical forms of its associated logical formulas. It is interesting to have both canonical forms of a set of formulas because they can be used together as a generalized inference rule, giving rise to a complete logical inference method [3]. As the cost of generating both canonical forms of a large number of logical formulas is prohibitive, the system maintains both forms for, usually small and carefully chosen, subsets of formulas: the theories. If more than one theory is to be used, the cost of combining together canonical forms of two different theories is always less than the cost of generating both canonical forms of the union of the two original theories [2].

A hypercube of dimension n is a graph where the vertices are the set of all n-tuples whose elements belong to the set $\{0, 1\}$ and the edges connect any two vertices whose representations differ only at one position (e.g., [21]). Consider such a hypercube, where n is the number of predicate symbols that occur in the clauses and dual clauses that define the current theories. Each vertex of this hypercube corresponds to a certain combination of predicates given by those coordinates of the vertex that are not zero. A (dual) clause is associated with vertex $(k_1, \ldots, k_n)$ if, for all $k_i \neq 0$, the predicate P_i appears in some literal of the (dual) clause and, for all $k_i = 0$, the predicate P_i does not appear in any literal of the (dual) clause.

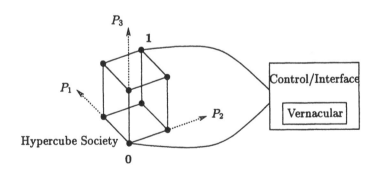

Fig. 1. The Architecture

The knowledge base contents, i.e., the clauses and dual clauses that repre-

---

[1] Actually, there are many subtleties in this process. In what follows, we assume that the dual forms are generated by a transformation from W to W_c, including variable renaming and skolemization steps [6], followed by a transformation from W_c to W_d, preserving the variable names.

sent the theories, are distributed through the hypercube in such a way that each (dual) clause of each theory is stored into its associated vertex. Using this hypercube architecture, it is possible to define concurrent processes that perform clause subsumption calculation, transformation between canonical forms, theory combination and logical inference. These processes are defined in such a way that they can be tackle by a society of agents, resident in the vertices of the hypercube, where communication is restricted to adjacent vertices. The complete architecture of the system consists of this *hypercube society* and a *control/interface* agent, which is responsible for the treatment of the TELL and ASK primitives. An instance of the architecture, for the case there are only three predicate symbols, is shown in Fig. 1.

3 The Hypercube Society

The vertices of the hypercube contain, for each theory, special representations for their associated clauses and dual clauses that include the theory context, i.e., numbers that indicate, for each literal, in which clauses it occurs and which clauses present literals that subsume or are subsumed by it. These special representations are defined below.

Consider a theory T_k with m clauses. Let us use the notation $\alpha \rightsquigarrow X$ to indicate that the expression α occurs in the definition of the mathematical object X. A *quantum*[2] – denoted by $\phi_i^{(F,S)}$ – is a mathematical object that consists of three elements: a literal $\phi_i \in \mathcal{F}_i$ and two sets of integers $F, S \subseteq \{1, \ldots, m\}$. The set F of *fixed coordinates* indicates which clauses C_j contain the literal ϕ_i, i.e.:

$$F = \{j \mid \phi_i \rightsquigarrow C_j\}$$

The set S of *subsumed coordinates* indicates which clauses C_j contain literals $\phi_i' \in \mathcal{F}_i$ subsumed by the literal ϕ_i, i.e.:

$$S = \{j \mid \phi_i \succ \phi_i' \text{ and } \phi_i' \rightsquigarrow C_j\}$$

where the symbol $\succ$ means "subsumes".

A quantum is intended to be a compact representation of the context information about each literal that occurs in the clause set of theory T_k. Each quantum has its *dual*, that represents the context information of the associated literal with regard to the dual clause set of T_k.

The mathematical object *(dual) particle* is defined simply as a set of quanta: $\gamma = \{\phi_i^{(F,S)}\}$ and it is intended to represent a (dual) clause and its context in the theory. Given a theory T_k, we can associate with each clause a particle in a set Φ_k of particles and with each dual clause a dual particle in a set Ψ_k. These two sets are a kind of "holographic" representation of each other. Each particle in Φ_k

---

[2] The metaphoric notation adopted to name the defined mathematical objects (quantum, particle, wave, etc.) are intended to facilitate the understanding and do not have any further connotation.

consists of a combination of all dual particles in Ψ_k and, conversely, each dual particle in Ψ_k consists of a combination of all particles in Φ_k. Furthermore, the structure of this combination is represented through the sets F and S associated with the quanta in Φ_k and Ψ_k.

The behavior of the agents in the hypercube society, although complex, is deterministic. At each moment, there are a set of global computations occurring in parallel. Each of these computations is assigned its own agents, one per vertex. These agents execute all the same procedure, specified by the control/interface agent when the global computation is initiated. This procedure is a data driven process, depending, at each vertex, on the arrival of information from lower vertices. The agents communicate with each other through messages that contain *wave packages*, where a *wave* is also simply a set of quanta. The communication paths are restricted to hypercube edges.

Typically, the procedure to be executed by each agent at each vertex consists of the following steps: the agent waits until all wave packages associated with its assigned global computation arrive from lower vertices, performs the necessary manipulations, possibly changing the contents of the (dual) particles associated with the vertex, and, finally, emits the appropriate wave packages to its successors. Each theory can be manipulated by just one global computation at a time to avoid conflict. There is no global control: in general, a computation is started by wave packages sent out of vertex **0** that propagates asynchronously through the hypercube vertices until the wave front reaches the vertex **1**.

4 The Control/Interface Agent

The control/interface agent contains all global knowledge of the system, in particular, the names and contents of the defined theories and the list of predicate symbols that occur in these theories. It also contains a table, called *vernacular*, (see Fig. 1), where the entries, indexed by the literal set $\mathcal{F}$, have the following information, called the *syntagma* of the literal:

Signal $\sigma \in \{T, F\}$
Predicate $P_i^{(k)} \in P$
Matrix $(t_1, \ldots, t_k), t_j \in \mathcal{T}$
Subsume $S_{\succ} \in \mathcal{F}$
Subsumed $S_{\prec} \in \mathcal{F}$
Contradict $\{(\phi, \theta), \phi \in \mathcal{F}, \theta$ a substitution$\}$
Instances $\{(T_k, \tau, F_c, S_c, F_d, S_d), T_k \in \aleph, \tau$ a substitution, $F_c, S_c, F_d, S_d \in I\!N\}$

where, $P_i^{(k)}$ in the ith predicate symbol (with arity k). The variables that occur in the terms t_j have standard names, in such a way that literals that are alphabetic variants of each other are stored in the same entry in the table.

The elements of the sets $S_{\succ}$ and $S_{\prec}$ refer to other entries in the table. $S_{\succ}$ indicates which entries have literals that are subsumed by the current literal and $S_{\prec}$ indicates which entries have literals that subsume the current literal. Where the current literal is that associated with the current entry of the table. This literal can be constructed using the first three attributes of the entry. The elements of the set $\{(\phi, \theta)\}$ indicates which literals – ϕ – contradict the current literal and with which substitution – θ. Finally, each six-tuple $(T_k, \tau, F_c, S_c, F_d, S_d)$ in the set at the last line of the syntagma represents an instance of the literal. More formally, it means that, in theory T_k, the current literal – $\phi = \sigma\, P_i^{(k)}(t_1, \ldots, t_k)$ – is represented at least by a pair of dual quanta:

$$(\phi\, \tau)^{(F_c, S_c)} \quad \text{and} \quad (\phi\, \tau)^{(F_d, S_d)}$$

The only expensive operation in the vernacular table is the inclusion of a new literal, when it must be tested for subsumption[3] and contradiction. On the other hand, operations such as the subsumption between clauses can be performed using just primitive set operations.

The control/interface agent is itself controlled by the TELL and ASK primitives. To perform the necessary operational manipulations in the internal representation in such a way that the intended semantics of these primitives is respected, the control/interface agent disposes of a set of global operations that can be submitted to the hypercube society. These operations act on theories, changing previously existing ones or creating new ones. The operations are executed asynchronously by the agents in the hypercube vertices. To avoid conflict, each operation has exclusive access to the (dual) particles of the theories it manipulates. When an operation ends, the information in the vernacular table about the theories it has manipulated is updated. The global operations are described below.

4.1 Subsumption

The subsumption operation is used, in the TELL primitive, as a filter to eliminated subsumed clauses inadvertently introduced into theory definitions. It is also used when two or more theories are combined together and, therefore, it is also used during the inference operation.

If a clause subsumes another, the set of predicate symbols which occur in it must be a subset of the set of predicate symbols which occur in the subsumed clause. This implies that, if we place all particles in the set Ψ_k in their associated vertices in the hypercube, then, given one particle (and its associated clause), all particles subsumed by it (i.e., all particles associated with clauses that are subsumed by its associated clause) should lie in the same hypercube vertex or in some upper vertex.

The subsumption elimination process consists of the propagation of wave packages upward through the hypercube. At each vertex, a new wave is created for each particle associated with the vertex. To synchronize the vertex processes, an empty wave package is emitted, if there is no particle associated with the vertex. When all the wave packages associated with a given vertex arrive, the

---

[3] The subsumption concept is extended to include the subsumption between literals by considering a literal as a unitary clause.

subsumption procedure is executed. This procedure eliminates the subsumed particles of the vertex, taking into account the input waves. The operation stops when the vertex 1, which has no successors, is reached.

The last step is to renumerate the new particles and update accordingly the F and S sets associated with each quantum in the dual particle set Ψ_k. This process can be performed concurrently in all vertices of the hypercube, because it only involves local data, i.e., each vertex in the hypercube can update its own dual particles. It is important to note that all quanta whose F sets become empty, because the particles which they represented were eliminated through subsumption, should also be eliminated from the dual particle set.

4.2 Dual Transformation

The dual transformation operation is used to implement the part of the TELL primitive that calculates both canonical representations of the input theory. It consists of the transformation from one canonical form into the other. The intuitive idea of the operation that calculates the dual particle set $-\Psi_k$ -, given the particle set $-\Phi_k$ - (the reverse transformation being totally symmetric), is the following. Let m be the number of particles in the set Φ_k. Each dual particle to be generated can be imagined as a wave with m slots, one for each particle in the set Φ_k. These slots, called the *spectrum* of the wave, should be filled in with quanta (i.e., with literals) that come from the corresponding particle. Once all the slots of a wave are filled, a set of complete dual particles can be generated by taking one literal from each slot. If we only take literals that are not subsumed by any other, then no subsumed particles will be generated.

Initially, a new wave is created for each literal that occurs in the initial particle set. These waves – because they contain only one literal and therefore only one predicate – are associated with vertices $(k_1, \ldots, k_n)$, where only one k_i is different from zero. Consider all the waves associated with one of these vertices. They contain literals built up from the same predicate. If one of these literals subsumes another literal that comes from a different particle, then we can build a new wave that contains the former literal at its corresponding slot and, at the slot corresponding to the latter literal, put some mark indicating that it is trivially filled. This new wave can be used to build all the dual particles that contain the subsuming literal. In fact, any dual particle that contains both the subsuming and the subsumed literals, or any other literal that comes from the same particle as the subsumed literal, will be subsumed by some particle that contains only the subsuming literal. Actually, the picture is a little more complex because the same literal may appear in more than one of the original particles. Therefore, we will have waves with more than one slot filled in with the same literal. The waves that contain literals which are neither subsuming nor subsumed by others can be combined into a single wave. This wave represents all the dual particles that can be constructed by selecting one literal from each slot of the wave.

The operation proceeds by propagating these waves through the hypercube along its edges. At each vertex, the waves that arrive from the lower dimension vertices are combined together. Those combinations that contain at least one instance of each of the predicates associated with the vertex are examined. The remaining combinations are ignored since each dual particle should be generated at the vertex corresponding to its predicates. Each time a wave is filled up, the corresponding dual particles are generated and its propagation stops, preventing the generation of subsumed dual particles; because the latter have more predicates, they would necessarily be generated at (and only at) vertices with a higher dimension. When finally the vertex 1 is reached, all dual particles are already created in their associated vertex.

4.3 Combination

The combination operation is the base for the inference operation, because it is used both to combine together the hypothesis theories, in the ASK primitive, and to add to the original theories the new generated theorems.

Consider a set of theories $T_1, \ldots, T_N$ and let T be the combined theory associated with this set. Each theory T_k is associated with a set of particles – Φ_k – and a set of dual particles – Ψ_k. The sets Φ and Ψ that define the combined theory T are defined as follows: the set Φ contains one new particle for each of the particles in $\Phi_1 \cup \cdots \cup \Phi_N$ and the set Ψ contains one new dual particle for each element in the Cartesian product of the dual particle sets: $\Psi_1 \times \cdots \times \Psi_N$. The new particle and dual particle sets may contain subsumed (dual) particles and to find out whether it is the case we must analyze each possible pair of (dual) particles, what would make the cost of the combination operation exponential.

Fortunately, there is another solution: the particle and dual particle representation of the N theories can be viewed as a intermediate solution of a dual transformation process applied on the combined theory T, where the problem was initially divided into N subproblems. The proposed operation just combines the subproblem solutions.

Initially, all particles in the sets Φ_k's are placed on their associated nodes in the hypercube and the subsumption global operation is executed. Next, the vernacular table is used to verify, whether literals associated with quanta in the dual particle sets Ψ_k's subsume or are subsumed by any literals associated with quanta of a different theory $T_{k'}$, $k \neq k'$. If it is the case, the updated F and S sets associated with these quanta are sent to the appropriate vertices, in order to update the dual particle representations.

Finally, each dual particle in the sets Ψ_k's is transformed into a wave with identical attributes and propagated through the hypercube. At each node, the procedure verifies whether a combination of propagating waves generates a *saturated* wave, i.e., one with all the slots in its spectrum filled. Each of these saturated waves give rise to one or more dual particles of the combined theory. Again, when the vertex 1 is reached, all dual particles are already created.

4.4 Inference

The inference operation supports the deductive capabilities of the ASK primitive and it makes use of all three previously defined operations. Instead of defining a specific proof strategy, we present a nondeterministic procedure that can be instantiated into several different strategies if its nondeterministic choices are fixed. Intuitively, the inference operation consists of the following steps:

- Detection of potentially contradictory dual particles and determination of the set of substitution fragments that actualize these contradictions.
- Combination of these substitution fragments into a set of independent substitutions.
- Application of these substitutions to the dual particle set.
- Generation of the particle sets associated with these instances of the dual particle set.
- Creation of a new theory represented by these particle and dual particles sets.

The particles in the new theory created at the last step represent new theorems. This new theory can be combined with the original theory or additionally with other infered new theories – through the combination operation – and the cycle may be repeated. Besides these undetermined control flow, the second and third steps of the operation involve external choices, characterizing a nondeterministic behavior. It can be proved that at least one of the execution paths of this operation leads to a complete theorem proving method.

The goal of the second step of the inference operation is to build the set of substitutions that will be used to generate the new theorems. This set can be noted by: $\Omega = \{ \langle \omega, J \rangle \}$, where each substitution ω transforms all the dual particles $j \in J$ into explicit contradictions. The set Ω is constructed from the set: $\Theta = \{\langle \theta, J, \phi_i^{(F,S)}, \phi_i'^{(F',S')} \rangle\}$, determined in the first step of the operation, where, each substitution θ – the most general unifier of ϕ_i and ϕ_i' – makes all dual particles $j \in J$ contradictory. The brute force method to calculate the set Ω is to determine $\mathcal{P}(\Theta)$, where $\mathcal{P}$ stands for the set of all subsets of a set. The problem with this method is that, analogously to the *Level Saturation* strategy of the resolution inference method, it includes *all* valid combinations of substitutions in $\mathcal{P}(\Theta)$. One way to refine this strategy is to use the extra information contained in the vernacular table and in the particle and dual particle sets to chose a more sensible subset of these possible combinations.

Another efficiency problem with the inference operation is that its last step uses the dual transformation operation, which is expensive. This can be avoided using the properties of the particle representation. The basic idea is the following: if some of the dual particles in the set Ψ_k are contradictory, they can be eliminated. The effect of this elimination on the set Φ_k is that, in each of its particles, the spectrum slots associated with the contradictory dual particles are no longer necessary and can also be eliminated. The instances of the resulting reduced particles, when the associated substitutions are applied, give us directly the new theorems. This means that the particles and dual particles associated with a theory can be thought of as a "compiled" representation of this theory, that can be used as a complex inference rule.

5 Conclusion

We described a hierarchical heterogeneous multi-agent society based on a hyper-cube parallel architecture able to manage a first-order logic knowledge base and to draw inferences from it. A prototype of the proposed knowledge representation system, where concurrence is sequentially simulated, has been implemented in the Common Lisp language [22] using the object-oriented extension CLOS.

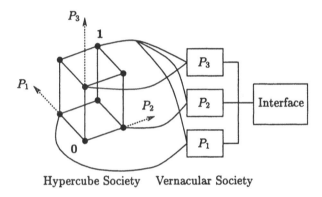

Fig. 2. The Distributed Architecture

To facilitate the presentation, we didn't explore all concurrence possibilities of the proposed architecture. In fact, the vernacular table can be partitioned into several tables, one for each predicate symbol, because the pointers in the syntagma refer always to the same subset F_i to which the current literal belongs. Therefore, the control/interface agent can be exploded into a *vernacular society* and an *interface agent*, see Fig. 2. The function of the interface agent is to maintain the theory definitions and to redirect the input to the relevant vernacular agents, the global control being obtained through the cooperation between these agents. The interface functions could also be distributed. If we assume that some predicate symbols are semantically interpreted as perceived facts and others as action commands, then the input and output flows of information could be connected directly to the hypercube nodes that contain the relevant (dual) particles combining together the activated perception/action predicates. This will leave only the theory maintenance function at the interface agent.

The script of a query to the knowledge base gives an idea of the complexity of the interaction between the agents in this extended architecture: the interface agent receives an ASK primitive establishing the literal ϕ as the current goal. This generates a message to the associated vernacular agent, i.e., that that shares the predicate symbol with ϕ. The vernacular agent consults ϕ's syntagma and finds out in which theories it occurs and starts a concurrent combination of (some of) these theories and a theory build up from the negation of the goal, whose canonical forms are both equal to $\neg\phi$. Eventually, the combination process will lead to contradictions in some vernacular agents, which can cooperate in order to combine their associated substitutions. The goal owner can coordinate this cooperation informing which dual particles it would like to be contradictory in order to prove its goal. The interface process plays the role of a *blackboard* [13] where the shared knowledge about theory definitions is maintained. Every time a substitution is applied a new theory is created. In the case of a refutation proof, the process stops when some substitution is found that eliminate all (dual) particles of the current theory.

The proposed knowledge representation system can also be provided with a *reflexive* capacity in a rather smooth way: it is enough to extend the language L to $L^1(P \cup P^1, F \cup F^1, C \cup C^1)$, where P^1, F^1 and C^1 are sets of predicate, function and constant symbols whose semantic domain is augmented to include the set of theory names $\aleph$. In particular, the set C^1 is interpreted as the set $\aleph$ itself. The resulting knowledge base could again be structured into *second order* theories, whose names could form a new set of theory names that could be used as the semantic domain of a new set C^2, giving rise to a *third order* logical language L^2, and successively. At each level, a special *computable* predicate – $Use(T)$, where T is a theory – could be introduced in order to articulate the inference mechanisms of the different levels. This reflexive capacity can be used to improve the cooperation efficiency through the use of the knowledge representation and inference power of the architecture to reason about its own proof strategies.

The proposed knowledge representation system is part of a wider project based on a generic model for a *cognitive agent* that integrates the logical approach to the connectionist and evolutionary computation approaches [4].

Acknowledgments

The authors are grateful to all those that helped in the development of this paper, in particular the LCMI team and the anonymous referees. The first author is partially supported by *Conselho Nacional de Desenvolvimento Científico e Tecnológico (CNPq)*, grant No. 352017/92-9.

References

1. W. Bibel. *Automated Theorem Proving*. Vieweg Verlag, 1987.
2. G. Bittencourt. Boxing theories (abstract). *Workshop on Logic, Language, Information and Computation (WoLLIC'96), Journal of the Interest Group in Pure and Applied Logics (IGPL), Imperial College, London and Max-Planck-Institut, Saarbrücken*, 4(1):479–481, 1996.

3. G. Bittencourt. Concurrent inference through dual transformation. *Journal of the Interest Group in Pure and Applied Logics (IGPL)*, in press, 1997.

4. G. Bittencourt. In the quest of the missing link. In *Proceedings of IJCAI 15*, 1997.

5. R.J. Brachman and H.J. Levesque, editors. *Readings in Knowledge Representation*. Morgan Kaufmann Publishers, Inc., Los Altos, CA, 1985.

6. C.-L. Chang and Lee R.C.-T. *Symbolic Logic and Mechanical Theorem Proving*. Academic Press, Computer Science Classics, 1973.

7. J. Chassin De Kergommeaux and P. Robert. An abstract machine to implement or-and parallel prolog efficiently. *The Journal of Logic Programming*, 8(3):249–264, May 1990.

8. W.-T. Chen and M.-Y. Fang. An efficient procedure for theorem proving in propositional logic on vector computers. *Parallel Computing*, 17:983–5, 1991.

9. A. Ciepielewski, S. Haridi, and B. Hausman. Or-parallel prolog on shared memory multiprocessors. *The Journal of Logic Programming*, 7(2):125–147, September 1989.

10. N. Eisinger. What you always wanted to know about clause graph resolution. In *Proceedings of the 8th ICAD, Springer-Verlag LNCS No. 230*, pages 316–336, 1986.

11. M. Fitting. *First-Order Logic and Automated Theorem Proving*. Springer-Verlag, New York, 1990.

12. L. Gasser. Boundaries, identity and aggregation: Plurality issues in multiagent systems. In Eric Werner and Yves Demazeau, editors, *Decentralized Artificial Intelligence*, pages 199–212. Elsevier Science Publishers, Amsterdam, NL, 1992.

13. B. Hayes-Roth. A blackboard architecture for control. *Artificial Intelligence*, 26(3):251–321, July 1985.

14. C.E. Hewitt. Open information system semantics for distributed artificial intelligence. *Artificial Intelligence (Special Volume Foundations of Artificial Intelligence)*, 47(1-3):79–106, January 1991.

15. M.N. Huhns and D.M. Bridgeland. Multi-agent truth maintenance. *IEEE Transactions on Systems, Man and Cybernetics*, 21(6):1437–1445, 1991.

16. R. Loganantharaj and R.A. Mueller. Parallel theorem proving with connection graphs. In *Proceedings of the 8th ICAD, Springer-Verlag LNCS No. 230*, pages 337–352, 1986.

17. B. Malheiro, N.R. Jennings, and E. Oliveira. Belief revision in multi-agent systems. In A. Cohn, editor, *Proceedings of ECAI 11*. John Wiley & Sons, Ltd., 1994.

18. T.R. Martinez and J.J. Vidal. Adaptative parallel logic networks. *Journal of Parallel and Distributed Computing*, 5(1):26–58, February 1988.

19. C. Mason and R. Johnson. Datms: A framework for distributed assuption based reasoning. In L. Gasser and M.N. Huhns, editors, *Distributed Artificial Intelligence Vol. II*, pages 293–317. Elsevier Science Publishers, Amsterdam, NL, 1989.

20. B. Moulin and B. Chaib-Draa. An overview of distributed artificial intelligence. In G.M.P. O'Hare and N.R. Jennings, editors, *Foundations of Distributed Artificial Intelligence*, chapter 1, pages 3–55. John Wiley & Sons. Inc, 1996. http://iris.ift.ulaval.ca/publications/moulin/pub-96/pub-96.html.

21. M.J. Quinn. *Desingning Efficient Algorithms for Parallel Computers*. McGraw-Hill International Editions, 1987.

22. G.L. Steele Jr. *Common LISP, the Language*. Digital Press, Burlington, 1984.

Modelling Dynamic Aspects of Intentions

Michael da Costa Móra[2,1] *, Gabriel Pereira Lopes[1] **, Helder Coelho[3] ***,
and Rosa M. Viccari[2] †

[1] CENTRIA/DI – Universidade Nova de Lisboa
Quinta da Torre – 2825 Monte da Caparica – Portugal
[2] CPGCC – II – Universidade Federal do Rio Grande do Sul
Bloco IV – Campus do Vale – Av. Bento Gonçalves 9500 – Porto Alegre – RS – Brasil
[3] DI - FCUL – Universidade de Lisboa
Bloco C5, Piso 1 – Campo Grande – 1700 Lisboa – Portugal

Abstract. In this paper, we define a formal model of intentions that
accounts for both static and dynamic aspects of intentions. By static
aspects, we mean its relation with desires and beliefs and the properties that this relation has (namely, consistency and avoidance of side-
effects). By dynamic aspects, we mean establishing criteria, other than
those derived from commitment, to drop intentions (namely, based on
the cause-effect relation between desires and intentions) and mechanisms
that triggers the reasoning process without imposing a significant additional burden on the agent. Our approach is to define those conditions
that make the agent start reasoning about intentions as constraints over
its beliefs.

Keywords: intentions; mental states modeling; agent architectures; distributed
artificial intelligence; logic programming.

1 Introduction

When we model agents using mental states as beliefs, desires and intentions, one
of the hardest tasks is to represent dynamic aspects of the agent's behavior. We
illustrate these aspects in the following example.

Example 1. Mike has two distinct programmes for his evening. He may go to
the local opera house or to a soccer game, at the local stadium. Both events
start at the same time. Mike cannot go to both the opera and the soccer game.
Therefore, he has to *choose* one of them. Mike may make this choice considering

---

* PhD student at the CPGCC/UFRGS, in Brazil. Currently at the CEN-
TRIA/DI/UNL, in Portugal. Supported by CAPES/Brazil and project
DIXIT/JNICT. E-mail: mdm@di.fct.unl.pt .
** Researcher at the CENTRIA/DI/UNL, in Portugal. Supported by project
DIXIT/JNICT. E-mail: gpl@di.fct.unl.pt .
*** Professor at the DI/FCUL/UL. E-mail: hcoelho@di.fc.ul.pt .
† Professor at the CPGCC/UFRGS, in Brazil. Supported by CNPq/Brazil. E-mail:
rosa@inf.ufrgs.br .

many factors, like his preferences (he may be more fond of opera than soccer, for instance), costs (tickets for the opera cost three times as much as those for the soccer game; the stadium may be several kilometers far from his home while the opera house is 15 minutes walk distance) or others. Suppose that, after all these considerations, Mike chooses to go to the opera. As he is a rational person, we expect him to plan actions and to act in order to accomplish his intents to go to the opera. We also expect that, since he has already considered the pros and cons of his options, he does not reconsiders again and again his previous choice. That is, we expect that, after he decides what to do, he commits to that decision. Meanwhile, he receives a call from a colleague telling him the term paper they believed was due to the end of the month is, in fact, due to the next morning. Although Mike had already decided to go to the opera, we expect him to reconsider his choices, as he is now in presence of new facts that pose him a new important situation that was not previously present.

Although this behavior may be characterized as rational and it is what one would expect of a rational agent, most of the existing formal models of agents are not capable of capturing it. These models follow Bratman's analysis[Bra90], where he describes the relation among the three basic mental states that compose an agent — beliefs-desires-intentions (BDI)[1]. Bratman argues that, since agents are assumed to be resource-bounded, they cannot continuously evaluate their competing beliefs and desires in order to act rationally. After some reasoning, agents have to commit to some set of choices. It is this choice followed by a commitment that characterizes intentions. Thus, intentions are viewed as a compromise the agent assumes with a specific possible future that is abandoned only in certain circumstances, namely when the agent believes it is satisfied or when it believes it is impossible to achieve it. This means that, once an intention is adopted, the agent will pursue that intention, planning actions to accomplish it, re-planning when a failure occurs, and so. Also, it means that intentions will constrain the adoption of future intentions, i.e., they will form a *screen of admissibility*[Bra90] for adopting new intentions, preventing the agent to make new choices that are not consistent with those previously made. Therefore, with intentions as a kernel mental attitude, agents have a general strategy that prevent them from having to reconsider all of their mental states every time, in order to know what to do.

But this characterization of intentions lead to some strange behavior. For instance, in our example, as Mike had already adopted as intention to go to the Opera, this intention would constrain the adoption of new ones. Therefore, when he is notified about the real due date of his term paper, he would not adopt *to finish the paper tonight* as an intention, since it would be contradictory with a previous one, namely *to go to the Opera*.

In this paper, we show how to model these dynamics aspects of the agent's behavior, namely how an agent decides to break commitment to satisfy previous

---

[1] In fact, Bratman stresses on the relation between intentions and beliefs. He mentions that desires would constitute a set of options where the agent would pick up his intentions, but he does not focus on this mental state and its relations with the others.

intentions and re-evaluate its competing mental states in order to decide what to do, without having to constantly engage in this expensive reasoning process.

Recall that, in existing models (like [CL90,Sin94]), after committing to some intention, agents will only re-evaluate their choices when they believe that an intention has been satisfied or that an intention is impossible to satisfy. Those models specify these conditions, but they do not model how an agent may detect that such conditions hold and that it is relevant, at a certain time, to reconsider its decisions. We do this by modelling them as constraints that are part of the agent's beliefs set and that, when violated, trigger the intention revision process. Having defined how an agent detects relevant situations and how it triggers its reasoning process, we define additional triggering conditions, based on the causal relation between desires and intentions, that relax the notion of commitment and avoids the type of behaviors described above.

Our model focus on the formal definition of mental states and on how the agent behaves, given such mental states. Initially we define the three basic mental states and the static relations between them, namely constraints on consistency among those mental states. Afterwards, we advance with the definition of how agents select their intentions among its competing desires. Desires are schemas of properties agents will eventually want to bring about. Differently from intentions, agents are not committed to their desires, i.e., agents do not necessarily act in order to satisfy all of its desires. Instead, they select among their (possibly contradictory) desires those that are relevant and that they believe may be achieved. We rely on the logical formalism, namely Extended Logic Programming with the Well-Founded Extended Semantics to detect and remove contradiction, as well as to perform several types of non-monotonic reasoning, namely defeasible and abductive reasoning.

As the reasoning mechanisms provided by ELP are at the very core of our model, in the next sections we start by briefly describing the syntax and semantics of extended logic programming, as well as how to use it to perform the necessary non-monotonic reasoning (section 2) and to deal with action and time using an extension of the Event Calculus[Mes92,QL97](section 3). Afterwards, we present the formal definition of our model of intentions (section 4). Finally, we draw some conclusions and point to some future work.

2 Extended Logic Programming

Differently of normal logic programs, where negative information is only stated implicitly (i.e., a proposition is false only if it cannot be proved to be true), extended logic programs have a second kind of negation that allows us to explicitly represent negative information. If, on one hand, this second negation increases the representational power of the language, it may also introduce contradictory information in programs. Therefore, it is necessary to attribute some meaning to contradictory programs and to be able to deal with contradiction. The paraconsistent version of the $WFSX$ semantics, $WFSX_P$, attributes meaning to contradictory programs and is used as a tool by the revision mechanism that restores consistency to contradictory programs. This revision mechanism may be used to perform several kinds of reasoning, as we will see bellow.

An extended logic program (ELP) is a set of rules $H \leftarrow B_1, \ldots, B_n, not\ C_1,$ $\ldots, not\ C_m$ (m,n $\geq$ 0), where $H, B_1, \ldots, B_n, C_1, \ldots, C_m$ are objective literals. An objective literal is either an atom A or its explicit negation $\neg A$. The symbol not stands for negation by default and $not\ L$ is a default literal. Literals are either objective or default literals and $\neg\neg L \equiv L$. The language also allows for integrity constraints of the form $A_1 \vee \ldots \vee A_l \Leftarrow B_1, \ldots, B_n, not\ C_1, \ldots,$ $not\ C_m$ (m,n $\geq$ 0; l $\geq$ 1) where $A_1, \ldots, A_l, B_1, \ldots, B_n, C_1, \ldots, C_m$ are objective literals, stating that at least one of the A_i (i $\geq$ 1), should hold if its body $B_1, \ldots, B_n, not\ C_1, \ldots, not\ C_m$ (m,n $\geq$ 0) holds. Particularly, when $A = \bot$, where $\bot$ stands for *contradiction*, it means that a contradiction is raised when the constraint body holds. The set of all objective literals of a program P is the extended Herbrand base of P denoted by $\mathcal{H}(P)$. In order to attribute meaning to ELP programs, we need to the notions of interpretation of ELP clause[2]. Roughly, an interpretation of an ELP program is a set of literals that verifies the coherence principle: if $\neg L \in T$ then $L \in F$. A literal L is true in an interpretation I if $L \in I$, L is false in I if $not\ L \in I$, and L is undefined, otherwise. An interpretation I is a model for program P iff, for every clause L in P, $I \models_P L$.

2.1 Program Revision and Non-Monotonic Reasoning

As we stated before, due to the use of explicit negation, programs may be contradictory. In order to restore consistency in programs that are contradictory with respect to $WFSX$, the program is submitted to a revision process that relies on the allowance to change the truth value of some set of literals. This set of literals is the set of *revisable literals*, and can be any subset of $\mathcal{H}$ for which there are no rules or there are only facts in the program. No other restriction is made on which literals should be considered revisable. They are supposed to be provided by the user, along with the program. The revision process changes the truth value of revisable literals in a minimal way and in all alternative ways of removing contradiction. *Minimally revised programs* can be defined as those programs obtained from the original one after modifying the subsets of revisable literals.

The ability to represent negative information, along with a well-defined procedure that restores consistency in logic program, makes ELP suitable to be used to perform different forms of non-monotonic reasoning [AP96]. In particular, we are interested in two of these forms of non-monotonic reasoning, namely *defeasible reasoning* and *abductive reasoning*.

Defeasible Reasoning A defeasible rule is a rule of the form *Normally if A then B*. ELP allows us to express defeasible reasoning and to give meaning to a set of rules (defeasible or not) when contradiction arises from the application of the defeasible rules. To remove contradiction, we revise the truth value of revisable literals in the body of the defeasible rules

---

[2] For a formal definition, see [AP96].

We use defeasible reasoning to select a consistent subset of the agent's desires that will constitute its intentions (in section 4).

Abductive Reasoning Abductive reasoning consists of, given a theory T and a set of observations O, to find a theory Δ such that $T \cup \Delta \models O$ and $T \cup \Delta$ is consistent. In the ELP context, an abductive framework P' is a tuple $\langle P, Abd, IC \rangle$, where P is an extended logic program, Abd is the set of abducible literals and IC is the set of integrity constraints. An observation O has an abductive explanation Δ iff $P' \cup \Delta \models_P O$ and $P \not\models_P \Delta$. We may abduce a theory Δ that explains such observations making each of these observations O a new integrity constraint $O \Leftarrow$ and revising the program with revisable set Abd (recall that a program is contradictory iff for some literal L in program P, $P \models L$ and $P \models \neg L$, or a constraint is not satisfied). We use abductive reasoning to determine if an agent believes there is a possible course of actions that satisfies a desire (in section 4).

Preferred Revisions Sometimes, it may be necessary to state that we do not only want the minimal revisions provided by the formalism, but also that we prefer revisions that have a certain fact only after finding that no other revisions including other facts exist. The ELP formalism allows us to express preferences over the order of revisions using a labeled directed acyclic and/or graph defined by rules of the form[DNP94] $Level_0 \ll Level_1 \wedge Level_2 \wedge \ldots Level_n (n \geq 1)$. $Level_i$ nodes in the graph are preference level identifiers. To each of these levels is associated a set of revisables denoted by $\mathcal{R}(Level_i)$. Rules like the one above for $Level_0$ state that we want to consider revisions for $Level_0$ only if, for some rule body, its levels have been considered and there are no revisions at any of those levels. The root of the preference graph is the node denoted by **bottom**.

We use preference specification when selecting the most appropriate subset of desires that will be adopted as intentions (in section 4).

3 The Event Calculus

When we reason about pro-attitudes like desires and intentions, we need to deal with properties that should hold at an instant of time and with actions that should be executed at a certain time. Therefore, in order to represent them and to reason about them, we need to have a logical formalism that deals with actions and time. In this work, we use a modified version of the Event Calculus (EC) proposed in [Qua97,QL97]. This version of the EC allows events to have a duration and an identification, instead of being instantaneous and identified to the instant of time the event occurs, as in [Mes92]. As a consequence, events may occur simultaneously.

The predicate *holds_at* defining the properties that are true at a specific time is:

$$holds\_at(P, T) \leftarrow happens(E, T_i, T_f), \tag{1}$$
$$initiates(E, T_P, P), T_P < T, T_P >= T_i,$$

$$persists(T_P, P, T).$$

$$persists(T_P, P, T) \leftarrow not\ clipped(T_P, P, T). \tag{2}$$

$$clipped(T_P, P, T) \leftarrow happens(C, T_{ci}, T_{cf}), terminates(C, T_C, P), \tag{3}$$
$$T_C >= T_{ci}, not\ out(T_C, T_P, T).$$

$$out(T_C, T_P, T) \leftarrow (T \leq T_C); (T_C < T_P). \tag{4}$$

The predicate $happens(E, T_i, T_f)$ means that event E occurred between T_i and T_f; $initiates(E, T, P)$ means that event E initiates P at time T; $terminates\ (E, T, P)$ means that event E terminates P at time T; $persists(T_P, P, T)$ means that P persists since T_P until T (at least). We assume there is a special time variable Now that represents the present time. Note that a property P is true at a time T ($holds\_at(P, T)$), if there is a previous event that initiates P and if P persists until T. P persists until T if it can not be proved by default the existence of another event that terminates P before the time T. We need additional rules for the relation between not holding a property and holding its negation and we also need to define the relation between the two kinds of negation:

$$holds\_at(\neg P, T) \leftarrow \neg holds\_at(P, T). \tag{5}$$

$$\neg holds\_at(P, T) \leftarrow not\ holds\_at(P, T). \tag{6}$$

The predicates that will be abduced need to be related by some integrity rules, namely:

$$\perp \Leftarrow happens(E, T_{1i}, T_{1f}), happens(E, T_{2i}, T_{2f}), \tag{7}$$
$$not(T_{1i} = T_{2i}, T_{1f} = T_{2f}).$$

$$\perp \Leftarrow happens(E, T_i, T_f),\ not(T_f < T_i). \tag{8}$$

$$\perp \Leftarrow happens(E, T_i, T_f), not(act(E, A)). \tag{9}$$

that state, respectively, that events cannot be associated to different time intervals, that events cannot have a negative duration and that events must have an associated action.

The EC allows us to reason about the future, by hypothetically assuming a sequence of actions represented by $happens/3$ and $act/2$ predicates and verifying which properties would hold. It also allows us to reason about the past. In order to know if a given property P holds at time T, the EC checks what properties remain valid after the execution of the actions that happened before T. We are now ready to define the agent's model.

4 The Model of Intentions

In this section, we present our model of agents. We take a mentalistic approach, i.e., we define agents in terms of their mental states and we characterize the agent's behavior in terms of these mental states. Initially, we define what mental states agents posses and how these mental states relate to each other. Afterwards, we characterize the dynamic aspects of agents' behavior, namely how agents decide what to do (how they choose their intentions) and how and when agents reconsider their decisions.

4.1 The Mental States

Mental states are divided in two major categories: *information attitudes* and *pro-attitudes*[Sea84]. Information attitudes relate to the information an agent has about the environment where it lives, those that tend to reflect the state of the world, precisely *knowledge* and *beliefs*. Pro-attitudes are those that are related to actions and somehow lead the agent to act, that tend to make the agent modify the world in order to fit its mental states, i.e., attitudes like desires, intentions, obligations and so on. What exact combination of such mental states is adequate to describe an agent in a certain environment is no consensus. Very often, in the philosophical literature (see [Sea84], for instance), desires and beliefs have been used as the two basic mental states to define an intelligent agent. All the explanations of rational actions, and consequently all the other mental states, could be reduced to them. Nevertheless, according to Bratman[Bra87,Bra90], a third mental state, *intentions*, should be considered. In his detailed analysis, where he describes the relation among those three mental states — beliefs-desires-intentions (BDI), Bratman argues that, since agents are assumed to be resource-bounded, they cannot continuously evaluate their competing beliefs and desires in order to act rationally. After some reasoning, agents have to commit to some set of choices. It is this choice followed by a commitment that characterizes the intentions.

We start by defining desires. Desires are related to the state of affairs the agent eventually wants to bring about. But desires, in the sense usually presented, does not necessarily drive the agent to act. That is, the fact of an agent having a desire does not mean it will act to satisfy it. It means, instead, that before such an agent decides what to do, it will be engaged in a reasoning process, confronting its desires (the state of affairs it wants to bring about) with its beliefs (the current circumstances and constraints the world imposes). It will choose those desires that are possible according to some criteria it will act upon them. In other words, desires constitute the set of states among which the agent chooses what to do. Notice that, since agents are not committed to their desires, they need not to be consistent, neither with other desires nor with other mental states.

Definition 2 (Desires Set). The *desires* of an agent is a set $\mathcal{D}$ of ELP sentences of the form $desires(D, P, T, A) \leftarrow Body$, where D is the desire identification, P is a property, T is a time point and A is list of attributes. *Body* is any conjunction of literals. An agent desires that a property P holds at time T iff $desires(D, P, T, A) \in \mathcal{D}$, for some D and some A.

Our definition of desires allows the agent to have a desire that a certain property holds (or does not hold) in a specific instant of time (when T is instantiated). *Desires/4* clauses may be facts, representing states the agent may want to achieve whenever possible, or rules, representing states to be achieved when a certain condition holds. The attributes associated to each desire define properties, like urgency, importance or priority[Bea94] that are used by to agent to choose the most appropriate desire (see bellow).

Beliefs constitute the agent's information attitude. They represent the information agents have about the environment and about themselves. Such information includes time axioms and action descriptions (see 3, along with agent capabilities.

Definition 3 (Beliefs Set). The *beliefs* of an agent is a consistent extended logic program $\mathcal{B}$, i.e. $\forall b \in \mathcal{B}.\mathcal{B} \not\models_P b$. An agent believes L iff $\mathcal{B} \models_P L$.

We assume that the agent continuously updates its beliefs to reflect changes it detects in the environment. Describing the belief update process is beyond the scope of this paper. We just assume that, whenever a new belief is added to the beliefs set, consistency is maintained.

As we stated before, intentions are characterized by a *choice* of a state of affairs to achieve, and a *commitment* to this choice. Thus, intentions are viewed as a compromise the agent assumes with a specific possible future. This means that, differently from desires, an intention may not be contradictory with other intentions, as it would not be rational for an agent to act in order to achieve incompatible states. Also, intentions should be supported by the agent's beliefs. That is, it would not be rational for an agent to intend something it does not believe is possible. Once an intention is adopted, the agent will pursue that intention, planning actions to accomplish it, re-planning when a failure occurs, and so. These actions, as means that are used to achieve intentions, must also be adopted as intentions by agents.

Definition 4 (Intentions Set). The *intentions* of an agent is a set $\mathcal{I}$ of ELP sentences of the form *intends_that*(I, P, T, A) or of the form *intends_to*(I, Act, T, A), where I is the intention identification, P is a property, T is a time points, A is a list of attributes and Act is an action, and such that

1. $\forall intends\_that(I, P, T, A) \in \mathcal{I}.(Now \leq T)$
2. $\forall intends\_to(I, Act, T, A) \in \mathcal{I}.(Now \leq T)$
3. $\forall intends\_to(I, Act, T, A) \in \mathcal{I}.(\mathcal{B} \not\models_P (happens(E, T, T_F), act(E, Act)));$
4. $\exists \Delta.(P' \cup \Delta \not\models_P \bot)$, where
   - P' is the abductive framework $\langle \mathcal{B}, \{happens/3, act/2\}, IC(\mathcal{I})\rangle$
   - $IC(\mathcal{I})$ is set of constraints generated by intentions, defined as
     - "$holds\_at(P, T) \Leftarrow$", for every *intends_that*(I, P, T, A) in $\mathcal{I}$;
     - "$happens(E, T, T_f) \Leftarrow$" and "$act(E, Act) \Leftarrow$" for every *intends_to*$(I, Act, T, A)$ in $\mathcal{I}$;

An agent intends that a property P holds at time T iff *intends_that*$(I, P, T, A) \in \mathcal{I}$. A agent intends to do an action Act at time T iff *intends_to*$(I, Act, T, A) \in \mathcal{I}$.

The definition of intentions enforces its rationality constraints. Conditions 1 and 2 state that an agent should not intend something at a time that has already past. Condition 3,the non-triviality condition[CL90] states that an agent should not intend something it believes is already satisfied or that will be satisfied with no efforts by the agent. Condition 4 states that an agent only intends something it believes is possible to be achieved, i.e., if it believes there is a course of actions that leads to the intended state of affairs.

Notice that we take some measures to avoid the *side-effect problem*[Bra90]. Bratman states that *an agent who intends to do a α an believes that doing α would require it to do β does not have to also intend β*. In our definition, an agent does not intend the *side-effects* of its intentions, as the side-effects are not in the intentions set[3]. To fully avoid this problem, it is also important, when we define dynamic aspects of intentions, namely how to originate intentions and how and when to revise them, that we characterize commitment in a way that side-effects of adopted intentions do not prevent agents from adopting intentions, neither that side-effects make agents revise their intentions.

4.2 Originating Intentions

Once we have characterized intentions and related mental states, it is necessary to define its dynamic aspects, namely how agents select intentions and when and how agents revise selected intentions. In order to illustrate the forthcoming definitions, we introduce the following example.

---

[3] This is similar to the belief base approach, but it is simpler because we do not have to include the derivations in the base, as with belief bases.

Example 5 (The Office Robot). In a building with several offices, there is a robot that transport mail from one office to another, when it is ordered to. Also, the robot has to be careful not to let his battery go out of charge, what would prevent it from performing its tasks. The robot's desires and beliefs are:

Desires

$$desires(1, exec\_order(O), T, [0.6]).$$
$$desires(2, charged, T, [1.0]).$$

Beliefs

$$initiates(E, exec\_order(O), T) \leftarrow holds\_at(is\_order(O), T),$$
$$holds\_at(O, T).$$
$$initiates(E, movemail(Orig, Dest, Mail), Tf) \leftarrow holds\_at(took\_mail(Mail, Orig), Ti),$$
$$happens(E, Ti, Tf),$$
$$act(E, leave(Mail, Dest)).$$
$$initiates(E, took\_mail(Mail, Origin), Tf) \leftarrow happens(E, Ti, Tf),$$
$$act(E, get(Mail, Orig)).$$
$$terminates(E, took\_mail(Mail), Tf) \leftarrow happens(E, Ti, Tf),$$
$$act(E, leave(Mail, Dest)).$$
$$initiates(E, charged, Tf) \leftarrow holds\_at(low\_charge, T),$$
$$happens(E, Ti, Tf),$$
$$act(E, full\_charge).$$
$$terminates(E, charged, Tf) \leftarrow senses(low\_charge, Ti, Tf).$$
$$initially(charged).$$
$$initially(is\_order(movemail(A, B, C))).$$
$$\bot \Leftarrow exec\_order(O), bat\_charged.$$

Agents choose their intentions from two different sources: from its desires and as a refinement from other intentions. We start by defining the creation of intentions from desires.

Intentions as Selected Desires By definition, there are no constraints on the agent's desires. Therefore, an agent may have contradictory desires, i.e., desires that are not jointly achievable. Intentions, on the other hand, are restricted by rationality constraints (as shown in the previous section). Thus, agents must select only those desires that conform to those constraints. We start by defining those desires that are eligible to be chosen and the notion of candidate desires set.

Definition 6 (Eligible Desires). Let $\mathcal{D}$ be the agent's desires. We call *eligible desires* the set $\mathcal{D}' = \{desires(D, P, T, A) \ / \ [(desires(D, P, T, A) \leftarrow Body) \in \mathcal{D}] \land Now \leq T \ (\mathcal{B} \models_P Body)\}$

Eligible desires are those desires the agent believes are not satisfied. Recall that, according to rationality constraint $1 - 2$ in section 4, its is not rational for an agent to intend something it believes is already achieved or that is impossible. Notice that if a desire is conditional, then the agent should believe this condition is true.

As the initial set of desires, eligible desires may also be contradictory. Therefore, it is necessary to determine those subsets of the eligible desires that are jointly achievable. In general, there may be more than one subset of the eligible desires that are jointly achievable. Therefore, we should indicate which of these subsets are preferred to be adopted as intentions. We do this through the preference relation defined bellow.

Definition 7 (Desires Preference Relation $<_{Pref}$). Let $\mathcal{D}$ be the agent's desires, $\mathcal{D}'$ the set of eligible desires from $\mathcal{D}$, $\mathcal{P}(\mathcal{D}')$ the power set of $\mathcal{D}'$ and $R, S \in \mathcal{P}(\mathcal{D}')$; $imp(R)$ the set of importances of the desires subset R. We say that $R <_{Pref} S$ iff, for $T = max(imp(R))$ such that $\exists X \in imp(S).(X = T)$ and $T' = max(imp(S))$ such that $\exists Y \in imp(R).(Y = T')$, $T' < T$ or $(\exists T \lor \exists T') \land (\#S < \#R)$. We say that R is an *antecedent* of S iff $\exists T \in \mathcal{P}(revisable).[(R <_{Pref} T) \land (T <_{Pref} S)]$

According to this definition, the agent should prefer to satisfy first the most important desires. Additionally to preferring the most important ones, the agent adopts as much desires as it can.

Example 8. Given the set $\mathcal{D}' = \{desires(1, a, U, [0.5]), desires(2, b, U, [0.3]), desires(3, c, U, [0.3]), desires(4, d, U, [0.2])\}$ of eligible desires: (1) for $d_1 = \{desires(2, b, U, [0.3]), desires(4, c, U, [0.2])\}$ and $d_2 = \{desires(1, a, T, [0.5])\}$, we have $(d_2 <_{Pref} d_1)$. That is, d_2 is less preferred than d_1, since $T = 0.5$ for d_2 and $T' = 0.3$ for d_1; (2) for $d_3 = \{desires(3, c, U, [0.3])\}$, we have $d_3 <_{Pref} d_1$, as $T = 0.2$ for d_1 and there is no T' for d_3, but $\#d_3 < \#d_1$.

Notice that the preference relation is not an order relation. For instance, if an agent were to choose between $d_4 = \{desires(2, b, U, [0.3])\}$ and $d_5 = \{desires(3, c, U, [0.3])\}$, based only on the importance of desires and maximization of desires satisfied, it would not prefer either of them. And, indeed, according to the preference relation, we have that neither $(d_4 <_{Pref} d_5)$ nor $(d_5 <_{Pref} d_4)$. Based on this preference order, we define the preference graph that will be used to revise the mental states and the revision process.

Definition 9 (Desires Preference Graph). Let $\mathcal{D}$ be the agent's desires and $\mathcal{D}'$ the set of eligible desires from $\mathcal{D}$. Let *Revisable* be the set $\{unsel(D) \; / \; \exists \; desires(D, P, T, A) \in \mathcal{D}'\}$ and $index : \mathcal{P}(Revisable) \longrightarrow \aleph^+$ a function from the power set of *Revisable* to natural numbers (zero excluded) that attributes a level number to elements of $\mathcal{P}(Rev)$. The *desires preference graph* is the graph defined by

1. $Rev(\text{bottom}) = \{happens(E, T_i, T_f), act(E, A)\}$;
2. $Rev(i) = R \cup \{happens(E, T_i, T_f), act(E, A)\}$, where $R \in \mathcal{P}(Revisable)$ and $i = index(R)$;
3. $i \ll \text{bottom}$, where $i = index(R)$, $R \in \mathcal{P}(Revisable)$ and $\exists S \in \mathcal{P}(Revisable)$. $(S <_{Pref} R)$;
4. $j \ll k_1, \ldots, k_n$, where $j = index(R)$, $k_i = index(S_i)$ $(1 \leq i \leq n)$, $R, S_i \in \mathcal{P}(Rev)$ $(1 \leq i \leq n)$ and R is an antecedent of S.

For the example 8, the preference graph for eligible desires would be:

$Rev(\text{bottom}) = \{happens/3, act/2\}, Rev(1) = \{unsel(4)\}$
$Rev(2) = \{unsel(2)\}, Rev(3) = \{unsel(3)\}$
$Rev(4) = \{unsel(2), unsel(4)\}, Rev(5) = \{unsel(3), unsel(4)\}$
$Rev(6) = \{unsel(2), unsel(3)\}, Rev(7) = unsel(2), unsel(3), unsel(4)$
$Rev(8) = \{unsel(1)\}, Rev(9) = \{unsel(1), unsel(4)\}$
$Rev(10) = \{unsel(1), unsel(3)\}, Rev(11) = \{unsel(1), unsel(2)\}$
$Rev(12) = \{unsel(1), unsel(3), unsel(4)\}, Rev(13) = \{unsel(1), unsel(2), unsel(4)\}$
$Rev(14) = \{unsel(1), unsel(2), unsel(3)\}$
$Rev(15) = \{unsel(1), unsel(2), unsel(3), unsel(4)\}$
$(1 \ll \text{bottom}), (2 \ll 1), (3 \ll 1), (4 \ll 2, 3), (5 \ll 2, 3), (6 \ll 4)$
$(6 \ll 5), (7 \ll 6), (8 \ll 6), (9 \ll 8), (10 \ll 9), (11 \ll 9)$
$(12 \ll 11, 10), (13 \ll 11, 10), (14 \ll 13), (14 \ll 12), (15 \ll 14)$

and every $R(i)$ united with $Rev(\textbf{bottom})$. That is, when revising the eligible desires set, the preferred revisions are those that eliminate first the less important desires, and the least possible amount of desires, as shown in the definition bellow.

Definition 10 (Candidate Desires Set). Let $\mathcal{D}$ be the agent's desires and $\mathcal{D}'$ the set of eligible desires from $\mathcal{D}$ with a preference graph associated to it. We call *candidate desires set* any set $\mathcal{D}'_C = \{desires(D,P,T,A) \; / \; (desires(D, P, T, A) \in \mathcal{D}') \wedge [\exists \; \Delta \; .$ $(\mathcal{B} \cup \Delta \models_P (holds\_at(P, T), \; not \; unsel(D))) \wedge (P' \cup \Delta \not\models_P \perp)]\}$ where $(1)P'$ is the abductive framework $\langle \; \mathcal{B}, \; \{happens(E, T_i, T_f), \; act(E, Act), \; unsel(D)\} \; , IC \rangle$; (2) IC is a set of constraints of the form

- $\{holds\_at(P,T) \Leftarrow Body, not \; unsel(D)\}$ for every $desires(D,P,T,A)$ in $\mathcal{D}'$;
- the constraints $IC(\mathcal{I})$ generated by intentions (see definition 4).

In the revision process, we mix abductive reasoning with defeasible reasoning, where the literal $unsel(D)$ is defeasible. Its intuitive meaning is *"Desire D should not be selected as an intention"*. If the agent believes it is possible to satisfy all of its desires (if it can abduce actions that satisfy all desires and satisfy all constraints), it will find a revision that contains only *happens*/3 and *act*/2. This is enforced by the preference graph with $Rev(\textbf{bottom}) = \{happens(E, T_i, T_f), act(E, A)\}$. When constraints may not be all concurrently satisfied, it means that the adoption of all desires as intentions leads to contradictions, i.e., they are not jointly satisfiable.

Notice that contradictions do not arise if the actions necessary to satisfy two different intentions have contradictory effects. Recall that, according to the EC axioms, a property P holds if there is an action that initiates it or, alternatively, if $\neg P$ implicitly does not hold, and vice-versa for $\neg P$. Therefore, actions that make contradictory properties hold in fact just cancel each other. This allows us to avoid the *side-effect problem*[Bra90]. If we allowed for this kind of situations to raise contradictions, we would be making the agent preclude intentions that have contradictory consequences, but that are not directly contradictory with each other, and making the agent intend the logical consequences of its intentions. On the other hand, if an action necessary to satisfy an intention cancels a property that is also an intention, a constraint is violated and that course of action is rejected. In this case, the revision will try to defeat intentions, changing the truth value of $unsel(D)$ literals. According to the preference graph, it will try to defeat those constraints that represent the less important desires, trying to preserve the maximum of the most important ones.

As we mentioned before, the desires preference relation is not an order relation. Therefore, it is possible to have more than one candidate set after a revision. However, if we consider only achievability and desires atributes as decision criteria, it makes no difference for the agent to adopt any of the candidate desires set[4][JLS93][BH97].

Definition 11 (Primary Intentions). Let $\mathcal{D}$ be the agent's desires, $\mathcal{D}'_C$ a candidate desires set from $\mathcal{D}$. The *primary intentions* of an agent is the set $\{intends\_that(D, P, T, A) \; / \; desires(D, P, T, A) \in Des'_C)\}$

---

[4] The revision process provided by the ELP framework defines a *sceptical revision*[AP96], that is the revision formed by the union of all the minimal program revision. This kind of approach prevents the agent from having to choose one of the minimal revisions. However, for intentions, this is not adequate, since we would like our agents to try to satisfy all the eligible desires it can.

Example 12 (contd. from 5). Suppose the robot has received two orders, *movemail* (101, 105, *letter*) and *movemail* (102, 108, *magazine*). Initially, the robot (who had no intentions) is going to select, among its desires, its intentions. Its eligible desires are

$$desires(1, exec\_order(movemail(101, 105, letter)), T, [0.6]).$$
$$desires(2, exec\_order(movemail(102, 108, magazine)), T, [0.6]).$$
$$desires(3, bat\_charged, T, [1.0]).$$

as all of then have their (null) bodies true and are in time. It is now necessary to verify which desires can be jointly satisfied, computing the candidate desires sets. The preference graph derived from the importance attribute is

$$Rev(\text{bottom}) = \{happens/3, act/2\}, Rev(1) = \{unsel(1)\}$$
$$Rev(2) = \{unsel(2)\}, Rev(3) = \{unsel(1), unsel(2)\}$$
$$Rev(4) = \{unsel(3)\}, Rev(5) = \{unsel(3), unsel(1)\}$$
$$Rev(6) = \{unsel(3), unsel(2)\}, Rev(7) = \{unsel(1), unsel(2), unsel(3)\}$$
$$(1 \ll \text{bottom}), (2 \ll \text{bottom}), (3 \ll 1, 2), (4 \ll 3), (5 \ll 4), (6 \ll 4), (7 \ll 6, 5)$$

with every $Rev(i)$ united with $Rev(\text{bottom})$. There is one candidate desires set, namely $D'_C = \{desires(1, exec\_order(movemail(101, 105, letter)), T, [0.6]), desires(2, exec\_order (movemail (102, 108, magazine)), T, [0.6])\}$, as the robot believes it can perform the following sequence of actions

$$happens(E, T_1i, T_1f), act(E, get(101, letter))$$
$$happens(E, T_2i, T_2f), act(E, get(102, magazine))$$
$$happens(E, T_3i, T_3f), act(E, leave(letter, 105))$$
$$happens(E, T_4i, T_4f), act(E, leave(magazine, 108))$$
$$T_1i < T_1f < T_2i < T_2f < T_3i < T_3f < T_4i < T_4f$$

that brings about both desires. Notice that the robot does not select "charged" to be an intention because its initiation depends on the battery being low, which is not the case. Thus, its primary intentions will be that only candidate desires set.

Intentions as Refinements from Intentions Once the agent adopts its intentions, it will start planning to achieve those intentions. During planning, the agent will form intentions that are relative to pre-existing intentions. That is, they "refine" their existing intentions. This can be done in various ways, for instance, a plan that includes an action that is not directly executable can be elaborated by specifying particular way of carrying out that action; a plan that includes a set of actions can be elaborated by imposing a temporal order on that set[KP93]. Since the agent commits to the adopted intentions, these previously adopted intentions constrain the adoption of new ones. That is, during the elaboration of plans, a potential new intention is only adopted if it is not contradictory with the existing intentions and with beliefs.

Definition 13 (Planning Process, Relative Intentions). Let $\mathcal{I}_P$ be the set of primary intentions. A *planning process* is a procedure that, for each $i \in \mathcal{I}_P$, will generate a set of temporal ordered actions $\mathcal{I}_R$ that achieve i, such $B \cup \mathcal{I}_P \cup \mathcal{I}_R$ is non-contradictory. The set $\mathcal{I}_R$ are the *relative intentions* of the agent.

The non-contradiction condition enforces again the notion of commitment, i.e., once an intention is adopted it constrains the adoption of new intentions.

4.3 Revising Intentions

In the previous section, we defined how the agent chooses its intentions. As we have seen, weighing motivations and beliefs means finding inconsistencies in competing desires, checking valid desires according to beliefs and intentions, resolving constraints imposed by intentions and desires, i.e., very expensive reasoning activities. It is now necessary to define *when* the agent should perform this process.

We argue that it is not enough to state that an agent should revise its intentions when it believes a certain condition holds, like to believe that an intention has been satisfied or that it is no longer possible to satisfy it, as this suggests that the agent needs to verify its beliefs constantly. Instead, we take the stance that it is necessary to define, along with those conditions, a mechanism that triggers the reasoning process without imposing a significant additional burden on the agent. Our approach is to define those conditions that make the agent start reasoning about intentions as constraints over its beliefs. Recall that we assume that an agent constantly has to maintain its beliefs consistent, whenever new facts are incorporated.

Definition 14 (Trigger Constraints from Intentions). Let B be the agent's beliefs set and I its intentions. We add to B the following *trigger constraints*: (1) ($\perp \Leftarrow Now > T$, *not* *rev_int*), for each (*intends_that*(I, P, T, A), *intends_to*(I, *Act*, T, A)) $\in I$; (2) ($\perp \Leftarrow happens(E, T_i, T_f)$, *act*($E$, *Act*), *not rev_int*, for each *intends_to*(I, *Act*, T, A)) $\in I$.

The literal *rev_int* is part of the revisable set of beliefs, and its initial value is *false*. Whenever the agent revises its beliefs and one of the conditions for revising beliefs hold, a contradiction is raised. We identify such contradiction by testing if *rev_int* is in the selected revision for the beliefs set, i.e., if it has to have its truth value modified in order to restore consistency. The intention revision process is triggered when one of these constraints is violated.

Trigger Constraints from Desires The conditions we have defined so far are the usual ones defined by formal models of agents. As we have seen before, this characterization of intentions may lead to some fanatical behavior. Therefore, we need to adopt additional constraints that will avoid those unwanted behaviors. We take the stance that the same reasons that originated intentions may be used to break commitment associated to them[Bra92]. If we accept that an intention is originated from desires, it is reasonable to state that it is not rational to persist with an intention whose reasons are superseded by more urgent or important ones. The agent's normal behavior would be to weigh its competing desires and beliefs, selecting its intentions. The agent would commit to these intentions and they would constitute the filter of admissibility for other intentions. Also, the agent would try to satisfy those intentions, until successful accomplishment, impossibility (as usually defined), or *until some of his other desires that were not selected before would become eligible*, or *until the desires that originated them would not be eligible anymore*, re-activating the revision process that would weigh (again) competing desires and beliefs. Since the notion of commitment is preserved, the agent would not start this process every time there is a change in beliefs, but only if relevant conditions trigger the intention revision process, changing the agent's focus of attention[BC96]. These triggers are determined by the desires pre-conditions. We model this triggers using an approach similar to the normative constraints in [SMP97,Wag96].

Definition 15 (Trigger Constraints from Desires). Let D be the agent's desires and D' the set of eligible desires from D. We define *trigger constraints from desires* as

1. For every $desires(D,P,T,A) \leftarrow Body \in (\mathcal{D} - \mathcal{D}')$ with importance A bigger that the biggest importance in intentions, we define a trigger constraint $\bot \Leftarrow Body$, $not\ rev\_int$;

2. given the set of actions Δ abduced by the agent (see definition 10), for each $desires(D,P,T,A) \in (\mathcal{D}' - \mathcal{D}'_C)$ with importance A bigger that the biggest importance in intentions, we define a trigger constraint $\bot \Leftarrow C_1, \ldots, C_n, not\ rev\_int$, where $Cond_i$ $(1 \leq i \leq n)$ are the conditions the agent could not bring about when selecting the candidate desires set.

The first constraint trigger is formed by the the pre-conditions of those desires that were not eligible and that are more important than those that were evaluated. It means that if the pre-conditions of such desires become true, these desires (that were not considered during reasoning) become eligible. Therefore, it is necessary to re-evaluate desires and beliefs to check if this new desire may be brought about. The second constraint is formed by the pre-conditions of those eligible desires that, although more important, were not relevant when the agent made his choice. Notice that there are no triggers for those desires that were eligible but that were ruled out during the choice of a revision. This is so because they had already been evaluated and they have been considered less important than the other desires. Therefore, it is of no use to trigger the whole process again (i.e., to shift the agent's attention) to re-evaluate them.

Example 16 (contd. example 5). Suppose that, while executing his orders, the robot senses a low battery condition. We would expect him to interrupt his tasks and proceed to recharge. Indeed, as "charged" was an eligible desire but it was not selected as a candidate desire, a trigger constraint of the form $\bot \Leftarrow holds\_at(low\_charge, T), not\ rev\_int$ is added to the robot beliefs set. When it updates its beliefs with "*senses (low_charge, T_i, T_f)*", the constraint is violated, rev_int is the revision that restores consistency and, therefore, the role reasoning procedure to decide what to do starts again.

5 Conclusion and Further Work

The main contribution of this paper is to provide a formal model of intentions that accounts for both static and dynamic aspects of intentions. By static aspects, we mean its relation with desires and beliefs and the properties that this relation has (namely, consistency and avoidance of side-effects). By dynamic aspects, we mean establishing criteria, other than those derived from commitment, to drop intentions (namely, based on the cause-effect relation between desires and intentions). We also define where intentions come from and how the agent chooses its intentions.

We may compare our work to other models of intentions in the literature. The classical model is due to Cohen and Levesque[CL90]. In this model, the authors do not address the question of where and how the agent chooses its intentions, neither they overcome the fanatical behavior caused by the commitment strategy. The same may be said about other models that followed Cohen and Levesque's and that tried to overcome some of its theoretical problems: Rao and Georgeff[RG91] tried to solve the side-effect problem present in [CL90] introducing the notions of strong and weak realism; Konolidge and Pollack[KP93] also tried to solve the side-effect problem using non-normal modal logics, where the solution were embedded in the semantics; Singh[Sin94] introduces the notion of know-how and defines communication and multi-agent interaction using its model, but he does not treat the question of the origins of intentions nor how to relax commitment. Van Linder et ali[vLvdHM95] model the origin and choice of intentions and provide a formalism that can be extended to model other pro-active attitudes, but they do not provide any improvements on the notion of commitment. All these works have also in common the fact that their models are based on modal logics and, therefore, may be just used to specify agents. We are, on the other hand, heading to define a computational theory of agency that has an underlying architecture, the one partially described here. This computational theory will allow us to specify and prove properties about the agents, as well as to execute such an specification to test if the agents behave like expected. Our choice of the logical formalism has been deeply influenced by this long term goal, since it is formal and computationally tractable. This concern with the computational aspects of the agent models can also be found in [Rao96].

Our work has many similarities with the one of Gaspar et ali[GC95]. Although they use a different formalism (that is not so computationally tractable as ours), both works have many objectives in common: to address the question of the origin of intentions, to have a computational model, to revise intentions. While we concentrate on the relation between desires and intentions and use this relation to relax commitment, they focus on the evolution of plans and communication, and on how this affects the stability of intentions. In order to have a complete treatment of these issues, both aspects are important and must be integrated. This is our next step in the development of our model.

References

[AP96]   J.J. Alferes and L.M. Pereira. *Reasoning with Logic Programming*. Springer-Verlag, Berlin, DE., 1996. Lecture Notes in Artificial Intelligence Series (LNAI 1111).

[BC96]   L.M. Botelho and H. Coelho. Agents that rationalize their decisions. In *Proceedings of the II International Conference on Multi-Agent Systems*, Kyoto, Japan, 1996. AAAI Org.

[Bea94]   L. Beaudoin. *Goal Processing in Autonomous Agents*. PhD thesis, Birmingham University, Birmingham, UK, august 1994.

[BH97]   J. Bell and Z. Huang. Dynamic goal hierarchies. In *Proceedings of the Second Workshop on Practical Reasoning and Rationality*, London, England, 1997. AISB Workshop Series.

[Bra87]   M.E. Bratman. *Intentions, plans and practical reasoning*. Harvard University Press, Cambridge, MA, 1987.

[Bra90]   M.E. Bratman. What is intention? In P.R. Cohen, J.L. Morgan, and M. Pollack, editors, *Intentions in Communication*, chapter 1. The MIT Press, Cambridge, MA, 1990.

[Bra92]   M. Bratman. Planning and the stability of intentions. *Minds and Machines*, 2:1–16, 1992.

[CL90]   P.R. Cohen and H.J. Levesque. Intention is choice with commitment. *Artificial Intelligence*, 42:213–261, 1990.

[DNP94]   C. Damásio, W. Nejdl, and L.M. Pereira. Revise: An extended logic programming system for revising knowledge bases. In *Knowledge Representation and Reasoning*. Morgan Kaufmann inc., 1994.

[GC95]   G. Gaspar and H. Coelho. Where do intentions come from?:a framework for goals and intentions adoption, derivation and evolution. In C. Pinto-Ferreira and N.J. Mamede, editors, *Proceedings of the Seventh Portuguese*

Conference on *Artificial Intelligence (EPIA'95)*, Berlin, Germany, 1995. APIA, Springer-Verlag. Lecture Notes on Artificial Intelligence (LNAI 990).

[JLS93]   P.N. Johnson-Laird and E. Shafir. The interaction between reasoning and decision making: an introduction. *Cognition*, 49:1–9, 1993.

[KP93]   K. Konolige and M. Pollack. A representationalist theory of intentions. In *Proceedings of the XII International Joint Conference on Artificial Intelligence (IJCAI'93)*, Chambéry, France, 1993. IJCAI inc.

[Mes92]   L. Messiaen. *Localized abductive planning with the event calculus*. PhD thesis, Katholieke Universiteit Leuven, Leuven (Heverlee), 1992.

[QL97]   J. Quaresma and J.G. Lopes. A logic programming framework for the abduction of events in a dialogue system. In *Proceedings of the Workshop on Automated Reasoning*, London, England, 1997. AISB Workshop Series.

[Qua97]   P. Quaresma. *Inferência de Atitudes em Dialogos*. PhD thesis, Universidade Nova de Lisboa, Lisbon, Portugal, june 1997. In Portuguese.

[Rao96]   A.. Rao. Agentspeak(1): Bdi agents speak out in a logical computable language. In *Proceedings of the European Workshop on Modelling Autonomous Agents and Multi-Agents Worlds 1996 (MAAMAW'96)*, Berlin, Germany, 1996. Springer-Verlag.

[RG91]   A.S. Rao and M.P. Georgeff. Modelling rational agents within a bdi-architecture. In R. Fikes and E. Sandewall, editors, *Proceedings of the Knowledge Representation and Reasoning'91 (KR&R'91)*, San Mateo, CA., 1991. Morgan Kauffman Publishers.

[Sea84]   J. Searle. What is an intentional state? In H. Dreyfuss and H. Hall, editors, *Husserl, Intentionality and Cognitive Science*, volume 42, pages 213–261. 1984.

[Sin94]   M. Singh. *Multiagent systems: a theoretical framework for intentions, know-how, and communications*. Springer-Verlag, Heidelberg, Germany, 1994. Lecture Notes in Artificial Intelligence (LNAI 799).

[SMP97]   M. Schroeder, I.A. Móra, and L.M. Pereira. A deliberative and reactive diagnosis agent based in logic programming. In *Proceedings of the Intelligent Agents III: Agent Theories, Architectures and Languages*, Budhapest, Hungary, 1997. ECAI Org. Lecture Notes in Artificial Intelligence (LNAI 1193).

[vLvdHM95]   B. van Linder, W. van der Hoek, and J.-J.C. Meyer. Formalising motivational attitudes of agents: on preferences, goals and commitments. In *Proceedings of the Intelligent Agents II: Agent Theories, Architectures and Languages*, Montreal, Canada, 1995. IJCAI Org. Lecture Notes in Artificial Intelligence (LNAI 1037).

[Wag96]   G. Wagner. A logical and operational model of scalable knowledge and perception-based agents. In *Proceedings of the European Workshop on Modelling Autonomous Agents and Multi-Agents Worlds 1996 (MAAMAW'96)*, Berlin, Germany, 1996. Springer-Verlag.

Multi-agent Negotiation Algorithms for Resources Cost Estimation: A Case Study

José Manuel Fonseca[1]   Eugénio de Oliveira[2]   Adolfo Steiger-Garção[1]

[1] Departamento de Electrotécnia da Universidade Nova de Lisboa
2825 Monte de Caparica, Portugal
{jmf,asg}@uninova

[2] Departamento de Electrotécnia da Universidade do Porto
Rua dos Bragas, 4099 Porto, Portugal
eco@garfield.fe.up.pt

Abstract. In this paper we describe appropriate negotiation protocols we have developed for a multi-agent system whose aim is to advice on distributed resources selection, as well as cost estimation, in big civil construction companies. Prices of each specific resource have an influence on the results of the negotiation algorithm which leads to the best agents (resources) coalition for a given task. Moreover, several interesting problems have been addressed in order to make agents negotiation strategies more competitive and adequate. This is the case of the "self depreciation problem" which arises when an agent (a resource) belongs to more than one coalition which alters its own behaviour during the competition between those coalitions. Our negotiation protocol and agents strategies are able to provide the company with a precise idea about the respective importance of each resource and reach a solution, i.e. find the best set of resources, to deal competitively with the task in hands. Another important factor our approach takes into account during agents negotiation, is the influence of time (date of task announcement, starting and ending task dates) which may guide each agent negotiation strategy according with a forecast of their own employment possibilities in the future. We conclude the paper with a description of a realistic example in the civil construction domain, which illustrates the concepts we have developed.

1 Introduction

The increase on communication facilities strongly characterises the final decade of this century. The commercial barriers are nowadays decreasing both by political and technological reasons with electronic commerce promising to radically transform business [Kam97]. These facts lead companies to the necessity of an increasingly optimised management due to the harder and harder competition in a more and more global market. This is true also in the Civil Construction sector. The solution is often the optimisation of the internal processes and sometimes even the radical change of the existing ones. This problem is addressed by the BPR (Business Process Re-engineering) science [Cou94]. However, implemented in an incremental or in a revolutionary way, BPR always stress the necessity of improvement of the existing technology and the introduction of new technology.

Resource management and budget estimation are very important activities for a Civil Construction company. The high price of the involved resources and the unpredictability of the environment turn this problem specially hard. The usual solution nowadays in many companies in this field of activity is to select an "appropriated" resource and estimate an overprice that can cover any surprises. This process must be revised because it means that the competitiveness of the company is highly prejudiced. As it is explained in the next paragraph, MACIV project is dedicated to the development of a Multi-Agent System (MAS) for resources management and price estimation specially for that kind of companies.

In this paper we are dedicating special attention to the price calculation mechanism to be used by agents in the framework of a multi-agent system developed for the MACIV project [Fon96]. The economical options are presented and justified, as well as the negotiation algorithm specially designed for the adaptation of costs calculation to the company economical conditions. Finally, some small examples are used to illustrate the results obtained with agents including the described algorithms.

2 MACIV project overview

MACIV project is dedicated to the development of a Multi-Agent System for resource management and budget estimation on civil construction companies. This is usually a highly complex problem due to the great number of heterogeneous entities, geographically distributed over a wide area constituting a fertile scenario for the application of Distributed Artificial Techniques. In fact, this is an inherently distributed problem because all medium and large building companies have many different building storing and managing sites, geographically distant from each other. There is usually a great resources diversity giving the opportunity for a very rich and interesting modelling. Moreover, the agents functions multiplicity, the high dynamics of the environment and the easy task decomposition are challenging characteristics that appeal to the appliance of a MAS based system.

The goal of our system is real-time resources management and the achievement of a correct budget evaluation as well as an adequate resources utility estimation. The system's input is the output of the planning department (a sequence of tasks to be performed) and its result, the set of the more appropriated resources to execute those tasks together with a price estimation for the tasks execution. The system will also support the replanning of the tasks when unexpected occurrences happen as well as when new demands introduced by any user in the system. To achieve our goals we opted for a very detailed modelling - we use one software agent per each physical resource - which allows us to introduce in the system a large amount of information about each resource leading to a great optimisation in the use of each equipment or worker. This leaded us to a system that can be compared to a society of artificial agents behaving in a market oriented style [Wel94].

It is a current strategy for the great majority of large companies to decentralise control as well as economical management. Usually, each construction site has its own local economic parameters and tries to decide in a competitive way regarding all other sites, trying to maximise its own profits. In our systems we even follow this strategy more deeply. Through the use of detailed models, each resource also has its own "economic parameters". Therefore, a market-like behaviour is expected from the agents that compete to get the most adequate tasks for the best possible price.

In such a system, there are usually a large number of entities. The large number of agents that represent these entities, has motivated the introduction of communication facilitators [Gen94; Oli95], one in each site, in order to reduce the communication overhead. Their main function is the routing of messages to the adequate agents.

When any single agent is created, it must declare to its local facilitator all its capabilities. Also, when a new site becomes active, the respective facilitator announces its presence to all other facilitators. When a new announcement is sent out, it can be sent out by means of the announcing agent to the local facilitator which has then the responsibility to convey it both to the other facilitators and to the local agents which previously have declared interests on the subject (capabilities to execute that specific task). By means of this Facilitator-based structure, a large number of possible messages is avoided when compared to the classical broadcasting protocols. The agents in our systems are mainly characterised by a great autonomy, self-interest, truthfulness and mobility. This system, which encompasses our main application requirements, was the motivation for the development of the algorithms presented in this paper and will be the immediate target for their application.

As we will see, the final result of the system will be the best resource to perform the requested activity and a set of three prices: the ideal price, the absolute minimum price and the negotiated price. This latter value gives the operator an idea about the economical cost of the activity thus reflecting the importance of the involved resource on the companies' internal market not just at that moment but also having in mind the remaining period until that particular activity takes place.

3 Individual price calculation

Accordingly to the Net Present Value (NPV) criterion [Pin95], a resource is considered worthwhile, if the present value of the expected cash-flows in the future is higher than it's actual cost:

$$NPV = -C + \frac{\pi_1}{(1+R)} + \frac{\pi_2}{(1+R)^2} + \ldots + \frac{\pi_N + V_r}{(1+R)^N} = -C + \sum_{i=1}^{N} \frac{\pi_i}{(1+R)^i} + \frac{V_r}{(1+R)^N} > 0 \qquad (1)$$

where C is the amount of investment, R the discount rate that is used to discount the future stream of profits (it can be a market interest rate or some other rate), N the number of years that we expect the investment to generate profits, π_i the profit of year i and V_r the residual value of the equipment after N years of usage.

In order to simplify the previous equation, we can consider the annual profits constant along the life time of the investment ($\forall_{i \in [1.N]} \pi_i = \pi$). Using this simplification the minimum value for the annual incoming will be:

$$\pi > R \frac{C(1+R)^N - V_r}{(1+R)^N - 1} \qquad (2)$$

For this analysis the inflation and the risk of the investment have also to be taken into account. Inflation is automatically considered provided that the annual cash flow π and the discount rate R are both nominal or real values[1]. The risk of investment is usually considered by the increase of the discount rate by adding a risk premium to the risk-free rate R. Therefore, equation 2 can be maintained unchanged.

In order to guarantee any machine a minimum annual cash flow of π, a daily *fixed cost* for each resource in the company, independent of its activity, and equal to the value π divided by the number of usual working days in the year must be introduced.

---

[1] The real interest rate is the nominal interest rate minus the rate of inflation [Sam92].

Therefore, the accounting cost for the activity of any resource will be calculated as:

$$AC = FC + VC + P \qquad (3)$$

where AC is the accounting cost, FC the fixed cost, VC the variable cost of the resource and P the expected profits from that activity. Variable costs are the costs in consequence of the activity - fuel consumption, tyres degradation, etc. The profits P are the way for the resources to compensate the loses caused by inactivity periods due to maintenance programs or unemployment.

Although the accounting cost is correct from the accountant point of view, the economist and managers must have a forward-looking concerning the firm. They also should be concerned about the opportunity cost, the cost associated with opportunities that are foregone by not putting the firm's resources to their highest value use [Pin95]. Therefore, when evaluating what we call the *economical cost - EC -* of performing any activity, we must also consider the two possible alternatives to the present activity: the unemployment with a probability of p_u (where it will get a loss of $FC+P$) or other alternative activity with probability $(1-p_u)$ (where the resource could get an additional profit of $AC-EC$). Therefore, the equation for the economical cost will come:

$$EC = AC + (1 - p_u)(AC - EC) - p_u(FC + P) \qquad (4)$$

Two extreme cases can be pointed out to exemplify the significance of the last equation. Suppose that $p_u=0$ meaning that the resource can be sure that it will get in the future an alternative task. In this case $EC=FC+VC+P$ what is exactly the accounting cost (see equation 4). On the opposite case, $p_u=1$ means that there is no probabilistic chance to get any other task than the current one. In this case $EC=VC$ which means that in the costs calculation for employing that particular resource on that task, only the variable costs must be paid. From the economical point of view, a resource can perform any task (it is suitable for) since it is paid higher than its economical cost. This tell us that a resource will have a negotiation margin between its accounting cost, which we can consider an ideal revenue, and its economical cost that can be seen as a minimum allowable value.

Expressing the activity profit as a percentage p_p of the total cost, $P=p_p(FC+VC)$, equation 4 will became:

$$EC = \frac{FC\left(2 - 2p_u + 2p_p - 2p_u p_p\right) + \left(2 - p_u + 2p_p - 2p_u p_p\right)}{2 - p_u} \qquad (5)$$

As it can easily be seen, the unemployment probability is fundamental in the economical cost calculation. In the next figure the evolution of EC according to the value of p_u for two different agents A and B with $FC=100$, $VC=150$, $P=0\%$ and $FC=300$, $VC=50$, $P=0\%$ respectively is shown.

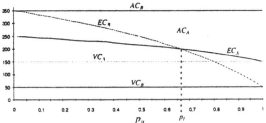

Fig. 1 - Economic cost variation with p_u for two different agents.

To calculate the unemployment probability p_u we propose the following formula:

$$\begin{cases} \text{if } N_c - 1 > N_a \Rightarrow p_u = 1 - \dfrac{N_a}{N_c - 1} \\ \quad \text{if } N_c - 1 \le N_a \Rightarrow p_u = 0 \end{cases} \tag{6}$$

where N_a represents the expected number of new announcements and N_c the number of agents competing for the announced task. This formula is very easy to interpret. If the number of expected announcements is higher than the number of agents competing for its execution it is expected to have activities for all of them and therefore the unemployment probability is zero. Otherwise, only N_a of them will get a task what will lead to the value $1-N_a/(N_c-1)$. While the number of competitors can be supplied by the announcer, the expected number of announcements may be estimated based on the past activities of the system. For this propose, the last years of activity should be registered and analysed in order to get a correct estimation for that parameter.

We may consider our work near to Sandholm's recent work [San95; San96]. However, some differences can be pointed out: we are not only interested on assembling coalitions of agents for getting the best price but our main concern is first to assemble a good coalition to execute the announced task, an then try to calculate a fair price having also in mind each agent's interests as well as the interest of the multi-agent system (a company). Moreover, we have a significant difference in the way we are calculating coalition bids for an announced task. Once we are proposing a price for a presumable future task execution, we are taking into account the dynamics of the environment like, for instance, future agents' opportunities. This concern leads us to the calculation of an agent's economical cost, where some of these factors are reflected, and not just the marginal costs, as it seems to be the case with Sandholm.

4 The negotiation algorithm

We can look at the accounting and economical costs as maximum and minimum acceptable costs for a task execution. In order to adjust the cost accordingly to the company internal market situation, we adopted an iterative algorithm that can be considered as an extension of the well known Contract Net Protocol [Smi80,Dav83]. This protocol is composed by six successive steps:

• 1st step - announcing - the announcer agent sends the task announcement to all the potentially interested agents.

• 2nd step - task evaluation - the interested agents compute the estimated price for the task execution and sends it out to the announcer.

• 3rd step - selection phase - the announcer collects the bids and rejects those coming from agents that don't fulfil (from his point of view) the basic pre-conditions for election. The announcer must then calculate all the possible agents coalitions that can solve the problem. Notice that our concept of coalition comes from the functional point of view. At this stage, our main interest is not to maximise the profits of the agents like in [Ket93,Zlo93,Ros94] but the constitution of teams that only together can solve the problem. The individual profits will result from the negotiation process.

The calculation of all the possible teams is a computationally heavy process. However, it can be efficiently computed for a large number of agents. If the number of agents is too high, a simple selection based on the initial cost/performance ratio can be used to dramatically reduce the number of coalitions under consideration (see [Oli96] for a more detailed discussion).

In every approved coalition one of its members is designated as "coordinator" and will be responsible for the intra-coalition negotiation. This election will be done trying to distribute evenly the responsibilities between all the agents in the process. Finally, the announcer must send out to all coordinators the information that they are coordinators of a coalition, the composition of the coalition team, the individual prices proposed by each of the agents in that coalition and the best price achievable at this stage. In the limit, it will also be possible to have "coalitions" of one single agent.

• 4th step - market manipulation - the announcer sends out to the coordinators the best bid achievable at this stage.

• 5th step - price adjusting - the coordinator of each coalition evaluates the possibility to improve the actual coalition offer. For that, he establishes an intra-coalition negotiation with the coalition partners, as we will see later. If it is not possible to obtain a price lower than the currently best one, the agent quits the coalition from the process sending out a message to the announcer communicating this fact. If a lower price is achievable it sends out the new offer to the announcer.

• 6th step - price selection - the announcer, after receiving all the bids from all the coordinators (offering better conditions or quitting), evaluates the best offer.

The last three steps are repeated until just one coalition remains active or some timeout is reached.

5 The self depreciation problem

With this negotiation protocol we have just described, an interesting problem arises. Suppose that an agent simultaneously belongs to two or more coalitions.

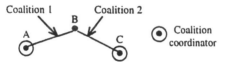

Fig. 2 - The multi-coalition problem.

According to the last section protocol, agent B will participate in the dispute between coalition 1 and coalition 2. Therefore, it will reduce its price whenever it is asked by any of the coordinators (A and C), until it reaches its own lower limit. This is quite unnatural because, if the agent belongs to both coalitions, it should keep its price and try to force the other agents to argue between them. To solve this problem, we adopted what we call the frozen costs solution.

This solution is based on the simple saying "when we are leading, we have no reason to change". Following this tactics, the leading coalition elements will keep their prices without changes until they are approved or they loose the leading position.

Suppose that we are in the situation illustrated in Fig. 2 and the proposed prices for A, B and C respectively are 20, 50 and 30. Coalition 1 generates the best offer (70) and is leading the process. This implies that agents A and B freeze their costs. In this situation, agent C, coordinator of coalition 2, will try to ask to agent B to reduce its price in order to get a better offer than the actual best one, 70. Because B is cost frozen, it disagrees and keeps the initial value. This means that agent C must reduce its own price. Suppose that C can reduce it from 30 to 10 (50+10). The new coalition 2 bid will therefore be 60. Coalition 2 is now leading and agent A must try to beat this new offer. It will then ask B to lower its value but B will deny because it is still in the leading coalition. To overcome that value, agent A must reduce to less than 10 which (let us assume it) is impossible for it. The negotiation process finishes with the victory of coalition 2 proposing the value 60. Note that agent B didn't reduce his value along all the process what is exactly what it was intended because it is considered to be a critical resource which is absolutely needed for that specific task execution.

6 The cost of being important

If this negotiation algorithm is applied to a set of isolated agents a result equivalent to a Vikrey auction [Vic61], where the best offer gets the second best price will be achieved. However, if coalitions are considered and the frozen costs policy is adopted, the results can be quite different. Actually, the final price found by this negotiation algorithm can be quit different from the absolute minimum of all the offers. Let us illustrate our point with a short example:

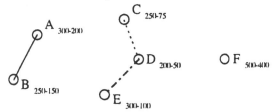

Fig. 3 - A small example of negotiation.

In this example, six agents are competing for a task with maximum and minimum prices as shown in the next table:

Agent	Initial value	Minimum value
A	300	200
B	250	150
C	250	75
D	200	50
E	300	100
F	500	400

Table 1 - Agent's maximum and minimum prices.

The initial values are the values that the agents facing a new announcement and without any information about the offers from the other agents, are proposing to the announcer. The minimum values are the lower acceptable values for each agent. Therefore, these two values represent the upper and lower negotiation limits. Suppose that based on the agents offers, four coalitions have been designated by the announcer: {A,B}, {C,D}, {D,E} and {F} the coordinators being respectively A, C, E and F. Let us see how the coalitions prices evolve along the negotiation process (see Table 2).

To simplify the example all the coordinators adopted a very simple strategy for each new offer: to lower the current best offer in 50 cost units. Due to this very simple strategy, draws happen in almost all the rounds. Notice that, even with any other strategy this situation can always happen. To decide between drawn coalitions, a simple heuristic was adopted: the coalition with a lower initial offer is chosen; if the initial offers are equal the coalition with lower number of elements is chosen; if the number of elements is equal the choice is random.

Coalition	1	2	3	4	5	6
A.B	550	400	350	Quit		
C,D	450	-	350	-	250	-
D.E	500	400	350	300	-	Quit
F	500	400	-	Quit		

Table 2 - Prices evolution along the negotiation process[2].

As it can be seen in the last table, after six negotiation rounds, coalition {C,D} gets the task with a final offer of 250 cost units.

It is interesting to compare the final value achieved by our negotiation algorithm with the absolute minimum values that could be offered by the different coalitions.

Coalition	Minimum value
A.B	350
C.D	125
D.E	150
F	400

Table 3 - Coalitions absolute minimum values.

As it can easily be seen, the winner coalition on our negotiation algorithm has a final price of 250 while the sum of it's elements minimum values is 125. Moreover, coalition {D,E} has a minimum value of 150 and in our algorithm it gives up from beating the value 250. Why? The reason is the presence of agent D on both coalitions. When coalitions {A,B} or {F} are leading the negotiation, agent D agrees with both C and E to lower it's price accordingly to their proposals because it also needs to "fight" against the common competitors. However, when just the two coalitions containing agent D remain, this agent is always on the leading coalition and continuously refuses to lower its price. Therefore, after the withdrawal of the other coalitions, just C and E will lower their prices while D keeps it constant until the end of the process.

This negotiation process seems very interesting to us because, contrary to the well known Vickrey algorithm, it automatically calculates the economical cost of the agents activity accordingly to their social importance. Using this tactics, the company can get a precise idea about the importance of each resource reflecting it on the prices asked to the external entities. This is important for budget estimation when the company is trying to bid for new tasks. However, because it is based on expectations, this choice must be revised later, when the execution date is approaching. Returning to the example presented in figure 1, we have the comparison between two agents where agent A has low fixed costs and high variable costs and agent B has high fixed costs but low variable costs (for simplicity we considered profits zero for both).

As it can be seen, if $p_p=1$, the economical cost of agent A is significantly higher than the cost of agent B. However, if $p_p=0$, agent B has much better economical cost than agent A. Therefore, p_p is below the value p_l agent A represents a better choice than A but not before that. It means that two different situations can be distinguished. When a

---

[2] Leading coalitions don't bid (-).

new task is announced with a significant antecedence the best offer must be selected (based on the economical costs resulting from the presented negotiation algorithms) and the resource reserved for that activity. When the execution date is approaching, the situation must be revised and a new evaluation of the situation must be done. From the new results of the negotiation at that time we will get the resource that will really perform the task.

7 An application example

To exemplify the protocol we described, we will now present a synthetic example containing all the process from the announcement to the final task assignment.

Suppose that, in February 1996 one agent announces the task "Excavation 900m3/hour along 3 weeks starting in the 1st December 1996". This announcement is sent to the facilitators that broadcast it to the potentially interested agents. Due to the current conditions of the company, the following agents are available for the execution of the required task:

Agent	Initial investment	Capacity [m3/hour]	Fixed Costs (Fc)	Variable costs (Vc)	Desired profits	Initial bid
A	5000	360	22.22	4.81	2.70	29.73
B	4000	280	17.77	11.54	2.93	32.24
C	2500	160	11.11	7.21	1.83	20.15
D	6000	280	26.66	5.77	3.24	35.67
E	3500	360	15.55	10.10	2.56	28.21
F	3000	260	13.33	8.65	2.20	24.18

Table 4 - Agents characteristics.

Notice that all the agents shown on the previous table are able to perform the specified task because they declared such capability when they inscribed themselves on the respective facilitator. The calculated costs for this activity as calculated by each agent are shown on the column "Initial proposal". For the fixed costs calculation a residual value (V_r) of 20% of the initial investment was used. As it can be seen in the previous table, none of the agents can actually solve the problem alone. Therefore, the announcer calculates all the interesting coalitions of agents that working together can effectively solve the task. The approved coalitions to solve the problem are shown in the first column of table 8. Notice that all other possible coalitions are redundant (contain at least one superfluous element) or not capable (not powerful enough). The initial bid of each one of the coalitions present on the second column is simply the sum of the individual costs of its agents.

Agent	Pu [%]	Ec/Week
A	55	20.27
B	45	26.23
C	35	17.41
D	40	28.19
E	60	20.45
F	40	20.30

Table 5 - Agents economical costs.

When the announcement is received, the agents also calculate their economical costs that will be their minimum values along the negotiation process (see Table 5). In this table, p_u should have been calculated based on the historical data accessible by the system. However, the values presented here have been manipulated in order to improve comprehensibility on the example.

Coalition	Team	Initial bid	1st round	2nd round	3th round	4th round
1	A,B,D	97.64	Quit			
2	A,B,E	90.18	Quit			
3	A,D,E	93.61	Quit			
4	B,D,E	96.12	Quit			
5	A,B,F	86.15	80.14	72.12	-	Quit
6	A,D,F	89.58	82.10	73.89	Quit	
7	B,C,D,F	112.24	Quit			
8	A,E,F	82.12	-	73.91	66.52	-
9	B,E,F	84.63	78.62	-	70.86	Quit
10	D,E,F	88.06	80.59	Quit		

Table 6 - Bids evolution along the negotiation process.

After the calculation of the coalitions teams and bids, the announcer chooses the coordinators (signalled bold on the coalition teams column) and communicates to them the composition of their teams as well as the best initial offer (82.12). Then, intra-coalitions negotiation starts with the coordinators trying to reduce their own coalitions offers. In this example, the strategy chosen for the coordinators was: "just try to reduce the last offer in 10% steps". From table 7 we can see that five of the ten coalitions quit in the first round. Looking at the coalition 1, if we add up the minimum values for agents A, B and D we get 74.70 which is lower than 82.12. However, this coalition quits. This is because agent A is frozen (it is participating on the leading coalition) and the minimum prices for agents B and D (26.23+28.19) added up to the offer of agent A in the previous round (29.73) is 84.15 which is higher than 82.12. A similar situation happens with all other coalitions quitting in the first round. In this first round four coalitions make new offers. Notice that the leading coalition in one round doesn't bid in the next one. The negotiation process keeps going until just one coalition remains and wins the task. In this case coalition 8 wins having a cost of 66.52. This value is therefore considered to be the minimum acceptable cost for the task execution.

This way, the expert using the system will get the information that any price for the activity going from this minimum value 66.52 to the ideal value 82.12 (or even higher) is worthwhile for the company. Expert final decision must be taken accordingly to his own knowledge of the external market and the company strategy. This cost estimation, calculated a long time prior to the task execution, is based on beliefs about the future activity and will be used for the company to bid externally for new tasks. If the task is awarded to the company the resources that presented the best bid (in this example A, E and F) will be reserved for the task execution.

As we previously said, when the execution date arrives, the problem should be revised. The best resources to execute the task can be different from those that presented the best offer in the budget estimation step. This can happen due to two different reasons: the scenery changed (new machines were acquired, machines went out of service, etc) or the agents beliefs have not be confirmed. When we are really close to the execution date, the unemployment probability of disposable resources is around one. Therefore, the economic cost is close to the variable or marginal cost. This means that the final decision must be based on the variable costs. This means that, in this example, if the resources available at the execution date are the same as they were at the first announcement date (A,B,C,D,E and F) it will be coalition 6, comprising elements A, D and F to win the re-announcement. This new agents coalition will be chosen to perform the task because its marginal cost 19.2 (4.81+5.77+8.65) is the best of all produced by other coalitions.

We believe that this is an interesting result because the costs are initially calculated taking into consideration the opportunities of future commitments that, as they are future events, have to be estimated on a probabilistic basis. Of course that the future can not be predicted exactly and therefore, whenever it is possible, revisions must be done to adjust the estimations to reality. This is what is achieved with this costs revision step at the execution task date.

8 Conclusions and future work

We have here presented what we believe that constitutes a consistent cost calculation framework well suited for task oriented distributed systems including expensive resources as it is the case with typical civil construction companies. To achieve a correct cost estimation, an appropriate negotiation algorithm was introduced and justified.

The introduction of different negotiation strategies and the analysis of the sensibility of the final results to this strategies have been studied. The simulation of a large period of systems life, taking into account possible future opportunities and the evaluation of the individual economical results can allow interesting conclusions about the evaluation of the resources value for the company.

The prediction of the agent's unemployment probability by the system is another interesting research topic. The introduction of induction and linear prediction to the estimation of each resource unemployment probability based on the historical data of the company, seems to be an important point for the correctness of the final results.

The extension of the proposed multi-agent system architecture to include more than one company in what is usually called a virtual enterprise seems to be very promising. Due to the potential opposite interests of the different companies, some of the assumptions which are included in the current model such as "agents truthness" should be removed and the negotiation protocols have to be adapted to this new challenging conditions.

9 References

[Cou94] Coulson-Thomas, C. (1992). Transforming the company. Kogan Page Limited. London.

[Dav83] R. Davis and R. G. Smith, "Negotiation as a Metaphor for Distributed Problem Solving," Artificial Intelligence, vol. 20, pp. 63-109, 1983.

[Fon96] Fonseca J. M., Oliveira E., Steiger-Garção A. (1996). MACIV - A DAI Based Resource Management System. Proceedings of PAAM'96, pages 263-277, London, UK, April 1996. Also to be published on the International Journal of Applied AI.

[Gen94] Genesereth, M., Ketchpel, S. (1994). Software Agents. Communications of the ACM, Vol. 37, No 7, July 1994, Pp. 48-53.

[Kam97]   Kambil, A. (1997). Doing Business in the Wired World. IEEE Computer. May 1997, pp. 56-61.

[Ket93]   Ketchpel, S. 1993. Coalition Formation Among Autonomous Agents. Lecture Notes in Artificial Intelligence 957, pp. 73-88. Springer Verlag.

[Oli95]   Oliveira, E., Garrido, P. (1995). Cognitive Cooperation Facilitators. Proceedings of IEEE Int. Conf. On System, Man and Cybernetics, Vancouver, Canada.

[Oli96]   Oliveira, E., Fonseca, J. M., Steiger-Garção, A. (1996). Agent coalitions, negotiation and strategy adaptation. Proceedings of the 1st Iberoamerican Workshop on Distributed Artificial Intelligence and Multiagent Systems. Pp. 99-108. Xalapa, Mexico.

[Pin95]   Pindyck, R., Rubinfeld, D. (1995). Microeconomics. Prentice Hall International. New Jersey.

[Ros94]   Rosenschein J. R., Zlotkin G. (1994). Rules of Encounter. MIT Press.

[San95]   T. W. Sandholm and V. R. Lesser, "Coalition Formation among Bounded Rational Agents" Conference on Artificial Intelligence (IJCAI-95), Montreal, Canada, pp. 662-669.

[San96]   T. W. Sandholm (1996). "Negotiation among self-interested computationally limited agents". PhD Dissertation. University of Massachusetts at Amherst.

[Smi80]   R. G. Smith and R. Davis, "The Contract Net Protocol: High-Level Communication and Control in a Distributed Problem Solver," in *Transactions on Computers*: IEEE, 1980, pp. 1104-1113.

[Vic61]   Vickrey, W. (1961). Counter speculation, auctions, and competitive sealed tenders. Journal of Finance, 16:8-37.

[Wel94]   Wellman M. P. (1994). Market-oriented programming: some early lessons. Department of Electrical Engineering and Computer Science, University of Michigan. Ann Arbor.

[Zlo93]   Zlotkin G., Rosenschein J. S. (1993). One, Two, Many: Coalitions in Multi-Agent Systems. Proceedings of the Fifth European Workshop on Modelling Autonomous Agents in a Multi-Agent World, Neuchatel, Switzerland.

Parla: A Cooperation Language for Cognitive Multi-agent Systems

A. C. P. L. da Costa   G. Bittencourt

Laboratório de Controle e Microinformática
Departamento de Engenharia Elétrica
Universidade Federal de Santa Catarina
88040-900 - Florianópolis - SC - Brazil
E-mail: { loureiro | gb }@lcmi.ufsc.br

Abstract. One of the main goals of *Distributed Artificial Intelligence* is to devise methods to join a community of *Computational Agents* into a *Multi-Agent System*, where these agents can cooperate to reach common goals. Cooperation in a *Cognitive Agent* community is usually supported by an *Agent Communication Language (ACL)* which allows the agents to exchange knowledge and information through a computer network. In this paper, we propose *Parla*, a high level agent communication language to cognitive multi-agent systems. This language is based on a standard message format, that contains the necessary information for the message integrity, network security and groupware services to be implemented. These services can either be performed by the lower layers of the system or be included in the high level agent communication support. This message format has a specific slot to store the cooperation language expressions. These expressions consist of a primitive name and an argument, which should be a valid expression of a knowledge representation formalism supported by the cognitive agent. The following aspects of the Parla language are presented: language layers, agent communication support requirements, message format, primitive set and primitive semantics. To demonstrate the language use, a cooperation example among four agents is presented. In this example, each agent has its own specific domain of knowledge but, because of global interdependences, cooperation is necessary. This example refers to the recomposition of part of the South Brazil's electrical network.

Content Areas: Agent-Oriented Programming, Distributed AI, Expert Systems, Planning and Scheduling.

1 Introduction

The problem that has originally motivated our research in cognitive multi-agent systems [10] is the recomposition of an electricity transmission network after a blackout has affected part of the network [4]. This task is performed usually by sub-station operators that should follow a pre-determined procedure according to the specific situation of the sub-station in the network. Each of these procedures can be independently codified into an expert system. For practical reasons, these procedures minimize the communication between operators, in detriment of optimal operation of the network. In this kind of problem, each electricity sub-station has its own domain of knowledge. Indeed, given sub-station A, it is not important if it is receiving the necessary electrical energy from unite C or D, the point is whether the received electrical energy is sufficient or not. In the case it is not, the preoccupation is to find out some other station to supply the rest of the necessary electrical energy in this moment. On the other hand, there are global priorities and restrictions that depend on external parameters such as the season, day of the week and hour of the day. Then in our case the question is how Cognitive Agents, with a local domain of knowledge but a global interdependence, should interact and interoperate to perform an intelligent behavior.

Interaction and interoperation among Cognitive Agents to reach common goals require more than a common language understood by these agents. Objectively, the Cooperative behavior in an Agent Community effectively requires the following three elements: a common language; a common understanding of the knowledge and/or information exchanged; and, finally, the ability to exchange whatever is included in the two last elements [6]. In Cognitive Agents Communities, the two last elements refer directly to the knowledge base and knowledge communication mechanisms present in each Agent. In this case, a common knowledge representation formalism is paramount to allow these elements to be effective. The first element, a common language, usually consists in a primitive set, known by all Agents in the community, that informs what is being exchanged and what should be done with this knowledge or information.

Some ACL have already been developed, e.g., *KQML* [6], a language that provides a message format and message handling protocol supporting run-time knowledge sharing and interaction among agents. Exist yet another ACL, Coordination Language *COOL* [1], based on *KQML*, that includes describing coordinator protocol describing. But *KQML* requires special agent to provide some functions as: association of physical address with symbolic names; registration of databases and/or services offered and sought by agents; and communication services. Beside this a three layers structure is adopted in this language, content layer, message layer and communication layer. The content layer bears the actual content of the message, the knowledge or informations. The communication level encodes a set of message which describe the lower level communication parameters (e.g., sender, recipient and communication identifier). The message layer determines the kind of interaction the agents perform. Then another message format and layer attributions is proposed in Parla Language allowing that *the special agent* features, required by *KQML*, should be reduced and this new requirement should take part of Agent Communication Support or to use a distributed programming environment, like ISIS toolkit [2], to play this role.

This paper presents an ACL called Parla. This language is part of a public domain environment for the development of Cognitive Multi-Agent Systems, called *Expert-Coop* [3] [5]. This environment has been used to implement a Cognitive MAS to recompose an electricity transmission network after a blackout has affected part of network. The paper presents the syntax and semantics of the language primitives, the agent communication support requirements and the language layer. Finally, a cooperation example among four agents is presented. In this example, each agent has its own specific domain of knowledge but, because of global interdependences, cooperation is necessary. This example refers to the recomposition a part, called *'Area 1*, of the South Brazil's electrical network.

2 Cooperation Language

2.1 Message Format

The communication process in the Agent Community is performed by message exchange. All these messages are built according to a standard message format.

```
(MESSAGE (TO ...)(FROM ...)(TIME-STAMP ...)
         (ROUND ...)(BODY ...)
         (GRADE ...)(PRIORITY ...)(ALPHA ...))
```

This format consists in a message object with the following slots:

- **from** - the sender agent name.
- **to** - the recipient agent name or group name.
- **time-stamp** - the message time stamp.
- **body** - Any valid Parla primitives followed by one knowledge Representation formalism.
- **round** - contract competition identifiers, when using Contract Competition as cooperation strategy.
- **grade** - a grade, or one of uncertainty representation, to be associated with a given proposal during Contract Competition.
- **priority** - the priority level of the contract competition.
- **alpha** - The Alpha slot is used to associate an alpha cut to a contract competition. Once this alpha cut is associated to a contract competition, the winner proposal must have been a *Grade* higher than the respective alpha value.

Among these slots, **to, from, time-stamp** and **body** must be present in all messages and the others – **grade, round, alpha** and **priority** – are optional. The syntax of the Parla Messages is the following:

```
┌─────────────────────────────────────┐
│                                     │
│           Message Layer             │
│                                     │
└─────────────────────────────────────┘

┌─────────────────────────────────────┐
│                                     │
│         Communication Layer         │
│                                     │
└─────────────────────────────────────┘
```

Fig. 1. Message Layer Structure

2.2 Language Layer

The Parla Language presents two layers (figure 1) : the message layer and the communication layer, like most of the ACL's. The message layer holds a language primitive (e.g., request, announce, confirm, etc) followed by one argument that should be one of knowledge representation formalism supported by the *MAS* environment. In Expert-Coop's case, first-order logic, frames or semantic network formalisms are supported. These primitives inform the Agent what should be done with the knowledge passed as an argument. The message layer holds the logical address of the message target. This address can be an agent's name point-to-point communication, an agent's group name for a multicast, or all to make a broadcast. Then from the message layer view point, that is same Agent view point. The Parla language supports all the ACL communication types: broadcast, multicast and point-to-point. Three other messages slots are held by the message layer: *Round (Rd)* that consists in the *Contract Competition* identification, *Grade (Gd)*, a numerical or fuzzy, like in the Expert-Coop [5] environment, evaluation that is associated to a *Contract Competition Proposal* and *Alpha* an alpha cut [9] associated to a *Contract Competition*. The communication layer encodes some message features which describe the low level communications parameter, such as message's sender and message time stamp.

2.3 Agent Communication Support Requirements

There are some requirements on the Agent Communication Support, to ensure the following assumptions: (i) Total Event Ordering to guarantee that messages will be handle according to the "first in, first out" order [8]; Realiable Broadcast [7], to ensure that messages will be received by all active agents; and a System Fault Tolerance Algorithm to keep an active agents list in all agents. These requirements should be implemented in the Agent Communication Support, such as in Expert-Coop. On the other hand this requirements could be guaranteed using a distributed programming environment, like the ISIS Toolkit [2]. When using a distributed programming environment, the environment primitives should be invoked by the Agent Communication Support.

2.4 Primitives

The Parla Language is composed by the following primitive set:

```
{ ACCEPT, ANNOUNCE, CONFIRM, REFUSE, INFORM
  REQUEST, REPLY, RECALL, SUBSCRIBE, UNSUBSCRIBE}
```

The expressions of the language consists in one of these primitives, followed by an argument. The argument should be a knowledge or information fragment represented in one of knowledge representation formalisms supported by the Agent Community. Each primitive treats its argument according to its function.

- **ANNOUNCE** - The Announce primitive is used to communicate to all active Agents that a Contract Competition was opened. The Contract Competition's Object is passed as argument and it should be represented in one of knowledge representation formalism supported by the Agent Community. This primitive automatically requires that value ALL is attributed to the TO slot and the current time stamp to the $ROUND$ slot.
- **ACCEPT** - the Accept primitive is used by the Agents to inform the Agent that has broadcasted a given *Announce*, that the announced Contract Competition Object may be accepted. When an Agent uses the ACCEPT primitive, he should attribute to the $ROUND$ slot the value received in the respective ANNOUNCE message. An evaluation grade or a fuzzy value, should be associated to the $GRADE$ message slot. Finally, the appropriate knowledge or information fragment about the Contract Competition Object must be passed as argument.
- **CONFIRM** - the Confirm primitive is used, by the Agent who has opened a Contract Competition, to inform another Agent that it wins the Contract Competition identified be $ROUND$ slot value. As in ACCEPT primitive knowledge or information about Contract Competition Object must have be passed as argument.
- **REFUSE** - the Refuse primitive is used by the Agents to inform the Agent that has broadcasted a given *Announce*, that the announced Contract Competition Object was not accept. When an Agent uses the Refuse primitive, he must attribute to the $ROUND$ slot the value received in the respective ANNOUNCE message. In this case, a $GRADE$ slot value is not necessary. A knowledge or information fragment about the Contract Competition Object must be passed as argument.
- **INFORM** - The Inform primitive is used to communicate a fact, information or knowledge. This primitive do not require an answer. The respective knowledge or information fragment must be passed as argument.
- **REQUEST** - Request primitive is used to solicit an information or knowledge from another *agent*. The solicited external information or knowledge, must be passed as argument.
- **REPLY** - Reply primitive is used to return an information or knowledge, solicited by another *agent*. The information or knowledge must be passed as argument.

- **RECALL** - the Recall primitive is used by the Agent, who has opened a Contract Competition, to inform another Agent that it lost the Contract Competition identified be *ROUND* slot value. As in the Recall primitive as knowledge or information fragment about the Contract Competition Object must be passed as argument.

- **SUBSCRIBE** - the Subscribe primitive is used by an external Agent to ask one of the active Agents of the Community to take part of the Community as a member. Two important informations must be passed in the knowledge or information fragment: the new Agent's name and its host name.

- **UNSUBSCRIBE** - the Unsubscribe primitive is used by an Agent to ask another active Agent of the Community to leave the Community. In this case, only the agent's name is necessary to be passed in the knowledge or information fragment.

3 Example

To illustrate the Parla Language use as a ACL in a Cognitive Multi-Agent Community, an cooperation example among four Agents is presented. In this example, each agent has a specific domain of knowledge, but they have a global interdependence that makes cooperation necessary. This example refers to the recomposition of part of the South Brazil's electrical network, after a blackout has affected this area.

Part of the, so called, *Area 1* electrical network is represented in figure 2. Three plants – *Salto Santiago (UHSS)*, *Segredo (SGD)* and *Governador Bento Munhoz (GBM)* – and two substations – *Areia (ARE)* and *Ivaporã (IVP)* – are represented. All these plants have four electrical generators. According to the fluent recomposition process, to send electrical energy from *UHSS* to *IVP* the plant operator must be sure that at least four of twelve electrical generators have been synchronized, that the transmission lines *LT-SGD, LT-ITA, LT-ARE* and *LT-ARE-1* have been turned on and that the connection between *LT-ARE* and *LT-ARE-1* has been made by *ARE*.

The proposed recomposition Cognitive Multi-Agent System consists in the allocation of an agent in *Ivaporã IVP*, and one in each of the following plants: *Segredo SGD, Governador Bento Munhoz GBM* and *Salto Santiago UHSS*.

Once the request to recompose the *IVP* transmission line is made by the *IVP agent*, the *UHSS* agent requests information from *GBM agent* and *SGD agent* about the state of their electrical generators. If the synchronized electrical generators number, in the agent community, is not enough *(e.g., UHSS 1, SGD 1 and GBM 1)* a contract competition is opened by *UHSS agent* and, once a winner has been chosed to supply the necessary number of synchronized electrical generators, they are turned on, then the *IVP agent* request is replayed and the *IVP* transmission line is recomposed. The complete sequence of messages exchanged during one of the situations above described is shown in table 1.

Message Body	From	To	Rd	Gd	T.S.
(REQUEST ((logic (recompose lt uhss-ivp))))	IVP	UHSS			1
(REQUEST ((logic (synchronized-generators x y))))	UHSS	PLAN			8
(REPLY ((logic (synchronized-generators sgd 0))))	SGD	UHSS			12
(REPLY ((logic (synchronized-generators gbm 0))))	GBM	UHSS			15
(ANNOUNCE ((logic (synchronize-generator x 2))))	UHSS	PLAN	26		28
(ACCEPT ((logic (synchronize-generator gbm 2))))	GBM	UHSS	26	1.0	35
(ACCEPT ((logic (synchronize-generator sgd 2))))	SGD	UHSS	26	0.7	37
(ACCEPT ((logic (synchronize-generator uhss 2))))	UHSS	UHSS	26	0.8	42
(CONFIRM ((logic (synchronize-generator gbm 2))))	UHSS	GBM	26	0.8	44
(RECALL ((logic (synchronize-generator x 2))))	UHSS	LOOSERS	26	0.6	48
(REQUEST ((logic (synchronized-generators x y))))	UHSS	PLAN			59
(REPLY ((logic (synchronized-generators sgd 0))))	SGD	UHSS			62
(REPLY ((logic (synchronized-generators gbm 2))))	GBM	UHSS			65
(ANNOUNCE ((logic (synchronize-generator x 2))))	UHSS	PLAN	72		74
(REFUSE ((logic (synchronize-generator gbm 2))))	GBM	UHSS	72		79
(REFUSE ((logic (synchronize-generator sgd 2))))	SGD	UHSS	72		82
(REFUSE ((logic (synchronize-generator uhss 2))))	UHSS	UHSS	72		84
(RECALL ((logic (synchronize-generator x 2))))	UHSS	PLAN	72	0.6	89
(ANNOUNCE ((logic (synchronize-generator x 1))))	UHSS	PLAN	96		98
(ACCEPT ((logic (synchronize-generator gbm 1))))	GBM	UHSS	96	0.6	103
(ACCEPT ((logic (synchronize-generator sgd 1))))	SGD	UHSS	96	0.6	106
(ACCEPT ((logic (synchronize-generator uhss 1))))	UHSS	UHSS	96	0.8	108
(CONFIRM ((logic (synchronize-generator uhss 1))))	UHSS	UHSS	96	0.8	110
(RECALL ((logic (synchronize-generator x 1))))	UHSS	LOOSERS	96	0.6	114
(REQUEST ((logic (synchronized-generators x y))))	UHSS	PLAN			123
(REPLY ((logic (synchronized-generators sgd 0))))	SGD	UHSS			126
(REPLY ((logic (synchronized-generators gbm 2))))	GBM	UHSS			129
(ANNOUNCE ((logic (synchronize-generator x 1))))	UHSS	PLAN	137		139
(ACCEPT ((logic (synchronize-generator gbm 1))))	GBM	UHSS	137	0.6	143
(ACCEPT ((logic (synchronize-generator sgd 1))))	SGD	UHSS	137	0.8	147
(ACCEPT ((logic (synchronize-generator uhss 1))))	UHSS	UHSS	137	0.6	149
(CONFIRM ((logic (synchronize-generator uhss 1))))	UHSS	SGD	137	0.8	151
(RECALL ((logic (synchronize-generator x 1))))	UHSS	LOOSERS	137	0.6	155
(REQUEST ((logic (synchronized-generators x y))))	UHSS	PLAN			163
(REPLY ((logic (synchronized-generators sgd 1))))	SGD	UHSS			166
(REPLY ((logic (synchronized-generators gbm 2))))	GBM	UHSS			169
(REPLY ((logic (recomposed lt uhss-ivp))))	UHSS	IVP			174

Table 1. UHSS Message Log

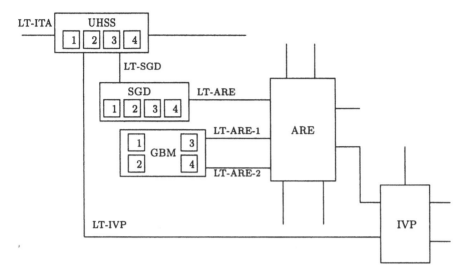

Fig. 2. Fragment of the Electrical Network *Área 1*

4 Conclusion and Future Works

The Parla is presented here as an ACL to Cognitive Agents Communities. The initial primitive set has been developed to an Cognitive Multi-Agent System that uses Contract Competition as cooperation strategy. The language primitive set should be esily encreased to cover other situations. We intend to include new primitives in Parla Language to make it able to cover another agents cooperation strategies. The main advantage of Parla Language is that network services and group services should be implemented either in Agent Communication Support or use a distributed environment programming to play this role. Parla Language is part of Expert-Coop, a public domain environment to Cognitive Multi-Agent System implementation using Contract Competition as agent cooperation strategy. This environment has been used to implement a Cognitive *MAS* to solve electricity network recomposition problem, like the presented example.

Acknowledgments

The authors are grateful to all those that helped in the development of this paper, in particular the LCMI team, the Eletrosul staff and the anonymous referees. The second author is partially supported by *Conselho Nacional de Desenvolvimento Científico e Tecnológico (CNPq)*, grant No. 352017/92-9.

References

1. M. Barbuceanu and M. S. Fox. Cool:a language for describimg coordination in multi agent. *EIL working paper*, pages 1–15, 1994.
2. K. Birman. The process group approach to realiable distributed computing. *Communications of the ACM*, 36(12):37–53, 1993.
3. G. Bittencourt and A.C.P.L. Costa. Expert coop: An environment for cognitive multi-agent system. *Accepted in IFAC'97*, March 1997.
4. D. Cockburn and N. R. Jennings. Archon: A distributed artificial intelligence system for industrial applications. *Foundations of Distributed Artificial Intelligence*, pages 319–344, 1996.
5. A.C.P.L. Costa. *Expet Coop: Um Ambiente para Desenvolvimento de Sistemas Multi-Agente Cognitivos*. Master Thesis, Universidade Federal de Santa Catarina, Laboratório de Controle e Micro Informática, Brazil, 1997.
6. T. Finin, Y. Labrou, and J. Mayfield. *KQML as an Agent Communication Language*. MIT Press, Cambridge, 1995.
7. P. Jalote. *Fault Tolerance in Distributed System*. PTR Prentice Hall, Englewood Cliffs, New Jersey, 1994.
8. L. Lamport. Time, clocks, and ordering of events. *Communications of ACM*, 21(7):558–565, July 1978.
9. S. Sandri, D. Dubois, and H. Prade. Elicitation, pooling and assessement of expert judments using possibility theory. *IEEE Transactions on Fuzzy Systems*, 1995.
10. J.S. Sichman, Y. DEMAZEAU, and O. BOISSER. When can knowledge-based systems be called agents? *Anais do IX Seminario Brasileiro de Inteligencia Artificial*, pages 172–185, Outubro 1992. ISSN 0104-6500.

Vivid Agents Arguing about Distributed Extended Logic Programs*

Michael Schroeder[1], Iara Móra[2], and José Julio Alferes[2,3]

[1] Institut für Rechnergestützte Wissensverarbeitung, University of Hannover, Lange Laube 3,
30159 Hannover, Germany, schroede@kbs.uni-hannover.de
[2] CENTRIA, Universidade Nova de Lisboa, 2825 Monte de Caparica, Portugal,
{idm,jja}@di.fct.unl.pt
[3] D.M., Univ. Évora, Largo dos Colegiais, 7000 Évora, Portugal

Abstract. Argumentation semantics in extended logic programming has been defined in [5,12] for a single agent which determines its believes by an internal argumentation process. In this paper we extend the initial argumentation framework to a multi-agent setting including both argumentation and cooperation. We define inference for multi-agent systems and define an algorithm for inference. We sketch an argumentation protocol and line out by an example how it is implemented using vivid agents [15,13].

Keywords: Multi-Agent Systems, Argumentation, Logic Programming

1 Introduction

In the last 5-10 years researchers have been devoting much work to the semantics of logic programs. Among the different approaches that usually either emphasise an operational or a declarative view argumentation semantics turned out to be a very intuitive approach. Rather than defining a semantics in technical terms argumentation semantics uses the metaphor of argumentation as used in politics, law, discourse, etc. and formalizes a part of it sufficient to give a meaning to extended logic programs. Intuitively, argumentation semantics treats the evaluation of a logic program as an argumentation process, where a goal G holds if all arguments supporting G cannot be attacked anymore. Thus, logic programming is seen as a discourse involving attacking and counterattacking arguments.

While argumentation in rhetorics comprises a variety of figures logic programming can be described in terms of two figures: Reductio ad absurdum- and ground-attack [6] or equivalent rebut and undercut [12]. The former classifies an argument that leads to a contradiction under the current believes and arguments, and the latter an argument that falsifies the premise of one of the current arguments. Argumentation semantics in extended logic programming has been defined in [5,12] for a single agent which

---
* Thanks to Luis Moniz Pereira, Wolfgang Nejdl, Daniela Plewe, and Gerd Wagner. The work is financially supported by JNICT project ACROPOLE PBIC/TIT/2519/95, the Europeu project BMFB/JNICT, and the Brasilian CAPES.

determines its believes by an internal argumentation process. In this paper we extend the initial argumentation framework to a multi-agent setting including both argumentation and cooperation. We define inference for multi-agent systems and define an algorithm for inference. We sketch an argumentation protocol and line out by an example how it is implemented using vivid agents [15,13].

2 Basic Definitions

Since Prolog became a standard in logic programming much research has been devoted to the semantics of logic programs. In particular, Prolog's unsatisfactory treatment of negation as finite failure led to many innovations. Well-founded semantics [8] turned out to be a promising approach to cope with negation by default. Subsequent work extended well-founded semantics with a form of explicit negation and constraints [11,4] and showed that the richer language, called WFSX, is appropriate for a spate of knowledge representation and reasoning forms [9,10,3].

Definition 1. Extended Logic Program, Integrity Constraint
An extended logic program is a (possibly infinite) set of rules of the form $L_0 \leftarrow L_1, \ldots, L_l, \text{not } L_{l+1}, \ldots, \text{not } L_m$ $(0 \le l \le m)$ where each L_i is an objective literal $(0 \le i \le m)$. An objective literal is either an atom A or its explicit negation $\neg A$. Literals of the form $\text{not } L$ are called default literals. The set of all objective literals is called the herbrand base $\mathcal{H}(P)$. A rule with head $L_0 = \bot$ is called *integrity constraint*. The symbol $\bot$ stands for falsity. A program P is inconsistent iff $P \models \bot$, otherwise it is consistent.

The following definitions for argumentation are based on [5,12]. In contrast to the latter we do not distinguish between strict and defensible rules. However, our results can be extended to this direction.

Definition 2. Argument
Let P be an extended logic program. An argument for a conclusion L is a finite sequence $A = [r_n, \ldots r_m]$ of ground instances of rules $r_i \in P$ such that

1. for every $n \le i \le m$, for every objective literal L_j in the antecedent of r_i there is a $k < i$ such that L_j is the consequent of r_k.
2. L is the consequent of some rule of A;
3. No two distinct rules in the sequence have the same consequent.

A sequence of a subset of rules in A being an argument is called subargument. A rule $r \in P$ is called partial argument.

Definition 3. Undercut, Rebut
Let A_1 and A_2 be two arguments, then

- A_1 *undercuts* A_2 iff A_1 is an argument for L and A_2 is an argument with assumption $\text{not } L$, i.e. there is an $r: L_0 \leftarrow L_1, \ldots, L_l, \text{not } L_{l+1}, \ldots, \text{not } L_m \in A_2$ and a $l+1 \le j \le m$ such that $L = L_j$.
- A_1 *rebuts* A_2 iff A_1 is an argument for L and A_2 is an argument for $\neg L$.

– A_1 *attacks* A_2 iff A_1 undercuts or rebuts A_2.

Definition 4. Coherent, Conflict-free

An argument is coherent if it does not contain subarguments attacking each other. A set *Args* of arguments is called conflict-free if no two arguments in *Args* attack each other.

Definition 5. Defeat, Acceptable

Let A_1 and A_2 be two arguments, then

– A_1 *defeats* A_2 iff A_1 is empty and A_2 incoherent or A_1 undercuts A_2 or A_1 rebuts A_2 and A_2 does not undercut A_1.
– A_1 *strictly defeats* A_2 iff A_1 defeats A_2 but not vice versa.
– A_1 is *acceptable* wrt. a set *Args* of arguments iff each argument undercutting A_1 is strictly defeated by an argument in *Args*.

Our notion of acceptability deviates from Prakken and Sartors definition [12] where an argument A_1 is accepted if each *defeating* argument is accepted. Our notion is more credolous and leads to more intuitive results.

Example 6. Consider the program $P = \{a \leftarrow not\ b; b \leftarrow not\ a; \neg a\}$, then $\neg a$ and $b \leftarrow not\ a$ are acceptabel, whereas $a \leftarrow not\ b$ is not. For Prakken and Sartors definition of acceptibility there is no acceptabel argument which contradicts the intuition of $\neg a$ being a fact.

Definition 7. Characteristic Function

Let P be an extended logic program and S be a subset of arguments of P, then $F_P(S) = \{A \mid A$ is acceptable wrt. $S\}$ is called *characteristic function*.

1. A is *justified* iff A is in the least fixpoint of F_P.
2. A is *overruled* iff A is attacked by a justified argument.
3. A is *defensible* iff A is neither justified nor overruled.

Argumentation is closely related to logic programming. While Dung uses argumentation to define a declarative semantics for extended logic programs, Prakken and Sartor's work is driven by their application in legal reasoning. To relate argumentation and extended logic programming, we review WFSX [4], a semantics for extended logic programs.

Definition 8. $\models$ Let P be an extended logic program, then

$$P \models L \text{ iff } P, \emptyset, \emptyset, t \models L$$
$$P, M \models L \text{ iff } P, \emptyset, \emptyset, M \models L$$
$$P, LA, GA, M \models true$$
$$P, LA, GA, M \models (L_1, L_2) \text{ iff } P, LA, GA, M \models L_1 \ \& \ P, LA, GA, M \models L_2$$
$$P, LA, GA, M \models not\ L \text{ iff } P, GA, GA, M \models \neg L \text{ or}$$
$$M = t \ \& \ P, \emptyset, GA, tu \not\models L \text{ or}$$
$$M = tu \ \& \ P, GA, GA, t \not\models L$$
$$P, LA, GA, t \models L \text{ iff } L \notin LA \ \& \ L \leftarrow L_1, \ldots, L_l, not\ L_{l+1}, \ldots, notL_m \in P \ \&$$
$$P, LA \cup \{L\}, GA \cup \{L\}, t \models L_1, \ldots, L_l, not\ L_{l+1}, \ldots, notL_m$$
$$P, LA, GA, tu \models L \text{ iff } L \notin LA \ \& \ P, GA, GA, t \not\models \neg L \ \&$$
$$L \leftarrow L_1, \ldots, L_l, not\ L_{l+1}, \ldots, notL_m \in P \ \&$$
$$P, LA \cup \{L\}, GA \cup \{L\}, tu \models L_1, \ldots, L_l, not\ L_{l+1}, \ldots, notL_m$$

The inference operator has three parameters M, LA, and GA, where M is either t or tu indicating that we want to prove verity (t) and non-falsity (tu), respectively, LA and GA are lists of local and global ancestors that allow to detect negative and positive loops which lead to inference of non-falsity and failure, respectively; for details see [1,2,4]. For consistent programs the above inference operator yields the same results as the argumentation process:

Proposition 9. *Relation of $\models$ and Argumentation*
Let P be consistent. $P,t \models L$, iff L is a conclusion from a justified argument. $P,t \models notL$, iff L is a conclusion from an overruled argument. $P,t \not\models L$ and $P,tu \models L$ iff L is a conclusion from a defensible argument.

Proof sketch: Inference by argumentation is equivalent to WFSX given by bottom-up evaluation of extended logic programs [12], which is in turn equivalent to top-down inference [4]. For inconsistent programs argumentation semantics and WFSX slightly differ. By WFSX a and $\neg a$ can be inferred from the inconsistent program $\{a, \neg a\}$ which is not the case for argumentation semantics [12].

3 Multi-Agent Argumentation

There are two main reasons to extend the single-agent to a multi-agent approach:

1. Given an extended logic program, we want to distribute the program and its evaluation over a network. A semantics for implicitly parallel extended logic programs in terms of argumentation may be promising to be close to an operational semantics, since argumentation is naturally distributed.
2. Given several extended logic programs corresponding to agents with their individual view of the world we want to obtain their global believes.

I.e. in the first case, we partition a program and compute its semantics distributely to solve more complex problems or speed up evaluation. In the second case we exchange parts of several independent or overlapping programs and want to obtain a consensus among the programs concerning inference of literals.

Both approaches need an inference operation for MAS, the only difference being that in the first case we wish that the MAS proof procedure coincides with the single-agent one.

Definition 10. Multi-Agent System
Let Ag_i be extended logic programs, where $1 \leq i \leq n$. Then the set $\mathcal{A} = \{Ag_1, \ldots, Ag_n\}$ is called multi-agent system.

Definition 11. $\models_i$ Let $\mathcal{A} = \{Ag_1, \ldots, Ag_n\}$ be a MAS, then

$$\mathcal{A} \models_i L \text{ iff } \mathcal{A}, \emptyset, \emptyset, t \models_i L$$
$$\mathcal{A}, LA, GA, M \models_i true$$
$$\mathcal{A}, LA, GA, M \models_i (L_1, L_2) \text{ iff } \mathcal{A}, LA, GA, M \models_i L_1 \text{ \& } \mathcal{A}, LA, GA, M \models_i L_2$$
$$\mathcal{A}, LA, GA, M \models_i not \ L \text{ iff } \mathcal{A}, GA, GA, M \models_i \neg L \text{ or}$$
$$M = t \text{ \& } \mathcal{A}, \emptyset, GA, tu \not\models_i L \text{ or}$$
$$M = tu \text{ \& } \mathcal{A}, GA, GA, t \not\models_i L$$
$$\mathcal{A}, LA, GA, t \models_i L \text{ iff } L \notin LA \text{ \& } L \leftarrow L_1, \ldots, L_l, not \ L_{l+1}, \ldots, not L_m \in Ag_i \text{ \&}$$
$$\text{f.a. } 1 \leq k \leq l \text{ ex.} 1 \leq j \leq n \text{ s.t.}$$
$$\mathcal{A}, LA \cup \{L\}, GA \cup \{L\}, t \models_j L_k \text{ \&}$$
$$\text{f.a. } l+1 \leq k \leq m \text{ f.a.} 1 \leq j \leq n:$$
$$\mathcal{A}, LA \cup \{L\}, GA \cup \{L\}, t \models_j not L_k$$

$$\mathcal{A}, LA, GA, tu \models_i L \text{ iff } L \notin LA \text{ \& } \text{f.a.} 1 \leq j \leq n: \mathcal{A}, GA, GA, t \not\models_j \neg L \text{ \&}$$
$$L \leftarrow L_1, \ldots, L_l, not \ L_{l+1}, \ldots, not L_m \in Ag_i \text{ \&}$$
$$\text{f.a. } 1 \leq k \leq l \text{ ex.} 1 \leq j \leq n \text{ s.t.}$$
$$\mathcal{A}, LA \cup \{L\}, GA \cup \{L\}, tu \models_j L_k \text{ \&}$$
$$\text{f.a. } l+1 \leq k \leq m \text{ f.a.} 1 \leq j \leq n:$$
$$\mathcal{A}, LA \cup \{L\}, GA \cup \{L\}, tu \models_j not L_k$$

$$\mathcal{A} \models L \text{ iff } \{ \bigcup_{i=1}^{n} \mathcal{A} \} \models L$$

While 1. to 4. of $\models_i$ are identical to $\models$ items 5. and 6. differ. Item 5 states that an agent can infer L if it has a rule for L whose body can be proven with the help of the other agents. This cooperative prove means that any objective literal in the body has to be proven by a least one agent, whereas default literals have to be infered by all of them, i.e. to infer L no agent should object to the default assumptions. Item 6. is similar to 5. for mode tu. Multi-agent inference is closely related to the single agent semantics. For $n = 1$, i.e. $\mathcal{A} = \{Ag_1\}$, $\models$ and $\models_1$ coincide. But in general this is not the case. The main difference being that for multi-agent inference default assumptions are treated locally, whereas conclusions via arguments are subject to global consensus.

Proposition 12. $\models$ *is not equivalent to* $\models_i$.

Example 13. For $Ag_1 = \{a \leftarrow not \ b\}$, $Ag_2 = \{b\}$ and $\mathcal{A} = \{Ag_1, Ag_2\}$ we have $\mathcal{A} \models_1 not \ b, not \ a$, $\mathcal{A} \models_2 b$, and $\mathcal{A} \models b, not \ a$. At first sight it seems puzzling that Ag_1 does not infer a. The reason is that concluding a requires Ag_2 to agree to $not \ b$ which is obviously not the case.

However, if an agent has complete knowledge about a literal single and multi-agent semantics are equivalent.

Definition 14. Partial and Complete Definition
Let $\mathcal{A} = \{Ag_1, \ldots, Ag_n\}$ be a MAS. Ag_i *defines L partially* iff $L \in \mathcal{H}(Ag_i)$. Ag_i *defines L completely*, iff Ag_i is the only agent defining L partially.

Proposition 15. *Let Ag_i be an agent that defines L completely, then $\mathcal{A} \models L$ iff $\mathcal{A} \models_i L$.*

Proposition 16. *Let* $\{a_1, \ldots, a_m\}$ *be all indices of agents partially defining* L, *then* $\mathcal{A} \models L$ *iff ex. j such that* $\mathcal{A} \models_{a_j} L$.

Since previous approaches did not tackle multi-agent argumentation there was no need for cooperation. With two or more agents involved in the process it may be the case that an agent needs the support of another one in order to counter-argue. For example, in a trial a prosecutor may need the help of a witness to defeat the arguments of the defender.

Definition 17. Successful Cooperation
Let $\mathcal{A}$ be a MAS. Agent $Ag_i \in \mathcal{A}$ successfully cooperates wrt. a partial argument $A \in Ag_i$ iff for all objective literals L in the body of A there is an agent $Ag_j \in \mathcal{A}$ such that $\mathcal{A} \models_j L$.

Proposition 18. *If an agent successfully cooperates wrt. a partial argument A and A' is equal to A with all objective literals removed from A's body, then A' is an argument.*

To infer conclusions the agents have to agree on the justified arguments. To obtain one any possible attack has to be overruled.

Proposition 19. *A is justified iff any attack is overruled.*

The above proposition is the core for an algorithm. Additionally we make use of a dialogue tree [12] where each agent stores the dialogues it has been involved in. To fully implement the algorithm sketched below, the dialogue trees have to be extended to include dialogues on cooperation.
Algorithm:
Proponent, Argumentation:
1. On receipt of a query to infer L, cooperate for arguments for L and then propose these arguments
2. On receipt of an agreement, add it in the dialogue tree and check tree's leaves
3. On receipt of an oppose, cooperate for counter-arguments and then propose them. If there are none, answer initial request negatively
Opponents, Argumentation:
1. On receipt of a proposal, cooperate for counter-arguments and then oppose. If there are none, then agree with proposal
Both, Cooperation for L:
1. For all objective literals L' in the body of a partial argument for L ask all agents to infer L'
2. On receipt of a reply, update cooperation process.
To implement the above algorithm we need agents with an expressive knowledge system and reaction rules such as vivid agents [15,13].

4 Vivid Agents

A *vivid agent* is a software-controlled system whose state is represented by a knowledge base, and whose behavior is represented by means of *action* and *reaction rules*. Following [14], the state of an agent is described in terms of mental qualities, such as beliefs and intentions. The basic functionality of a vivid agent comprises a knowledge system (including an update and an inference operation), and the capability to represent and perform actions in order to be able to generate and execute plans. Since a vivid agent is 'situated' in an environment with which it has to be able to communicate, it also needs the ability to react in response to perception events, and in response to communication events created by the communication acts of other agents. Notice that the concept of vivid agents is based on the important distinction between action and reaction: actions are first planned and then executed in order to solve a task or to achieve a goal, while reactions are triggered by perception and communication events. Reactions may be immediate and independent from the current knowledge state of the agent but they may also depend on the result of deliberation. In any case, they are triggered by events which are not controlled by the agent. A vivid agent without the capability to accept explicit tasks and to solve them by means of planning and plan execution is called *reagent*. The tasks of reagents cannot be assigned in the form of explicit ('see to it that') goals at run time, but have to be encoded in the specification of their reactive behavior at design time.

We do not assume a fixed formal language and a fixed logical system for the knowledge-base of an agent. Rather, we believe that it is more appropriate to choose a suitable knowledge system for each agent individually according to its domain and its tasks. In the case of diagnosis agents, extended logic programs proved to be an appropriate form of the knowledge base of an agent because it is essential for model-based diagnosis to be able to represent negative facts, default rules and constraints.

4.1 Specification and Execution of Reagents

Simple vivid agents whose mental state comprises only beliefs, and whose behavior is purely reactive, i.e. not based on any form of planning and plan execution, are called *reagents*. A reagent $R = \langle X, EQ, RR \rangle$, on the basis of a knowledge system K consists of

1. a knowledge base $X \in L_{KB}$,
2. an event queue EQ being a list of instantiated event expressions, and
3. a set RR of *reaction rules*, consisting of epistemic and physical reaction and interaction rules which code the reactive and communicative behavior of the agent.

A multi-reagent system is a tuple of reagents $S = \langle R_1, \ldots, R_n \rangle$

Operational Semantics of Reaction Rules Reaction rules encode the behavior of vivid agents in response to perception events created by the agent's perception subsystems, and to communication events created by communication acts of other agents. We distinguish between epistemic, physical and communicative reaction rules, and call the latter *interaction rules*. We use L_{PEvt} and L_{CEvt} to denote the perception and communication event languages, and $L_{Evt} = L_{PEvt} \cup L_{CEvt}$. The following table describes the different formats of epistemic, physical and communicative reaction rules:

$$Eff \leftarrow \text{recvMsg}[\varepsilon(U), S], Cond$$
$$do(\alpha(V)), Eff \leftarrow \text{recvMsg}[\varepsilon(U), S], Cond$$
$$\text{sendMsg}[\eta(V), R], Eff \leftarrow \text{recvMsg}[\varepsilon(U), S], Cond$$

The event condition recvMsg[$\varepsilon(U), S$] is a test whether the event queue of the agent contains a message of the form $\varepsilon(U)$ sent by some perception subsystem of the agent or by another agent identified by S, where $\varepsilon \in L_{Evt}$ represents a perception or a communication event type, and U is a suitable list of parameters. The epistemic condition $Cond \in L_{Query}$ refers to the current knowledge state, and the epistemic effect $Eff \in L_{Input}$ specifies an update of the current knowledge state.

Physical Reaction: do($\alpha(V)$) calls a procedure realizing the action α with parameters V.

Communicative Reaction: sendMsg[$\eta(V), R$] sends the message $\eta \in L_{CEvt}$ with parameters V to the receiver R.

Both perception and communication events are represented by incoming messages. In general, reactions are based both on perception and on knowledge. Immediate reactions do not allow for deliberation. They are represented by rules with an empty epistemic premise, i.e. $Cond = true$. Timely reactions can be achieved by guaranteeing fast response times for checking the precondition of a reaction rule. This will be the case, for instance, if the precondition can be checked by simple table look-up (such as in relational databases or fact bases).

Reaction rules are triggered by events. The agent interpreter continually checks the event queue of the agent. If there is a new event message, it is matched with the event condition of all reaction rules, and the epistemic conditions of those rules matching the event are evaluated. If they are satisfiable in the current knowledge base, all free variables in the rules are instantiated accordingly resulting in a set of triggered actions with associated epistemic effects. All these actions are then executed, leading to physical actions and to sending messages to other agents, and their epistemic effects are assimilated into the current knowledge base.

5 Argumentation Protocol

To implement the MAS's inference operation, the agents evolve an argumentation process. In the light of speech act theory and subsequent agent communication languages such as ACL, KIF, or KQML [7] we can identify five relevant speech acts of the dialogues:

1. An agent requests inference of a literal L by sending a token $ask(L)$,
2. and replies to a request by $reply(L)$.
3. An agent proposes a conclusion L to other agents by sending the token $propose(L, A, LA, GA, M)$ where A is the agent's argument A for conclusion L. LA, GA, and M are parameters for local and global ancestors and the mode due to definition 11
4. An agent opposes an argument by $oppose(L, A, LA, GA, M, L', A', LA, GA', M')$ where $L' \leftarrow A'$ is an argument attacking the previously received $L \leftarrow A$.
5. In case the received argument is acceptable the agent acknowledges this by sending $agree(L)$, where L is the conclusion of A.

Using the above speech acts we define an argumentation protocols in terms of reaction rules. We assume that a proposing agent sends its conclusion to all agents, but the opposition against a conclusion occurs only between the proponent and the opposer.

Consider a trial with a judge, a defender, a prosecutor and a witness. The judge has no knowledge, while the defender knows that the accused is by default not guilty ¬guilty ← not guilty, i.e. explicit negation is derived by default. The prosecutor knows that the accused is guilty if there is evidence given by a witness: guilty ← seen. Finally the witness saw the accused committing the crime and knows therefore seen. If the judge asks the defender to defend the accused an argumentation process as shown on the right evolves.

The defender proposes not guilty by its default assumption. The prosecutor asks the witness to cooperate by asking whether the witness saw the accused. With the subsequent testimony the prosecutor generates the counter-argument that the accused is guilty because he/she was seen. The defender cannot attack the counter-argument anymore and therefore answers to the judge accordingly.

To implement the above scenario we assume two meta predicates argument/2 and partial_argument/3. If the defender receives a query of the judge it generates an argument for its conclusion and proposes it to the prosecutor (see figure 1 rule 1), the prosecutor asks the witness for cooperation in case it receives a proposal by the defense and has a partial argument that needs further elaboration (2). If the witness is asked and can serve the query it responds accordingly (3). The prosecutor assimilates testimonies of the witness and informs itself to check arguments in the light of the new testimony (4). On the receipt of the check-message the prosecutor verifies whether there are open proposals of the defense and arguments to counter-attack the proposal, which are then sent. If the defense receive an oppose to its proposal it reports to the judge its failed proposal.

If executed the example leads to a trace as shown in figure 2. Though the example is small it gives a favor of the full implementation. It contains proposing, opposition and cooperation. For the sake of simplicity it does not consider full dialogue of repeated proposal and opposition and it does not implement the full semantics. However, the example shows how dialogues can be easily expressed by reaction rules which are executable. For the full implementation of the algorithm the concept of dialogue trees [12] has to be generalized to include multiple agents and cooperation. Vivid agents have a further advantage as tested for implemented legal reasoning. They are formally underpinned, which allows to verify protocols. In the proof theory lined out in [15,13] we can prove the following proposition stating that inference by $\models_i$ is equivalent to a reply transition eventually reached by the vivid agent:

Proposition 20. Let $\mathcal{A} = \{Ag_1,\ldots,Ag_n\}$ be a MAS. Then $\mathcal{A} \models_i L$ iff $(Ag_i, RR_i, [ask(L)|EQ]) \rightarrow^{* \ \overset{reply(L)}{\longrightarrow}} (Ag_i, RR_i, EQ')$.

1. $send(propose(L,B), prosecutor)$,
   $proposed(L,B) \longleftarrow$
   $recv(ask(L), judge)$,
   $i\_am(defender)$,
   $argument(L,B)$.

2. $send(ask(C), witness)$,
   $open\_proposed(L,B) \longleftarrow$
   $recv(propose(L,B), defender)$,
   $i\_am(prosecutor)$,
   $partial\_argument(L,B,C)$.

3. $send(reply(B),A) \longleftarrow$
   $recv(ask(B),A)$,
   $i\_am(witness), B$.

4. $send(check\_for\_oppose, prosecutor), B \longleftarrow$
   $recv(reply(B), witness)$,
   $i\_am(prosecutor)$.

5. $send(oppose(L,B,C,D), defender) \longleftarrow$
   $recv(check\_for\_oppose, prosecutor)$,
   $i\_am(prosecutor)$,
   $open\_proposed(L,B)$,
   $member(not\ C,B)$,
   $argument(C,D)$.

6. $send(reply(notL), judge) \longleftarrow$
   $recv(oppose(L,B,C,D), prosecutor)$,
   $proposed(L,B)$.

Fig. 1. Reaction rules of the trial.

1.	*defender*	$\longleftarrow$ *judge*	$ask(\neg guilty)$
2.	*defender*	$\longrightarrow$ *prosecutor*	$propose(\neg guilty, [not\ guilty])$
3.		*defender*	*assimilates* $proposed(\neg guilty, [not\ guilty])$
4.	*prosecutor*	$\longleftarrow$ *defender*	$propose(\neg guilty, [not\ guilty])$
5.	*prosecutor*	$\longrightarrow$ *witness*	$ask(seen)$
6.		*prosecutor*	*assimilates* $open\_proposed(\neg guilty, [not\ guilty])$
7.	*witness*	$\longleftarrow$ *prosecutor*	$ask(seen)$
8.	*witness*	$\longrightarrow$ *prosecutor*	$reply(seen)$
9.	*prosecutor*	$\longleftarrow$ *witness*	$reply(seen)$
10.	*prosecutor*	$\longrightarrow$ *prosecutor*	$check\_for\_oppose$
11.		*prosecutor*	*assimilates seen*
12.	*prosecutor*	$\longleftarrow$ *prosecutor*	$check\_for\_oppose$
13.	*prosecutor*	$\longrightarrow$ *defender*	$oppose(\neg guilty, [not\ guilty], guilty, [seen])$
14.	*defender*	$\longleftarrow$ *prosecutor*	$oppose(\neg guilty, [not\ guilty], guilty, [seen])$
15.	*defender*	$\longrightarrow$ *judge*	$reply(not\ \neg guilty)$
16.	*judge*	$\longleftarrow$ *defender*	$reply(not\ \neg guilty)$

Fig. 2. Trace of the trial example.

6 Comparison and Conclusion

The work presented in this paper is based on work by Dung [5,6] and Prakken and Sartor [12] on argumentation. Dung defines a declarative semantics for extended logic programs using the metaphor of argumentation. Our work continues this line of research in that we extend the single-agent approach to a multi-agent one. Prakken and Sartor are motivated by legal reasoning and define a rigorous and concise framework similar to Dung's. Prakken and Sartor also deal only with a single agent and therefore do not tackle the issue of cooperation. Defeasible priorities as used in [12] can be easily added in the implementation by defining the meta predicate *argument* accordingly. In contrast to ours, Dung's and Prakken and Sartor's work is not implemented.

In this article we showed the connection between top-down inference of WFSX and bottom-up argumentation. We extended top-down inference from single to multi-agent and discussed the relation. We designed an argumentation language to specify argumentation protocols for multi-agent systems and implemented multi-agent inference by vivid agents. For a full implementation dialogue trees have to be extended to include cooperation.

References

1. J. J. Alferes, C. V. Damásio, and L. M. Pereira. Top-down query evaluation for well-founded semantics with explicit negation. In A. Cohn, editor, *Proc. of the European Conference on Artificial Intelligence'94*, pages 140-144. John Wiley & Sons, August 1994.

2. J. J. Alferes, C. V. Damásio, and L. M. Pereira. A top-down derivation procedure for programs with explicit negation. In M. Bruynooghe, editor, *Proc. of the International Logic Programming Symposium'94*, pages 424-438. MIT Press, November 1994.

3. J. J. Alferes, C. V. Damásio, and L. M. Pereira. A logic programming system for non-monotonic reasoning. *Journal of Automated Reasoning*, 14(1):93-147, 1995.

4. J. J. Alferes and L. M. Pereira. *Reasoning with Logic Programming*. (LNAI 1111), Springer-Verlag, 1996.

5. P. M. Dung. An argumentation semantics for logic programming with explicit negation. In *Proc. of the 10th International Conference on Logic Programming*, pages 616-630. MIT Press, 1993.

6. P. M. Dung. On the acceptability of arguments and its fundamental role in nonmonotonic reasoning, logic programming and n-person games. *Artificial Intelligence*, 77(2):321-357, 1995.

7. T. Finin, J. Weber, G. Wiederhold, M. Genesereth, R. Fritzson, D. McKay, J. McGuire, R. Pelavin, S. Shapiro, and C. Beck. Specification of the KQML agent communication language. Technical report, The DARPA Knowledge Sharing Initiative, External Interfaces Working Group, Baltimore, USA, 1993.

8. Allen Van Gelder, Kenneth Ross, and John S. Schlipf. Unfounded sets and well-founded semantics for general logic programs. In *Proceeding of the 7th ACM Symposium on Principles of Database Systems*, pages 221-230. Austin, Texas, 1988.

9. L. M. Pereira, J. N. Aparício, and J. J. Alferes. Non-monotonic reasoning with logic programming. *Journal of Logic Programming. Special issue on Nonmonotonic reasoning*, 17(2, 3 & 4), 1993.

10. L. M. Pereira, C. V. Damásio, and J. J. Alferes. Diagnosis and debugging as contradiction removal. In L. M. Pereira and A. Nerode, editors, *2nd Int. Workshop on Logic Programming and Non-Monotonic Reasoning*, pages 334–348, Lisboa, Portugal, June 1993. MIT Press.

11. Lu's Moniz Pereira and José Júlio Alferes. Well founded semantics for logic programs with explicit negation. In *B. Neumann (Ed.), European Conference on Artificial Intelligence*, pages 102–106. John Wiley & Sons, 1992.

12. Henry Prakken and Giovanni Sartor. Argument-based extended logig prpgramming with defeasible priorities. *Journal of Applied Non-Classical Logics*, 1997.

13. Michael Schroeder, Rui Marques, Gerd Wagner, and José Cunha. CAP - Concurrent Action and Planning: Using PVM-Prolog to implement vivid agents. In *Proceedings of the fifth Conference on Practical Applications of Prolog*, 1997. to be published.

14. Yoav Shoham. Agent-oriented programming. *Artificial Intelligence*, 60(1):51–92, 1993.

15. Gerd Wagner. A logical and operational model of scalable knowledge-and perception-based agents. In *Proceedings of MAAMAW96, LNAI 1038*. Springer-Verlag, 1996.

Approximate Reasoning

Helmut Prendinger

University of California, Irvine
Irvine, California 92717-4555
E-mail: hprendin@benfranklin.hnet.uci.edu

Abstract. In this paper, we investigate approximate forms of deductive and nonmonotonic reasoning. In the case of approximate deductive reasoning, we propose a logic programming approach that combines features of the 'limited inference' approach of Schaerf and Cadoli [21] with a notion of 'relevance' as introduced by Brüning and Schaub [1]. It is argued that approximate reasoning is more appropriate if *nonmonotonic* logics are considered. For this case, we present the *guided inference* strategy. It relies on distinguishing preconditions from default conditions in antecedents of default rules (Elkan [8], Ginsberg [10,12]). While preconditions are treated as ordinary subgoals in a logic program clause, default conditions of format not A can be left partly unproved. The FIRE-AND-REMEMBER mechanism that is part of the strategy may take advantage of incomplete proofs and speed up subsequent computations of similar queries. The main contribution of our paper is twofold. First, we show that approximate deductive reasoning can be seen as a form of *relevant* reasoning. Second, we describe a strategy for approximate nonmonotonic reasoning that is robust for dynamically changing knowledge bases.

1 Introduction

Logical reasoning has high computational complexity, even in the propositional case. One motivation for the development of formalizations of nonmonotonic reasoning originates from the need of intelligent systems to draw conclusions quickly without having access to all the relevant information. It was supposed that some sort of default inference will *speed* commonsense reasoning. But after years of considerable theoretical progress made in the area of nonmonotonic reasoning, implementations of systems with nonmonotonic reasoning capabilities are almost lacking [11]. After all, the computational properties of nonmonotonic logics are far worse than those of classical (monotonic) logics [13].

Recently, Schaerf and Cadoli [21] proposed a form of *approximate* reasoning to make reasoning tractable. Basically, they suggest to restrict the classical notions of (propositional) entailment and satisfiability to a subset S of the language. In [2], their approximation method is applied to default logic and circumscription. Computational savings are immediate, *provided* a favorable set S is readily found; yet they demonstrate no way how to generate the set S of predicates relevant for proving or disproving a given query. Brüning and Schaub

[1] address this problem by introducing a notion of *relevance* via 'reachability relations'. We discuss the limited inference approach in a logic programming setting. When theorem proving is restricted to Horn theories, a minor modification of the semantics of programs is able to cover all the flexibility of the limited inference approach to approximate reasoning. Thereby, the 'relevance problem' is solved without extra effort.

For the nonmonotonic case, we motivate our own approach that is called the *guided inference* approach to approximate reasoning. It is based on two ideas: the 'negation-as-failure to prove so far' idea and the FIRE-AND-REMEMBER mechanism. Answers to queries are 'approximate' in the sense that they are allowed to depend on *unproved* assumptions [8,16,10]. Naturally, assumptions that are responsible for the consistency check are only incompletely performed: these (default) assumptions may *guide* inference by pruning the search space. In nonmonotonic systems that use Prolog technology, the *negation-as-failure* operator marks an interruption point where the computation may be suspended. Following Ginsberg [12] we suggest to change the interpretation of negation in Prolog from "negation as failure to prove" to "negation as failure to prove *so far.*" The FIRE-AND-REMEMBER mechanism proposes to focus attention to default conditions *after* at least one intended outcome of the knowledge base is reported. Roughly speaking, it maintains a table of *constraints* that are built up during the reasoning process, and uses this table when the same (or a similar) query is encountered again. This paper is organized as follows. In Section 2, we first introduce the 'limited inference' approach of Schaerf and Cadoli [21] and the concept of reachability relations due to Brüning and Schaub [1]. Then both ideas are combined in a uniform logic programming framework. In Section 3, we briefly describe how the limited inference approach applies to the nonmonotonic case. The main part of Section 3 presents the guided inference approach to nonmonotonic approximate reasoning. The strategy is illustrated by means of Ginsberg's [12] 'voyage' example. Finally, in Section 4, we summarize the paper and discuss future and related work.

2 Approximation in Deductive Reasoning

2.1 Limited Inference and Relevant Reasoning

The limited inference procedure of Schaerf and Cadoli [21] yields a form of *local* reasoning. When dealing with large knowledge bases, it is reasonable (on grounds of tractability) to take into account only an 'interesting' part of the alphabet. Assume a finite set P^0 of propositional variables; S denotes a (not necessarily proper) subset of P^0.

Definition 1. An *S-3-interpretation* of P^0 is a truth assignment v which is a standard 2-valued interpretation for variables $p \in S$ and does not map both variables $p \in P^0 \backslash S$ and their negations $\neg p$ into 0. An *S-1-interpretation* of P^0 is a truth assignment v which is standard for $p \in S$ and maps every variable $p \in P^0 \backslash S$ and their negations into 0.

Informally, S-3-interpretations allow models that contain contradictions as long as these contradictions originate from variables that are (so far) ignored; S-1-interpretations take ignored variables and their negations to be false. A formula A is S-3-satisfiable if there exists an S-3-interpretation v that satisfies A. $\Delta \models_S^3 A$ iff every S-3-interpretation that satisfies Δ also satisfies A; Δ a set of formulas. The notions of S-1-satisfiability and S-1-entailment are defined analoguously. All formulas are put to Negation Normal Form. The following theorem is proven in [21].

Fact 2 (monotonicity). For any S and S' where $S \subseteq S' \subseteq P^0$: (1) if $\Delta \models_S^3 A$ then $\Delta \models_{S'}^3 A$, hence $\Delta \models A$; (2) if $\Delta \not\models_S^1 A$ then $\Delta \not\models_{S'}^1 A$, hence $\Delta \not\models A$.

In case (1) we say that the relation $\models_S^3$ is a *sound* approximation of the classical entailment relation $\models$, and in case (2) $\models_S^1$ is a *complete* approximation of $\models$. Approximation is defined as an incremental process that checks the entailment relation for increasing subsets $S_i \subseteq P^0$.

A major problem of the 'limited inference' strategy in [21] is the way in which the set S of 'interesting' predicates is to be selected. The approach implies non-standard proof procedures and heuristics for a sensible choice of S have to be formulated. A principled method requires, for instance, to choose a subset $S \subseteq P^0$ that is *relevant* for (dis)proving A. Brüning and Schaub [1] combine their approach to approximate reasoning with a *relevance* concept. Approximate reasoning in [1] utilizes existing theorem-proving techniques, a combination of the (possibly incomplete) unit-resulting resolution and reasoning by cases. As opposed to the non-obvious choice of 'interesting' predicates in the approximation technique of [21], reasoning there is query-sensitive. This is accomplished by defining so-called *reachability relations*. The motivation behind the definition is the following: a literal K is reachable from a literal L if the derivation of a clause containing K could be used in a proof to refute L.

2.2 Approximate Reasoning with Horn Theories

We argue that logic programming with Horn clauses solves the 'relevance problem' immediately. The semantic foundation of approximate computations is given by employing standard (2-valued) completion semantics [3] for definite (Horn) logic programs. The following statement applies to the language of (propositional) Horn clauses.

Observation 3. The set of literals reachable from a literal p is identical to the set of literals resolved upon in the refutation mechanism of SLD-resolution with query $? - p$, provided the whole search tree is explored.

What this observation actually tells us is that instead of computing the reachability relation, we can execute a logic program and be confident that only relevant literals are resolved upon.

Our semantic account of approximation is closely related to the notion of completion as introduced by Clark [3], but is generalized to (possibly) incompletely processed Horn programs. Consider the following definite logic program

$P = \{p :- q; q :- r; r\}$ with query ?- p. The Clark completion of P is $comp(P) = \{p \leftrightarrow q, q \leftrightarrow r, r \leftrightarrow \top\}$. Obviously, $comp(P) \models p$. On the other hand, if $S = \{p, q\}$, then $comp(P_S^\perp) \not\models p$, where $comp(P_S^\perp) = \{p \leftrightarrow q, q \leftrightarrow \perp\}$. Note that r is treated as an 'undefined' predicate since it does not occur in the head of any clause.

Definition 4. Let P be a definite logic program, and S the set of predicates so far resolved upon.

- $comp(P_S^\perp)$ is like the Clark completion $comp(P)$ of P with all atoms $p \in P^0\backslash S$ (atoms not occurring in the head of any clause) replaced by $\perp$. A Prolog interpreter will report "failure" in this case. We call $comp(P_S^\perp)$ an *optimistic* Clark completion of P with respect to S.
- $comp(P_S^\top)$ is like the Clark completion $comp(P)$ of P with all atoms $p \in P^0\backslash S$ replaced by $\top$. $comp(P_S^\top)$ is called a *pessimistic* Clark completion of P with respect to S.

Instead of resorting to non-standard forms of interpretations $\Delta \models_S^k A$ ($k \in \{1, 3\}$) [21], we use the standard entailment relation with modified knowledge bases Δ_S^l ($l \in \{\top, \perp\}$).

Theorem 5 (equivalences [19]). *For any definite logic program P, $A \in \mathcal{L}(S)$ a set of atoms and any set $S \subseteq P^0$: (1) $P \models_S^3 A$ iff $comp(P_S^\perp) \models A$; (2) $P \models_S^1 A$ iff $comp(P_S^\top) \models A$.*

Corollary 6 (monotonicity in logic programming [19]). *For any definite logic program P, $A \in \mathcal{L}(S)$ a set of atoms, and any S and S' where $S \subseteq S' \subseteq P^0$: (1) if $comp(P_S^\perp) \models A$ then $comp(P_{S'}^\perp) \models A$, hence $comp(P) \models A$; (2) if $comp(P_S^\top) \not\models A$ then $comp(P_{S'}^\top) \not\models A$, hence $comp(P) \not\models A$.*

This corollary seems to show that we can do sound and complete deductive reasoning with less effort, that is, by taking into account only part of the knowledge base. But this is misleading since we have to consider at least a *relevant* part of the knowledge base. For instance, in the case of a sound approximation of the entailment relation, the set S cannot be smaller than the smallest set R of predicates relevant to prove the query. As pointed out, for instance, by Schurz [22], the interesting problem is to find the *shortest* derivation path among all (weakly) relevant derivation paths.

3 Approximation in Nonmonotonic Reasoning

3.1 Limited Inference for Default Logic

Cadoli and Schaerf [2] suggest a form of approximate reasoning within default logic [20] that relies on modifying the classical consequence relation in the definition of extensions. The first modification of Reiter's notion of extension, S-3-extension, is obtained by 'weakening' conditions (involving the consequence relation) in the original definition, while in S-1-extensions the respective conditions are 'strengthened'.

Without giving the details of their definition of extensions, we argue that the argument against the limited (deductive) inference strategy applies to default inference too, that is, there is no immediate way to find the letters that are relevant to the computations.

3.2 Guided Inference

Our approach to approximation by reasoning with unproved assumptions is dubbed the 'guided inference' strategy. Nonmonotonic logic may *guide* inference since it makes explicit by syntactic form (at least, in some of the most famous systems) which antecedents of rules should be computed exhaustively and which antecedents may be left partly unproved. Antecedents of the first sort are called *preconditions* of rules and antecedents of the latter sort are called *default conditions*. Only conditions of the second kind may be left unproved. For instance, in the default rule $fly :- bird, \text{not} \, not\_fly$[1] the literal *bird* is a precondition and **not** *not_fly* is a default condition. Recalling the motivation for nonmonotonic reasoning mentioned in the Introduction, this procedure seems justifiable from an intuitive point of view: from *bird* we 'jump to the conclusion' *fly* and do the consistency check as time permits.

The Negation-as-failure-to-prove-so-far Idea We develop the 'guided inference' strategy as a method of approximate reasoning within a logic programming setting. The main reason for the computational benefits of the logic programming language Prolog is that SLD-resolution (the refutation mechanism underlying Prolog), in a depth-first fashion, only resolves upon relevant (reachable) literals. We employ the consecutively bounded depth-first algorithm [23] to select clauses for resolution in a balanced way. The algorithm performs exhaustive depth-first search repeatedly for increasing depth bounds $1, 2, ..., n$. In the guided inference strategy, the method is only applied to default conditions, that is, goals of format **not** A. Recall that according to the negation-as-failure idea [3], the goal **not** A succeeds iff the goal A finitely fails.

Example 7 (Fred's voyage). Consider the following story [12].

> Fred fell out of an airplane over a farmer's field. The good news is that he was wearing a parachute. The bad news is that the parachute didn't open. The good news is that there was a haystack in the field. The bad news is that there was a pitchfork in the haystack. The good news is that Fred missed the pitchfork. The bad news is that he also missed the haystack.

The knowledge base for this example (as a normal logic program) is given in Table 1. Approximate reasoning becomes important if one does not have the time to analyze a situation in detail. The key problem of approximate reasoning is to make reliable inferences when the knowledge base is only partly processed.

Table 1. Fred's vogage program

(r1)	dead(X) :- fall_onto(X,Y), not good_para(X), not soft(Y).
(r2)	good_para(X) :- wearing_para(X,P), not broken(P).
(r3)	soft(Y) :- haystack(Y,H), not ouch(H), not missed(H).
(r4)	ouch(H) :- pitchfork(H,P), not missed(P).
(f1)	fall_onto(fred,field).
(f2)	wearing_para(fred,parachute).
(f3)	broken(parachute).
(f4)	haystack(field,haystack).
(f5)	pitchfork(haystack,pitchfork).
(f6)	missed(pitchfork).
(f7)	missed(haystack).

The goal $demo(dead(fred), D)$ succeeds for every depth bound except $d = 2$. At depth 2 $wearing\_para(fred, para)$, $haystack(field, hayst)$ and **not** $ouch(hayst)$ are satisfied, while **not** $broken(para)$ and **not** $missed(hayst)$ did not yet fail. We may say that although literals for further consideration are selected in a principled way, it is not guaranteed that answers improve, whatever one can mean by "improving a yes/no answer". Below, we suggest to combine the 'negation-as-failure to prove so far' idea with a mechanism that does indeed take advantage of partly explored proofs.

The Fire-and-Remember Mechanism The FIRE-AND-REMEMBER mechanism as a component of the guided inference approach to approximate nonmonotonic reasoning proposes to focus attention to default conditions *after* at least one intended outcome of the knowledge base is reported, for instance, $dead(fred)$. That is, rather than hoping to infer the correct answer right away, we begin by computing some minimal-effort answer to the query, thereby recording the sets of *constraints* corresponding to default conditions. For instance, at depth 0 in the voyage example, the constraint set Γ is

$$\Gamma(0) = \{ \text{ not good\_para(fred), not soft(field) } \}.$$

The FIRE-AND-REMEMBER mechanism is a way to utilize information gained by an approximate reasoning process in subsequent computations. In the following, the general idea is illustrated by means of the voyage example. A more systematic treatment of the mechanism will be given below.

Assume that for some reason (in fact, to stick to the given example), we want to know whether people die when they are paradropped onto a field. Actually, we expect them to die since our knowledge base contains the default rule that a person usually dies if s/he falls onto a field (clause r1). In the *first* step, we

---

[1] This is our representation of Reiter's [20] *normal* defaults $\frac{A:B}{B}$.

predict that Fred will die based upon the (rather sloppy) exploration of the knowledge base until depth 0; and observe that he really dies. At this point, we know that the circumstances were favorable to kill Fred but we do not know why, that is, we do not know what facts brought about the effect $dead(fred)$. All we can tell is that the constraint $\Gamma(0)$ must have been satisfied. It is important to see that we need a 'positive example' in order to proceed. In the *subsequent* step, when dropping another person, say Bob, off the plane, we only partly recompute the goal $dead(bob)$. All we have to worry about is whether the constraints are still satisfied. In order to do that, observations concerning Bob are made and their effect upon the current inference is checked. For instance, we might observe $wearing\_para(bob, para)$ and conclude that Bob dies since this observation does not violate the constraints.

The conclusion that Bob dies is based on the following assumptions. Informally, we assume a *similarity* between (the source) Fred and (the target) Bob, or whoever is dropped off the plane [5]. This allows generalization of arguments for predicates involving the class of objects under consideration, here $wearing\_para(X, para)$.[2] On the other hand, *queries* are similar if they contain the same predicates but have pre-defined argument positions bound to (possibly) different constants. The queries $dead(fred)$ and $dead(bob)$ are similar in this sense. The inference that Bob dies is based on the

Assumption of total awareness. Whenever some fact changes its truth-value, it is reported to the reasoner.

In other words, all facts that can possibly defeat a conclusion must be known, otherwise the inference is unsound. For simplicity, we assume (i) that all facts are in the language of *operational* predicates [17], and (ii) that observations are restriced to 'representative' facts: assumption (i) guarantees that observations are easily evaluated, whereas (ii) circumvents the so-called *ramification* problem, the problem of stating the indirect consequences of actions or states. For instance, $loaded(fred)$ is not representative in the sense that it is a consequence of $wearing\_para(fred)$. In general, there is no limit to what can be observed in a situation. The restriction avoids the problem to deal with fluent-triggered [14] consequences of representative facts.

Now suppose that we learn that $broken(para)$ is not satisfied by the knowledge base (f3 is absent). First, we try to identify a rule that has $broken(para)$ in its body and find rule (r2). Since $broken(para)$ fails, not $broken(para)$ succeeds by negation-as-failure. The other body literal of (r2), $wearing\_para(bob, para)$, can be proved by matching it with $wearing\_para(X, para)$ so that all subgoals of (r2) are satisfied. Next, we *forward-chain* on rule (r2) and establish $good\_para(bob)$ as provable, with the result that the constraint $\Gamma(0)$ is violated. As a consequence, $dead(bob)$ is not provable.

---

[2] The fact that we have to assume similarity between individuals is a complication peculiar to the voyage example. Normally, we want to pose the same query at subsequent instances of time, for instance, "Is Fred (still) safe?"; for obvious reasons, it makes no sense to ask whether Fred is still dead.

The FIRE-AND-REMEMBER mechanism provides a general way to take advantage of partly proved default assumptions. It assumes that iterative deeping is performed starting with constraints that initially have the form

$$\Gamma(0,0) = \{\text{not } L_1, ..., \text{not } L_n\}$$

where the first zero symbol refers to the *(search) depth* of the constraint and the second zero symbol refers to the *level* of the constraint. These notions are defined as follows.

Definition 8 (search depth and level). The *depth* d of a literal L is the number of (or-)nodes on the path between the root node of the search tree (the original query) and the node that contains L. The depth of the root node of the tree is set to 0. By convention, we take the depth of a node containing an unnegated literal A as $m + 1$ if the depth of the node containing the negated literal not A is m. The operation that generates a positive literal from a negative literal is called a *positive switch*. The *level* l of a literal L is the number of positive switches performed on the path between the root node of the tree and the node that contains L.

Now we define an operation on constraints that produces a set of more accurate constraints, that is, constraints that can be more easily matched against new observations.

Definition 9 (Γ-splitting). Let $\Gamma_k(i,j)$ be a constraint of the (general) form

$$\Gamma_k(i,j) = \{A_1, ..., A_m, \text{not } A_{m+1}, ..., \text{not } A_n\}$$

where i refers to the depth of Γ_k and j refers to the level of Γ_k. The *Γ-splitting* operation transforms $\Gamma_k(i,j)$ in the following way: For each *atomic* literal A_u, construct a constraint $\Gamma_{u_k}(i+1,j) = \{L_1, ..., L_n\}$ where A_u unifies with the head of a normal clause $A :- L_1, ..., L_n$. For each *negative* literal not A_t, construct a constraint $\Gamma_{t_k}(i+1,j+1) = \{A_t\}$. We say that Γ_k *splits to* Γ_{l_k}. The resulting set of constraints is called the Γ_k-*successor set*. A *Γ-dependency graph* $\mathcal{D}$ is defined as follows: $\langle \Gamma_{s_k}, \Gamma_k \rangle \in \mathcal{D}$ iff Γ_{s_k} is in the successor set of Γ_k. The relation D (depends on) is the reflexive and transitive closure of the inverse of the 'splits to' relation. Γ_1 *immediately* depends on Γ_2 if $\langle \Gamma_1, \Gamma_2 \rangle \in \mathcal{D}$ and there is no Γ_3 such that $\langle \Gamma_1, \Gamma_3 \rangle \in \mathcal{D}$ and $\langle \Gamma_3, \Gamma_2 \rangle \in \mathcal{D}$. A set $\{L_1, ..., L_n\}$ is called an *and-split* constraint. If A_u unifies with the head of m clauses, the generated set $\{\{L_{1_1}, ..., L_{n_1}\}, ..., \{L_{1_m}, ..., L_{n_m}\}\}$ is called an *or-split* constraint set.

The FIRE-AND-REMEMBER mechanism constructs all successor sets for each not A_i in the original constraint $\Gamma_{top} = \{\text{not } A_1, ..., \text{not } A_n\}$ until a certain (preferably high) depth bound is met for which the result of applying the default rules is the same as the observed outcome. At this stage, the mechanism has produced some odd-level and even-level constraints. The dependency graph of the voyage example is given in Fig. 1.

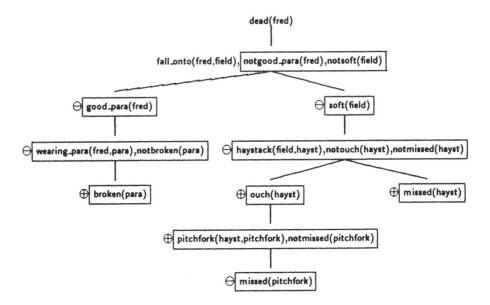

Fig. 1. The dependency graph of Fred's voyage example. Constraints are boxed. The symbols ⊖ and ⊕ indicate odd-level and even-level constraints, respectively.

Theorem 10 ([19]). *The (original) constraint Γ_{top} succeeds if, for a given depth d, the following conditions hold for the successor set of each **not** A_i in Γ_{top} (else Γ_{top} is not satisfied).*

1. *If Γ is a member of an or-split constraint set that is generated by an (unnegated) odd-level literal A, then all (odd-level) constraints Γ fail.*
2. *If Γ is a member of an or-split constraint set that is generated by an (unnegated) even-level literal A, then at least one (even-level) constraint Γ succeeds.*
3. *If Γ immediately depends on an odd and-split constraint (that is supposed to fail), then (i) at least one odd-level constraint Γ fails, or (ii) at least one even-level constraint Γ succeeds.*
4. *If Γ immediately depends on an even and-split constraint (that is supposed to succeed), then (i) every odd-level constraint Γ fails, and (ii) every even-level constraint Γ succeeds.*

The more time we spend for constructing the successor set, the 'closer' (in terms of node count) the constraints will be to new observations since more specific constraints are generated. In the limit, the proof tree is computed completely and $\Gamma(n) = \emptyset$ for some depth n. Unfortunately, the construction is expensive in terms of *space* (memory), but when similar queries are posed multiple times, savings in *time* are immediate since only a small part of the knowledge base is processed. This is achieved by forward-chaining (and possibly backward-chaining) on the given observation until the result of rule applications can be checked for (in)consistency with a constraint.

4 Summary and Discussion

In this paper, we describe approximate forms of reasoning. In the context of deductive reasoning we have shown that the inference mechanism of SLD-resolution guarantees that only relevant literals are resolved upon. Sound and complete approximations are obtained by appropriate definitions of the Clark-completion of a program. In our opinion, approximate deductive reasoning is only reasonable if it is understood as an effort to generate least-effort solutions to problems. So, as far as deductive reasoning is concerned, we suggest to concentrate on *relevant* reasoning rather than approximate reasoning. Regarding nonmonotonic reasoning, the guided inference approach to approximate reasoning does not introduce a new logic; rather a technique (or strategy) is developed that is intended to be integrated within some existing form of nonmonotonic reasoning, for instance Horn logic augmented by negation-as-failure.

To our knowledge, Elkan [8] and Ginsberg [10,12] give the most direct statement of the ideas underlying the 'negation-as-failure to prove so far' idea. The concept of computing default conditions in a resource-bounded way is already present in the 'variable precision logic' of Michalski and Winston [16]. In a recent paper, Etherington and Crawford [9] provide preliminary experiments aimed at the empirical validation for nonmonotonic reasoning with incomplete consistency checks. In general, the 'negation-as-failure to prove so far' mechanism is neither sound nor complete; on the other hand, it is complete with respect to SLDNF-resolution if the program is a translation of a default theory where defaults d are of the form $(: C/C)$, so-called *elementary* defaults. In this particular case, an atom A is derivable from $comp(P_S^\perp)$ iff A is in at least one S-1-extension of P.

The second component of the strategy is the FIRE-AND-REMEMBER mechanism. Since it requires that we already know the answer to a query it does not stand in direct competition to other nonmonotonic formalisms. The intuition behind utilizing a given 'positive' example is drawn from explanation-based learning [17] where a positive example of the target concept is assumed as given. Yet repeated querying of a changing knowledge base naturally occurs in many domains, and most nonmonotonic frameworks perform query-answering from the scratch. At this point, it is unclear to us whether the *lemma* default rules of Linke and Schaub [15] are re-usable. Several important technical and practical issues remain open: *First*, our approach needs to be described in terms of the intended semantics, for instance, well-founded semantics. *second*, we make the assumption that that the reasoner is informed about *all* changes in the world, and similar to other nonmonotonic approaches, we also assume that we have correct and complete knowledge of the domain. Eventually, we have to restrict the assumption of total awareness to a manageable set of facts that are 'relevant' to the current query. *Third*, the FIRE-AND-REMEMBER mechanism seems to share some intuitions with the *tabulated evaluation* strategy in logic programming [24], in particular with tabling of negative goals. The exact nature of this relationship has to be investigated. *Finally* and most importantly, in order to validate the computational gain of our approach, we have to implement the strategy as a Prolog program and perform experiments with large-size examples.

The guided inference strategy can also be applied to other forms of non-monotonic reasoning such as *abductive* reasoning [4]. Given a logic program T and goal G, the abductive mechanism searches for sets Δ_i such that $T \cup \Delta_i \models G$. In our voyage example, $fall\_onto(fred, field)$ would be abduced immediately. As a first approximation, default conditions need not be executed at all. They are accumulated in a constraint set, $\Gamma(0)$, and given more time, fleshed out to a higher level of detail, possibly abducing more goals (see Prendinger [18] for details). We also plan to apply the strategy to abductive *planning* [7] and explanation-based *learning* [17]. Planning this way is 'anytime' [6] since the plan generation process can be terminated at any time to provide at least an approximate answer. Plans are gradually refined if more computational resources are available. If an approximate but correct (working) plan exists, new facts can be efficiently checked against the current (plan) constraint set to find out about the plan correctness.

Acknowledgements

The author is indebted to the anonymous referees for their competent and guiding comments. The author is supported by the Salzburg/Austria-Irvine/USA exchange program, and by grants from the *Österreichische Forschungsgemeinschaft* and the *Stiftungs- und Förderungsgesellschaft*, Salzburg.

References

1. Stefan Brüning and Torsten Schaub. Using classical theorem-proving techniques for approximate reasoning: A revised report. In B. Bouchon-Meunier, R. Yager, and L. Zadeh, editors, *Advances in Intelligent Computing*, pages 389–398. Springer, 1995.
2. Marco Cadoli and Marco Schaerf. Approximate inference in default logic and circumscription. *Fundamenta Informaticae*, 21:103–112, 1994.
3. Keith L. Clark. Negation as failure. In H. Gallaire and J. Minker, editors, *Logic and Data Bases*, pages 293–322. Plenum Press, New York, 1978.
4. Luca Console, Daniele Theseider Duprè, and Pietro Torasso. On the relationship between abduction and deduction. *Journal of Logic and Computation*, 1(5):661–690, 1991.
5. Todd R. Davis and Stuart J. Russell. A logical approach to reasoning by analogy. In *Proceedings 10th International Joint Conference on Artificial Intelligence (AAAI-87)*, pages 264–270, 1987.
6. Thomas Dean and Mark Boddy. An analysis of time-dependent planning. In *Proceedings of the Seventh National Conference on Artificial Intelligence*, pages 49–54, 1988.

7. Marc Denecker, Lode Missiaen, and Maurice Bruynooghe. Temporal reasoning with abductive event calculus. In *Proceedings ECAI-92*, 1992.
8. Charles Elkan. Incremental, approximate planning. In *Proceedings of the Eighth National Conference on Artificial Intelligence AAAI-90*, pages 145–150, 1990.
9. David W. Etherington and James M. Crawford. Toward efficient default reasoning. In *Proceedings 13th National Conference on Artificial Intelligence (AAAI-96)*, pages 627–632, 1996.
10. Matthew L. Ginsberg. The computational value of nonmonotonic reasoning. In James Allen, Richard Fikes, and Erik Sandevall, editors, *Proceedings of the Second International Conference On Principles of Knowledge Representation and Reasoning*, Cambridge, Massachusetts, 1991.
11. Matthew L. Ginsberg. AI and nonmonotonic reasoning. In *Handbook of Logic in Artificial Intelligence and Logic Programming, Volume 3, Nonmonotonic and Uncertain Reasoning*, pages 1–33. Clarendon Press, 1994.
12. Matthew L. Ginsberg. Modality and interrupts. *Journal of Automated Reasoning*, 14(1):43–91, 1995.
13. Georg Gottlob. Complexity results for nonmonotonic logics. *Journal of Logic and Computation*, 2:397–425, 1992.
14. Fangzhen Lin. Embracing causality in specifying the indirect effects of actions. In *Proceedings IJCAI-95*, pages 1985–1991, 1995.
15. Thomas Linke and Torsten Schaub. Lemma handling in default logic theorem provers. In *Proceedings of the Workshop on Applications and Implementations of Nonmonotonic Reasoning Systems (IJCAI-95 Workshop)*, 1995.
16. Ryszard S. Michalski and Patrick H. Winston. Variable precision logic. *Artificial Intelligence*, 29:121–146, 1986.
17. Tom M. Mitchell, Richard M. Keller, and Smadar T. Kedar-Cabelli. Explanation-based learning: A unifying view. *Machine Learning*, 1:47–80, 1986.
18. Helmut Prendinger. Approximate abductive reasoning. Submitted to Conceptus, 1997.
19. Helmut Prendinger. Approximate common sense reasoning. Technical Report, University of Salzburg, Austria, 1997.
20. Raymond Reiter. A logic for default reasoning. *Artificial Intelligence*, 13:81–132, 1980.
21. Marco Schaerf and Marco Cadoli. Tractable reasoning via approximation. *Artificial Intelligence*, 74:249–310, 1995.
22. Gerhard Schurz. Relevance criteria for deductive reasoning. Technical report, University of Salzburg, 1996.
23. Mark E. Stickel and W. Mabry Tyson. An analysis of consecutively bounded depth-first search with applications in automated deduction. In *Proceedings of the Ninth International Joint Conference on Artificial Intelligence*, pages 1073–1075, 1985.
24. David S. Warren. Memoing for logic programs. *Communications of the ACM*, 35(3):93–111, 1992.

New Results About Sub-Admissibility for General Families of Heuristic Search Algorithms

Henri Farreny

Institut de Recherche en Informatique de Toulouse (IRIT),
118 Route de Narbonne, 31 062 Toulouse cedex, France. Email : Henri.Farreny@irit.fr

Abstract : We propose a formal generalization for various works dealing with Heuristic Search in state graphs. This generalization focuses on the properties of the evaluation functions, on the characteristics of the state graphs, on the notion of path length, on the procedures that control the choices of the node expansions, on the rules that govern the updating operations. Consequently, we present new theorems about the sub-admissibility. These theorems widely extend the analogous results previously published concerning Nilsson's A* algorithms and diverse successors due to Pohl (HPA), Harris (particular A), Martelli (B), Pearl and Kim (A$_\varepsilon^*$), Ghallab and Allard (A$_\varepsilon$), Bagchi and Mahanti (C), Pearl (BF*), Mero (B'), Korf (IDA*), Mahanti and Ray (D), Dechter and Pearl (A**). They provide a theoretical support for using diverse kinds of Heuristic Search algorithms in enlarged contexts.

1 Position of this Work

According to Simon [28], Search and Reasoning are two complementary ways to view Problem Solving : « A logic taken by itself may be viewed as a non deterministic algorithm for finding all of the consequences of a set of premises... Then the logic must be supplemented by some kind of control structure. A search strategy must be superimposed upon it... In this sense, reasoning processes are a subset of search processes ; the subset that uses rules of inference as the sole operators ». Generally, Search algorithms are guided by heuristics ; commonly, the heuristics use numeric values and functions in order to evaluate and to compare different perpectives. So, Heuristic Search is a possible approach for representing some kinds of knowledge and for managing some kinds of reasoning.

Heuristic Search algorithms are studied from about thirty years. [29] lists one thousand papers concerning this topic, of which several hundreds refer to Heuristic Search in *state graphs*. What is our contribution here ? We do not describe another particular algorithm or a new experimentation. But we propose an unifying and generalizing point of view and we explain how the constraints usually respected by the Heuristic Search algorithms in state graphs, in order to assure the admissibility or the sub-admissibility, can be widely relaxed. More precisely, we present original theorems that can be applied to obtain sub-admissibility formulas when working with more general state graphs, or with more general evaluation functions, or with more general path lengths or with more general algorithmic mechanisms ; for instance, the arc costs and the heuristic estimates may be not exclusively positive, the arc costs of a path may be aggregated by other operations than the addition, the heuristic estimate of any node may be a variable rather than a constant. In particular, these theorems can be applied to rediscover and *extend* the results about admissibility or sub-admissibility concerning Nilsson's A* [15, 20, 21] and many of its successors.

2 Admissibility : Previous Results, Ways for Extensions

First we recall the definitions of Nilsson's A and A* and we report under which precise conditions it has been established that A* terminates by discovering a minimal solution. Then, we recall precise results about the admissibility or sub-admissibility of various descendants of A or A* ; but we do not recall neither the complete definitions nor the other interesting properties of these algorithms.

Finally, we discern several attractive ways to relax the definitions and running conditions of Heuristic Search algorithms.

2.1 Algorithms A

The algorithm described in Fig. 1 is widely known as *algorithm A* [21]. It searchs a goal node by progressively expliciting the state graph from the start node « s ». The state graph is supposed to be *son-finite*, that is to say : the number of sons of any node is finite. A *cost* denoted $c(m,n)$ is associated to each arc (m,n) from a node « m » to a node « n ». The notation A* [20] is considered further.

```
1   procedure A-of-Nilsson
2       open ← {s} ; closed ← {} ; g_memo(s) ← 0 ; f_memo(s) ← h(s)
3       until open = {} repeat
4           m ← best-firt-extraction
5           if m ∈ T then edit-reverse-path stop endif
6           open ← open – {m} ; closed ← closed + {m}
7           for each n son of m repeat
8               g_neo ← g_memo(m) + c(m,n)
9               if n ∈ open and g_neo < g_memo(n) then update-father&g_memo&f_memo endif
10              if n ∈ closed and g_neo < g_memo(n) then   update-father&g_memo&f_memo
11                                                         open ← open + {n}
12                                                         closed ← closed – {n} endif
13              if n ∉ closed and n ∉ open then   update-father&g_memo&f_memo
14                                                open ← open + {n} endif
15          endrepeat
16      endrepeat
17  procedure edit-reverse-path
18      until m = s repeat write m ; m ← father(m) endrepeat ; write "s"
19  procedure update-father&g_memo&f_memo
20      father(n) ← m ; g_memo(n) ← g_neo ; f_memo(n) ← g_memo(n) + h(n)
21  procedure best-first-extraction
22      return node n* of open such as f_memo(n*) = min_{q ∈ open} f_memo(q)
```

$$f_{memo}(n^*) = \min_{q \in open} f_{memo}(q)$$

Fig. 1. Algorithm A of Nilsson.

The set of the goal nodes is denoted by « T » (line 5) ; if a goal is discovered, the algorithm writes the reversed node list of a path from the start node to the found goal (lines 17, 18) and terminates (stop in line 5). Possibly, the algorithm terminates without discovering any goal node (test in line 3), even if such a node exists in the considered state graph. Possibly, it does not terminate. The execution of the algorithm is constituted by node *extractions* (lines 4 to 6) followed by the *expansions* of the extracted nodes (lines 7 to 15). At the beginning of each execution of the loop 3-16, « open » is the set of the nodes that are available for the next step of the search ; « closed » is the set of the nodes previously extracted and expanded that are not available now. The algorithm uses an *evaluation function* « f » to direct the choice of the node that must be extracted from open and then expanded. We denote « $f_x(n)$ » the later value of the evaluation function at the node « n » when the extraction « x » is about to be executed ; the index « x » is aimed to recall that the same node « n » may be successively evaluated in different ways, according to the successive *extractions* (lines 4 to 6). The algorithm systematically extracts from « open » (lines 4 and 21-22) one of the nodes that own the minimal evaluation ; this mechanism may be interpreted like this : the more the evaluation of a node is small, the more we hope that this node leads a path to a goal. The sons of the extracted node are evaluated (for the first time or afresh) ; any new son is put in « open » ; if a son is already in « closed » and if its present evaluation is less than its previous evaluation then the node is got out from « closed » and put in « open » again.

By definition of algorithms A, the values $f_x(n)$ are calculated using the following formula : $f_x(n) = g_x(n) + h(n)$, where $g_x(n)$ is the *standard term* while $h(n)$ is the *heuristic term*. The *standard function* g is recursively defined hereafter :

Before any extraction (x = 0), only the start node s has appeared. Let $g_0(s)$ be equal to 0. At the time of the extraction of rank x,

    for each son n of node m extracted at rank x

        if n has already appeared before extraction x then $g_x(n) = \min(g_{x-1}(n), g_{x-1}(m) + c(m,n))$

        else $g_x(n) = g_{x-1}(m) + c(m,n)$

    for each node n, appeared before extraction x, which is not a son of m, $g_x(n) = g_{x-1}(n)$

Clearly : for any node n, $g_x(n)$ measures the length of a path[1] from s to n in the state graph and $g_x(n)$ decreases (not strictly) when x increases ; thus, when n is fixed, we may consider $g_x(n)$ as a decreasing overestimate of the minimal path length, if any, from s to n (this minimum is denoted $g^*(n)$ below). In Fig. 1, $g_{memo}(n)$ keeps track of the minimum of values $g_x(n)$ calculated until now for node n ; likewise, $f_{memo}(n)$ memorizes the minimum of values $f_x(n)$ calculated until now for n ; father(n) records the father node whose expansion led to fix the later value $g_{memo}(n)$. So, any node in « open » is the end of a path from s, whose length is $g_{memo}(n)$ and that only includes expanded nodes ; in addition, any path from s to n whose length is smaller has to include a node not yet expanded.

Heuristic term $h(n)$ only depends on node n at which *heuristic function* h is applied and not of the extraction rank. For this reason, we say that the heuristic function h is *static* while we say that the standard function g (and the evaluation function f) is *dynamic*. Moreover, Nilsson's A algorithm (and most of its successors) supposes that the heuristic h is positive. The measure (according to the length function ; here : $\mathcal{L}_{add}$) of a minimal path, if any, from n to the set T of goal nodes, is denoted $h^*(n)$; so, $h^*(s)$ is the length of a minimal path, if any, from the start node to the set of goals. Commonly, $h(n)$ is considered as an estimate of $h^*(n)$.

2.2 Algorithms A*

For Nilsson [21] and other authors[2], algorithms A are designated by A* when the state graph $\mathcal{G}$ and the heuristic function h satisfy the relation : for any node n of $\mathcal{G}$, $h(n) \le h^*(n)$. We say that h is a *lower-bounding* function[3].

2.3 Admissibility for A*

An algorithm of Heuristic Search in state graphs is called *complete* if and only if it is guaranteed that it terminates finding a path from the start node (s) to the set of goal nodes when such a path exists. An algorithm is called *admissible* if and only if it is complete and the length of the found path is $h^*(s)$. The admissibility of A* is proved in [15, 20, 21, 23] supposing that, at once : 1) $\mathcal{G}$ is son-finite and it contains at least one goal, 2) $\exists\ \delta > 0$, $\forall$ (m,n) arc of $\mathcal{G}$, $c(m,n) \ge \delta$ (this property characterizes the so-called δ-graphs), 3) $h \ge 0$. Under the same conditions, algorithms A are complete.

2.4 Admissibility or Sub-Admissibility for Other Algorithms

Later on we shall refer to various successors of Nilsson's A and A*, but without recalling their definitions : Pohl's HPA [25], Pohl's extended A [26], Harris' A [14], Martelli's B [18], Pearl-Kim's A_ε^* [24], Ghallab-Allard A_ε [11, 12], Bagchi-Mahanti's C [1, 2], Pearl's BF* [23, 3, 4], Mero's B' [19], Korf's IDA* [16], Mahanti-Ray's D [17], Dechter-Pearl's A** [3, 4].

---

[1] For Nilsson, the length of a path $\mathcal{C}$ is the sum of its arc costs. We denote it : $\mathcal{L}_{add}(\mathcal{C})$.
[2] In [20], notation A is not yet used and notation A* does not depend on the fact that « h » is *lower-bounding* or not.
[3] Several authors say that h is *admissible* rather than lower-bounding.

An algorithm is *sub-admissible* if and only if it terminates finding a path from s to T whose length is *near to* h*(s). According to the relations that concretize the « *near to* » notion, the *sub-admissibility* has different meanings. Fig. 2 reports previous results concerning the admissibility of HPA, B, C, IDA*, A** and the sub-admissibility of Harris'A, Pohl's extended A, A_ε^*, A_ε, B', BF* and D ; for a while, it is sufficient to consider columns 1 and 9.

2.5 Several Interesting Ways to Relax A* and Other Algorithms

Fig. 2 suggests several ways to relax A* and various other algorithms, *while preserving diverse forms of sub-admissibility*.

Constraints About State Graph and Length Functions

Consider columns 2 to 4. All the mentioned algorithms refer to δ-*graphs* (possibly infinite) or finite graphs ; note : in the first case, all the costs are *strictly* positive and in the both cases they are positive[4]. The length of a solution path is always calculated as the *sum* of the costs of its arcs[5]. We shall relax these constraints.

Constraints About Heuristic Functions and Evaluation Functions

Consider column 5 and 6. Most authors associate admissibility with heuristic functions that are at once positive, static and lower-bounding. Nevertheless, we remark that B', A** and D algorithms can assure minimal solutions using non-static heuristic functions. We observe a form of sub-admissibility for Harris'A and for A_ε while these algorithms use non-lower-bounding heuristic functions. We observe also a form of sub-admissibility for Pohl's extended A while this algorithm uses a non-static and non-lower-bouding heuristic function. Moreover, except for BF* and A**, the evaluation function f is always calculated as the sum (or a linear combination, for HPA) of two functions : the standard function g used by Nilsson's A and a heuristic function (the h of algorithm A or a variant h'). From these examples, we shall propose a more general point of view ; because, in some circumstances, the arc costs (thus the functions f, g, h) may be non-positive (see [10]) ; because, it may be natural to adjust, at least for some nodes n, the quantity h(n) in proportion as the algorithm is running ; because it may be easier to know (or more attractive to use) a non-lower-bounding heuristic function ; because it may be pertinent to examine the interest of other forms of f than a linear combination of g and h or h'.

Constraints About Extraction Modes

Consider column 7. Most algorithms execute *best-first* extractions : as A* does, they systematically extract one of the nodes of open that presently minimize the evaluation function. The A_ε^* and A_ε relax this mechanism. We shall offer more possibilities ; so, the choice of the nodes to expand may be controlled according to a secondary criterion, as previously suggested by [24, 12].

Constraints About Updating Types

Consider column 8. An important (and perhaps undervalued) difference between algorithms lies in the manner to update the values and the pointers associated to each node. The difference appears if we compare the algorithms that use static h with those that use dynamic h : the latter can dissociate the lowerings of g and f. The difference also appears when an algorithm (for instance : BF*) does not exploit the g values : then the pointers are updated if and only if the f values are lowered. We shall develop this topic in Para. 3.1 and 3.3.

---

[4] [10] gives a condition for guarantying admissibility of A* when the state graphs contain non-positive arc costs. We do not know another work dealing with this problem.
[5] Nevertheless the interest of other forms of length is suggested in [27, 23] and illustrated in [30, 6, 13].

1 Name	2 Arc costs	3 Length function	4 State graphs	5 Heuristic function	6 Evaluation function	7 Extraction mode	8 Updating type	9 Length of the discovered path
A*	> 0	$\mathcal{L}_{add}$	δ-graphs	h : static $0 \leq h \leq h^*$	$g + h$	best-first	1&2&3	$= h^*(s)$
HPA	> 0	$\mathcal{L}_{add}$	δ-graphs	h : static $0 \leq h \leq h^*$	$(1 - \omega)g + \omega h$ $[0 \leq \omega \leq 1]$	best-first	1&2&3	$= h^*(s)$ [only if $\omega \leq 1/2$]
ext. A of Pohl	≥ 0	$\mathcal{L}_{add}$	finite graphs	dynamic and positive h' derived from static h $0 \leq h \leq h^*$	$g_X(n) + h'_X(n)$ $= g_X(n) + h(n) +$ $\lambda(1 - \dfrac{depth_X(n)}{N})h(n)$ $(0 \leq \lambda)$	best-first	3	$\leq (1 + \lambda)h^*(s)$
A of Harris	> 0	$\mathcal{L}_{add}$	δ-graphs	h : static $0 \leq h$ $h \leq h^* + H$ $(H \geq 0)$	$g + h$	best-first	1&2&3	$\leq h^*(s) + H$
B	> 0	$\mathcal{L}_{add}$	δ-graphs	h : static $0 \leq h \leq h^*$	$g + h$	best-first	1&2&3	$= h^*(s)$
A^*_ε	> 0	$\mathcal{L}_{add}$	δ-graphs	h : static $0 \leq h \leq h^*$	$g + h$	n_X if $f_X(n_X) \leq$ $(1 + \varepsilon)f_X^*$ $(\varepsilon \geq 0)$	1&2&3	$\leq (1 + \varepsilon)h^*(s)$
A_ε	> 0	$\mathcal{L}_{add}$	without infinite path whose length is finite	h : static $0 \leq h$ $h \leq (1+\alpha)h^*$ $(\alpha \geq 0)$	$g + h$	n_X if $f_X(n_X) \leq$ $(1 + \varepsilon)f_X^*$ $(\varepsilon \geq 0)$	1&2&3	$\leq$ $(1 + \varepsilon)(1 + \alpha)h^*(s)$
C	> 0	$\mathcal{L}_{add}$	δ-graphs	h : static $0 \leq h \leq h^*$	$g + h$	best-first	1&2&3	$= h^*(s)$
B'	> 0	$\mathcal{L}_{add}$	δ-graphs	dynamic and positive h' derived from static h $0 \leq h \leq h^*$	$g + h'$	best-first	3	$= h^*(s)$
BF*	> 0	$\mathcal{L}_{add}$ but ideas for extension	δ-graphs	dynamic and positive h' derived from static h $0 \leq h \leq h^*$	$f_X(n) =$ $\Psi(\mathcal{L}(P_{X,n}))$ (Ψ strictly increasing)	best-first	1	$\leq \Psi^{-1}(M)$ (M = min for all paths $\mathcal{P}$ from s to T of $\max\limits_{p \in \mathcal{P}} f(\mathcal{P}_p)$
A**	> 0	$\mathcal{L}_{add}$	δ-graphs	dynamic and positive h' derived from static h $0 \leq h \leq h^*$	$f_X(n) =$ $\max\limits_{p \in \mathcal{P}_{X,n}}$ of $\{g_X(p) + h(p)\}$	best-first	3	$= h^*(s)$
IDA*	≥ 0	$\mathcal{L}_{add}$	finite graphs	h : static $0 \leq h \leq h^*$	$g + h$	best-first	1&2&3	$= h^*(s)$
D	> 0	$\mathcal{L}_{add}$	δ-graphs	dynamic and positive h' derived from static and positive h	$g + h'$	best-first	3	$=$ minimal length of paths $\mathcal{P}$ from s to T minimizing $\max\limits_{p \in \mathcal{P}}$ $\{\mathcal{L}_{add}(\mathcal{P}_p) + h(p)\}$ [Note: if $h \leq h^*$, this quantity is $h^*(s)$]

Fig. 2. Admissibility/sub-admissibility of diverse Heuristic Search algorithms. $depth_x(n)$: minimal number of arcs from s to n, known at rank x ; N : an upperbound for all x and n. $P_{x,n}$: pointer path of node n at rank x (see Para. 3.8). Updating types : see Para. 3.1 and 3.3. Extraction modes : see Para. 3.4. At rank x, n_x is the extracted node and f_x^* is the min of $f_x(n)$ for all n in open. $\mathcal{P}_p$: the part of $\mathcal{P}$ from s to p. Actually, some results reported in last column were originally established with more restrictive hypothesis not explicited here (it is the case for Harris'A, BF*, A**).

3. Formalizations and Generalizations

Hereafter we present an unifiying formalization. This formalization leads to general theorems, presented in Section 4, which allow to rediscover completely and to extend the table of Fig. 2.

3.1 Algorithms ρ of Type 1

We call *basic algorithm ρ for Heuristically-Ordered Search* the code presented in Fig. 3. Later, we shall make the algorithm more precise (to remove the non determinism of the procedures called in lines 4, 8, 9, 10) and we shall consider the application circumstances (what evaluation functions ? what kind of path length ? what state graphs ?). The reference to the evaluation function f is only done in the assignment instructions of the lines 2, 8 and 13 in order to fire 1) an evaluation *now* according to n and according to the execution of the algorithm up to *now*, then 2) an assignment for the variables « $f_{memo}(s)$ », « evolution » and « $f_{memo}(n)$ ».

When a node n appears for the first time (line 13), the evaluation of n is assigned to $f_{memo}(n)$; so for s, in line 2. When n appears again, value $f_{memo}(n)$ may be modified by the update procedure (lines 9 and 10) not yet specified.

According to the manner to make the line 4 more precise, we may define different *extraction modes* (see Para. 3.4). The lines 7 to 15 realize the expansion of the extracted node. Each extracted node that it is not a goal (test in line 5) is immediately *expanded* : *all* its sons are considered (the *partial* expansions are not allowed in this approach). The lines 7 to 15 correspond to the first appearance or eventually a new appearance of the sons of node m lately extracted of open when executing the lines 4 and 6.

```
1   procedure basic-algorithm-ρ
2       open ← {s} ; closed ← {} ; f_memo(s) ← f_x(s)
3       until open = {} repeat
4           m ← extract-node-of-open-according-to-values-f_memo-for-the-nodes-in-open
5           if m ∈ T then edit-reverse-path ; stop endif
6           open ← open – {m} ; closed ← closed + {m}
7           for each n son of m repeat
8               evolution ← according-to-characteristics-of-n-including-f_x(n)
9               if evolution and (n ∈ open) then update endif
10              if evolution and (n ∈ closed) then  update
11                                      open ← open + {n}
12                                      closed ← closed – {n} endif
13              if n ∉ closed and n ∉ open then  father(n) ← m ; f_memo(n) ← f_x(n)
14                                      open ← open + {n} endif
15          endrepeat
16      endrepeat
17  procedure edit-reverse-path
18      until m = s repeat write m ; m ← father(m) endrepeat ; write "s"
```

Fig. 3. Basic algorithm ρ

The procedures called in lines 4, 8, 9 and 10 are not yet precisely determined.

The execution of the line 8 assigns « true » or « false » to « evolution » according to whether it is decided or not that value $f_{memo}(n)$, or pointer father(n), must evolve ; this decision may take into account the value of the function f at n *now* , i.e. : $f_x(n)$; but we may also exploit other characteristics of the current node. According to the manner for governing the evolution of $f_{memo}(n)$ and father(n) in lines 8 to 10, we may define different *types* for algorithms ρ .

Basic algorithm ρ includes partially determined updating orders, (lines 9 and 10 in Fig. 3). We say that algorithm ρ is *of type 1* when the updating orders comply with the following rules : at the time of the expansion of any node m and for any son n of m, 1) $f_{memo}(n)$ receives $f_x(n)$ except if the $f_{memo}(n)$ value was already smaller and 2) father(n) receives m except if $f_{memo}(n)$ is not lowered by the step 1.

Remarks about the obtained generalization : Clearly, algorithms A and A* are particular cases of algorithms ρ of type 1. It may be easily verified that HPA's

Pohl, Harris'A, Martelli's B, Pearl-Kim's A^*_ε, Ghallab-Allard's A_ε, Bagchi-Mahanti's C, Pearl's BF* and Korf's IDA* are also of type 1.

Algorithms ϱ and algorithms ρ of type 1 do not refer to any cost of arc or path : they may be applied to graphs whose arcs are not valued. When the arcs of the state graph are valued we may be interested in the length of the paths from s to T which are possibly discovered. Nevertheless, if we do not know anything about the relations between the evaluation values of the nodes in open and the length of the paths from s to these nodes, it will be *a priori* difficult to compare the length of the found path with respect to the length of a minimal path. At the contrary, we shall further propose some formulas of sub-admissibility for some algorithms ρ of type 1 because these algorithms exploit particular evaluation functions. We shall also present some ϱ, called of type 2 or 3, whose codes explicitly refer to costs of arcs and paths. Before, we propose a broadened definition for the *length* of paths.

3.2 Generalization of the Notion of Path Length

Commonly the length of a path is calculated as the sum of the costs of its arcs (see column 3 of Fig. 2). However, Pearl [23] looks at other path lengths, especially the maximal cost of the arcs defining the path. For instance, Yager [30] deals with a family of problems where the path length is calculated as the minimum of the arc costs ; the work described by Dubois, Lang and Prade [6] refers to this family ; Gonella [13] aggregates the arc costs by multiplication. Hereafter we propose a general definition for the lengths of paths. This definition includes the ordinary length $\mathcal{L}_{add}$ and many other particular lengths such as those considered by Pearl, Yager and Gonella ; we shall see in Section 4 that this definition is compatible with interesting properties related to the admissibility or sub-admissibility of Heuristic Search algorithms.

In essence, the operation + and the set $\mathbb{R} =]-\infty,+\infty[$, involved in the definition of the classical length $\mathcal{L}_{add}$, can be respectively replaced by any two place operation Θ and any subset $\mathbb{V}$ of $\mathbb{R}$, provided that : $\mathbb{V}$ is closed under Θ and Θ is associative, increasing in the wide sense (in right and left places) and admits an identity element in $\mathbb{V}$. Now, here is a formal presentation. Let $\mathbb{V}$ be a subset of $\mathbb{R}$ which forms a monoid[6] $(\mathbb{V},\Theta)$ with a two place operation Θ increasing in the wide sense (in right and left places). $\mathbb{C}_{\mathbb{V}}$ denotes the set of all the sequences of arcs that are valued in $\mathbb{V}$, completed by the empty sequence. c denotes a function which associates to each arc u in $\mathbb{C}_{\mathbb{V}}$ a value c(u) in $\mathbb{V}$. $\mathbb{C}_{\mathbb{V}}$ forms a monoid with the operation of concatenation of finite arc sequences. We call *length associated to the monoid $(\mathbb{V},\Theta)$ and to the function c*, the function $\mathcal{L}$ whose domain is $\mathbb{C}_{\mathbb{V}}$, whose range is $\mathbb{V}$ and that respects the following rules : 1) $\forall$ u arc of $\mathbb{C}_{\mathbb{V}}$, $\mathcal{L}(u) = c(u)$, 2) $\mathcal{L}$ (empty sequence of arcs) = e_n (identity element of the monoid), 3) $\forall S',S'' \in \mathbb{C}_{\mathbb{V}}$, $\mathcal{L}(S'_\circ S'') = \Theta(\mathcal{L}(S'),\mathcal{L}(S''))$.

Remarks about the obtained generalization : Taking $\mathbb{V} = \mathbb{R}$ or $\mathbb{R}^+$ or $\mathbb{Q}$ (rational numbers) or $\mathbb{Q}^+$ or $\mathbb{Z}$ (relative numbers), or $\mathbb{N}$ (integer numbers), and $\Theta = +$, we recognize the current forms of the length $\mathcal{L}_{add}$. Other lengths may be made with $\Theta = \times$ and $\mathbb{V} = [0,+\infty[$ or $]0,+\infty[$ or $[1,\infty[$ (also with the restrictions to $\mathbb{Q}$ or $\mathbb{N}$) or $[0,1]$ or $]0,1]$. For instance too, if x and y denote two arc values and if a *is a positive number*, we can use Θ such as : min(x,y), max(x,y), $x + y - a \cdot x \cdot y$, $\sqrt{x^2+y^2}$, min (a, x + y), max (0, x + y − a), $x \cdot y / \max(x,y,a)$.

Now, we can define a *generalized standard term* g_x : if $(\mathbb{V},\Theta)$ is the monoid associated to the current length $\mathcal{L}$ then we substitute operation Θ to operation + in the previous definition of g_x (see Para 2.1). It may be verified yet, that for any node n : 1) $g_x(n)$ measures the length $\mathcal{L}(\bar{C})$ of a path $\bar{C}$ from s to n existing in the state graph and 2) $g_x(n)$ decreases in the wide sense when x increases.

---

[6] $\mathbb{V}$ is closed under Θ, Θ is associative and admits an identity element (e_n) in $\mathbb{V}$.

The minimal path length from s to n (if it exists) will be also denoted g*(n) ; the minimal path length from n to T (if it exists) will be also denoted h*(n).

3.3 Other Types of Updating — Algorithms ρ of Type 2 or 3

Below we distinguish two types of updating mechanisms that depend on the generalized standard term g. Other updating types could be conceived. We specially consider the types 1, 2 and 3 for the following reasons : 1) all the Heuristic Search algorithms we know use at least one of these updating types[7], 2) for the three types we have obtained results [6, 8] concerning the completeness property, 3) for the type 3 we can present a result[8] concerning the admissibility / sub-admissibility, 4) for the three types we can present a result[9] concerning the length of the possible discovered paths

We shall speak of algorithms ρ *of type 2* if and only if : at the time of the expansion of any node m and for any son n of m : 1) $f_{memo}(n)$ receives $f_x(n)$ except if the $f_{memo}(n)$ value was already smaller and 2) father(n) receives m except if the value of $g_{memo}(n)$ is not lowered when m is expanded. We shall speak of algorithms ρ *of type 3* if and only if : at the time of the expansion of any node m and for any son n of m : 1) $f_{memo}(n)$ receives $f_x(n)$ except if the value of $g_{memo}(n)$ is not lowered when m is expanded 2) father(n) receives m except if the value of $g_{memo}(n)$ is not lowered when m is expanded.

Remarks about the obtained generalization : Column 8 of Fig. 2 indicates the updating type of the particular algorithms to which we refer from the beginning. Nilsson's A and A* algorithms are simultaneously of types 1, 2 and 3, because for any node n, the staticity of the heuristic term (function h) leads $f_{memo}(n)$ and $g_{memo}(n)$ to be lowered at the same time. For the same reason, it may be easily verified that Pohl's HPA, Harris' A, Martelli's B, Pearl-Kim's A_ε^*, Ghallab-Allard's A_ε, Bagchi-Mahanti's C and Korf's IDA* are simultaneously of types 1, 2 and 3. Pearl's BF* is a particular algorithm ρ of type 1. Pohl's extended A, Mero's B', Mahanti-Ray's D and Dechter-Pearl's A** are particular algorithms ρ of type 3. We have not met, in the literature of the field, any particular algorithm that is purely of type 2. However, when the updating type is 2, the interesting property of « homogeneity » (defined just below) is satisfied. So, one may suppose that particular algorithms of type 2 will be proposed sooner or later.

Property of « Homogeneity »

For any algorithm ρ , for any rank of extraction x and for any appeared node n, we call *pointer path of node n at rank x* the path from s to n determined by reversing the sequence n, father(n), father(father(n)),..., s. We denote it $C_{x,n}$. For any updating type, we have : $\mathcal{L}(C_{x,n}) \geq g_x(n)$. For algorithms ρ of type 2 or 3, it may be easily verified that : $\mathcal{L}(C_{x,n}) = g_x(n)$. We shall say that the *property of homogeneity* is satisfied when for any x rank of extraction, for any n node already appeared *and situated on a path from s to T*, $\mathcal{L}(C_{x,n}) = g_x(n)$. Clearly : algorithms ρ of type 2 or 3 satisfy the property of homogeneity. *A priori* that is not the case for ρ's of type 1 ; nevertheless, it may be verified that the specific constraints considered by Pearl imply that its algorithm BF* satisfy the property of homogeneity. This property will be exploited for proving a theorem (Para. 4.5) which provides a general relation concerning the lengths of the solution paths.

3.4 Extraction Modes

Line 4 in Fig. 1 (Nilsson's A) orders a *best-first extraction* that is described in lines 21-22. Many other Heuristic Search algorithms use the same extraction mode.

---

[7] More details are proposed below.
[8] A theorem about the existence and the length of a solution path is given in Para. 4.4.
[9] A theorem concerning the length of a possible solution path is given and proved in Para. 4.5.

The best-first extraction has an intuitive motivation when the algorithms use the evaluations given by g + h in order to guide the search. Indeed, for any node n, $g_x(n)$ may be interpreted as an estimate of $g^*(n)$ and h(n) may be interpreted as an estimate of $h^*(n)$; so $g_x(n)$ + h(n) may be interpreted as an estimate of $g^*(n)$ + $h^*(n)$, that is to say : the length of a shortest path from s to T passing by n ; finally, the minimal value of $g_x(n)$ + h(n), for any n in « open », may be interpreted as an estimate of the length of a shortest path from s to T ; which leads to respect the « best-first constraint » : extract a node ñ of « open » such as : $f_{memo}(ñ) = \min_{q \in open} f_{memo}(q)$. However, according to the application context, it may seem not pertinent to choose ñ only by virtue of this formula ; Ghallab-Allard [11, 12] and Pearl-Kim [24, 23] have proposed to relax the « best-first » constraint : given a positive number ε, ñ may be extracted seeing that $f_{memo}(ñ) \leq (1 + ε) \cdot \min_{q \in open} f_{memo}(q)$; this extraction mode allows to use a secondary criterion, depending on the application, in order to complete the choice of ñ. Hereafter we propose a generalization of the previous extraction modes. We shall see that this generalization is also compatible with interesting properties concerning the lengths ot the solution paths.

Let a function $f \mid x \in D \subset \mathbb{R} \rightarrow f(x) \in \mathbb{R}$. We shall say that *f is overpassed on* D when : $\forall x \in D, \exists y \in D, f(x) \leq y$. Consider a particular application of an algorithm ρ. $\mathbb{W}$ denotes the range of the evaluation function f. Suppose that there exists a function $\mathcal{E}$ widely increasing and overpassed on $\mathbb{W}$, such as during this application, for any rank of extraction :

$$\mathcal{E}(\min_{q \in open} f_{memo}(q)) \geq \min_{q \in open} f_{memo}(q).$$ Suppose that the algorithm systematically extracts a node ñ of « open » such as : $f_{memo}(ñ) \leq \mathcal{E}(f_{memo}(n^*))$.

We shall say that this algorithm uses $\mathcal{E}$-*extraction*

Remarks about the obtained generalization : The best-first extraction is a particular case of $\mathcal{E}$-extraction : take $\mathcal{E}$ equal to the identity function $\mathcal{I}$. Many known algorithms (see column 7 of Fig. 2) use the best-first extraction too : HPA, A of Harris, extended A of Pohl, BF* (note : in « BF* », « BF » means Best-First), B', D and A**. Algorithms $A_ε^*$ and $A_ε$ use another simple form of $\mathcal{E}$-extraction : take $\mathcal{E} = (1 + ε) \cdot \mathcal{I}$. It may be verified that algorithms B, C, IDA* use other particular (and less evident) forms of $\mathcal{E}$-extraction.

3.5 Algorithms Ã

In order to define this sub-family of algorithms ρ we suppose that a length $\mathcal{L}$ is available. Thus there exists a monoid $(\mathbb{V}, \Theta)$ such that Θ is the operation used by $\mathcal{L}$ and any arc of the considered state graphs is valued by a number taken in $\mathbb{V}$.

An algorithm Ã is an algorithm ρ whose evaluation function satisfies the following constraint : for any rank of extraction x, for any son n of the node that is extracted at rank x, $f_x(n) = \Theta(g_x(n), h_x(n))$, where $g_x(n)$ is the standard term defined in Para 2.1, while $h_x(n)$ is a value of $\mathbb{V}$ (called *heuristic term*).

For any x and any n, $h_x(n)$ may always be *interpreted* (well knowing or not, according to the context), as *an estimate* of the length of a minimal path, if any, from n to T.

Note : if the monoid $(\mathbb{V}, \Theta)$ is a group, any ρ may be seen as an algorithm Ã : it is sufficient to take $h_x(n) = \Theta(g'_x(n), f_x(n))$ where $g'_x(n)$ is the inverse of $g_x(n)$ in the monoid $(\mathbb{V}, \Theta)$; if $(\mathbb{V}, \Theta)$ is not a group we may define some ρ 's that are not algorithms Ã : then Ã's form a *proper* subset of the set made by the ρ 's.

Remarks about the obtained generalization : Nilsson's A is a particular algorithm Ã that uses a static heuristic term. It may be easily verified that the following algorithms are particular Ã too : extended A of Pohl, B, C, $A_ε^*$, $A_ε$, B', D. At first sight, the evaluation functions of algorithms BF* and A** have not the form required for algorithms Ã ; but BF* and A** are defined on the monoid $(\mathbb{R}^+, +)$ and use evaluation functions f such as : $f \geq g$; thus, the evaluation function f may be formulated as a sum g + h (with h ≥ 0) and so we can conclude that BF* and A** are particular algorithm Ã. Algorithm HPA behaves as an Ã, because its evaluation function is *proportional* to the evaluation function of an Ã. It may be verified that algorithm IDA* behaves as an Ã *during each iteration*.

We may distinguish algorithms Ã whose updating type is 1, 2 or 3. We call Ã$_\mathcal{E}$ (possibly of type 1, 2 or 3) the Ã's that work with $\mathcal{E}$-extraction.

3.6 More Possibilities for Functions h and f

We propose to relax the constraints commonly required for the evaluation function f and for the heuristic function h. In this less constrained context we propose general results concerning the admissibility or sub-admissibility ; so, it will be possible to use a larger variety of functions f or h and thus the field of applications will be potentially extended. Still we denote by $\mathbb{V}$ the domain of the arc values (a length $\mathcal{L}$ is defined on $\mathbb{V}$, the range of h is included in $\mathbb{V}$), by $\mathbb{W}$ the range of f and by $\mathcal{G}$ the state graph dealt with. Given a Heuristic Search algorithm $\mathcal{A}$ and a state graph $\mathcal{G}$, we denote by S($\mathcal{A}$,$\mathcal{G}$) the set of the nodes n such that : 1) h*(n) is defined and 2) n is evaluated during the application of $\mathcal{A}$ to $\mathcal{G}$.

Covered h or f

We say that the heuristic function h of an algorithm Ã is *covered by F when the algorithm is applied to* $\mathcal{G}$, if and only if : there exists a function F whose domain is S(Ã,$\mathcal{G}$),whose range is $\mathbb{V}$ and for any node n of S(Ã,$\mathcal{G}$), if n is evaluated at rank x then $h_x(n) \leq F(n)$. We say that the evaluation function f of an algorithm ρ is *covered by F when the algorithm is applied to* $\mathcal{G}$, if and only if : there exists a function F whose domain is S(ρ,$\mathcal{G}$),whose range is $\mathbb{V}$ and for any node n of S(ρ,$\mathcal{G}$), if n is evaluated at rank x then $f_x(n) \leq F(n)$.

Remarks about the obtained generalization : The preceding constraint widely extends the basic constraint respected by Nilsson's A* and many successors : $h(n) \leq h*(n)$ (in this particular case we said that the *static* heuristic term was « lower-bounding » or « admissible », see Para. 2.2). We can immediately propose several general examples of covered heuristic functions : 1) the h's that are upper-bounded (i.e., $\exists M \in \mathbb{V}$, for any node n evaluated at any rank x : $h_x(n) \leq M$), 2) the h's that are *semi-static* (i.e., for any evaluated node n, $h_x(n)$ is allowed to take only a finite number of distinct values), 3) the h's that are simply *static* (i.e., for any evaluated node n, for any i and j ranks for which n is evaluated : $h_i(n) = h_j(n)$), 4) or still the h's that satisfy relations such as : for any node n evaluated at any rank x, $h_x(n) \leq (1 + \alpha)\cdot h*(n) + H$, where the constants α and H are positive or zero (but note : h is not necessarily static). Now, algorithms A, HPA, B, C, A$_\mathcal{E}^*$, A$_\mathcal{E}$ and IDA* use static (thus covered) heuristic functions (see column 5 in Fig. 2) ; moreover, A$_\mathcal{E}$ satisfy a relation of the form $h \leq (1 + \alpha)\cdot h*$, while the particular algorithm A due to Harris satisfy a relation of the form $h \leq H$. It may be verified that the extended A of Pohl uses a semi static (thus covered) h and that the algorithms B' and D use other particular forms of covered h's. It may be verified that A** use a covered f.

Finitely-decreasing h or f

Given a node n, we denote $[h_x(n)]_x$ the sequence of values taken by the heuristic function h for the successive ranks of extraction x for which n is evaluated. We say that the heuristic function h is *finitely-decreasing when an algorithm Ã is applied to* $\mathcal{G}$, if and only if : for any evaluated node n of $\mathcal{G}$, there does not exist any infinite sub-sequence of $[h_x(n)]_x$ that is strictly decreasing. Likewise, we say that the evaluation function f is *finitely-decreasing when an algorithm ρ is applied to* $\mathcal{G}$, if and only if : for this application, for any evaluated node n of $\mathcal{G}$, there does not exist any infinite sub-sequence of $[f_x(n)]_x$ that is strictly decreasing

Remarks about the obtained generalization : The *finite-decrease* of h or f is a rather soft constraint. Indeed, it seems often natural that for any node n the estimates $h_x(n)$ cannot decrease indefinitely. Obviously, all the semi-static functions and therefore all the static functions are finitely decreasing. It may be easily verified that A, HPA, extended A of Pohl, B, A^*_ε, A_ε, C, B', IDA* and D use finitely decreasing h (most of them use a static or semi static h ; see Column 5 in Fig. 2).

Quasi-coincident h

We say that heuristic function h is *quasi-coincident when an algorithm $\tilde{A}$ is applied to $\mathcal{G}$*, if and only if : $\exists\, m_T \in \mathbb{V}$, $\exists\, m'_T \in \mathbb{V}$, $\Theta(m_T, m'_T) \geq e_n$ (e_n : identity element), for any evaluated goal node t, $h_x(t) \geq m_T$.

Remarks about the obtained generalization : It may be easily verified that A, HPA, extended A of Pohl, B, A^*_ε, A_ε, C, B', IDA*, D, SDW are quasi-coincident ; indeed, all these algorithms use $\mathbb{V} = \mathbb{R}+$, $\Theta = +$ ($e_n = 0$) and a heuristic function h that is positive or zero.

3.7 A Larger Family of State Graphs

We identify now a wide family of state graphs : the $\mathcal{L}$ -*standard* state graphs. It includes, at least, all the state graphs considered in the literature related to A, HPA, extended A of Pohl, B, A^*_ε, A_ε, C, BF*, B', IDA*, D and A**.

$\mathcal{L}$ -uncompressibility

Let $\mathcal{L}$ be the used length[10]. We say that a state graph $\mathcal{G}$ is $\mathcal{L}$ -*uncompressible* if and only if : $\forall\, M \in \mathbb{V}$, $\exists\, k \in \mathbb{N}$, $\forall\, \mathcal{C}$ elementary[11] path of $\mathcal{G}$ from s, $\mathcal{N}(\mathcal{C}) > k \Rightarrow \mathcal{L}(\mathcal{C}) > M$, where $\mathcal{N}(\mathcal{C})$ denotes the number of arcs of $\mathcal{C}$.

Remarks about the obtained generalization : Clearly : any δ-graph (see Para 2.3) is $\mathcal{L}_{add}$-uncompressible and any finite graph is $\mathcal{L}$ -uncompressible (whatever is $\mathcal{L}$). All the algorithms above-mentioned, except A_ε, have been analyzed by their authors in case of application to δ-graphs (see Column 4 in Fig. 2) ; Ghallab and Allard have defined and studied A_ε when it is applied to graphs less constrained than δ-graphs, but these graphs are still particular $\mathcal{L}_{add}$-uncompressible graphs.

$\mathcal{L}$ -standard State Graphs

We say that a state graph is $\mathcal{L}$ -*standard* if and only if it satisfies the four following conditions : it is son-finite, it contains at least a goal, it is $\mathcal{L}$ -uncompressible, it does not contain any absorbant circuit[12]. It may be easily verified that any $\mathcal{L}$ -standard graph owns at least one minimal path (in the sense of $\mathcal{L}$) from s to T.

Remarks about the obtained generalization : All the above-mentioned algorithms have been analyzed by their authors in case of application to particular $\mathcal{L}$ -standard graphs.

4. General Results to Approach the Sub-admissibility

Within the preceding formal framework, we can prove various general results. So, the five original properties presented below form a set of tools to establish formulas of sub-admissibility. The arguments of the proofs are given in [8]. For general results about the *termination finding a path to a goal*, see [9]. Let $\mathcal{G}$ be a goal-accessible state graph at which an algorithm $\tilde{A}$ is applied. It is easily verified that : at the time of any extraction i, on any path of $\mathcal{G}$ from s to T, there exists a node belonging to « open » whose predecessors along the path belong to « closed »; this node is called : *input of the path for the ith extraction*.

4.1 Lemma

Let $\mathcal{G}$ be a state graph at which is applied an algorithm $\tilde{A}$ of type 1, 2 or 3 whose heuristic term h is covered by F . Let $\mathcal{C}$ be a path of $\mathcal{G}$ from s to T such as, $\forall\, i$ rank of extraction, $g_{i-1}(e_i) = \mathcal{L}(\mathcal{C}_{e_i})$ and h(e_i) is defined, where e_i is the input of*

---

10 Length relative to some monoid $(\mathbb{V},\Theta)$; the arc values are taken in $\mathbb{V}$ (see Para. 3.1).
11 i.e. : without repeating any state.
12 Absorbant circuit : whose length $< e_n$ (identity element of the monoid of arc values).

$\check{C}$ at the time to decide the ith extraction and $\check{C}_{e_i}$ is the part of $\check{C}$ from s to e_i. Then : $f_i(e_i) \leq \Theta(\mathcal{L}(\check{C}_{e_i}), F(e_i))$, where $f_i(e_i)$ is the evaluation value fastened to e_i at the ith extraction. This result generalizes « lemma 3.1 » proposed[13] in [20] (also : « result 2 » in [21] and « lemma 1 » in [23]).

4.2 Theorem

Let $\mathcal{G}$ be a state graph without absorbant circuit. Suppose that Θ is strictly increasing in the left place[14]. Let an algorithm ρ of type 3 applied to $\mathcal{G}$. Let n be any node of $\mathcal{G}$. Let $\check{C}$ be any minimal path from s to n. Denote $\check{C} = n_0, ..., n_t$ where $n_0 = s$ and $n_t = n$. $\forall i$ rank of extraction, if $n \notin$ closed, let $n_k (k \in \mathbb{N}, 0 \leq k \leq t)$ be the input of $\check{C}$ at the time to decide the ith extraction. Then : $\forall j \in \mathbb{N}, 0 \leq j \leq k \Rightarrow g_{i-1}(n_j) = g^*(n_j)$. This result generalizes the « lemma 2 » proposed[15] in [23].

4.3 Theorem

Let $\mathcal{G}$ be a state graph without absorbant circuit and that contains at least one goal. Let an algorithm $\tilde{A}_\mathcal{E}$ of type 3 applied to $\mathcal{G}$, which terminates. Suppose that, when the algorithm is applied, heuristic function h is covered by F and quasi-coincident (thus : $\exists m_T \in \mathbb{V}, \exists m'_T \in \mathbb{V}, \Theta(m_T, m'_T) \geq e_n$). Suppose that Θ is strictly increasing in the left place. Then, at the time of the termination, the algorithm has found a path $\check{C}$ from s to T such as : $\mathcal{L}(\check{C}) \leq \Theta(\mathcal{E}(\Theta(g^*(e_i), F(e_i))), m'_T)$, where e_i is the input, when the ith and last extraction is decided, of any minimal path from s to T in $\mathcal{G}$. In the following theorem, the termination of the algorithm is not an hypothesis but a part of the conclusion.

4.4 Theorem of Sub-Admissibility

Let $\mathcal{G}$ be a $\mathcal{L}$-standard state graph at which is applied an algorithm $\tilde{A}_\mathcal{E}$ of type 3, whose heuristic function h is covered by F during the application, quasi-coincident (thus : $\exists m_T \in \mathbb{V}, \exists m'_T \in \mathbb{V}, \Theta(m_T, m'_T) \geq e_n$) and lower-bounded by an element m of $\mathbb{V}$ such as $\exists m' \in \mathbb{V}, \Theta(m', m) \geq e_n$. Suppose that Θ is strictly increasing in the left place. Then, the algorithm terminates finding a path $\check{C}$ of $\mathcal{G}$ from s to T such as : $\mathcal{L}(\check{C}) \leq \Theta(\mathcal{E}(\Theta(g^*(e_i), F(e_i))), m'_T)$, where e_i is the input, at the time to decide the ith and last extraction, of any minimal path from s to T in $\mathcal{G}$.

This result generalizes « theorem 3.1 » proposed[16] in [20] (also : « result 4 » in [21] and « theorem 2 » in [23]).

4.5 Theorem of the Found Path

Let $\mathcal{G}$ be a state graph that contains at least one goal. Let an algorithm ρ of type 2 or 3, that is applied to $\mathcal{G}$ and terminates at the time of the ith extraction ; let $extract_i$ be the ith extracted node. Suppose that there exists a function Ω, whose domain is the range T_f of $f_x(n)$ when n runs on T such as : for any evaluated goal node t, $g_x(t) \leq \Omega(f_x(t))$. Then, at the time of the termination the algorithm has found a path $\check{C}$ from s to T such as : $\mathcal{L}(\check{C}) \leq \Omega(f_i(extract_i))$. This theorem holds for the algorithms ρ of type 1 when the property of homogeneity is satisfied.

This result generalizes the « theorem 2* » proposed by Pearl[17] in [23].

---

[13] Statement of « lemma 3.1 » in [20] : « If $\hat{h}(n) \leq h(n)$ for all n, then at any time before A* terminates and for any optimal path P from node s to a goal, there exists an open node n′ on P with $\hat{f}(n') \leq f(s)$ ».

[14] For instance, this property is true if $(\mathbb{V}, \Theta)$ is a group rather than a simple monoid.

[15] Statement of « lemma 2 » in [23] : « Let n′ be the shallowest OPEN node on an optimal path $P_{s-n''}$ to any arbitrary node n″, not necessarily in Γ. Then : $g(n') = g^*(n')$, stating that A* has already found the optimal pointer-path to n′ (i.e., n′ is along $P_{s-n''}$) and that path will remain unaltered throughout the search ».

[16] Statement of « theorem 3.1 » in [20] : « If $h(n) \leq h(n)$ for all nodes n, and if all arc costs are greater than some small positive number δ, then algorithm A* is admissible ».

[17] Statement of « theorem 2* » in [23]: « BF* is $\Psi^{-1}(M)$-admissible, that is, the cost of the solution path found by BF* is at most $\Psi^{-1}(M)$ ».

Remarks about some rediscoveries and generalizations : Nilsson's A* algorithm is also a particular case of $\tilde{A}_{\mathcal{C}}$ of type 3 ; its heuristic function h is covered by F = h*. The state graphs considered by Nilsson contain at least one goal and do not admit absorbant circuits. The heuristic function is quasi-coincident (take $m_T = m'_T = 0$). The operation Θ (that is to say +), is strictly increasing in the left place. Thus we may apply theorem 4.4 : $\mathcal{L}_{add}(\mathcal{C}) \leq g*(e_i) + h*(e_i)$, where $\mathcal{L}_{add}(\mathcal{C})$ is the length of the found path $\mathcal{C}$ from s to T while e_j is the final input of any minimal path $\mathcal{C}_0$ from s to T[18]. Because e_i belongs to $\mathcal{C}_0$ (minimal) : $g*(e_i) + h*(e_i) = \mathcal{L}_{add}(\mathcal{C}_0)$. Thus $\mathcal{L}_{add}(\mathcal{C}) = h*(s)$: the admissibility of A*'s is thus rediscovered. The admissibility may be still proved when some constraints applied to Nilsson's A* are relaxed ; indeed, providing that the updates remain of type 3, theorem 4.4 is yet applicable to monoids $(\mathbb{V}, \Theta)$ other than group $(\mathbb{R}+, +)$, to state graphs that are not necessarily δ-graphs, to heuristic functions h that are not necessarily static or positive. Moreover, theorem 4.4 gives some formulas of sub-admissibility for extraction modes which may be not best-first and for h which may be not lower-bounding. If we relax Nilsson's A* algorithms towards $\tilde{A}$'s of type 1 or 2, we can establish some formulas of sub-admissibility by combining the theorem 4.5 with the general results about completeness given in [9]. Likewise, we have applied[19] theorems 4.1 to 4.5 for extending the known results about the admissibility or the sub-admissibility concerning HPA, extended A of Pohl, B, A^*_ε, A_ε, C, BF*, B', IDA*, D and A**.

5. Concluding Remarks and Perspectives

We have proposed a formalization concerning the Heuristically-Ordered Search in state graphs. We have considered 5 dimensions : 1) the notion of length to measure the paths between nodes, 2) the characteristics of the state graphs dealt with, 3) the choices of the nodes to expand, 4) the kinds of updating to realize, 5) the properties of the evaluation functions that guide the search. We have employed this formalization to present several general theorems about the admissibility or sub-admissibility. These theorems allow to extend the availability of Heuristic Search algorithms (yet existing or not) ; thus, the field for applications is potentially enlarged. Moreover, the proposed analysis allows an unifying and comparative presentation (just suggested here by lack of space) of various classical algorithms ; this analysis facilitates a better understanding of the key points, the limitations and the non exploited potentialities.

We have supposed that the cost of a move from any node to another one is a real number ; it may be interesting to extend our formalization for dealing with other kinds of values, namely fuzzy numbers or fuzzy intervals (see chapter 5 of [7] and [5] for a basic study of Heuristic Search in an imprecise environment). Our work may be also developed in order to tackle the problems of completeness, admissibility or sub-admissibility for other variants of Heuristic Search algorithms (such as real-time algorithms, restricted-memory algorithms or algorithms for dynamic environnements) or to extend the results relative to the bidirectional algorithms (see [8], chapter 8, for preliminary work).

References

1. A. Bagchi and A. Mahanti, Search algorithms under different kinds of heuristics — A comparative study, *J. ACM* 30 (1) (1983) 1-27.
2. A. Bagchi and A. Mahanti, Three approaches to heuristic search in networks, *J. ACM* 32 (1) (1985) 1-27.
3. R. Dechter and J. Pearl, Generalized best-first search strategies and the optimality of A*, *J. ACM* 32 (3) (1985) 505-536.

---

[18] For any $\mathcal{L}$-standard graph, there exists a minimal path from s to T.
[19] We don't give the details by lack of place.

4. R. Dechter and J. Pearl, The optimality of A*, in: L. Kanal and D. Kumar, eds, *Search in Artificial Intelligence* (Springer-Verlag, 1988) 166-199.

5. D. Dubois, H. Farreny and Henri Prade, Combinatorial search with fuzzy estimates, in : J. Kacprzyk and S. A. Orlowski, eds, *Optimization models using fuzzy sets and possibility theory* (D. Reidel publishing company, 1987) 171-185.

6. D. Dubois, J. Lang and H. Prade, Theorem proving under uncertainty. A possibility theory-based approach, in : *Proceedings 10th IJCAI*, Milan, Italy (1987) 984-986.

7. D. Dubois and H. Prade, *Possibility theory - An Approach to Computerized Processing of Uncertainty*, (Plenum, 1988).

8. H. Farreny, *Recherche Heuristiquement Ordonnée — Algorithmes et propriétés*, (Masson, Paris, 1995).

9. H. Farreny, Une généralisation pour la Recherche Heuristiquement Ordonnée : les algorithmes ρ et la propriété d'arrêt avec découverte de solution, in : *Proceedings of RFIA 96*, Rennes, France (1996) 225-234.

10. D. Gelperin, On the optimality of A*, *Artificial Intelligence* 8 (1) (1977) 69-76.

11. M. Ghallab, Optimisation de processus décisionnels pour la robotique, Thèse de Doctorat d'Etat, Université Paul Sabatier, Toulouse, France (1982).

12. M. Ghallab and D. G. Allard, A_ε : An efficient near admissible heuristic search algorithm, in : *Proceedings 8th IJCAI*, Karlsruhe, Germany (1983) 789-791.

13. R. Gonella, Diagnostic de pannes sur avions : mise en oeuvre d'un raisonnement révisable, Thèse de l'École Nationale Supérieure de l'Aéronautique et de l'Espace, Toulouse, France (1989).

14. L. R. Harris, The heuristic search under conditions of error, *Artificial Intelligence* 5 (3) (1974) 217-234.

15. P. E. Hart, N. J. Nilsson and B. Raphael — A formal basis for the heuristic determination of minimal cost paths, *IEEE Trans. SSC* 4 (1968) 100-107.

16. R. E. Korf, Depth-first iterative-deepening : an optimal admissible tree search, *Artificial Intelligence* 27 (1985) 97-109.

17. A. Mahanti and K. Ray, Network search algorithms with modifiable heuristics, in : L. Kanal and D. Kumar, eds, *Search in Artificial Intelligence*, (Springer-Verlag, 1988) 200-222.

18. A. Martelli, On the complexity of admissible search algorithms, *Artificial Intelligence* 8 (1) (1977) 1-13.

19. L. Mero, A heuristic search algorithm with modifiable estimate, *Artificial Intelligence* 23 (1) (1984) 13-27.

20. N. J. Nilsson, *Problem-solving methods in artificial intelligence*, (Mc Graw-Hill, 1971).

21. N. J. Nilsson, *Principles of artificial intelligence*, (Tioga, 1980).

22. J. Pearl, Some recent results in heuristic search theory, *IEEE Trans. on PAMI* 6 (1) (1984) 1-12.

23. J. Pearl, *Heuristics : intelligent search strategies for computer problem solving* (Addison-Wesley, 1984).

24. J. Pearl and J. H. Kim, Studies in semi-admissible heuristics, *IEEE Trans. on PAMI* 4 (4) (1982) 392-400.

25. I. Pohl, First results on the effect of error in heuristic search, in : B. Meltzer and D. Michie, eds, *Machine Intelligence 5* (Edinburgh University Press, 1969) 219-236.

26. I. Pohl, The avoidance of (relative) catastrophe, heuristic competence, genuine dynamic weighting and computational issues in heuristic problem solving, in : *Proceedings 3d IJCAI*, Stanford, USA (1973) 12-17.

27. M. J. Schoppers, On A* as a special case of ordered search, *Proc. 8th IJCAI*, Karlsruhe, Germany (1983) 783-785.

28. H. A. Simon, Search and Reasoning in Problem Solving, *Artificial Intelligence* 21 (1-2) (1983) 7-29.

29 B. Steward, C. F. Liaw and C. C. White III, A bibliography of Heuristic Search Research Through 1992, *IEEE transactions on Systems, Man, and Cybernetics* 24 (2) (1994) 268-293.

30. R. R. Yager, Paths of least resistance in possibilistic production systems, *Fuzzy sets and systems* 19 (1986) 121-132.

Fixed Point Classification Method for Qualitative Simulation

Martin Takáč

Institute of Informatics, Faculty of Mathematics and Physics,
Comenius University, Mlynská dolina, 84215 Bratislava,
Slovak Republic

Abstract. Qualitative simulation has become a successful method for predicting qualitatively distinct behaviors of physical systems. Yet it is quite weak in providing a global view on a system's behavior, e.g. its stability.
Another approach to reasoning about qualitative properties of dynamic systems is based on Qualitative System Theory of Y. Ishida, deriving global properties of the system from its graphical representation.
This paper presents a Qualitative System Theory based method for fixed point classification in QSIM-like qualitative models and discusses its applicability to qualitative reasoning.

Content areas: Qualitative reasoning, dynamic systems

1 Introduction

Qualitative simulation [8] is an important method of reasoning about the behavior of incompletely specified dynamic systems. However, it can give spurious results or even get stuck by intractable branching, especially for large-scale systems. Although valuable for obtaining detailed view on behavior as a sequence of discrete states ordered in time, qualitative simulation is unable to determine global properties of the system, such as stability, periodicity, and observability.

Qualitative analysis [5] is a common name for variety of techniques for determining system properties by analysis of qualitative structures of the system's model. It covers comparative analysis of Weld [13], qualitative phase portrait composition of Kuipers and Lee [9], fixed point analysis of Sacks [11] and Qualitative System Theory of Ishida [3, 4, 5].

As complementary techniques, both qualitative simulation and qualitative analysis are important for intelligent qualitative reasoning [14]. In this paper we present a Qualitative System Theory based method for fixed point classification in QSIM[1] models and discuss its application to QSIM-based reasoning. Section 2 intoduces basic concepts of dynamic systems, qualitative simulation and Qualitative System Theory. Section 3 presents our main results and describes individual steps of the fixed point classification method. Section 4 gives a few

---

[1] QSIM is the well-known qualitative simulation algorithm of Kuipers [8].

remarks on implementation and experiments. The remaining sections discuss possible applications, related works, and topics for future research.

2 Underlying Concepts

The state of a dynamic system at any time t can be described by a set of values of time-dependent variables $\{x_1, \ldots, x_n\}$. The variables that fully determine the overall state of the system[2] are called *phase variables*. The variables whose values are fixed by mechanisms outside the particular system under consideration, are called *exogenous,* or *independent variables.* They are assumed to be constant during qualitative simulation [2], thus we will treat them as parameters and exclude them from the set of phase variables. As qualitative models cannot explicitly reference time in most qualitative reasoning formalisms, they represent *autonomous systems* – systems whose behavior is governed only by the values of phase variables [1].

Autonomous systems are usually described by a system of first-order ordinary differential equations (ODE)

$$\dot{x}_i = f_i(x_1, \ldots, x_n), \quad i = 1, \ldots, n \tag{1}$$

where x_i are phase variables. One can convert higher-order equations to first-order ones by introducing new variables as synonyms for higher derivatives. We will sometimes use shorter vector form $\dot{x} = f(x)$ of equation (1).

The *phase space* is a Cartesian product of the x_i's domains, points in the phase space represent states of the system. As the system evolves in time, the state traces out a path in the phase space called *trajectory*. The topological and geometric properties of trajectories characterize the qualitative behavior of solutions to (1). For example, a point trajectory, called a *fixed point,* indicates a constant solution, while a closed curve indicates a periodic solution.

Fixed point (equilibrium) is a point x^* in the phase space of (1), such that $f(x^*) = 0$. Fixed points can be either *sinks* (where trajectories only terminate), *sources* (where trajectories only emerge), *saddles* (where some trajectories emerge and some terminate), and *centers* (where trajectories neither emerge nor terminate) [9].

a   b   c   d

Fig. 1. Examples of fixed points in two-dimensional phase space: (a) source, (b) saddle, (c) center, (d) sink.

---

[2] We mean the *minimal* set of variables that fully determine the state of the system.

Qualitative reasoning applies to domains where exact equations and analytical solutions are unknown or too complex. In QSIM formalism incompletely known variable values are described in terms of their relations with a discrete set of *landmark values*. Each variable has its own finite totally ordered set of landmarks – the *quantity space*. The structure of a system is expressed by a set of *constraints* that variable values must satisfy in every time-point t, e.g.

(add x y z) $\equiv x(t) + y(t) = z(t)$

(mult x y z) $\equiv x(t) \cdot y(t) = z(t)$

(minus x y) $\equiv y(t) = -x(t)$

(d/dt x y) $\equiv \frac{d}{dt}x(t) = y(t)$

(constant x) $\equiv \frac{d}{dt}x(t) = 0$

(M+ x y) $\equiv y(t) = f(x(t)), \quad f'(x(t)) > 0$

(M- x y) $\equiv y(t) = f(x(t)), \quad f'(x(t)) < 0.$

The M^+ and M^- constraints express monotonic functional relationship. Each constraint can be associated with a set of *corresponding values* – tuples of landmark values that the variables in the constraint can take on at the same time. Qualitative description of a system in terms of qualitative variables, quantity spaces and constraints is called qualitative differential equation (QDE).

QDE representation has been extended also with non-monotonic function constraints, e.g. U^+ and U^- represent continuously differentiable functions concave up and concave down, respectively, monotonic on each side of an extreme point[3] [8].

Qualitative simulation, given initial qualitative values for variables, generates the set of *behaviors* – sequences of qualitatively described states consistent with the constraints.

2.1 Qualitative System Theory

The Qualitative System Theory (QST) of Ishida [4] studies the properties of incompletely specified linear or linearized dynamical systems

$$\dot{x} = Ax, \quad A \in R^{n \times n}. \tag{2}$$

The available information is often insufficient to identify exact values of the elements of A, hence a triple valued *sign matrix* A_s, whose elements are defined as

$$(A_s)_{ij} = \begin{cases} + \text{ if } (A)_{ij} > 0 \\ 0 \text{ if } (A)_{ij} = 0 \\ - \text{ if } (A)_{ij} < 0 \end{cases}$$

---

[3] For example, $y = U^+_{(a,b)}(x)$ means that $y = f(x)$ where $f(a) = b$, $f'(x) < 0$ for $x < a$, and $f'(x) > 0$ for $x > a$.

is considered instead of A. We can view the sign matrix A_s as a class of all real-valued matrices having the sign pattern identical to that of A_s. We say the property of the matrix A_s is *sign (potential)*, if all (some of) instances of A_s satisfy the property.

Most of the qualitative properties of sign matrices, e.g. sign stability[4] and observability, can be checked by investigating their graphical expression – *signed digraph* (cf. Fig. 2). Signed digraph of a matrix $A \in R^{n \times n}$ is a graph of n nodes and arcs corresponding to non-zero elements of A. An arc directed from node j to i is labelled $+(-)$, when $a_{ij} > 0$ (< 0). A *circuit* is a closed path where the path is a graph connecting many nodes by arcs of the same direction sequentially. The *sign* of a circuit is a multiplication of all the signs of the arcs included in the circuit. The *length* of the circuit is the number of arcs included in the circuit. The circuit of length 1 is called *loop*.

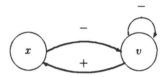

Fig. 2. Signed digraph for damped spring model $\dot{x} = v$ and $\dot{v} = -f(x) - g(v)$, where $f, g \in M^+$. The model satisfies sufficient and necessary conditions for sign stability.

Our fixed point classification method utilizes results of the following theorem [3]:

Theorem 1 Necessary and sufficient conditions for sign stability. *The matrix A_s is sign stable if and only if its graph satisfies the following conditions:*

1. *All the loops must have non-positive signs, and at least one loop must have a negative sign.*
2. *All the circuits of length two must have non-positive sign.*
3. *There must be no circuits of length greater than two.*
4. *The graph does not pass the color test and passes the matching test.*

Model satisfying conditions (1) (2) and (3) is known not to have divergent solutions. The condition (4) ascertains the model does not have periodic or constant solutions (i.e., its matrix does not have pure imaginaries or zero as its eigenvalues). Color and matching tests are defined in [5].

---

[4] Matrix A_s is *sign stable*, if every instance of A_s is stable (that is, the real part of every eigenvalue of the matrix is negative).

3 QST-based Method for Stability Checking

We have proposed an algebraic method for a classification of fixed points of a system modeled with a QDE – the usual input to QSIM. The method works in the following steps:

1. Take a QSIM-like QDE and generate a canonic equation $\dot{x} = f(x)$ for it.
2. Determine fixed points of the canonic equation by setting $f(x) = 0$.
3. Obtain the Jacobian matrix $J(x)$ in a general point x by symbolic differentiation of the canonic equation.
4. Determine the sign pattern J_s of the matrix $J(x^*)$ for each fixed point x^*.
5. Determine the type of the fixed point by considering the sign properties of $J_s(x^*)$.

3.1 QDE Canonization

The input to this step is a QDE description of a system as used in QSIM define-QDE macro [8]. Unlike in QSIM, we require the quantity space for each variable contain zero, so that the signs of all landmarks can be uniquely determined. We allow hybrid quantity spaces containing both numeric and symbolic landmarks. Numeric landmarks are treated as numbers where possible (see Sect. 3.3).

QDE constraints can consist of add, mult, minus, d/dt, M+, M-, U+, U- and constant clauses. The QDE model must contain at least one d/dt constraint, i.e. it must express dynamics of the modeled system.[5] QDE can also contain an optional clause independent, which identifies exogenous variables.

By canonization we mean the process of transforming a given QDE to a set of equations[6]

$$\dot{x}_i = f_i(x_1, \ldots, x_n), \quad i = 1, \ldots, n, \tag{3}$$

where x_i are qualitative variables of the original QDE identified as *phase variables*, f_i are defined in terms of addition, multiplication, division, opposite, M+, M-, U+, U- constraints, and raising to a constant (non-negative integer) power. Operands to these operations must be phase variables, independent variables, variables appearing in constant constraint, or numbers.

The canonization algorithm identifies variables appearing as the first argument in a (d/dt x y) constraint as *phase variables* and expresses their derivatives in terms of constants and phase variables. Appropriate expressions are

---

[5] Equlibrium equations not containing derivatives are used under *steady-state assumption* [2] in comparative analysis.

[6] In fact, these equations are not canonic, because any mathematically equivalent form of the equations obtained by commutation, distribution, factorization, etc., satisfying the above stated conditions could be a legal result of the canonization process. What we mean by canonization, is actually a process of eliminating auxiliary variables and can be viewed as a kind of inverse process to structural abstraction from ODE to QDE.

derived from the constraints of the original QDE by a constraint satisfaction algorithm SO based on variable separation and substitution [12].

3.2 Fixed Point Determination

Fixed points of the QDE model can be obtained by setting left sides of all equations in the canonic form to zero and solving the resulting equations.[7]

We can use the SO algorithm to express phase variables from these equations, and Q-EVALUATE algorithm (cf. Sect. 3.5) to obtain qualitative interval bounds for fixed points. However, mostly because of the weak separation procedure, SO algorithm gets blocked for sufficiently complicated simultaneous equations. More sophisticated fixed point determination remains for future work.

In some applications fixed point determination is not necessary, because fixed points are recognized during qualitative simulation and marked as *quiescent states* [8].

3.3 Jacobian Matrix in a General Fixed Point

To obtain the Jacobian matrix, we symbolically partially differentiate the expression $f_i(x_1, \ldots, x_n)$ of the canonic QDE by phase variable x_j for each $i, j = 1, \ldots, n$, using simple transcription rules, e.g.

1. $\neg contains(E, x) \rightarrow \frac{\partial E}{\partial x} \Rightarrow 0$
2. $\frac{\partial(E+F)}{\partial x} \Rightarrow \frac{\partial E}{\partial x} + \frac{\partial F}{\partial x}$

As we can see in the first rule, transcription can make numbers appear in expressions. The simplification rules[8] for hybrid (numeric-symbolic) expressions are applied when possible, e.g. $0 + E \Rightarrow E$.

3.4 Sign Pattern Determination

In general, resulting elements of the Jacobian matrix obtained in the previous step are symbolic expressions in phase variables, constants and numbers. To determine their signs, we must substitute appropriate values for constants and for phase variables in each fixed point.

In QSIM formalism a variable can have a qualitative magnitude l_i, where l_i is a landmark, or (l_i, l_j), where l_i, l_j are *adjacent* landmarks. However, during sign pattern determination we often need to express incompletely known qualitative magnitudes, e.g. when some of the fixed point coordinates are not known. Thus we represent qualitative magnitudes as landmark intervals (l_i, l_j), where l_i, l_j need not to be adjacent. We distinguish between open and closed interval, using the notation (l_i, l_j) for open, and $\langle l_i, l_j)$ for closed interval (half-open intervals

---

[7] Due to incompletely specified functions in QDE models, this is not possible in general. For example, the variable x cannot be separated from the equation $x + M^+(x) = 0$.

[8] For complete set of rules for partial differentiation and simplification see [12].

(l_i, l_j) and $\langle l_i, l_j \rangle$ are allowed as well). Single landmark qualitative magnitude l_i is used instead of the closed interval $\langle l_i, l_i \rangle$. Numbers appearing in partially differentiated qualitative expressions are treated as landmarks.

In order to express ordinal relation between a qualitative magnitude and a landmark in their respective quantity space, we define the following sign operator $[\![\cdot]\!]$:

Definition 1 *Let a, x be landmarks, Q be a quantity space containing a, x. We define*

$$[\![x]\!]_a = \begin{cases} [+] & \text{if } x > a \text{ in } Q \\ [0] & \text{if } x = a \text{ in } Q \\ [-] & \text{if } x < a \text{ in } Q. \end{cases}$$

By definition, $x < \infty$ for each $x \neq \infty$, and $x > -\infty$ for each $x \neq -\infty$. The ordinal relation between ∞ and ∞ ($-\infty$ and $-\infty$, respectively) is indefinite, i.e. $[\![\infty]\!]_\infty = [\![-\infty]\!]_{-\infty} = [?]$.

Let y be a landmark in Q, and $x < y$. We define

$$[\![(x, y)]\!]_a = \begin{cases} [+] & \text{if } x \geq a \text{ in } Q \\ [-] & \text{if } y \leq a \text{ in } Q \\ [?] & \text{otherwise} \end{cases}$$

$$[\![\langle x, y \rangle]\!]_a = \begin{cases} [+] & \text{if } x > a \text{ in } Q \\ [0+] & \text{if } x = a \text{ in } Q \\ [-] & \text{if } y < a \text{ in } Q \\ [0-] & \text{if } y = a \text{ in } Q \\ [?] & \text{otherwise} \end{cases}$$

$$[\![(x, y)]\!]_a = \begin{cases} [+] & \text{if } x \geq a \text{ in } Q \\ [-] & \text{if } y < a \text{ in } Q \\ [0-] & \text{if } y = a \text{ in } Q \\ [?] & \text{otherwise.} \end{cases}$$

$[\![\langle x, y \rangle]\!]_a$ *is defined by analogy.*

Reader can see that $[\![x]\!]_0$ corresponds to usual mathematical $sign(x)$. If $[\![x]\!]_0 \in S = \{[-], [0], [+]\}$, the sign of x is uniquely determined, $[0-]$, $[0+]$ represent partially known[9] $sign(x)$, $[?]$ means $sign(x)$ is indeterminate. We will call S the *Domain of Signs* and $S_E = S \cup \{[0-], [0+], [?]\}$ the *Extended Domain of Signs*. Qualitative addition and multiplication are defined over the Domain of

---

[9] In particular, $[\![x]\!]_a = [0-]$ means $x \leq a$, and $[\![x]\!]_a = [0+]$ means $x \geq a$.

Signs (cf. e.g. [8] p. 49). We define qualitative addition, multiplication, opposite, and absolute value operators $\oplus$, $\otimes$, $\ominus$, $\| \, \|$ over S_E:

$\oplus$	[-]	[0-]	[0]	[0+]	[+]	[?]
[-]	[-]	[-]	[-]	[?]	[?]	[?]
[0-]	[-]	[0-]	[0-]	[?]	[?]	[?]
[0]	[-]	[0-]	[0]	[0+]	[+]	[?]
[0+]	[?]	[?]	[0+]	[0+]	[+]	[?]
[+]	[?]	[?]	[+]	[+]	[+]	[?]
[?]	[?]	[?]	[?]	[?]	[?]	[?]

x	$\ominus x$	$\|x\|$
[-]	[+]	[+]
[0-]	[0+]	[0+]
[0]	[0]	[0]
[0+]	[0-]	[0+]
[+]	[-]	[+]
[?]	[?]	[?]

Multiplication operator is defined by analogy.

3.5 Sign Propagation Across Constraints

Quantity spaces in QSIM are completely unrelated structures. Landmarks in different quantity spaces have no *a priori* relation, even if they have the same names. Thus, any intended relationship among landmarks across quantity spaces must be made explicit in corresponding values of suitable constraints ([8] p. 66). We use corresponding value tuples for sign propagation across constraints.

Constraint	Proposition	Validity Conditions
$z = x + y$	$[z]_{z^*} = [x]_{x^*} \oplus [y]_{y^*}$	
$z = x \cdot y$	$[z]_0 = [x]_0 \otimes [y]_0$	except $[\pm\infty \cdot 0]_0 = [?]$
$z = \frac{x}{y}$	$[z]_0 = [x]_0 \otimes [y]_0$	$[y]_0 \notin \{[0], [0+], [0-]\}$
		$\wedge \, y \neq \pm\infty$
	$[z]_0 = [x]_0 \otimes [+]$	$[y]_0 = [0+]$
	$[z]_0 = [x]_0 \otimes [-]$	$[y]_0 = [0-]$
	$[z]_0 = [0]$	$x \neq \pm\infty \wedge y = \pm\infty$
$y = -x$ or $y = M^-(x)$	$[y]_{y^*} = \ominus[x]_{x^*}$	
$y = M^+(x)$	$[y]_{y^*} = [x]_{x^*}$	
$y = x^k$ where $k > 0$ integer	$[y]_0 = [x]_0$	$odd(k)$
	$[y]_0 = \|[x]_0\|$	$even(k)$
$y = U^+_{(a,b)}(x)$	$[y]_{y^*} = [x]_{x^*}$	$x \geq a \wedge x^* \geq a$
	$[y]_{y^*} = \ominus[x]_{x^*}$	$x < a \wedge x^* \leq a$
$y = U^-_{(a,b)}(x)$	$[y]_{y^*} = \ominus[x]_{x^*}$	$x \geq a \wedge x^* \geq a$
	$[y]_{y^*} = [x]_{x^*}$	$x < a \wedge x^* \leq a$

Table 1. Summary of propositions holding for each corresponding value tuple (x^*, y^*, z^*) or (x^*, y^*) associated with the constraint.

The qualitative magnitude of a compound expression can be determined by induction in two steps:

1. Substitute qualitative magnitudes for all variables in the expression. If the qualitative magnitude for some variable is unknown, substitute the maximal closed interval of the variable's quantity space.[10]
2. Let E be a (sub-)expression with qualitative magnitudes substituted for all its arguments. Obtain the list $C = \{(lmark, sign), \ldots\}$ by applying propositions from Table 1 for each corresponding value tuple associated[11] with E. Each pair in C expresses the ordinal relation between the E's magnitude and some landmark appearing in a corresponding value tuple.

   Treat C as a conjunction of elementary inequalities to obtain the tightest bounds for E. Substitute the resulting interval for qualitative magnitude of E.

These two steps form the body of our algorithm Q-$evaluate(E\ Subst)$, where E is an expression and $Subst = \{(var, qmag), \ldots\}$ determines the known qualitative magnitudes of the variables in E.

The sign pattern of the Jacobian matrix $J(x^*) = (a_{ij}(x^*))_{i,j=1}^n$ is

$$J_s(x^*) = ([\![Q\text{-}evaluate(a_{ij}, Subst_{x^*})]\!]_0)_{i,j=1}^n,$$

where $Subst_{x^*}$ determines the known values of constants and coordinates of the fixed point x^*.

3.6 Fixed Point Classification

The obtained matrix need not to be fully sign determinate, i.e. it can contain $[0+]$, $[0-]$, or $[?]$ elements. For each element $e = [0+]$ ($[0-]$) we must consider two possibilities $e = [0] \vee e = [+]$ ($e = [0] \vee e = [-]$, respectively). For $e = [?]$ we must consider even three possibilities $e \in \{[-], [0], [+]\}$. We say that indeterminate sign matrix A_s satisfy the property $\mathcal{P}$, if $\mathcal{P}$ is satisfied by *each* possible sign determinate instance of A_s.

We can classify the fixed point x^* in the following manner:

1. If Jacobian sign matrix $J_s(x^*)$ is sign stable, then x^* is a stable fixed point (sink).
2. If $\ominus J_s(x^*)$ is sign stable, then x^* is an unstable fixed point (source).

We determine sign stability by testing the conditions of Theorem 1. The $\ominus J_s(x^*)$ is the sign version of $-J(x^*)$. If $\ominus J_s(x^*)$ is sign stable, then $-J(x^*)$ has all eigenvalues with negative real parts, hence $J(x^*)$ is sign unstable and x^* is a repellent fixed point (source).

---

[10] Maximal closed interval for the quantity space $\{l_1, \ldots, l_n\}$ is $\langle l_1, l_n \rangle$.

[11] The tuple $(0, 0, 0)$ is implicitly associated with the add constraint and $(0, 0)$ with the minus constraint.

If neither $J_s(x^*)$ nor $\ominus J_s(x^*)$ is sign stable, we cannot conclude x^* is non-stable (saddle), as J_s and $\ominus J_s$ could fail sign stability test simply because some of their instances were stable while others were unstable.

As stated in Sect. 2, the set of phase variables fully determining the state of the system should be minimal, i.e., none of the phase variables can be expressed in terms of constants and other phase variables. System containing dependent phase variables is *redundant*, and redundancy prevents stable systems from being sign stable. The FPA algorithm of Sacks [11] ameliorates this problem by eliminating linear dependences. We assume the input model of the considered system be correct, in that its phase variables are mutually independent.

The stability properties obtained from the Jacobian matrix are local, in that they are valid only in the neighborhood of the considered fixed point. However, in case the considered system is *monostable*, the obtained information is sufficient to determine global phase portrait. System is monostable, if all its trajectories approach a single fixed point. A sufficient condition for monostability is that the matrix $J(x)$ be stable for every x [11]. Our method can test monostability by computing $J_s(x)$ for a general fixed point, i.e. for fixed point whose coordinates are unknown and hence supplemented by their maximal intervals. If the matrix $J_s(x)$ in a general fixed point x is sign stable, then the system is monostable, i.e. it has a single stable fixed point.

4 Implementation and Experiments

To prove viability of the above described method, we have been implementing SAMST – Simple Algebraic Manipulator for Stability Test. The fixed point determination has not been implemented yet, hence fixed point coordinates must be given as input to the program. The SAMST's current output is the sign matrix, and its sign properties must be determined manually.

We have tested SAMST performance on twenty examples from QSIM Sample Library, including various tanks, controllers, Lienard and Van der Pol equations, equilibrium mechanisms in kidney, and pressure regulator. SAMST derived canonic equations for all the twenty models. It computed fully determined sign matrices in nineteen cases, in one case (pressure regulator) sign matrix contained one [?] element. In two cases (U-tube and Starling equilibrium) SAMST did not identify stable equilibrium (sink) because of the flabby models with mutually dependent phase variables (cf. Sect. 3.6). Sinks and sources could be identified from computed sign matrices in fourteen out of the seventeen remaining models.

5 Possible Applications

Comparative Analysis

Comparative analysis ([8] p. 151, [13]) studies behavior of systems that are always at, or very near, a point of stable equilibrium. It is concerned with the relation between an initial equilibrium state and the state resulting from small perturbation to values of exogenous variables. The [8] presents QSIM-based comparative analysis method that works correctly, provided the considered equilibrium is stable. To check stability of the equilibrium, our method can be used.

Qualitative Phase Portrait Composition

Kuipers and Lee [9] describe QSIM-based program QPORTRAIT that constructs phase portraits for autonomous two-dimensional systems with non-degenerate fixed points.[12] They check non-degeneracy of fixed points manually. Our method can be used for that purpose, as well as for fixed point classification of sinks and sources.

6   Related Works

Most closely related to our work is FPA[13] algorithm of Sacks [11]. It computes Jacobian matrix in each fixed point and derives signs of the elements with BOUNDER inequality reasoner [10]. If the stability cannot be determined from sign information, Routh-Hurwitz stability criterion [3] is applied for magnitudes. FPA applies to qualitative models of a generic form, while our method is designed to work with QSIM-like models, e.g. we handle models containing U^+, U^- constraints. Major differences in the value bounding strategies are the following:

- We distinguish between open and closed intervals, while BOUNDER always returns closed ones.
- BOUNDER assumes all variables be mutually comparable by having common domain $\Re$. In QSIM formalism quantity spaces are unrelated structures, hence any ordering relationship between variables can be determined only from corresponding value information.[14]

7   Limitations and Future Work

Our method draws conclusions from sign stability – condition too strong for most systems. However, although the method uses only sign information, it computes *interval* matrices first, hence its performance could be improved by considering stability of the interval Jacobian matrix. Ishida [6, 7] describes methods for investigating some properties of interval matrices.

---

[12] Fixed point x^* is non-degenerate if all eigenvalues of the Jacobian matrix $J(x^*)$ have non-zero real parts.

[13] FPA means Fixed Point Analysis.

[14] Recent version of QSIM implements an experimental feature – hierarchical quantity spaces, where partial ordering between landmarks from different quantity spaces can be defined.

Another drawback of the method is that results obtained for linearized systems are valid only locally. Global synthesis of linearization results, along with the limit cycle detection, location of separatrices, etc. would be a valuable contribution to qualitative analysis of non-linear systems.

The stability properties of the system computed by our method could help to filter out spurious behaviors in qualitative simulation. Provided a system is stable and given a qualitative expression for the Lyapunov function of the system, we could filter out behaviors violating stability. However, this is a topic for future research.

Acknowledgements

Many thanks to Ján Šefránek for help and for reading drafts of this paper, Milan Medved' for consultations on dynamic systems, and Mikuláš Popper for advices.

References

1. Arrowsmith, D. K., Place, C. M.: *Ordinary differential equations: A qualitative approach with applications.* Chapman and Hall, London New York (1982)
2. de Kleer, J., Brown, J. S.: Theories of Causal Ordering. *Artificial Intelligence* **29** (1986)
3. Ishida, Y., Adachi, N., Tokumaru, H.: Some Results on the Qualitative Theory of Matrix. *Trans. of SICE*, Vol. 17, No. 1 (1981)
4. Ishida, Y.: Using Global Properties for Qualitative Reasoning: A Qualitative System Theory. *Proceedings IJCAI-89.* Morgan Kaufmann, San Mateo, CA (1989)
5. Ishida, Y.: A Qualitative Analysis on Dynamical Systems: Sign Structure. Memoirs of Kyoto University, Vol. 54, No. 1 (1992)
6. Ishida, Y.: Structural Analysis on Interval Matrices by Signed Digraph: Determinant Maximization and Singularity. Technical Report NAIST-IS-TR 95032, Nara Institute of Science and Technology, Nara (1995)
7. Ishida, Y.: Structural Analysis on Interval Matrices by Signed Digraph: Structural Perturbation Principle. Technical Report NAIST-IS-TR 95033, Nara Institute of Science and Technology, Nara (1995)
8. Kuipers, B. J.: *Qualitative Reasoning: Modeling and Simulation with Incomplete Knowledge.* MIT Press, Cambridge, MA (1994)
9. Lee, W. W., Kuipers, B. J.: A Qualitative Method to Construct Phase Portraits. *Proceedings of AAAI-93.* MIT Press, Cambridge, MA (1993)
10. Sacks, E.: Hierarchical Reasoning about Inequalities. *Proceedings of AAAI-87.* Seattle, Wash (1987)
11. Sacks, E.: A Dynamic Systems Perspective on Qualitative Simulation. *Artificial Intelligence* **42** (1990)
12. Takáč, M.: *A Qualitative System Theory Based Method for Stability Checking and Its Applicability to Qualitative Reasoning.* Diploma thesis, Institute of Informatics, Faculty of Mathematics and Physics, Comenius University, Bratislava (1997)
13. Weld, D. S.: Comparative Analysis. *Artificial Intelligence* **36** (1988)
14. Weld, D. S., de Kleer, J. (eds.): *Readings in Qualitative Reasoning about Physical Systems.* Morgan Kaufmann, San Mateo, CA (1990)

Contextual Logic of Change and the Ramification Problem *

Pedro A. Matos and João P. Martins

Secção de Sistemas/DEM
Instituto Superior Técnico
Technical University of Lisbon
1096 Lisboa Codex, Portugal
{pedro,jpm}@gia.ist.utl.pt

Abstract. In this paper we discuss CLOC, an approach for reasoning about action and change, which is an alternative to the situation calculus and circumscription. In our approach, inspired by the possible worlds approach, change is modeled as changing the theory that describes the world. CLOC extends first order logic by representing changes, defining predicates about the execution of change and defining new inference rules that handle change. We also present a rule of inference, $EX_P\mu$, that is used for concluding what propositions hold after the execution of change. We study the ramification problem and conclude that our approach presents the correct solution for the example Baker uses to show that his approach doesn't solve the ramification problem. We also show that our method is highly sensitive to the choice of formulation used to describe the situations involved, since some variations would be enough to make our method suffer from the ramification problem. We conclude that this is a problem of choosing adequate formulation of both situations and actions. We identify the conditions under which our method solves this problem and make suggestions for avoiding it.

1 Introduction

Situation calculus [18] is a formalism for reasoning about action and change. In this formalism, propositions refer situations and, therefore, need to be reformulated after changing the situation. This problem is strongly related to the frame problem, the problem of deciding which propositions hold after change has occurred.

One of the approaches used to try to solve the frame problem is to use circumscription [19,20,14], a method for performing common-sense reasoning. The circumscription of a predicate relative to a theory minimizes the extent of that predicate. McCarthy [20] proposes the use of simple abnormality theories, whose

---

* We thank Prof. Carlos Pinto Ferreira, the anonymous reviewers and the members of GIA for their for their helpful comments. This work was partially supported by Junta Nacional de Investigação Científica e Tecnológica and by PRAXIS XXI under grant 2/2.1/TIT/1568/95.

general facts are described using the predicate *Ab*, for abnormal. The circumscription of predicate *Ab*, relative to the theory, with all predicates variable, would presumably be enough to model common-sense reasoning and solve the frame problem. However, as McCarthy realized, this was not the case.

Hanks and McDermott [6] present an example, the Yale shooting problem, which shows that the solutions presented by the use of the circumscription method do not correspond to the intended solution. Several approaches have been proposed to expand and correct the simple abnormality theories approach, including [8,12,1,15,7].

However, the specificity of these approaches still raises some problems. Lifschitz, for example, mentions the difficulties in dealing with the multitude of choices that these methods allow, claiming that this is "the main reason why circumscription is not applied today in knowledge representation as widely as would be expected" [15]. He proposes the use of nested abnormality theories instead, which introduces blocks and embedding of blocks, about which he writes "...each block can be viewed as a group of axioms that describes a certain collection of predicates and functions, and the embedding of blocks reflects the dependence of these descriptions on each other" [15]. This dependence relation among propositions goes against our understanding of McCarthy's ideas, namely that "the general facts of common sense are described by a collection of sentences that are not oriented in advance to particular problems" [20, Section 11], which we subscribe.

Another approach to the problem of formalizing change is what Sandewall and Shoham [23] named the meta-level approach. In this approach, propositions do not include the identification of situations and change is modeled as changing the set of propositions that hold in situations. Ginsberg and Smith's possible worlds approach [5] is based in these ideas. However, this approach has been criticized by Winslett [26], who proposes the possible models approach, according to which the models, rather than the formulas, are to be changed. We argue, in a forthcoming paper, that change may be modeled using syntactic approaches.

Mutation logic (ML) [21,22], is one example of the meta-level approach. In this logic, the execution of change is modeled as changing the set of propositions that hold before change is executed into a new set. Change is represented by a proposition describing its pre-conditions and post-conditions. However, this logic has limitations affecting its expressive power, in particular, there is no way to express side-effects of change and the language of the logic does not allow the representation of plans.

Contextual logic of change (CLOC), the logic we are developing, is an extension of first order logic (FOL), augmenting the expressive power of ML, using some ideas from the possible world approach and belief revision techniques.

When using our method, propositions do not refer situations. We may think of situations as belief spaces of contexts (a *context* is a set of hypotheses and a *belief space* of a context is the set of derivable propositions from the context) and are not represented explicitly by any object in the language. A consequence of this representation is the limitation of the expressive power of the language, since we are no longer able to represent propositions about situations.

The execution of change in CLOC is modeled by altering the set of propositions that describes the situation before change is executed, to the set of propositions that describes the situation after change is executed (in the framework of predicate calculus, we may think of changing the value of some predicates as we change the situation being represented).

CLOC expands FOL by: i) introducing new terms that represent change; ii) defining new functions on these terms that are used to represent structured changes; iii) introducing predicates about change, for example $\mathcal{X}_P$, which is applied to a term representing change, and means that it has been executed; and iv) adding inference rules that change the context description when change is known to have been executed.

CLOC solves the frame problem as presented by McCarthy and Hayes because propositions are not explicitly associated with situations as in situation calculus.

Reasoning about action and change, using our approach, is modeled as reasoning in different contexts. We found that this kind of reasoning is best described using a non-traditional proof system, the contextual proof [17], which is a generalization of traditional proof systems [3,10,19].

In this paper, we present our approach to the ramification problem, which is the problem of knowing what are the effects of a change. One of the problems of reasoning about action and change is that executing an action may lead to states that are not completely specified. Baker [1] refers one such example, which he finds himself unable to solve.

We present that example and show that CLOC may solve it, depending on the formulation used to represent both the situation and change. In fact, we show that the problem is: i) solved, if we use a given formulation; ii) unsolved, if a minor change on the formulation is considered, even though the set of derivable propositions is the same for both the original and changed formulation; and iii) solved again, if we also consider an altered change representation. We, therefore, conclude that the ramification problem is really one of the adequacy of change representation given the situation representation.

In Section 2, we present part of the CLOC logic, including the representation of change and an inference rule. In Section 3, we motivate the need and then present contextual proofs. In Section 4, we discuss our approach to the ramification problem, and finally, in Section 5, we present the conclusions.

2 Contextual Logic of Change

In this section, we discuss the contextual logic of change, the logic we propose to handle change, and present one of its rules of inference.

CLOC expands first order logic by: i) introducing terms to represent change, the *mutations*; ii) introducing operations for building structured changes (also called plans); iii) introducing new predicates about changes; and iv) defining inference rules that handle change.

A *mutation* corresponds to an atomic change. A mutation μ_i is described by two sets of propositions, the pre-conditions, $\Psi(\mu_i)$, and post-conditions, $\Phi(\mu_i)$, and is written as $\mu(\Psi(\mu_i); \Phi(\mu_i))$. The set $\Psi(\mu_i) - \Phi(\mu_i)$ contains propositions that are no longer known to be true after the execution of change. For example, moving a robot from room R_1 to room R_2 might be represented by the mutation $\mu(\{At(Robot, R_1)\}; \{At(Robot, R_2)\})$.

We define *change* as a generalization of mutation. There are two different kinds of changes: *elementary changes*, that corresponds to mutations, and *structured changes*, that corresponds to the composition of mutations and simpler structured changes. We consider two types of structured changes: (1) sequential execution plans and (2) unordered execution plans. Given changes Π_1 and Π_2, then $\Pi_1 - \Pi_2$ represent the sequential execution of Π_1 and Π_2, and $\prec \Pi_1, \Pi_2 \succ$ represent the unordered execution of Π_1 and Π_2.

The advantage of representing change as a term is that propositions about change can now be written. One example of such a proposition is that the change represented by a term has been executed in the past. These propositions are represented using the predicate $\mathcal{X}_P$. When considering only one change, the proposition "the mutation μ has been executed" is written as $\mathcal{X}_P(\mu)$. Some of the extended inference rules use these propositions to justify the conclusion on the effects of change.

We now present a sketch of one rule of inference of CLOC, *Elimination of Execution of a Mutation in the Past*, $E\mathcal{X}_P\mu$, that governs changes in contexts due to the execution of an elementary change. We will be interested, in the rest of this paper, in the theories that Lifschitz [13] called "theories of a single action", in which only one elementary change is considered. In order to present the rule $E\mathcal{X}_P\mu$, we define the *support* of a derivation as the set of hypotheses that are used in the derivation.

Consider a context, that represents the initial situation, and a mutation μ, that represents a change from the initial situation into another situation. Suppose that there is a derivation of the conjunction on the pre-conditions of change, $\bigwedge(\Psi(\mu))$. Then the representation of the situation resulting from the execution of change may be derived.

We may introduce hypothesis $\mathcal{X}_P(\mu)$, meaning that change has been executed, and then the execution of rule $E\mathcal{X}_P\mu$ has the following effects: i) removes a set of hypotheses from the context such that both the pre-conditions in $\Psi(\mu)$ that are not post-conditions in $\Phi(\mu)$, and negations of the post-conditions, are no longer derivable, and the set of removed hypotheses is minimal relative to set inclusion; and ii) derives the post-conditions with support $\{\mathcal{X}_P(\mu)\} \cup Sup(\bigwedge(\Psi(\mu)))$, where $Sup(\bigwedge(\Psi(\mu)))$ is the support of the derivation of $\bigwedge(\Psi(\mu))$ (for clarity, in step i, we are ignoring propositions such as "the mutation μ *will be* executed", which should also be removed from the belief space after executing change μ).

When considering a execution of rule $E\mathcal{X}_P\mu$, no hypotheses should be added to the proof after the execution of rule $E\mathcal{X}_P\mu$, except other hypotheses describing the execution of change. However, since we are only interested in theories of a single action in this paper, we will not concern ourselves with such hypotheses.

Notice that rule $E\mathcal{X}_P\mu$ changes a minimum set of hypotheses, which is a way to obtain a behavior consistent with extended STRIPS assumption, which says, using STRIPS terms, that "any formula that is satisfied in the initiating state and does not belong to the delete list will be satisfied in the resulting state, *unless* it is inconsistent to assume so" [4] (original emphasis).

3 The Nonmonotonic Nature of Change

In this section, we argue that reasoning about action and change is nonmonotonic by nature, and because of this, contextual proof [17] is more appropriate than traditional proofs to be used when describing a proof in CLOC.

Consider a situation in which a robot is in room R_1. This situation is represented by the context containing the proposition $At(Robot, R_1)$. Suppose that the robot moved to room R_2. Mutation $\mu(\{At(Robot, R_1)\}; \{At(Robot, R_2)\})$ represents this change and the proposition that this change has been executed is represented as $\mathcal{X}_P(\mu(\{At(Robot, R_1)\}; \{At(Robot, R_2)\}))$. If we add this as an hypothesis and apply the rule of inference $E\mathcal{X}_P\mu$, we change the situation description and conclude that $At(Robot, R_1)$ should no longer be derivable and $At(Robot, R_2)$ should become derivable.

The logic is nonmonotonic because, according to the $E\mathcal{X}_P\mu$ rule of inference, we may no longer conclude a proposition that was derived in the previous situation, as happens with $At(Robot, R_1)$ in the example.

Traditional proof systems are not appropriate to be used with this logic because of the nonmonotonic behavior. McCarthy [19] defines "a proof from the premises A is a sequence of sentences each of which is either a premise, an axiom, or follows from a subset of the sentences occurring earlier in the proof by one of the rules of inference". This proof definition is not adequate to represent CLOC proofs because there is no way to distinguish propositions that hold in a situation and propositions that don't hold any more.

Figure 1 presents an example of a natural deduction proof using Lemmon's proof [10] in which each line contains: the support; the number of line; the proposition; and the inference rule. In this proof, we prove the conjunction of propositions $At(Robot, R_1)$ and $At(Robot, R_2)$. This conjunction should not be derived, since if $At(Robot, R_2)$ was derived, $At(Robot, R_1)$ should have been removed from the belief space.

We extended this proof definition and introduced the contextual proof [17], where lines may be struck, meaning that they should not be used in any further derivation, at least until the strokes were removed. The strokes are associated with the line that caused them. Using this new proof definition, presumes changing the inference rules so that only lines that were not struck are considered.

$\{1\}$ 1 $At(Robot, R_1)$ Hyp

$\{2\}$ 2 $\mathcal{X}_P(\mu(\{At(Robot, R_1)\}; \{At(Robot, R_2)\}))$ Hyp

$\{1, 2\}$ 3 $At(Robot, R_2)$ $1, 2, E\mathcal{X}_P\mu$

$\{1, 2\}$ 4 $At(Robot, R_1) \wedge At(Robot, R_2)$ $1, 3, \wedge I$

Fig. 1. Example of inappropriate proof in CLOC.

$\cancel{\{1\}}$ $\cancel{1}$ $\cancel{At(Robot, R_1)}$ ———————————————— Hyp 2

$\{2\}$ 2 $\mathcal{X}_P(\mu(\{At(Robot, R_1)\}; \{At(Robot, R_2)\}))$ Hyp

$\{1, 2\}$ 3 $At(Robot, R_2)$ $1, 2, E\mathcal{X}_P\mu$

Fig. 2. The same example using contextual proof.

Referring to CLOC, when a proposition is removed from the belief space, the line where it appears in the proof is struck and the number of the line where the hypothesis of execution of change was raised is associated with the stroke.

Rule $E\mathcal{X}_P\mu$ application lines must follow the execution of change hypotheses it refers to, so only one elimination execution of change may be applied for each execution of change hypothesis.

In Figure 2, we present the proof of last example using contextual proof, and observe that since the line where hypothesis $At(Robot, R_1)$ was raised has been struck by Line 2, we are no longer able to derive $At(Robot, R_1) \wedge At(Robot, R_2)$.

4   CLOC and the Ramification Problem

In this section, we discuss the ramification problem and how our approach may be used to prevent it. We present an example that Baker [1] uses to show that his approach doesn't solve the ramification problem, and then show that our approach solves it.[1] However, our solution is dependent on the formulation we use for describing both the situation and the change. We discuss these dependencies and identify the necessary conditions to solve the ramification problem.

The ramification problem is the problem of knowing what are the effects of a change. We model a situation as the belief space of a given set of hypotheses, and we model change in the world by a term, the mutation, which describes the pre-conditions of change, the propositions to be added to the belief space, and implicitly describes the propositions that should be removed from the belief space. Inadequate change description might result in multiple scenarios, a problem that also appears in other approaches, such as in Baker's approach.

Baker introduced the robot and ice-cream example, where a robot, known to be in room R_1 and to be holding an ice-cream, changes its location to room

---

[1] We deliberately simplified Baker's formulation because of size of the proofs. Moreover, we changed the implication in $\forall(r)(At(Robot, r) \rightarrow At(IceCream, r))$ to an equivalence so that the alternative formulation which presents the unexpected conclusions could be created.

~~{1}~~	~~1~~	~~At(Robot, R₁)~~	Hyp	5
{2}	2	$\forall(r)(At(Robot, r) \leftrightarrow At(IceCream, r))$	Hyp	
{2}	3	$At(Robot, R_1) \leftrightarrow At(IceCream, R_1)$	$2, \forall E$	
~~{1,2}~~	~~4~~	~~At(IceCream, R₁)~~	$1, 3 \equiv E$	5
{5}	5	$\mathcal{X}_P(\mu(\{At(Robot, R_1)\}; \{At(Robot, R_2)\}))$	Hyp	
{1,5}	6	$At(Robot, R_2)$	$1, 5, E\mathcal{X}_P\mu$	
{2}	7	$At(Robot, R_2) \leftrightarrow At(IceCream, R_2)$	$2, \forall E$	
{1,2,5}	8	$At(IceCream, R_2))$	$6, 7 \equiv E$	

Fig. 3. Baker's example using CLOC.

R_2. After moving the robot from room R_1 to room R_2, his method concludes that either the ice-cream moves along with the robot or the ice-cream remains in room R_1. However, according to him, the first scenario is preferable to the second, but his method is unable to choose between these scenarios, and so the ramification problem is not solved yet.

Our approach, when applied to this problem, proposes the expected solution. This happens because we distinguish the set of hypotheses that originated the belief space from the other propositions considered in the belief space, as we will show. The dependency of the correctness of reasoning about action and change in the selection of some set of propositions is not new. Several other formalisms depend on the selection of a special set of propositions, including Lifschitz's *essentials* [11], Lifschitz's *primitive fluents* [12] and Pinto-Ferreira's *primitive propositions* [22].

4.1 Baker's Example

In Figure 3, we extend the proof of last example to present Baker's example. We add the hypothesis $\forall(r)(At(Robot, r) \leftrightarrow At(IceCream, r))$ to the initial situation description, meaning that the robot is in the same room where the ice-cream is, which allows us to derive that the ice-cream is also in room R_1 in the initial situation.

The situation description that results from moving the robot to room R_2 is obtained by adding the hypothesis that $\mu(\{At(Robot, R_1)\}; \{At(Robot, R_2)\})$ was executed and applying the $E\mathcal{X}_P\mu$ inference rule, according to which the lines where $At(Robot, R_1)$ is raised as hypothesis and its consequences are struck, and the proposition $At(Robot, R_2)$ is derived. The proposition saying that the ice-cream was in room R_2 is then derived.

The derivation of proposition $At(IceCream, R_1)$ was struck because this proposition is one of the consequences of a proposition whose derivation was struck. Therefore, the unwanted scenario that Baker consider doesn't hold.

We observe that we don't have the undesirable scenario because the formulation of both the situation and the change are such that there is only one way both to remove the proposition $At(Robot, R_1)$ from the initial situation representation and to add the proposition $At(Robot, R_2)$ to the resulting belief space.

~~{1}~~ ~~1~~ ~~At(IceCream, R₁)~~ — Hyp 5
{2}   2 $\forall(r)(At(Robot, r) \leftrightarrow At(IceCream, r))$ Hyp
{2}   3 $At(Robot, R_1) \leftrightarrow At(IceCream, R_1)$ $2, \forall E$
~~{1,2}~~ ~~4~~ ~~At(Robot, R₁)~~ — $1, 3 \equiv E$ 5
{5}   5 $\mathcal{X}_P(\mu(\{At(Robot, R_1)\}; \{At(Robot, R_2)\}))$ Hyp
{1,2,5} 6 $At(Robot, R_2)$ $4, 5, E\mathcal{X}_P\mu$
{2}   7 $At(Robot, R_2) \leftrightarrow At(IceCream, R_2)$ $2, \forall E$
{1,2,5} 8 $At(IceCream, R_2))$ $6, 7 \equiv E$

Fig. 4. Desirable scenario for Baker's example using CLOC with the alternative formulation of the initial situation.

{1}   1 $At(IceCream, R_1)$ Hyp
~~{2}~~ ~~2~~ ~~$\forall(r)(At(Robot, r) \leftrightarrow At(IceCream, r))$~~ — Hyp 5
~~{2}~~ ~~3~~ ~~$At(Robot, R_1) \leftrightarrow At(IceCream, R_1)$~~ — $2, \forall E$ 5
~~{1,2}~~ ~~4~~ ~~$At(Robot, R_1)$~~ — $1, 3 \equiv E$ 5
{5}   5 $\mathcal{X}_P(\mu(\{At(Robot, R_1)\}; \{At(Robot, R_2)\}))$ Hyp
{1,2,5} 6 $At(Robot, R_2)$ $4, 5, E\mathcal{X}_P\mu$

Fig. 5. Undesirable scenario for Baker's example using CLOC with the alternative formulation of the initial situation.

4.2 Alternative Formulation of the Initial Situation

One of the points we want to make is that the ramification problem in our framework is strongly dependent on the choices we make when describing the world and formalizing change. We consider the same representation of change and present an alternative formulation of the initial situation, and show that in this case a problem similar to the one that Baker found arises when using our method.

Consider the alternative formulation of the initial situation, where we assume the hypothesis $At(IceCream, R_1)$ instead of $At(Robot, R_1)$. The proposition $\forall(r)(At(Robot, r) \leftrightarrow At(IceCream, r))$ ensures that $At(Robot, R_1)$ is derivable and therefore belief spaces that represent the initial situation in both formulations contains the same propositions.

However, if we execute the change $\mathcal{X}_P(\mu(\{At(Robot, R_1)\}; \{At(Robot, R_2)\}))$, we will obtain both the desirable and the undesirable scenarios that Baker obtained using his method. These two scenarios are represented in Figures 4 and 5.

In the example presented in Figure 3, there are no multiple scenarios because the proposition that is to be removed from the belief space depends only on itself, and there is only one way to remove it from the belief space, which is to remove the hypothesis itself.

The multiple scenarios appear in the alternative formulation example, presented in Figures 4 and 5, because the derivation of the proposition that will be removed from the belief space depends on more than one hypothesis. Removing any of the hypotheses underlying this derivation would be enough to prevent

$$
\begin{array}{llll}
\{1\} & 1 & \sout{At(IceCream, R_1)} & Hyp & 6 \\
\{2\} & 2 & \forall(r)(At(Robot, r) \leftrightarrow At(IceCream, r)) & Hyp & \\
\{2\} & 3 & At(Robot, R_1) \leftrightarrow At(IceCream, R_1) & 2, \forall E & \\
\{1, 2\} & 4 & At(Robot, R_1) & 1, 3 \equiv E & 6 \\
\{1, 2\} & 5 & At(Robot, R_1) \land At(IceCream(R_1)) & 1, 4 \land I & 6 \\
\{6\} & 6 & \mathcal{X}_P(\mu(\{At(Robot, R_1), At(IceCream, R_1)\}; & & \\
& & \quad \{At(Robot, R_2), At(IceCream, R_2)\})) & Hyp & \\
\{1, 2, 6\} & 7 & At(Robot, R_2) & 5, 6, E\mathcal{X}_P\mu & \\
\{1, 2, 6\} & 8 & At(IceCream, R_2)) & 5, 6, E\mathcal{X}_P\mu & \\
\end{array}
$$

Fig. 6. Baker's example using CLOC with the alternative formulation of both initial situation and change.

the derivation of this proposition, and therefore, multiple scenarios should be considered. The problem may be even harder if there are multiple derivations of the proposition being removed.

4.3 Alternative Formulation of the Initial Situation and Change

The existence of multiple scenarios depends on the formulation of the world. We have concluded that a given formulation of the world may not have multiple scenarios but they may appear when using a logical equivalent representation of the world. We next show that a given formulation of the world may or may not result in multiple scenarios, depending on the change representation.

Given the alternative formulation of the initial situation presented above, suppose we consider another representation for the change and include the proposition $At(IceCream, R_1)$ in the set of pre-conditions and $At(IceCream, R_2)$ in the set of post-conditions, as shown in the proof in Figure 6.

According to rule $E\mathcal{X}_P\mu$, we should remove both propositions $At(Robot, R_1)$ and $At(IceCream, R_1)$ from the belief space. Since $At(IceCream, R_1)$ only depends on itself, there is only one way to remove it from the belief space. Furthermore, its consequences, including $At(Robot, R_1)$, are also removed from the belief space. The rule further derives the post-conditions.

Since there is only one way of removing the propositions that are to be removed, there are no multiple scenarios, and we may conclude that given a formulation of the initial situation, we might have or not have multiple scenarios depending on the representation for change.

4.4 Avoiding Multiple Scenarios

From the examples discussed above, it is clear that executing change might or might not result in multiple scenarios depending on the formalization of both the situation and change.

Given a formulation of a situation, choosing a formulation of the change such that the propositions that are to be removed from the belief space depends only on one proposition avoids the existence of multiple scenarios. However, choosing another formulation in which change is modeled removing a proposition from the belief space that has at least one derivation depending on multiple hypotheses leads to the existence of multiple scenarios, and therefore, to the ramification problem.

Another technique to minimize the number of multiple scenarios is to use axioms to model the initial situation. Axioms are used to represent propositions that are not questionable and correspond to Ginsberg and Smith's domain constraints [5].

5 Concluding Remarks

We present an alternative approach to situation calculus [18] and circumscription [19,20,14] for modeling change, the CLOC approach. It is based in the possible worlds approach [5], according to which situations are represented by sets of propositions, instead of being reifyed. As a consequence of this lack of expressiveness, the frame problem, as presented by McCarthy and Hayes [18], is solved.

CLOC is an extension of first order logic, introducing new terms representing change, operations to build structured representations of change, a new predicate which describe the changes that were executed from the initial situation, and inference rules that describe how to change the situation description. We presented part of its proof theory, namely the $E\mathcal{X}_P\mu$ rule, the inference rule that describes the derivation of the consequences of the execution an action. The semantic theory has not been developed yet, and, therefore, the semantics of the logic is still informal.

When using CLOC, the nonmonotonic nature of this logic drives us to the conclusion that proofs in this logic are best described using contextual proof [17].

We studied the ramification problem using CLOC and show that it results from inadequate combination of situations and change formulations. We presented an example in which there is only one scenario resulting from the execution of change, changed its initial situation formulation and although its belief space was preserved, we now have multiple scenarios resulting from executing the same change. An appropriate alteration in the change representation results in having our method proposing only one scenario, which shows that our method is sensitive to situation and change formalization. We proposed methods for obtaining single scenarios resulting from the execution of change.

CLOC is a result of project we are developing to extend the SNePS system [25,24]. In this project, we are going to integrate three descendants of logic SWM [16], the logic underlying the SNePS, which are: the mutation logic [21,22], a logic for dealing with change, as described above; the logic SWMC [2], a logic for default reasoning underlying SNePSwD, a version of the SNePS system using defaults; and the OK BDI formalism [9], the formalism underlying the SNePS actuator. The logic CLOC results from the integration of mutation logic with OK

BDI formalism. The resulting system will be used to perform reasoning about action and change using incomplete information.

References

1. Andrew Baker. Nonmonotonic reasoning in the framework of situation calculus. *Artificial Intelligence*, 49:5–23, 1991.
2. Maria dos Remédios Cravo and João P. Martins. SNePSwD: A Newcomer to the SNePS Family. *Journal of Experimental and Theoretical Artificial Intelligence (JETAI)*, 5(2&3):135–148, 1993.
3. Frederic Brenton Fitch. *Symbolic Logic – An Introduction*. The Ronald Press Company, New York, 1952.
4. Michael P. Georgeff. Planning. *Ann. Rev. Comput. Sci*, 2:359–400, 1987. Reprinted in James Allen, James Hendler, and Austin Tate, eds., *Readings in Planning*, Morgan Kaufmann Publishers, Inc., San Mateo, CA, 1990.
5. Mathew L. Ginsberg and David E. Smith. Reasoning about Action I: A Possible Worlds Approach. *Artificial Intelligence*, 35:165–195, 1988.
6. Steve Hanks and Drew McDermott. Nonmonotonic Logic and Temporal Projection. *Artificial Intelligence*, 33:379–412, 1987.
7. G. Neelakantan Kartha and Vladimir Lifschitz. Actions with Indirect Effects (Preliminary Report). In *International Conference on Knowledge Representation and Reasoning*, pages 341–350, 1994.
8. Henry Kautz. The logic of persistence. In *Proceedings of the Fifth National Conference on Artificial Intelligence*, pages 401–405, 1986.
9. Deepak Kumar and Stuart C. Shapiro. Acting in Service of Inference (and viceversa). In Douglas Dankel II, editor, *Proceedings of the Seventh Florida Artificial Intelligence Research Symposium (FLAIRS-94)*, May 1994.
10. E. J. Lemmon. *Beginning Logic*. Van Nostrand Reinhold (International), 1965.
11. Vladimir Lifschitz. On the semantic of STRIPS. In *Proceedings of the 1986 Workshop on Reasoning about Actions and Plans*, pages 1–9. Morgan Kaufmann, 1986.
12. Vladimir Lifschitz. Formal theories of action. In F. Brown, editor, *The Frame Problem in Artificial Intelligence: Proceedings of the 1987 Workshop*, pages 35–58. Morgan Kaufmann Publishers, 1987.
13. Vladimir Lifschitz. Frames in the Space of Situations. *Artificial Intelligence*, 46:365–376, 1990.
14. Vladimir Lifschitz. Circumscription. In Dov Gabbay, C. J. Hogger, and J. A. Robinson, editors, *Handbok of Artificial Intelligence and Logic Programming*, volume 3, pages 287–352. Oxford University Press, 1993.
15. Vladimir Lifschitz. Nested abnormality theories. *Artificial Intelligence*, 74, 1995.
16. João P. Martins and Stuart C. Shapiro. A Model for Belief Revision. *Artificial Intelligence*, 35:25–79, 1988.
17. Pedro A. Matos and João P. Martins. Contextual Logic of Change and Contextual Proofs. In *Proceedings of the 4th Workshop on Temporal Representation and Reasoning (TIME-97)*. IEEE Press, 1997.
18. John McCarthy and P. Hayes. Some philosophical problems from the standpoint of artificial intelligence. In *Machine Intelligence*, volume 4, pages 463–502. Edinburg University Press, 1969. Reprinted in James Allen, James Hendler, and Austin Tate, eds., *Readings in Planning*, Morgan Kaufmann Publishers, Inc., San Mateo, CA, 1990, 393–435.

19. John McCarthy. Circumscription – A Form of Non-Monotonic Reasoning. *Artificial Intelligence*, 13:27–39, 1980.
20. John McCarthy. Application of Circumscription to Formalizing Common-Sense Knowledge. *Artificial Intelligence*, 28:89–116, 1986.
21. Carlos Pinto-Ferreira and João P. Martins. A Formal System for Reasoning about Change. In *Proceedings of the Ninth European Conference on Artificial Intelligence*, pages 503–508, London, 1990. Pitman Publishing.
22. Carlos Pinto-Ferreira and João P. Martins. The strict assumption – a propositional approach to change. *Journal of Experimental Theoretical Artificial Intelligence*, 5(2&3):215–224, 1993.
23. Erik Sandewall and Yoav Shoham. Non-monotonic Temporal Reasoning. In Dov Gabbay, C. J. Hogger, and J. A. Robinson, editors, *Handbok of Artificial Intelligence and Logic Programming*, volume 4, pages 439–498. Oxford University Press, 1994.
24. Stuart C. Shapiro and William J. Rapaport. The SNePS family. *Computers & Mathematics with Applications*, 23(2–5):243–275, January–March 1992.
25. S. C. Shapiro and W. J. Rapaport. SNePS Considered as a Fully Intensional Propositional Semantic Network. In N. Cercone and G. McCalla, editors, *The Knowledge Frontier*, pages 263–315. Springer–Verlag, New York, 1987.
26. Marianne Winslett. Reasoning about action using a possible models approach. In *Proceedings of the Seventh National Conference on Artificial Intelligence*, pages 89–93, 1988.

Temporal Reasoning about Actor Programs

Susanne Schacht & Udo Hahn

(ⒸⒻ) Computational Linguistics Lab, Freiburg University
Werthmannplatz 1, D-79085 Freiburg, Germany
http://www.coling.uni-freiburg.de

Abstract. We present an approach to reasoning about actor programs based on temporal logic. This formal framework allows more sophisticated abstraction mechanisms to be introduced into actor specifications. Such mechanisms turn out to be a major prerequisite for the use of actor systems in large-scale applications.

1 Temporal logic for actor computations

Actor systems [5] have been developed as a convenient vehicle for combining concurrency and object-oriented programming principles. The spectrum of work being done ranges from hardware implementations of actor systems [15,21] over various actor programming languages [2] to semantic specifications of the actor computation model — either operational or denotational ones [3,8]. Usually, formal considerations of actors systems rely upon quite primitive, low-level constructs that can hardly be applied to complex real-world problems.

Looking for a more appropriate formal framework which allows for enhanced abstraction mechanisms, temporal logics seem to be a good choice. Whereas purely operational or denotational semantics are too fine-grained, temporal logics render a level of formalization that is sufficiently abstract to make useful assertions about the overall behavior of a complex distributed and concurrent system. Using a temporal logic framework, safety properties (invariants like partial correctness, absence of deadlock, mutual exclusion) and liveness properties (termination, total correctness, cycles, etc.) of concurrent programs can be shown without having to take implementation details into account [18,6]. Another advantage of temporal logic specifications is their incrementality. New features can simply be added, thus decreasing the set of possible models, i.e., implementations. However, most temporal logic proof systems for concurrent computations rely on imperative language constructs. They take only a simple action language as a basis to build the program's states and entirely ignore the creation of processes and the dynamic configuration of communication channels, issues that are crucial for object-oriented programming, in particular, the actor model of computation.

In order to fill this gap, we here present an approach to reasoning about actor programs on the basis of temporal logic, called Temporal Actor Logic *(TAL)*. In Section 2, we introduce a general temporal logic system. In Section 3, we will briefly sketch the actor model and introduce a simple syntax for actor programs. Next, we adjust the general proof system to the description of actor computations in Section 4. Finally, the application of this framework is demonstrated in Section 5 by a definition of receipt handlers which manage the termination recognition of subcomputations.

2 A basic proof system

In this section, we give a basic proof system for discrete and linear[1] temporal logic, following [13]. We will first introduce a set of temporal-logic *future* operators:

"next", $\bigcirc A$, "*A* will hold at the next state"
"eventually", $\Diamond A$, "*A* holds now or at least at one of the following states"
"always", $\Box A$, "*A* holds now and at all following states"
"until", $A \mathcal{U} B$, "*A* will hold up to the first state at which *B* holds"
"atnext", $A \mathcal{N} B$, "*A* will hold at the first state at which *B* holds"

The semantics of a linear first-order temporal logic language is given by a structure **K** which consists of a structure for the first-order kernel (all formulae containing no temporal operators) and a sequence of variable valuations. $\mathbf{K}_i(F)$ is the valuation of a formula F (in state i) as in FOL and, additionally, for the temporal operators:

$\mathbf{K}_i(\bigcirc A) = \mathbf{t}$ iff $\mathbf{K}_{i+1}(A) = \mathbf{t}$
$\mathbf{K}_i(\Diamond A) = \mathbf{t}$ iff $\mathbf{K}_j(A) = \mathbf{t}$ for some $j \geq i$
$\mathbf{K}_i(\Box A) = \mathbf{t}$ iff $\mathbf{K}_j(A) = \mathbf{t}$ for every $j \geq i$
$\mathbf{K}_i(A \mathcal{U} B) = \mathbf{t}$ iff $\mathbf{K}_j(B) = \mathbf{t}$ for some $j \geq i$ and $\mathbf{K}_k(A) = \mathbf{t}$ for every $k, i \leq k < j$
$\mathbf{K}_i(A \mathcal{N} B) = \mathbf{t}$ iff $\mathbf{K}_j(B) = \mathbf{f}$ for every $j > i$
$\qquad$ or $\mathbf{K}_k(A) = \mathbf{t}$ for the smallest $k > i$ with $\mathbf{K}_k(B) = \mathbf{t}$

A is *valid in* or *satisfied by* **K**, $\models_{\mathbf{K}} A$, if $\mathbf{K}_i(A) = \mathbf{t}$ for every $i \geq 0$. A is *valid* if $\models_{\mathbf{K}} A$ for every **K**. This actually means that a valid formula must be true in *every* possible state. *B follows from A*, i.e., $A \models B$ if $\models_{\mathbf{K}} B$ for every **K** with $\models_{\mathbf{K}} A$. In contradistinction to the correspondence between the semantic satisfiability $\models$ and the syntactic implication $\rightarrow$, i.e., $A \models B$ iff $\models A \rightarrow B$ in classical logic, in temporal logic implication applies only locally to states, and $A \models B$ is equivalent to $\models \Box(A \rightarrow B)$; this can also be written as "$\Rightarrow$" (*entailment*): $\Box(A \rightarrow B)$ iff $A \Rightarrow B$. Accordingly, the notion of equivalence, $\leftrightarrow$, is captured by that of *congruence*: $\Box(A \leftrightarrow B)$ iff $A \Leftrightarrow B$.

	modus ponens:
$\neg \bigcirc A \Leftrightarrow \bigcirc \neg A$	$A, A \rightarrow B$
$\bigcirc(A \rightarrow B) \Rightarrow (\bigcirc A \rightarrow \bigcirc B)$	$\overline{B}$
$\Box A \Rightarrow (A \wedge \bigcirc \Box A)$	*next:*
$\bigcirc \Box \neg B \Rightarrow A \mathcal{N} B$	A
$A \mathcal{N} B \Leftrightarrow \bigcirc(B \rightarrow A) \wedge \bigcirc(\neg B \rightarrow A \mathcal{N} B)$	$\overline{\bigcirc A}$
$\forall x \bigcirc A \rightarrow \bigcirc \forall x A$	*induction:*
$A \rightarrow \bigcirc A$	$A \rightarrow B, A \rightarrow \bigcirc A$
	$\overline{A \rightarrow \Box B}$

Fig. 1. Axioms and inference rules for first-order temporal logic

---

[1] Branching-time logics (cf., e.g., [9]) are much more complex than linear ones, as their models are graphs. This extra amount of complexity is not needed in our application. Hence, we concentrate on sets of sequences that can be adequately described by linear temporal logic.

The axioms and inference rules in Fig. 1, together with all FOL tautologies, build our proof system for temporal logic. All As and Bs are formula schemata; axioms can be instantiated with any *wff*, while for the rules' premises instantiations occur with already derived formulae. The soundness of the deduction system, stating that any derivable formula is valid, can be proven by induction over the derivation of A.

3 The actor model

An actor system consists of several concurrently processing objects, the *actors*, which communicate by asynchronous message passing. Message processing is required to be *fair*, i.e., all sent messages are eventually received and consumed. An actor *program* contains a set of actor definitions, as well as some initially created actors and messages sent to them. Actor definitions contain the declaration of internal variables (the actors' *acquaintances*) and the method definitions describing the actors' reaction to incoming messages (the actors' *behavior*) for their instances. Each instantiated actor has a unique *mail address*. Upon the reception of a message, an actor performs a composite action. This consists of sending further messages to other actors it knows about (`send`), creating new actors from actor definitions, thus supplying their initial acquaintances (`create`), or specifying a new behavior and/or new acquaintances for itself (`become`). The replacement behavior defined by a `become` action – only one replacement can be performed per method – is effective for the next message the actor accepts. If only some of the actor's acquaintances are updated, we use a restricted `become`(name:value$^+$) statement. Additionally, we include a `let` expression for binding actors to local variables as well as conditional statements (Fig. 2).

```
program      ::= { actorDef }* action
actorDef     ::= defActor actorType (acquaintance*) methodDef*
                 endActor
methodDef    ::= meth messageKey(parameter*) (action) endMeth
action       ::= action; action
               | send actor messageKey (actor*)
               | if cond then (action) [else (action)]
               | let variable be actor in (action)
               | become actorType(actor*)
               | become ({ acquaintance:actor }+ )
actor        ::= self | nil | value | acquaintance | parameter
               | variable | (create actorType(actor*))
actorType    ::= identifier
acquaintance ::= identifier
parameter    ::= identifier
variable     ::= identifier
value        ::= integer | boolean | ...
```

Fig. 2. Syntax of a basic actor language

Several kinds of formal semantics have been proposed for the actor model, usually based on the notion of events (processing of a single message at an actor) and tasks (pending events). Agha's operational semantics [3] assigns a tree of *configurations* related by transitions to each program as its meaning. A configuration consists of a *local states function* and a set of unprocessed *tasks*, where the local states function maps actor addresses to behaviors. Tasks are functions as well, mapping a unique tag (an identifier created in order to distinguish between similar tasks) to pairs consisting of a target actor address and a message. Transitions between configurations are determined by choosing one of the unprocessed tasks for execution. The effects of the processing of this task's message at its target are evaluated, giving a set of new tasks, a set of newly created actors and the replacement behavior for the target actor. This semantics depends on the existence of one (of several possible) global view(s) of the system: the configurations describe all actors involved. As with the denotational semantics [8], it does not allow for abstract propositions about *parts* of the system's computations that could be combined. Mechanisms for abstraction over the total ordering of events, as well as abstraction over specific details of a configuration are needed to make comprehensive statements about the overall system behavior or that of selected parts.

More recently, Agha et al. [1] have proposed a λ-calculus-based semantics of functional languages in terms of transitions modeled as reduction rules. The functional language is extended by actor primitives like send, become, newAddress, and initBehavior, the latter building create. To specify *open* systems, a configuration states internal recipient actors which are able to receive messages from the outside and from external actors that do not belong to the actors in the configuration, but can be addressed by them. Although partial descriptions of an actor system become feasible in this approach, its semantics is not meant to increase the abstraction level of actor computations. This is due to the fact that message processing is further decomposed into its constituent parts at the cost of introducing additional specification details.

4 Temporal Actor Logic

In order to adapt the system from Section 2 to the actor model and to construct the domain part of the proof system, the actor language must provide the elements for building local, non-temporal propositions about pending tasks and the actors involved. These will serve as basic state descriptions. Sequences of states will then be defined by determining the effects of one of the pending tasks. We assume a standard FOL plus identity for propositions about the bindings between identifiers and values (i.e., actor addresses and basic values) and between actors and their definitions. Accordingly, we use unary predicates to indicate whether a term denotes an instance of a certain actor definition and binary predicates named after acquaintance or variable names to indicate an actor's acquaintances. A name can be used as a function symbol, taking the actor as a parameter and denoting the acquaintance's or variable's value, thus forming a term.

For tasks, we use the notation (a, m), with a denoting an actor address and m denoting a unique message. The predicate task states whether a task is an element of the set of unprocessed tasks, *tasks*. This way, a state proposition in the underlying logic consists of *SP*, a conjunction of basic propositions about bindings of identifiers to values (addresses or basic values) and actors to definitions, and *TP*, which combines task(i) for every task i by conjunction. The effects of processing a task turn up as the creation of new tasks and changes affecting the binding properties. A formal definition for the state transition is given below. Meanwhile, we express the effects of processing a task (a, m) on *SP* and *TP* as *effects*$(a, m)(SP, TP)$, or simply as *effects*(a, m). *effects*$(a, m)(SP)$ denotes the local state proposition *SP* after (a, m) has been processed, *effects*$(a, m)(TP)$ denotes the new proposition about tasks.

The following axiom *(single transition)* states that as long as there are unprocessed tasks, exactly one of them, (a, m), is processed at each step and no changes on *SP* and *TP* are made other than those caused by (a, m):

$$
\begin{aligned}
&\exists(c, r) : \text{task}(c, r) \leftrightarrow \\
&\quad \exists(a, m) : \forall(b, n) : \text{task}(b, n) \leftrightarrow (\text{task}(a, m) \land SP \land TP \land \\
&\quad \bigcirc(\neg\text{task}(a, m) \land (\text{task}(b, n) \lor (a, m) = (b, n)) \land \textit{effects}(a, m)(SP) \\
&\quad \land \textit{effects}(a, m)(TP)))
\end{aligned}
$$

Fairness must also be included as an axiom of the proof system — any pending task will stay pending, until eventually it is chosen for execution. Then, in the next state, it will be removed from *tasks* and its effects can be observed. Since no pending task can be cancelled, this axiom *(fairness)* is sufficient to guarantee fair computations.

$$
\forall(a, m) : \text{task}(a, m) \leftrightarrow \text{task}(a, m) \, \mathcal{U} \, (\text{task}(a, m) \land \bigcirc(\textit{effects}(a, m) \land \Box\neg\text{task}(a, m)))
$$

From this, we can conclude:

$$
\forall(a, m) : \text{task}(a, m) \rightarrow \Diamond(\text{task}(a, m) \land \bigcirc\textit{effects}(a, m)) \tag{1}
$$

since $\quad \mathbf{K}_i(A \, \mathcal{U} \, (A \land \bigcirc(B \land C))) = \mathbf{t} \Rightarrow \mathbf{K}_j(A \land \bigcirc(B \land C)) = \mathbf{t}$ for some $j > i$
$\leftrightarrow \mathbf{K}_i(\Diamond(A \land \bigcirc(B \land C))) = \mathbf{t} \quad \Rightarrow \mathbf{K}_i(\Diamond(A \land \bigcirc B)) = \mathbf{t} \; \blacksquare$

To reason about a particular program, existing actors and sent messages, as well as the program's actor definitions must be accounted for. The local state propositions about actors are determined by their binding to actor definitions and the values of their acquaintances, both forming the state propositions *SP*. For tasks (a, m), from a's method definition for m's message key, we take the combined action to determine m's effects. The bindings of m's parameters can be found in *SP*, as they must have been either acquaintances or variables of m's sender or newly created actors known from the previous steps of computation. If no identifier of an actor is available (e.g., if it is created anonymously), we use a variable which can be considered existentially quantified. With these conventions, *effects*$(a, m)(SP, TP)$ can be defined in a straightforward way. The effects of performing (a, m) on the set of pending tasks, *tasks*, are determined by identifying all send actions in the method's definition that are actually performed (depending on a's state). The receivers and messages are combined to tasks and then added to *tasks*. Below, $act(a, m)$ denotes the action that is the body of m's definition at a ("\" denotes the set complement operator).

$$
\textit{effects}(a, m)(\textit{tasks}) := \textit{tasks} \setminus \{(a, m)\} \cup \textit{newTasks}(act(a, m))
$$

with: $newTasks(act(a,m)) :=$

$$\begin{cases} \{(b,n)\} & \text{if } act(a,m) = \texttt{send b n} \\ newTasks(\text{act}) & \text{if } act(a,m) = \texttt{let <var> be <actor> in act} \\ newTasks(\text{act}_1) \cup newTasks(\text{act}_2) & \text{if } act(a,m) = \texttt{act}_1 \texttt{ ; act}_2 \\ newTasks(\text{act}_1) & \text{if } act(a,m) = \texttt{if cond then act}_1 \texttt{ else act}_2 \\ & \text{and cond is true} \\ newTasks(\text{act}_2) & \text{if } act(a,m) = \texttt{if cond then act}_1 \texttt{ else act}_2 \\ & \text{and cond is false} \\ \emptyset & \text{else} \end{cases}$$

The proposition TP is defined via $tasks$: $TP := \bigwedge_{i \in tasks} task(i)$ and therefore:

$$effects(a,m)(TP) := \bigwedge_{i \in effects(a,m)(tasks)} task(i).$$

The effects on the local state propositions, SP, concern newly created actors via `create` actions and changes on a via become. For any actor b created from a definition D with initial acquaintances aqc_i bound to a_i, $D(b)$ and $\text{Aqc}_i(b, a_i)$ are added to SP. Also, we refer to a_i as $acq(b)$, and extend the function as well as the predicate notation to local variables where necessary. All elements of SP concerning a itself are changed according to the occurrence of a `become` action.

$$effects(a,m)(SP) := SP \cup created(act(a,m)) \cup new(act(a,m)) \backslash old(act(a,m))$$

with the following definitions of *created*, *new*, and *old*, respectively:

$$created(act(a,m)) := \begin{cases} \{D(\text{var}(a)), \text{Aqc}_1(\text{var}(a), a_1), \ldots, \text{Aqc}_n(\text{var}(a), a_n)\} \\ \quad \text{if } act(a,m) = \texttt{let var be create D(a}_1..\texttt{a}_n)\texttt{in}.. \\ \text{and analogously for other occurrences of } \texttt{create} \end{cases}$$

$$new(act(a,m)) := \begin{cases} \{D(a), \text{Aqc}_1(a, a_1), \ldots, \text{Aqc}_n(a, a_n)\} \\ \quad \text{if } act(a,m) = \texttt{become create D(a}_1 \ldots \texttt{a}_n) \end{cases}$$

$$old(act(a,m)) := \begin{cases} \{D_{prev}(a), \text{Aqc}_1(a, b_1), \ldots, \text{Aqc}_k(a, b_k)\} \\ \quad \text{if } act(a,m) = \texttt{become create D(a}_1 \ldots \texttt{a}_n) \text{ and} \\ D_{prev}(b_1 \ldots b_k) \text{ the previous definition of } a \end{cases}$$

For the initial configuration, *tasks* and SP are determined from the initially created actors and sent messages in the program.

To summarize, a TAL proof system Θ for a program P as shown in Fig. 2 is a quadruple $\langle \Sigma^\Theta, Op, R_b, R_p \rangle$, consisting of a signature Σ^Θ, the set Op of the usual first-order and temporal logic operators, and two sets of rules and axioms. The set R_b contains the axioms and rules of the basic proof system (cf. Section 2). The set R_p consists of the rules taken from P by instantiating the axioms for fairness and single transition. This is achieved by evaluating the *effects* function on the methods (cf. Section 5 for an example). The signature Σ^Θ is defined as (V, K, O, M, F, P) with V the set of variables, K and O constants and operators for arithmetics and set theory, M a set of function symbols of various arities, F a set of unary function symbols, and P a set of unary and binary predicate symbols as mentioned above. M contains the `messageKeys` in P, F contains symbols that appear in P as `variable`, `acquaintance` or `parameter`; P consists of the symbol `task` and of the symbols that appear as `actorType` and as `acquaintance`. By convention, we write predicate symbols starting with a capital letter and functions with a lower-case letter. Terms and formulae are inductively defined:

Any element of V and K is a term.
Any element of F and O applied to terms is a term.
Any element of M applied to terms is a message term.
Given a term s and a message term m, task(s, m) is a formula.
Given a term s and an element P of P, P(s) is a formula.
Given a variable v and a formula G, $\forall v : G$ and $\exists v : G$ are formulae.
Given formulae G and H, then
$(G), G \wedge H, G \vee H, G \rightarrow H, \neg G, \square\, G, \diamond\, G, \bigcirc G, G\, \mathcal{U}\, H, G\, \mathcal{N}\, H$ are formulae

The main application of TAL is to study given actor programs and to show properties about them that are more general than those that can be directly derived from the program code. To show that a given actor program P is a model of a TAL formula F, it is necessary to construct F from P. For this purpose, one has to build the formulae for every actor definition in P and for the initial actors and messages as shown above and combine them by $\wedge$. This is demonstrated in the next section.

5 Example: Partial termination detection

Due to its fine granularity, the asynchronous actor mode of message passing does not easily fit with complex real-world applications. Especially, synchronization constructs are needed (for suggestions, cf. [11,4]). As an example for applying the temporal logic system, we will discuss a programming scheme for 'partial termination'. Instead of detecting the termination of arbitrary processes, we focus on a characteristic subset of computations which are obliged to signal their termination to their initiators without considering other activities of the actors involved. We use a set of *acknowledged* messages the sending of which forms the subcomputation under consideration: Any message involved sends a receipt that may carry unique descriptions (so-called *tags*) of further receipts that have to be expected. Special actors, `ReceiptHandlers`, accept the receipts and manage the tags already received, as well as those still to be expected, in two separate sets, `tagsRec` and `tagsExp`, respectively, and, finally, send a `terminated` message to their creator `replyDest`. Assuming `ReceiptHandlers` with initially empty sets, a computation process is considered terminated, if both sets are empty and if at least one receipt message has arrived (since no spontaneous computation can occur in an actor system). As a safety property, we expect no `terminated` message to be sent (i.e., being an element of *tasks* in the next state), if both sets are non-empty. This can be expressed as:

$$\square(\bigcirc(\text{task}(\text{replyDest}(x), \text{terminated}) \rightarrow (\exp(x) = \emptyset = \text{rec}(x)))) \qquad (2)$$

ReceiptHandlers are defined as below.[2] From this definition, we can derive the formulae in Fig. 3. After having received a receipt message, both sets exp and rec will be calculated. If and only if for both sets the result equals the empty set, the terminated message will be issued. Therefore, the invariant (2) holds. From the definition of ReceiptHandler itself no (useful) liveness properties can be derived, since they depend on the respective application of ReceiptHandlers.

```
defActor ReceiptHandler (tagsExp tagsRec tag replyDest)
  meth receipt (rtag furtherTags)
    let exp be ((tagsExp ∪ (furtherTags \ tagsRec)) \ {rtag})
      in let rec be (tagsRec ∪ {rtag}) \ (furtherTags ∪ tagsExp)
        in if ((exp = ∅) and (rec = ∅))
          then (send replyDest terminated; become Inactive)
          else (become ReceiptHandler (exp rec tag replyDest))
  endMeth
  meth generateTag (returnAddress)
    send returnAddress return (tag+1);
    become ReceiptHandler (tag: tag+1)
  endMeth
endActor
```

$$(\text{ReceiptHandler}(x) \wedge \text{task}(x, \text{receipt}(t \, set))) \rightarrow$$
$$\Diamond \, (\text{ReceiptHandler}(x) \wedge \text{TagsExp}(x, set_1) \wedge \text{TagsRec}(x, set_2) \wedge \text{Tag}(x, n)$$
$$\wedge \text{ReplyDest}(x, y) \wedge \text{task}(x, \text{receipt}(t \, set))$$
$$\wedge ((\exp(x) = (set_1 \cup (set \setminus set_2)) \setminus \{t\} = \emptyset$$
$$\wedge \text{rec}(x) = (set_2 \cup \{t\}) \setminus (set \cup set_1) = \emptyset$$
$$\wedge \bigcirc (\text{task}(y, \text{terminated}) \wedge \text{Inactive}(x)))$$
$$\vee (\exp = (set_1 \cup (set \setminus set_2)) \setminus \{t\} \neq \text{rec} = (set_2 \cup \{t\}) \setminus (set \cup set_1)$$
$$\wedge \bigcirc (\text{ReceiptHandler}(x) \wedge \text{TagsExp}(x, \exp(x))$$
$$\wedge \text{TagsRec}(x, \text{rec}(x)) \wedge \text{Tag}(x, n) \wedge \text{ReplyDest}(x, y)))))$$

$$(\text{ReceiptHandler}(x) \wedge \text{task}(x, \text{generateTag}(z))) \rightarrow$$
$$\Diamond \, (\text{ReceiptHandler}(x) \wedge \text{TagsExp}(x, set_1) \wedge \text{TagsRec}(x, set_2) \wedge \text{Tag}(x, n)$$
$$\wedge \text{ReplyDest}(x, y) \wedge \text{task}(x, \text{generateTag}(z))$$
$$\wedge \bigcirc (\text{task}(z, \text{return}(n + 1)) \wedge \text{ReceiptHandler}(x) \wedge \text{TagsExp}(x, set_1)$$
$$\wedge \text{TagsRec}(x, set_2) \wedge \text{Tag}(x, n + 1) \wedge \text{ReplyDest}(x, y)))$$

Fig. 3. Effects of messages to ReceiptHandlers

We will now demonstrate how to use ReceiptHandlers by considering a rather simple recursive computation, *viz.* the printing of the structure and the contents of a tree in a depth-first manner as defined in Fig. 4.[3] The objects involved in this example are

---

[2] For the purpose of readability, we use set-algebraic operators instead of low-level message-passing expressions.

[3] Two notational conventions have to be added: ask expressions denote rpc-like communications, and for <var> in <collection> do abbreviates an enumeration of the ele-

```
defActor TreeNode(parent children contents)
  meth printAll (printer)
    let tag be 1 in (let rhActor be
      (create ReceiptHandler(∅ ∅ tag self) in
        (send self printChildren(printer rhActor tag);
        send rhActor receipt(nil {tag}))))
  endMeth
  meth printChildren (printer returnDest rtTag)
    send printer print (contents);
    let tagSet be (create Set) in
      (if (children ≠ ∅)
        then (let tag be (ask returnDest generateTag) in
          (for child in children do
            (ask tagSet add(tag);
            send child printChildren(printer returnDest tag))));
        send returnDest receipt(rtTag tagSet))
  endMeth
```

Fig. 4. Application of ReceiptHandler: Recursive printing of tree contents

not very active ones, but our partial termination detection scheme has also been implemented in a distributed natural language parser [12,17], a serious real-world application of actor computations.

Fig. 5 depicts a graphical representation of the objects and messages involved. All of the messages, except for the generation of tags, operate asynchronously. After a ReceiptHandler has been created, every non-leaf tree node's daughter are asynchronously accessed and printed. At each node, for each daughter node a receipt tag is computed and sent to the daughter as a parameter of the printChildren message (rtTag). With the receipt message sent to the receipt handler, the set of all these tags is returned as those which

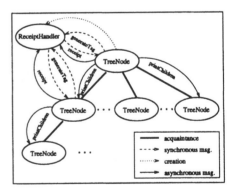

Fig. 5. Printing trees

are to be expected (furtherTags) and the node's own receipt tag as that tag which is hereby received (rtag).

In order to prove the termination we have to show that *(a)* if the tags transmitted as 'received' are exactly those transmitted as 'expected', the sets will eventually be empty, and *(b)* given *(a)*, the terminated message will be sent, and *(c)* that *(a)* and *(b)* are guaranteed to happen. First, we prove that the bookkeeping of tags is *correct*. Assuming

---

ments of <collection>. Both can be expanded to patterns of asynchronously communicating actors.

a collection of receipt messages $r_i(t_i\ S_i)$ with $1 \le i \le k$, t_i pairwise distinct, S_i pairwise distinct or empty, and $\{t_1 \ldots t_k\} = \bigcup_{i=1}^{k} S_i$ sent to a ReceiptHandler, with initially empty sets tagsExp$_1$ and tagsRec$_1$. At each arrival of a message r_i, tagsExp$_{i+1}$ and tagsRec$_{i+1}$ are calculated as follows:

$$\text{tagsExp}_{i+1} := (\text{tagsExp}_i \cup (S_i \setminus \text{tagsRec}_i)) \setminus \{t_i\}$$
$$\text{tagsRec}_{i+1} := (\text{tagsRec}_i \cup \{t_i\}) \setminus (\text{tagsExp}_i \cup S_i)$$

tagsExp$_{k+1}$ will amount to the empty set, since all t_i that became an element of it via S_j, $j < i$, will be eventually excluded, and tagsRec$_{k+1}$ will be empty, too, since all elements t_i that might have been added have been an element of tagsExp$_l$, $l < i$, or of S_j, $j \ge i$, and therefore have been already removed.

Next, the *liveness* property must be shown, i.e., that the sets will eventually be empty and a terminated message is really sent to the creator of the ReceiptHandler. This can be described as

$$\Diamond(\text{Exp}(x, \emptyset) \wedge \text{Rec}(x, \emptyset) \wedge \bigcirc(\text{task}(\text{replyDest}(x), \text{terminated}))) \tag{3}$$

The methods defined for TreeNodes are formalized as:

(TreeNode(u) $\wedge$ task(u, printAll(pr))) $\rightarrow$
  $\Diamond$(task(u, printAll(pr))
    $\wedge\bigcirc$(ReceiptHandler(rhActor) $\wedge$ task(u, printChildren(pr rhActor 1))
    $\wedge$task(rhActor, receipt(nil $\{1\}$)))))

(TreeNode(u) $\wedge$ task(u, printChildren(pr rhActor tag))) $\rightarrow$
  $\Diamond$((task(u, printChildren(pr rhActor tag)) $\wedge$ Children(u, $\emptyset$)
    $\wedge\bigcirc$(task(rhActor, receipt(tag $\emptyset$))))
  $\vee$(task(u, printChildren(pr rhActor tag)) $\wedge \neg$Children(u, $\emptyset$)
    $\wedge\bigcirc(\forall v : v \in$ children(u) $\leftrightarrow$ ($\exists$vt : vt $= i \wedge$ vt $\in$ tagSet
    $\wedge$task(v, printChildren(pr rhActor vt))) $\wedge$ task(rhActor, receipt(tag tagSet)))))

The newly generated tags i are assumed to be pairwise distinct, which can be easily ensured by an appropriate name server. Given the above formalizations of Receipt-Handler (Fig. 3) and TreeNode, an initial set *tasks* = $\{$(tree, printAll(prt))$\}$, and TreeNode(tree), we can derive (3) by the following deduction. The formula (4) is derived from an instantiation of the formula (1) which was derived from the fairness axiom. Given the single transition axiom, the only available task is immediately chosen for execution, and in the next step its effects occur (the creation of the Receipt-Handler *rh* and the sending of the messages printChildren(prt rh 1) and receipt(*nil* $\{1\}$)).

TreeNode(tree) $\wedge$ task(tree, printAll(prt)) $\rightarrow$
  $\bigcirc$(ReceiptHandler(rh) $\wedge$ exp $= \emptyset \wedge$ rec $= \emptyset$ (4)
  $\wedge$ task(tree, printChildren(prt rh 1)) $\wedge$ task(rh, receipt(*nil* $\{1\}$))))

Now, we can derive the effects of the two new elements of *tasks*:

$$\ldots \rightarrow$$
$$\Diamond((\text{ReceiptHandler(rh)} \wedge 1 \notin \text{tagsRec(rh)} \wedge \text{exp} = \text{tagsExp(rh)} \cup \{1\} \neq \emptyset)$$
$$\wedge \bigcirc(\text{ReceiptHandler(rh)} \wedge 1 \in \text{tagsExp(rh)}))$$
$$\vee(\text{ReceiptHandler(rh)} \wedge 1 \in \text{tagsRec(rh)} \wedge \text{rec} = \text{tagsRec(rh)} \setminus \{1\}) \qquad (5)$$
$$\wedge \bigcirc(\text{ReceiptHandler(rh)} \wedge 1 \notin \text{tagsRec(rh)} \wedge 1 \notin \text{tagsExp(rh)}))$$
$$\wedge \Diamond((\text{Children(tree, } \emptyset) \wedge \bigcirc \text{task(rh, receipt(1 } \emptyset)))$$
$$\vee(\neg\text{Children(tree, } \emptyset) \wedge \bigcirc(\exists T : A \wedge \text{task(rh, receipt(1 T))))))$$

with $A \equiv \forall c : c \in \text{children(tree)} \leftrightarrow (\exists cTag : cTag \in T \wedge \text{task}(c, \text{printChildren(prt}$ rh cTag))). Transitively from (4) and the first disjunction of (5), we can conclude that whether the *receipt(nil* $\{1\}$) or the *receipt*(1 X) message arrives first at *rh*, "1" will be excluded from both sets, *tagsExp* and *tagsRec*. This holds analogously for all elements of T in the second disjunction of (5), until both sets are empty again ∎

6 Discussion

A substantial body of knowledge has already been accumulated in the field of applying temporal logics to concurrent program specification. The seminal work of Manna and Pnueli (cf., e.g. [16]) has led to elaborated specification languages based on temporal logics such as TLA [14] or UNITY [7]. They all have in common that they concentrate on the temporal part of the specification and do not provide a deeper treatment of single states. This is, however, crucial for actor programming, since an actor system, as a whole, cannot be described simply by sequences of atomic states or events. Adequate descriptions of actor systems such as the proposal we have made in this paper must account for the complexity of objects and connections between objects. Closest to our formal view on the proper description of object-oriented distribution and concurrency is the work on METATEM, a directly executable temporal logic language [10]. However, its computation model is not based on point-to-point communication (as actors are) but on broadcasting (disallowed in actor systems). Furthermore, the underlying logic is a dense temporal logic instead of a discrete one, on which our approach is based.

The importance of properly accounting for the complexity of objects and connections between objects, a basic motivation for actor systems, of course applies to systems of intelligent agents, too — perhaps, even more. This becomes evident when one considers, e.g., the AGENT programming language [20]. It is deeply concerned with mental states ascribed to computational agents such as beliefs, capabilities and commitments. While these issues are treated in a rather informal way in AGENT, the BDI logic framework [19] provides an interesting formalization of epistemic primitives such as beliefs, desires and intentions. These pragmatic notions are treated in considerable depth, but the BDI theory lacks a serious account of formal properties inherent in distribution and concurrency. This is where the actor model, and our contribution in particular, comes in and may complement the theoretical foundations of intelligent agencies.

We have shown how a general proof system for discrete linear temporal logic can be tailored to describe the behavior of actor systems. The specialized proof system has been applied to an extension of the basic actor communication mode that allows for the detection of the termination of partial computations. Temporal logics turn out to be a suitable formal framework for reasoning about systems of distributed autonomous agents that can easily modelled by actors.

References

1. G. Agha, I. A. Mason, S. F. Smith, and C. L. Talcott. A foundation for actor computation. *Journal of Functional Programming*, 7:1–72, 1997.
2. Gul Agha. *Actors: a Model of Concurrent Computation in Distributed Systems*. MIT Press, 1986.
3. Gul Agha. The structure and semantics of actor languages. In J.W. de Bakker et al., editors, *Foundations of Object-Oriented Languages*, pp. 1–59. Springer, 1990.
4. Gul Agha et al. Abstraction and modularity mechanisms for concurrent computing. In Gul Agha et al., editors, *Research Directions in Concurrent Object-Oriented Programming*, pp. 3–21. MIT Press, 1993.
5. Gul Agha and Carl Hewitt. Concurrent programming using actors. In A.Yonezawa and M.Tokoro, editors, *Object-Oriented Concurrent Programming*, pp. 37–53. MIT Press, 1987.
6. Howard Barringer. The use of temporal logic in the compositional specification of concurrent systems. In A. Galton, editor, *Temporal Logics and their Applications.*, pp. 53–90. Academic Press, 1987.
7. K. Many Chandy and J. Misra. *Parallel Program Design*. Addison-Wesley, 1989.
8. W.D. Clinger. *Foundations of Actor Semantics*. PhD thesis, MIT, Dept. of Mathematics, 1981.
9. E.A. Emerson and J. Y. Halpern. 'Sometimes' and 'Not Never' revisited: on branching time versus linear time temporal logic. *Journal of the ACM*, 33(1):151–178, 1986.
10. Michael Fisher. A survey of Concurrent METATEM: the language and its applications. In *Proc. of the First International Conference on Temporal Logic (ICTL)*, 1994.
11. Svend Frølund. Inheritance of synchronization constraints in concurrent object-oriented programming languages. In *ECOOP '92 – European Conf. on Object-Oriented Programming*, pp. 185 – 196, 1992
12. U. Hahn, S. Schacht, and N. Bröker. Concurrent, object-oriented dependency parsing: the *ParseTalk* model. *Int'l. Journal of Human-Computer Studies*, 41(1/2):179–222, 1994.
13. Fred Kröger. *Temporal Logic of Programs*. Springer, 1987.
14. Leslie Lamport. The temporal logic of actions. *ACM Transactions on Programming Languages and Systems*, 16(3):872–923, 1994.
15. Henry Lieberman. An object-oriented simulator for the Apiary. In *AAAI '83 – Proc. of the National Conf. on Artificial Intelligence*, pp. 241–246, 1983
16. Zohar Manna and Amir Pnueli. *The Temporal Logic of Reactive and Concurrent Systems*. Springer, 1992.
17. Peter Neuhaus and Udo Hahn. Restricted parallelism in object-oriented lexical parsing. In *COLING '96 - Proc. of the 16th Intl. Conf. on Computational Linguistics*, pp. 502–507, 1996.
18. Susan Owicki and Leslie Lamport. Proving liveness properties of concurrent programs. *ACM Transactions on Programming Languages and Systems*, 4(3):455–495, 1982.
19. A.S. Rao and M.P. Georgeff. Modeling rational agents within a bdi-architecture. In *Proc. of the 2nd Int'l. Conf. on Principles of Knowledge Representation and Reasoning*, pp. 473–484, 1991
20. Yoav Shoham. Agent-oriented programming. *Artificial Intelligence*, 60(1):51–92, 1993.
21. M. Yasugi, S. Matsuoka, and A. Yonezawa. ABCL/onEM-4: a new software/hardware architecture for object-oriented concurrent computing on an extended data-flow computer. In *Proc. ACM Int'l. Conf. on Supercomputing*, pp. 93–103, 1993.

A CLP Model to the Job Sequencing Problem

Nuno Filipe da Fonseca Bastos Gomes
Instituto Superior de Engenharia do Porto
Rua S. Tomé, 4200 Porto

1 Introduction

The Scheduling problem can be seen as a decision-making process, where we want to know which resource should perform a determined task and, when to do it. Considering the type of production, the resources and the degrees of freedom of scheduling the tasks, we can distinguish three broad families of problems: *Pure Resource Allocation Problems* (e.g., allocation of crews to planes or trains); *Joint Scheduling* and *Pure Scheduling Problems* (e.g., Job-Shop Scheduling). In this last family we can identify several groups of problems according to the number of resources and activities, the flow model and the optimisation criteria. One of these groups is the aim of this work, and it can be named **Job Sequencing**.

2 The Job Sequencing Problem

The Pure Job Sequencing Problem can be seen as a type of Scheduling Problem, where we have one instead of several resources. The problem is to perform all the activities in this unique resource in order to minimise or maximise some cost function. Usually, the set-up time among activities depends on the order in which they are scheduled. Furthermore, the magnitude of the set-up times when compared with production times can be such, that the problem's optimisation criteria are to minimise the overall time spent in set-up, and consequently, maximise the resource utilisation rate. The objective is to find the best sequences among activities so that we can find the best Job Sequencing. A few variations can be considered according to the characteristics of the problem.

Generally, the Job Sequencing Problem is more important than it seems at a first glance. It is true that in most of the real scheduling problems we have more than one resource, precedence constraints between activities, etc. In some cases however, we can consider all the production lines as one single resource with unit capacity. A good example of this case appears in the glass industry. Even in the general Job Shop Scheduling it is possible to identify one or more bottlenecks. A good schedule of these bottlenecks can increase a great deal the efficiency of the global production line. In this way we can transform a big and complex Job Shop Scheduling Problem in a set of simpler Job Sequencing Problems.

Once proved the importance of the JSP, it is desirable to find a good way to solve it, and consequently to model it. This objective is not new. Roughly speaking, we can distinguish two fields of research that address scheduling problems. They are *Operations Research* (OR) and *Artificial Intelligence* (AI). Each of these areas represents a different school in scheduling. One more dedicated to efficiency, but at the same heavily dependent on the problem structure, and the other less efficient but more flexible and less problem dependent. It seems then that if we find a new paradigm that includes the flexibility and generality of AI and the good performance of OR, we have the ideal approach. This new problem solving paradigm is *Constraint Programming*.

3 Constraint Programming

As previously stated, we need some flexibility in the modelling process. We also need a good solving method, or efficient *problem solving*. Montanari defined the *Constraint Satisfaction Problem* (CSP) [2] in which the problem is modelled with a set of domain variables and a set of constraints on those variables. The idea is to find a value in the domain of each variable that can satisfy all constraints simultaneously. Solving a scheduling problem within the constraint programming paradigm requires the performance of two tasks. First, we must formulate the problem in terms of variables and constraints; then the right constraint handling techniques must be applied in order to obtain a solution for the given problem. A new form of constraint handling emerged within the *Constraint Logic Programming paradigm* (CLP). The CLP Scheme [3], is a generalisation of logic programming where constraints are handled by a *Solver*. When we speak of finite constraint problems, constraint solving is normally replaced by constraint propagation. Constraint propagation is an incomplete method: it does not always detect inconsistencies. So, in order to achieve completeness it is necessary to add some variable labelling procedures.

4 The Job Sequencing model for CLP

In order that a solution can be found, we first we need to formulate the problem in terms of variables and constraints . In other words, we need to find a *Constraint Model*.

As we have just seen in the JSP, we want to know the best sequence for a set of tasks. More than that, we also want to know the duration of each task. Naturally we have two related but quite different problems. In our model we treat each of these problems independently. In each period (e.g., a trimester) we need to have some quantity of each product. The set-up times are highly undesirable (during the set-up process we do not produce). Naturally, if in the first period we produce the total quantity of one product needed for all the periods, we reduce the total set-up time by eliminating the subsequent changes to that product. Another fact is that in most cases there exists some relation between set-up times and the tasks. This means that, normally the product A_1 is similar to A_2, so we just have to make a few changes in the machine in order to process A_2 after A_1. Considering this, we can say that there are great probabilities that the best sequence will be not very different from the one based on the similarities of the products. At most, a few permutations could take effect on the final solution.

Considering the relation between the set-up times referred above, we want to establish a sequence for all the tasks that will minimise the sum of the set-up times. The task duration is the same for all the tasks, and we do not have any constraints at all on the tasks. We just want to build a stretch that passes once through all the tasks. This problem could be modelled as a simple *Travelling Salesman Problem* (TSP). The resolution of this problem is well known in AI, and will not be discussed in this paper. The base for the second problem is the solution of the current one. Note that dividing the JSP by these means raises great practical difficulties in proving the optimality of a solution.

4.1 The quantities problem

Once we have the sequence, we need to know the quantity to be produced of each product in each period (the sequence is the same for all the periods) in order that: All the needs of each product must be fulfilled at the end of each period; The resource capacity can never be exceeded; Some constraints on the *est* of one task can be considered; The resource utilisation will be maximised; The total set-up time will be minimised;Some other optimisation criteria can be taken into account. The idea is to solve this search problem (we restricted ourselves to combinatorial ones) using a constraint system and its constraints handling tools. In order to do that we need to put the problem in terms of variables and constraints. For example $\{r_{ij}$-*Requirements of product i in the period j (in processing time); s_{ij}-Time needed to change production from the product i to the product j; cp_i-Resource capacity for the period i; f_i-Estimated down time for the period i; $\{p_n,...,p_m\}$-Production sequence returned by the first problem}*.

Quantity to produce The quantity that we should produce of each product in each period is represented by the variable QP_{ij}. Note that if we know the sequence, the quantity (in terms of processing time) to be produced of each product, and the set-up times among activities, naturally we know the starting and ending time for each task.

Requirements Constraints As mentioned above, for each period we need a certain quantity of each product (it can be 0). Nevertheless, we can produce in one period more than we need, so that in the subsequent periods the product requirements decrease. This can be represented in terms of constraints by $QP_{ij} \geq r_{ip} - (\sum_{j=0}^{p-1} QP_{ij} - \sum_{j=0}^{p-1} r_{ij})$. In other words, the quantity that we must produce of product i in the period j, must be equal or greater than, the requirements of that product for that period minus the remainder quantity from the antecedent periods.

Capacity Constraint In this model the minimum schedule is for one period, so we can set the capacity constraint for each period. In order to impose this constraint over the variables we need to know which of them are equal to 0.

Obviously, if one variable is 0, then we do not need to include in the schedule the set-up time of the corresponding task. We represent this fact by a Boolean variable B_{ijp}. This variable takes the value 0 if the tasks P_i and P_j are 0 for the period p, and 1 otherwise. Considering that, we can represent the Capacity Constraint by $\sum_i QP_i + \sum_{ij}(s_{ij} \times B_{ijp}) \leq cp - f$.

Temporal Constraints Usually in this type of problems the requirements and capacity constraints are the important ones. There are not precedence constraints, and the temporal ones are rare. Anyway, in some situations it is useful to have some kind of temporal constraints.

In our model, the starting and ending time of each activity is not directly determined. As we saw before, we do not define any particular variable for that. So, for example, consider the task sequence $\{P_1, P_2, P_3\}$, and suppose that the earliest starting time of P_3 is 8. One way to impose this constraint is by saying that, the sum of the production times and set-up times until P_3 must be equal or greater than 8. Imposing the constraint in this way raises some problems because it automatically constrains the duration of P_1 and P_2. The sum of this two tasks cannot be 0. In a real situation, if for some reason one task takes some time to start then it is necessary to wait. in order to solve the above problems, we introduce a new variable in the beginning of our task sequence. This variable is a fictitious task that can take the value of the delay time, if necessary. Considering this new task (variable), we can represent the temporal constraints by $\sum_i^{t-1}(QPf + QP_i) + \sum_{ij}^{t-1}(s_{ij} \times B_{ijp}) \leq est_i$. Where QP_f-*Fictitious task* and *est_i-Earliest starting time of the task t*. The fictitious constraints can be used to model other issues. For example, if in a specific period we estimate that the machine will be down for a period of time between two values, we can represent this easily by: $QP_f \geq L_l$ and $QP_f \leq U_l$. Where L_l and U_l are the lower and upper limits. Naturally QP_f is a fictitious task for a specific period.

Value and Variable selection strategies Once we have the variables and the constraints, it is necessary to find a solution, using some constraint propagation techniques. As discussed above, constraint propagation is an incomplete method. It does not always detect inconsistencies. So, it is necessary, in order to achieve completeness, to add some variable labelling procedures. First, we must choose a variable from the set of the uninstantiated variables, and then choose a value of its domain. These strategies can be considered labelling heuristics, and can be used to converge the search for the best solution. Usually, in the JSP, the optimisation criterion is to minimise the total set-up time, and consequently to increase the resource utilisation. At a first glance, if we produce the maximum possible quantity in the first periods, we can eliminate some tasks in the subsequent ones, and consequently reduce the total set-up time. We can implement this idea in our model through the value selection strategy. We should choose the greater value in domain's variable. This last approach is somewhat naive. The results can be bad depending on the variables domains upper limit. The question is, how can we reduce that limit?

Initially, we can set the upper limit of each variable to the value of the machine capacity for one period. This corresponds to saying that only one task is processed in one period. Naturally, this is not a good approach. In practice, the highest value for the limit of one variable is equal to the capacity of the machine for one period, minus the sum of the minimum values of all the other variables of the same period. Considering this, we can impose a new constraint for each variable that reduces its domain, and allows implementation of the above strategy $QP_{ij} \leq cp_j - \left[\sum_{k \neq i} QP_{kj} + \sum_{k \neq i;\, j} (s_{kj} \times B_{kj})\right]$.

When we mentioned the JSP characteristics we referred that the model can include more than one optimisation criteria. In spite of each problem having its own characteristics we can use the variable selection strategy in order to make the solution converge to an optimal one. In a large number of problems that we intend to model, the products produced are to constitute stock. The production sequence is not solely based on set up time; for instance, it is usually desirable to firstly produce products with lower stocking cost. This issue can be included in the final cost function, but it can also be considered in the variable selection strategy.

This selection strategy is accomplished by first selecting the variable which represents the product with lower stocking cost. Having chosen the variable and initialising it with the highest value of its domain, we are sure that the product that is stocked for a longer period is the one with lower stocking cost. This is not the only situation that can be modelled by this means. Suppose we are solving the JSP for a bottleneck resource. This bottleneck resource feeds a production line with set up times different from those of the bottleneck. Some products have large set up times associated with them. In these conditions it is desirable to produce the largest possible quantity of these products at the same time. This situation can be solved by choosing firstly the variables that correspond to those products. The above situations are just a few examples of the variety of situations that can be modelled. This proves that our model is flexible enough to be used in a great number of practical situations.

5 Model Advantages

The JSP has been largely studied [6, 5, 4]. Most of the works are based on the model of the *Travel Salesman Problem* (TSP). Some of them consider an extension of that problem, becoming a *Travel Salesman Problem with Time Windows* (TSPTW). The aim of the pure TSP, is to find the shortest path between N cities. This path should start and end in the same city, and should pass only once through each city. Additionally in the TSPTW a time window is considered. This window corresponds to the period in which each city should be visited. Considering the TSPTW, we can establish a parallelism with JSP, that will be called *Job Sequencing Problem with Time Windows and Set-up* (WINSET).

This model is identical for all the works referred above. The difference is in the solving method. In [6] a simple Local Search method is presented. Although not being an efficient method, it produces better results and in a shorter time than the manual methods do. In [4] the Local Search method is discussed in a broad sense. A great disadvantage is pointed out in that method and its variants. It cannot escape *Local Minimums*.

In order to solve that problem some meta-heuristics such as *Simulated Annealing* and *Tabu Search* are presented. All these meta-heuristics help to find the optimal solution, or at least a good solution to a specific problem, but all of them need an initial solution to start with. The final results are strongly dependent on this initial solution. Independently of the method used, the main question is how the problem is modelled. We might have a method capable of achieving the optimal solution. However if the model does not represent the problem correctly, the solution will obviously not be as valid as desirable. Therefore the model of a problem should be capable of representing all of its structure. The WINSET model to represent a real JSP, may be not the more adequate in some cases.

The model presented in this paper is being used to represent a real JSP from the *Paper Transforming Industry*. In this problem we have a resource that is the bottleneck to a complete production line. This line produces about 50 types of products that must fulfil the commercial demand. The schedule is based in the forecasting demand for one year, that is divided into 4 periods (trimesters). More than fulfil the demand, we try to optimise the set up times, stock costs, and some production requirements. Considering this, we can easily see that it is not possible to represent this problem using the WINSET model. The WINSET model imposes that we know at the start the duration of each task, but in our problem this is one of the questions. Ideally in order to optimise the set up times, we should produce the entire year requirements for each product at the same time. Naturally this is not possible, because we must fulfil the demand for each product and the machine capacity is finite. In sum, in our problem we have a large number of sub-problems to solve, that can not be explicitly represented and handled by the WINSET model. The presented model easily represents these sub-problems. Moreover, it also allows us to add new constraints and change existing ones in a interactive manner.

References

1. K. R. Baker, *Introduction to Sequencing and Scheduling*. Wiley & Sons, 1974.
2. U. Montanari, Networks of constraints: fundamental properties and applications to picture processing. *Information Sciences*, 7, 95–132, 1974.
3. J. Jaffar and J.-L. Lassez, Constraint Logic Programming. In *Proceedings of 14th ACM Symposium on Principles of Programming Languages*, 1987.
4. Ana Madureira, João Jorge Pinho de Sousa, Aplicação de Meta-Heurísticas a problemas de escalonamento de uma unica máquina. *In Publicações APDIO*, 1996.
5. Fernando Vieira, Um sistema informático de apoio ao sequenciamento de tarefas. In *Publicações APDIO*, 1992.
6. M. Savelsbergh, Local search in routing problems with Time Windows. In Anneals of Operation Research 4, 285–305, 1985/86.

A New Approach for Extracting Rules from a Trained Neural Network

Castellanos A.L.*, Castellanos J., Manrique D., Martinez A.*.
Departamento de Inteligencia Artificial
Facultad de Informatica - Universidad Politecnica de Madrid
Campus de Montegancedo s/n - 28660 Boadilla de Monte - Madrid - Spain
E-mail: jcastellanos@fi.upm.es
*Escuela Universitaria de Ingenieros Técnicos Forestales
Universidad Politecnica de Madrid
Ciudad Universitaria s/n 28040 Madrid - Spain

Abstract--Artificial Neural Networks perform adaptive learning. This advantage can be used to complete and improve the knowledge acquisition in knowledge engineering by rule extraction from a trained neural network. This paper proposes a new rule extraction method based on MACIE algorithm, which has been improved so that it can be used in neural networks with continuous inputs and outputs, obtaining a global and continuous set of production rules in a very efficient way. An application example to obtain the average load demand of a power plant is also shown.

1. Introduction

Knowledge acquisition is the bottle-neck in knowledge engineering. Besides being a time-consuming process that make expert systems very difficult to build, the quality of the acquired knowledge also depends on many aspects, such as the availability of the domain experts, their expertise, their ability and attitude to express their expertise, the relationship between knowledge engineers and domain experts, and so on.

That is the reason why artificial intelligence searches in extracting symbolic knowledge from a neural network that has learned to perform a certain task, such as production rules extraction, that can then be used to complete the extracted knowledge from an expert to build an expert system[3][4][6].

This paper proposes a new method used for production rules extraction from a trained neural network, using two techniques together: first, a sensitivity analysis is used to determinate which are the most important variables for the prediction. This will guide the rule extracting process so that the set of rules to be extracted later will have fewer antecedents and so be maximally general. In the second place, an algorithm based on MACIE[5] algorithm is applied. This new algorithm allows rule extraction from neural networks with continuous inputs and outputs, so that it can be applied to a higher number of cases, improving the efficiency and quality of the rules obtained with MACIE.

2. Problem Description

Once a neural network that has been trained to perform a certain task, symbolic knowledge can be extracted from it as production rules. Those rules should be maximum general as much as possible, so that they can be applied to a greater number of cases. It is also necessary that those rules have significant antecedents; so those input network variables that really influence in its output must be chosen.

One of the most efficient algorithms for production rule extraction is the MACIE algorithm, which extracts rules from the trained neural network starting from its weights and training patterns. This algorithm is only valid with discrete inputs and outputs; so antecedents and consequents in the rules are composed of discrete variables with only two possible values.

This algorithm is intended to be improved, taking advantage of its efficiency and good quality of the rules obtained, to be used when both inputs and outputs are continuous. So, it can be applied to a greater number of real cases, getting rules where both antecedents and the consequent are variables whose values belong to a preestablished interval.

To perform this task, first of all a division of the initial set of training patterns is made according to their outputs, later, a neural network is designed for each set of training patterns. This way the output domain is divided into ranges, with a specialized neural network in every one of these intervals.

A sensitivity analysis for each specialized trained neural network for each output interval is necessary to be carried out to get significant antecedents and make the process efficient.

Finally, the rule extraction for every net is made, obtaining a subset of rules for each output. Assembling all rule sets, the final set for the knowledge base in the expert system is formed.

3. Procedure of Rule Extraction

3.1 Initial Pattern Set Division

First of all, it is necessary to standarize the set of training patterns in the interval $[-1,1]$, so that the maximum corresponds to 1 and the minimum to -1.

The output is divided into intervals k units wide, obtaining $2/k$ training subsets from each output interval $I_1..I_{2/k}$, where $I_1=[-1,-1+k)$, ... $I_{2/k}=(1-k,1]$. Those intervals will be the consequents of the extracted rules.

For each interval I_i, a training set S_i is considered, which output is I_i. For each training set related to the output I_i, an independent neural network is trained, as shown in fig.1, obtaining a set of rules R_i.

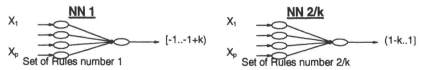

Fig. 1. Architecture of the trained neural networks

3.2 Finding the Most Important Variables

A program for obtaining the most important variables, which is the aim of this step, is implemented, so that the rule extraction process will be guide for making it more efficient and for obtaining rules with more quality. The program implements an algorithm called Point Sensitivity Index (PSI) [2][7], which gives for each input network variable a weight of importance for all the values of the domain for these inputs. Finally, A graph is obtained showing which is the importance of the variable (vertical axe) for all the values of the domain (horizontal axe).

The algorithm works as follows: for a network with i training examples of dimension d, and with a single output O. To compute the sensitivity along the domain, an x is taken for all the values of the domain and so PSI_{dx} is calculated, then an importance values matrix is obtained, the rows will be the input variables and the columns, the importance of an input variable in a point x of the domain: PSI_{dx} is calculated following the equation: $\forall i, PSI_{dx} = \sum \left| O_i(I_d = x) - O_i(I_d = x + \Delta) \right|$ where $O_i(I_d = x)$ is the output of the network for the training example i with its dth input replaced by the x value. The same for $O_i(I_d = x + \Delta)$, but the dth input is replaced by $x + \Delta$ where Δ is a small value added to the dth input.

3.3 Variable Analysis

Once the most important variables have been determined, it is necessary to find, for each subset of training set, rules with the minimum number of antecedents, studying the variation of those antecedents so that the consequent covers the net's whole output range. Also it is important to bear in mind that only consequents resulting from the union of several non adjacent ranges should not be considered due to these are not global rules that can be used.

In this process, antecedents should be chosen in order of importance, in such way that the number of chosen antecedents verify the following:
1) Each set of antecedents from each rule must be disjoined, for each output range, with the set of antecedents that come from rules belonging to other output range.
2) The output from each rule is a whole range I_k, but in some cases it corresponds to the union of adjacent ranges $I_k \cup I_{k+1}$. The reason is that the training patterns are related to consecutive sets in their output order, and they present characteristic data more homogeneous than in the rest of the training sets.

3.4 Rule Extraction

It is necessary to get a set of rules covering the input's domain as much as possible, to give an output in any case. To do so, a new MACIE algorithm has been implemented to allow a continuous input and output.

The objective of the MACIE algorithm is to reach: $w_{i,0} + \Sigma\ w_{i,j}u_j >$ UNKNOWN, where $w_{i,o}$ is the output neuron bias, w_i are the weights of the output neurons connections with the previous layer, and u_j represents the input values to the variables j.

When trying to show the inference $C^i = \{-1,1\}$, the input u_j will contribute only if $C^i w_{ij} u_j \geq 0$, where each of the variables $u_j \in$ CURRENT will play the role of the rule antecedent. The consequent in MACIE could be OUTPUT=1 or OUTPUT=-1.

To implement this new method with continuous inputs and outputs, it is necessary to select the net to extract the rules from; this way the range of the output I_i is determined, and so the rule's consequent. Then, the most important variables are chosen (obtained from the Sensitivity Analysis), and the input variables domain which will be positive or negative depending on $C^i w_{ij} u_j \geq 0$ is studied for each rule.

The range I_i from which the rules are being extracted, decides the sign of the input variable which will be the antecedent of the rule. Thus, for example if the output is negative, it is necessary to consider the sign of the weight in the variable that participates in the antecedent of the rule: in case of a negative weight and a negative inference, the variable whose weight is being considered must participate in the antecedents with positive values $uj \in (0,1]$. Once known this information (that is, the maximum range of the antecedent), it can be studied in which range of allowed values of the variable, along with the other variables that contribute in the rule, is possible to obtain the whole output range which is being studied. The range of the antecedents would never be $[-1,1]$, due to the sign of the weights will determine if the variable will be positive or negative.

Using the function f as the activation function in the continuous output, the following operations are added to the ones included in MACIE:

$$W_{i,0} + \Sigma \, w_{i,j} u_j - f^{-1}(I_i) > \text{UNKNOWN} \qquad (\textit{for positive inference}) \qquad (1)$$

$$-(W_{i,0} + \Sigma \, w_{i,j} u_j) - |f^{-1}(I_i)| > \text{UNKNOWN} \; (\textit{for negative inference}) \qquad (2)$$

In case of positive inference, a rule is activated by some determined variables if the sum of the weights multiplied by their corresponding inputs minus each of the values $J_i = f^{-1}(I_i)$ is greater than the sum of the weights of the variables that do not contribute (UNKNOWN), being I_i the range of outputs corresponding to the net from which the rules are extracted. It is necessary to check which set of continuous values of the variables:
$$u_{i,} \in (a,b) \qquad (3)$$
exceed the sum of:

$$\textit{Unknown} + f^{-1}(x_i) \textit{ where } x_i \textit{ covers all the values of } I_i$$

That set of values for the input variables (3) shows the ranges of variation of the antecedents for the output range selected, using (1) or (2) according to the type of the inference (positive or negative). It is considered that the rules are more general if the variables with more contribution have the maximum variation amplitude.

4. Example of Application

The above theoretical results have been used in the construction of a rule-oriented knowledge base, applied on a system to predict the load demand for the next day in a power plant[1].

The data used to design the training and test sets has been supplied by one of the most important Spanish load suppliers on a specific format, that is featured by providing for each day the load demand data sampled for each hour measured in Mw., and the mean temperature of the day measured in °C for two years. The input variables considered for the network were the maximum, minimum, average load demand and temperature for the current day. The output variable was the average load demand for the next day.

The data was standarized in the range [-1,1] and the output was divided in intervals of 0.2 units wide, obtaining 10 different training subsets from each output interval $I_1..I_{10}$ where $I_1=[-1,-0.8)$, $I_2=[-0.8,-0.6)$ ... $I_{10}=[0.8,1]$. In this case $S_2=\varnothing$, there are not training patterns which output belongs to the interval I_2, so, there are a total of 9 neural networks.

The sigmoid function defined in the range [-1,1] was chosen as activation function because of its best learning rate. The function is defined as:

$$f(x) = \frac{1 - e^{-x}}{1 + e^{-x}} \; ; \; f^{-1}(y) = Ln(1+y) - Ln(1-y) \; ; \; y \in I_i$$

The networks were trained using the backpropagation learning algorithm. Learning was considered completed when the mean square error reached the value of 0.01 in the worst case of the 9 neural networks.

To make Sensitivity Analysis, the chosen value for Δ was 0.01 and the values of x=-1.0, -0.9, -0.8, ..., 0, 0.1, ..., 1.0. The results for each variable in net 7 (for example) are shown in the figure 2, where it cat be seen how the most important variable for the output (range [0.2,0.4]) is the maximum followed by the mean load demand of the current day. The temperature is not very important and finally the minimum has no influence. It can be also seen how the temperature has a constant importance through the domain of possible values but maximum and average are softly decreasing.

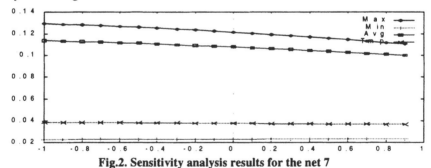

Fig.2. Sensitivity analysis results for the net 7

Table 1 shows how there is a correspondence between the importance of the variables given by the sensitivity analysis, and the absolute value of the weight for that variable in the trained neural network 7 used as an example.

Output	w_0	w_1	w_2	w_3	w_4
next day demand	BIAS	MAX	MIN	AVERAGE	TEMPERATURE
[0.2 , 0.4)	0.4966	0.3178	-0.0632	0.283	0.0956

Table 1. Correspondence between sensitivity analysis and weights of the net

Using section 3.4, the following rules have been obtained:

IF $Avg \in [15,18.5]$ and $Max \in [44.1,49.3]$ IF $Avg \in [20.1,37.3]$ and $Max \in [28.6,-0.6]$
  and $Min \in [20.6,25.1]$ and $Min \in [14.7,18]$
THEN $Output \in [-17,18)$ THEN $Output \in [18,20.1)$
IF $Avg \in [21.6,24]$ and $Max \in [47.2,49.3]$ IF $Avg \in [24,37.3]$ and $Max \in [43.1,49.3]$
  and $Min \in [14.7,17.5]$ and $Min \in [14.7,16.9]$
THEN $Output \in [20.1,21.6)$ THEN $Output \in [20.1,23)$
IF $Avg \in [24,37]$ and $Max \in [43.1,49.3]$ and $Temp \in [6.7,14]$ THEN $Output \in [23,24.5)$

5. Conclusions

A new method to extract rules from a neural net has been elaborated, improving the MACIE algorithm, so that it allows both antecedent and consequent of a rule to take continuous values, instead of being only discrete and making it capable of being applied to a greater number of cases.

In this way, the rules obtained will allow to complete the knowledge that could be extracted from an expert when building the knowledge base for an expert system. In the proposed method, first the problem is divided in output ranges; then a set of rules are extracted from each interval, and finally the solution (set of rules) is globalized. A Sensitivity Analysis algorithm that allows to know which are the most important variables has been introduced in the process. This algorithm leads the process of rule extraction for doing it more efficient and easy to control.

6. References

[1] Carpintero A., Castellanos J., Mingo L.F., Rios J., "Short-Term Load Demand with a Mixed Neural Network System" Proceedings of ICICS'96, Tehran pp. 60-63, 1996.
[2] Castellanos J., Pazos A., Rios J., Zafra J.L., "Sensitivity Analysis on Neural Networks for Metereological Variable Forecasting" Neural Networks for signal processing IV. Proceedings of the 1994 IEEE workshop, New York pp. 587-595, 1994.
[3] Craven M. and Shavlik J.,"Learning Symbolic Rules using Artificial Neural Networks", Proceedings of the 10th International Conference on Machine Learning, 1993, pp.73-80.
[4] Síma J.,"Neural Expert Systems", Neural Networks, Vol 8, No. 2, pp. 261-271, 1995.
[5] Gallant S. I. "Neural Network Learning and Expert Systems", MIT Press, Massachusetts, 1993.
[6] Fu L.M. "Rule Generation from Neural Networks". IEEE Transactions on Systems, Man, and Cybernetics, 24(8), 1994, pp. 1114-1124.
[7] Zurada J.M., Malinowski A., Cloete I., "Sesitivity Analysis for Minimization of Input Data Dimension for Feedforward Neural Network", IEEE International Symposium on Circuits and Systems, London, 1994.

Bayesian Networks, Rule Induction and Logistic Regression in the Prediction of Women Survival Suffering from Breast Cancer

P. Larrañaga[1], M. J. Gallego[1], B. Sierra[1], L. Urkola[2], M. J. Michelena[3]

[1] Department of Computer Science and Artificial Intelligence, University of the Basque Country
[2] Department of Economics, University of the Basque Country
[3] Oncological Institute of Gipuzkoa

Abstract. In this paper we present an empirical comparison between several paradigms coming from Statistics and Artificial Intelligence for solving a supervised classification problem. The empirically compared paradigms are Bayesian Networks, Rule Induction and Logistic Regression. The problem to tackle is the prediction of women survival diagnosed with breast cancer taking into account four predictor variables gathered at the moment of the diagnosis. The data file includes 1000 diagnosed cases at the Oncological Institute of Gipuzkoa (Basque Country). The validation of the paradigms was carried out using the 10-fold cross-validation method.

1 Introduction

Supervised classification is one of the most frequent tasks carried out by the so-called Intelligent Systems. Thus, a large number of paradigms developed either by Statistics (Logistic Regression, Discriminant Analysis, K-N-N) or by Artificial Intelligence (Neural Networks, Rule Induction, Classification Trees, Bayesian Networks) are capable of carrying out classification tasks.

Three of the previous paradigms have been selected in this work - Bayesian Networks, Rule Induction and Logistic Regression - in order to compare their performance in a real Oncological problem. In order to avoid obtaining an estimate too optimistic in the percentage of well-classified for each model, this parameter has been estimated with the 10-fold cross-validation method.

While both, the Logistic Regression approach as well as the Rule Induction algorithm used - CN2 - are well known, there are several new approaches that are related with the automatic learning of the Bayesian Networks. In these approaches, the search of the best structures of the Bayesian Networks is carried out by means of Genetic Algorithms.

* This work was supported by the Diputación Foral de Gipuzkoa, under grant OF 92/1996, by the grant UPV 140.226-EA186/96 from the University of the Basque Country, and by the grant PI 95/52 from the Gobierno Vasco - Departamento de Educación, Universidades e Investigación.

2 The Prediction of the Survival of Women Suffering from Breast Cancer

Breast cancer is the most frequent malignant tumor which affects women in Spain, just as the rest of Europe. More than a quarter of the cases of tumors which affect the female population in Spain is Breast Cancer. According to the Cancer Register of the Basque Country in 1990 the rate of incidence in Gipuzkoa, was 52.5 for every 100000 people.

There are several risk factors involved in the aetiology and pathogenesis of the disease. None of them, when isolated, can predict its appearance and its prognosis is still uncertain. Survival is one of the best guides for measuring the achieved progress. This is why, among other reasons, we have decided to analyze the survival in breast cancer in Gipuzkoa where, there has been a Populational Based Cancer Register since 1983. This register collects information about all types of tumours that arise in the population, no matter where they have been diagnosed or treated. All cases of invasive breast cancer diagnosed in the female population of Gipuzkoa for the first time between the first of January, 1983 and the 31 of December, 1988 and microscopically confirmed has been included.

The database contains 1000 cases, and we have information about seven variables in each of them. The four predictor variables are: age (5 categories), phase-stage (4 categories), tumor size (4 categories) and the number of positive nodes (4 categories). The rest of the variables, called survival-1year, survival-3years and survival-5years, are the variables to predict, and each one has two categories, taking into account respectively if the woman survives or not after one, three or five years of being diagnosed with breast cancer. For the construction of the five variables models, the four predictor and the corresponding variable to predict for each model, have been taken into account.

3 Searching Bayesian Network Structures by Genetic Algorithms

While the first attempts to building Expert Systems regarded probabilities as an underlying formalism, the large number of parameters to estimate - $2^n - 1$ for the case of n dichotomic variables - forced the researches to reject this massive approach and instead of it to use probabilistic models based on the hypothesis of independence among variables. These models presented the advantage of their simplicity but they could not give good solutions to problems with a high degree of interdependence among variables.

As a consecuence of these extreme positionings the probability was not taken into account in the building of Expert Systems until the late 80s when Lauritzen and Spiegelhalter [12] developed an algorithm for the propagation of the evidence. This algorithm allows probabilistic reasoning within graphical models which represent conditional independencies among the variables of the system. The most popular approach to the model search in Bayesian Network is based on score and search. In it a measure of the goodness of fitness (likelihood, entropy, well-classified percentage) of a particular structure is defined as well as, a searching procedure over the space of all possible structures of Bayesian Networks. This searching procedure usually works like a greedy algorithm. Our approach will use Genetic Algorihms[5] (GA) as an intelligent metaheuristic in the searching process.

In our approach, the individuals of the Genetic Algorithm will be Bayesian Network structures. A Bayesian Network structure, for a fixed domain with n variables, can be represented by an $n \times n$ connectivity matrix C, where its elements, c_{ij}, can be defined as:

$$c_{ij} = \begin{cases} 1 \text{ if } j \text{ is a parent of } i, \\ 0 \text{ otherwise.} \end{cases}$$

In our genetic approach, we represent an individual of the population by the string:

$$c_{11}c_{21} \cdots c_{n1}c_{12}c_{22} \cdots c_{n2} \cdots c_{1n}c_{2n} \cdots c_{nn}.$$

As it can be seen, in the case of a total order among the variables is assumed, [7] the usual genetic operators are closed operators with respect to the DAG conditions. In the more general case in which there is no assumption of order among the variables [8] the usual genetic operators are not closed operators and to assume the closeness we introduce a repair operator, which aim is to transform the child' structure that does not verify the DAG conditions into DAGs, by randomly eliminating the edges that invalidate the DAG conditions.

In our problem, although the cardinality of the searching space is not too large, the previous approach will be used. See [9] in order to consult another approach about the problem of structural learning of Bayesian Network in which an individual is a cyclic permutation of n considered variables, and the Genetic Algorithm uses crossover and mutation operators developed for the Traveling Salesman Problem.

Genetic Algorithms have been used as optimizers in other combinatorial problems that arise from the Bayesian Networks context. Thus, for example, in [10] they obtain good decompositions of the moral graph associated with the propagation algorithm proposed by Lauritzen and Spiegelhalter. Finally in [11] the problem of the fusion of Bayesian Network proposed by different authors, seeking the consensual BN is handled.

We have considered four diferents approaches to the model search:

(i) *The a posteriori most probable structure. CH - GA.* This approach evaluates the goodness for each of the structures proposed by the GA during the search process using the metric proposed in [3]. This approach does not take into account the existence of a variable to predict, a question present in the rest of the considered paradigms.

(ii) *Tree Augmented Naive - Bayes. TAN - GA.* Several authors - see, for instance [4] - have tried to construct models that starting from a Bayesian Network structure in which all variables are conditionally independent given the variable to predict, successively add arcs to the structure in a greedy way. These arcs will reflect correlations among variables and its inclusion maximizes the posteriori probability of the outcoming structure. In our approach the search of the model is made using Genetic Algorithms. Although the TAN structure takes into account the existence of a variable to predict, the score used for searching the appropiate model still uses the a posteriori probability.

(iii) *Markov Blanket of the variable to be predicted. MB - GA*. Taking into account that in a Bayesian Network any variable is only influenced by its Markov Blanket, that is, its parent, children variables and the parent variables of his children variables it seems to be intuitive to search in the set of structures that are Markov Blanket of the special variable. In this approach, individuals in the Genetic Algorithms are Markov Blankets for the variable to be classified. We have introduced one operator that guarantees that the obtained children comply with a Markov Blanket of the variable to be classified. On the other hand, the score used to search for the best Markov Blanket uses the percentage of well-classified individuals obtained by applying the evidence propagation feature of the HUGIN [1] software.

(iv) *The Naive Bayes Classifier NB*. In spite of the strong assumptions related to the conditional independence of the predictor variables given the variable to predict, over which the so-called Naive Bayes classifier is constructed, the empirical results are good.

4 Rule Induction

In the task of constructing expert systems, systems for inducing concept descriptions from examples have proved useful in easing the bottleneck of knowledge acquisition. One of these induction systems, CN2 [2], has been used as representative of the approach called Machine Learning. CN2 was designed for the efficient induction of simple, comprehensive production rules in domains where problems of poor description language and/or noise may be present.

The learning algorithm of CN2 works in an iterative fashion, each iteration searching for a complex covering a large number of examples of a single C class and few of other classes. Having found a good complex, those examples it covers are removed from the training set and the rule "if complex then predict C" is added at the end of the rule list. This process iterates until no more satisfactory complexes can be found.

5 Logistic Regression

Logistic Regression [6] is a method coming from Statistics which aim is to obtain a functional relationship between a transformation - from a cualitative variable - called logit and p predictor variables which can be either quantitatives or qualitatives. In this work, we have used the PROC LOGISTIC procedure of the SAS software for the empirical comparison.

6 Experimental Results

In order to give a proper estimate of the classifier accuracy, several methods - train and test, bootstrap, cross-validation - are usually employed. In this case a variation of the last one has been used, the 10-fold cross-validation. In this method the cases are randomly divided into 10 mutual exclusive test partitions of approximately equal size. The cases that are not found in each test partition are used for training and the resulting classifier is tested on the corresponding test partition. The average error rates over all 10 partitions is the 10-fold cross-validation error rate.

If we ignore the computational complexity and the transparency of the generated rules and only take into account the accuracy of the different paradigms, the conclusion we get to that there are no differences significant among the predictive capacity of the several paradigms regarded. It is worth of noticing the good behaviour of the Bayesian Network approach (CH-GA) in which the training is accomplished without regards to the latter use of the paradigm. This kind of training lets the learnt structures be more robust than if they had had a specialized training (MB-GA) in which the risk of overfitting is greater.

Survival with Breast Cancer			
	1 year	3 years	5 years
Bayesian Networks CH - GA	94.4%	80.4%	72.0%
Bayesian Networks TAN - GA	93.7%	79.0%	70.9%
Bayesian Networks MB - GA	92.0%	78.8%	71.5%
Bayesian Networks NB	93.7%	79.0%	70.9%
Rule Induction	93.7%	78.9%	70.2%
Logistic Regression	95.0%	80.0%	69.0%

Table 1. Accuracy of the different approaches for the prediction of survival one-year, thee-years and five-years after being diagnosed.

7 Conclusions and Futher Research

An empirical comparison of several classifying paradigms, - Bayesian Networks, Rule Induction and Logistic Regression -, in a real Oncological problem has been made. According to the obtained results there is no significant different behaviour among the various paradigms.

In the future we are interested in developing algorithms that will integrate the information coming from various classifiers. Another problem of interest for our group is the one connected with the developing of classifiers that use longitudinal information obtained from different time spaces in an efficient way.

References

1. Andersen, S.K., Olesen, K.G., Jensen, F.V. and Jensen, F. (1989) HUGIN - a shell for building Bayesian belief universes for expert systems.*Eleventh International Joint Conference on Artificial Intelligence*, vol. I, pp. 1128-1133.
2. Clark, P., and Niblett, T. (1989) The CN2 Induction Algorithm, *Machine Learning*, 3 (4), pp. 261-283.
3. Cooper, G.F., and Herskovits, E.A. (1992) A Bayesian method for the induction of probabilistic networks from data. *Machine Learning*, vol. 9, no. 4, pp. 309-347.
4. Friedman, N., and Goldszmidt, M. (1996) Building Classifiers using Bayesian Networks. *Proceedings of AAAI-96*.
5. Goldberg, D.E. (1989) *Genetic Algorithms in Search, Optimization and Machine Learning*. Addison-Wesley, Reading, MA.
6. Hosmer, D. W., and Lemeshow, S. (1989) *Applied Logistic Regression*. Wiley Series in Probability and Mathematical Statistics.
7. Larrañaga, P., Murga, R., Poza, M., and Kuijpers, C. (1996) Structure Learning of Bayesian Networks by Hybrid Genetic Algorithms. *Learning from Data: AI and Statistics V, Lecture Notes in Statistics 112*. D. Fisher, H.-J. Lenz (eds.), New York, NY: Spriger-Verlag, pp. 165-174.
8. Larrañaga, P., Poza, M., Yurramendi, Y., Murga, R., and Kuijpers, C. (1996) Structure Learning of Bayesian Networks by Genetic Algorithms: A Performance Analysis of Control Parameters. *IEEE Transactions on Pattern Analysis and Machine Intelligence*, 18, pp. 912-926.
9. Larrañaga, P., Kuijpers, C., Murga, R., and Yurramendi, Y. (1996) Bayesian Network Structures by searching for the best ordering with genetic algorithms. *IEEE Transactions on System, Man and Cybernetics*. Vol 26, no. 4, pp. 487-492.
10. Larrañaga, P., Kuijpers, C., Poza, M., and Murga, R. (1997) Decomposing Bayesian Networks by Genetic Algorithms. *Statistics and Computing*. In press.
11. Larrañaga, P., Kuijpers, C., Murga, R., Yurramendi, Y., Graña, M., Lozano, J.A., Albizuri, X., D'Anjou, A., and Torrealdea, F.J. (1996) Genetic Algorithms applied to Bayesian Networks. A. Gammerman (ed.) *Computational Learning and Probabilistic Reasoning*. John Wiley, pp. 211-234.
12. Lauritzen, S.L., and Spiegelhalter, D.J. (1988) Local computations with probabilities on graphical structures and their application on expert systems. *J.R. Statist. Soc. B*, vol. 50, no. 2, pp. 157-224.

Controlling for Unexpected Goals when Planning in a Mixed-Initiative Setting

Michael T. Cox and Manuela M. Veloso
Computer Science Department. Carnegie Mellon University
Pittsburgh, PA 15213-3891
{mcox; mmv}@cs.cmu.edu

A mixed-initiative setting is where both human and machine are intimately involved in the planning process. We have identified a number of challenges that occur for traditional planning frameworks as humans are allowed more latitude. In this paper we will examine the types of unexpected goals that may be given to the underlying planning system and thereby how humans change the way planning must be performed. Users may want to achieve goals in terms of actions as well as states, they may specify goals that vary along a dimension of abstraction and specificity, and they may mix both top-level goals and subgoals when describing what they want a plan to do. We show how the Prodigy planning system has met these challenges when integrated with a force deployment tool called For-MAT and describe what opportunities this poses for a generative planning framework.

1 Introduction

The objective of mixed-initiative planning is to fully engage the user in automated planning processes. Yet such situations add unexpected challenges to current technologies. Incorporation of the user into an existing automated planner is not accomplished by simply presenting to the user the option of making any decision the system would otherwise make itself, because some decisions a machine might consider may not be appropriate for or understandable to a human user. For instance, the formalism of operator postconditions and preconditions (or a specific hierarchical action decomposition) may not be natural to a user, and the relationship of these conditions to goals and subgoals (or level of refinement) may not be obvious. So it is not realistic to assume that the user will either be familiar with the planning formalisms or willing to learn them. Moreover, the planning system may actually be embedded as an unobtrusive subcomponent of a larger system whose task is only obliquely relevant to planning, so the user's awareness of the planning facility may be marginal. Therefore, a user view must be presented that abstracts the details of the underlying planner. Our belief is that the focus should be upon what the user sees (the interface), what the user wants (the goals), and what the user does (the task). But given such user-centered objectives, the user will inevitably violate the implicit assumptions and expectations of the planner. To compensate, the planner will have to be smart and robust.

As a concrete example of these challenges, we will examine the specification of a user's objectives and their transformation into planning goals. Normally the goals given to a planning system by a knowledgeable and sympathetic user are in a well-structured format. But goals provided by a more realistic and less restrained user present at least three problems to traditional planning systems: (1) *input goals may actually be specified as actions rather than state conditions;* (2) *they may be abstract rather than grounded;* and (3) *they may include subgoals along with top-level goals.* This paper will describe the control exerted by the planner to manage such problems. The second section will introduce the mixed-initiative planning system from which we extrapolate our experience. The subsequent sections describe these three problems and their implementation- and domain-independent solutions. The paper concludes with a brief discussion.

2 Prodigy/Analogy — ForMAT Integration

ForMAT [6, 7] is a case-based planning tool that supports military deployment planning through the acquisition of user-built deployment cases (plans), query-driven browsing of past plans, and functional analysis primitives for evaluating new plans. However, human performance while creating force deployment plans using ForMAT varies as a function of the military experience of the user. This variance appears to be due (in part) to ForMAT's lack of automated support for adapting similar past plans in the context of new planning problems. The more experienced user can accomplish the adaptation task manually, whereas the novice cannot as easily. A technology integration experiment was established between ForMAT and Prodigy/Analogy [9, 11] in order to explore mixed-initiative plan development and adaptation support for force deployment users (see [10, 12] for details).

Prodigy/Analogy is a fully-automated planner that combines generative and case-based planning. The current Prodigy system employs a state-space nonlinear planner and follows a means-ends analysis backward-chaining search procedure that reasons about both multiple goals and multiple alternative operators from its domain theory appropriate for achieving such goals. A domain theory is composed of a hierarchy of object classes and a suite of operators and inference rules that change the state of the objects. A planning problem is represented by an initial state (objects and propositions about the objects) and a set of goal expressions to achieve. Planning decisions consist of choosing a goal from a set of pending goals, choosing an operator to achieve a particular goal, choosing a binding for a given operator, and deciding whether to commit to a possible plan ordering and to get a new planning state or to continue subgoaling for unachieved goals. Different choices give rise to different ways of exploring the search space. These choices can be guided by either control rules, by past problem-solving episodes (cases), or by domain-independent heuristics.

Under a case-based replay mode, Prodigy/Analogy creates plans, interprets and stores planning episodes, and retrieves and reuses multiple past plans that are found similar to new problems. Stored plans are annotated with plan rationale, and reuse involves adaptation driven by the plan rationale. Research to integrate Prodigy/Analogy and ForMAT has investigated sophisticated methods for providing plan modification guidance to the For-MAT user. Guidance from Prodigy suggests to the user how to modify the elements of a past plan to fit the current situation. The sequence of events is as follows.

A ForMAT user receives the description of a new mission. Selecting attributes from the mission description to serve as probes into memory, the user queries ForMAT's database of past plans in search of relevant exemplars with which to build a plan. While browsing, the user refines the mission statement in terms of specific objectives (i.e., goals to be achieved) utilizing a domain-specific goal language. Using past plans as a template, the user edits the old case, substituting new features and values for old, deleting irrelevant old plan steps, and adding necessary new ones. As plan construction proceeds, the user can perform consistency checks on specific aspects of the plan to ensure plan integrity. During these actions, ForMAT sends messages to Prodigy/Analogy, capturing the history of the user actions.

When the mission goals are entered by the user, ForMAT reports this information to Prodigy/Analogy. Given the mission goals, Prodigy retrieves similar past solutions from its own database of plans (a mirror of the ForMAT database in a state-space representation) or creates a new plan generatively given an empty retrieval. It then identifies useful modifications for the past plans as a function of the new and past missions' rationale. Suggestions are sent to the ForMAT user that specify relevant past plans, additional retrieval probes, and potential modifications that the user should perform when building the plan.

3 Goal Specification

One of the obstacles to integrating ForMAT and Prodigy was that ForMAT's user goals were implicit in textual mission statements provided by commanders. State-space planners, such as Prodigy however, need well-defined goals and an initial state description from which to create plans. The goals describe the desired world in an unambiguous manner, specifying the states of the world that must be true after an agent executes the steps of the plan starting with those conditions present in the initial state. Plan creation is accomplished by some combination of forward chaining from the initial state and/or backward chaining from the goal state using operators and inference rules present in the domain theory. To provide Prodigy with goal input we required that ForMAT be modified to explicitly represent the user goals and that these goals be passed to Prodigy. In response, a goal editor was added to ForMAT. Nonetheless, unrestrained users will still specify goals in surprising ways. A user is given a planning problem in the form of a commander's mission statement. The following statement is an example description of a military objective along with guidance towards its achievement.

> *Need a Hawk unit and the 21st Division Ready Brigade to send to Pacifica to secure an airport. Also want to provide security police to keep the airbase secure so that a squadron of A-10As can be forward deployed there.*

The ForMAT user represents these statements in the system's goal editor. The goals specify the military planning objectives and may or may not bear close resemblance to the kind of goals Prodigy expects. When the user saves the goals from the editor, the goals are automatically sent to Prodigy in the representation shown by Figure 1.

```
(:GOALS
 (g-146 :SEND-SECURITY-POLICE (GEOGRAPHIC-LOCATION PACIFICA))  )
 (g-145 :SEND-BRIGADE ((FORCE 21ST-DIVISIONREADYBRIGADE)
                       (GEOGRAPHIC-LOCATION PACIFICA))  )
 (g-144 :SEND-HAWK    ((FORCE HAWK-BATTALION)
                       (GEOGRAPHIC-LOCATION PACIFICA))  )
 (g-143 :DEPLOY-A10A  ((GEOGRAPHIC-LOCATION PACIFICA)
                       (AIRCRAFT-TYPE A-10A)) )  )
```

Fig. 1. ForMAT output to Prodigy

For a generative planner, this input presents a number of problems. First, the goals are represented as actions to accomplish, rather than as states to achieve. For example, the input includes goals to send units to Pacifica, rather than to achieve the state of such units' locations being in Pacifica. Second, some goals pertain to particular unit instances (e.g., the 21st Division Ready Brigade); whereas, others pertain to unspecified units of a particular combat type (e.g., a Hawk anti-aircraft unit). Third, both top-level goals and subgoals are sent simultaneously without discretion. In Figure 1, deploying the squadron of A-10A aircraft is the top most goal, while all other goals are in support of this objective. The underlying subgoal structure to a resulting plan in Prodigy is partially shown in Figure 2.

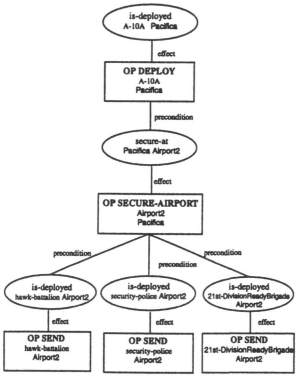

Fig. 2. Prodigy goal tree

4 Goals as Actions

Initially, the impulse was to convince human planners that goals should be represented as desired states of the world, and attempted to provide examples. We claimed that "to send" was an action corresponding to a planning operator that resulted in effects on the world. An operator effect constituted a proper goal. It became apparent, however, that such change would be resisted by users accustomed to thinking in terms of actions and that insisting on such changes might jeopardize the willingness of users to use the system. So the solution was to bypass such a conflict altogether and to build a preprocessor instead that made the transformation to a state representation automatically and in the background.

The preprocessor simply parses each ForMAT goal and obtains the corresponding Prodigy operator from a table. The primary effect of such operators then becomes the translated goal. To some extent, this solution finesses the more general problem of understanding user intent and desire [8]. For example, the translation heuristic assumes that the user does not wish the action to be accomplished due to a side-effect the operator can produce. However, for the purposes of the integration experiment and within the limited domain for which it is used, this solution proves sufficient.

A larger open question exists as to whether humans plan better in terms of actions or states (cf., [4]). Some hierarchical planners support task level specification of goals. See, for example, [13] for an application of hierarchical planning in a mixed-initiative setting for military operations planning. Nevertheless, in the military domain, the key notion of *objective* is important in high level planning, and this concept is often cast in terms of state. In either case, an automated planning component should allow humans to express goals in natural and familiar terms consistent with their language of manual planning.

5 Goal and Operator Hierarchies

In a traditional state-space planner, goals are represented as literals that have a predicate and an arbitrary number of arguments. Thus goal g-145 from Figure 1 can be represented as the literal (is-deployed 21st-DivisionReadyBrigade Pacifica). However, the FORCE argument of g-144 is a type identifier rather than an instance. In the Prodigy system, this is easily represented by specifying an existentially quantified goal such as (exists ((<hwk> hawk-battalion)) (is-deployed <hwk> Pacifica)). The goal is solved if some unit that is an element of the class hawk-battalion is deployed in Pacifica.

However given a hierarchy of types, a difficulty is that different operators may apply to goals up and down the abstraction hierarchy. For instance, the operator SECURE-AIR-PORT is used to make secure a specific airport (see Figure 3); whereas a more general SECURE operator is used to make secure objects such as hills for which no specialized operators exist. The difference between the two is that the second operator does not have an <air-defense> variable (nor the precondition associated with it) and the variable <obj> is of type OBJECT, rather than a more specific type AIRPORT (and thus the effect and preconditions are more abstract).[1] The first operator can be used to achieve (secure-at Pacifica Airport2), while the second is appropriate when achieving either a literal such as (secure-at Pacifica Hill21) or an existentially quantified goal such as (exists ((<obj> OBJECT)) (secure-at Pacifica <obj>)).

The advantage of reasoning about such an operator hierarchy is that when achieving novel goals, the more general operator can be applied when no specialized operator is available.[2] However, when the user wants to secure Airport2, both operators are now licensed because Airport2 is a member of the class AIRPORT, but is also a member by transitivity

---

1. In general an operator can be made be more widely applicable by dropping preconditions and by abstracting its variables.

2. They can also be applied when preconditions for the more specific operator is unsatisfied. If additional information arrives at planning time or during execution, then such general operators can be specialized dynamically.

```
secure-airport (<obj>, <loc>)
   <loc>: type LOCATION
   <obj>: type AIRPORT
   <internal-security>: type POLICE-FORCE-MODULE
   <external-security>: type TROOPS
   <air-defense>: type ANTI-AIR-MODULE
   Pre:  (loc-at <obj> <loc>)
         (is-deployed <internal-security> <obj>)
         (is-deployed <air-defense> <obj>)
         (is-deployed <external-security> <obj>)) )
   Add:  (secure-at <loc> <obj>)))) )
```

Fig. 3. Secure operator (representation adapted from [11])

of the class OBJECT. Thus, the effect of either operator will unify with the goal and so both are applicable. But clearly the planner should choose the more specific operator.

Thus it is useful to think of an existing hierarchy of operators that depends on the semantics of their effects. To formalize this notion, consider that one goal may be an ancestor of another goal. We have already mentioned that both literal and quantified goals exist in the Prodigy framework. But in more general terms we want to argue for the notion that the goal (is-deployed HAWK-BATTALION Pacifica) is more specific than (i.e., is a descendent of) the goal (is-deployed ANTI-AIR-MODULE COUNTRY), given that the first goal is a short-hand notation for the existential goal introduced earlier.

Abbreviation 1: Given G = (predicate arg1 .. argn) *such that* predicate $\in$ Existing-Predicates *and given type hierarchy graph* H = (V, E) *where* V *is the set of class vertices and* E *is the set of incident edges* $<x\ y>$ *such that* x *is a member of the class set* y. *Then* G *above is an abbreviation for the expression*

$$\forall\ arg_{i=1..n}\ |\ arg_i \in V, \exists\ x_i\ |\ x_i \in arg_i, (predicate\ x_1\ x_2\ ..\ x_n).$$

Definition 1: *Given that* $Arg(G, i)$ *is the ith argument of goal* G *as abbreviated above, we define goal* G_1 *to be an* **ancestor** *of* G_2 (G_2 *is a* **descendant** *of* G_1) *in hierarchy* H *iff*

(1) arity(G_1) = arity(G_2) = n
(2) predicate(G_1) = predicate(G_2)
(3) for i=1..n, Arg(G_1, i) $\geq$ Arg(G_2, i) *in* H

where the relation "$\geq$" between arguments is defined as equivalence or class inheritance such that a path exists through H *from* $Arg(G_2, i)$ *to* $Arg(G_1, i)$. *That is, the edges* $<Arg(G_2, i)\ e_1>\ <e_1\ e_2>\ ...\ <e_k\ Arg(G_1, i)>$ *are all elements of edge list* E.

Knowing this property, the planner can control its choice of operator when solving goals in a hierarchy. Given a goal such that two or more operators apply to the goal, if one operator is an ancestor of another, then Prodigy should prefer the more specific operator. Control rule Prefer-More-Specific-Op in Figure 4 implements this preference. Two operators to be compared are bound to the rule using the standard meta-predicate `candidate-operator` [1]. The function `is-ancestor-op-of-p` is a user defined meta-predicate that returns t *iff* the primary effect [2] of both operators are not equal and the primary effect of the first operator is an ancestor of the primary effect of the second operator (as specified by the "$\geq$" relation of Definition 1).

```
(CONTROL-RULE Prefer-More-Specific-Op
  (if (and (candidate-operator <OP1>)
           (candidate-operator <OP2>)
           (is-ancestor-op-of-p <OP1> <OP2>)))
  (then prefer operator <OP1> <OP2>) )
```

Fig. 4. Given two applicable operators from which to choose, prefer the more specific one

6 Top-level Goals Versus Subgoals

Finally, the goal information ForMAT sends to Prodigy always contains a mix of top-level goals and lower level constraining information. Myers [5] considers such information to be constraint advice, although in the context of state-space planning, we view this advice as simply a subgoal specification. Given that the user provides both subgoals and top-level goals within an agenda, two decisions need to be addressed by a mixed-initiative system. First, for which class of goals should the system plan first? Should it proceed bottom up or top down and why? Second, given that it goes top down, how should the system serendipitously take advantage of the existing information the subgoals provide?

6.1 Order of Planning

Given two goals such as $G-143$ = (is-deployed A-10A Pacifica) and its subordinate goal $G-145$ = (is-deployed 21st-Division-Ready-Brigade Pacifica), a planner will first plan for one and then the other. If the subordinate goal is achieved first, thus establishing the brigade in Pacifica, then the precondition of operator SECURE-AIRPORT having <external-security> in <loc> will already be true when planing for the superodinate goal (review Figures 2 and 3).

The problem with this approach, however, is twofold: First, we want to make sure that if more than one operator exists to achieve the subordinate goal, then the plan chosen is consistent with the goals above it in the goal tree so that backtracking is avoided and the plan remains consistent. The top-level goals need to provide guidance to their subgoals.

Second, in this domain, the user should view the planning process and the evolving plan in an understandable, top-down way, rather than in a disjoint fashion as subgoals are randomly assembled. Successive-refinement planning is appropriate in domains that exhibit hierarchical structure, when time is a scarce resource, and when reliable abstract plans exist in the domain [3]. So given a choice of goals to achieve, we want to choose the one highest in the subgoal tree. That is, Prodigy should choose the one that is a supergoal of the other.

Definition 2: G_2, *is a subgoal of* G_1, *(or alternatively,* G_1 *is a supergoal of* G_2) iff

(1) *a backward operators chain exists* $OP_1 \; .. \; OP_n$ *from* G_1 *to* G_2 *such that* $\forall OP_{i=1..n-1}$
     $\exists p, e \mid p \in pre(OP_i), e \in eff(OP_{i+1}), p$ *unifies with* e *under substitution* σ
(2) $\exists p \mid p \in pre(OP_n),$ *and* p *unifies with* G_2 *under* σ
(3) $\exists e \mid e \in eff(OP_1),$ *and* e *unifies with* G_1 *under* σ .

In the case of $n=1$, a single operator, OP, exists whose effects includes the effect $e \in eff(OP)$ that unifies with G_1 under the simple substitution, σ, and whose preconditions includes $p \in pre(OP)$ that unifies with G_2 also under σ.

Given Definition 2, control rule Prefer-Top-Most-Goal in Figure 5 can choose goals bound to supergoal <G1> over any of its subgoals bound to <G2> when the meta-predicate subgoal-of-p returns t. This occurs when some operator in Prodigy's subgoal tree for <G1> also achieves <G2> earlier in the plan.

```
(CONTROL-RULE Prefer-Top-Most-Goal
    (if (and (candidate-goal <G1>)
             (candidate-goal <G2>)
             (subgoal-of-p <G2> <G1>)))
    (then prefer goal <G1> <G2>) )
```

Fig. 5. Given two goals, prefer one if making the other true solves one of the preconditions for an operator that results in the preferred

In a large domain, a direct implementation of this control rule will result in inefficiency because when two goals are independent, the metapredicate must search the entire space of plans for both goals. To alleviate exponential search, a heuristic can be incorporated into the metapredicate that either places a bound on, n (the number of operators in the chain specified in condition 1 of Definition 2), or it can refer to a cache table maintained during past planning episodes that map goal-subgoal relations.

6.2 Opportunistic Planning

The policy established by Prefer-Top-Most-Goal creates another problem. If a top level goal is established first, such as G-143, then no guarantee exists that bindings established in plan operators such as SECURE-AIRPORT will agree with deferred subgoals. In the plan for deploying the A-10A, external security may be established by binding <external-security> with an instance of type TROOPS other than the 21st Division Ready Brigade.

Figure 6 shows a control rule that watches for propitious opportunities to optimize a plan by preferring bindings that also achieve additional pending goals. Given candidate bindings for the current operator in the search tree, meta-predicate match-constraining-goals identifies pending subgoals that unify with preconditions of the current operator. New bindings are then generated that satisfy this goal. Out of the candidate bindings, therefore, the control rule distinguishes ones that are consistent and are not consistent with such pending goals, preferring the former to the latter.

```
(CONTROL-RULE Prefer-Bindings-Opportunistically
    (if (and (current-operator <OP>)
             (candidate-bindings <CB>)
             (match-constraining-goals <G> <OP>)
             (generate-new-bindings <NB> <G> <OP>)
             (identify-worse-bindings <CB> <NB> <WB><OP>)
             (identify-better-bindings <CB> <NB> <BB><OP>)))
    (then prefer bindings <BB> <WB>))
```

Fig. 6. Given current operator and candidate set of bindings, prefer bindings that opportunistically solve another pending goal

7 Conclusion

The success of these control rules in managing the variety of goal types provided to Prodigy by the ForMAT user has been established and validated through trials conducted in real-time across the internet with Prodigy/Analogy operating from CMU in Pittsburgh and ForMAT from Mitre in Boston. (see [12]). Military planners have used the system in a limited fashion, but one that combines all three situations described herein.

Our observation is that a major trade-off exists between the goal of maintaining the simplifying assumptions of traditional planning systems and the goal of allowing the user more control and decision-making flexibility in mixed-initiative systems. Experience from the technology integration experiment performed between the Prodigy and ForMAT planning systems shows that even simple tasks presents challenges to the automated component. The underlying planning system must be flexible enough to allow the user to express desires and goals in terms most natural to the user and, therefore, cannot unconditionally expect to impose all of its decision-making representation on the user community if it is to be effective. The choice for the system developer then is to choose the right user restrictions on which to insist (e.g., requiring the user to explicitly represent their planning goals). Here we have discussed three potential problems that the technology can manage with internal control, thus avoiding user compromise altogether.

Specifically we examined problems faced by traditional planning systems when obtaining goal input from the user. Most planning systems make three implicit assumptions that the user will invariably negate. These assumptions are (1) the goal input is in terms of desired states of the world; (2) these goal states are literals grounded in specific instances; and (3) the goals are strictly top-level goals. In mixed-initiative planning systems, however, the user will present goals to the planner in terms of actions, the goals will range in specificity along the domain's abstraction hierarchy, and the user will mix both subgoals and top-level goals in the input. Our solutions to these problems have been a mix of preprocessing and internal planning control. Preprocessing is used to translate actions into states. Control rules prefer appropriate abstract operators for the given level of goal abstraction. Control rules also prefer top-level goals before lower-level goals and then prefer bindings for operators that opportunistically solve user-provided subgoals.

Unexpected goals are not simply problems to be overcome; rather, they represent user-provided hints on how to construct good plans. The use of abstract goals can allow the system to avoid overfitting the plan. Most automated planners construct plans that are too specific for subsequent plan steps when uncertainty exists as to the outcome of previous plan steps. Managing relative plan abstraction is essential for effective planning given substantial temporal extent. Moreover, the subgoal constraint information that users provide often originates from details outside the transitive closure provided by the domain theory. Given a more detailed domain theory, the planner could infer these constraints directly, but at the cost of considerable search. Thus, being able to handle constraint information from the user allows the planner to be more efficient in practical problems. The challenge involved with mixed-initiative systems is to engineer a more robust mechanism that is flexible with respect to user needs. The opportunity is to leverage user experience.

Acknowledgments

This research is sponsored as part of the DARPA/RL Knowledge Based Planning and Scheduling Initiative under grant number F30602-95-1-0018. The authors thank Eugene Fink, Alice Mulvehill, and Gary Pelton for comments and suggestions on earlier drafts of this publication.

References

[1] Carbonell, J. G.; Blythe, J.; Etzioni, O.; Gil, Y.; Joseph, R.; Kahn, D.; Knoblock, C.; Minton, S.; Pérez, A.; Reilly, S.; Veloso, M. M.; and Wang, X. 1992. *PRODIGY4.0: The Manual and Tutorial*, Tech. Rep., CMU-CS-92-150, Deptartment of Computer Science, Carnegie Mellon University.

[2] Fink, E, and Yang, Q. in press. Automatically Selecting and Using Primary Effects in Planning: Theory and Experiments. *Artificial Intelligence.*

[3] Hayes-Roth, B., and Hayes-Roth, F. 1979. A Cognitive Model of Planning. *Cognitive Science* 3: 275-310.

[4] McDermott, D. 1978. Planning and Acting. *Cognitive Science* 2: 71-109.

[5] Myers, K. L. 1996. Strategic Advice for Hierarchical Planners. In *Proceedings of the 5th International Conference on Principles of Knowledge Representation and Reasoning*, 112-123. San Francisco: Morgan Kaufmann.

[6] Mulvehill, A. 1996. Building, Remembering, and Revising Force Deployment Plans, In A. Tate ed. *Advanced Planning Technology*, 201-205. Menlo Park, CA: AAAI Press.

[7] Mulvehill, A., and Christey, S. 1995. *ForMAT - a Force Management and Analysis Tool.* Bedford, MA: MITRE Corporation.

[8] Pollack, M. E. 1990. Plans as Complex Mental Attitudes. In P. R. Cohen, J. Morgan and M. E. Pollack eds. *Intentions in Communication*, 77-104. Cambridge,MA: MIT Press.

[9] Veloso, M. M. 1994. *Planning and Learning by Analogical Reasoning.* New York: Springer-Verlag.

[10] Veloso, M. M. 1996. Towards Mixed-Initiative Rationale-Supported Planning. In A. Tate ed. *Advanced Planning Technology*, 277-282. Menlo Park, CA: AAAI Press.

[11] Veloso, M.; Carbonell, J.; Pérez, A.; Borrajo, D.; Fink, E.; and Blythe, J. 1995. Integrating Planning and Learning: The PRODIGY Architecture. *Journal of Experimental and Theoretical Artificial Intelligence* 7(1): 81-120.

[12] Veloso, M.; Mulvehill, A.; and Cox, M. in press. Rationale-Supported Mixed-Initiative Case-based Planning. To appear in *Proceedings of the Ninth Annual Conference on Innovative Applications of Artificial Intelligence.* Menlo Park, CA: AAAI Press.

[13] Wilkins, D., and Desimone, R. 1994. Applying an AI Planner to Military Operations Planning. In M. Zweben and M. Fox eds. *Intelligent Scheduling*, 685-709. San Mateo, CA: Morgan Kaufmann.

Cooperative Memory Structures and Commonsense Knowledge for Planning

P.V.S.R. Bhanu Prasad   Deepak Khemani

Department of Computer Science and Engineering
Indian Institute of Technology, Madras
Madras - 600036
India
bhanu@iitm.ernet.in   khemani@iitm.ernet.in

Abstract. Here we present a memory-based planning system in which the memory is divided into three components namely the memory of *skeletons*, the memory of *properties*, and the memory of *secondary objects*. The planning and domain knowledge is distributed over these components which interact with each other in producing a plan. A skeleton is organized using a *packaging hierarchy*. An *abstraction hierarchy* is used in organizing the other two memories. A plan is generated in a hierarchical fashion by unfolding a suitable skeleton with the aid of the other two memories. The culinary domain has been taken up for system's implementation. The system utilizes some commonsense knowledge of the domain to adapt known plans to user requirements. This knowledge is represented in the form of rules.

1 Introduction

Experience is a crucial factor for expert performance. But experience alone does not fully account for expert performance: people with comparable levels of experience may exhibit very different levels of skill [1, 4, 12]. Likewise, sufficient memory is only one of the many requirements for successful performance in memory-based systems; other crucial factors are its organization, retrieval, and adaptation strategies.

We have developed a memory-based hierarchical planning model, BAWARCHI. It is implemented in a program with the same name. Vegetarian cooking in the South-Indian style is the domain of implementation. BAWARCHI is mainly based on packaging and abstraction hierarchies [14], and some commonsense knowledge [3] of the domain. We believe that, especially in structured domains, experience as acquired by *cases* [10, 11] should get assimilated into more general memory structures. This is in accordance with Schank's [15] notion of how people may acquire scripts. This work is an exploration of how such memory could be structured. The motivation for taking up the culinary domain for the system implementation stems mainly from its wide access and also due to its structured nature. Cooking domain is well represented in the memory-based reasoning community [6, 7].

The schematic diagram of BAWARCHI is shown in figure 1. In this figure, the arcs represent data flow.

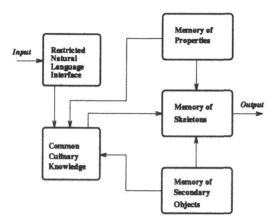

Fig. 1. Schematic Diagram of BAWARCHI

2 Memory Organization

The basic assumption regarding our memory organization is that there exists distinct and identifiable styles of cooking such as *fry, curry* etc. In BAWARCHI each such style is accessed via the root node of a packaging hierarchy. The root node itself is reached by a simple indexing mechanism [14]. Unfolding the packaging hierarchy results in a hierarchical plan expansion, and this expansion is guided by the knowledge of the ingredients. Plan generation, therefore essentially uses three separate memories: the memory of properties, the memory of secondary objects, and the memory of skeletons.

2.1 Memory of Properties

The memory of properties is the system's knowledge of the primary domain objects, in our case, vegetables. This memory organizes the vegetables and their properties using an abstraction hierarchy. Culinary information such as the size of the pieces, cooking time, boiling time etc. is associated with the nodes in this memory. A node in this memory is implemented as a *frame*. Details on the memory of properties are available in [2, 8, 9].

2.2 Memory of Secondary Objects

The memory of secondary objects organizes the information regarding the secondary ingredients and their properties. This memory is used to capture a different dimension of the use of ingredients, that is, for flavoring. It is orthogonal to the memory of properties, and together the two determine the contents and the flavoring combination. This memory is again organized using an abstraction hierarchy. Culinary information regarding the quantities of the secondary ingredients is associated with the nodes in this memory. A node in this memory is represented as a *frame*, in which the nodes are the indexes. Quantities of the secondary ingredients are represented as slots in these frames. This information is indexed by the properties of the vegetables and the cooking styles too. Details on the memory of secondary objects can be found in [2].

2.3 Memory of Skeletons

The memory of skeletons organizes the planning knowledge of the system. This knowledge is organized based on the fact that there are distinct recipe styles, but within the same style different vegetables can be cooked in a similar way. For example, the recipe for *biangan* (brinjal) fry is very different from *biangan bharta*, but quite close to potato fry. For each style we build a skeleton. In other words, this memory recognizes the existence of different cooking styles which have some characteristic action patterns. More details regarding the memory of skeletons can be found in [2, 8, 9].

3 Input Representation and Refinement

The system developed so far organizes known plans (recipes) in a structured fashion. However it is somewhat inflexible and brittle in its performance. If the user specifies that some ingredients should be present and/or absent, the system will not be able to create a proper plan. The same is true for taste requirements like *spicy*, *bland*, *sour* etc.

To overcome these drawbacks, some recipe independent culinary knowledge is incorporated into the system. This "commonsense" knowledge is used for adapting known plans to user specifications. This knowledge is explained in the following subsection. We believe that many important kinds of commonsense knowledge are domain specific. A search for completely domain-independent principles of commonsense knowledge can provide useful techniques (eg., non-monotonic logic, context logic), but misses much of the important substance of the problem of commonsense knowledge. Commonsense reasoning as envisaged in this work is neither the study of the recurrent, domain independent basic forms or patterns [3, 13] that are applicable across a wide range of domains (if such forms are believed to be existing) nor the study of finding out such forms portable over a class of similar domains. An attempt is made to utilize commonsense knowledge in order to make the system robust.

A user may specify the names of the vegetables involved in the dish and the style of cooking. However, he may desire variations in the standard recipe to suit his taste. These variations may involve such things as whether a vegetable should be pre-boiled or not, whether a secondary ingredient is required or not, the quantities in which the ingredients should be present and so on. To accept such specifications, a restricted natural language interface is implemented in the system. The restricted natural language interface accepts a sentence from the user as input, processes it, and interprets the keywords in terms of a set of symbols whose functionality is pre-defined. This generated set of symbols captures the meaning of the input. For example, the sentence, "a dish that contains potato and cinnamon and which does not contain garlic" is converted into the following form. {(without-sec-ingr garlic) (with-sec-ingr cinnamon)(with-vegetable potato)}. The predicate set is sent to the *input refinement mechanism* which is explained below.

3.1 Input Refinement Knowledge

The predicate set generated by the restricted natural language interface needs to be refined before further processing. For example, a fried dish with less amount of oil needs to have its vegetables chopped in smaller pieces. The input refinement mechanism is used to interpret the requirements and it generates specifications for the planner. It accepts the predicate set supplied by the restricted natural language interface and refines it using the commonsense rules. The resultant set of predicates is used by the memory of skeletons for plan generation. The refinement may involve addition of predicates to the existing set.

The input refinement mechanism is a *forward chaining rule-based system* [5]. The *fact part* consists of all tuples of the form *(a v)* where *v* is a vegetable in the memory of properties and *a* is an abstraction of *v*. In addition, the fact part contains tuples of the form *(a s)* where *s* is a secondary ingredient and *a* is an abstraction of *s*. Apart from these tuples, the fact part contains the predicate set supplied by the restricted natural language interface. The *rule part* contains the commonsense rules. The variables in these rules are ranged over the set of all vegetables. Following is one such rule corresponding to the style *fry*: *(with-large-pieces ?x)* → *(more-oil ?x)*.

Once the *inferences* are derived for a given input, the *working memory* is added to the input predicate set and the resultant (or refined) predicate set is sent to the memory of skeletons for plan generation. More details on the input refinement mechanism can be be found in [2].

4   The Planning Algorithm

To generate a plan, the root node of a suitable skeleton is selected using the indexing mechanism. It is then expanded along the packaging links. On this plan, the modification knowledge associated with the root node is applied. This is repeated for each of the operators in this plan until a ground-level plan is generated.

1. /* RECEIVE INPUT */
   Accept user input supplied in the form of a natural language sentence and convert it into a set of predicates.

2. /*REFINE INPUT */

Refine the predicate set using the input refinement mechanism and supply the resultant set to the memory of skeletons.

3. /* SELECT SKELETON */

Select the operator that represents the root node of the required skeleton.

4. /* INITIALIZE */

For each level i in the hierarchy of that skeleton, create a list *plan-list-i* to store the operator identifiers at that level. Initialize each list to NULL. Add the root node to *plan-list-0*. Set $i \leftarrow 0$.

From the memory of properties, retrieve the information regarding the size of the pieces, boiling time, cooking time etc. that corresponds to the style and the vegetable which are there in the user input.

5. /* EXPAND AND MODIFY */

For each of the operators (from left to right) in *plan-list-i* do the following in the specified order.

(a) If it is a high-level operator then
   i. Generate its next-level plan using the packaging links.
   ii. Modify the plan using the appropriate modification rules associated with the operator.

(b) If the operator is a ground-level one then
   i. If the operator has a variable which is not instantiated then compute the value of the variable. Instantiate the variable with that value.
   ii. If either the template does not have a variable or the variables in the template are already instantiated then leave the operator unchanged.

(c) Append the modified next-level plan or the ground-level operator to *plan-list-(i+1)*.

6. /* DESCEND */

If any of the elements in *plan-list-(i+1)* is not an instantiated ground-level one then set $i \leftarrow (i+1)$ and go to step 5. Else output the ground-level plan.

A more detailed algorithm and comparisons with some existing systems can be found in [2].

5 References

[1] Bareiter, C.; Scardamalia, M. 1993. *Surpassing Ourselves: An Inquiry into the Nature and Implications of Expertise.* Open Court, Chicago.

[2] Bhanu Prasad, P.V.S.R. 1997. *Planning With Cooperative Memory Structures.* Ph.D. Thesis, Department of Computer Science and Engineering, Indian Institute of Technology, Madras.

[3] Davis, E. 1990. *Representations of Commonsense Knowledge.* Morgan Kaufman Publishers, San Mateo, CA.

[4] Ericsson, L.; Smith, J. (editors). 1991. Prospects and Limits of the Empirical Study of Expertise: An Introduction. In *Toward a General Theory of Expertise,* Cambridge, NY.

[5] Golshani, F. 1990. *Rule-Based Expert Systems,* Chap. 2 of *Knowledge Engineering: Fundamentals.* H. Adeli (editor), McGraw-Hill, NY.

[6] Hammond, K.J. 1989. *Case-Based Planning: Viewing planning as a memory task.* Academic Press, Inc, NY.

[7] Hinrichs, T.R.; Kolodner, J.L. 1991. The Roles of Adaptation on Case-Based Design. In *Proceedings of AAAI.*

[8] Khemani, D.; Prasad, P.V.S.R.B. 1995a. *A Memory-Based Hierarchical Planner,* Case-Based Reasoning Research and Development, M. Veloso and A. Aamodt (editors.), Lecture notes in Artificial Intelligence, Springer-Verlag, 1010, Berlin.

[9] Khemani, D.; Bhanu Prasad, P.V.S.R. 1995b. A Hierarchical Memory-Based Planner, *Proceedings of the IEEE International Conference on Systems, Man, and Cybernetics,* Canada.

[10] Kolodner, J. 1993. *Case-Based Reasoning.* Morgan Kaufmann, San Mateo, CA.

[11] Leake, D.B. (editor). 1996. *Case-Based Reasoning: Experiences, Lessons, and Future Directions.* The MIT Press, MA.

[12] Lesgold, A. et al. 1988. *Expertise in a Complex Skill.* In *The Nature of Expertise,* M. Chi et al. (editors), Lawrence Erlbaum, NJ.

[13] McCarthy, J. 1968. Programs With Commonsense. In *Semantic Information Processing,* M. Minsky (editor), MIT Press, Cambridge, MA.

[14] Riesbeck, C.K.; and Schank, R.C. 1989. *Inside Case-Based Reasoning.* Lawrence Erlbaum Associates, NJ.

[15] Schank, R.C. 1982. *Dynamic Memory: A Theory of Learning in Computers and People.* Cambridge University Press.

Diagonalization and Type Rewriting in Clam

Jerônimo Pellegrini and Jacques Wainer

Institute of Computing
Unicamp - Brazil

Abstract. In this paper, we show an implementation of Cantor's Diagonalization Process in the Oyster-Clam theorem proving system. To achieve that, we have extended the Oyster logic with comparison and induction on types, and developed a method and some rewrite rules. The rewrite rules deal with types, what was not supported yet in the Oyster-Clam system, and some modifications were done to make that possible.

1 Introduction

In [7], Huang and Kerber present three theorems proved by diagonalization as examples of analogy-driven proof planning. We have implemented diagonalization proof techniques in the Oyster-Clam system using a different approach. Some rewrite rules specially related to types and a Clam method were developed. Some theorems were proved using them, which we describe in the last section of this paper.

1.1 Cantor's Diagonalization Process

Diagonalization is a proof technique used to prove statements of the form:

$$\neg surj(f, \alpha, \beta) \tag{1}$$

$$greater\_than(\alpha, \beta) \tag{2}$$

That is, (1) "the function $f : \alpha \to \beta$ is not surjective", and (2) "the cardinality of α is greater than the cardinality of β".

Some theorems like these are: $|I\!N| < |I\!R|$, $\forall x, |x| < |\mathcal{P}(x)|$, the existence of a non-computable function, the unsolvability of the halting problem, and many other theorems in Computability theory.

To prove (1) by diagonalization, we proceed as follows: given the function $f : \alpha \to \beta$, if we know that β is equipotent to a set of functions [1] $\alpha \to \gamma$ (see figure 1), and $|\gamma| > 1$, then we may find a function *diff* that, for each element of γ, returns a different one. Now, let δ be $\lambda x.diff(f(x)(x))$. The element δ is a function from α to γ, that is in the codomain of f, but not in its image (since $diff(x) \neq x$). Hence, f is not surjective. The idea is to take the diagonal and build an element from it which differs from each line in the matrix, as shown in figure 1.

---

[1] We will use the notation $\alpha \to \gamma$ for γ^α, the set of all functions from α to γ

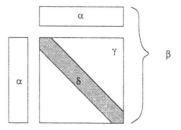

Fig. 1. Cantor's Diagonalization

As an example, consider the theorem $\forall x, \forall f : x \to \mathcal{P}(x)$, f is not surjective ($\mathcal{P}(s)$ denotes the powerset of s). Here we have $\alpha = x, \beta = \mathcal{P}(x), \gamma = \{0,1\}$.

If we pay attention to figure 1, it's easy to see that when $|\beta|$ is equipotent to some set $\theta \to \gamma$, with $|\theta| < |\alpha|$, the picture would have a different shape, and we would not be able to find the counter-example δ, since the elements in the bottom of it wouldn't be in the diagonal.

1.2 The Oyster-Clam System

In [2], Bundy argues that theorem proving would be best done using the processes that mathematicians use rather than using the well known theorem proving algorithms existent until then. This idea led to the development of the *proof planning* paradigm for automated theorem proving.

The first proof plan-based theorem proving system was Oyster-Clam [1]; Oyster [5] is a proof development environment, in which the user builds proofs. After stating a theorem, the user may apply Oyster's inference rules to prove it. While inference rules are applied, a λ-term is being automatically created. This λ-term is called the *extract term*, and it is the algorithm underlying the constructive proof. Rules may be grouped in commonly used sequences, called tactics, which make it much easier to work. Oyster's logic is a variation of Martin-Löf's Type Theory [10]; it is sequent-based, and reasoning is backwards in the system.

Clam [4] is built on top of Oyster, and given a conjecture, tries to determine automatically which tactics should be applied in order to build a proof. A proof plan is built using descriptions of the tactics available (this descriptions are called methods). Oyster-Clam is, then, a fully automated theorem proving system.

1.3 Diagonalization and Reasoning About Types in Other Systems

Although other two systems, Isabelle [11] [12] and Coq [9], support reasoning about types, none of them seem to have been used with proof planners as Clam.

As far as we know, there is only one theorem proving system based on proof planning which performs proofs by diagonalization - Ω-MKRP [8]. Some diagonalization proofs are given as example of the use of meta-methods in this system in [7]: the *powerset* theorem, a theorem about cardinality of $I\!R$ and $I\!N$, and the undecidability of the halting problem. In Ω-MKRP, methods have a declarative part: a proof sketch. Theorems are proved in this system using the same basic idea, i. e., one original proof, which is reformulated by the so-called meta-methods, generating new methods (with new proof sketches). However, meta-methods will generate new methods to prove similar theorems, and that may take some time. With one single method, we have proven some theorems by diagonalization. Although we point to this advantadge of our approach, we do not intend to invalidate the one used in the Ω-MKRP system, namely analogy driven proof planning: it is a powerful technique, which is also being incorporated in the Oyster-Clam system, and which we expect to be used in other systems as well.

In the next sections, we show the implementation of a simple formalization of the diagonalization process in Oyster-Clam.

2 Our Approach

We have shown two kinds of statements in last section; our method will try to turn them into a statement of the form $\exists diff : \gamma \to \gamma, \forall c \in \gamma, diff(c) \neq c$, which our rewrite rules will try to reduce to an elementary goal, usually $s(x) \neq x$ or $x + 1 \neq x$, which Clam can deal with. If γ is a unary type (and in this case the conjecture is not true), Clam will not find reduction rules for *diff*.

Our method deal with goals of the expanded form of (1), and others, like $\beta \sim (\alpha \to \gamma) \Rightarrow \forall f : \alpha \to \beta, \exists \delta : \alpha \to \gamma, f(a) \neq \delta$ [2] The method is not very complex; most of the work is done via rewriting.

For goals of the form (2), we have only a single rewrite rule: $greater\_than(\alpha, \beta) \Rightarrow \forall f : \alpha \to \beta, \neg surj(f, \alpha, \beta)$, that will turn them into goals of form (1).

Other ways of proving that one set is greater than another may be added, by adding other equations to the definition of *greater than*.

2.1 Extending Oyster

Oyster is a type theory (a variation of Martin-Löf's); the basic types are all members of a universe called $u(1)$, and each universe is also a type, and member of all higher universes, i. e., $l < m \to u(l) \in u(m)$. Hence, we have transitivity of $\in$ for types, and an infinite number of universes, which are built inductively.

Besides the basic types, e.g., *int*, *pnat* (natural numbers with Peano postulates), there are compound types. In [6], a version of Oyster which has induction on types is described by Horn and Smaill. However, the version of Oyster (release 1) available at Edinburgh does not have that principle. Comparison between types is also not possible in this version of Oyster.

We have added some inference rules to Oyster, so that an *elim* rule may be applied to any variable of type $u(i)$ in the hypothesis list of a sequent, generating several subgoals, one for each type, and generating a type induction term

---

[2] The symbol $\sim$ denotes equipotency between sets.

as extract term. Decision rules and operators for types were also included (as shown below). All these extensions follow the patterns already existent in Oyster, so that it will be easier to adapt the whole Oyster-Clam system to cope with reasoning about types.

These two extensions allows us to define a unique *diff* function for all types, thus avoiding reasoning about types within methods and keeping Clam as nearly theory-free as it was before[3].

As an example, if there is a variable in the hypothesis list called $v0$, we may apply the **decide** rule to it, splitting the proof in two cases: $v0 = int$ and $v0 \neq int$[4]. The extract term is `type_eq(v0,int,_,_)`, a decision procedure that compares $v0$ to int and evaluates one of other two extract terms.

2.2 The *diff* Function

Clam's rewrite system was originally implemented to deal only with terms of the types int, pnat and lists of these; with types specifically, although the `sym_eval` method would behave correctly, its tactic would fail. However, types themselves are terms over universes, and since we have extended Oyster with the treatment of types as terms, we have also improved the well-formedness tactics used by the `sym_eval` tactic, which were not built to deal with types as terms. As long as we treat types correctly as terms in this way, we may add rewrite rules for them in Clam's term rewriting system.

Recursive definitions are implemented in Clam as *defeqn* objects. These have three components:

- a *synth* object, a theorem whose extract term is exactly the function being defined;
- a *def* object – an Oyster definition that is like
  `f(x_1,x_2, ..., x_n) <==> term_of(f) of x_1 of x_2 ... of  x_n`;
- a set of *eqn* objects – the rewrite rules that will be used by Clam in the proof planning process.

The set of rewrite rules below implements the *diff* function. Note that we are using type rewriting. As an example, the rule `element(x list) :=> nil` is understood as "$\forall x \in u(1)$", `element(x list) :=> nil`, i. e., for any type in universe $u(1)$, a list of elements of that type may be rewritten as an empty list.

The reader familiar to the *rippling* [3] heuristic will recognize the use of "*rippling in*" here.

```
element(int)    :=> 0
element(pnat)   :=> 0
element(atom)   :=> atom(a)
element(x list) :=> nil
```

---

[3] See F. V. Harmelen's note on Clam's manual about that
[4] If the **decide** rule is applied at universe level l, there are two more goals generated, and the user will have to prove that both $v0$ and int are in u(l)

```
element(unary) :=> unit
element(t#t2) :=> (element(t)#element(t2))
element(t\t2) :=> inr(element(t2))in(t\t2)
element(t\t2) :=> inl(element(t))in(t\t2)


diff(x,int) :=> x+1
diff(x,pnat) :=> s(x)
diff(atom(a),atom) :=> atom(b)
(x=atom(a)in atom=>void) => diff(x,atom) :=> atom(a)
diff(x,t list) :=> element(t)::x
diff(e&e2,t#t2) :=> (diff(e,t)&diff(e2,t2))
diff(inl(e),t\t2) :=> inr(element(t2))
diff(inr(e),t\t2) :=> inl(element(t))
```

The function *element* is necessary, since Clam normally does not prove goals of the form $\exists x, x \in T$, except in unfrequent cases.

Note that *diff* is not defined for all possible types. In the case of *void* and *unary* this is intentional, since we want *diff* not to be reduced, causing the symbolic evaluation method of Clam not to be applicable.

In the case of other types, we have decided not to implement any rules (although we think it would be very useful). It will probably not be easy to find rules for the subset types, for example. Also, the more rules in the rewrite system, the greater will be the time required for Clam to load them.

Besides diagonalization proofs, rewriting of types is clearly useful in other occasions; the `element` function may be used, as an example, when proving existentially quantified theorems and base case of induction.

2.3 Some Theorems Proved

The following theorems were proved using the method and rules described:

- *Powerset*: This ($\forall x, |\mathcal{P}(x)| > |x|$) theorem and some instances of it, such as $|\mathcal{P}(int)| > |int|$. $\mathcal{P}(x) = x \to \mathcal{B}$, where $\mathcal{B}$ is a binary set (type); we have chosen to use *unary* \ *unary* as $\mathcal{B}$.
- *Existence of a Non-Computable Function*: This theorem has as extract term a function that, given an enumeration of all computable functions, returns a non-computable one.
- $|I\!N| < |I\!R|$: This theorem, and a variant, $\forall f : \mathbb{Z} \to I\!R, \neg surj(f, \mathbb{Z}, I\!R)$, were easily proved.

3 Conclusions

We have presented a very simple though efficient formalization of diagonalization; it was implemented in the Oyster-Clam system through a method and some rewrite rules. The Oyster logic was modified to cope with type induction and comparison among types, in order to allow a more efficient use of the rewrite system, allowing type rewriting. Some theorems were proved using the method and rules described.

Acknowledgements

The authors would like to thank the reviewers for their comments and suggestions, and Prof. Flávio Soares C. da Silva, from IME/USP, for the use of computational resources. The first author was partially supported by CAPES; the second author was partially supported by CNPq grant 301245/95-9.

References

1. A. Bundy, F. van Harmelen, C. Horn, and A. Smaill. The Oyster-Clam system. In M. E. Stickel, editor, *Proceedings of the 10th CADE*, number 449 in LNAI, pages 647–648. Springer-Verlag, 1990.
2. Alan Bundy. A science of reasoning. In J. L. Lassez and G. Plotkin, editors, *Computational Logic: Essays in Honor of Alan Robinson*, pages 178–198. MIT Press, 1991. Also available from Edinburgh as DAI Research paper 445.
3. Alan Bundy, A. Stevens, F. van Harmelen, Andrew Ireland, and Alan Smaill. Rippling: A heuristic for guiding inductive proofs. *Artificial Intelligence*, 62:185–253, 1993. Also available from Edinburgh as DAI Research Paper No. 567.
4. Frank Van Harmelen and the Dream group. *The Clam Proof Planner*. Dept. of Artificial Intelligence, Univ. of Edinburgh, 1997. Clam is available with its manual at ftp://dream.dai.ed.ac.uk.
5. Christian Horn and Alan Smaill. Theorem proving with Oyster. Research Paper 505, Dept. of Artificial Intelligence, Edinburgh, 1990.
6. Christian Horn and Alan Smaill. From meta-level tactics to object-level programs. In S. McKee J. Johnson and A. Vella, editors, *Artificial Intelligence in Mathematics*, pages 135–146. Claredon Press, 1994.
7. Xiaorong Huang, Manfred Kerber, and Lassaad Cheikhrouhou. Adapting the diagonalization method by reformulations. In Alon Levy and Pandu Nayak, editors, *Proceedings of the Symposium on Abstraction, Reformulation, and Approximation, SARA-95*, Ville d'Esterel, Canada, 1995.
8. Xiaorong Huang, Manfred Kerber, Michael Kohlhase, Erica Melis, Dan Nesmith, Jörn Richts, and Jörg Siekmann. Ω-MKRP: A proof development environment. In Alan Bundy, editor, *Automated Deduction — CADE-12*, Proceedings of the 12th International Conference on Automated Deduction, pages 788–792, Nancy, France, 1994. Springer-Verlag, Berlin, Germany. LNAI 814.
9. Gerard Huet, Gilles Kahn, and Christine Paulin-Mohring. The coq proof assistant : A tutorial : Version 6.1. Technical Report 0204, INRIA, 1997.
10. Per Martin-Löf. Constructive mathematics and computer programing. In *6th International Congress for Logic, Methodology and Philosophy of Science*, pages 153–175, Hannover, August 1982. Published by North Holland, Amsterdam.
11. Lawrence C. Paulson. Introduction to Isabelle. Technical Report 280, University of Cambridge, Computer Laboratory, 1993.
12. Lawrence C. Paulson and Tobias Nipkow. Isabelle tutorial and user's manual. Technical Report 189, University of Cambridge, Computer Laboratory, January 1990.

Granularity for Explanation

Sanjay Poria and Roberto Garigliano

Department of Computer Science, University of Durham,
South Road, Durham, DH1 3LE, UK

Abstract. Most people would agree that a formalisation of granularity in natural language should involve notions of *abstraction* and *detail*. However in reality, this concept has proved difficult to capture formally. In this paper we examine the role of granularity in constructing explanations. This role is clarified by providing several dimensions along which any explanation task can be characterised. We argue that a combination of these dimensions can be used to define a notion of coherence in texts. This notion of coherence gives rise to search heuristics when solving non-trivial language engineering problems such as reference resolution.

1 Introduction

Intuitively shifts in granularity correspond to the ability of an individual to see the same concept through different perspectives depending upon the current needs. However this notion has proved difficult to capture rigourously, and in the cases where a formal characterisation has been given few implementations have emerged.

We initially show that the study of granularity in AI is an important field of research by introducing a model of the explanation construction process, and illustrating the role of granularity within it.

We argue that the introduced model of explanation helps us to define a type of regularity/coherence often found in texts. The formalisation of granularity within the explanation model can be used impose search limits in natural language understanding systems.

This work is in the process of being implemented in the Natural Language Processing system LOLITA[1][5]. We hope to apply the introduced theory to common language understanding tasks; in particular reference resolution.

2 Explanation

Explanation, with particular application to expert systems, is a well studied topic of research in AI, perhaps the most well known work being that based on the MYCIN system. However it is the real world explanation of events that is of interest to us here. As Leake [3] recognises, the construction of explanations

---

[1] Large Scale Object Based Linguistic Interactor Translator and Analyser

is a key process in human understanding, having many applications from internal tasks such as learning through to external ones such as diagnosis and plan recognition.

Since explanation construction is ubiquitous in all areas of AI we believe that not only will any intelligent reasoning system benefit from an *explicit* notion of granularity but it is essential if the system is to model the explanation capability of humans. For example, given the knowledge:

John was in a hurry to get to the airport and was killed in a car accident.
He hit his head on the steering wheel with great force.

then consider the following possible explanations for why *"John was killed"*

1. because he was in a hurry,
2. because he was involved in a car accident,
3. because he hit his head on the steering wheel with great force
4. because Johns brain received a shock

and so on. The important point to note is that while all the explanations above may be simultaneously true, a coroner would typically be interested in the last two reasons. However an explanation at this level detail would be inappropriate to give to John's relatives to inform them of his death. In this case the second explanation would seem more appropriate.

The required level of granularity of an explanation is only one constraint that influences the explanation selection (choosing the desired explanation amongst candidates) process. Below we outline several other considerations which arise when an explanation is being selected. The identification of these orthogonal primitives gives rise to a new model of explanation construction and evaluation. The focus of this paper on granularity means that this whole model can only be sketched.

The identification of each primitive is accompanied by possible values it may take in the case of everyday commonsense explanation. We claim that different situations may well require different values of the introduced primitives if the constructed explanation is to be useful. To illustrate the flexibility of the model we show how some[2] of the primitives have corresponding notions (to explanation) in a vastly different domain - that of *proof explanation*.

Type – Explanations can be of various types in particular domains. In the commonsense domain, given some observation, humans can often construct a physical explanations or explanations involving goals of the actors involved or explanations involving emotions [4], *e.g.*, In the example given above the first explanation involves John's goals (of getting to the airport), while the third is purely physical. In the domain of proof explanations this primitive might correspond to forward or backward explanation of proofs.

---

[2] obviously commonsense explanation being more general than proof explanation.

Modality – refers to the precise relationship between the explained and explaining event. In the commonsense domain where cause is the notion of explanation then the modality of the cause may be necessary, sufficient or simply statistical. In the domain of proof explanation there may exist only one modality based on a notion of derivability.

Granularity – an explanation may be conceptualised/viewed in many different ways. However the best explanation for a task may prefer one view over another (as in the example above). In proof explanation one may require an explanation of a theorem at the level of different theories which are involved in its proof, *e.g.*, at the level of logical connectives, at the level of set theory, at the level of group theory and so on.

Strength – no explanation in the real world is ever certain[3]. Different tasks require different levels of certainty for the explanation to be useful. For example, a doctor before making a decision to operate on a patient will require a lot more certainty in his diagnosis of the problem than someone deciding whether to take an umbrella with them in case it rains.

Distance – explanatory chains can often be traced arbitrarily far back from the conclusion being explained. In the commonsense domain this primitive refers to the distance along the causal chain in which some relevant cause is chosen and given as the explanation for the event. For example, an explanation for why *"John died"* could always be that *"John was born"*, but a policeman at the scene of the crime is unlikely to be interested in an explanation that sits so far away from the effect. In the domain of proof explanation it is chains of inferences (proof steps) that are of interest. Only certain steps may be of interest in the chain, *e.g.*, those justified by the the application of a definition or theorem.

These primitives partition explanations into categories, each category being further partitioned by particular values of the primitive under consideration. Hence each primitive may be viewed as a variable, which, for a particular explanation, is instantiated to some value taken from the predefined set.

Below we discuss more clearly (through examples) the role of granularity in commonsense explanations and show how it can be further characterised.

3 Granularity of Commonsense Explanations

In the previous section we gave an intuitive example of commonsense explanations at differing levels of granularity without specifying what granularity is. Below we offer some more concrete insights.

Let us suppose that our knowledge of why the ball moved was that John had kicked it whilst playing football, and that, firstly, a physical explanation is required. Then the event may be explained in a number of different ways, including:

---

[3] with the exception of tautologies which hold in a definitional sense

1. his shoe hit the ball
2. his foot hit the ball
3. the point of his foot hit the ball
4. his muscles around his knee joint stretched and contracted applying a force to the joint...

If, secondly, an explanation which involves an actor's goals is required, at various levels of conceptualisation, then possible explanations might include:

1. he wants to make money and one way of achieving this is to be a successful footballer, which involves impressing the scouts...
2. he wants to gain a dominant position in the attack
3. he wants to win the game

A change in granularity takes place when a concept is viewed differently. This change manifests itself with a change in language (with the exclusion of synonymous statements) hence each view is taken to be a different concept. Thus, changes in granularity and changes in language are inherently linked; granularity is identified with a switch in language. A change in granularity is not an "all or nothing" phenomenon; there is a gradual change from small variations to a total change. These changes in language can be classified as belonging to one of the following types:

descriptive change – this is a change in granularity of the smallest possible type. It involves the substitution of a term[4] by a collection of others. However the original term is still present in this set of new terms and used as a reference, *e.g.*, the shift from 2 to 3 in the first example above, represents a descriptive change; the original term in 2 *"the foot"* has been changed to *"the point of the foot"*.

substitution of terms – involves the direct substitution of one term for another different one, *e.g.*, the shift from 1 to 2 in the first example, "shoe" is substituted with "foot".

change in terminology – The process of continuous substitution of terms, can result in a total shift in the language used to express something. The boundaries representing such a shift are extremely distinctive. In the first example, a change from 1,2 or 3 to 4 falls into this category because while the first three express statements in the language of parts of the leg the latter uses terminology related to muscles and joints.

While the first statement in the latter example uses the language of peoples' global goals (Schank [6] may call this a "theme") the next two are both in the context of language that may be used to describe a typical game of football.

Clearly it is not simply arbitrary terms that may be substituted into an explanation to convert it to a differing level of granularity.

---

[4] the notion of a term is left undefined for the time being.

Changes in granularity for commonsense explanations occur along two dimensions;*abstraction* and *aggregation*. Abstraction corresponds to shifts in focus from general to specific or vice versa; and aggregation corresponds to shifts in focus through part whole relationships. Below we characterise changes in granularity by providing a set of inference rules which enable a change in focus along the two mentioned dimensions.

4 Language Understanding

The problem of text comprehension involves connecting causally related events and is consequently viewed as a special case of abduction [2, 1]. Since we have shown that explanations can vary in many dimensions, the search space for potential explanations in a large scale NLP system is likely to be extremely large, resulting in a search intensive process. Below we introduce a property of coherent text that enables this search space to be restricted.

4.1 Language and Coherence

Coherent text is written such that it requires minimal effort for the reader to understand. In this work we claim that the coherence of text is greatly reduced in cases where consecutive events in the passage *vary* or *change* in any of the dimensions introduced in the explanation model[5]; distance, modality, causal type and granularity. In addition exaggerated changes in one or more of these dimensions can be used to produce certain stylistic effects such as humour.

Of course this claim is a large one to make and one that is not entirely obvious. I hope to convince the reader by providing some examples where text seems to be incoherent precisely for the reason mentioned above:

1. Tom was killed by the bullet puncturing his lung because John Major failed to ban all firearms.
2. John ordered a taxi because he wanted to go home. He stretched his hand out grasped the door handle and turned it to open the door of the taxi. He was soon at home.
3. John damaged his knee in the car accident because Mary had been drinking before she got into the car.

In the first and third cases a causal chain is visualised in which the distance between the first and second event is much longer than the second an third, *e.g.*, in 3, one may infer that the time (specified by the distance dimension) between having an accident and injuring oneself is extremely short compared to the time between drinking alcohol and then getting into a car and driving.

In the second case the sudden change to a very low level of granularity seems strange as might be done to focus attention on some aspect of the text. It is

---

[5] We ignore for the time being that these consecutive events may not be explanation and explained event.

examples like 2 in which changes of granularity lead to difficulty in comprehension for the reader. Indeed we do not expect this to happen unless the writer is trying to focus on some part of a scenario (this case is not dealt with here).

Although in the second example the consecutive events are not causal the example serves to illustrate a useful heuristic; one should first search for an explanation at a similar level of granularity when trying to do some non-trivial task such as pronoun resolution, *before* looking at explanations at differing levels of granularity.

5 Conclusions

In this paper we have examined a generalised notion of explanation by providing various primitives which influence the explanation construction process. Of particular interest is one of these primitives; *granularity*, which is based upon ideas of *abstraction* and *detail*. Granularity is an important concept and its study/formalisation can provide us with great benefits due to the ubiquity of explanation in AI.

In the field of language understanding we are able to use this notion of granularity to provide search heuristics for correct explanations. This can be done because we observe that the uniformity of consecutive events in terms of granularity is required if the text is to be coherent.

References

1. Eugene Charniak and Drew McDermott. *Introduction To Artificial Intelligence.* Addison-Wesley, 1985.
2. Jerry R. Hobbs, Mark E. Stickel, Douglas E Appels, and Paul Martin. Intrepretation as abduction. *Artificial Intelligence*, 63:69–142, 1993.
3. David B. Leake. Focusing construction and selection of abductive hypotheses. In *Proceedings of the Eleventh International Joint Conference on Artificial Intelligence*, pages 24–29, Chambéry, France, 1993.
4. Derek Long and Roberto Garigliano. *Reasoning by Analogy and Causality: A model and application.* Artificial Intelligence. Ellis Horwood, 1994.
5. Richard Morgan, Roberto Garigliano, Paul Callaghan, Sanjay Poria, Mark Smith, Agnieszka Urbanowicz, Russell Collingham, Marco Costantino, Chris Cooper, and the LOLITA Group. Description of the lolita system as used in muc-6. In *The Sixth Message Understanding Conference*, pages 71–87, Nov 1995.
6. R. C. Schank and R. P. Abelson. *Scripts, Plans, Goals and Understanding.* Erlbaum, 1977.

Object Model of Intelligent Tutoring Shell

Ljubomir Jerinic[1], Vladan Devedzic[2], Marijana Lomic[1] and Danijela Radovic[3]

[1] Institute of Mathematics, University of Novi Sad,
Trg Dositeja Obradovica 4, 21000 Novi Sad, Yugoslavia
[2] FON - School of Business Administration, University of Belgrade,
Jove Ilica 154, 11000 Belgrade, Yugoslavia
[3] University of Kragujevac, Technical Faculty Cacak
Svetog Save 65, 32000 Cacak, Yugoslavia

Abstract. The difficulty of designing and developing intelligent tutoring systems (ITSs) has caused a recent increase in the interest of the AI researchers in realization of some new approaches in that field. Our starting point and perspective on developing ITSs shell is motivated by issues of pragmatics and usability. Considering commercially available and widely used authoring systems for traditional computer-based teaching, we try to give the next step, the next paradigm shift that is needed to enable some of the advantages of ITSs. The paper describes an object-oriented model of ITS shell in which the enduser (teacher) could make their own ITS lessons, alone. The model enables the developing of more flexible software environments for building of the ITS, significantly increasing their reusability.

1 Introduction

Intelligent Tutoring Systems (ITSs) [1, 2] are used for giving computer-based instruction to students in a particular domain. They have the possibility of presenting the appropriate content to the user (student), monitoring his/her reactions and the learning process, generating problems and tasks for the user in order to check his/her knowledge, etc. Relying on a particular model of each student, the control mechanism of an ITS can suit the tutoring process for each individual user.

Traditional ITSs are concentrated on the fields (domains) they are supposed to present, hence their control mechanisms are often domain-dependent. More recent ITSs pay more attention to generic problems and concepts of the tutoring process, trying to separate architectural, methodological, and control issues from the domain knowledge as much as possible. This was also one of the main ideas behind the ITS shell (environment) called **EduSof** [3, 4], designed to allow fast prototyping of ITSs in different domains.

However, the original design of **EduSof**'s mechanisms for representing domain and control knowledge has proved to be fragile in maintenance and further development. Therefore, a new version of **EduSof** has been designed, considering a new model of ITS we developed using object-oriented approach. It is called **GET-BITS** (**GE**neric **T**ools for **B**uilding **ITS**s), and is essentially a specific extension of a more general, recently developed model of knowledge bases, called **OBOA** (**OB**ject-Oriented Abstraction).

2 Models of Knowledge Representation for ITS Shells

Currently, we can consider grouping of systems or ITS shells [5, 6] in two different classes. First, there are the commercial systems like Authorware, ToolBook, Icon Author and Smarttext. These systems have a number of advantages over programming languages such as help in lesson planning, and built-in widgets which make instructional presentation easier. What they lack is any AI. All adaptive behavior has to be programmed in by an experienced user. The other class of systems are the different research tools, such as IDE (Russell et al, 1988), ID Expert (Merrill, 1989), KAFITS (Murray and Woolf, 1992), COCA (Major and Reichgelt, 1992), GTE (Van Marcke, 1992), RIDES (Munroe et al., 1994), Byte-sized Tutor (Bonar et al., 1986) and EON (Murray 1996). These systems come with knowledge base structure and interpreter much like and expert system shell. Their difficulty is knowing how much flexibility to offer to the teacher and how to make that acquisition process as easy as possible. These systems have not made it out of the lab or seen wide use in multiple domains, and according to T. Murray that happened because of one or more of these factors:

- They are based on a specific instructional approach;
- Domains of application are limited because the system was modeled from an existing task-specific intelligent tutor and generalized to similar domains;
- They are too complex, because they are based primarily on theoretical concerns or AI techniques;
- They provide tools for structuring and using of knowledge, but not for creating appealing student interface or learning environment.

In general, these ITSs, though some are fairly powerful and general, were not designed with significant user input, and did not address the practical issues encountered when educators actually have used them (with the exception of COCA, which underwent some user testing).

We tried to solve these problems with authoring tools and ITS shells, by using object-oriented approach in designing of new version of the **EduSof** shell, instead of a component architecture for ITS shell. Also, the previous version of **EduSof** suffered from some deficiencies, which we tried to overcome in the new version. First, different kinds of knowledge in its modules were designed separately, although all of them conceptually had much in common. Second, decomposing the system functionally to the above modules made it hard to make additional changes and extensions when they were needed. Adding of new knowledge representation techniques when needed required substantial changes in several modules. Finally, whenever there was a need for a change, not much of the relevant software could be used without any changes.

By applying the principles of the **OBOA** model, we can define appropriate class hierarchies for developing of ITS. That is what **GET-BITS** is about. It also starts from the concept of knowledge element, and derives meaningful subclasses that are needed for building a wide range of ITSs. However, classes for knowledge representation are not the only tools needed for an object-oriented ITS to be built. Apart from knowledge of various kind, in each such ITS there must also exist some control objects that functionally connects the system modules, handle messages, control each session with the system, monitor student's reactions, etc. In other words, such objects provide control and handle dynamics of ITS. The **GET-BITS** also specifies classes of these control objects. Due to space limitations, we describe only the most important classes specified in the **GET-BITS** for representing various kinds knowledge in ITS. They are illustrated in Figure 1.

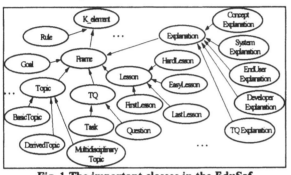

Fig. 1 The important classes in the EduSof

Obviously, many key classes are derived from the Frame class (Lesson and Topic - lessons and topics the user learns; *TQ* - an abstract class used to derive the classes representing questions the student has to answer, tasks and problems the system generates for him/her, etc.; *Explanation* - explanations that the system generates on request from various classes of users (end-users and system developers), as well as topic- and concept-oriented explanations). Additional attributes of these classes make them semantically different and more specific than ordinary frames, although they are actually implemented as more specific frames. The names of the other classes are easily interpreted.

The most important elements of knowledge for designing the intelligent tutoring lesson is the model of **Lesson**, and this is basic class needed for modeling the learning process. Any lesson is consisted of one or more issues, modeled by the class **Topic** in the **OBOA** model. We assume that the student must learn these issues, during mastering that lesson. The basic attributes of the lesson are: the name (**Name**), current topic (**CurrentTopic**, the issue or the problem introduced, defined and/or explained in the present moment), the task that is currently solved, the level of prerequisites for the student (**StudentLevel**), and so on.

Name:	**Lesson**	
Visibility:	**Exported**	; visible outside the encl. class category
Cardinality:	**n**	; there can be more than one such object
Base class:	**Frame**	; in general, a list of base classes
Derived classes:	**FirstLesson, LastLesson, HardLesson, EasyLesson**	
Interface		
Operations:	**SetTopic, GetTopic, UpdateTopic, DeleteTopic, CreateTopicCollection, GetTopicCollection,...**	
Implementation		
Uses:	**Topic, Goal,...**	; in general, a list of classes used by this one
Fields:	**Title, CurrentTopic, CurrentGoal, StudentLevel, TopicCollection_Ptr [],..**	
Persistency:	**Static**	; disk files

The issues that student must learn (class Topic) are realized with separate type of knowledge elements in the **EduSof** system. Any topic could be introduced with text information (**Information**), graphically (the pictures and/or the diagram - **Image**), and/or with the simulation of some event (**Simulation**). Also, the additional or further explanation (**Explanation**) for that theme, or some suggestions (**Hints**) could .be defined. The class **Topic** in **EduSof** is made for specifying and defining the issues or notions needed for lesson creation.

Abstract class TQ served for description of common elements for two comparable and connected classes, one for the definition of tasks or assignments (class **Task**) and the other class for the realization of questions or problems (class **Question**). The instances of that class are given to the student during the learning process.

Another important type of knowledge is explanations generated by the system or required from the user. **EduSof** differs between several kinds of explanations (those presented to end-users - *EndUserExplanation*, those presented to ITS developers - *DeveloperExplanation*, those required from students when checking their knowledge - *StudentExplanation*, those concerned with explaining the system's functioning - *SystemExplanation*, those explaining various concepts or topics - *ConceptExplanation* and *TopicExplanation*, etc.). In generating explanations, **EduSof** can use knowledge from various kinds of knowledge elements (rules, frames, knowledge chunks, etc.). The corresponding *Explanation* class is designed as follows:

Name:	**Explanation**	
Visibility:	**Exported**	; visible outside the encl. class category
Cardinality:	*n*	; there can be more than one such object
Base class:	**Frame**	; in general, a list of base classes
Derived classes:	**EndUserExplanation, DeveloperExplanation,**	
	StudentExplanation, SystemExplanation,	
	TQExplanation, TopicExplanation,...	
Interface		
Operations:	**SetExplanation, GetExplanation, UpdateExplanation,...**	
Implementation		
Uses:	**Rule, Frame, K_chunk, Goal, Topic,...**	
Fields:	**CannedText, TopicCollection_Ptr [], RuleCollection_Ptr [],...**	
Persistency:	**Static/Dynamic**	; disk files for some parts only

3 An Example

The **EduSof** shell is used in developing FORALG, an ITS in the domain of formal theory of algorithms (Turing machines, Markov algorithms etc.). The idea of the FORALG project is to develop software that supports systematic introduction of students into the system domain, in accordance with both the logical structure of the domain and individual background knowledge and learning capabilities of each student. The system is discussed here only from the **EduSof** perspective. The Expert module contains all of the domain-dependent knowledge:

- the concepts, topics, facts and domain heuristics the student has to learn;
- a database of examples used to illustrate the domain concepts, topics, etc.; and
- the pedagogical structure of the domain.

The pedagogical structure of the domain is considered a part of the domain knowledge rather than a part of the tutor module, as well as in [3]. In FORALG, pedagogical structure of the domain is defined as a set of directed graphs showing explicitly precedence relationships of knowledge units within each lesson and among the topics of different lessons.

FORALG always operates in one of the following three modes of operation: teaching, examination, and consulting. It is actually the **EduSof**'s Tutor module that operates in one of these three modes. FORALG's Explanation module tightly co-operates with the Tutor module in the consulting mode, in order to answer the student's questions and provide desired explanations. Student model in **EduSof** and in FORALG is an object of a class derived from the corresponding GET-BITS class.

The following example illustrates how GET-BITS has been used in designing **EduSof**'s classes in order to adapt the shell to support development of FORALG. A *lesson* in FORALG is a meaningful subset of concepts, topics, facts and domain heuristics. These items in a lesson are closely coupled but they can refer to items in other lessons. Some important attributes of each FORALG's lesson are sets of objectives and goals, sets of topics, concepts, facts, theorems, etc. taught in that lesson, a set of the corresponding teaching rules, and a set of associated problems (tests, questions and exercises). The class *Lesson*, as specified in GET-BITS and included in the current version of **EduSof**, supports most of the above attributes. However, when structuring the domain knowledge for implementing it in FORALG, it turned out that many lessons could be better organized if the *Lesson* class had some additional features. Therefore a new class, *T-Lesson*, has been designed and included in the version of **EduSof** which is used for the development of FORALG. The *T-Lesson* class supports using theorems in presenting a lesson and fine-tuning of the presentation by showing/hiding theorem proofs, lemmas and corollaries:

Name:	*T-Lesson*
Base class:	*Lesson*
Derived classes:	*FirstLesson, LastLesson, HardLesson, EasyLesson,...*
Interface Operations:	*SetTheorem, GetTheorem, DeleteTheorem,*
	CreateTheoremCollection,GetTopicCollection, ...,
	SetSkipProofs_Flag, SetSkipLC_Flag
Implementation	
Uses:	*Theorem*
Fields:	*SkipProofs_Flag, SkipLC_Flag*
Persistency:	*Static* ; disk files

This example simultaneously illustrates how computer-based tutoring and learning based on the **GET-BITS** model can be easily adapted to closely reflect the way human-based instruction is done in a given domain and given the student's background knowledge and goals. It is possible to control the setting of *SkipProofs_Flag* and *SkipLC_Flag* from the rules of the Tutor module. Among the other conditions and heuristics, pedagogical rules use the values of the relevant attributes of the student model in order to adapt the lesson presentation to each individual user.

4 Conclusions

The present model of intelligent tutoring systems, presented in the paper, allows for easy and natural conceptualization and design of a wide range of ITS applications, due to its object-oriented approach. It suggests only general guidelines for developing of ITSs, and is open for fine-tuning and adaptation to particular application. ITSs developed by using this model are easy to maintain and extend, and are much more reusable than other similar systems and tools.

The **GET-BITS** model of intelligent tutoring system, presented in the paper, allows easy and natural conceptualization and design of a wide range of ITS applications, due to its object-oriented approach. It suggests only general guidelines for developing of ITS, and is open for fine-tuning and adaptation to particular applications. The model is particularly suitable for use by ITS shell developers. Starting from a library of classes for knowledge representation and control needed in the majority of ITSs, it is a straightforward task to design additional classes needed for a particular shell.

Further development of the **GET-BITS** model is concentrated on development of appropriate classes in order to support a number of different pedagogical strategies. The idea is that the student can have the possibility to select the teaching strategy from a predefined palette, thus adapting the ITS to his/her own learning preferences. Such a possibility would enable experimentation with different teaching strategies and their empirical evaluation. Another objective of further research and development of **GET-BITS** is the support for different didactic tools which are often used in teaching.

References

1. Frasson, C., Gauthier, G., Lesgold, A., (Eds.): Intelligent Tutoring Systems. Proceedings of Third International Conference ITS '96, LNCS Vol. 1086, Springer Verlag (1996).
2. Greer, J., (Ed.): Proceedings of AI-ED 95, World Conference on Artificial Intelligence in Education, AACE Press, Charlottesville, VA, USA (1995).
3. Jerinic, Lj., Devedzic, V.: The EduSof Intelligent Tutoring System. Proceedings of the II International Conference on Graphics Education, EDUGRAPHICS'95, (1995) 185-192.
4. Jerinic, Lj., Devedzic, V.: An object-oriented shell for intelligent tutoring lessons. LNCS Vol. 1108, Springer Verlag (1996) 69-77.
5. Major, N., Murray, T., Bloom, C., (Ed.): AIED '95 Workshop on Authoring Shells for Intelligent Tutoring Systems. Washington, DC, WWW Conference, (1995).
6. Murray, T., (Ed.): ITS '96 Workshop on Architectures and Methods for Designing Cost-Effective and Reusable ITSs. Montreal, WWW Conference, (1996).

Resource Allocation on Agent Meta-Societies

Alcino Cunha and Orlando Belo

Departamento de Informática, Universidade do Minho
Largo do Paço, 4709 Braga Codex, PORTUGAL
{alcino,obelo}@di.uminho.pt

Abstract. This paper is concerned with the formalization of a automated contracting mechanism that enables a society of cooperative resource allocation agents to negotiate rationally in a self-interested meta-society. Such environments induce agents to adopt different social behaviors according to the negotiation partner. This problem may be solved by taking an economic perspective in all the decisions, namely, by using utility based agents, through the use of marginal utility calculations, and defining dynamically the market extent for a task. The risk attitude and reactivity of each agent can be parameterized in order to achieve different negotiation strategies. The framework presented in this paper can be applied in a wide variety of situations, ranging from electronic commerce on virtual economic markets, to load distribution problems.

1 Introduction

One of the major debates in the multi-agent community is concerned with the social attitude of individual agents [3]. Some researchers argue that agents, being artificial, should behave as cooperative entities whose main objective is to maximize the society's overall goal. Others think that agents should be self-interested, with coordination emerging as a sub-product of their self satisfaction maximization attitude. A similar debate may be found in modern social science between the advocates of the atomistic model of human society and the advocates of the organic model [5]. The former views the society as a group of individuals ruled by the law of maximization of one's rational self-interest, and the latter argues that individuals are products of their society and can only realize themselves inside it.

Such debate could be avoided if we consider any society as a single organism recursively partitioned into several sub-organisms whose behavior is similar to the global organism [4]: from the actions and interactions of a group of societies, a new meta-society emerges which can be viewed as a single entity acting in a coherent manner when reacting to events that occur in its environment. At different levels in this hierarchy of societies, different social attitudes can be found. The study of coalition formation [9][13] provides examples of how selfish agents can eventually coordinate their actions and form an atomistic society that interacts in an also atomistic meta-society.

Resource allocation in a single and homogeneous society is one of the major interest areas of research in multi-agent community [6]. Cooperation mechanisms and protocols for both self-interested and cooperative societies have already been proposed. However, a negotiation mechanism for a meta-society requires that the agents assume, simultaneously, a dual behavior: self-interested when dealing with others agents from external societies and cooperative within their society. This problem has already been addressed, but not solved, in [7]. In this paper we formalize a negotiation mechanism for automated contracting under such circumstances. The presented mechanism works among utility-based agents and is supported by marginal utility calculations in order to guarantee the rational behavior of the society when reacting to its environment. A simpler version was already used in a practical application for load distribution in multi-enterprise environments [2], and extended in a generic framework for resource allocation on multi-agent enterprises [1].

2 A Meta-Society Framework

Each society integrated in a self-interested meta-society is a set of cooperative utility-based agents. A definition of an utility function provides the ability to quantify the monetary compensation that the society is willing to tradeoff for the remote execution of a task. This trading of services and resources for money is typical in negotiation protocols of real economic markets. By using a similar economic approach in the design of the meta-societies, it is possible to enlarge the possibilities of their practical application.

Let $C(t)$ be a function that represents the available cash in an instant t, let $P_i(t)$ be a function that assesses the value of a specific parameter i that influences the level of satisfaction of the society, and let Np denote the number of parameters of the utility function ($C(t)$ is not included in this number), the utility function of a society is given by $U(C(t), P_1(t), ..., P_{Np}(t))$. $C(t)$ must always exist because of the need to quantify the monetary compensations. In the presented equations, we assumed that inflation does not exists. The utility function is replicated in all the agents of the society. The cooperativeness exists because they assess the value of its parameters in the all community and not because all the agents have the same utility function. Let $A_I(P_i(t))$ denote the set of agents where agent I evaluates the level of parameter $P_i(t)$, a set S of agents is a organic society iff

$$\forall I \in S \quad A_I(C(t)) = S \quad \wedge \quad \forall 1 \leq i \leq Np \quad A_I(P_i(t)) = S \qquad (1)$$

and is a atomistic society iff

$$\forall I \in S \quad A_I(C(t)) = \{I\} \quad \wedge \quad \forall 1 \leq i \leq Np \quad A_I(P_i(t)) = \{I\}. \qquad (2)$$

Similar conditions can be applied to the definition of meta-societies behavior. These conditions only cater for the extreme social attitudes. It is possible to define, at least in theory, other types of society that do not fit in these definitions (such investigation is reserved to future work). In this paper only this two types will be considered. Our meta-society is characterized by condition 2 and its internal societies by condition 1.

Each agent of an organic society is an allocation agent that contains the knowledge related to a set of tasks to be allocated, and has the ability to control a set of resources and services. A task can be executed locally, in a member of the same society, or in an external society when profitable. In the last situation a monetary compensation must be payed. The cooperation process is achieved through the establishment of direct communication channels among agents. When an agent is cooperating within its own society a protocol similar to the Contract Net Protocol (CNP) [11] is used and the negotiation process is task oriented. Each agent can control the answers to its messages through the specification of eligibility conditions and can request remote information in order to update the global society status. When negotiating with external societies, an extension to CNP, similar to the one proposed in [10], is used. The original CNP can not be used in this context because it did not deal, explicitly, with the self-interestness of the agents. The major innovation of this extension is the use of multiple levels of commitment with penalties associated to decommitment.

It is possible to characterize the behavior of the agents according to two parameters: risk attitude and reactivity. The risk attitude is determined by α $(0 < \alpha < 1)$. A low value of α stands for a risk-seeking agent, that, for instance, will expect higher returns from contract announces. A high value of α characterizes a risk-averse agent. The reactivity is determined by R, the size of the agent memory. A low value for R will make the agent more reactive because its memory is smaller and only keeps record of the more recent experiences. One can also see α as defining the agent exploratory behavior. In fact, a risk-seeking agent sends announces to larger groups of agents and societies and thus searches a larger task allocation solution space.

The presented automated contracting mechanism is based on marginal utility calculations. It provides rational behavior to an organic society by guaranteeing that all its agents make decisions that maximize the expected value for the marginal utility. To avoid local optima, tasks can be clustered and negotiated together and lower decommitment penalties can be used in order to search a larger task allocation space [10].

3 Automated Contracting Through Negotiation

When an agent receives a new task, either created in its society or as result of a contract with another society, it must decide if it will be executed locally or if the task will be announced for remote execution. In the latter case it is also necessary to decide if the task will be announced only to its society or if it will be negotiated abroad. Additionally, it is necessary to define precisely to which agents and societies the announce of the task will be sent. This decision process depends mainly on three factors: the cost of executing locally the task, the communication costs of sending the announces and the results of past interactions. The former can also be stated as the influence of the task execution in the society global level of satisfaction, or, more precisely, the marginal utility of adding the task to the local plan of the agent.

To handle transparently such kind of decisions, a new mechanism is presented: the dynamic definition of the task market extent. Every time a new task allocation process begins, the allocation agent determines the set of agents and societies to which the contract will be announced. If the determined set is empty then the task is executed locally. If it contains only agents from the same society then the cooperation process will be very simple, being the task assigned without negotiation to the agent which offers lower execution costs. If other societies are present in the set, then an iterative negotiation process will begin, in order to determine if the remote execution of the task is profitable.

The market of a set of tasks T is defined as $M(T)$. This set results from the maximization of the expected return of an announcement and is determined as

$$\max_{M(T) \subseteq Others} \mathcal{E}(\Delta U^{M(T)}(T)), \tag{3}$$

where $Others$ is a set which contains the remaining allocation agents of the announcing agent society and all the external societies known to it; $\mathcal{E}(\Delta U^{M(T)}(T))$ is the expected change in utility if the tasks in T are announced to the set of agents and societies $M(T)$.

Let $\mathcal{E}(\Delta U^{O}_{with\_off}(T))$ be the expected change in utility if the set of agents O make a valid offer and $\Delta U^{M(T)}_{comm}(T)$ be the change in utility caused by the communication costs of sending announces to all the agents in $M(T)$, then for any task set T and for any set of entities $M(T)$, $\mathcal{E}(\Delta U^{M(T)}(T))$ is bounded below by

$$\mathcal{E}^{-}(\Delta U^{M(T)}(T)) = \min_{O \subseteq M(T)} (\mathcal{E}(\Delta U^{O}_{with\_off}(T)) + \Delta U^{M(T)}_{comm}(T)),$$

and above by

$$\mathcal{E}^{+}(\Delta U^{M(T)}(T)) = \max_{O \subseteq M(T)} (\mathcal{E}(\Delta U^{O}_{with\_off}(T)) + \Delta U^{M(T)}_{comm}(T)).$$

Between $\mathcal{E}^{-}(\Delta U^{M(T)}(T))$ and $\mathcal{E}^{+}(\Delta U^{M(T)}(T))$ there is a wide range of values that could be used to estimate $\mathcal{E}(\Delta U^{M(T)}(T))$. Each agent must decide which of these values will be used in its calculations. Since a risk-seeking agent expects a higher return from the announce, the expected change in utility, if T is announced to $M(T)$, can be determined by

$$\mathcal{E}(\Delta U^{M(T)}(T)) = \mathcal{E}^{+}(\Delta U^{M(T)}(T)) - \alpha \times (\mathcal{E}^{+}(\Delta U^{M(T)}(T)) - \mathcal{E}^{-}(\Delta U^{M(T)}(T))).$$

$\mathcal{E}(\Delta U^{O}_{with\_off}(T))$ is determined by

$$\mathcal{E}(\Delta U^{O}_{with\_off}(T)) = \begin{cases} \Delta U_{add}(T) & \text{if } O = \emptyset \\ \max_{Winner \in O} (\mathcal{E}(\Delta U^{Winner}_{ex}(T)) + \Delta U^{Winner}_{send}(T) \\ \qquad + \Delta U^{O-\{Winner\}}_{dec}(T)) & \text{otherwise,} \end{cases} \tag{4}$$

where $\mathcal{E}(\Delta U_{ex}^{Winner}(T))$, $\Delta U_{send}^{Winner}(T)$, $\Delta U_{dec}^{O-\{Winner\}}(T)$ and $\Delta U_{add}(T)$ are, respectively, the expected change in utility, if the task is executed by $Winner$, the change in utility caused by the communication costs of sending the task to $Winner$, the change in utility caused by the penalties that must be payed to the remaining agents, whose offers must be rejected, and the marginal utility of adding the tasks in T to the local plan of the announcing agent. When $O = \emptyset$, the task will not be announced but executed locally. This is the reason why the expected change in utility when $O = \emptyset$ is equal to $\Delta U_{add}(T)$. This also guarantees that equation 3 returns an empty set if the announcement is not profitable.

The values of $\Delta U_{comm}^{M(T)}(T)$ and $\Delta U_{send}^{Winner}(T)$ do not require further formalization because they simply accounts for the communication monetary costs, which are very well defined. The determination of $\Delta U_{add}(T)$ is achieved through similar calculations and is partially based on the specification presented in [8]. The values of $\mathcal{E}(\Delta U_{ex}^{Winner}(T))$ and $\Delta U_{dec}^{O-\{Winner\}}(T)$ are estimated based on past values stored in the agent memory and thus are directly influenced by R, the parameter that defines the agent reactivity.

The transparency concerning the social attitude of the agents in $M(T)$ is achieved because, when an agent belongs to the same society, parameters like $\Delta U_{send}(T)$ or $\Delta U_{dec}(T)$ have values very close to zero or even zero. This characteristic guarantees that equation 3 implicitly gives priority to the agents of the same society when building $M(T)$. However, it is important to remember that all the decisions are taken in an economic perspective and try to maximize the expected utility of the consequent action. So, if the execution in an external society is expected to be more profitable, even with all the costs associated to the remote negotiation, that society will be included in $M(T)$.

To complete the specification of the automated contracting strategy it is also necessary to define how agents will assess the global value of the various parameters which contribute to the society utility function. The adopted solution is based on the periodic exchange of the utility function parameters between the allocation agents and was presented in detail in [1].

4 Conclusions

This paper presents the formalization of an automated contracting mechanism that can be used to build a rational cooperative society of utility based agents that interacts coherently in a self-interested meta-society. The use of a negotiation mechanism based on marginal utility calculations and the dynamic definition of the market extent for an announce provide the agents with the ability to manage transparently the dual behavior that they must have in such environments. The presented approach also allows the implementation of different negotiation strategies inside the same society just by changing the parameters that define the risk attitude and reactivity of its agents. Such possibility facilitates the task of the system designer when setting up the system. Since almost every computational problem can be modeled in a resource allocation fashion

[12], the presented framework can be applied in a wide variety of situations, ranging from load balancing problems to distributed factory production plans.

References

1. Alcino Cunha and Orlando Belo. An electronic commerce framework for resource allocation among multi-agent entreprises. In *Proceedings of The 10th International FLAIRS Conference (FLAIRS97)*, pages 362–366, Florida, USA, May 1997.
2. Alcino Cunha and Orlando Belo. A multi-agent based approach for load distribution in multi-enterprise environments. In *IASTED International Conference on Applied Informatics (AI-97)*, Innsbruck, Austria, February 1997.
3. Edmund H. Durfee. What your computer really needs to know, you learned in kindergarten. In *Proceedings of the 10th National Conference on Artificial Intelligence*, pages 858–864, July 1992.
4. Brian R. Gaines. The collective stance in modelling expertise in individuals and organizations. Technical report, Knowledge Science Institute, University of Calgary, Calgary, Alberta, Canada T2N 1N4, August 1995.
5. Robert Hollinger. *Postmodernism and the social sciences: A thematic approach*, volume 4 of *Contemporary social theory*. Sage Publications, Inc., 1994.
6. Victor R. Lesser. Multiagent systems: An emerging subdiscipline of ai. *ACM Computing Surveys*, 27(3):340–342, September 1995.
7. Tuomas Sandholm and Victor R. Lesser. On automated contracting in multi-enterprise manufacturing. In *Improving Manufacturing Performance in a Distributed Enterprise: Advanced Systems and Tools*, pages 33–42, Edimburgh, Scotland, 1995.
8. Tuomas W. Sandholm. An implementation of the contract net protocol based on marginal cost calculations. In *Eleventh National Conference on Artificial Intelligence (AAAI-93)*, pages 256–262, Washington D.C., 1993.
9. Tuomas W. Sandholm and Victor R. Lesser. Coalition formation among bounded rational agents. In *14th International Joint Conference on Artificial Intelligence (IJCAI-95)*, pages 662–669, Montereal, Canada, 1995.
10. Tuomas W. Sandholm and Victor R. Lesser. Issues in automated negotiation and electronic commerce: Extending the contract net framework. In *First International Conference on Multiagent Systems (ICMAS - 95)*, pages 328–335, San Francisco, 1995.
11. Reid G. Smith. The contract net protocol: High-level communication and control in a distributed problem solver. *IEEE Transactions on Computers*, C-29(12):1104–1113, December 1980.
12. Michael P. Wellman. The economic approach to artificial intelligence. *ACM Computing Surveys*, 27(3):340–342, September 1995.
13. Gilad Zlotkin and Jeffrey S. Rosenschein. Coaliation, cryptography, and stability: Mechanisms for coalition formation in task oriented domains. In *The AAAI 1994 Spring Symposium on Software Agents*, pages 87–94, Stanford, California, March 1994.

Diagnostic Information at Your Fingertips !

Oskar Dressler

OCC'M Software GmbH, 82041 Deisenhofen, Gleissentalstr. 22, Germany

Abstract

The paper calls for attention to the following points:

- There is a rapidly opening gap between available computational resources in all kinds of technical devices and useful on-board applications for the end user. This means opportunities for creating *embedded artificial intelligence systems* of all sorts, in particular on-board model-based diagnosis in cars.

- In the case of model-based diagnosis relevant technology has been available for years. This is demonstrated by sketching a minimal on-board diagnosis system using rather *old* components. Based on this latter experience we emphasize the need for real examples even in the early stages of a research program. It helps focusing one's efforts both on a personal as on a community level. Despite the successes so far, diagnosis is an *open* problem. More, not less *basic* research is needed to solve the problems arising in industrial environments.

- There are many other tasks in a technical product's life cycle where a model-based approach is suitable (both on-board and off-board), but where even more basic research is needed.

1 Introduction

New products and services .....

The simultaneous implosion and explosion of computer hardware in terms of size and cost on the one and speed and memory on the other hand opens huge opportunities for *embedded artificial intelligence systems*. The software side of the story, however, is almost entirely blank. Traditionally, computers are used for displaying data and checking thresholds, but advanced interpretation of data and acting are rare. Instead of simply triggering an alarm, a detailed on-board diagnosis, i.e. interpretation of the data, could assess the situation and imply certain actions. The potential impact misdiagnoses and wrong situation assessments have on the safety of people and on the environment stresses the importance of powerful diagnosis systems. The applications could be numerous.

Your car could check its state continuously, detect malfunctions early on, do diagnosis under the exact conditions of the malfunction happening, limit the use of the vehicle (e.g. limp home, but not faster than 30 km/h), advice you and later on in the service bay the mechanic, get in contact with the garage etc. Office equipment could warn not the end user, but the supplier when early signs of malfunction are detected and do diagnosis. The supplier would schedule an earlier maintenance visit carrying the right items needed for repair (hopefully even before an actual breakdown). Depending on cost considerations devices could carry redundant subsystems which would be automatically activated when their counterparts are diagnosed to be broken. And so on ...

.... old processes ...

Imagine yourself in a top management position of a supplier to e.g. the automotive industry. You are producing complete subsystems including embedded software. There are well established ways of how your products are built. The process for developing a new product X starts with an informal description written in natural language. It reflects input from marketing, technical sales, support, service, and maintenance people. This way they try to convey their thoughts on what the product should look like. Engineers then collect a set of potential designs and start evaluating them according to various informal methods. As a next major step a preliminary best design is chosen for which a system failure mode and effects analysis is carried out. Risks are evaluated and the design is improved in order to reduce risks where critical. For safety critical parts additional investigations like fault tree analysis and event tree analysis are undertaken.

Successful termination of the above steps triggers more detailed design activities including numerical calculations followed by a design failure mode effects and analysis and again an evaluation of risks. Finally, documents for the manufacturing process are produced and handed over to manufacturing people.

After the start of series production, fault search instructions and repair manuals for the field are prepared. In this phase quick learning about occurred faults is essential. On the one hand, when the new product is introduced to the market, the repair personnel are left without adequate manuals; on the other hand these manuals are only available through feedback from the field.

These steps have to be repeated at least partially for new versions of the device. This creates the variants dilemma: while the basic design and components are very similar, no complete system design is the same for most systems delivered to different manufacturers. As a consequence the individual steps in the design process are per variant repeated over and over again. The average overlap between variant designs is estimated to be greater than 90%, which means that up to 90% of the associated work is redundant. There are more than 100 variants of X. In addition support of old variants is needed for up to ten years after the end of production. For all of the variants requirements, specifications, CAD diagrams, circuit diagrams, reliability and safety analysis reports, technical documents for repair shops, etc. are produced *manually* more or less independently from other variants. You estimate that more than 50% of the installed engineering capacity are occupied in this way.

If you could improve a little, say 2%, on any of the involved tasks, this would help in fighting your competition. In a desperate move you have already agreed on future productivity increases in your contracts, that are currently not backed up by implemented production plans and machinery. In order to achieve them you need to boost your design and production processes. However, the processes have been in place for years now. They have been continually optimized by local changes because you were forced to strive for total quality management as the competition does. Feel helpless ?

... and a new technology on the horizon ...

There is an emerging technology that could help you with some of your problems:

- it gives you new functionalities that add to the value of your products and outperform the competition
- it provides an explicit, compositional representation of behavior and structure of technical devices as a common basis for various important tasks thus reducing your design and production costs.

BEGIN Dreaming ... Input from marketing, technical sales, support, service, and maintenance people is formalized by using a vocabulary of high level functional language elements in order to describe the intended functions of a new product or product variant. Engineers then embark on finding designs that meet these functional requirements. Where possible they (re)use behavioral models of components from libraries by parameterizing them appropriately. They can add new component models when necessary, subject to peer review. By running a qualitative simulation of the assembled aggregate they make sure the intended functions are achieved. A formal verification can be added when required.

The model of the new variant allows generating various documents, e.g. documents for various failure mode and effects analyses in the product's life cycle, fault tree analysis, event tree analysis etc. Other business functions can interface with the design process by examining models of design variants. They can provide valuable input, e.g. perform a cost analysis.

Furthermore, models are re-used for diagnosis and repair. Preparation of repair manuals no longer critically depends on feedback from the field but starts right after finishing the design and *before* series production. At the end of the production line rigorous testing and diagnosis based on models greatly improves product quality as experienced by the end user.

END Dreaming ... here the scenario ends at the latest because no manager on this earth - not even the most desperate one - will take the risk and re-engineer the whole business around an unproved technology. In order to make any progress in building a ·market one must demonstrate success on a per task basis.

This is very hard indeed. In order to qualify for the application of the more revolutionary aspects of the new technology, like re-use of models across different tasks, one has to optimize one step within a large business process that has been subject to optimization for years. So one has to look for suitable subtasks where the available state of the art applies, where the integration with the existing processes is feasible given a limited budget and where it will meet people's interests, or at least not disrupt them doing *their* work, where the benefit of the whole exercise can be clearly demonstrated to management, meaning: can be spelled in $$$ *now*, and where there is a migration path to other tasks once there is success at some point in the future. A plus would be if one could offer new services to the end user, meaning new business to management. Difficult.

Nevertheless, we believe that diagnosis is one such task. It has visible economic effects and in the on-board case even offers new services. On the downside, there has been an unfortunate first generation of diagnosis expert systems coming from AI. It has had some successes but overall it has failed to deliver an economically viable technology.

The next section will sketch the common ground for model-based systems: an explicit, compositional representation of physical behavior and structure. The then following sections will first give an idea of what could be a minimal on-board diagnosis system, and then look at some other related tasks in the product life cycle.

2 Representing Structure and Behavior

Model-based systems offer their services on the basis of an explicit representation of structure *and* behavior. In technical the system under investigation is often viewed as a set of components that map to things such as valves, pipes, electronic control units, wires, switches, etc. but also to steps within a process. The modeled structure reflects the possible interaction paths between these components. Hierarchical abstraction allows one to handle large structures in the way system designers are used to do it. However, use of an explicit representation of structure alone does not characterize model-based systems as we discuss them here. An explicit representation of behavior must also be present. It captures *how things work*. Such a behavior description should not be confused with a simple listing of component parameters, e.g. the descriptions one finds in the data sheet of an integrated circuit. A behavior model of e.g. an integrated circuit describes the relations between the signals at its different pins; it captures the behavior of the physical object *as deemed relevant by the modeler*.

There is no official way of modeling. System engineers from technical domains will normally equate models with differential equations over the real numbers. This is not excluded, but normally not intended in our contexts. The modeler chooses what the objects (system constituents) and their behaviors are. Depending on the task and of course the modeler the outcome of the efforts can be quite different although we all adhere to the illusion that we are interacting with the same physical objects.

From an economic viewpoint a behavioral model of a complete system as one huge chunk, say a big set of unstructured equations, is almost useless: it could be applied to just one variant of a technical device. Obviously, smaller pieces - centered on the components - that can be re-used for different variants of a device and even for different devices, are a far more attractive solution. This requires that the

- overall behavior can be reproduced by interacting component models, and that
- components are modeled in a 'context free', local manner.

The models in a model library should be as re-usable as their counterparts in the physical world for an intended range of applications. This implies that the author of a *good* model library shares the views of the modeler population using the library. If these requirements are met a model of a device can be assembled from structural information and a model library automatically.

In diagnosis applications compositional, local, and context-free models are especially important for two additional reasons:

- Analysis of discrepancies between the model and the real world can trace back to constituent behaviors and assumptions about their presence.
- Making implicit assumptions about a functioning context when modelling a component behavior could be fatal, i.e. lead to wrong diagnoses; in diagnosis we are dealing with *malfunctions* which by definition can invalidate the assumptions, thus rendering the models invalid.

Nevertheless, knowledge about the intended function of a consituent within a design is valuable also in diagnosis. But functional models capturing purpose and intended interactions between constituents are inherently non-local. What they should look like and how we could integrate them in automated diagnosis is an open research issue.

A controlled violation of the above requirements is possible. Introducing and keeping track of simplifying and modeling assumptions allows one to ground conclusions on explicitly made assumptions. This makes feasible the exploration of e.g. diagnostic hypotheses such as 'single faults only' without losing control when the assumptions were wrong ([Struss 92], [Böttcher, Dressler 94]). This leads to multiple modeling, i.e. the separate representation of different aspects of component behaviors, often at multiple hierarchical levels of abstraction.

On a technical level the common denominator across different model-based systems with respect to formalisms for representing behavior is propositional logic and constraints. Behavior is described by mathematical relations and functions between variables and parameters of constituents. Logic is used to tie these descriptions to behavioral mode assumptions about the component in consideration or to its internal state. A typical example is

$$ok(valve) \rightarrow (valve.status = closed \rightarrow valve.[i_1] = valve.[i_2] = 0)$$

where [.] denotes qualitative values for the flow in and out of a valve.

To make use of such behavioral descriptions constraint systems (see e.g. [Forbus, de Kleer 93]) determine solutions by local propagation: the results of applying a constraint locally are handed over to neighbor constraints. Since each component is represented by a set of constraints, it is easy to trace what effects where caused by which components. Constraint systems can handle static relations, which describe equilibrium states in devices. By adding temporal indices state changes can be treated as well. Because the relations and their underlying domains are not fundamentally restricted in any way they can be used especially for qualitative predictions. Symbolic values, intervals, fuzzy values, and orders of magnitude are all possible choices.

3 A minimal model-based on-board diagnosis system

On-board, instead of being manually activated when a malfunction occurs, an automatic diagnosis system as a first task has to decide whether there actually is a problem. Does the behavior as seen via the sensors deviate from the specified normal operation? Only then the diagnosis process will start. Thus, *a preceding monitoring phase is required.*

Once the faulty components have been identified, an integrated monitoring and diagnosis system may be allowed to switch back to monitoring mode interpreting the measurements coming from the sensors under the hypotheses that the identified components are broken. *Monitoring and diagnosis may be interleaved.*

We sketch a minimal on-board diagnosis system that consists of two rather old components, GDE ([de Kleer, Williams 87])and MCTCP ([Dressler, Freitag 89]). There are several remarks to make about this apparently outdated combination:

- It indeed constitutes a minimal on-board diagnosis system, and it is simple to describe and implement.
- More elaborated versions of these techniques are available. For example, where GDE might be capable of diagnosing a circuit with say 50 components, focused Sherlock ([de Kleer 91]), DDE ([Dressler,Struss 94]), etc are capable of diagnosing circuits of up to several thousand components, more precisely - and this is an important difference - digital circuits: simple And-, Or- , Nand- Gate, inverters and buffers.
- However, already GDE suffices to handle systems that are of interest in the real

world e.g. to the automotive industry: anti-lock braking systems, electronic diesel control, central locking, etc. These systems do not consist of thousands of digital gates, but are composed of subsystems with typically less than 50 components: wires, valves, electronic control units, simple motors, and the likes.

- The difference lies in the models. Models of these components constitute *qualitative* views of electric and hydraulic circuits, i.e. deal with important behavioral distinctions in the physics of the devices instead of the rather idealized and trivial digital gates.

- As will be shown in the following two subsections the major tasks in the diagnosis and monitoring cycle can all be delegated to an assumption-based truth maintenance system (ATMS, [de Kleer 86]). This makes the *ATMS a micro-kernel* for this type of system. This even holds for the more elaborated versions: they are using focused and non-monotonic ATMS's.

In conclusion of these remarks: we could have done this ten years earlier, but certainly not in the automotive domain because of the involved costs of computer hardware at the time. Nevertheless, research went astray, solving diagnosis problems of artifical nature, refusing to develop rock-solid and suitable (i.e. qualitative) models of basic physics phenomena that are used in everyday devices.

3.1 The General Diagnosis Engine GDE

In 1987, de Kleer and Williams described a diagnosis framework that subsequently influenced almost all work in the field of model-based diagnosis. With GDE, they made several important contributions:

- Candidates for diagnosis are computed from minimal sets of component correctness assumptions that together with the system description and observations are not satisfiable (*minimal conflicts*).

- In contrast to previous systems, diagnoses are no longer limited to single faults.

- A de-coupled ATMS identifies conflicting assumption sets, and provides the basis for a

- probabilistic method for determining optimal probing points.

Four distinguished major phases are organized in a cycle: prediction, conflict detection, candidate generation and ranking, and discrimination between diagnoses by additional measurements.

Prediction

During prediction the system description (SD) and observations (OBS) are used to derive conclusions about variable values. The process is centered around the device components, COMPS. Whenever sufficient information about variables at a component is available, conclusions about other variables of the same component are drawn. Each of the conclusions is justified by variable values and assumptions about the correct behavior. For example, from given values for a valve, new values are computed and justified:

value(valve.Status, open) $\wedge$ value(valve.[i₁], +) $\wedge$ ok(valve) $\rightarrow$ value(valve.[i₂], -)

The GDE predictor makes use of the ATMS as a repository for inferences. It caches them as propositional horn clauses called *justifications*.

$$\alpha_1 \wedge \ldots \ldots \wedge \alpha_n \rightarrow \beta$$

A distinguished subset ASSM of the occurring propositional atoms PROP is called assumptions: ASSM ⊆ PROP. Component modes like e.g. ok(valve) are treated as assumptions. The set of atoms derivable from a set of assumptions (environment) E is called (logical) context of E and denoted by cxt(E). All environments which allow deriving the constant ⊥ are considered inconsistent.

Reasoning in multiple contexts can be characterized as considering all consistent contexts cxt(E) of all subsets E ⊆ ASSM of the given assumptions. All propositions are labeled with the complete set of minimal (w.r.t. set inclusion) consistent environments from which they are derivable. I.e. for a proposition p its (logical) label is defined as

$$LL(p) = \{E \subseteq ASSM \mid (E \text{ consistent} \wedge p \in cxt(E) \wedge \forall E' \subset E. \ p \notin cxt(E))\}$$

Justifications are used to record the inferences as performed by a problem solver, in GDE's case the predictive engine, a constraint system. The label of a proposition is computed by propagating and combining environments in the network of justifications using basic set operations. By caching inferences as justifications, an inference is done once for the first context. It automatically holds in each context that is characterized by a superset of its environments. Whenever the antecedents hold in another context this causes just an update of the label of the consequent proposition. Thus, expensive recomputation is avoided. As we will see in the monitoring section this can also be exploited with respect to different temporal contexts. However, labels the ATMS must compute can grow big and hamper larger applications. Focusing on interesting contexts ([Dressler, Farquhar 90]) avoids this problem while maintaining the essential properties of assumption-based truth maintenance.

Conflict Detection

Whenever a variable v takes on contradictory values, say a and b, in the same logical context, the supporting assumption set must be identified as a nogood, i.e. an inconsistent environment. This is achieved by creating justifications of the form

$$\text{value } (v, a) \wedge \text{value } (v, b) \rightarrow \perp$$

The ATMS computes and maintains a database of minimal nogoods. Therefore, the identification of minimal conflicts is trivial for the diagnosis engine; they are simply determined by the minimal nogoods.

Candidate Generation and Candidate Ranking

In a sense minimal conflicts contain the essence of the detected discrepancies between model and artifact behavior. The diagnostic information in a single conflict is that at least one of the involved components is misbehaving. A candidate for diagnosis must thus hypothesize a fault for at least one of them. Given minimal conflicts $CONFL_1, \ldots, CONFL_n$ a minimal diagnosis FAULTY turns out to be a minimal hitting set of the respective sets of suspect components

$$COMPS_i := \{Cj \in COMPS \mid \neg \ ok(Cj) \in CONFL_i\}$$

i.e. a) $\forall \ i. \ FAULTY \cap COMPS_i \neq \varnothing$ (hitting set)

and b) $\forall \ i. \ FAULTY' \subset FAULTY \Rightarrow$

$\exists \ COMPS_i. \ FAULTY' \cap COMPS_i = \varnothing$ (minimality).

In the worst case both the set of minimal conflicts and the set of minimal diagnoses grow exponentially in the number of device components. The following construction illustrates this point. The elements of a conflict disjunctively support the respective conflict node and the conflict nodes conjunctively support the resulting candidate node Γ_1 (Fig. 1).

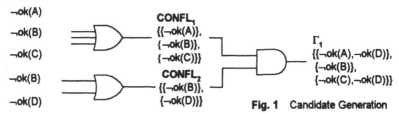

Fig. 1 Candidate Generation

Now the resulting And-Or-tree is labeled. Each conflict element is labeled with the set containing itself, e.g. ¬ok(A) is labeled with {{¬ok(A)}}. These labels ar omitted in the figures. Conflict nodes are labeled with the set of its antecedents' labels, e.g.

$$\text{label(CONFl}_1) = \{\{ \neg ok(A)\}, \{ \neg ok(B)\}, \{ \neg ok(C)\}\}.$$

Candidate nodes are labeled with the minimal set covers of their antecedent nodes, e.g. label(Γ_1) = {{ ¬ok(A), ¬ok(D)}, { ¬ok(B)}, { ¬ok(C), ¬ok(D)}}.

The And-Or construction can be implemented my means of the ATMS. Conflict nodes are (disjunctively) justified by multiple justifications of the form

$$\neg\, ok(.) \rightarrow conflict\ node$$

where ¬ok(.) is an element of a conflict. Candidate nodes are (conjunctively) justified by a single justification:

$$candidate\text{-}node \wedge new\text{-}conflict\text{-}node \rightarrow new\text{-}candidate\text{-}node$$

Additional conflicts are handled incrementally. First, a conflict node is formed as above. In a second step the new conflict node and the last candidate node, Γ_1 in fig. 2, conjunctively support a new candidate node Γ_2. Labeling proceeds as before. Fig. 2 shows the labeling with a third conflict {¬ok(C), ¬ok(D)}.

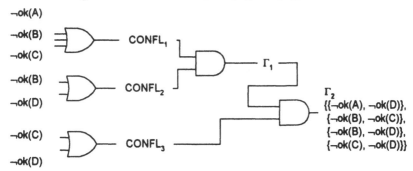

Fig. 2 Candidate Tree Labeling

It is easily verified that the label of the last candidate node is exactly the set of minimal candidates, four double faults in fig.2. Intuitively, each candidate node selects one element from each antecedent conflict. This is both an easy and efficient way to implement *incremental candidate generation*.

In practice, the potential exponential blow up of the minimal candidate sets hurts less than the trained AI theoretician would expect. The main reason seems to be that the number of components involved in conflicts is usually quite small. One possible explanation is that the devices to be diagnosed were designed by humans. Therefore the complexity of the device is limited by our capability to evaluate its design.

Probe selection

Measurement proposal is of lesser interest in the on-board case. There tend to be very few sensor values available, but at zero cost. So one will use what one can get right from the beginning. Any remaining ambiguity can only be resolved over time by processing more data samples which is discussed in the next section.

3.2 Monitoring

When GDE does not detect any discrepancy, it responds with a single diagnosis: all components are ok. It could thus be a monitoring engine, too. Just use it repeatedly or let it process more data samples from different times. A straightforward approach is to use ATMS assumptions not only for component mode assumptions but also as time index. This works, however, at a prohibitive computational cost. Even focused ATMS's bog down after a few samples taken at different times. The reason is that inferences are re-done over and over again, just at different times.

With respect to time the behavioral models in SD, observations OBS, and assumptions fall into two different classes. The behavioral models are time invariant in the sense that they describe behavior independent of the specific time at which it takes place. Observations and assumptions, however, may change their truth value over time. Therefore, instead of re-doing inferences based on the models, we can factor out the relevant computations (and do them only once!). This can be done by *caching* inferences made for a specific time and *generalizing* them to other times. We start from statements like proposition α holding at time t_i, $\alpha@t_i$, , which we call *temporally indexed statements*. The temporal extent of α, TE (α), denotes the set $\{t_i \mid \alpha$ holds at $t_i\}$. Omitting delays for consequences, the derivation of α can be generalized from the single time index t_i to sets of time indices. A set GS of time variant formulae is called *ground support* for ϕ iff there exists a subset SD' of the models SD such that SD' $\cup$ GS $\models \phi$. If GS is a ground support for ϕ then $\bigcap_{\alpha \in GS} TE(\alpha) \subseteq TE(\phi)$. This means we can generalize a derivation of ϕ at a specific time t_i to the intersection of temporal extents of ϕ's support. Whenever all the propositions in GS hold at some time $t_j \neq t_i$ we know without re-deriving ϕ that it holds at t_j, too.

For those propositions α that may occur in the ground support of derived formulae we introduce symbols TE_α to represent TE(α). These propositions α are exactly the propositions for which temporally indexed statements are available, i.e. observations and assumptions. Symbols like TE_α are called *temporal base symbols*. Using these symbols each atom ϕ is labeled with a *unique* symbolic representation of its temporal extent (*temporal label*) like e.g.

$$TL(\phi) = \{\{TE_{a11}, ..., TE_{a1n}\}, ..., \{TE_{am1}, ... , TE_{amk}\}\}.$$

The similarity to "logical" labels in the ATMS is not accidental. The ATMS can do both temporal and logical labels, and even mix them. Therefore we can handle data samples indexed by time without re-doing inferences unnecessarily. An inference made at a specific time in the past "generalizes" to the same inference made at *all* possible times. There is no need to ever make an inference twice. Consequently, prediction can be much faster when relevant previous inferences have been made. Due to the use of qualitative models this happens all of the time. Intuitively, only when a monitored variable changes its qualitative value, i.e. an important behavioral change occurs, *new* predictions have to be made. And exactly this happens, nothing more. Furthermore, the And-Or construction we have used to delegate the candidate generation task to the ATMS carries over to the time enhanced GDE, except there is no need to enter identical conflicts at different times. Because the assumptions have temporal labels, the diagnoses read off from the candidate nodes have them, too, --- - --- automatically, informing us about the temporal extends of diagnoses.

This completes the sketch of this minimal on-board diagnosis system, but by no means the research necessary to really built on-board diagnosis systems. For instance, the range of applicability of this kind of diagnosis, call it state-based, is not known and subject to on-going research ([Dressler 96],[Struss 97], for an overview and introduction to the consistency-based approach to diagnosis see [Dressler,Struss 96]).

4 Other Tasks

Diagnosis has been a prominent theme in artificial intelligence and various engineering communities for years. As such it appears as an abstraction of just one random sample from the activities carried out in a product's life cycle. There are many more that deserve more attention. Below are comments on a few of them. Solutions to individual subtasks will necessarily have to take into account other tasks. The goal of diagnosis, for example, changes from identifying the broken components to localizing (and probably identifying) the fault(s) such that the device's purpose can be re-established when we take into account that the device will be repaired. This focuses the diagnosis process and avoids discrimination among diagnoses that would all lead to the same repair ([Friedrich et al 91]).

Repair

Our minimal embedded diagnosis system is capable of listening to the device, automatically start diagnosis, and switch back to monitoring mode when the diagnosis is found. But today's embedded system software, e.g. in a motor controller, is more sophisticated. It includes certain *repair actions* as hard coded heuristics. A missing sensor value, for instance, can be substituted by estimated values calculated from other sensors' values: a *virtual sensor*. Closing the loop by acting in real time within one motor cycle on the basis of the computed diagnoses is certainly beyond the capabilities of even the fastest available model-based diagnosis engine. Triggering prepared actions at later times like various forms of limp home modes or similar restrictions, however, is possible.

Failure Modes and Effects Analysis (FMEA)

FMEA as a side effect prepares the ground for such software. *Automated* FMEA ([Hunt et al 93]) makes use of the fact, that known modes of component failures can be described in behavioral models as well. As long as these models respect the principles outlined before, they can be combined with the ok- and fault- models of other components, and thus predict the behavior of faulted devices.

A straight forward approach to include repair actions could simulate the effects of faults and use a model-based diagnosis engine to diagnose them *off-line*. During the diagnosis sessions the probing points suggested by the diagnosis engine would be recorded. Together with the given initial values at the start of a session they determine the diagnosis. The relation between these values and the diagnosis would then be enhanced by repair actions and compiled into a table or other suitable data structure, that can be checked on-board in real time.

The advantage in comparison to existing processes lies in the automation of a large part of the activities and the fact that a completeness guarantee with respect to a catalogue of known component failure modes can be given.

Verification and Testing

Verifying a device is an extremely difficult and cost intensive task. In principle a device could be working correctly under the myriad of all possible input combinations but fail in one. Think of Intel's famous FDIV Bug in the Pentium processor. In a safety critical subsystem of a car or airplane one would want absolute safety. A close look is scary, especially where software is involved. The systems' complexity is increasing at an explosive rate, in particular for the even more complex continuous - in contrast to - discrete-valued systems. Use of formal methods that would guarantee at least a certain degree of absence of faults in the design are *practically* not existing. An enormous amount of engineering hours is spent on 'validating' designs by use of informal methods such as event tree analysis etc.

Even if a design is flawless, the product could be faulted due to broken components or failing interactions between them. Automatically preparing a minimal set of tests off-line that guarantees absence of e.g. single faults is one theme discussed under the subject title of 'Testing'. Selecting an appropriate test within a diagnosis session in order to discriminate between possible diagnoses is a different but related task. The currently available methods for the latter are much too weak. Including cost considerations, necessary setup actions, safety aspects, availability of test equipment, etc. are all practical requirements that are met by writing hard coded heuristics, if at all.

For digital hardware (and even small scale software programs) verification and testing techniques are well advanced ([Burch et al 90], [Roth 80]). Extending them to other technical domains requires discrete models with finite variable domains. Qualitative models obeying the principles discussed in section 2 are good candidates for achieving this goal ([Struss 94], [Kuipers, Shults 94]).

Characterization of Results

Model-based diagnosis has been not only quite successful in developing systems, but also provided a rigorous theoretical foundation leading to formal characterizations of the expected results of the diagnosis process and its subtasks. This puts us in a unique position. Our algorithms can be *formally* verified. Their specifications are already there. Not only is this an advantage in the context of safety critical systems. It also allows checking of implementations on a test case basis given us a handle on improving software quality following the common, more pragmatic approach.

5 Speculation about a possible future

The list of discussed tasks is by no means complete. In fact, the large variety of tasks within the product life cycle where models can be applied suggests that model-based reasoning may indeed one day play a major role in corporations where design and production of technical devices takes place. Today we see serious attempts aiming at various isolated tasks. The full effect of model-based systems, however, will only be visible when most of the tasks are handled in a model-based way, when models can be re-used on *different* variants, *different* products, *different* tasks, and most importantly by *different* people at *different* times and *different* locations.

This requires re-engineering the business and the relations with its partners and customers. The interaction patterns between the involved people change.

As a result there will be fewer people in the processes which is one reason why this - given the current economic rules - might happen: it will allow corporations to further cut down on their production costs when almost all of the real production has finally been transfered to whatever low-wage country offers so called *favorable* conditions (to the corporations, *not* to the people here or there).

References

[Böttcher, Dressler 94] Böttcher, Dressler. A Framework for Controlling Diagnosis Systems with Multiple Actions Annals of Mathematics and Artificial Intelligence, 11(1-4), 1994. Special Issue on Model-based Diagnosis.

[Burch et al. 90] Burch, Clarke, McMillan. Symbolic model checking: 10^{20} states and beyond. 5th Annual IEEE Symposium on Logic in Computer Science, IEEE, New York, pp. 428 - 439

[de Kleer 86] de Kleer, J., An Assumption-based Truth Maintenance System. Artificial Intelligence, 1986

[de Kleer 91] de Kleer. Focusing on Probable Diagnoses. Proc. AAAI'91. MIT Press, 1991

[de Kleer, Williams 87] de Kleer, Williams. Diagnosing Multiple Faults. Artificial Intelligence, 1987

[Dressler, Freitag 89] Dressler, Freitag. Propagation of Temporally Indexed Values in Multiple Contexts. In GWAI'89, Springer, 1989

[Dressler, Farquhar 90] Dressler, Farquhar. Putting the problem solver back in the driver's seat: contextual control of the ATMS. Springer Lecture Notes on AI, 1990

[Dressler, Struss 94] Dressler,Struss.Model-based diagnosis with the default-based diagnosis engine: effective control strategies that work in practice . Proc. ECAI'94, Wiley, 1994

[Dressler, Struss 96] O. Dressler, P. Struss. The Consistency-based Approach to Automated Diagnosis of Devices. In G.Brewka (Ed.), Principles of Knowledge Representation, pages 267 - 311, CSLI Publications, Stanford 1996

[Dressler 96] Dressler.On-line Diagnosis and Monitoring of Dynamic Systems based on Qualitative Models and Dependency-based Diagnosis Engines Proc ECAI'96, Wiley, 1996.

[Forbus, de Kleer 93] Forbus, de Kleer. Building Problem Solvers. MIT Press, 1993

[Friedrich et al 91] Friedrich, Gottlob, Nejdl. Formalizing the repair process. Proc. EPIA '91, Springer Lecture Notes on AI, 1991

[Hunt et al 93] Hunt, Price, Lee. Automating the FMEA Process. Intelligent Systems Engineering, 2:119 -132, 1993

[Kuipers, Shults 94] Kuipers, Shults. Reasoning in Logic about Continuous Systems, Proc. KR '94, Morgan Kaufmann Publishers

[Roth 80] Roth, P. Computer Logic, Testing, and Verification. Pitman Publishing, 1980

[Struss 92] Struss. What's in SD ? in Hamscher, Console, de Kleer (Eds.) Readings in Model-based diagnosis, Morgan Kaufmann, 1992

[Struss 94] Struss, P. Testing Physical Systems, Proc. AAAI 94, MIT Press, 1994

[Struss 97] Struss, P. Fundamentals of Model-based Diagnosis of Dynamic Systems. Proc. IJCAI'97, Morgan Kaufmann, 1997

Reasoning about Actions with Abductive Logic Programming

Luís Moniz Pereira[1] and Renwei Li[1]
{lmp,renwei}@di.fct.unl.pt

Centro de Inteligência Artificial
Universidade Nova de Lisboa
2825 Monte de Caparica
Portugal

Abstract. In order to construct a computer-based system which can reason and act intelligently in the real world, we have to develop a computational but provably correct methodology and its related software system which can reason about actions and changes in dynamic domain. For this purpose we propose to use abductive logic programming paradigm as the computational mechanism. Technically, we make use of a simple, but extensible if needed, action description language to describe the domain in question. Then we use a sound and complete translation algorithm to transform domain descriptions into abductive logic programs. And thus reasoning about actions is reduced to abductive queries against abductive logic programs. In this paper we will only address three important issues: knowledge assimilation, refinement of action theories, and concurrent actions. For the task of knowledge assimilation we will introduce a formal and computational methodology, called the possible causes approach, in contrast to Ginsberg's possible worlds approach and Winslett's possible models approach. For the refinement of a possibly incomplete action theory, we use tests on the domain, and then abductively refine the original domain description to a new one which is closer to the domain in reality. For concurrent actions, we introduce a new semantics by using three-valued fluents to resolve conflicts among atomic actions.

1 Introduction

The development of computer-based systems, or so-called intelligent agents, which are able to observe, reason and act intelligently is one of the most challenging efforts ever made by Artificial Intelligence workers. It is hence no surprise that knowledge representation and reasoning techniques have become a focol topic in this field. Due to their declarative semantics and efficient execution, logic programs have become a more and more important tool for knowledge representation and reasoning. In this paper we will show the usefulness of abductive logic programming in reasoning about actions.

Basically, an intelligent agent consists of at least three components: sensor for observing, effector for acting, and a processor for reasoning. The task of an intelligent agent can roughly be represented by an algorithmic loop:

- Select a goal G among all its intentions;
- Generate a (partial) plan P for the selected goal G;
- Perform an action in the plan P;
- Revise its knowledge base appropriately.

A central issue in the above loop is how to automate reasoning about actions and changes. In this paper we will address three related problems: knowledge assimilation, refinement of action theories, and concurrent actions. The result of this paper is currently used in constructing situated agents [21]. Technically, we start with a simple, but extensible if needed, action description language to describe the domain in question. Then we use a sound and complete translation algorithm to transform domain descriptions into abductive logic programs. And thus reasoning about actions is reduced to abductive queries against abductive logic programs. For the task of knowledge assimilation we will introduce a formal and computational methodology, called the possible causes approach (PCA), in contrast to Ginsberg's possible worlds approach (PWA) and Winslett's possible models approach (PMA). For the refinement of action theories, we start with a possibly incomplete action theory, use tests on the domain, and then abductively refine the original domain description to a new one which is closer to the domain in reality. For concurrent actions, we introduce a new semantics by using three-valued fluents to resolve conflicts among atomic actions.

2 Domain Descriptions

When reasoning about actions and changes, we often assume that an action theory has been given and described in a formal language or in a framework, e.g. situation calculus [24], event calculus [19], action description languages $\mathcal{A}$ [14] and ADL [25], the fluent-features framework (FFF) [29], and their variants or extensions.

In this section we introduce an action description language $\mathcal{A}^+$, an extension to $\mathcal{A}$ of [14]. And thus $\mathcal{A}^+$ is one of $\mathcal{A}$ family languages. The reason we choose $\mathcal{A}$ is simply that $\mathcal{A}$ has been shown to be a simple, extensible and expressive action description language, and to be equivalent to other three major formalisms [18] proposed by Pednault [25], Reiter [28] and Baker [6], respectively.

$\mathcal{A}^+$ will be directly used to represent a possibly incomplete action theory to be refined. A complete action theory can be represented in $\mathcal{A}$. And hence $\mathcal{A}$ will be used for knowledge assimilation. We will also extend $\mathcal{A}$ with concurrent actions later.

2.1 Syntax

We begin with three disjoint non-empty sets of symbols, called *proposition names*, *fluent names*, and *action names*, respectively. For convenience we will also use parameterized names. *Actions* and *propositions* are defined to be action names and proposition names, respectively. A *fluent expression*, or simply *fluent*, is defined to be a fluent name possibly preceded by $\neg$. A fluent expression is also called a *positive fluent* if it only consists of a fluent name; otherwise it is called a *negative fluent*.

In $\mathcal{A}^+$, a domain description is defined to be a set of effect assertions and constraints. An effect assertion is defined to be a statement of the form

$$A \text{ causes } F \text{ if } P_1, \ldots, P_m, Q_1, \ldots, Q_n$$

where A is an action, each of F, P_1, ..., P_m $(m \geq 0)$ is a fluent expression, and each of $Q_1, \ldots, Q_m$ $(n \geq 0)$ is a proposition name. If $m = n = 0$, then we will simply write it as A **causes** F. A constraint is defined as follows:

- A proposition name is an atomic constraint.
- A statement of the form

$$F \text{ after } A_1, \ldots, A_n$$

where F is a fluent and A_i is an action, is an atomic constraint, also called *value assertion*. When $n = 0$, the value assertion above is abbreviated to **initially** F.
- If C_1 and C_2 are constraints, then $\neg C_1$, $C_1 \wedge C_2$, $C_1 \vee C_2$ are constraints, called complex constraints. Other propositional connectives can be defined in terms of them as derived connectives.

It can be seen that $\mathcal{A}^+$ is an extension of $\mathcal{A}$ by allowing propositions and more types of constraints.

2.2 Remarks

It seems that we would increase the expressive power if we defined the effect assertions in the following way: (1) A basic effect assertion is a statement of the form A **causes** F **if** $C_1, \ldots, C_n$; (2) An effect assertion is a statement of the form $(E_{11} \wedge \ldots \wedge E_{1m_1}) \vee \ldots \vee (E_{n1} \wedge \ldots \wedge E_{nm_n})$, where each E_{ij} is a basic effect assertion. In fact, combining with proposition names, we can reduce the above complex effect assertion to simpler ones of $\mathcal{A}^+$. We can systematically do so by introducing a few new proposition names and then transform effect assertions. For example, consider:

$$(A_1 \text{ causes } F_1 \text{ if } C_{11}, \ldots, C_{1n_1})$$
$$\vee \ldots$$
$$\vee (A_m \text{ causes } F_m \text{ if } C_{m1}, \ldots, C_{mn})$$

Let h_i, $1 \leq i \leq m$ be m new proposition symbols. Then, the above complex effect assertions can be transformed into m basic effect assertions and a new constraint as follows:

$$A_1 \text{ causes } F_1 \text{ if } C_{11}, \ldots, C_{1n_1}, h_1$$
$$\ldots$$
$$A_m \text{ causes } F_m \text{ if } C_{m1}, \ldots, C_{mn}, h_m$$
$$h_1 \vee \ldots \vee h_m$$

On the other hand, it also seems that we would increase the expressive power if we allowed general well-formed propositional formulas in the preconditions of effect assertions. For example, let A be an action, P_1 a fluent, and Q_1, Q_2, Q_3 be proposition names. Consider

$$A \text{ causes } F \text{ if } P_1, (Q_1 \wedge Q_2) \vee \neg Q_3$$

This kind of seemingly more expressive effect assertions can also be reduced to effect assertions in $\mathcal{A}^+$. Let Q_4 be a new proposition name. The following effect assertion and a constraint is equivalent to the above assertion:

$$A \text{ causes } F \text{ if } P_1, Q_4$$
$$Q_4 \leftrightarrow (Q_1 \wedge Q_2) \vee \neg Q_3$$

2.3 Semantics

The semantics of a domain description is defined by using proposition assignment, states, and transitions.

A proposition assignment α is a set of proposition names. Given a proposition name P and an assignment α, we say that P is true if $P \in \alpha$, and $\neg P$ is true if $P \notin \alpha$. A *state* is a set of fluent names. Given a fluent name F and a state σ, we say that F holds in σ if $F \in \sigma$; $\neg F$ holds in σ if $F \notin \sigma$. A *transition function* Φ is a mapping from the set of pairs (A, σ), where A is an action expression and σ is a state, to the set of states.

An *interpretation structure* is a triple (α, σ_0, Φ), where α is an assignment, σ_0 is a state, called the *initial state* of (σ_0, Φ), and Φ is a transition function. For any interpretation structure $M = (\alpha, \sigma_0, \Phi)$ and any sequence of action expressions $A_1; \ldots; A_m$ in M, by $\Phi(A_1; \ldots; A_m, \sigma_0)$ we denote the state $\Phi(A_m, \Phi(A_{m-1}, \ldots, \Phi(A_1, \sigma_0) \ldots))$.

Given an interpretation structure (α, σ_0, Φ), a constraint C is said to be true with respect to it iff

- if C is a proposition name, then $C \in \alpha$;
- if C is a value assertion of the form F **after** $A_1, \ldots, A_n$, then F holds in the state $\Phi(A_1; \ldots; A_n, \sigma_0)$;
- if C is a complex constraint, then it is true according to the usual propositional connective evaluation methods.

An interpretation structure (α, σ_0, Φ) is a *model* of a domain description D iff

- Every constraint is true with respect to the interpretation structure.
- For every action A, every fluent name F, and every state σ: (i) If D includes an effect assertion A **causes** F **if** $P_1, \ldots, P_m, Q_1, \ldots, Q_n$, such that fluents $P_1, \ldots, P_m$ hold in σ and propositions $Q_1, \ldots, Q_n$ are true with respect to (α, σ_0, Φ), then $F \in \Phi(A, \sigma)$; (ii) If D includes an effect assertion A **causes** $\neg F$ **if** $P_1, \ldots, P_m, Q_1, \ldots, Q_n$, such that fluents $P_1, \ldots, P_n$ hold

in σ and propositions $Q_1, \ldots, Q_n$ are true with respect to (α, σ_0, Φ), then $F \notin \Phi(A, \sigma)$; (iii) If D does not include any such effect assertions, then $F \in \Phi(A, \sigma)$ iff $F \in \sigma$.

A domain description is *consistent* if it has a model. A domain description is *complete* if it has exactly one model. A domain description D entails a value assertion V if V is true in all models of D. It can be shown that different models of the same domain description differ only in different initial states and/or proposition assignments. In addition, the interpretation of a proposition name is independent of states.

In reality a practical domain should have only one model. The task of refining domain descriptions is to construct a new domain description which has fewer models than the original domain description. We will achieve this purpose by first performing some actions and observing their outcome, then we will abductively infer the truth values of propositions and initial states. We will make use of abductive logic programming for the purpose of abductive reasoning.

3 Abductive Logic Programming

As will be seen, the translations of domain descriptions will be acyclic, and thus In this paper we will follow Denecker [12] and use Console's predicate completion semantics by only completing defined predicates and leaving abducible predicates open.

An abductive logic program is a triple $< P, IC, \Delta >$, where P is a set of logic programming rules, IC is a set of first-order sentences as integrity constraints, and Δ is a set of predicates, called abducible predicates. A logic programming rule is of the form

$$A \leftarrow B_1, \ldots, B_m, not\ B_{m+1}, \ldots, not\ B_n$$

where A and each B_i are atoms, and *not* is the negation-as-failure operator.

An abductive answer δ to a query Q in $< P, IC, \Delta >$ is a finite subset of instances of Δ such that (i) $Q \in SEM(P \cup \{a \leftarrow\ : a \in \delta\}, IC)$; (ii) $P \cup \{a \leftarrow\ : a \in \delta\}, IC)$ is consistent according to definition of SEM; (iii) δ is minimal in the sense that no subset of it satisfies the previous two conditions, where $SEM(P, IC)$ denotes the semantics of the program P with constraints IC.

There have been a few competing semantics for logic programs in the literature: predicate completion semantics, stable model semantics [13], and well-founded model semantics [31]. All of them can be extended for abductive logic programs. As is known, for acyclic programs [1] [5], their predicate completion models coincide with both the stable models and the well-founded models. In

---

[1] Let P be a normal logic program, and B_P the set of ground atoms of P. A *level mapping* for a program P is a function $\lambda : B_P \to N$ from ground atoms to natural numbers. For $A \in B_P$, $\lambda(A)$ is the *level* of A; Given a level mapping λ, we extend it to ground negative literals by letting $\lambda(\neg A) = \lambda(A)$; A clause of P is called *acyclic with respect to* a level mapping λ, if for every ground instance $A \leftarrow L_1, \ldots, L_n$ of it,

the case of abductive logic programs, the semantical coincidence still holds, as shown by Denecker [10]. In this paper we will only use acyclic logic programs, and will define the semantics of logic programs as the predicate completion semantics. For abductive logic programs, we will complete all predicates except the abducible ones [8].

Example 3.1 *Consider an abductive logic programming framework* $FOO = (P, A, I)$, *where*

$$P = \left\{ \begin{array}{l} p \leftarrow a \\ p \leftarrow b \\ q \leftarrow b \end{array} \right\}, \quad A = \{a, b\}, \quad I = \{false \leftarrow p, q\}$$

Then, we have

$$COMP(P; A) = \left\{ \begin{array}{l} p \leftrightarrow a \vee b \\ q \leftrightarrow b \end{array} \right\}$$

The semantics of FOO is $COMP(P; A) \cup I$, *which is equivalent to the following first-order theory*

$$\{p \leftrightarrow a \vee b, q \leftrightarrow b, \neg(p \wedge q)\}$$

Suppose that we want to evaluate a query $? - p$. *Then* $\{a\}$ *is an abductive answer, since it satisfies the following three conditions:*

- $COMP(P; A) \cup I \cup \{a\} \models p$;
- $COMP(P; A) \cup I \cup \{a\}$ *is consistent.*
- *There is no proper subset of* $\{a\}$ *satisfying the above two conditions, and hence* $\{a\}$ *is a set-inclusion minimal subset satisfying the above two conditions.*

Note that $COMP(P; A) \cup I \cup \{b\}$ *is not consistent. Thus,* $\{b\}$ *is not an abductive answer to* $? - p$ *in FOO. Now suppose that we want to evaluate a query* $? - q$. *It can be shown that there is no abductive answer to it.*

There have been many proposals, e.g., [11, 30], for abductive query evaluation procedures for abductive normal logic programs. The work reported in this paper has been experimented with the latest version of the REVISE system [9], an extended logic programming system for revising knowledge bases. It is based on logic programming with explicit negation and integrity constraints and provides a two- or three-valued assumption revision to remove contradictions from the knowledge base. The latest version of the REVISE system is based on a top-down query evaluation procedure [2] of well founded semantics with explicit negation (WFSX) [26, 4]. If explicit negation is not used, then the WFSX semantics coincides with the WFS semantics. Thus, the use of REVISE is not essential for the purpose of this paper.

---

we have $\lambda(A) > \lambda(L_i)$, for every $1 \le i \le n$. A program P is called em acyclic with respect to a level mapping λ, if all its clauses are. P is called *acyclic* if it is acyclic with respect to some level mapping.

4 Refinement of Action Theories

4.1 Motivation

When reasoning about actions and changes, we often assume that a complete action theory has been given and described in a formal language. But sometimes no complete action theory is available in practice. We may need to do some tests and perform some reasoning in order to have a complete action theory. For example, let's consider Vladimir Lifschitz' challenge problem[2]:

> The room has two lamps, say Big and Small, and two light switches, say Left and Right. A switch controls one and only one light. Both lights are off. Initially we don't know whether the wiring is this way or the other way around, but we can find out by toggling a switch.

In this example, we have two actions: to toggle the left switch and to toggle the right switch, denoted by $toggle(left)$ and $toggle(right)$, and we have two fluents: the big light is on and the small light is on, denoted by $on(big)$ and $on(small)$. If we knew the way in which the circuit is connected, then we could generate plans, predict the future, or explain the past. The problem is that no such an immediately available theory is available. An intelligent agent should be able to perform some tests and then obtain a complete action theory. In this paper we will present an abductive methodology for reasoning about actions and changes starting from an incomplete action theory, i.e., an action theory with more than one model, then refining it by testing and abductive reasoning so as to have a complete action theory, which can then be used for planning, predicting and explaining depending on specific needs. Our methodology consists of a high-level action description language $\mathcal{A}^+$, a translation from $\mathcal{A}^+$ to abductive logic programs, and an abductive logic programming system used as the underlying inference engine for refinement. We will return to this problem later.

4.2 Translation into Abductive Programs

In this section we will present a translation from domain descriptions in $\mathcal{A}^+$ into abductive logic programs.

Let D be a domain description. The translation πD includes a set of programming rules and a set of constraints defined as follows:

1. Initialization: $holds(F, s_0) \leftarrow initially(F)$.
2. Law of Inertia:

$$holds(F, result(A, S)) \leftarrow holds(F, S), not\ noninertial(F, S, A).$$

where not is the negation-as-failure operator. By the law of inertia, F is true at a new situation by doing A on S if it was true at S.

---

[2] Vladimir Lifschitz's email message to lmp@di.fct.unl.pt and renwei@di.fct.unl.pt on March 25, 1996.

3. Each effect assertion a **causes** f **if** $p_1, \ldots, p_m, q_1, \ldots, q_n$, with f being positive, p_i being a fluent, and q_i being a proposition, is translated into

$$holds(f, result(a, S)) \leftarrow holds(p_1, S), \ldots, holds(p_m, S), q_1, \ldots, q_n.$$

where $holds(\neg p, S)$ with p being positive stands for $not\ holds(p, S)$. This convention is also used in the rest of this paper.

4. Each effect assertion a **causes** $\neg f$ **if** $p_1, \ldots, p_m, q_1, \ldots, q_n$, with f being positive, p_i being a fluent, and q_i being a proposition, is translated into

$$noninertial(f, a, S) \leftarrow holds(p_1, T), \ldots, holds(p_m, T), q_1, \ldots, q_n.$$

5. For every constraint C of D: (i) if C is a proposition name, $\pi C = C$; (ii) if C is f **after** $a_1, \ldots, a_n$ with f being positive, then $\pi C = holds(f, result(a_1; \ldots; a_n, s_0))$; (iii) if C is $\neg f$ **after** $a_1, \ldots, a_n$, with f being positive, then $\pi C = \neg holds(f, result(a_1; \ldots; a_n, s_0))$; (iv) $\pi(\neg C_1) = \neg(\pi C_1)$, $\pi(C_1 \wedge C_2) = \pi C_1 \wedge \pi C_2$, $\pi(C_1 \vee C_2) = \pi C_1 \vee \pi C_2$.

We will define abducible predicates to be $initially(F)$ and all proposition names. The semantics of πD, denoted by $Comp(\pi D)$, is defined to be the first-order theory by completing all predicates except $initially(F)$ and proposition names, jointly with Clark's theory of equality, and the constraints [8].

Theorem 4.1 *Let D be any domain description in $\mathcal{A}^+$. πD is an acyclic logic program with first-order constraints in the sense of [5].*

Corollary 4.2 *The completion semantics $Comp(\pi D)$ of πD agrees with its generalized stable model semantics [17] and generalized well-founded model semantics [27].*

The above corollary means that the result of this paper can be experimented with any abductive logic programming system with one of the three major semantics. The detailed proof follows from [10].

4.3 Soundness and Completeness

In general it is very difficult to reason about actions in $\mathcal{A}^+$. The purpose of the translation is to reduce the reasoning work in $\mathcal{A}^+$ to abductive querying in an abductive logic programming system. This section will show that reasoning in $\mathcal{A}^+$ is equivalent to abductive querying.

Theorem 4.3 *The translation π is sound. That is, for any domain description D and any value assertion V, if $Comp(\pi D) \models \pi V$, then D entails V.*

Definition 4.4 *A domain description D is effect consistent iff for each pair of effect assertions,*

$$A \text{ causes } F \text{ if } C_1, \ldots, C_m$$
$$A \text{ causes } \neg F \text{ if } C_{m+1}, \ldots, C_n$$

in D, there exists i, $1 \leq i \leq m$, and j, $m + 1 \leq j \leq n$, such that C_i is the complement of C_j.

Theorem 4.5 *The translation π is complete for any effect consistent domain descriptions. That is, for any effect consistent domain description D and any value assertion V, if D entails V, then $Comp(\pi D) \models \pi V$.*

The requirement for a domain description to be effect consistent is necessary. If a domain description D is not effect consistent, no transition functions exist to satisfy its effect assertions, thus it has no models, and hence it entails every value assertion. On the other hand, its translation is consistent and thus has at least one model which entails a proper subset of what D entails.

The above soundness and completeness theorems signify that our translation can actually be used for the general purposes of reasoning about actions and changes such as abductive planning, prediction, explanation. That is to say, our result of this paper goes beyond refinement of action theories. But we will not delve into detailed discussion on how to use our translation for abductive planning, temporal prediction and explanation. In the next section we will concentrate on refinement of action theories.

4.4 Refinement

Let D be a domain description. D may have more than one model. If D has more than one model, we may only predict a disjunctive future instead of a definite future. That is to say, after a sequence of actions is done, we cannot predict whether a fluent is definitely true or not. When a domain description is complete, we can always predict whether a fluent is true or not after an action is done. This is sometimes a very important factor in reasoning about actions, as shown as in [22].

When a domain description is not complete, all its models differ in their initial states and/or proposition assignments. In order to determine initial states and proposition assignments, one may perform some tests: doing some actions, observing their effects, and then abductively determining initial states and proposition names.

Definition 4.6 *Let D_1 and D_2 be two domain descriptions. D_2 is said to be a refinement of D_1 iff every model of D_2 is a model of D_1.*

Now suppose that we are given a domain description D_0. We want to refine it. The way to do it, as said as before, is to perform some actions and observe their effects. This process is called *test*. The purpose of tests is to generate new value assertions. And thus we can formally define a test to be a set of value assertions.

Definition 4.7 *A test in an action domain is a set of value assertions. Let D be a domain description. The pair (D, τ) is called a refinement problem.*

Theorem 4.8 *Let D be a domain description, and τ a test. Then, $D \cup \tau$ is a refinement of D.*

The above theorem means that simply adding tests to a domain description will definitely refine a domain description. But syntactically $D \cup \tau$ is more complicated than D. We may prefer simpler and finer descriptions. Note that in an interpretation structure, all proposition names will be either true or false. In the reality, all these proposition names can and can only be either true or false. When we do enough tests, the refinement of the domain will be closer and closer to a complete domain description. The above corollary implies that the complete domain description is a limit of all refinements of domain descriptions. When the domain description has only one model, all proposition names can be removed from the domain description by substituting them with their truth values, and thus syntactically simplifying the domain description. Hence, the previous definition of refinements is modified as follows.

Definition 4.9 Let D_1 and D_2 be two domain descriptions. D_2 is said to be a refinement of D_1 iff the following conditions are satisfied:

- Every model of D_2 is a model of D_1;
- There is no proposition name in D_2 which is true in every model of D_2;
- There is no proposition name in D_2 which is false in every model of D_2.

In what follows we want to show how to compute refinements with abductive logic programming. In Section 4.2 we presented a translation from domain descriptions to abductive logic programs. However, many existing abductive logic programming systems do not directly support our constraints. Instead, they support constraints of the form

$$\bot \leftarrow L_1, \ldots, L_n$$

First we need to translate all constraints into the above form.

The translation, still denoted by π, is as follows. Let C be a constraint in the program πD. Then C can be equivalently transformed into a conjunctive normal form:

$$(C_{11} \vee \ldots \vee C_{1m_1}) \wedge \ldots \wedge (C_{m1} \vee \ldots \vee C_{mn})$$

Then, it will be translated into

$$\bot \leftarrow not\ C_{11}, \ldots, not\ C_{1m_1}$$

$$\ldots$$

$$\bot \leftarrow not\ C_{m1}, \ldots, not\ C_{mn}$$

where $not\ \neg L$ is taken as L.

After constraints are translated into a logic program, we can run it in any abductive logic programming system. Before proceeding, we need to guarantee that the correctness of the translation is preserved.

Theorem 4.10 The translation π is both sound and complete for any effect consistent domain descriptions.

Note that above translation does not change completions of non-abducible predicates. On the other hand, the completion of $\bot$ is logically equivalent to $\neg C$. Therefore, the semantics of new programs is the same as before.

Let $\tau = \{V_1, \ldots, V_n\}$ be a test. Then, τ can be transformed into a query:

$$\leftarrow \pi V_1, \ldots, \pi V_n$$

where for each i, πV_i is defined as follows: Let V_i be F **after** $A_1, \ldots, A_n$ in τ. If F is positive, then πV_i is defined to be $holds(F, result(A_1; \ldots; A_n, s_0))$; if F is negative and equal to $\neg G$, then πV_i is defined to be $not\ holds(G, result(A_1; \ldots; A_n, s_0))$.

Submitting the query to an abductive logic programming system, we will get abductive answers to it. In what follows we will write $\mathcal{R}(D, \tau)$ to stand for the set of all abductive answers to the query $\leftarrow \pi \tau$ against the abductive logic program πD. Now we are in a position to define the procedure of refining action theories.

Definition 4.11 *Let D be a domain description and τ a test. Let $\mathcal{R}(D, \tau) = \{R_1, \ldots, R_n\}$. Perform:*

1. *For every proposition name P, if $P \notin R_1 \cup \ldots \cup R_n$, remove from D all effect assertions containing P in the precondition list, and replace P with false in every constraint of D;*
2. *For every proposition name P, if $P \in R_1 \cap \ldots \cap R_n$, remove P from all effect assertions of D, and replace P with true in every constraint of D;*
3. *Simplify constraints of D in the usual way by using of true and false in the formulas. For example, if C is of the form $\neg false$ or $C_1 \vee true$, C is removed.*

Then, define $S(D, \tau)$ to be the set of the resulting effect assertions, constraints, and the test τ.

The following theorem says that the new domain description $S(D, \tau)$ is a refinement of D.

Theorem 4.12 *Let D be a domain description, τ a test. Then, $S(D, \tau)$ is a refinement of D.*

4.5 An Example

Now we return to the example in the Introduction. Let $controls(S, L)$ be a parameterized proposition name to denote that switch S controls light L. Then, we can have the following domain description D:

$controls(left, small) \leftrightarrow controls(right, big)$
$controls(left, big) \leftrightarrow controls(right, small)$
$controls(left, small) \dot{\lor} controls(left, big)$
$controls(right, small) \dot{\lor} controls(right, big)$
$toggle(left)$ **causes** $on(small)$ **if** $\neg on(small), controls(left, small)$
$toggle(left)$ **causes** $\neg on(small)$ **if** $on(small), controls(left, small)$
$toggle(right)$ **causes** $on(small)$ **if** $\neg on(small), controls(right, small)$
$toggle(right)$ **causes** $on(small)$ **if** $\neg on(small), controls(right, small)$
$toggle(left)$ **causes** $on(big)$ **if** $\neg on(big), controls(left, big)$
$toggle(left)$ **causes** $\neg on(big)$ **if** $on(big), controls(left, big)$
$toggle(right)$ **causes** $on(big)$ **if** $\neg on(big), controls(right, big)$
$toggle(right)$ **causes** $on(big)$ **if** $\neg on(big), controls(right, big)$
initially $\neg on(big)$
initially $\neg on(small)$

Then, we have an abductive logic program πD. Now suppose we have a test τ = $\{on(big)$ **after** $toggle(left)\}$. Then, evaluate the following query against the abductive logic program πD:

$$\leftarrow holds(on(big), result(toggle(left), s_0))$$

An abductive logic programming system should correctly output the following unique abductive answer $\mathcal{R}(D, \tau)$:

$$\{\{controls(right, small), controls(left, big)\}\}$$

Then, by definition we have the following new domain description $\mathcal{S}(D, \tau)$:

$$toggle(right) \textbf{ causes } on(small) \textbf{ if } \neg on(small)$$
$$toggle(right) \textbf{ causes } on(small) \textbf{ if } \neg on(small)$$
$$toggle(left) \textbf{ causes } on(big) \textbf{ if } \neg on(big)$$
$$toggle(left) \textbf{ causes } \neg on(big) \textbf{ if } on(big)$$
$$\textbf{initially } \neg on(big)$$
$$\textbf{initially } \neg on(small)$$
$$on(big) \textbf{ after } toggle(left)$$

Thus we have obtained a complete domain description which enables us to generate plan, to predict the future, or to explain the past, as what we expected and intended.

5 Knowledge Assimilation

5.1 Motivation

Knowledge assimilation is a process of reasonably incorporating new knowledge into an existing knowledge base. It is not always clear how different knowledge assimilation and belief revision/update. Existing approaches to belief revision/update can be roughly classified into postulate-based approaches such as AGM theory [1], syntax-based approaches such as the possible worlds approach PWA [16], and semantics-based approaches such as the possible models approach PMA [32]. The AGM theory is rooted in philosophical logic, and the syntax/semantics-based approaches seem to be currently favored in the AI community since they can be immediately used to solve some practive problems such as reasoning about actions, diagnosis, counterfactual query, etc.

Now consider a domain where there are two people: *Tom* and *Mary* , and two objects: *Money* and *Book*. In the beginning, say November 1, 1995, *Tom* has *Book* while *Mary* has *Money*. Assume that either of the two people can buy *Book* from the other if he/she has *Money* and the other has *Book*; either can give *Book* or *Money* to the other; either can steal an object from the other. Suppose that *Mary* is found to have *Book* later, say November 5, 1995.

Applying either PWA or PMA, we will only have the following knowledge base [20]:

$$\{\neg has(Tom, Book), \neg has(Tom, Money), has(Mary, Book), has(Mary, Money)\}$$

However, in practice there is another possible new knowledge base:

$$\{\neg has(Tom, Book), has(Tom, Money), has(Mary, Book), \neg has(Mary, Money)\}$$

Intuitively, the former corresponds to the possible cause: *Tom* gives *Book* to *Mary* or *Mary* steals *Book* from *Tom*, while the latter corresponds to the possible cause: *Mary* buys *Book* from *Tom* with Mary's *Money*. These two possible causes should be equally possible. In our PCA approach, both of the new knowledge bases can be found.

We will make use of the following sub-langage of $\mathcal{A}^+$ to describe a domain. The effects of actions are described by effect assertions of the form

$$A \text{ causes } F \text{ if } P_1, \ldots, P_n$$

The initial conditions are described by the value assertions of the form

initially F

A domain description is a set of the above two types of assertions.

Note that such a domain description can be obtained through refinement of action theories. In the following we first translate such a domain description into abductive logic programs including a time dimension.

5.2 Translation into logic programs

In the following we present a new translation π from domain descriptions to abductive logic programs, where a time dimension is incorporated so that one can represent and reason about narratives, actions and time. Let D be a domain description, the translation πD consists of the following logic programming rules:

1. Time dimension:
   In this paper we assume that time is structured on points, represented by a totally linearly-ordered set $(TP, \prec, succ, init)$, where TP is an infinite set of time points, $init \in TP$, and $succ(T) \in TP$ for any $T \in TP$. We will often use natural numbers which have a straightforward correspondence to terms for time points: $init$ corresponding to 0, $succ(init)$ to 1, etc.
2. Initialization: $holds(F, init) \leftarrow initially(F)$.
3. Law of Inertia:

$$holds(F, succ(T)) \leftarrow holds(F, T),$$
$$not\ noninertial(F, T).$$

   where not is the negation-as-failure operator. By the law of inertia, a fluent F is true at a time point T if it was true earlier and inertial then.
4. Each e-proposition a **causes** f **if** $p_1, \ldots, p_n$, with f being positive, is translated into

$$holds(f, succ(T)) \leftarrow happens(a, T),$$
$$holds(p_1, T), \ldots, holds(p_n, T).$$

5. Each e-proposition a **causes** $\neg f$ **if** $p_1, \ldots, p_n$,
   with f being positive, is translated into

$$noninertial(f, T) \leftarrow happens(a, T),$$
$$holds(p_1, T), \ldots, holds(p_n, T).$$

6. Each v-proposition **initially** f or **initially** $\neg g$, where f and g are positive, is respectively translated into

$$false \leftarrow not\ holds(f, init).$$
$$false \leftarrow holds(g, init).$$

The above two logic programming rules function as integrity constraints.

5.3 Representation of Knowledge Bases

In this section, we we will use the above translation to represent temporal knowledge bases about domains of actions.

5.4 Temporal knowledge bases

Given a domain description D, we want to determine whether a fluent holds at a particular time point after some actions have happened in the past. We start with the concept of histories, then employ abductive logic programming for the representation of temporal knowledge.

A domain history H is a finite set of pairs (A, T) for action A and time T. By $(A, T) \in H$ we mean that A happens at T. In this paper we do not consider concurrent actions. Thus we assume that for any $T \in TP$ there is at most one action A such that $(A, T) \in H$.

A domain evolution E is a pair (D, H), where D is a domain description and H a history. Given a domain evolution (D, H), we can have an abductive logic program $KB(D, H)$ defined as follows:

$$KB(D, H) = \pi D \cup \{false \leftarrow not\ happens(a, t) : (a, t) \in H\}$$

The logic program $KB(D, H)$ will be simply called *the knowledge base generated from D and H*. The literal $false$ is always interpreted as logical falsity, and all rules with $false$ as heads function as integrity constraints. The predicates $initially(F)$ is taken as an abducible predicate used to capture the incomplete knowledge about the initial situation/time. The semantics of $KB(D, H)$ is defined to be the union of the integrity constraints, the Clark Equality Theory, and the first-order theory obtained by completing all the non-abducible predicates (all predicates except $initially(F)$). We will simply write $COMP(KB(D, H))$ to denote the semantics of of $KB(D, H)$, and often write $KB(D, H) \models Q$ to stand for $COMP(KB(D, H)) \models Q$. The following two results justify the above semantics definition.

Proposition 5.1 $KB(D, H)$ *is an acyclic logic program.*

Corollary 5.2 *The semantics $COMP(KB(D, H))$ of the abductive logic program $KB(D, H)$ coincides with its generalized stable model semantics and generalized well-founded model semantics.*

5.5 Soundness and completeness

Given a history H, we can have a unique sequence of actions $A_1; A_2; \ldots; A_m$ and a unique sequence of time points $T_1 \prec T_2 \prec \ldots \prec T_m$ such that $H = \{(A_i, T_i) : 1 \leq i \leq m\}$. The sequence of actions $A_1; A_2; \ldots; A_m$ will be called *the trajectory generated from H*, denoted by $Traj(H)$. A pre-history of H is defined to be a subset H' of H such that $Traj(H')$ is a prefix of $Traj(H)$.

Given an interpretation structure $M = (\sigma_0, \Phi)$, a history H and a time point T, we can derive a state S as follows: if $H' = \{(A_1, T_1), \ldots, (A_k, T_k)\}$ is a pre-history of H such that $T_k \prec T$ and there is no time point Tx and action Ax with $T_k \prec Tx \prec T$ and $(Ax, Tx) \in H$, then $S = \Phi(A_1; A_2; \ldots; A_k, \sigma_0)$, called *the state generated from H and T in M*, denoted by $GS_M(H, T)$. If T is a time point such that $(A, T) \notin H$ for any action A, and $(A, Tx) \notin H$ for any action A and any time point Tx with $T \prec Tx$, then the state $GS_M(H, T)$ is called *the state* *generated from H in M*, denoted by $GS_M(H)$. For example, let $M = (\sigma_0, \Phi)$ be an interpretation structure, and $H = \{(a, 1), (a, 6), (b, 4), (c, 10)\}$ a history. Then, $GS_M(H, 5) = \Phi(a; b, \sigma_0)$ and $GS_M(H) = \Phi(a; b; a; c, \sigma_0)$.

Proposition 5.3 *Given an interpretation structure M, a history H, and a time point T, the state $GS_M(H, T)$ generated from H and T in M is unique.*

Note that $\mathcal{A}$has an infinite tree-like time structure. Given a history H, the translation π only takes into account a special path in the tree corresponding to H. In order for π to be correct, we require that π be correct with respect to any history.

Definition 5.4 *Let D be a domain description, and H a history. The logic program $KB(D, H)$ is said to be sound with respect to H iff, for every model M of D, fluent F and time T, if $KB(D, H) \models holds(F, T)$, then $F \in GS_M(H, T)$. The translation π is said to be sound iff, for every history H, $KB(D, H)$ is sound with respect to H.*

Definition 5.5 *Let D be a domain description, and H a history. The logic program $KB(D, H)$ is said to be complete with respect to H iff, for every fluent F and time T, if $F \in GS_M(H, T)$ for every model M of D, then $KB(D, H) \models holds(F, T)$. The translation π is said to be complete iff, for every history H, $KB(D, H)$ is complete with respect to H.*

Theorem 5.6 (Soundness) *Assume that D is a domain description. For any history H, model I of D, fluent F, and time T, if $KB(D, H) \models holds(F, T)$, then $F \in GS_I(H, T)$.*

A domain description D is *e-consistent* [12] iff for each pair of e-propositions a **causes** f **if** $p_1, \ldots, p_n$ and a **causes** $\neg f$ **if** $p_{n+1}, \ldots, p_m$ in D, there exist i and j such that p_i is the complement of p_j.

Theorem 5.7 (Completeness) *Assume that D is an e-consistent domain description. For any history H, fluent F, and time T, if $F \in GS_I(H, T)$ for any model I of D, then $KB(D, H) \models holds(F, T)$.*

5.6 Possible Causes Approach

For easy reference, we will simply write $KB(D, H) \oplus N$ to informally denote all the possible new knowledge bases obtained by incorporating N into $KB(D, H)$ before we formally define it later. For convenience, we often write $N = L$ if $N = \{L\}$.

Suppose that $N = holds(F, T)$ is a newly observed fact. In the process of incorporating N into $KB(D, H)$, first the agent should check whether N is already stored in her knowledge base $KB(D, H)$, i.e., whether $KB(D, H) \models N$. If it is so, the agent will do nothing. In this case, $KB(D, H) \oplus N \equiv KB(D, H)$. Suppose that N is not stored in the knowledge base, that is, $KB(D, H) \not\models N$.

In this case, either the fluent F was true and inertial at the last time point or an action has happened at the last time point and a initiates F. After a careful analysis, it can be seen that the v-propositions **initially** F and occurrences of actions which initiate N or recursively initiate preconditions of actions which initiate N are possible causes for N in $KB(D, H)$.

Let (D, H) be a domain evolution, and Δ the set of instances of $initially(F)$ and $happens(A, T)$. For any finite subset δ of Δ we will write $KB(D, H) \dotplus \delta$ to stand for $KB(D', H')$, where $D' = D \cup \{ \text{ initially } F : initially(F) \in \delta\}$ and $H' = H \cup \{(A, T) : happens(A, T) \in \delta\}$. We assume that no concurrent actions appear in H'. We will often omit $initially(F)$ from δ when both **initially** $F \in D$ and $initially(F) \in \delta$.

Definition 5.8 *Let D be a domain description, H a history, and N a set of literals. A possible cause for N in $KB(D, H)$ is a subset δ of Δ such that (i) $KB(D, H) \dotplus \delta \models N$; (ii) $KB(D, H) \dotplus \delta$ is consistent; (iii) For any time T, there are no different actions A and B such that $(A, T), (B, T) \in H \cup \{(C, T) : happens(C, T) \in \delta\}$; (iv) δ is minimal in the sense that no subset δ' of δ exists such that δ' satisfies the first three conditions. We will write $KB(D, H) \uparrow N$ to stand for all the possible causes for N in $KB(D, H)$.*

As an example, consider the Stolen Car Problem:

$$D_{scp} = \{ \text{ initially } \neg Stolen. \; Steal \text{ causes } Stolen.\}$$

and $H_{scp} = \emptyset$. Suppose that the car is missing from the parking lot at time 3. Then there are three possible causes for $holds(stolen, 3)$ in $KB(D_{scp}, H_{scp})$:

$$\delta_1 = \{happens(steal, 0)\},$$
$$\delta_2 = \{happens(steal, 1)\},$$
$$\delta_3 = \{happens(steal, 2)\}$$

In order to incorporate N into $KB(D, H)$, if there is a possible cause δ for N in $KB(D, H)$, then we can simply add δ into the knowledge base to have a new knowledge base. Now we have to question about whether there is always a possible cause δ for N in $KB(D, H)$. The answer turns out to be negative.

Proposition 5.9 *Let D be a domain description, and H a history. Let N be a set of literals. It does not hold that there is always a possible cause for N in $KB(D, H)$.*

For incorporation of N into $KB(D, H)$, when there is no possible cause for N in $KB(D, H)$, we will simply discard N because N cannot be explained.

Definition 5.10 *Given a knowledge base $KB(D, H)$, and a set of new facts N, all the possible new knowledge bases $KB(D, H) \oplus N$ are defined to be*

$$\{KB(D, H) \dotplus \delta : \delta \in KB(D, H) \uparrow N\}$$

The operator $\oplus$ is called the PCA knowledge incorporation operator.

For example, $KB(D_{scp}, H_{scp}) \oplus holds(stolen, 3)$ includes, in the Stolen Car Problem,

$$KB(D_{scp}, \{(steal, 0)\}), \ KB(D_{scp}, \{(steal, 1)\}), \ \text{and} \ KB(D_{scp}, \{(steal, 2)\}).$$

Note that the new knowledge N is not directly added to the knowledge base. This can be problematic in general. As discussed in its long version, there is a simple way to modify the above definition so that both new knowledge and its possible causes are incorporated, described as follows. For each fact $holds(F, T)$ and $\neg holds(G, T)$ in N, we add the following two constraints, respectively:

$$false \leftarrow not \ holds(F, T)$$
$$false \leftarrow holds(G, T)$$

Then, N is kept permanently in the knowledge base.

The PCA knowledge incorporation operator can also be used to evaluate counterfactual queries: if F_1 were true at time T_1, would F_2 be true at time T_2? This amounts to evaluate the query "$? - holds(F_2, T_2)$" in $KB(D, H) \oplus holds(F_1, T_1)$. The details are omitted.

5.7   Computational considerations

The critical step in the PCA approach is the computation of the possible causes. In this section we show how to compute them with abductive logic programming and how to improve computational efficiency.

First we introduce a new predicate $occurs(A, T)$, for action A and time T, and add a new programming rule to $KB(D, H)$:

$$happens(A, T) \leftarrow occurs(A, T) \tag{1}$$

Now we define the abducibles to be $initially(F)$ and $occurs(A, T)$. The above rule means that if action A is abduced to occur at time T, it happens at T. As said before, this paper does not consider concurrent actions. Thus we add the following rule:

$$false \leftarrow A_1 \neq A_2, happens(A_1, T), happens(A_2, T) \tag{2}$$

The definitions for $A1 \neq A2$ should also be added such that every two syntactically different actions are not equal. However, later we will find that the above rule is redundant and can be removed for efficiency improvement. Let $KB_{occurs}(D, H) = KB(D, H) \cup \{(1), (2)\}$. It is easy to see that KB_{occurs} is still acyclic. It can also be shown that possible causes for N become abductive answers to N in $KB_{occurs}(D, H)$.

Proposition 5.11 $\delta \in KB(D, H) \uparrow N$ iff $\{initially(F) : initially(F) \in \delta\}$ $\cup \{occurs(A, T) : happens(A, T) \in \delta\}$ is an abductive answer to N in the abductive logic program $KB_{occurs}(D, H)$.

In what follows we develop some techniques to improve the search efficiency.

Proposition 5.12 *Let δ be any abductive answer to $holds(F_n, T_n)$ in the program $KB_{occurs}(D, H)$. Then, for any $occurs(A, T) \in \delta$ we have $T \prec T_n$.*

Thus it is not necessary to consider predicate instances $occurs(A, T)$ for $T \not\prec T_n$. The second observation is that we have assumed that no concurrent actions have happened in histories. Thus, if $(A, T) \in H$, we need not consider $occurs(B, T)$ for any other action B.

Proposition 5.13 *Let δ be any abductive answer to N in $KB_{occurs}(D, H)$. If $occurs(a, t) \in \delta$, then there is no other action b such that $(b, t) \in H$.*

The third observation is about the consistency check. $KB(D, H) \dot{+} \delta$, by Definition 5.8, needs to be consistent for δ to be a possible cause. To check the consistency of a knowledge base is very expensive. In the following we give a sufficient and cheap technique to check the consistency.

Proposition 5.14 *Let D be an e-consistent domain description. If D is not consistent, then there are two value propositions* **initially** F *and* **initially** G *such that $F = \neg G$ or $G = \neg F$.*

By the above proposition, the consistency check can be done in the following way: For each fluent F, we add a new programming rule to $KB(D, H)$:

$$false \leftarrow holds(F, init), not \ holds(F, init)$$

All the examples of this paper and a few more benchmark examples have been experimented with the latest version of the REVISE system [9].

6 Concurrent Action

6.1 Motivation

In reality, occurrences of many actions overlap in time, which complicates temporal prediction and explanation in AI. For definite goals some actions may be planned to be carried out at the same time in order to save time, or to decrease production cost, or for other context-dependent purposes.

A concurrent action is understood as a finite nonempty set of atomic actions, which happen at the same time. A nonempty subset of a concurrent action is called a subaction of the concurrent action. For example, opening a door and switching on a light at the same time is a concurrent action consisting of two atomic actions: opening a door and switching on a light. In common sense, the effect of a concurrent action is the aggregation of those of its subactions. For example, after one opens a door and switches on a light at the same time, the door is open and the light is on, which is the aggregation of the effects of opening the door and switching on the light.

The effect relationship between an action and its subactions was first discussed by Gelfond, Lifschitz and Robinov in the framework of the situation calculus [15], and further explored by Lin and Shoham [23], and Baral and Gelfond [7]. According to [23, 7], essentially, a concurrent action *usually* inherits effects of its subactions. There is no problem with such a default when a concurrent action does not include atomic actions with conflicting effects. When a concurrent action includes atomic actions with conflicting effects, they may give intuitively undesired results. According to [23], the epistemological completeness implies that in any situation one can always decide whether a fluent is true or not. Thus, if the door is initially closed, then the door will still be closed after $\{Open, Close\}$ is done; if the door is initially open, then the door will still be open after $\{Open, Close\}$ is done. According to [7], after $\{Open, Close\}$ is done, the resulting situation does not exist and $\{Open, Close\}$ is not executable.

In this paper we will introduce a cautious semantics to concurrent actions. When subactions of a concurrent action do not have conflicting effects, it can be proved that our semantics coincides with Lin-Shoham's and Baral-Gelfond's. When two subactions of a concurrent action have conflicting effects, the truth value of all fluents affected by the two subactions will be left undefined. For example, the fluent denoting the status of the door will be left undefined after $\{Open, Close\}$ is done.

6.2 Domain Descriptions

Syntax of $\mathcal{AC}$ The syntax of $\mathcal{AC}$ is similar $\mathcal{A}$ except that an action expression is a finite set of atomic actions. Thus, a domain description in $\mathcal{AC}$ is a set of effect assertions of the form A **causes** F **if** $P_1, \ldots, P_n$, and value assertions of the form F **after** $A_1, \ldots, A_m$, where $A, A_1, \ldots, A_m$ may be a set of atomic actions.

Example 6.1 (Mary's Soup [15]) *Whenever Mary lifts the bowl with only one hand, she will spill the soup. But when she lifts the bowl with two hands, she will not spill the soup. Let LL and LR to denote lifting the bowl with the left hand and the right hand, respectively. Then, the domain can be described as follows:*

$$D_{soup} = \left\{ \begin{array}{l} \textbf{initially} \ \neg Spilled. \\ LL \ \textbf{causes} \ Spilled. \\ LR \ \textbf{causes} \ Spilled. \\ \{LL, LR\} \ \textbf{causes} \ \neg Spilled. \end{array} \right\}$$

Semantics of $\mathcal{AC}$ The semantics of $\mathcal{AC}$ is defined by using states and transitions.

A *state* σ is a pair of sets of fluent names $\langle \sigma^+, \sigma^- \rangle$ such that σ^+ and σ^- are disjoint, i.e., $\sigma^+ \cap \sigma^- = \emptyset$. Given a fluent name F and a state σ, we say that F holds in σ if $F \in \sigma^+$, F does not hold in σ if $F \in \sigma^-$, and it is not known whether F holds in σ otherwise. Given a fluent name F, we also say that $\neg F$ holds in σ if F does not hold in σ. Sometimes we also say that F is true in σ if $F \in \sigma^+$, F is false in σ if $F \in \sigma^-$, and F is undefined in σ otherwise.

A *transition function* Φ is a mapping from the set of pairs (A, σ), where A is an action expression and σ is a state, into the set of states.

A *structure* is a pair (σ_0, Φ), where σ_0 is a state, called the *initial state* of the structure, and Φ is a transition function. For any structure $M = (\sigma_0, \Phi)$ and any sequence of action expressions $A_1; \ldots; A_m$ in M, by $\Phi(A_1; \ldots; A_m, \sigma_0)$ we denote the state $\Phi(A_m, \Phi(A_{m-1}, \ldots, \Phi(A_1, \sigma_0) \ldots))$. A v-assertion of the form F **after** $A_1, \ldots, A_m$ is satisfied in a structure $M = (\sigma_0, \Phi)$ iff F holds in the state $\Phi(A_1; \ldots; A_m, \sigma_0)$.

We say that the execution of an action A in a state σ *immediately initiates* a fluent expression F if there is an e-proposition A **causes** F **if** $P_1, \ldots, P_m$ in the domain description such that for each $1 \leq i \leq m$, P_i holds in σ. Moreover, we say that the execution of A in σ *initiates* a fluent expression F if A immediately initiates F, or there is a $B \subseteq A$ such that execution of B in σ *immediately initiates* F and there is no C such that $B \subset C \subseteq A$, where execution of C in σ immediately initiates $\neg F$.

Let F be positive. When A initiates $\neg F$, we will say that A terminates F. We define two set-ranged functions as follows:

$$Initiate(A, \sigma) = \{F \;:\; F \in \Sigma_f \text{ and } A \text{ initiates } F \text{ in } \sigma\}$$
$$Terminate(A, \sigma) = \{F \;:\; F \in \Sigma_f \text{ and } A \text{ initiates } \neg F \text{ in } \sigma\}$$

Note that $Initiate(A, \sigma)$ and $Terminate(A, \sigma)$ are not necessarily disjoint. We also need a set-ranged function $Cause(F, \sigma, A)$, (for fluent name F, state σ, and action expression A), which is defined to contain and only contain all the *set-inclusion minimal* subactions B of A satisfying: B immediately initiates F (or $\neg F$, resp.) in σ and there is no C such that $B \subset C \subseteq A$, where C immediately initiates $\neg F$ (or F, resp.) in σ. If $B \in Cause(F, \sigma, A)$, we will say that B is a cause for the change in truth values of the fluent name F in σ when A is done. The truth value of the fluent name F may change in two ways: from *true* to *false* and from *false* to *true*. Note that the subaction B is set-inclusion minimal among all subactions which satisfy one of the two conditions above.

For later purpose we also need one more auxiliary functions:

$$\Delta(A, \sigma) = \bigcup_{B \in W} (Initiate(B, \sigma) \cup Terminate(B, \sigma))$$

where

$$W = \bigcup_{F \in Initiate(A, \sigma) \cap Terminate(A, \sigma)} Cause(F, \sigma, A)$$

Intuitively speaking, $\Delta(A, \sigma)$ denotes those fluents influenced by subactions of A which have conflicting effects. All of the fluents influenced by these subactions will be made undefined in the new situation resulting from doing A.

Definition 6.2 (Model) *A structure (σ_0, Φ) is a model of a domain description D iff*

- *Every v-proposition of D is satisfied in (σ_0, Φ).*

- For every action expression A and every state σ,

$$\Phi(A, \sigma) = \langle S^+, \quad S^- \rangle$$

where

$$S^+ = (\sigma^+ \cup Initiate(A, \sigma)) \setminus Terminate(A, \sigma) \setminus \Delta(A, \sigma)$$
$$S^- = (\sigma^- \cup Terminate(A, \sigma)) \setminus Initiate(A, \sigma) \setminus \Delta(A, \sigma)$$

A domain description is consistent if it has a model. A domain description is complete if it has exactly one model. We will use $Mod(D)$ to denote the set of all models of D.

Definition 6.3 (Entailment) A v-proposition is entailed by a domain description D if it is satisfied in every model of D.

All of D_{YSP}, D_{door}, and D_{soup} defined before are complete since they have only one model, respectively.

6.3 Translation into Abductive Logic Programs

In order to automate temporal reasoning in $\mathcal{A}$, now we present a sound and complete translation from domain descriptions in $\mathcal{AC}$ to abductive logic programs. The familiarity with abductive logic programming is assumed. imm stands for "immediately" in $imm\_initiates(A, F, S)$ and $imm\_terminates(A, F, S)$. In the translation, all the predicates are either self-explanatory or mirror the definitions of Subsection 6.2. The symbol not in logic programs denotes the negation-as-failure operator.

Let D be a domain description in $\mathcal{AC}$. The translation πD consists of a normal logic program and a set of constraints, defined as follows:

1. Auxiliary predicates about subactions:
   Assume given standard rules for set-theoretical predicates $member(A, S)$, $subseteq(S_1, S_2)$. Sets can be represented by lists. Using these predicates we can define $subacteq(S_1, S_2)$ and $subact(S_1, S_2)$ about subactions in logic programming rules.
2. Initialization:

$$is\_true(F, s_0) \leftarrow initially\_true(F). \qquad (3)$$
$$is\_false(F, s_0) \leftarrow initially\_false(F). \qquad (4)$$

where s_0 is a new symbol to denote the initial situation. $initially\_true(F)$ and $initially\_false(F)$ are taken to be abducible predicates. If a fluent name F is abduced to be true (false, resp.) initially, then it is true (false, resp.) in the initial situation s_0.

3. Auxiliary Predicates:

These predicates will be used to define two main predicates $is\_true(F, S)$ and $is\_false(F, S)$, indicating whether fluent F is true or false in situation S.

$$initiates(A, F, S) \leftarrow imm\_initiates(A, F, S).$$
$$initiates(A, F, S) \leftarrow subacteq(B, A), imm\_initiates(B, F, S),$$
$$not\ clip\_initiates(F, B, A, S).$$

$$terminates(A, F, S) \leftarrow imm\_terminates(A, F, S).$$
$$terminates(A, F, S) \leftarrow subacteq(B, A), imm\_terminates(B, F, S),$$
$$not\ clip\_terminates(F, B, A, S).$$

$$causes(F, S, A, B) \leftarrow subacteq(B, A), imm\_initiates(B, F, S),$$
$$not\ clip\_initiates(F, B, A, S),$$
$$not\ clip\_cause1(F, B, A, S).$$
$$causes(F, S, A, B) \leftarrow subacteq(B, A), imm\_terminates(B, F, S),$$
$$not\ clip\_terminates(F, B, A, S),$$
$$not\ clip\_cause2(F, B, A, S).$$

$$delta(A, S, F) \leftarrow initiates(A, G, S), terminates(A, G, S),$$
$$causes(G, S, A, B), initiates(B, F, S).$$
$$delta(A, S, F) \leftarrow initiates(A, G, S), terminates(A, G, S),$$
$$causes(G, S, A, B), terminates(B, F, S).$$

$$clip\_initiates(F, B, A, S) \leftarrow subact(B, C), subacteq(C, A),$$
$$imm\_terminates(C, F, S).$$

$$clip\_terminates(F, B, A, S) \leftarrow subact(B, C), subacteq(C, A),$$
$$imm\_initiates(C, F, S).$$

$$clip\_cause1(F, B, A, S) \leftarrow subacteq(B, A), subact(C, B),$$
$$imm\_initiates(C, F, S),$$
$$not\ clip\_initiates(F, C, A, S).$$

$$clip\_cause2(F, B, A, S) \leftarrow subacteq(B, A), subact(C, B),$$
$$imm\_terminates(C, F, S),$$
$$not\ clip\_terminates(F, C, A, S).$$

4. Main Predicates:

The following predicates are used to determine whether a fluent is true or false in a situation.

$$is\_true(F, result(A, S)) \leftarrow is\_true(F, S), not\ terminates(A, F, S),$$
$$not\ delta(A, S, F).$$
$$is\_true(F, result(A, S)) \leftarrow initiates(A, F, S), not\ terminates(A, F, S),$$
$$not\ delta(A, S, F).$$

$$is\_false(F, result(A, S)) \leftarrow is\_false(F, S), not\ initiates(A, F, S),$$
$$not\ delta(A, S, F).$$
$$is\_false(F, result(A, S)) \leftarrow terminates(A, F, S), not\ initiates(A, F, S),$$
$$not\ delta(A, S, F).$$

5. Domain-Specific Predicates

The syntax and semantics of the following predicates depend on domain descriptions. Let F be a fluent name, i.e., $F \in \Sigma_f$. Then, we write $Holds(F, S)$ to stand for $is\_true(F, S)$ and write $Holds(\neg F, S)$ for $is\_false(F, S)$.

- For each effect proposition a **causes** f **if** $p_1, \ldots, p_n$ in D, where f is positive, we have a logic programming rule:

$$imm\_initiates(a, f, S) \leftarrow$$
$$Holds(p_1, S), \ldots, Holds(p_n, S).$$

- For each effect proposition a **causes** $\neg f$ **if** $p_1, \ldots, p_n$, where f is positive, we have a logic programming rule:

$$imm\_terminates(a, f, S) \leftarrow$$
$$Holds(p_1, S), \ldots, Holds(p_n, S).$$

The integrity constraints, denoted by IC_D, are defined as follows: For each value proposition F **after** $A_1; \ldots; A_m$, we have:

$$Holds(F, result(A_1; \ldots; A_m, s_0)) \tag{5}$$

As we will use the predicate completion semantics, the above integrity constraint can be equivalently transformed into

$$false \leftarrow not\ Holds(F, result(A_1; \ldots; A_m, s_0)).$$

Note that we cannot abduce a fluent to be both true and false. For this purpose we add the following domain-independent constraint:

$$false \leftarrow is\_true(F, S_0), is\_false(F, S_0). \tag{6}$$

The literal $false$ is always interpreted as logical falsity, and all rules with $false$ as heads function as integrity constraints. The predicates $initially\_true(F)$ and $initially\_false(F)$ are taken as abducible predicates used to capture the incomplete knowledge about the initial situation. The semantics of πD is defined to be the union of the integrity constraints, the Clark Equality Theory, and the first-order theory obtained by completing all the non-abducible predicates [8]. The definition for abducible predicates $initially\_true(F)$ and $initially\_false(F)$ are left open. We will write $COMP(\pi D)$ to denote the semantics of of πD. The following two results justify the above semantics definition.

Proposition 6.4 πD *is an acyclic program with first-order constraints in the sense of [5].*

Corollary 6.5 *For the abductive logic program* πD, $COMP(\pi D)$ *coincides with its generalized stable model semantics [17] and generalized well-founded model semantics [27].*

The following two technical results are proved in the long version of this paper.

Theorem 6.6 (Soundness) *Let D be any domain description. For any value proposition Q, if* $COMP(\pi D) \models \pi Q$, *then D entails Q.*

Theorem 6.7 (Completeness) *Let D be a domain description. For any value proposition Q, if D entails Q, then* $COMP(\pi D) \models \pi Q$.

Since our translation is both sound and complete, we can reduce temporal reasoning in $\mathcal{AC}$ to abductive query evaluaiton in logic program πD. The work reported in this paper has been experimented with the latest version of the REVISE system [9]. The use of the REVISE system is not essential, and other abductive query evaluaiton procedures for normal logic programs such as SLD-NFA [11] and that in [30] should also work. If for every fluent name F, one and only one of **initially** F and **initially** $\neg F$ appears in a domain description, then PROLOG can be used for temporal projection after (3), (4), and (6) are removed and the integrity constraitns are represented only in the form of (5). For example, temporal reasoning in the Yale Shooting domain D_{YSP} can be done in PROLOG. Furthermore, if we introduce more propositions, say observation propositions, we can abductively diagnose action domains when there! is a discrepancy between predicted propositions and observed propositions. For the sake of space limitation, we will not go into deeper discussions.

6.4 An Unsolved Problem

Now let's condider the following so-called Poor Street Musician Problem: Suppose there is a poor street musician with a violin and a money bag. While he plays the violin in the street, the by-passers may throw some money into the money bag. It is often the case that two or more by-passers may throw their money at the same time. For simplicity, we write $Money(x)$ to denote that he has x dollars in the bag, and $Gives(x)$ to denote that a by-passer gives x dollars to the musician. Then, the domain can be described as something like this:

initially $Money(0)$
$Gives(x)$ **causes** $Money(x+y)$ **if** $Money(y)$
$Gives(x)$ **causes** $\neg Money(y)$ **if** $Money(y)$

Then, what's the effect of the concurrent action $\{Gives(1), Gives(2)\}$. The intuitive answer should be that there are three more dollars in the bag. However, it can be found that neither of the above three inheritance-based semantics works in this example.

An alternative semantics would be expected to be based on so-called *interleaving trace* of concurrent actions [3].

However, the interleaving trace based semantics does not work well if one slightly modifies Gelfond-Lifscitz-Robinov's Mary's Soup example: Suppose that Mary wants to lift a bowl of soup to serve a guest. Whenever she lifts the bowl with only one hand, she will spill the soup to the floor. But when she lifts the bowl with two hands, she will not spill the soup. What will be the effects of $\{sing, liftwithleft-hand, liftwithrighthand\}$? It can be seen that the interleaving- trace-based semantics does not work for this example.

Now the problem is whether there is any elegant semantics for concurrent actions which can uniformly deal with both Poor Street Musician Problem and Modified Mary's Soup Problem?

7 Concluding Remarks

In this paper we have addressed three problems related to development of intelligent agents: refinement of action theories, knowledge assimilation, and concurrent actions. All the three problems can be solved in part by using abductive logic programs. The declarative semantics and efficient execution of abductive logic programs have made it possible to develop a formal, provably correct with respect to action theories in a high-level action description language ($\mathcal{A}$ family language), and yet computational methodology for reasoning about actions. In fact, abductive logic programmming can also be applied in many other occasions: intention recognitions of other agents, diagnosis, planning, etc., which are some of our current research topics in progress.

Acknowledgement

This work was partially supported by JNICT of Portugal under MENTAL project PRAXIS 2/2.1/TIT/1593/95 and PRAXIS XXI/BPD/4165/94.

References

1. C. Alchorrón, P. Gärdenfors, and D. Makinson. On the logic of theory change: Partial meet contraction and revision functions. *Journal of Symbolic Logic*, 50(2):510 – 530, 1985.
2. J. J. Alferes, C. V. Damásio, and L. M. Pereira. SLX - a top-down derivation procedure for programs with explicit negation. In M. Bruynooghe, editor, *International Logic Programming Symposium*. MIT Press, 1994.
3. J. J. Alferes, R. Li, and L. M. Pereira. Non-atomic actions in the situation calculus. In N. Mamede and C. Pinto-Ferreira, editors, *Progress in Artificial Intelligence, LNAI 990*, pages 273–284. Springer, 1995.
4. J. J. Alferes and L.M. Pereira. *Reasoning with Logic Programming, LNAI 1111.* Springer, 1996.

5. K. R. Apt and M. Bezem. Acyclic programs. In *Proc. of ICLP 90*, pages 579–597. MIT Press, 1990.

6. A. B. Baker. Nonmonotonic reasoning in the framework of situation calculus. *Artificial Intelligence*, 49:5–23, 1991.

7. C. Baral and M. Gelfond. Representing concurrent actions in extended logic programming. In *Proc. of IJCAI'93*, pages 866–871. Morgan Kaufmann, 1993.

8. L. Console, D. T. Dupré, and P. Torasso. On the relationship between abduction and deduction. *Journal of Logic and Computation*, 1(5):661–690, 1991.

9. C. V. Damásio, L.M. Pereira, and W. Nejdl. Revise: An extended logic programming system for revising knowledge bases. In *Proc. of KR'94*, 1994.

10. M. Denecker. Knowledge representation and reasoning in incomplete logic programming. Ph.D. thesis, Department of Computer Science, K.U.Leuven, 1993.

11. M. Denecker and D. De Schreye. SLDNFA: an abductive procedure for normal abductive programs. In K. R. Apt, editor, *Logic Programming: Proc. of 1992 Int'l Joint Conference and Symposium*, pages 686–700. MIT Press, 1992.

12. M. Denecker and D. de Schreye. Representing incomplete knowledge in abductive logic programming. In *Logic Programming: Proc. of the 1993 Int'l Symposium*, pages 147–163. MIT Press, 1993.

13. M. Gelfond and V. Lifschitz. The stable model semantics for logic programming. In R. Kowalski and K. Bowen, editors, *Proc. of 5th Logic Programming Symposium*, pages 1070–1080. MIT Press, 1988.

14. M. Gelfond and V. Lifschitz. Representing action and change by logic programs. *Journal of Logic Programming*, 17:301–322, 1993.

15. M. Gelfond, V. Lifschitz, and A. Rabinov. What are the limitations of the situation calculus? In R. Moore, editor, *Automated Reasoning: Essays in Honor of Woody Bledsoe*, pages 167–179. 1991.

16. M. Ginsberg. Counterfactuals. *Artificial Intelligence*, 30(1):35 – 79, 1986.

17. A.C. Kakas and P. Mancarella. Generalized stable models: A semantics for abduction. In *Proc. of ECAI'90*, 1990.

18. G.N. Kartha. Soundness and completeness theorems for three formalizations of action. In *Proc. IJCAI93*, pages 712–718. MIT Press, 1993.

19. R.A. Kowalski and F. Sadri. The situation calculus and event calculus compared. In *Proc. of ILPS 94*, pages 539–553. MIT Press, 1994.

20. R. Li and L.M. Pereira. Knowledge assimilation in domains of actions: A possible causes approach. *Journal of Applied Non-Classical Logic*, Special issue on Inconsistency Handling in Knowledge Systems (guest editor: G. Wagner), 1997.

21. R. Li and L.M. Pereira. Knowledge-based situated agents among us. In J. P. Muller, M. J. Wooldridge, and N. R. Jennings, editors, *Intelligent Agents III – Proc. of the Third International Workshop on Agent Theories, Architectures, and Languages (ATAL-96), LNAI 1193*, pages 375–389. Springer, 1997.

22. F. Lin and Y. Shoham. Provably correct theories of actions: preliminary report. In *Proc. of AAAI-91*, 1991.

23. F. Lin and Y. Shoham. Concurrent actions in the situation calculus. In *Proc. of AAAI-92*, pages 590–595, 1992.

24. J. McCarthy and P.J. Hayes. Some philosophical problems from the stand-point of artificial intelligence. In B. Meltzer and D. Michie, editors, *Machine Intelligence*, volume 4, pages 463–502, Edinburgh, 1969.

25. E. P. D. Pednault. Adl: Exploring the middle ground between strips and the situation calculus. In R. J. Brachman, H. Levesque, and R. Reiter, editors, *Proc. of KR'89*, pages 324–332. Morgan Kaufmann Publishers, Inc., 1989.

26. L. M. Pereira and J. J. Alferes. Well-founded semantics for logic programs with explicit negation. In B. Neumann, editor, *Proc. of ECAI'92*, pages 102–106. John Wiley & Sons, 1992.

27. L. M. Pereira, J. J. Alferes, and J. N. Aparício. Nonmonotonic reasoning with well founded semantics. In K. Furukawa, editor, *Proc. of 8th ICLP*, pages 475–489. MIT Press, 1991.

28. R. Reiter. The frame problem in the situation calculus: A simple solution (sometimes) and a completeness result for goal regression. In V. Lifschitz, editor, *Artificial Intelligence and Mathematical Theory of Computation: Papers in Honor of John McCarthy*, pages 359–380. Academic Press, San Diego, CA, 1991.

29. E. Sandewall. *Features and Fluents: The Representation of Knowledge about Dynamic Systems, Vol. 1*. Oxford University Press, 1994.

30. K. Satoh and N. Iwayama. A query evaluation method for abductive logic programming. In K. R. Apt, editor, *Logic Programming: Proc. of 1992 Int'l Joint Conference and Symposium*, pages 671–685, 1992.

31. A. Van Gelder, K. Ross, and J.S. Schlipf. The well-founded semantics for general logic programs. *J. ACM*, 38:620–650, 1991.

32. M. Winslett. Reasoning about action using a possible models approach. In *AAAI'88*, pages 89 – 93, 1988.

Dimensions of Embodiments: Possible Futures for Cognitive Science

(Abstract)

Francisco J. Varela

CNRS, Paris

Cognitive science has evolved over the last ten years at a dramatic pace. From a very dogmatic adherence to the idea of cognition as a semantic representation of world feature in 1960s, then into a new wave of interest in implicit continuous representation introduced by connectionism in 1970s, and finally over the last decade into its most recent phase emphasizing situated, embodied cognition. In this last phase what is suspended is the dogma of a cognitive agent's relation to its world as being cast into a semantic frame: a state of the world is represented by a symbolic token (be it discrete or continuous) inside the agent. Instead the key emphasis is placed on the active coupling with the agent's world so that pertinence is an emergent process. I have been a fervent defender of such situated approach from early on, starting with my work on autopoiesis in the 1970s, and more recently with an approach to cognition as enactive.

From this background my presentation will attempt to extend the situated, enactive to its next necessary stage of maturity. In fact, having regained the importance of the agent's physical embodiment in situation (its corps propre to use the phenomenological expression of Merleau-Ponty), it is essential to realize that both in animals and humans this bodily anchor is not isolated or decoupled from other members of the same species. From the recent research in primates and humans infants, it is quite clear that having a situated bodily scheme is possible if and only if it is established concurrent with the image of another. In fact the other serves as the mediator for the self-image. Given the recent interest in building collective intelligence through a group of interactive robots, the dialogue between the AI community and cognitive science can be interesting if one is willing to explore what is open beyond collective behavior by means of purely external interaction rules. What does it means for an artificial agent to create a self-image mediated by other? What kinds of bodily schemes and sensori-motor schemes can serve as basis?

Machine Learning Meets Natural Language

(Abstract)

Tom Mitchell

Carnegie Mellon University

The majority of the world's online data now exists in the form of text, rather than as numeric or symbolic data. It is therefore natural to seek better methods for automatically interpreting such text data. For example, consider the fact that your computer workstation can now retrieve up to 200,000,000 pages of text from the World Wide Web, but does not currently understand the content of any of these pages.

This talk considers how we might use machine learning methods to improve the ability of computers to interpret and process text data. First, we examine a class of learning algorithms that view each text document as a "bag of words", ignoring information about the sequence in which these words occur. Recently these methods have been shown to be surprisingly successful at learning to classify various types of documents. For example, we will describe our NewsWeeder system, which learns the reading interests of various individuals from training examples of news articles they have read and liked (or disliked) in the past. This learned interest profile is then used to recommend interesting new articles to the user.

Second, we consider the feasibility of using machine learning to automatically extract a symbolic, probabilistic knowledge base from the World Wide Web. The Internet, including the World Wide Web, electronic newsgroups, and commercial news feeds, has already become one of the most complete sources of up-to-date information in the world. Unfortunately for AI systems, this vast store of knowledge exists in text form, uninterpretable by computer systems. If it could be converted into an equivalent SYMBOLIC form, it would constitute a world-wide knowledge base of great value, that could form the basis for a wide range of knowledge-based AI systems.

We will describe our ongoing research on machine learning methods for automatically extracting symbolic information from hypertext on the World Wide Web. For example, after training on several thousand web pages from four universities, our system is currently able to extract symbolic descriptions of faculty members, students, courses, and research projects from new web sites, as well as relations among these entities such as Advisor-Of, Instructor-Of, etc. This talk will discuss several learning algorithms, experimental results demonstrating their effectiveness and limitations, and key directions for new research in this area.

Author Index

Springer
and the
environment

At Springer we firmly believe that an
international science publisher has a
special obligation to the environment,
and our corporate policies consistently
reflect this conviction.
We also expect our business partners –
paper mills, printers, packaging
manufacturers, etc. – to commit
themselves to using materials and
production processes that do not harm
the environment. The paper in this
book is made from low- or no-chlorine
pulp and is acid free, in conformance
with international standards for paper
permanency.

 Springer

Lecture Notes in Artificial Intelligence (LNAI)

Lecture Notes in Computer Science